Universit

ROBERT THOMAS

Serbia under Milošević

Politics in the 1990s

HURST & COMPANY, LONDON

Published in the United Kingdom by
C. Hurst & Co. (Publishers) Ltd.,
38 King Street, London WC2E 8JZ
© 1999 by Robert Thomas
Second impression, May 1999
Third impression, July 2000
All rights reserved.
Printed in Malaysia

ISBNs
1-85065-341-0 hardback
1-85065-367-4 paperback

Acknowledgements

I owe a particular debt of gratitude to Jadranka Porter and Svetlana Fleming for their help and encouragement during the writing of this book. I am also grateful to Milica Naumov and her family for their friendship and hospitality in Belgrade. I would like to thank the following people who provided helpful comments while the book was being written: Dušan Puvačić, Wendy Bracewell, Aleksa Djilas, Tim Evans and Stevan Pavlowitch. In addition I thank my parents for all the help that they have given over the years, and during the time the book was being written. Thanks, finally, to Michael Dwyer and Christopher Hurst for their help throughout the process of publication.

London,   ROBERT THOMAS
December 1998

Contents

Chronology of Events

1987

24 April   Slobodan Milošević visits Kosovo Polje. Intervenes on behalf of the Kosovo Serbs.

23 September   'Eighth Session' of Serbian Communist Party. Belgrade party chief, Dragiša Pavlović forced to resign. Milošević takes control of Serbian Communist Party.

1988

5 October   Vojvodina provincial leadership resigns in the face of mass demonstrations organised by pro-Milošević activist Mihalj Kertes.

7 October   Montenegrin party leadership resigns after mass protest organised by pro-Milošević faction led by Momir Bulatović.

1989

23 March   Kosovo provincial assembly votes itself out of existence after police and military intervention in the region.

28 June   Milošević addresses rally of 500,000 at Gazimestan in Kosovo Polje.

1990

6 January   Serbian National Renewal (SNO) founded at meeting in Novi Pazova with Mirko Jović as President and Vuk Drašković as Vice-President.

3 February   First meeting of Democratic Party (DS) held in Belgrade.

14 March   Serbian Renewal Movement (SPO) founded by Vuk Drašković and Vojislav Šešelj.

13 June   Seventy thousand people attend first joint opposition mass demonstration in Belgrade.

17 June   League of Socialist Youth of Serbia transform themselves into New Democracy – Movement for Serbia led by Dušan Mihailović.

18 June   Vojislav Šešelj establishes Serbian Četnik Movement. Authorities refuse to register it as a political party.

1/2 July   Referendum allows authorities to frame new Serbian constitution prior to the holding of multi-party elections.

12 July   Serbian Democratic Party formed in Bosnia under leadership of Radovan Karadžić.

16/17 July   League of Communists of Serbia and the Socialist Alliance of Working People hold 'unification congress' and form themselves into the Socialist Party of Serbia (SPS). Slobodan Milošević elected as party President.

29 September   Democratic Party national assembly elects Dragoljub Mićunović as party president.

19 November   League of Communists – Movement for Yugoslavia (SK-PJ) is founded. Key political role played by Mirjana Marković.

9 December   Parliamentary and Presidential elections. Socialists win parliamentary majority. Slobodan Milošević elected as President.

1991

22 January   Breakaway group from Democratic Party led by Nikola Milošević and Kosta Čavoški form Serbian Liberal Party.

23 February   Serbian Radical Party formed at a meeting in Kragujevac under the leadership of Vojislav Šešelj.

9 March   Street violence after opposition demonstration attacked by police. Authorities send Yugoslav National Army (JNA) tanks onto streets of Belgrade.

12/13 March   Vuk Drašković released from prison. Radmilo Bogdanović, Interior Minister, and Dušan Mitević, head of Serbian television dismissed from government.

25 March   Slobodan Milošević and Croatian President, Franjo Tudjman, hold secret talks at Karadjordjevo, Serbia.

2 May   Clashes between Serbian militia and Croatian police in Borovo Selo, Croatia.

22 May   Shortlived opposition coalition United Serbian Democratic Opposition (USDO) formed by Serbian Renewal Movement, Serbian Liberal Party, and New Democracy Movement for Serbia.

30 June   Vojislav Šešelj elected to the Serbian parliament representing Belgrade constituency of Rakovica.

20 November   Vukovar falls to Yugoslav National Army and Serbian paramilitary volunteer forces.

1992

15 January   European Union recognises Croatia and Slovenia.

6 April   European Union and United States recognise Bosnia-Hercegovina.

27 April Federal Republic of Yugoslavia promulgated as new state.

23 May DEPOS opposition coalition formed consisting of Serbian Renewal Movement, Serbian Liberal Party, New Democracy, pro-DEPOS faction of Democratic Party, and other smaller parties.

30 May United Nations Security Council imposes economic sanctions on Federal Republic of Yugoslavia.

10 June Civic Alliance of Serbia coalition formed led by Vesna Pešić.

15 June Dobrica Ćosić elected as President of Federal Republic of Yugoslavia.

14 July Milan Panić elected as Prime Minister of Federal Republic of Yugoslavia.

28 June DEPOS coalition initiates series of anti-government demonstrations (Vidovdan Sabor).

26 July Pro-DEPOS wing of Democratic Party forms itself into Democratic Party of Serbia (DSS) led by Vojislav Koštunica.

27/28 August London Peace Conference. Milan Panić and Slobodan Milošević in open conflict.

19 October Serbian police led by Mihalj Kertes seize control of federal Interior Ministry.

20 December Federal and republic level parliamentary and presidential elections in Serbia. Slobodan Milošević re-elected as President defeating challenge by Milan Panić. Serbian Radical Party makes substantial parliamentary gains.

1993

16 May Bosnian Serb referendum rejects Vance-Owen peace plan.

31 May Vote of 'no confidence' in Dobrica Ćosić passed in federal parliament.

1 June Vuk Drašković and his wife, Danica, are arrested and beaten by police after disturbances outside federal parliament.

15 July Vuk Drašković leaves hospital having been 'pardoned' by Slobodan Milošević.

20 September Serbian Radical Party moves vote of 'no confidence' in Socialist government.

20 October Slobodan Milošević dissolves Serbian parliament and calls new elections.

19 December Serbian parliamentary elections. Serbian Radical Party suffers losses but Socialists fail to win majority.

1994

12 January Slobodan Rakitić and ten DEPOS representatives in federal parliament defect from Serbian Renewal Movement. Rakitić later forms Assembly National Party.

24 January   Dragoslav Avramović introduces programme of financial and currency reform.

29 January   Zoran Djindjić replaces Dragoljub Mićunović as President of the Democratic Party.

23 February   Socialists form government headed by Mirko Marjanović supported by New Democracy.

24 March   League of Communists – Movement for Yugoslavia combines with other smaller parties to form Yugoslav United Left (JUL). Ljubiša Ristić is appointed as President of JUL, but real power resides with Mirjana Marković.

4 August   Slobodan Milošević imposes blockade on Bosnian Serbs after rejection of Contact Group peace plan.

29 September   Vojislav Šešelj arrested after spitting at the federal Prime Minister, Radoman Božović. Sentenced to four months in prison.

1995

19 January   *Naša borba* formed by a breakaway group of journalists after *Borba* is taken over by the authorities.

3 June   Vojislav Šešelj arrested at Gnjilane in Kosovo. Subsequently sentenced to two months in prison.

6 July   Bosnian Serb forces led by Ratko Mladić attack Srebrenica.

4 August   Croatian forces capture the Krajina. 165,000 Serbian refugees flee from the assault.

28 August   NATO campaign of air strikes against Bosnian Serb targets commences.

1 November   Peace negotiations begin at Dayton, Ohio.

3 December   Democratic Alliance coalition formed consisting of Democratic Party, Democratic Party of Serbia, Serbian Liberal Party, and Assembly National Party.

14 December   Peace agreement signed in Paris.

1996

15 February   Independent TV Studio B taken back into 'social ownership' by the Belgrade city authorities.

22 February   After expulsion from the Democratic Party Dragoljub Mićunović forms Democratic Centre grouping into new political party.

9 March   Joint rally held on Belgrade by Serbian Renewal Movement, Democratic Party, and Civic Alliance of Serbia. These three parties later form the Zajedno coalition.

22 April   Kosovo Liberation Army begins campaign of violence against Serbian police and civilian targets.

15 May   Dragoslav Avramović removed as head of the National Bank of Yugoslavia.

28 September   Dragoslav Avramović agrees to head election list for Zajedno coalition expanded to include Democratic Party of Serbia and Association of Free and Independent Trade Unions. On 7 October Avramović withdraws from the election for 'health reasons'.

3 November   Federal elections. Zajedno defeated by the 'left coalition' of Socialists, Yugoslav United Left, and New Democracy.

17 November   Zajedno wins local election victories in urban centres across Serbia. The attempt by the authorities to annul the elections triggers daily popular demonstrations.

24 December   Socialists and Yugoslav United Left organise counter-demonstration in Belgrade in attempt to provoke violent confrontation with Zajedno supporters.

1997

2 February   Police intervene using force to disperse Zajedno demonstrators in Belgrade.

21 February   Zajedno supporters celebrate recognition of their election victories. Zoran Djindjić becomes Mayor of Belgrade.

28 February   Agreement on Special Relations between Federal Republic of Yugoslavia and Republic Srpska. The agreement is supported by Momčilo Krajišnik and opposed by Biljana Plavšić.

10 April   Radovan Stojičić, Deputy Minister of the Interior, shot dead in Belgrade.

23 July   Slobodan Milošević elected as President of Federal Republic of Yugoslavia.

28 August   Serbian National Alliance (SNS) formed in Banja Luka by Biljana Plavšić.

21 September   Parliamentary and presidential elections in Serbia. Elections boycotted by Democratic Party, Democratic Party of Serbia and Civic Alliance of Serbia. Gains made by *Radicals*.

30 September   Zoran Djindjić ousted from position as Mayor of Belgrade by former allies in Serbian Renewal Movement working with Socialists and Radicals.

5 October   Presidential elections run-off between Vojislav Šešelj and Zoran Lilić declared invalid due to low turn-out.

19 October   Milo Djukanović elected as President of Montenegro defeating pro-Milošević candidate Momir Bulatović.

24 October   Zoran Todorović, General Secretary of Yugoslav United Left assasinated in Belgrade.

23 November Parliamentary elections ends Serbian Democratic Party (SDS) dominance of political life in the *Republika Srpska.*

7 December New Serbian presidential elections held.

21 December Milan Milutinović elected as President of Serbia in election run-off. Radical candidate Vojislav Šešelj alleges widespread election fraud.

1998

14 January Violence on the streets of Podgorica as supporters of Momir Bulatović attempt to prevent the inauguration of Milo Djukanović as President of Montenegro.

17 January Milorad Dodik elected as Prime Minister of Republika Srpska heading coalition government.

28 February Serbian security forces begin offensive against Albanian Kosovo Liberation Army insurgents in Drenica region of Kosovo.

24 March Coalition government formed by Socialists, Radicals, and Yugoslav United Left. Vojislav Šešelj appointed as Deputy Prime Minister.

23 April Referendum rejects foreign mediation over the crisis in Kosovo. Clashes on Kosovo/Albania border between Yugoslav National Army and Kosovo Liberation Army.

Regional Publications

Argument   Fortnightly newspaper which commenced publication in March 1994 and followed an anti-regime nationalist line. In the autumn of 1996 it ceased publication, but began again in March 1997.

Blic   Popular independent daily newspaper founded in September 1996.

Borba   Instituted in 1945 as the official daily journal of the League of Communists of Yugoslavia. Privatised in 1989 it sought to present an independent perspective on news. In November 1994 the Milošević government took control of *Borba* and imposed ideological orthodoxy on its new reporting. From then on *Borba*'s reporting did not deviate in its loyalty to the government-dictated line.

Demokratija   Founded in 1990 as the journal of the Democratic Party mainly circulating among party members. Reconstituted in November 1996 as an independent daily newspaper.

Demokratska stranka Srbije vesti   Journal of the Democratic Party of Serbia mainly circulating among party members.

Dnevni telegraf   Popular daily newspaper which began publishing in the spring of 1996 after *Telegraf* divided into daily and weekly editions.

Duga   Bi-weekly magazine mixing political reporting with general interest articles. Contributions include hardline nationalism and liberal critiques of nationalism. *Duga* was also renowned for carrying a diary column by Mirjana Marković, Slobodan Milošević's wife, before her departure in early 1997.

Glasnik   Bulletin of the Association of Free and Independent Towns and Opštinas (formed after Zajedno election victories of November 1996).

Glas Srpski   Bosnian Serb daily newspaper published in Banja Luka. Followed pro-Karadžić line during the 1997 intra-Serb conflict.

Gradjanin   Daily newspaper founded in April 1997, Edited by Aleksandar Tijanić, the former Minister for Information. It ceased publication later that year.

Intervju   Weekly news and general interest magazine. Until 1994, as part of the *Politika* publishing group, *Intervju* followed an editorial line effectively dictated by the authorities. Subsequently under the ownership of Bogoljub Karić it developed a policy of 'semi-independence' whereby coverage was given to opposition politicians and non-regime activities as long as these were not considered to pose a serious challenge to the government.

Istok   Montenegrin news journal based in Podgorica. Follows a pro-Serbian nationalist line but is opposed to the Milošević government.

Javnost   Bosnian Serb weekly journal published in Pale. First published in 19 October 1990 and closely connected with the Serbian Democratic Party.

Monitor   Independent Montenegrin journal published in Podgorica. Followed pro-Djukanović line during the 1997/1998 Montenegrin power struggle.

Naša borba   Founded in February 1995 by journalists who had defected from *Borba*. *Naša borba* has followed an editorial line which opposes the Serbian government from a liberal/civic perspective. It provides the most comprehensive and objective coverage of Serbian political news.

Nedeljni telegraf   Weekly newspaper which began publishing under this title after *Telegraf* was divided into weekly and daily edition in the spring of 1996.

Nezavisna svetlost   Independent weekly news journal published in Kragujevac. Founded after the local Socialist authorities took over the journal *Svetlost* in September 1995.

Nezavisne novine   Independent weekly current affairs journal based in Banja Luka.

NIN   Weekly news magazine founded in 1935. During the early years of Milošević's rule its editorial policy was firmly under the control of the government. It gradually, however, distanced itself from the regime, and currently follows an independent line strongly critical of the authorities.

Oslobodjenje   Daily newspaper published in Sarajevo. Founded in 1943, it was affiliated during the communist period to the Socialist Alliance of Working People. On 4 June 1990 it reconstituted itself as an independent publication being critical of all the contending nationalist factions.

Pogledi   Anti-regime journal with strong nationalist and royalist orientation. Founded in June 1987 by Miloslav Samardˇiˊc and other Kragujevac University students.

Politika   Founded in 1904 *Politika* established itself as the most widely read newspaper in Serbia. Since 1987, though formally a private enterprise, it has consistently followed a pro-government line.

Profil   Glossy bi-monthly magazine focussing on general interest and lifestyle articles. Began publication in October 1995.

Republika   Bi-weekly civic/liberal journal carrying articles which are often theoretical and academic in nature. Established in March 1989 and edited by Nebojša Popov of the Civic Alliance of Serbia.

Slobodna Bosna   Weekly independent news and current affairs journal published in Sarajevo.

Srpska reč   Journal, and publishing house, attached to the Serbian Renewal Movement and following the political line of that party. Founded in May 1990 under the directorship of Danica Drašković.

Srpska vojska   Journal of the Bosnian Serb Army.

Srpsko jedinstvo   Journal of the Serbian Unity Party of Željko Ražnatović 'Arkan'.

Stav   Weekly news and current affairs magazine published in Novi Sad.

Svedok   Weekly independent news and current affairs journal published in Belgrade.

Svet   Novi Sad-based weekly tabloid newspaper.

Večernje novosti   Pro-regime daily newspaper.

Velika Srbija   The journal of the Serbian Radical Party.

Vreme   Weekly independent news journal following an editorial line which is liberal and highly critical of Serbian government policy. Founded in autumn 1990 by dissident journalists from *NIN*.

Zemunske novine   Journal published by the local government in Zemun. After November 1996 its format and editorial line came to be dictated by the Serbian Radical Party who controlled the municipal government.

Organisations

Alliance of Reform Forces of Yugoslavia (*Savez reformskih snaga Jugoslavije* SRSJ) Founded 29 July 1990. Belgrade Main Committee headed by Vojin Dimitrijević.

Army of the Serbian Republic (*Vojska Republike Srpske* – VRS) Formed after official withdrawal of JNA from Bosnia. Chief-of-Staff from start of Bosnia war to November 1996: Ratko Mladić; November 1996-January 1998: Pero Čolić; January 1998: Momir Talić.

Assembly National Party: (*Saborna narodna stranka* – SNS) Founded 28 January 1995. President: Slobodan Rakitić.

Association for a Yugoslav Democratic Initiative (Udruženje za Jugoslovensku demokratsku inicijativu – UJDI) Founded 3 February 1989. Head of Belgrade branch: Nebojša Popov.

Christian Democratic Party of Serbia (Demohrišćanska stranka Srbije – DHSS) Founded 12 April 1997. President: Vladan Batić.

Civic Alliance of Serbia (Gradjanski Savez Srbije – GSS) Founded 10 June 1992. President: Vesna Pešić.

Croatian Democratic Union (*Hrvatska demokratska zajednica* – HDZ) Founded 17 June 1989. President Franjo Tudjman.

Democratic Alliance (*Demokratska alijansa* – DA) Opposition coalition. Founded 3 December 1995.

Democratic Centre (*Demokratski Centar* – DC) Formed after Dragoljub Mićunović's removal as President of the DS in 1994. Constituted as a political party on 22 February 1996.

Democratic Community of Vojvodina Hungarians (*Demokratska zajednica Vojvodjanskih Madjara* – DZVM) Founded 31 March 1990. President Andras Agoštan.

Democratic Movement of Serbia (*Demokratski Pokret Srbije* – DEPOS) Founded 23 May 1992. Chairman of Council: Matija Bećković.

Democratic Party (*Demokratska stranka* – DS) Founded 12 December 1989. First President: Dragoljub Mićunović. Zoran Djindjić elected as DS President, 29 January 1994.

Democratic Party of Serbia (*Demokratska stranka Srbije* – DSS) Founded 26 July 1992. President: Vojislav Koštunica.

Kosovo Liberation Army (*Ushtria Člirimatare e Kosoves* – UČK) Armed Albanian insurgent organisation. Began operations April 1996. Its name is Albanian, here with Serbian orthography.

League of Communists – Movement for Yugoslavia (*Savez Komunista Pokret za Jugoslaviju* – SK-PJ)   Founded 19 November 1990.

National Party (*Narodna stranka*) President: Milan Paroški.

National Peasants Party (*Narodna seljačka stranka* – NSS)   Founded 20 May 1990. President: Dragan Veselinov.

National Radical Party (*Narodna radikalna stranka* – NRS)   Founded 19 January 1990. President: Veljko Guberina.

New Democracy (*Nova demokratija* – ND)   Founded 17 June 1990. President: Dušan Mihailović.

Organisation for Security and Co-operation in Europe (OSCE).

Party of Democratic Action (*Stranke demokratske akcije* – SDA)   Founded in Bosnia-Hercegovina 27 March 1990; President: Alija Izetbegović. Founded in Sandžak (Serbia) 11 August 1990; President: Sulejman Ugljanin.

Serbian Četnik Movement (*Srpski četnički pokret* – SČP)   Founded 18 June 1990. President: Vojislav Šešelj.

Serbian Democratic Party (*Srpska demokratska stranka* – SDS)   Founded in Croatia 17 February 1990; President: Jovan Rašković. Founded in Bosnia 12 July 1990; President: Radovan Karadžić (1990-6); Aleksa Buha (1996-8).

Serbian Freedom Movement (*Srpski slobodarski pokret* – SSP)   Founded 23 January 1990. President: Vojislav Šešelj.

Serbian Guard (*Srpska garda* – SG)   Founded 6 July 1991. Commander: Djordje Božović 'Giška'. After Božović's death on 14 September 1991 the SG split into rival factions.

Serbian Liberal Party (*Srpska liberalna stranka* – SLS)   Founded 22 January 1991. President: Nikola Milošević.

Serbian National Alliance (*Srpski narodni savez*)   Founded 28 August 1997. President: Biljana Plavšić.

Serbian National Renewal (*Srpska naroda obnova* – SNO)   Founded 6 January 1990. President: Mirko Jović. Vice-Presidents: Vuk Drašković, Žarko Gavrilović.

Serbian Peasants Party (*Seljačka stranka Srbije* – SSS)   Founded 26 October 1990, President: Milomir Babić.

Serbian Radical Party (*Srpska radikalna stranka* – SRS)   Founded 23 February 1991. President: Vojislav Šešelj.

Serbian Renewal Movement (*Srpski pokret obnove* – SPO)   Founded 14 March 1990. President: Vuk Drašković.

Serbian Saint Sava Party (*Srpska Svetosavska stranka* – SSSS)   President Žarko Gavrilović.

Serbian Unity Party (*Stranka srpskog jedinstva* – SSJ)   Founded 2 November 1993. President: Željko Ražnatović 'Arkan'.

Serbian Volunteer Guard (*Srpska dobrovoljačka garda* – SDG)   Founded 11 October 1990. Commander: Željko Ražnatović 'Arkan'.

Serbian Volunteer Guard (*Srpska dobrovoljačka garda* – SDG)   Founded
11 October 1990. Commander: Željko Ražnatović 'Arkan'.

Socialist Party of Serbia (*Socialistička partija Srbije* – SPS)   Founded 17
July 1990. President: Slobodan Milošević.

Special Anti-terrorist Unit (*Specijalne anti-terorističke jedinice* – SAJ)   Commanded by Franko Simatović.

Stabilisation Force (SFOR)   NATO-led international force deployed
in Bosnia after Dayton agreement.

State Security Service (*Služba državne bezbednosti* – SDB)   Director: Jovica
Stanišić.

United Serbian Democratic Opposition (*Udružena Srpska demokratska
opozicija* – USDO)   Opposition coalition. Formed 22 May 1991.

Yugoslav Army (*Vojska Jugoslavije* – VJ)   Came into existence on 19
May 1992 after formal dissolution of JNA.

Yugoslav National Army (*Jugoslovenska narodna armija* – JNA).

Yugoslav United Left (*Jugoslovenska udružena levica* – JUL)   Founded 25
March 1995. President: Ljubiša Ristić.

Zajedno (Together)   Informal coalition of SPO-DS-GSS formed after
9 March 1996. Formally constituted on 2 September 1996 and widened
to include DSS on 28 September 1996. Fell apart during spring of
1997.

1. Introduction

In the late 1980s and early 1990s the Communist governments which had dominated political life in Central and Eastern Europe since the end of the the Second World War were overthrown, collapsed or negotiated themselves out of power. All of them adhered to a one-party *totalitarian* form of governance defined as being a state which has 'eliminated almost all pre-existing political, economic, and social pluralism, has a unified articulating and guiding utopian ideology, has intensive and extensive mobilisation, and has a leadership that rules, often charismatically, with undefined limits and great unpredictability for elites and non-elites'.[1]

In the subsequent years these countries have set out to deconstruct the mechanisms and institutions of complete social and political control which had characterised the old order. In their place they have sought to build and consolidate durable *democratic* and *pluralist* structures. Democratic governments vary in form from country to country, but can be expected to share a number of common attributes.[2] In a democracy, governments will be chosen by the periodic and regular consultation of the populace through the electoral process. The elections will take place within a framework whereby the contending parties enjoy clear legal equality. A viable democratic government will inevitably involve the dominance of a governing majority party or coalition over the minority opposition. The opposition agrees to occupy this subordinate status, provided that its own legal rights of association and action are respected, and that it can be guaranteed to have the chance, after a period of time, to reverse this situation. This 'democratic bargain'[3] depends on the actors in the democratic system 'having sufficiently long time horizons to conceive of future victory'.[4] Within this structure of 'contingent consent' the conflict and competition for power between rival parties is mitigated and contained within an accepted legal and institutional framework.[5] While the majority party is allowed to occupy the seat of power and direct the policies

1

pursued by public institutions, the structures and identity of the ruling party must remain separate from that of the state.

A democratic and *pluralist polity*, however, amounts to more than simply a functioning parliamentary system and an active political culture. Such a political system must be underpinned by the dispersal of power through the social and the economic spheres. The realm of plural social forces which are 'voluntary, self-generating, [largely] self-supporting, autonomous from the state, and bound by a legal order, or set of shared rules' is commonly described as 'civil society'.[6] In a democracy 'civil society' performs a number of key functions. It acts as a restraint on power 'strong enough to counterbalance the state and, while not preventing the state fulfilling its role of keeper of the peace and arbitrator between major interests, can nevertheless prevent it from dominating and atomising the rest of society'.[7]In addition this multiplicity of associations and civic initiatives serves as a stimulus for individual political involvement, an arena for the development of democratic values, a recruiting ground for future political leaders, and a means by which those not involved in mainstream political parties can enter public life. The freedoms which give vitality to civic society are invoked on a daily basis in contrast to the periodically available electoral choices. In particular a media sector independent of state control is a critical factor in allowing individual citizens to make informed political and social choices.

The concentration of economic power also acts as an inhibiting influence on the development of a democratic society. A *democratic* system will therefore be underpinned by a *plurality* of ownership and economic life conducted within an established legal framework.

The routes taken by various countries of Central and Eastern Europe towards achieving a system of governance based on these criteria have varied in their speed and have frequently been characterised by confusion and contradictions. Nevertheless almost all of these countries have made significant progress towards the consolidation of post-communist democracy. Even countries such as Romania and Bulgaria, whose political life was until recently characterised by a high degree of continuity with the old *totalitarian* order, can now be considered to be making significant progress towards the consolidation of democratic practice.

In Serbia, however, the shift away from one-party *totalitarianism* to *pluralism* has not been realised. Political life has seen the adoption of some of the formal attributes of *democracy* without the stable institutional underpinning associated with that system. Elections are held, but under conditions and rules which are determined by the ruling party. This political dominance of the electoral system whereby contests are weighted in favour of the ruling party means that the 'democratic bargain' does not function properly. Opposition parties have no guarantee that they will have a fair and legally equal chance of contesting the dominance of the political scene by the ruling party, which has fused its institutions and power-structures with those of the state. Civil society has remained weak and under constant harrassment by the state/ruling elite. Economic power has continued to be concentrated in the hands of the state or else is held by members of the state connected oligarchy. The economy continues to function according to rules which are social and bureaucratic rather than economic or legal.

In some senses the system operating in Serbia corresponds to the definition of *authoritarianism* given by Juan Linz and Alfred Stepan: it is said to be a system 'with limited, not responsible political pluralism, without elaborate and guiding ideology but with distinctive mentalities, without extensive or intensive political mobilisation, except at some points in their development, and in which a leader or a small group exercises power within formally ill-defined limits, but actually quite predictable ones.'[8]

This definition, however, does not capture the personal and highly unpredictable nature of power in Serbia where the ruling party and its leader Slobodan Milošević might be classified as what Linz and Stepan, following Max Weber, describe as a *sultanist* regime where the 'public and private are fused, there is a strong tendency towards familial power and dynastic succession, there is no distinction between state career and personal service to the ruler, there is a lack of rationalised impersonal ideology. [...] economic success depends on personal relationship to the ruler, the ruler acts only according to his own unchecked discretion.'[9] However, their description of *sultanism* and the examples given of such regimes would seem to leave little room for the competing political parties, independent media and civil initiatives which, despite their evident weaknesses, have been a part of Serbia's political life in the post-communist period. Instead Serbia exists in a classificatory limbo where stunted *democratic* institutions mix uneasily with *authoritarian* structures and both of these elements are overshadowed by the *sultanist* influence of the leader of the ruling party, Slobodan Milošević.

In the late 1980s it was by no means obvious to external observers that Serbia would be a country left behind in Eastern Europe's movement towards democracy. Sabrina Ramet analysed the changing political situation in Eastern Europe and its prospects for democratic development on the basis of the presence or absence of five factors (availability of information via the media, an active intelligentsia, the ability of citizens to organise, the presense of an active civic society, and a politically aware public), and classified Yugoslavia during this period, along with Poland and Hungary, as a 'strong society' in contrast to Bulgaria, a 'weak' society. She observed that the 'Slovenian, Croatian, and *Serbian* publics are organised and articulate, and have developed independent communication networks that bypass and make use of official networks.'[10] If civil society was 'weak' in Bulgaria during the later phases of communism it was effectively non-existent in Romania.[11]

This work therefore seeks to explain why Serbia failed to make the political leap from *totalitarianism* to *pluralism*. It seeks to demonstrate that while the inability of democracy to put down firm roots can be attributed in part to weaknesses and fault-lines within Serbian society, the decisions of individuals and personalities have also played a critical role both in the failure to bring about, or in actively seeking to thwart, the processes of democratic consolidation. It follows that if contingent factors played a role in the failure of democratic development in Serbia during the 1990s then there was no cultural inevitability to the triumph of *authoritarianism*.[12] The repeated failures of the opposition during the 1990s to achieve a 'democratic breakthrough' does not therefore mean that under the right circumstances stable democratic structures cannot be achieved in Serbia.

The work examines the critical role played by nationalism in Serbian politics during the 1990s. However, nationalism was a catalyst for change in countries across Eastern Europe, and acted in these countries as a force unique in its capacity to energise the masses and unite them against the old regime: the populations were mobilised and homogenised by nationalism into a *pre-political* movement capable of overthrowing the institutions of totalitarianism. This movement combined a vast array of diverse and even conflicting interests, united only by their desire to oust the regime. Nationalism often provided the political glue to bind together such loosely-aligned interests. With their political aims realised, however, such coalitions would under normal circumstances fragment, and competition would begin between the rival factions. In this way the new age of *pluralist* politics began in East European countries. The work shows how Milošević and his supporters from within the regime apparatus were not only able to use nationalism to cling to power at the end of the 1980s, but would continue throughout the 1990s to use 'nationalist mobilisation' as a means by which Serbian society could be kept in a state of 'permanent revolution'. The fact that the Serbian people were faced by a series of 'threats' and 'crises' meant that an ideological vacuum developed in political life where, in the eyes of a section of the electorate, the government was not held responsible for its failings and political suitability was assessed on the basis of dedication to the national cause.

Paradoxically, however, while the language of Serbian political discourse during the period was heavily laden with national symbolism and fervent declarations of unity, Serbia's democratic development was also inhibited by a lack of unifying national values. The most obvious of these factors which served to prevent national integration was the country's division along ethnic lines. In the case of the Albanian population of Kosovo, these divisions resulted in their complete withdrawal from the political processes. Other national minorities, however, also occupied a marginal position outside of the mainstream of political life. A situation where such a large section of the population could not identify themselves with the prevalent constitutional order inevitably had a corrosive effect and, in a worst-case scenario, carried with it the potential for internal violence.

The ethnic Serbian population of the state were, however, also divided among themselves. In a stable political democracy divisions occur as a natural consequence of political life, and these divisions are mitigated and made tractable by being subsumed into a common political/national identity. In Serbia ideological divisions are not necessarily connected with the pursuit of different policies; rather it is a matter of their adherence to or connection with different political traditions or cultures.[13] These cultures may not only have a differing political content but also a radically different understanding of history and vision of the nation underpinned by familial and collective memory. In Serbia this cultural schism particularly relates to the Partisan/Četnik and Socialist/anti-communist divide. This cultural and political chasm in the body politic is manifest in the use by contending parties of different national symbols, anthems and insignia. In practical terms this existence of alternative national political visions, which draw on the unresolved memories of civil war, means that there is no readily accepted 'legitimacy' for the dominance of either side. In these circumstances the terms of the 'democratic bargain' are prone to be called into doubt, the restraints on the bounds of political action are fragile, and political rhetoric tends to stray into the language of revolution.

As well as ethnic and ideological divisions there are also social/developmental divisions within the Serbian body politic which belie the rhetorical emphasis on national unity and destiny. These divisions reflect regional loyalties, the split between metropolitan and provincial areas, the historic split between rural and urban populations and the more modern split between established urban populations and recent migrants from the countryside. The aim of this work is to show that all these divisions not only served to define the language of politics but can also be utilised and exploited by rival political forces to strengthen their own positions or undermine the power of their opponents. Such a manipulation of the existing fault-lines in a divided society acted as an 'alternative' to charting a course of political and economic reform.

The work examines the way in the weaknesses of post-communist Serbian political culture have meant that voters have generally been mobilised not by the presentation of policies but rather by the manipulation and invocation of symbols and myths. According to Zdzislaw Mach, 'Symbols are not just a kind of sign. They have special qualities; they are emotionally loaded and are connected with ideas which are the most fundamental for human thought and culture, and the most difficult to grasp and express.'[14] Myths have been described as 'a set of beliefs usually put forth as a narrative held by the community about itself...it is the content of the myth that is important not its accuracy as a historical account.'[15] The importance of symbols and myths in politics has long been recognised, with the anthropologist Clifford Geertz observing that 'a world which is wholly demystified is wholly depoliticised.'[16]

All political institutions, including nations, states and parties are dependent on symbols and myths in order to define themselves. In Western political societies, however, the power of myths and symbols is 'curtailed by the existence of communities of reflexive communication, the rational organisation of political structures, and the universality of legal arrangements.'[17] In Serbia and other countries in 'transition' public life is less stable and the political rules are less clear, and 'with no understanding of politics people look for the simplest (and most dangerous) explanations: conspiracies, love and hate.'[18] In these circumstances myth and symbol comes to be the dominant form of communication and expression in political discourse.

In Serbia during the 1990s the language of politics saw the use of different categories of symbols. The first of these consisted of *national* symbols/myths relating to beliefs held by the whole Serbian ethnic national community. These symbols and myths were by used by the rival political forces to rhetorically outbid each other as guardians of the national interest. Symbolic mobilisation also revolved around *historic/political* symbols which have particular cultural/historical associations along the lines of 'left/right' and 'communist'/anti-communist'. The third category of symbolic mobilisation relates to what can be described as *historic/developmental* symbols. In this latter category there are on the one hand those symbols and myths which form part of a *neo-traditional* world-view which stresses the role of past historical institutions as a source of legitmacy. This *neo-traditional* world-view can also be described as a *national romantic* way of thinking because it projects on to contemporary politics an idealised image of past political life. The alternative form of political language used places great emphasis on the *modernising* mission inherent in politics. With its specifically *rational* understanding of politics this too represents an idealised representation of political life.

While both of these languages are *idealised*, this work demonstrates that they both have a certain cultural resonance within Serbia without which they would lack all relevance to contemporary politics. These symbolic systems and languages relate to the cultural context of Serbia where a rapid process of *modernisation* has transformed society, leading to a breakdown of *traditional* concepts of social and economic relations. This *modernisation* and its incomplete nature gives relevance to the *rationalist* form of political language. Although society has ceased to be *traditional*, the memory of the way of life remains sufficiently strong to make the *national romantic* form of symbolic rhetoric relevant. In this way rural symbols and images persist in urban environments. In the words of Eugene Hammel, 'The maps in the minds of men are the last thing to go.'[19]

The *modernist/rationalist* and *neo-traditionalist/national* to some extent corresponds to the distinction made by Tönnies between *Gesellschaft* (an orientation towards cosmopolitanism and peaceful evolutionary progress) and *Gemeinschaft* (an orientation towards organic and ethnic national solidarity and the sacralisation of tradition).[20] The political situation in Serbia was more complex and diverse than this categorisation implies, involving a linking of nationalism and ethnocentrism with traditionalism and cosmopolitanism with progressive rationalist language. It will be seen, however, that it was quite possible for individuals and groups using a highly *rationalist* language to adopt political attitudes which are strongly nationalist. Alternatively individuals and groups which use *neo-traditionalist* language can at times be seen to place themselves in opposition to nationalist policies. This complexity in classification is a reflection of the complexity observable in a society undergoing processes of transition.

In a newly *pluralised* political system symbols and myth play a critical role in binding together new political parties with fragile institutional identities, creating wider constituencies among the electorate and appealing to the uncommitted public. The continued dominance of symbolism over politics beyond the initial period of transition, however, has negative consequences for democratic development. Symbols and myths are by their nature *mobilisatory* rather than oriented towards problem-solving. A political language which remains dominated by myths and symbols also displays a tendency towards perpetuating a form of *issueless* politics. As countries pass through the process of transition towards pluralism, symbolism will come to take a secondary position to issues of policy as the concerns of the electorate shift from matters of identity to those of material concern. Political parties who continue to speak in a symbolic language, perhaps in an attempt to appeal internally to *activists*, when the priorities of the electorate have moved on will find themselves suffering at the polls.[21] The continued prevalence of primarily symbolic politics in Serbia is symptomatic of the unresolved nature of its democratic transition.

The *issueless* nature of Serbian politics is a product not only of ideological weakness but also of the institutional weakness of the political parties. The personality of the leader is emphasised, and the political language used by the party is often linked to his image. The power-structures inside the party are also constructed around the central personality of the leader. The personalised tone of Serbian politics was set at the end of the 1980s by Slobodan Milošević, whose 'anti-bureaucratic revolution' was in many senses a *populist* crusade in which he sought to establish a link between himself and the population transcending normal institutional politics. Such a *populist* movement has been described as follows: 'apolitical in ideology, it sees politics as bound up in a single apocalyptic and restorative need, not as an ongoing fallible and restorative need.'[22] The 'happening of the people' which brought Milošević to power might also be seen as what Ken Jowitt describes as a 'movement of rage' originating 'among provincial elites: men and women filled with hate for the culture of the capital city. And at the same time angered by their exclusion from it'.[23] Such a definition captures the negative characteristics of the 'anti-bureaucratic revolution' on the part of Milošević and the elements of the old regime who set these processes in motion. However, it is worth bearing in mind that the motives of some of those involved, even in such apparently negative movements, can be mixed and in the context of the time some people may have mistakenly seen the 'happening of the people' as genuinely heralding the advent of progressive change.

Since that time Milošević as an individual has cast a long shadow over Serbian politics: even as he has led the Serbian people from disaster to disaster, he has not lost his *supra-political* status in the eyes of at least part of the Serbian electorate. The opposition forces have been forced to find their own charismatic *supra-political* figure in order to compete with his iconic status. This has on occasion placed the opposition in a contradictory position whereby in order to present a programme of political reform they have had to appeal to the electorate on the basis of *supra-political* leadership.[24]

As has been observed, myths, symbols and leaders are key structural elements in any political society, but in a functioning democracy their role is kept in proportion by the existence of state and party institutions and the demands of political debate.

It will be a sign that Serbia has progressed towards a genuine democracy when myths, symbols and leaders are no longer the gigantic forms and images dominating the political landscape which they have been in the past. The forces wanting to prevent such change being effected remain strong, and in the past those committed to change have frequently found their position weakened by internal and external factors.

Notes

1. Juan Linz and Alfred Stepan, *Problems of Democratic Transition and Consolidation – Southern Europe, South America, and Post-Communist Europe*, Johns Hopkins University Press (Baltimore, MD), 1996, p. 40.
2. For analysis of different forms of democratic government see Arend Lijphart, *Democracies*, Yale University Press (New Haven), 1984.
3. *After the Revolution – Authority in a Good Society*, Yale University Press (New Haven), 1970.
4. Mary Ellen Fisher, *Establishing Democracies*, Westview Press (Boulder, CO), 1996, p. 3.
5. Philipe C. Schmitter and Terry Lynn Karl, 'What Democracy is and is Not...' in Larry Diamond and Marc F. Plattner (eds), *The Global Resurgence of Democracy*, Johns Hopkins University Press (Baltimore), 1996, p. 56.
6. Larry Diamond, 'Toward Democratic Consolidation' in Diamond and Plattner (eds), op. cit., p. 228.
7. Ernest Gellner, *The Conditions of Liberty – Civil Society and its Rivals*, Penguin (London), 1994, p. 5.
8. Linz and Stepan (1996), p. 38.
9. Ibid., p. 52.
10. Sabrina P. Ramet, *Social Currents in Eastern Europe – The Sources and Meaning of the Great Transformation*, Duke University Press (Durham, NC), 1991, p. 266.
11. Dennis Deletant, *Ceaușescu and the Securitate – Coercion and Dissent in Romania, ·1965-1989*, Hurst (London), 1996, pp. 235-93.
12. The idea that 'cultural' or 'civilisational' factors make some countries unsuitable for democratic development has been popularised by Samuel P. Huntingdon in *The Clash of Civilizations – Remaking the World Order*, Simon and Schuster (New York and London), 1996.
13. This 'cultural' and 'traditional' division in politics is not peculiar to Serbia and its prevalence in Bulgaria in the mid-1990s is discussed in Ivan Krastev, 'Party Structure and Party Perspectives in Bulgaria', *Journal of Communist Studies and Transition Politics*, March 1997.
14. Zdzislaw Mach, *Symbols, Conflict and Identity* Suny (New York), 1993, p. 25.
15. George Schöpflin, 'The Functions of Myth and a Taxonomy of Myths' in

George Schöpflin and Geoffrey Hosking (eds) *Myths and Nationhood*, Hurst (London), 1997, pp. 19-20.

16. Quoted in David Kertzer, *Ritual, Politics and Power*, Yale University Press (New Haven), 1988, p. 48.

17. Vladimir Tismaneanu, *Fantasies of Salvation – Democracy, Nationalism and Myth in Post-Communist Europe,* Princeton University Press, 1998, p. 25.

18. Stevan K. Pavlowitch, 'Who is "Balkanising whom?" The Misunderstandings Between the Debris of Yugoslavia and the Unprepared West', *Daedelus,* spring 1994.

19. Eugene Hammel, 'Urbanisation and Modernisation in Yugoslavia: Adaptive and Maladaptive Aspects of Traditional Culture' in Michael Kenny and David Kertzer (eds), *Urban Life in Mediterranean Europe*, University of Illinois Press (Urbana), 1983, p. 210.

20. F. Tönnies, *Community and Association*, (London), 1955.

21. Andras Körosényi in his analysis of the 1994 elections in Hungary attributes the failure of the centre-right political parties to an over emphasis on symbolic messages stating 'Matters of ideology and symbols are undoubtedly helpful for new parties without traditions in consolidating their identities and camps of political followers. But politics overtly grounded in ideology and values is ultimately better suited to retaining activists, and consolidating its own voters than to winning votes in large numbers.' In 'The Reasons for the Defeat of the Right in Hungary', *East European Politics and Societies*, winter 1995, p. 189.

22. Donald Macrae, 'Populism as an Ideology' in Ghita Ionescu and Ernest Gellner (eds), *Populism – Its Meaning and Characteristics*, Weidenfeld & Nicolson (London), 1969, p. 157.

23. *The New World Disorder – The Leninist Extinction*, University of California Press (Berkeley), 1992, p. 275.

24. Dragoslav Avramović was adopted as 'leader' by the opposition *Zajedno* coalition in September 1996 on account of his *supra-political* status as an icon for the populace and an economic 'miracle worker'. During his brief time at the head of the *Zajedno* list his message was 'rational' and centred on 'material' issues.

2. Serbia and the Past

The Serbs migrated to the Balkan peninsula in the early decades of the seventh century.[1] By the late eleventh century a number of Serbian kingdoms had been established of which Raška, in what is now the modern south Serbian region of the Sandžak, was pre-eminent. In 1167 Stefan Nemanja established himself as the ruler of Raška which he reigned over until his abdication in 1196. Nemanja's son, Sava (Rastko), created in 1219 the structures of the independent Serbian Orthodox church.[2] He was venerated by later generations as patron saint and culture-hero of the Serbian people. The Serbian kingdom reached its apogee under Stefan Dušan 'the Mighty' (1331-55) who extended his rule southwards taking territories from the Byzantines in Greece, Macedonia and Albania.[3]

The overlordship which Stefan Dušan had constructed flourished only briefly. Under his successors the Serbian lands were racked by internal dissension and came under increasing external pressure from the expanding power of the Ottoman Turks. On St Vitus's Day (*Vidovdan*), 28 June 1389, the most powerful of the Serbian princes, Lazar Hrebeljanović, and his allies, was defeated by an invading Ottoman army led by Sultan Murat on the Field of Blackbirds, Kosovo Polje.

While the exact result of the battle of Kosovo has been a matter of some historical controversy, and Serbia persisted as an Ottoman vassal principality until 1459, in Serbian historical memory the events on the plain of Kosovo came to mark a symbolic turning-point between independence and national servitude.[4] The medieval Serbian kingdom, however, was gone but not forgotten. In the Serbian Orthodox church, which was the sole organised representative of the Serbian people under the Ottoman *millet* system of rule, 'the memory of the medieval kingdom was worked into church ritual' and 'out of this emerged an amalgam which has been called the "Serbian faith" [*Srpska vera*]'.[5] This Serbian faith was also articulated through the symbols and ceremonies of enduring family rituals or *Slavas.*

Of perhaps even greater influence was the way in which the events of the battle of Kosovo were incorporated into, and elaborated in, a body of oral folk poetry which developed amongst the Serbian communities within the Ottoman empire. In these poems historical personages were transformed into mythic archetypes of virtue and villainy. The Serbian leader, Lazar, became the embodiment of saintly self-sacrifice. According to legend, on the eve of the battle of Kosovo, Lazar had been offered the choice between 'earthly' victory in battle against the Ottomans, or to suffer defeat and death thereby securing spiritual victory and the 'heavenly kingdom'. By choosing the latter course he sacrificed himself so that his people could attain future redemption. The poems also celebrated the exemplary heroism of Miloš Obilić. Before the battle Obilić had been accused of treason, and during the next day's fighting he had sought to redeem his own personal honour and avenge the defeat of the Serbian army by infiltrating the Ottoman camp and killing Sultan Murat before being slain himself. In Serbian folk tradition he was remembered as the epitome of warlike valour and a 'ruler over the shadows of heroes in the abode of dead heroes'.[6] While Obilić's conduct was celebrated that of Vuk Branković was deplored. Branković, a Serbian noble and Lazar's son-in-law, had betrayed his leader and his people by refusing during the battle of Kosovo to commit his fighters to the struggle. Vuk Branković would remain an enduring symbol of the dangers posed to the Serbian people by internal strife and disunity.[7]

These legends were formed in a time of migration and demographic change for the Serbian population. The Ottoman conquest sparked mass movements out of the old Serbian heartlands westwards into the mountains of Bosnia, Hercegovina and Montenegro. Movements also took place northwards into the lands of the Hungarian crown with Serbs settling in Croatia, Slavonia, Dalmatia and Southern Hungary (modern Vojvodina), where from 1553 until its dissolution in 1881 they were organised by the Habsburg authorities as part of a defensive military frontier (*Vojna Krajina*). When in 1690 the Serbian Patriarch, Arsenije III, led a mass trek of 30,000 Serbian families into Habsburg territory, an event remembered in Serbian history as the 'Great Migration', this was the culmination of an enduring process of folk movement. In Kosovo the departure of Serbs was followed by large scale Albanian immigration, encouraged by the Turkish authorities, resulting in the region gaining an Albanian majority by the eighteenth century.[8] After 1459 the flight from the central Serbian region of the Šumadija was so extensive that the area was considered to be depopulated. The name Šumadija itself was derived from the word for 'woodland', and in the early eighteenth century Lady Mary Wortley Montagu, an English traveller on her way to Constantinople, spoke of how she 'crossed the deserts of Servia almost quite overgrown by woods'.[9]

By the late eighteenth century, however, this process began to be reversed as the Šumadija received a new wave of settlers from the Dinaric mountains to the west. This population movement contained within it the seeds of the foundation of the modern Serbian state as many of these settlers were to play a key role in the Serbian uprisings against Ottoman rule. Chief among these figures was Karadjordje Petrović (Black George) a wealthy livestock farmer with military experience gained both in the Austrian army and as a rebel against Ottoman authority (*haiduk*), who raised the standard of revolt in 1804. The uprising began as an armed protest against the lawless nature of the Ottoman empire, but soon developed into a full scale bid for independence before being finally crushed by the Ottoman armies in 1813. The mantle of Serbian leadership then passed to the militarily less heroic but politically more astute figure of Miloš Obrenović. Obrenović initiated the Second Serbian Uprising in 1815 and was swiftly able to achieve a limited degree of self-government for a Serbian territory centred on the Ottoman *pashalik* of Belgrade. Miloš Obrenović demonstrated his readiness to protect his gains from Serbian rivals when, on his orders, Karadjordje was murdered. The ensuing feud between the Karadjordjević and Obrenović dynasties was a recurring theme in nineteenth century Serbian politics. Serbia's position as an autonomous principality, within the Ottoman empire, was confirmed in 1830.

From its initial boundaries Serbia gradually expanded, through a mixture of diplomatic guile and military exertion, southwards. In 1833 six districts were added to the Serbian territory by agreement with the Sultan, and in 1878, as a result of Serbia's participation with the Russians in the war against the Turks, a new swathe of land centred on the city of Niš and the towns of Leskovac and Vranje was gained under the terms of the Treaty of Berlin.

Serbia was also recognised under the Treaty of Berlin as an independent state, and in 1882 as a kingdom. In 1912-13 Serbia fought two Balkan Wars. The first pitted an alliance of Balkan national states, consisting of Serbia, Bulgaria, Greece and Montenegro against the forces of the Ottoman empire. In the second the victorious national states contended over the spoils of war when Bulgaria fought unsuccessfully against Serbia, Greece and Montenegro with additional interventions by the Romanians and the Ottomans. As a result of these wars Serbia almost doubled in size, gaining territory which included part of the Sandžak, Kosovo and a large proportion of Macedonia.

The territorial enlargement of the Serbian state was paralleled by a similar process of internal consolidation and modernisation. This programme of modernisation was in part state directed, but a key role was also played by the small, but growing, Serbian intelligentsia. In the early stages of the new state's development this educated class was largely made up of Serbs from Vojvodina. As the century progressed, however, a new formally educated strata of people was formed of Serbs who had studied in Western centres such as Paris or, as in the case of the future Serbian statesman Nikola Pašić, Zurich.

In line with this modernisation the size of the new state's capital, Belgrade, grew steadily with a population of 54,000 recorded in 1890 rising to 77,000 in 1905. Alongside this increase in population Belgrade also saw the gradual transformation in its appearance and urban infrastructure. In 1882 the monumental equestrian statue of prince Mihailo Obrenović designed by the Italian sculptor Enrico Pazzi, which stands in what is now the Republic Square, was unveiled. The old Turkish fortress of the Kalemegdan was re-styled as a park. In 1911 the first major modern boulevard in central Belgrade, the Terazije was opened. In 1882 electric lighting was installed in the capital and the first telephone system a year later. Such structural improvements were accompanied by the development of a thriving cultural and intellectual life.[10]

Measures were also taken to raise the level of education within Serbia, and by the end of the nineteenth century a national network of elementary schools had begun to take shape. In 1905 the Velika škola (High School) was renamed as Belgrade University; it had been founded in 1808 as an institution which provided basic education to students in the new insurgent Serbian state. The beginnings of a modern communications system in Serbia was marked in 1884 by the completion of the first railway line from Belgrade to Niš. When in 1888 this route was connected to the Bulgarian and Turkish railways it provided a vital economic connection for Serbia to central Europe, to the north, and the Middle East, to the south. During this period agricultural production also expanded with the Šumadija losing most of its woodland to the demands of arable farming. By the end of the century Serbia's small industrial sector was also showing signs of growth.[11]

Party politics also made its appearance in Serbian national life at this time. The first political faction or parliamentary grouping in Serbia came into being with the foundation of the 'constitutionalists' after 1838, but the activities of this loosely organised group, and other such political formations, remained largely the domain of the urban elite. In 1881 with the organisation of the National Radical Party, led by a group of young intellectuals, the first attempt was made to build a national political network which extended its activities to the peasantry in the villages. By the end of the nineteenth century a system of competing political parties had developed in Serbia in spite of resistance from the monarchy by whom popular political organisation was frequently regarded as a threat to its personal authority.[12]

Despite these efforts at modernisation and 'nation-building' Serbia remained an overwhelmingly agrarian country where local and regional ties could be more important in determining loyalties than the demands of national politics. The increasing 'Westernisation' of urban areas if anything served to heighten the traditional antagonisms between town and country.

This period of state formation cultivated the idea that the Serbs within Serbia formed one national community with those outside Serbia in the Vojvodina, Slavonia, Dalmatia, Croatia and Ottoman Bosnia-Hercegovina. Alongside such ideas, however, there developed a conscious sense of difference between those Serbs within Serbia (*Srbijanci*) and those outside of Serbia. Those Serbs from the Habsburg territories, and particularily Vojvodina, were described as *prečani* Serbs, a term which referred to the fact that they came from beyond the rivers Una, Sava, and Danube.

While Serbia had achieved gradual territorial expansion, at the expense of the ailing Ottoman empire, during the nineteenth century some political thinkers dreamed of more ambitious schemes whereby Serbia, as the 'Piedmont of the Balkans', would unite all the South Slav peoples in one state. One of the earliest political formulations of this idea was the *Načertanije* (Outline) drawn up in 1844 by Ilija Garašanin, who was at that time the Serbian Interior Minister (1843-52) and later First Minister and Foreign Minister (1852-3, 1861-7), but which remained unpublished until 1906. Under the pro-Austrian Obrenović dynasty such plans remained in the realms of political theory. In 1903, however, the unpopular monarch Aleksandar Obrenović and his wife Draga Mašin were assassinated by a group of disgruntled army officers led by Dragutin Dimitrijević who was also known as Apis. Petar Karadjordjević, at that time living in exile in Geneva, was invited to take his place:[13] he was a man of liberal political inclinations who counted among his achievements having fought under an assumed name as a volunteer in Bosnia during the revolt of 1875-8 and translating John Stuart Mill's work *On Liberty* into Serbian. Despite having come to power following a political murder, Petar achieved a working understanding with the veteran Radical politician, Nikola Pašić, and instituted a constitutional monarchy in Serbia. In Serbian popular historical memory the period from 1903-14 was remembered as a 'golden age' of parliamentary development.[14]

The rulers of the Austro-Hungarian empire, however, saw the liberalism of Petar I as dangerously attractive to the South Slav populations within the bounds of the empire, particularily those in Bosnia-Hercegovina and Croatia. The Treaty of Berlin in 1878 had placed Bosnia-Hercegovina under the control of Austria-Hungary although it remained formally a part of the Ottoman empire. The aim of Serbian political circles to act as a regional force was seen to clash with Austria-Hungary's need to exert its increasingly fragile European power status in the Balkans.[15] From 1903 to 1914 a number of events, including the Austro-Hungarian trade blockade of 1906-11, known as the 'Pig War', and the Habsburg annexation of Bosnia-Hercegovina in 1908, emphasised the growing hostility between Serbia and Austria-Hungary. The Serbian victories in the Balkan Wars were considered by Austria-Hungary to be a particularily ominous development which strengthened the hand of those within the Habsburg government who urged a 'preventive war' against Serbia. When on Saint Vitus's day, 28 June 1914, the young Bosnian student Gavrilo Princip assassinated

Archduke Franz Ferdinand while he was on an official visit to
Sarajevo, plunging Serbia and Austria-Hungary – and ultimately
the rest of Europe – into war, Princip was merely acting as a
catalyst for the long-mounting tensions between the two powers.[16]

The disintegration of the Habsburg empire at the end of the
First World War led to the union of its South Slav territories
with the kingdom of Serbia to form the kingdom of Serbs, Croats
and Slovenes. Yugoslav ideas, favouring South Slav unity had a
long predigree among the intellectual classes, but they had not
penetrated the thinking of the political establishment of these
territories which showed insufficient understanding of the demands
posed by the new circumstances. Serbia had emerged victorious
from the ordeal of the First World War, but a terrible price had
been paid for that victory. Losses had been suffered during the
war equivalent to 40 per cent of its military strength and 20 per
cent of the country's total population – proportionaly a greater
level of mortality than any other participant in the war.[17] These
sacrifices appear to have stiffened the Serbs' resolve not to abandon
their traditional forms of government. As a result the constitution
which came into effect on 28 June 1921 largely reflected established
Serbian political practice. Equally Stjepan Radić, the leader of
the main Croatian party, the Croatian Peasants Party (HSS), adopted
an attitude of ingrained opposition to, and confrontation with,
the new political framework in which he found himself operating.

The Serbian political landscape in the new kingdom was dominated
by the old Radical Party, which continued to be led by Nikola
Pašić until his death in 1926, and the Democratic Party. The
Democratic Party was formed in Sarajevo in February 1919 with
the merger of the Independent Radicals, who had split from the
Radical Party in 1901, led by Ljubomir Davidović, the *prečani*
Serb followers of Svetozar Pribićević, and several smaller Slovene
and Croat groupings. In March 1924 the Pribićević faction of
the Democrats broke away to form the Independent Democratic
Party. Davidović continued to lead the Democratic Party until
his death in 1940. His place was taken by the well-known Belgrade
theatre critic Milan Grol. In August 1920 the Agrarian Party was
formed led by Jovan Jovanović, a prominent former diplomat.
The party sought to appeal to the large Serbian peasant constituency,
but – unlike its counterparts in inter-war Bulgaria and Romania
– failed to secure significant political support within Serbia itself.

It did, however, attract pockets of support amongst the Serbs of Bosnia.[18] This inability to mobilise the peasantry appears to have been largely due to the continuing hold exerted by the Radical Party over the political loyalties of rural Serbia. The Communist Party polled well in Belgrade and other urban centres, during the local elections of 1920, but its banning in August 1921, following the terrorist murder of the Interior Minister, Milorad Drašković, effectively marginalised it as a political force. Despite being driven underground the Communist Party continued to attract recruits from amongst the young urban intelligentsia.

Notwithstanding the turbulence on the political scene inter-war Belgrade flourished as the capital of the new multi-national state. Between 1920 and 1929 the population of Belgrade rose from 112,000 to 226,000. The cultural life of Belgrade grew increasingly cosmopolitan and sophisticated, with strong connections to other Yugoslav and European centres. It was during this period that the newspaper *Politika*, which had first been published in 1904, established itself as Serbia's leading, independent daily.[19]

On 20 June 1928 the political and ethnic stalemate in Yugoslavia culminated violently when Stjepan Radić was shot and mortally wounded by Puniša Račić, a deputy from Montenegro, on the floor of the parliament. On 6 January 1929 King Aleksandar responded to this new crisis by installing a royal dictatorship. Aleksandar sought to rule the kingdom directly overturning the Vidovdan constitution and suspending the parliament. In an attempt to instill a Yugoslav identity an administrative reorganisation was undertaken dividing the kingdom into ten administrative districts or *banovinas*. On 3 September 1931 a new constitution was brought in which while formally restoring parliamentary life left political power effectively in the hands of the King and the royal administration. Croatian extremists known as the Ustaše (rebels), led by Ante Pavelić and with an ideology which was an amalgam of Croatian ultra-nationalism and European fascism, initiated a campaign of terrorism against the new regime. On 9 October 1934 they succeeded in assassinating King Aleksandar during a visit to Marseilles. The royal dictatorship, however, continued under Regent Pavle who governed in the place of Aleksandar's young son, Petar II.

In Serbia the effect of the royal dictatorship was to stultify political life and weaken party structures. After 1929 power was held first by a military clique around Aleksandar and then by a succession of 'state parties' starting with the cumbersomely named Radical Peasant Democratic Party (1932), and succeeded by the Yugoslav National Party (1933), and the Yugoslav Radical Union (1934). Attempts at forging a United Opposition coalition across ethnic boundaries foundered when in 1939 when Vladko Maček, Radić's successor as the leader of the HSS, came to an agreement or *sporazum* with the government whereby the prevailing constitutional arrangements were accepted in exchange for an autonomous Croatian *banovina*. On 27 March 1941 a group of officers, angered by the government's agreement to a pact with the Axis powers, overthrew the government. This coup was followed by mass displays of support as people came out onto the streets of Belgrade, other cities across Serbia, and places such as Split, outside of Serbia, in a spontaneous outburst of 'people power' Significantly the demonstrators chanted slogans calling for the democratisation of political life as well as condemning the pact with Nazi Germany.[20]

It was inevitable that, given the inbalance of forces involved, the Yugoslav armies would fail to halt the massive Axis assault which began on 6 April 1941 with the aerial bombardment of Belgrade. The victorious German forces, who regarded the Serbs as their principle opponents in Yugoslavia, proceeded to dismember the Serbian territory. The majority of Macedonia and some of southern Serbia fell under the control of the Bulgarians, Kosovo was annexed to Albania, parts of Vojvodina were assigned to Hungary and sections of the Banat (northern Serbia) were administered by the local German population (*Volksdeutsche*). The rest of Serbia fell under direct German military control aided by a puppet administration with limited powers, headed by General Milan Nedić. The Nazi occupation also hoisted Dimitrije Ljotić, and his Yugoslav National Movement, also known as the Zbor or 'Rally', to prominence. In the inter-war movement Ljotić's fascist movement, which had been founded in 1935 with the aim of achieving 'ethical restoration' and building a corporate state opposed to capitalism and communism, had been a marginal political force enjoying negligible electoral support. Under Nazi tutelage, however, Ljotić's Serbian Volunteer Corps, the military wing of Zbor acted as the most loyal auxillaries of the occupation.[21]

The chaotic conditions of the invasion and the destruction of legitimate central authority saw the devolution of power in the countryside onto local political and military units. The Četnik organisation led by Draža Mihailović, which was also known as the Yugoslav Home Army, and other royal officers who had refused to surrender, sought to weld these diverse elements into a single military force. The structure of the Četnik organisation in Serbia, however, remained decentralised throughout its existence resembling a 'territorial militia',[22] and Mihailović was able to exert even less control over the Serbian Četnik groups which had sprung up in Bosnia and Croatia in response to the campaign of mass terror being waged against the Serbian population in the newly-founded Independent State of Croatia (NDH) which was ruled by Pavelić's Ustaše.[23] Matteo Milazzo characterised the Četniks as 'local defence units, marauding bands of Serb villagers, anti-partisan auxiliaries, forcibly mobilised peasants, and armed refugees which a small group of uncaptured Yugoslav officers was attempting, without success, to mold into an organised fighting force.'[24]

Attempts were made by some of Mihailović's political advisers to give the organisation a radical flavour through the development of a political wing known as the Ravna Gora Movement after Mihailović's headquarters in the Šumadija. Mihailović's Četniks, however, remained essentially conservative being devoted to the monarchy and the pre-war social/political order, and steeped in the ideology and traditions of Serbian nationalism.[25] Strategically Mihailović was consistently pro-Allied and prepared his movement to aid any Western intervention in the region, but in the short term favoured a policy of relative passivity in order to avoid unnecessary civilian suffering and even limited tactical co-operation with the Axis forces in order to aid him in his struggle with the Communists whom he regarded, apart from the occupying Axis powers, as the major threat to Yugoslavia's future.[26] The Communist Partisans under Tito, the *nom de guerre* of Josip Broz, achieved organisational superiority over their Četnik rivals through their ability to deploy a degree of battlefield mobility and the fact that their activities were directed by a disciplined and ruthless ideology. Although the inter-war Communist Party had largely drawn its members from urban areas the recruits for Tito's Partisan army, which in the first years of the war was also a largely Serbian organisation, came mainly from amongst the poorest peasant high-landers from Bosnia and Croatia. Such people did not form part of a natural Communist constituency, but the conditions of war and the depredations of the Ustaše transformed them into willing recruits for Tito's Marxist guerillas.[27] For many of such fighters Tito, or *Stari* ('the old man') came to embody the archetypal patriarchal leadership figure of tradition. When Tito's army entered Belgrade in October 1944 the appearance and behaviour of these 'mountain men' was in stark contrast to the capital's traditions. The Communists moved swiftly to suppress opposition to their rule. Mihailović was captured, tried, and executed in July 1946. In the period 1945-7 many other lesser-known victims also went to their deaths. Tito sought to confirm his political dominance through early elections held on 11 November 1945. The Democratic, Radical and Agrarian parties formed a United Opposition electoral alliance in order to contest the elections against the Communist-dominated National Front. A campaign of intimidation, however, caused the United Opposition to withdraw from the elections. The Communist programme of repression was supervised by Aleksandar Ranković, Tito's wartime comrade and head of the secret police, OZNa, renamed as UDBa in March 1946. Milan Grol sought to maintain the Democratic Party journal, *Demokratija*, as an independent voice critical of the new regime, but his position was made increasingly difficult by the campaign of administrative harrassment and physical violence directed at him and his supporters by the authorities. Shortly afterwards opposition to the regime was finally curtailed with the imprisonment of the opposition leaders and the confiscation of party property.

The Communists sought not only to control the exercise of power in the present, but also to monopolise the interpretation of history. In this way the 'public' vision of the past, taught and cultivated by the authorities, portrayed the Second World War as a struggle of the whole people unified under the Partisan banner against the alien occupier. Those people who had opposed communism were stigmatised as 'reactionaries' or 'collaborators'. The authorities reinforced the Partisan myth through the ubiquitous monuments to the Partisans which dominated 'public space', and the political rituals associated with the public holidays celebrating Partisan anniversaries. The 'private' history held by individuals and families in Serbia, however, preserved the memory of a different and more complex reality.

Notes

1. For discussion of the original homeland from which the Serbs migrated and the controversies regarding their ethnic origins see John V.A. Fine, *The Early Medieval Balkans*, University of Michigan Press (Ann Arbor), 1983, pp. 49-59.
2. John V.A. Fine, *The Late Medieval Balkans*, University of Michigan Press (Ann Arbor), 1987, pp. 38-42.
3. George Christos Soulis, *The Serbs and Byzantium During the Reign of Tsar Stephen Dušan (1331-1355) and his Successors*, Dumbarton Oaks (Washington, DC), 1984.
4. The evidence regarding the battle of Kosovo is reviewed in Thomas A. Emmert, *The Serbian Golgotha – Kosovo 1389*, Columbia University Press (New York), 1990.
5. Michael B Petrovich, 'The Role of the Serbian Orthodox Church in the First Serbian Uprising 1804-1813' in Wayne S. Vucinich (ed.), *The First Serbian Uprising 1804-1813*, Brooklyn University Press (New York), 1982, p. 264.
6. Translations of the Kosovo poems are given in Anne Pennington and Peter Levi, *Marko the Prince – Serbo-Croat Heroic Songs*, Duckworth (London), 1984. The development of the epic tradition is discussed in Svetozar Koljević, *The Epic in the Making*, Clarendon Press (Oxford), 1980.
7. Jovan Brkić, *Moral Concepts in Traditional Serbian Epic Poetry*, Mouton (The Hague), 1961, p. 159.
8. Barbara Jelavich, *History of the Balkans – Eighteenth and Nineteenth Centuries*, Cambridge University Press, 1983, p. 93.
9. Lady Mary Wortley Montagu writing in 1717: Lord Wharncliffe (ed.), *The Letters and Works of Lady Mary Wortley Montagu*, Bickers (London) 1861, vol. 1, p. 282.
10. John R. Lampe, 'Modernisation and Social Structure – The Case of Pre-1914 Balkan Capitals', *South-Eastern Europe,* 5, 2 (1978), pp. 11-32.
11. Michael B. Petrovich, *A History of Modern Serbia 1804-1918*, Harcourt Brace Jovanovich (New York), 1976, pp. 510-32.
12. Gale Stokes, *Politics as Development – The Emergence of Political Parties in Nineteenth Century Serbia*, Duke University Press (Durham, NC), 1990.
13. Petrovich (1976), p. 540
14. Željan E. Šuster, 'Development of Political Democracy and Political Party Pluralism in Serbia 1903-1914', *East European Quarterly*, XXXI, 4 (Jan. 1998), pp. 435-47.
15. Alan Sked, *The Decline and Fall of the Habsburg Empire 1815-1918*, Longman (London), 1989, pp. 252-69.
16. Vladimir Dedijer, *The Road to Sarajevo*, Macgibbon and Kee (London), 1967.
17. Jozo Tomasevich, *Peasants, Politics, and Economic Change in Yugoslavia*, Stanford University Press, 1955, p. 55.
18. Ivan Avakumović, 'The Serb Peasant Party 1919-1945' in Ivan Volgoyes (ed.), *The Peasantry of Eastern Europe – Roots of Rural Transformation*, Pergamon Press (Oxford), 1979, pp. 57-69.

19. John R. Lampe, *Yugoslavia as History*, Cambridge University Press, 1996, pp. 142-5.
20. Aleksa Djilas, *The Contested Country – Yugoslav Unity and the Communist Revolution 1919-1935*, Harvard University Press (Cambridge, MA), 1991, p. 137.
21. Miloš Martić, 'Dimitrije Ljotić and the Yugoslav National Movement *Zbor* 1935-1945', *East European Quarterly;* 14, 2 (1980), pp. 219-39.
22. Lucien Karchmar, *Draža Mihailović and the Rise of the Četnik Movement 1941-1942*, Garlan Press (New York), 1987; and Jozo Tomasevich, *The Chetniks –War and Revolution in Yugoslavia 1941-1945*, Stanford University Press.
23. On the Uštase see Marcus Tanner, *Croatia – A Nation Forged in War*, Yale University Press (New Haven), 1997, pp. 141-67, and Djilas (1991), p. 103-27.
24. Matteo J. Milazzo, *The Četnik Movement and the Yugoslav Resistance*, Johns Hopkins University Press (Baltimore), 1975, p. 186.
25. Kosta Nikolić and Milan Vesović, *Ujedinjene srpske zemlje – Ravnogorski nacionalni program*, Vreme knjige (Belgrade), 1996
26. Walter W. Roberts, *Tito, Mihailović, and the Allies 1941-1945*, Duke University Press (Durham NC), 1987.
27. In his account of the Second World War Milovan Djilas describes how his Partisans entered a village where 'The local communists told us with malicious joy how the Ustashi had killed off the bourgeosie in the towns – priests, merchants, political party leaders – so that they were left with the people pure and simple.' Milovan Djilas, *Wartime*, Secker and Warburg (London), 1977, p. 205.

3. The Economy and Society of Serbia under Communism

The period after the Second World War saw massive economic and social changes in Serbia, and the rest of Yugoslavia. Having installed themselves in power, the Communists set in motion a programme of centrally-directed industrialisation. This phase of intensive industrial development, in the period 1950-80, was facilitated by the substantial inflow of resources from abroad in the form of foreign aid, war reparations and remittances from Yugoslav workers living abroad. From 1952 responsibility for economic policy moved increasingly away from the federal government and towards the republics and provinces, although the federal authorities remained responsible for investment in underdeveloped areas.

Alongside this devolution came the development of a system of workers 'self-management', which aimed to abolish the social divisions in the workplace through a framework of socialist democracy based on 'social ownership', as opposed to private or state ownership. These experiments in 'self-management' and 'social ownership', however, succeeded in massively bureaucratising, rather than democratising, the economic processes. Up until 1976 the form of 'self-management' was constantly being revised, but there was never any effective challenge to its basic characteristic, the domination of the political oligarchy over economic life. The lack of clear ownership criteria also meant that rational decision making was difficult and economic choices were frequently distorted. In the absence of economic criteria industries were frequently located in the areas considered to be most prestigous by the republican or local elite. These 'political factories,' most often from the heavy industry sector, showed all the worst symptoms of structural stagnation, poor management and inefficient utilisation of resources.[1] One of the best examples of this can be seen in the Smederevo steel plant on the Danube. Construction of the plant had begun in 1963, but by 1986 it had still not been completed. When it did, finally, begin production in 1987 it employed only 11,000 workers, of which 3,000-4,000 were deemed to be 'underemployed', rather than the 14,700 workers which had been projected. Despite losing more than 55 billion dinars in the first part of 1987 the completion of this project remained a key objective of the Serbian authorities.[2] It was symptomatic of the nature of the communist economic system, where managerial 'success' was measured by the ability to command subsidy and patronage rather than in terms of productivity, that political-economic control over this particularily gross example of failed development would be a source of political and social prestige.

During the 1980s the structural weaknesses of the Yugoslav economy were becoming increasingly evident. With the inflow of unilateral foreign resources having dried up the Yugoslav foreign debt had spiralled, standing by 1988 at $23 billion. At this time unemployment stood at 17 per cent with a further 20 per cent being classed as 'underemployed'. One-third of all Yugoslav industry was considered to be operating at between 40-50 per cent under capacity.[3] Parallel with this phase of post-war industrialisation there was an equally dramatic period of urban expansion. In 1953 the urban population in Serbia stood at 1,567,920 or 22.5 per cent of the population. By 1991 this had risen to 4,963,189 or 50.7 per cent of the population.[4] The primary recipient of these migrants to the town from the countryside was Belgrade. The population of Belgrade rose from 657,362 in 1961 to 1,168,454 in 1991. Many of these new arrivals settled in the post-war development of New Belgrade across the river Sava from the old city. The movement of such a large group of people over a limited period of time meant that many remained only partially assimilated in urban life. Such individuals have been collectively termed the 'peasant urbanites'.[5] It has been estimated that 50-60 per cent of those involved in non-agrarian occupations in Serbia have a rural origin. Within Belgrade the residential suburb of Dedinje was noted for being the home of the political, diplomatic and business elite. The Serbian capital not only received migrants from the rural interior, but also from Serb populated areas of Bosnia-Hercegovina and Croatia. Prior to the war of 1992-5 some 300,000 Serbian citizens had been born in Bosnia. During this same period other provincial Serbian towns also saw increases, albeit on a lesser scale, in their population.

While rural dwellers were arriving *en masse* in the towns urban ideas and attitudes were also arriving in the villages of the Serbian interior. The post-war period has been described as one characterised by the 'simultaneous urbanisation of the village and the peasantisation of the town'.[6] A new class of 'peasant-workers' came into being of villagers who worked in industry but continued to live in the countryside and remained enmeshed in a rural 'system of social relationships'.[7] The loss of population to the towns, however, left many rural villages facing problems of poverty and depopulation. The economic downturn of the 1980s served only to heighten the problems faced by rural society.

Serbia contained within its borders some of the most and some of the least developed areas of Yugoslavia. The federally-directed policies of development were intended to encourage greater economic equality between the regions. The poorly-formulated policies of investment and development, with their concentration on heavy industry, however, meant that the economic gap between the underdeveloped south and the relatively well developed north of Serbia increased significantly during this period. As a result Serbia under communism continued to be characterised by a series of regions with sharply differing economic, social and ethnic identities. The region of the highest development was the greater Belgrade area, the largest manufacturing centre in Yugoslavia, which was notable for its substantial consumer goods and food processing sector. Also at a high level of commercial development was Serbia's northern province of Vojvodina where there was a significant light manufacturing concentration, and exploitable reserves of oil. Alongside this relatively successful industrial base Vojvodina also attained a high level of urbanisation with, in 1991, 1,121,594 or 55.7 per cent of the population living in towns. The main urban centres in Vojvodina are the province's capital, Novi Sad, with a population of 180,000, Subotica on the Hungarian border, with 100,000, and the town of Pančevo to the north of Belgrade with a population of 73,000. Occupying a portion of the fertile Pannonian plain Vojvodina provided prime land for arable agriculture, and achieved renown as the 'breadbasket' of Yugoslavia specialising in corn, oats and wheat.

Vojvodina was also distinguished by its highly diverse ethnic profile. In 1991 Serbs made up 57.2 per cent of the population of Vojvodina and 63.2 per cent of the province's settlements had

Serbian majorities. Novi Sad has a large Serbian majority. Hungarians, concentrated in the north of the region, made up 16.9 per cent of the population comprising a majority in 17.2 per cent of settlements. The town of Subotica was the main Hungarian populated urban centre. Small but significant proportions of the population were also made up by Croats (3.7 per cent), Slovaks (3.2 per cent), Montenegrins (2.2 per cent), Romanians (1.9 per cent). Other nationalities, including Macedonians and Ruthenians/ Ukranians, made up some 14 per cent of the population. Over half of this 'others' category was comprised of people describing themselves as Yugoslavs – a fact, partly, accounted for by the large number of mixed marriages (15.9 per cent) recorded in Vojvodina. During the existence of Yugoslavia the ethnic composition of Vojvodina's population has been subject to considerable change. In the aftermath of the Second World War the Vojvodina Germans, who had made up over 20 per cent of the region's population, fled or were expelled.[8] The region also gained a progressively more Serbian character with the inflow of migrants, particularly after the First and Second World Wars, from economically less developed areas such as Hercegovina and Montenegro. Amongst the Serbian population of Vojvodina a distinction was made between those with a long tradition of settlement in the region, the *starosedeoci*, and the recent migrants or *kolonisti*.

To the south of Belgrade the generally heavily populated and relatively prosperous rural hill country of the Šumadija also provided an important centre of agricultural production with particular concentration on fruit and vegetables. The main urban centre in the Šumadija, Kragujevac, with a population of 147,000, developed as a major centre of manufacturing. Of particular importance were the Crvena Zastava plants with their facilities for the production of cars (the Yugo) and arms. The southern countryside, and particularily the lower Morava region, contained some of the poorest areas in Serbia. The urban centre of this southern region, Niš, with a population of 175,000, was also characterised by a strong concentration of industry including electronics and machine production. In areas adjacent to the Bulgarian border there was a significant minority of ethnic Bulgarians numbering around 36,000. While about 50,000 Albanians make up a substantial proportion of the population in the *opštinas* (regions) of Bujanovac, Medvedja and

Presevo. In south-east Serbia around the towns of Bor and Negotin there were also concentrations of ethnic Vlachs.[9]

The region of the Sandžak was divided in two by the Serbian/Montenegrin border. The six Serbian *opštinas* of the Sandžak were home to a large Muslim population. The designation of Muslim as a Yugoslav nationality was not recognised by the authorities until 1971. After this date, however, the proportion of the Sandžak population describing themselves in this way rose sharply. By 1991 the Serbian Sandžak had a population which was 59.6 per cent Muslim out of a total population of 440,000. The town of Novi Pazar, once the medieval Serbian capital Ras, by that time had a population which was only 23 per cent Serbian. In the same way, however, that many Serbs from Bosnia and Croatia migrated to Belgrade as their 'ethnic capital' many Sandžak Muslims sought to migrate to Sarajevo as Yugoslavia's main Muslim centre. Some of the outer suburbs of Sarajevo, such as Nedžari, became particularily noted for their high proportion of new arrivals from the Sandžak.[10] This connection between the Sandžak and Sarajevo was increasingly cultivated by Sandžak Muslim intellectuals who sought to define themselves as forming part of the same Bošnjak national body as the Muslims of Bosnia.[11]

The province of Kosovo was the most southerly in Serbia and it was also the least developed. When at the end of the 1980s economic recession engulfed Yugoslavia the rate of unemployment in Kosovo, at 54 per cent, was almost three times the national average. Kosovo, however, was not without natural resources, having deposits of magnesium, coal, zinc, lead and the largest lignite deposits in Europe. These assets, however, were characteristically poorly managed and exploited. By the end of the 1980s the Trepča plant, the largest lead and zinc producer in Europe, was facing spiralling debts and losses. In 1987 it was reported that Trepča's woes included poor organisation, low wages for workers, an 'irresponsible attitude to work' and excessive absenteeism. In a similar way the Ferronikl plant in Kosovo was by 1986 operating at only 70 per cent capacity. The nickel produced cost twice as much as that originating in a comparable plant in the United States. The plant was only able to continue to export due to extensive subsidies from the federal government.[12] The agricultural sector in Kosovo paralleled the failings of province's industry with

low yields and poor utilisation of land despite the region's burgeoning population.

This atmosphere of economic crisis formed the background to
an increasingly tense situation in Kosovo between the ethnic Serbian
and Albanian population. Censuses conducted in 1921 shortly
after the foundation of Yugoslavia showed Serbs as constituting
26 per cent of the population of Kosovo. Subsequent population
censuses, however, indicated a declining Serbian and increasing
Albanian population. By 1981 the Serbian population had fallen
to only 9.9 per cent compared to the Albanian 81.6 per cent of
the population. The dwindling Serbian proportion of the population
was accounted for by the high birth rate amongst Albanians and
the migration of Serbs from what they felt to be an increasingly
alien and hostile environment. The demographic marginalisation
of the Serbian population was illustrated by the fact that the
massive expansion of the town of Priština, from 38,593 in 1961
to 155,499, in 1981 had transformed it into a largely Albanian
town with Serbian settlement being increasingly confined to the
small towns and villages around its outskirts. Relations between
the Serbian and Albanian populations were soured by the memory
of historical events and conflicts, including Serbian authoritarian
inter-war rule, Albanian persecution of the Serbs during the Second
World War, and acts of Partisan revenge in its aftermath. In this
situation contact between the two communities was minimal,
despite their geographical inter-mixing, with the number of mixed
marriages recorded being the lowest of any area in Yugoslavia.

Notes

1.   Ljudomir Madžar, 'The Economy of Yugoslavia – Structure, Growth Record
     and Institutional Framework' in John B. Allcock, John J. Horton and Marko
     Milivojevic (eds), *Yugoslavia in Transition – Choices and Constraints*, Berg (Ox-
     ford), 1992, pp. 64–92.
2.   Harold Lydall, *Yugoslavia in Crisis*, Clarendon Press (Oxford), 1989, p. 84.
3.   Dijana Pleština, 'From "Democratic Centralism" to Decentralised Democracy?
     Trials and Tribulations of Yugoslavia's development' in Allcock *et al.* (eds),
     1992, p. 152.
4.   The figures for urban population and growth are taken from Svetlana
     Radovanović and Miroljub Račić, 'Urban Population and Demographic
     Components of Urbanisation', *Yugoslav Survey*, 2 (1996).

5. Andrei Simić, *The Peasant Urbanites – A Study of Rural-Urban Mobility in Serbia*, Seminar Press (New York), 1973.

6. Joel M. Halpern and Barbara Kerensky Halpern, *A Serbian Village in Historical Perspective*, Holt, Rinehart and Winston (New York), 1972, p. 67.

7. William G. Lockwood, 'The Peasant-worker in Yugoslavia' in Bernard Lewis (ed.), *The Social Structure of Eastern Europe – Transition and Process in Czechoslovakia, Hungary, Poland, and Yugoslavia*, Praeger (New York), 1976, p. 281.

8. Ethnic breakdowns of Serbian regions are taken from Srdjan Bogosavljević, 'Statistical Picture of Serbia, Montenegro and Parts of the Former Yugoslavia with a Serbian majority' in Dušan Janjić (ed.) *Serbia – Between the Past and the Future*, Institute of Social Sciences (Belgrade), 1995, pp 33-40.

9. Hugh Poulton, *The Balkans – Minorities and States in Conflict*, Minority Rights Publications (London), 1994, pp. 75-6 and 95-7.

10. Dušan Janjić, 'Bosna i Hercegovina – Otvorena pitanja državno-političkog identiteta multietniúcke i multikonfesionalne zajednice' in *Bosna i Hercegovina izmedju rata i mira*, Institute of Social Sciences (Belgrade), 1992, p. 24.

11. Perica Vučinić, 'Bošnjačka kahva', *Vreme*, 9 March 1996.

12. Lydall (1989), p. 85.

4. Dissent in Serbia under Communism

In post-war Yugoslavia all political activity fell within the embrace of the designated socio-political organisations of each republic. These organisations consisted of the League of Communists of Yugoslavia (previously the Communist Party of Yugoslavia), the Socialist Alliance of the Working People of Yugoslavia (formerly the National Front), the Trade Union Federation, the Veterans Federation, and the League of Socialist Youth. The line followed by all of these socio-political organisations was subordinate to that of the League of Communists.

Challenges to the Communist orthodoxy did, however, emerge from within the party itself. The first major schism within Communist ranks occurred in 1948 with the split between Tito and Stalin. During the period 1948-53, 16,288 Cominformists, pro-Soviet communists, were arrested and convicted. Of these 7,235, 44.42 per cent, were Serbs with many being veterans of the Partisan war for whom faith in Stalin and the Soviet Union had been part of their wartime creed.[1] Milovan Djilas, a key member of the Titoist wartime hierarchy from Montenegro, had, during the war and its aftermath, been noted for his austere ideological disposition and the fervour with which he denounced opponents of the revolution. After 1951, however, Djilas played a leading role in urging the liberalisation of Yugoslav political and cultural life. In January 1954, following a series of articles attacking the privileged way of life of the new party elite, Djilas fell from his position of grace among the party hierarchy. Further attacks on the structures of power and lack of democracy in Yugoslavia brought Djilas international renown but aroused the wrath of the authorities leading to his suffering two periods in prison in the subsequent years. Until his death in Belgrade in April 1995 he remained one of the most consistent and incisive critics of both the Titoist regime and its successors in Serbia.

Another member of Tito's 'old guard' was later also to be banished into the political wilderness. Aleksandar Ranković had built up a formidable political power-base as the head of UDBa, but in July 1966 he was removed from office by Tito. He was accused of having plotted to overthrow the leader although it has been suggested that the real reasons for his removal lay in the ongoing feud between UDBa and its rivals in military intelligence and Tito's personal security service.[2] Ranković's downfall was welcomed by Yugoslav liberals, who saw him as an opponent of economic liberalisation, and by Kosovo Albanians who had felt the oppressive influence of his secret police in the region.

In the ideological sphere party orthodoxies were also facing an active intellectual challenge. In the period after 1948 a degree of 'new thinking' among theoreticians and academics was welcomed by the authorities as it served to distinguish the Yugoslav brand of communism from the political rigidities of the Soviet Union. In 1964 this strain of 'socialist humanism' was given institutional form with the foundation of the journal *Praxis*. The journal drew on the contributions of sociologists, philosophers, and political theorists from across Yugoslavia. Among its Serbian luminaries were Mihailo Marković and Ljubomir Tadić, both lecturers in philosophy at Belgrade University whose Marxist intellectual development had followed on from their practical experience of the wartime Partisan struggle. As the *Praxis* group developed, during the 1960s it was joined by younger academics such as Dragoljub Mićunović, a lecturer in philosophy at Belgrade University of Montenegrin origin, and Nebojša Popov, a Belgrade University sociologist, whose formative political experience came not with the Second World War but rather with the student protests of 1968. As the writings of the *Praxis* group grew progressively more radical in their criticism of Yugoslav socialism the attitude of the authorities became less tolerant towards their activities. Subsequently many of the leading *Praxis* members were expelled from the League of Communists, deprived of their passports, and sacked from their jobs at Belgrade University. The journal itself was closed down in 1975.[3] In October 1972 Tito moved to purge the 'liberal' Serbian Communist leaders, Latinka Perović and Marko Nikezić. Their concentration on the independent internal development of Serbia was deemed by Tito to be a threat to his own position at the centre of the Yugoslav state. This move was paralleled by measures taken a year earlier against the leadership of the Croatian Communist Party.

During the late 1960s fears began to be expressed in Serbian intellectual circles that the policy of decentralisation being pursued by the federal authorities posed a threat to Serbia's territorial integrity. Between 1967 and 1971 three separate sets of constitutional amendments were passed handing powers down from the centre to the republics and provinces.[4] It was suggested that the strengthening of 'bureaucratic' institutions in Kosovo and Vojvodina would serve to separate these provinces from the rest of the Serbian body politic. The territorial provisions of the 1974 constitution served to further strengthen Serbian criticism of the *status quo*. The 1974 constitution gave the status of autonomous provinces to the regions of Vojvodina and Kosovo. The autonomous provinces had representation at the level of the Yugoslav Presidency equal with that of the other republics, including Serbia of which they were theoretically a territorial component. Objections were also raised to the fact that while the assemblies of the autonomous provinces were fully independent from Serbia, the autonomous provinces were represented in the Serbian parliament and could vote on republican legislation. Particular disquiet was expressed over the fact that the autonomy of the provinces placed the situation in Kosovo beyond Serbian control. It was widely believed that the status of the autonomous provinces was part of a deliberate attempt by Tito to weaken Serbia within Yugoslavia.

In the Yugoslav socialist state, however, Tito always acted as the final arbiter in defining which opinions were politically acceptable. During the 1970s his personal authority continued to act as a check on manifestations of discontent. Tito's death on 4 May 1980, which was greeted by apparently spontaneous displays of grief by all national groups, created a political vacuum with no immediately obvious successor to take his place. Political stagnation and uncertainty were coupled with a gathering sense of economic crisis. Yugoslavia had entered what Sabrina Ramet has described as a period of 'apocalypse culture' where the core values of the socialist state were increasingly being brought into question by dissident opinion and with the authorities being uncertain as to how they should respond.[5]

Following the fall of Ranković the mainly Serbian Partisan generation of Communist party officials in Kosovo had been replaced by a new generation of younger, mainly Albanian cadres. The Serbian population began to feel not only that they were under demographic pressure, but also that they were gradually being deprived of political power in the province. Relations between the two communities became further radicalised after the violent Albanian nationalist demonstrations of March and April 1981. In response groups of Serbian villagers and workers began to lobby the Serbian authorities in Belgrade, circumventing the provincial authorities, in order to draw attention to their plight.[6] The first such petition was circulated in early 1982 carrying the names of seventy-nine Serbs. At the end of 1985 a second petition was drawn up signed by 2,011 Serbs and Montenegrins. It soon became clear that the efforts of the Kosovo Serb activists had struck a chord with their compatriots in Belgrade. When Aleksandar Ranković died tens of thousands of Serbs attended his funeral in Belgrade on 20 August 1983 in what amounted to a spontaneous mass demonstration against government policy. In the eyes of these mourners Ranković had undergone a rehabilitation and was no longer, as he had been portrayed at the time of his downfall, a secret policeman and dedicated opponent of reform, but rather an 'honest Serb' who had tried to defend his people in Kosovo and had been consumed by the unfeeling party apparatus. In March 1986 a group of ninety-five Kosovo Serbs travelled to Belgrade in order to convey their grievances to the federal authorities in person. The provincial authorities, angered by this attempt to undermine their authority, arrested the leader of the delegation, Kosta Bulatović, an agricultural engineer of Montenegrin origin, accusing him of engaging in 'hostile propaganda'. In June 1986 several hundred Serbian villagers from the village of Batusi outside Priština sought to march to Belgrade in order to be present at the Thirteenth Party Congress being held in the Sava Centre. At the border between Kosovo and Serbia, however, they found their path blocked by local police.

The cause of the Kosovo Serbs was taken up by a broad range of intellectual opinion. Some intellectuals, such as the *Praxis* veterans, Ljubomir Tadić and Mihailo Marković, expressed this support in 'rational' terms deploring the nature of the 1974 constitutional arrangements. Tadić explained his position: 'The 1974 Constitution and the behind-the-scenes strategy of the political leadership revealed in a high-ranking Macedonian functionary's definition, "A weak

Serbia – A Strong Yugoslavia", have placed the Serbian Republic
in a paradoxical position within the Yugoslav constitutional system
which, I believe, has no equal in any other country's constitutional
history. The provinces of Kosovo and Vojvodina ostensibly within
Serbia, have all the rights – as well as their own representatives
– on the republican bodies, while the Serbian Republic itself,
so-called Serbia proper, has neither any rights nor any kind of
constitutionally guaranteed influence within "its" provinces. It is
because of this that the Serbian population in one of the provinces
of the Republic of Serbia [Kosovo] is exposed to drastic discrimination.'[7]

A similar critique was offered by Vojislav Koštunica, a lecturer
in law at Belgrade University who had lost his job at the faculty
in 1974 after signing a petition calling for the release of Mihajlo
Djurić, a fellow academic who had been imprisoned after criticising
the new constitution. Koštunica observed: 'One may rightly ask:
if territorial and political autonomy was to be established for the
Albanian minority, why has this been done only in the Serbian
federal unit, and not, for instance, in parts of Macedonia or Montengro that are also densely populated by the Albanian minority?
In the course of peripheralising developments in Yugoslav federalism,
with the federal units (both republics and provinces) acquiring
the basic features of national states and with increasing persecution
of Kosovo Serbs, the Serbs have been put in the paradoxical
situation of being reduced to the state of a national minority in
part of their own federal unit without at the same time enjoying
genuine minority rights.'[8]

Koštunica's broader analysis of the political system, however,
involved a rejection of socialism not present in the thinking of
the *Praxis* members. In Koštunica's work, written with Kosta
Ćavoški, *Stranački pluralizam ili monism* (Party Pluralism or Monism)
the way in which the Communists had come to power through
intimidation and suppression of the opposition was examined.
This work did not simply question the immediate constitutional
arrangements, but rather sought to repudiate the entire historical
legitimacy of the one party state, and its Marxist ideological foun-
dations.[9] His collaborator in this work, Kosta Ćavoški, had been
sentenced to five months in prison in 1973 for criticising the
Yugoslav legal system. Ćavoški lost his job in the law faculty of
Belgrade University, because of his political views, in 1975 shortly

after Koštunica had also been excluded from the University. Although once a member of the League of Communists he had left the party in 1968, and his academic specialisms, including Karl Popper and John Locke, emphasised his fundamental rejection of the 'left' stream of thought.[10] Also among those intellectuals expressing solidarity with the Kosovo Serbs and arguing for a fundamental re-examination of the historical basis of the Yugoslav state was the historian Veselin Djuretić, whose work *Saveznici i jugoslovenska ratna drama* (The Allies and the Yugoslav Wartime Drama) was published in June 1985. The work stressed the extent to which the Second World War in Serbia had been a civil war, between Četniks and Partisans, rather than a war of liberation, as was maintained in the official communist histories. As a result of this work he was expelled from the League of Communists in September 1985.[11] Serbian identification with their compatriots in Kosovo, however, had a dimension which went beyond constitutional theory or historical revisionism. The Serbian attachment to Kosovo was also, and most importantly, based on ideas of spirituality and emotional identity. The Communist authorities had never attempted to displace Kosovo as the 'master-symbol' in the Serbian mythos. Milovan Djilas captured the essence of this relationship: 'Wipe away Kosovo from the Serb mind and soul and we are no more...if there had been no battle of Kosovo the Serbs would have invented it for its suffering and its heroism.'[12]

Kosovo, as a spiritual symbol for the Serbs, had remained a central preoccupation of the Serbian Orthodox Church. In 1968 human remains excavated in 1926 in Prizren, and believed to be those of the emperor Dušan, were reburied at St Mark's church in Belgrade at a ceremony attended by tens of thousands of people. The Serbian Patriarch, German, told the congregation: 'We are placing them [the remains] here as a perpetual sentinel at this outpost of Orthodox Serbianism, to be a vigilant protector of religion and patriotism.' He assured his listeners of the continuing importance of Kosovo to Serbdom: 'A secret voice is still heard in Kosovo today, a powerful voice from a hallowed place.'[13] The fusion of Orthodox theology with national values (St Savaism) was a traditional element in the Serbian church which had been reinforced by the influential teachings of the inter-war theologian, Nikolaj Velimirović and the communist period religious dissident, Justin Popović. In the early 1980s priests of the Orthodox church sought to place themselves in the vanguard of those demanding solidarity with the Kosovo Serbs.[14] In April 1982 twenty-one priests signed an appeal, which was sent to the federal, republican and church authorities. Describing itself as 'a voice raised for the protection of the spiritual and biological essense of the Serbian people in Kosovo and Metohija', the appeal was critical of the policies pursued by the Communist authorities towards Kosovo stating that 'the question of Kosovo is a question of the spiritual, cultural and historical identity of the Serbian people...Kosovo is our memory, our hearth, the focus of our being.' Calls in the church journals *Pravoslavlje* and *Glas crkve*, by influential clerics such as Atanasije Jevtić and Žarko Gavrilović, for the church to take a more active role in 'old Serbia' became a frequent occurence. These articles and appeals often complained that monks, nuns, and Serbian monasteries and holy places had been attacked by Albanians. In 1983 Archpriest Božidar Mijač sought to explain the particular significance of Kosovo: 'Kosovo is not simply a physical dwelling place rather it is metaphysical creation. This Serbian homeland situated between the land and the sky translates a spiritual phenomonan into one of time and space. That is the greatest demonstration that ownership of a land cannot simply be reckoned in terms of numbers, or the composition of the mass of its inhabitants, but rather its is a spiritual concept which has come into being in an existential way. The process of ideogenesis is in this case the most important form of ethnogenesis.'[15] The concerns of Serbian clerics with the spiritual aspects of the Serbian national question were echoed by a group of 'national romantic' intellectuals. These writers and poets used traditional Serbian themes in their work, often referring back to the idiom of the villages or the regions. This conscious use of historical subjects and archaic forms was displayed in the poetry of Milan Komnenić, Slobodan Rakitić and Matija Bećković. Milan Komnenić, born in 1940, came originally from Pilatovci in Montenegro while Slobodan Rakitić, also born in 1940, had his origins in Raška (Sandžak). Both had studied literature at Belgrade University before beginning their literary careers. Matija Bećković, born in Vojvodina of Montenegrin parents, had risen to prominence as a poet, and in 1988 was elected as President of the Serbian Writers Association (UKS), despite the fact that he had faced occasional harassment by the authorities who drew attention to his father's Četnik background.[16]

The poetry and political statements of Gojko Djogo also drew upon the relationship between the Serbian people and the land which they occupied, with particular emphasis on his native Hercegovina. In 1981 a collection of Djogo's poems, *Vunena vremena* (Woolly Times), had aroused the wrath of the authorities who accused him of having 'sought to deprecate the achievements of the peoples and nationalities of this country in the post-war building of socialism, negated the gains of our revolution, and grossly offended the values and symbols of our society'.[17] Particularly galling for them was his poem 'Crnokrug na trgu republike' (The Viper on the Republic Square) which apparently described Tito as the 'old rat from Dedinje'.[18] Djogo was tried and jailed in September 1981 for two years, later reduced on appeal to one year, for this 'offence'. The novelist, Vuk Drašković, had worked as *Tanjug* journalist and press adviser to the head of the Yugoslav Trade Union Federation,[19] before beginning his literary career in 1981. Although he had been born in Serbia, in the Banat region, in 1946, Drašković's family roots were in eastern Hercegovina. Controversially he drew on these regional origins as inspiration for his work, particularly in his novel *Nož* (The Knife), using as literary background the Ustaše Second World War massacres of Serbian villagers. The use of such subject matter broke all the taboos on raising these national issues which had been cultivated, with the intention of preserving 'brotherhood and unity' in Titoist Yugoslavia. Drašković was forthright in declaring his support for the Kosovo Serbs. On 7 April 1986 Drašković asked a 'protest evening', held in the offices of the Serbian Academy of Arts and Sciences: 'Can we remove the knowledge that one whole nation, the Serbian nation in Kosovo and Metohija, are being subjected to a campaign of organised terror by their Albanian neighbours, and the government in that area, which is now only formally considered part of Serbia? Can we remove the knowledge of the soothing words and the promises of consolation which have been offered to the Kosovo Serbs so that we can tolerate the most brutal and most primitive outpouring of hatred and fascism and allow their Golgotha to continue under the double headed eagle, the banner of a foreign state?'[20] The novel *Knijga o Milutinu* (The Book about Milutin) by Danko Popović was published in 1986. This highly successful work related the life story of a Serbian peasant who, having lived through the experience of World War and the foundation of the Yugoslav state, finally dies in prison having failed to satisfy the economic demands of the new Communist rulers. For some critics it was clear that Milutin, as the 'salt-of-the-earth' countryman sceptical of, and suffering under, Yugoslav and Communist political 'experiments', was meant to represent an archetypal Serbian 'collective hero'.[21] The UKS provided an important institutional forum for the expression of such literary dissidence.

At this time Dobrica Ćosić was probably one of the best known and most widely respected of the Serbian national dissidents. Ćosić had been born in 1921 in the village of Velika Drenova near the Šumadijan town of Kruševac. While studying at an agricultural college he joined the Communist Party, and with the outbreak of the war in 1941 he became a Partisan commisar. For Ćosić, however, like other communists of his generation, a belief in the virtues of socialism was combined with a desire to promote and protect Serbian national interests. In May 1968 he was expelled from the League of Communists after he had criticised the Party's policy of political devolution in Kosovo and Vojvodina. After his exclusion from the Communist Party Ćosić's reputation as a novelist grew. His books dealt with epic historical themes such as the role of Serbia during the First World War and divisions among the Serbian people during the Second World War. Despite dealing with such 'heroic' national material and his split with the League of Communists Ćosić continued to consider himself to be a man of the 'left' maintaining close links with members of the *Praxis* group. The 1980s saw increasing moves towards collective organisation among Serbian intellectuals. In April 1984 a group of intellectuals were arrested after attending a meeting, in a Belgrade flat, addressed by Milovan Djilas. Although most of his group were released, six were subsequently re-arrested. In November 1984 a group of twenty-three prominent Serbian intellectuals, including Dobrica Ćosić, formed the Committee for the Defence of Free Thought and Expression. While the committee was a specific response to the arrest of the 'Belgrade Six' it also campaigned on behalf of dissidents of other nationalities. Kosovo, and the national question, however, increasingly pre-occupied the efforts of Serbian intellectuals. In January 1986, 212 Serbian intellectuals put their names to a petition expressing solidarity with the Kosovo Serbs. In the petition national and democratic issues mixed uneasily:

'We demand our right to spiritual identity, defence of the basis of Serbian national culture, and the physical existence of our nation in their own land. We demand decisive measures, based on the concern and desire of the whole of Yugoslavia to halt Albanian aggression in Kosovo and Metohija, that democratic reforms are established within a strong legal system with all citizens enjoying equal rights, that the undermining of Yugoslavia's borders should cease, and that through the guaranteeing of civic security and political freedom we regain the confidence, and win the support, of Europe and world.'[22]

In June 1985 the Serbian Academy of Arts and Sciences (SANU) appointed a committee, consisting of twenty-three of its members, to formulate a memorandum to 'raise the most important social, political, economic, educational and cultural problems' for Serbia and Yugoslavia. While the Memorandum was only ever completed in draft form on 24 and 25 September 1986, extracts were published in the newspaper *Večernje novosti*. The Memorandum presented a wide-ranging and radical analysis of Serbia's position in Yugoslavia. It attacked the 1974 constitution suggesting that it be replaced by 'democratic and integrative federalism where the principal of autonomy works in accordance with the principal of integration within the framework of a unified whole' and calling for 'democratisation and the radical renewal of cadres, authentic self-determination and equality for all nations, including the Serbs, and the full realisation of popular, civic and social-economic rights'. In its analysis of the national question the document not only stated that the Serbian population was threatened by 'neo-fascist aggression in Kosovo' but went on to suggest that the Serbs across Yugoslavia were facing discrimination at the hands of an 'anti-Serbian coalition' consisting of the republics of Croatia, Slovenia and the leadership of the autonomous province of Vojvodina. The divisive nature of the document's thesis ensured that it was swiftly condemned in the press both within Serbia and in the other republics as a nationalist text whose demands would lead to the breakup of Yugoslavia. The media campaign against the Memorandum, which lasted from the autumn of 1986 to the spring of 1987, was accompanied by demands that the SANU leadership and in particular its Vice-President, the writer Antonije Isaković, should resign.

While there was in Serbia during the 1980s a gathering sense of discontent with the political *status quo*, which focused on the national issue, it remained confined before 1987 to marginal or non-official groups. Fearful and increasingly militant groups of Kosovo villagers and workers, along with wider sections of Serbian public opinion, were finding support from institutions such as SANU and the Orthodox church which, while influential, were outside the essential bastions of official power. Slobodan Milošević was to be the critical actor in achieving the fusion between 'opinion' and 'power'.[23]

Notes

1. The Tito-Stalin split is dealt with in Ivo Banac, *With Stalin Against Tito – Cominformist Splits in Yugoslav Communism*, Cornell University Press (Ithaca, NY), 1988.
2. Marko Milivojević, 'The Role of the Yugoslav Intelligence and Security Community' in John B. Alcock, John J. Horton and Marko Milivojević (eds), *Yugoslavia in Transition – Choices and Constraints*, Berg (Oxford), 1992, pp. 210-12.
3. Gerson S. Sher, *Praxis – Marxist Criticism and Dissent in Socialist Yugoslavia*, Indiana University Press (Bloomington), 1977.
4. Audrey Helfant Budding, 'Yugoslavs into Serbs: Serbian National Identity, 1961-1971', *Nationalities Papers*, 25, 3 (1997), p. 414.
5. Pedro Ramet, 'Apocalypse Culture and Social Change in Yugoslavia' in Pedro Ramet (ed.), *Yugoslavia in the 1980s*, Westview Press (Boulder, CO), 1985, pp. 3-20.
6. Marina Blagojević, 'The Other Side of Truth – Migrations of Serbs From Kosovo' in Ger Duijzings, Dušan Janjić, and Shkelzen Maliqi (eds), *Kosovo – Confrontation and Co-existence*, Peace Research Centre (Nijmegen), 1996, pp. 70-81.
7. 'Nationocracy – A Surrogate' (Ljubomir Tadić interviewed by Tomo Ognjanović), *South Slav Journal*, autumn 1986.
8. Vojislav Koštunica, 'The Constitution and the Federal States' in Dennison Rusinow (ed.) *Yugoslavia – A Fractured Federalism*, Wilson Center Press (Washington, DC), 1988, pp. 78-92.
9. Kosta Čavoški and Vojislav Koštunica, *Party Pluralism or Monism? – Social Movements and the Political System in Yugoslavia 1944-1949*, Columbia University Press, East European Monographs, 1983.
10. Čavoski's explicit rejection of Communism can be seen in Kosta Čavoski, *The Enemies of the People*, Centre for Research into Communist Economies (London), 1986.
11. *Saveznici i jugoslovenska ratna drama*, Serbian Academy of Arts and Sciences (Belgrade), 1985.
12. Djilas quoted in Leonard Cohen, *The Socialist Pyramid – Elites and Power in Yugoslavia*, Tri-Service Press (London), 1989, p. 337.

13. Michael B. Petrovich, 'Yugoslavia – Religion and the Tensions of a Multi-National State', *East European Quarterly*, 6 (1972), p. 118-35.
14. Mirko Djordjević, 'Serbia's Ark in the Eye of the Storm', *War Report*: April 1996.
15. Radmila Radić, 'Crkva' i srpsko pitanje' in Nebojša Popov (ed.), *Srpska strana rata*, Republika (Belgrade), 1996, pp. 270-1.
16. While the Četnik background of Bećković's father had under communism made him a target for attack, it was celebrated by the royalist/anti-communist press in the early 1990s, e.g. in 'Moj otac komandant Vuk' (Matija Bećković interviewed by Aleksandar Popović), *Pogledi*, January 1992.
17. 'The Indictment of Gojko Djogo', *South Slav Journal*, autumn/winter, 1981.
18. Gojko Djogo, *Vunena vremena*, Naša reč (London), 1982, p. 65.
19. Drašković worked as press adviser to Mika Špiljak who was President of the Confederation of Trade Unions of Yugoslavia. Špiljak, a Croat, was Yugoslav State President, 1983-4.
20. Vuk Drašković 'Svi smo u zatvoru', in *Koekude Srbijo* (Collected Essays), Nova Knjiga and Glas Crkve (Belgrade), 1990, p. 17.
21. Mirko Djordjević, 'Književnost populističkog talas' in Popov (1996), pp. 394-418.
22. 'Zahtev za pravnim poretkom na Kosovu' in Aleksa Djilas (ed.), *Srpsko pitanje*, Politika (Belgrade), 1991, pp. 260-8.
23. Olivera Milosavljević 'Zloupotreba autoriteta nauke' in Popov (1996), pp. 306-15.

5. The 'Happening of the People': The Homogenisation of Serbian Opinion (1987–89)

On 24 April 1987 Slobodan Milošević, the Chairman of the Serbian Communist Party travelled south to Kosovo to attend a meeting of the Provincial Communist Party in the town of Kosovo Polje on the outskirts of Priština. Clashes broke out between the local police and some of the 15,000 Serbian demonstrators who gathered outside the building where Milošević was meeting local party leaders. The demonstration had been organised in advance by Milošević, in co-operation with Kosovo Serb activists, but eye-witnesses attested that Milošević appeared taken aback by the violence of the protest and the anger of the demonstrators.[1] He intervened, telling the demonstrators 'No one should dare to beat you.' A lengthy meeting followed ('the night of hard words') in which Milošević heard the manifold grievances of the protestors, and from that moment he obeyed the nationalist imperative and made the cause of the Kosovo Serbs his own. On returning to Belgrade he encapsulated his new priorities when addressing a meeting of the executive of the League of Communists: 'What we are discussing here can no longer be called politics, it is a question of the fatherland.' Milošević sought to place himself at the head of a mass movement ('the happening of the people') whose aims were ostensibly nationalist, seeking to restore Serbian central control over the provinces, and directed against the party establishment ('the anti-bureaucratic revolution'). In the process Milošević was to build for himself a political base from which he could hold the dominant position in Serbian politics. Milošević's first move was to gain control over the Serbian government. At the Eighth Session of the Serbian Communist Party, on 23 September, Milošević ousted Dragiša Pavlović, one of his main political opponents and head of the Belgrade Communist Party. On 14

December Ivan Stambolić, the Serbian President, whose support
for Pavlović in his struggle with Milošević had tied his political
fate to that of the Belgrade Party chief, was forced to resign.
Before these events the relationship between Milošević and
Stambolić had been particularly close. They had acted as *Kum* at
each other's weddings, a position broadly equivalent to 'best man'
but far stronger in nature and nearer to a form of fictive kinship
or 'blood brotherhood'. Such traditional niceties, however, did
not deter Milošević from overthrowing his former mentor.[2] In
consolidating his hold on power Milošević was aided by other
influential associates, such as Dušan Mitević who, crucially, was
head of Serbian state television (RTS). Mitević, whose origins
were in Montenegro, was like Milošević, with whom he had
studied law at Belgrade University, a young provincial party cadre
from the post-war generation of LCS officialdom.[3] The deposition
of Stambolić and his deputy, the Belgrade Communist chief Dragiša
Pavlović, marked the victory for Milošević's radical nationalist
faction in the League of Communists over their more cautious
and moderate policy of 'dialogue.'

This was followed by a series of mass demonstrations, organised
by Milošević and his supporters, attacking the governments of
the autonomous provinces, and neighboring Montenegro. The
declared aim of these meetings, also known as 'rallies for truth',
was to unite Serbia from 'Horgoš to Dragaš' (its most northerly
and most southerly points). Between July 1988 and the spring of
1989, 100 such meetings took place across Serbia involving an
estimated cumulative total of 5 million people. The slogans on
placards at meetings were frequently strident and nationalist in
tone: 'In all the places where there are Serbian souls, that is the
home and the hearth-place of my birth', 'We seek nothing new
– only the empire of Dušan', 'If necessary we will fight for freedom'
and 'We will not give up the land of Obilić without the shedding
of blood'. The Kosovo Serb activists, Miroslav Šolević and Kosta
Bulatović, founded in June 1988 the Organising Committee for
Participation of Kosovo Serbs and Montenegrins in Protest Rallies
Outside of the Region. Shortly afterwards this was joined by
another organisation, the Association for the Return of Serbs and
Montenegrins Exiled from Kosovo – Božur ('Peony')[5] headed by
Bogdan Kecman, a former boxer from Kosovo. This organisation
operated within the framework of the Socialist Alliance of Working

People of Serbia. Both of these groups were dedicated to mobilising and transporting Kosovo Serbs to rallies in locations across the country. However, observers noted the genuine enthusiasm with which the Kosovo Serbs were greeted by their fellow-Serbs in other regions of the country. In Vršac, Vojvodina, in September 1988 groups of Kosovo Serbs were received on their arrival by the region's Orthodox bishop, Amfilohije, bearing gifts of bread and salt, the traditional Serbian sign of greeting.[6] Another group of Kosovo Serbs, in October that same year, paused on their way to demonstrate in Belgrade to make a pilgrimage to the grave of Aleksandar Ranković.[7]

On 5 October 1988 the government of Vojvodina resigned in the face of mass demonstrations. During the demonstrations the assembly building in Novi Sad in which the provincial leadership was meeting was splattered with yoghurt by protesting farmers, causing these events to be remembered as the 'Yoghurt Revolution'. The demonstrators in Novi Sad were marshalled by Mihalj Kertes, a social worker of ethnic Hungarian origin and Secretary of the Communist Party in the small Vojvodinan town of Bačka Palanka. Along with his comrades and fellow-demonstrators, Radovan Pankov and Nedeljko Šipovac, Kertes was to rise high in the ranks of the new government as a result of his role in the 'Yoghurt Revolution'. On 7 October the Montenegrin government also caved in to popular pressure from the streets. A group of young Montenegrin Communists loyal to Milošević, and headed by Momir Bulatović, was raised up to take the place of the displaced rulers. This left the way open for Milošević to turn his attention to taking control of the province of Kosovo. Moves by Milošević to purge the Kosovo leadership, however, prompted Albanian popular resistance through strikes and demonstrations. Kosovo was finally brought under Milošević's control on 23 March 1989 when the Kosovo assembly voted itself out of existence following heavy deployments of Serbian police and troops of the Yugoslav National Army (JNA) and the arrest of the deposed Albanian provincial leader, Azem Vllasi.

The rallies and meetings which characterised the 'happening of the people' were cultivated by the Milošević controlled media, and provided with organisational and material support by the state authorities. Nevertheless the scale of the demonstrations and numbers of people involved clearly demonstrate that they were attracting support from across a wide section of Serbian society and opinion. Milošević was able to embrace a broad range of groups and interests within his movement due to the fact that, at that time, a relatively unknown quantity people could project their own priorities on to different aspects of his personality. In this respect, in Milošević the man and the moment were well met.

Milošević's primary, and most obvious, role in the 'happening of the people' was as a nationalist 'standard bearer for Serbdom.' While Milošević himself may not have been a Serbian nationalist by nature his background, coming from the small provincial town of Požarevac in eastern Serbia with a father who studied Orthodox theology, would have meant that he understood the habits and thought patterns of that creed.[8] There was a sense that Milošević, in his attacks on the autonomous provinces, was saying what had for long been considered unsayable under the prohibitions of the Titoist state. The political inconsistencies of the constitution served as an easily identifiable 'cause' for the multiplicity of ills afflicting post-Tito Serbia. For Serbs, therefore, the idea that central control needed to be reasserted over the provinces played the same role in homogenising diverse strands of opinion as did the drive to attain independence in the republics of Slovenia and Croatia.

For those desiring change in Serbia's crisis ridden economic and political system Milošević could also be viewed as a reformer. In 1986 when Milošević became Chairman of the League of Communists of Serbia he was, at the age of forty-five, a relatively young political figure, and his background was primarily in economic rather than political institutions. From 1966-8 he served as economic advisor to the Mayor of Belgrade before moving to the state Tehnogas company, where he became Director in 1973. In 1978 he moved to the Beobanka financial institution where he developed a wide range of international contacts, particularly in America. With such a profile Milošević could appear as a Western-oriented technocrat opposed to the unwieldy party apparatus built up by the Partisan generation. Milošević's emphasis on 'anti-bureaucratic' reform caught the mood of widespread public anger at the corruption and nepotism which pervaded the party structures. In terms of politics the active participation in demonstrations could be seen as a genuine expression of freedom set beside the controlled pluralism of self-management socialism. Even some of those who were alienated from the socialist system were able to persuade themselves that Milošević was no longer a real communist but only remained in the Communist Party for pragmatic reasons.

Viewed in a different light, however, Milošević could also be seen as a conservative and therefore an attractive figure for those who feared change in the uncertain times which Serbia had entered. They could take heart from his emphasis on reforming 'self-management' control mechanisms rather than abolishing them and stressed that 'the chief fundamental form of property under socialism remains social property.' In political terms Milošević talked of 'non-party' pluralism and as head of the Belgrade party he had made his name as an opponent of ideological deviation, in both its liberal and nationalist forms, from orthodox Marxist tenets.

During his lifetime Tito acted as the central source of authority within the Yugoslav system and cultivated his image as a 'father figure' overseeing the workings of the state. This patriarchal concept accorded both with communist 'power relations' and with South Slav folk traditions. By the end of the 1980s, however, Tito's death, and the increasingly tarnished nature of his memory created a psychological vacuum in the minds of the population which Milošević strove to fill. The intimacy of the relationship which Milošević established with his audiences was strengthened by his use of everyday patterns of speech and avoidance of the impersonal 'language of wood' used under socialism. His supporters reciprocated with a 'cult of personality', displaying his portrait prominently at rallies and including his name in songs and slogans. For many such people Milošević gained a reputation and authority which transcended all the normal considerations of party and politics. It was no coincidence that Milošević's most fervent supporters came from amongst the provincial party officialdom and the rural population amongst whom such traditional patriarchal imagery had the greatest potentcy. The slogans used by some of the demonstrators, with their reviling of the *foteljaši* or 'sitters in armchairs', also betrayed signs of the longstanding country-dwellers' contempt for the pampered urban officialdom.

Despite the obvious historical differences between the two countries it is nevertheless instructive to compare Serbia's 'anti-bureaucratic revolution' with Czechoslovakia's 'Velvet Revolution' which it pre-dated. In Czechoslovakia in 1989 a coalition formed consisting of an array of contradictory and normally incompatible interests and opinions. The only thing which kept this highly diverse alliance together was the desire to deconstruct the edifice of the 'old regime' and establish an environment in which normal political life was possible. This process of deconstruction was effected by the exertion of popular pressure on the streets, and under the leadership of anti-regime intellectuals. Once the immediate aim of the popular movement was achieved the *pre-political moment* passed and a natural process of political, 'left/right' differentiation took place.

In Serbia a similar coalition of social and political interests was formed, and 'people power' was deployed in order to change the system. In Serbia, however, leadership was not provided by independent dissident intellectuals, whose role became subsidiary, but rather by a product of the 'old order's' bureaucracy. In this way the force of popular will was diverted away from the main body of the old system – and towards an element which was represented as a threat to national integrity. In Serbia therefore the experience of 'people power' did not succeed in deconstructing the 'old regime' but rather in reconstructing it in a new guise. When the *pre-political moment* passed in Serbia, and political parties began to form they did so in conditions which would be constrained by many of the non-democratic conditions of the old order.

The Vidovdan rally of 28 June 1989, held at Kosovo Polje and marking the 600th anniversary of the Serbian defeat at the battle of Kosovo, was a victory celebration for the coalition which Milošević had assembled around him. For 'national romantic' intellectuals, such as Matija Bećković, it marked the triumph of claims over territory through 'historical right' over those of numerical self-determination. In March 1989 Bećković said: 'Six hundred years after the battle of Kosovo it is necessary for us to declare: Kosovo is Serbian and that fact depends neither on Albanian natality or Serbian mortality. There is so much Serbian blood and holy relics there that it will be Serbian even when not one Serb remains there.'[9] At the 28 June rally at the Gazimestan battlefield site he claimed that Kosovo should be seen as 'a Jerusalem in which the whole of Europe has its churches'. Human rights, he said, had been defended on the field of Kosovo six hundred years ago and now measures had been taken in Kosovo to once more defend human rights.[10]

The rally was presided over by Patriarch German and the Serbian Orthodox Church. The church too had cause to celebrate. Not only had they seen the territory around their holy places, which they perceived to be under threat, return to Serbian control, but they had also seen an apparently new relationship develop between themselves and the Serbian government. This rapproachement was manifest in the permission given by the government for work to resume on the building of the Saint Sava cathedral in the Vračar area of Belgrade, and in the meeting which took place on 15 June 1990 in which representatives of the church and the authorities met in order to regularise the relationship between the church and the state. In the autumn of 1988 and winter of 1989 the bones of the medieval Serbian leader, Lazar, under the supervision of the church, toured the holy places in Serbian-populated territories before being returned to their resting-place in the monastery Lazar founded at Ravanica. The arrivals of these relics in the months preceeding the Kosovo anniversary were occasions for excitement and veneration. In the mountainous Ozren region of central Bosnia 50,000 people turned out to await their arrival.

The greatest victor at this gathering, however, was Slobodan Milošević. His speech at Gazimestan mixed the rhetoric of socialist development with older and more powerful conceptions of heroism: 'The battle of Kosovo contains within itself one great symbol. That is the symbol of heroism. It is comemorated in our songs, dances, literature, and history. The heroism of Kosovo has for more than six centuries inspired our creativity, fed our pride, so that we did not forget that once we had a great army, courageous and proud, one of the few which despite its losses remained undefeated. Six centuries later we are again involved in battles, and facing battles. They are not battles with arms, but these cannot be excluded. But regardless of what form they take these battles cannot be won without decisiveness, courage, and sacrifice, without those good characteristics which long ago were present on the field of Kosovo. Our main battle today is for the realisation of economic, political, cultural and general social prosperity, and the successful advance towards the civilization in which people will live in the twenty-first century.'[11]

Although the meeting, attended by 500,000 Serbs from across Yugoslavia and beyond, was nominally organised as a federal Yugoslav event it effectively acted as a symbolic repudiation of the Titoist legacy. As Milošević addressed his audience portraits of

Lazar and Milošević were held aloft by members of the audience, the medieval monarch alongside the Communist *apparatchik*. Milošević, however, was soon to find his position as leader of the Serbs contested by new challengers.

Notes

1. For the organised nature of the meeting in Kosovo Polje see Laura Silber and Alan Little, *The Death of Yugoslavia*, Penguin (London), 1995, pp. 37-9. For Milošević's reaction to the demonstrations see Slavko Čuruvija and Ivan Torov, 'The March to War (1980-1990)' in Jasminka Udovički and James Ridgeway (eds), *Yugoslavia's Ethnic Nightmare*, Lawrence Hill (New York), 1995, pp. 82-3.
2. On the institution of *Kumstvo* see Eugene Hammel, *Alternative Social Structures and Ritual Relations in the Balkans*, Prentice Hall (Englewood Cliffs, NJ), 1968.
3. Slavoljub Djukić, *On, ona, i mi*, B-92 (Belgrade), 1997, p. 172.
4. Olivera Milosavljević, 'Jugoslavija kao zabluda' in Nebojša Popov (1996), p. 80.
5. The organisation takes its name from the red peonies which, according to legend, were said to have grown on the Kosovo battlefield where the fallen Serbian heroes had shed their blood.
6. Milan Milošević, 'Ratni Božić', *Vreme*, 13 January 1992.
7. Milan Milošević, 'Slobodane samo reči, letećemo kao meci', *Vreme*, 10 February 1992.
8. For Milošević's family background see Slavoljub Djukić, 'Izmedju slave i anateme', Filip Višnjić (Belgrade), 1994, pp. 13-20.
9. *Politika*, Matija Bećković, 5 March 1989, quoted in Dubravka Stojanović, 'Traumatični krug srpske opozicije' in Popov (1996), p. 511.
10. Milo Gligorijević, 'Srpski jerusalim', *NIN*, 2 July 1989.
11. Slobodan Milošević, 'Kosovo i sloga', *NIN*, 2 July 1989.

6. The Fragmentation of Serbian Politics and the Advent of Pluralism (January–October 1990)

The republic's League of Communists was reluctant to contemplate any moves towards genuine pluralist development within Serbia. In May 1989, however, the League of Socialist Youth of Serbia published a document entitled 'For the Young, Democracy and Socialism'. In this document it called for the recognition of rights of free association, freedom to gather and hold meetings, and liberalisation of the media. While these demands were not acted upon they did mark a departure from the party line on such matters. In July 1989 the League of Communists of Serbia issued its own wide-ranging examination of future development in Serbia in the report 'Basic Perspectives on Reform of the Political System'. It was conceded that 'working people and citizens' should have the right to freely form associations and alliances. In its view, however, such associations should be formed within the framework of the Socialist Alliance of Working People, and therefore, at one remove, under the indirect control of the League of Communists. At the XI Congress of the League of Communists of Serbia, pressurised by the process of pluralisation under way in the other republics, a change in policy took place with it being agreed that there should be 'direct and secret elections with a choice of candidates and the introduction of political pluralism'. Although these rights were not recognised in law until July 1990, these resolutions opened the way for the formation of independent political parties.[1]

On 6 January 1990 the Serbian National Renewal (SNO) was formed at a rally of 600 people held in the town of Nova Pazova.[2] The meeting's venue, Nova Pazova, was situated in Vojvodina, 40 km. north of Belgrade and known for its large number of inhabitants with origins in Bosnia and Kosovo. The President of the SNO was Mirko Jović, a local café-owner who had played an active role in the 'anti-bureaucratic revolution'. On 12 August 1988 Jović had founded the Saint Sava Society for the Preservation of Historical Truth, the Cyrillic Alphabet and the Defence of Kosovo.[3] The meeting of 6 January effectively marked the transformation of the Saint Sava Society into a political party. The SNO Vice-Presidents were the historical novelist, Vuk Drašković, and the Oxford-educated Orthodox priest and theologian, Žarko Gavrilović. The SNO adhered to what has been described as a 'nationalist opposition discourse' consisting of a number of key elements including the de-Titoisation of Serbia and repudiation of the Communist legacy, the rehabilitation of Draža Mihailović's Četnik movement, support for the return of the royal Karadjordjević dynasty, and advocacy of a new ('Great') Serbian state whose territorial limits were defined in maximal ethnic and historical terms.[4] Jović described the SNO, saying: 'We are not a classical political party. We are a Serbian monarchist, state-building movement.'[5] The SNO programme, written by Vuk Drašković, stated that it was 'a political party whose longstanding and unchanging aim is the creation of a democratic and multi-party state within its historical and ethnic borders. [...] The SNO will fight by democratic means to achieve these aims within the territory of contemporary Serbia, as a Piedmont of renewed liberation and unification, and will gain democratic support for these aims in all the Serbian regions of the present day Yugoslavia, and by the same means will work actively amongst Serbs from around the world.'[6] The date chosen for the foundation of the SNO, 6 January, was also significant as, being the Orthodox Christmas Eve, it corresponded to the ideas of spiritual 'rebirth' and 'renewal' which were important themes in radical Serbian nationalist ideology. A split, however, soon developed within the SNO between Mirko Jović and Vuk Drašković. During this schism, which culminated on 10 March with Drašković's departure from the SNO, Jović sought to highlight Drašković's background as a former member of the Communist Party. Shortly afterwards Žarko Gavrilović also left the SNO to form the Serbian Saint Sava Party (SSSS). Gavrilović's party defined itself as a 'movement for spiritual rebirth'. Gavrilović called for the re-introduction of religious studies into the educational system from primary to university level, and was particularly keen to see state backed observance of religious holidays, such as St

Sava's day, 27 January. Gavrilović said: 'We live in a godless state caught between Islam and Roman Catholicism' and defined the role of the SSSS as to fight 'against atheism, the secular state, the communists, religious sects, and other confessions who threaten the Orthodox faith'.[7] The formation of the SSSS was a clear, if largely unsuccessful, attempt to form an explicit clericalist party in Serbia. It was, however, a personal initiative on Gavrilović's part and did not enjoy the official backing of the church. Jović was left in control of the rump of his movement, but in October 1990 there were further defections from the SNO when Mihaijlo Mladenović and Aleksandar Spasić left to form the Serbian Royalist Bloc. This multiplicity of splits ensured that in electoral terms the SNO was, by the time of the December 1990 republican elections, a spent force securing only 0.8 per cent of the vote, and failing to have any representatives elected.

Following his split with the SNO Vuk Drašković merged his schismatic faction with the Serbian Freedom Movement (SSP) headed by Vojislav Šešelj to create the Serbian Renewal Movement (SPO) on 14 March 1990.[8] Vojislav Šešelj, the son of a railway worker from Sarajevo with family origins in eastern Hercegovina, had graduated from Belgrade University in 1979 as the youngest person in post-war Yugoslavia to be awarded a doctorate. His doctoral thesis was on 'the essence of fascism and militarism'. In his early years as a Communist Party member he reportedly enjoyed a reputation for such fervent ideological orthodoxy that he was nicknamed 'Stalin' by his fellow school students.[9] In 1981, however, while working as a lecturer in political science at Sarajevo University he was expelled from the League of Communists of Bosnia and Hercegovina, having been accused of spreading 'nationalist and anarcho-liberal ideas'. On 20 April 1984 he was arrested and accused of 'endangering the social order'.[10] His sentence of eight years in prison, subsequently reduced to four years, was served in the Zenica prison in central Bosnia.

Having moved to Belgrade, Šešelj founded his own political group, the SSP, which held its first congress on 23 January 1990. In contrast to the radical nationalism which characterised his later political ventures, the programme of the SSP was apparently moderate in tone, calling for 'Yugoslavia to be organised on a federative principle on the model that today exists in federative states in the civilized world such as the American or German federation'.

Resolutions at the SSP congress had called for the ending of the monopoly of power of the League of Communists, an end to censorship, free access to the media, and a 'revival of the national, spiritual, cultural, economic and political unity of the Serbian people and mutual understanding between Serb believers and Serb atheists as well as brotherhood of Serb-Catholics, Serb-Muslims and Serb-Protestants'. The SSP was intended as a 'supra-party' alliance, and throughout its short existence its numerical strength remained limited.[11] The two leaders of the newly founded Serbian Renewal Movement had been close associates, and Šešelj had acted as *kum* at the wedding of Vuk and his wife Danica.

Despite these connections Drašković and Šešelj proved unable to work together. A public dispute arose over a play, 'Saint Sava' by Siniša Kovačević, which its critics, including Žarko Gavrilović, claimed was derogatory to the reputation of the Serbian patron saint. Gavrilović called on other nationalist leaders, in the SNO and the SPO, to co-operate with him in organising the disruption of the play. While Šešelj responded positively to this request Drašković was hostile declaring that 'a theatre is not a place for shouting and howling' and that he would always 'fight against all censorship and for artistic rights'.[12] This particular disagreement, however, was representative of wider disputes over authority and party direction within the SPO. Although on 31 May Šešelj split from the SPO, a number of individuals who had been members of his SSP, including Slobodan Rakitić, Mladen Markov, Bogoljub Pejčić and Aleksandar Čotrić, remained with Drašković's movement.[13]

In this initial phase of its existence the SPO followed a strong 'Great Serbian' line with Drašković declaring that the new borders of Serbia would be 'where the Serbian concentration camps were, the places of most executions and the burned-down Serbian churches and villages'.[14] In accordance with this orientation the SPO sought to organise not only within Serbia, but also amongst the Serbian populations of Croatia and Bosnia. This created a problem for the SPO as to whether their relationship with the indigenous Serbian political organisations within these territories should be one of co-operation or competition. In Croatia the Zora (Dawn), Serbian cultural organisation, was formed by Jovan Opačić on 8 July 1989. After disturbances which took place at the Lazarica church, near the Dalmatian Kosovo Polje, on 9 July Opačić was arrested and sentenced to three months in prison by the Croatian authorities. His jailing made Opačić a hero in the eyes of many Serbs. On 17 February 1990 he co-operated with the psychiatrist Jovan Rašković in forming the Serbian Democratic Party (SDS) in Knin. On 12 July 1990 a Bosnian branch of the SDS had been founded under the leadership of another psychiatrist, Radovan Karadžić. A Bosnian branch of the SPO had been founded earlier that year, in April 1990. However, at the First World Congress of the SPO, held in Belgrade on 28-29 October 1990, Vladimir Srebrov, a writer and founding member of the Bosnian SDS who had defected to Drašković's movement, proposed that the SPO step up its activities in eastern Hercegovina and western Bosnia. This was rejected by Drašković, who said that such a move would only serve to divide the Serbian voters when the SDS 'is in fact a sister-party to our movement'.[15]

In the elections in Bosnia-Hercegovina in November 1990, the SPO did put up candidates but was effectively marginalised by the SDS, and received only 0.4 per cent of the vote. It gained one representative in the *opština* of Nevesinje in Eastern Hercegovina, near to Drašković's family home of Gacko. The failure of the SPO at the polls in Bosnia was followed by the departure of some of its key members, such as Miroslav Radovanović, who became an official of the SDS, and later Vice-President of the Bosnian Serbian Radical Party.[16] The SPO attracted some defectors from amongst the Croatian SDS including Dušan Zelembaba and Jovan Opačić, but were never in a position to seriously challenge the role of the SDS in this region.[17]

In Kosovo the SPO had even greater problems in establishing itself. The prestige which Slobodan Milošević had gained for himself, amongst the Serbian population, meant that any attempt to form a political alternative was regarded as tantamount to treason. Despite having secured the loyalty of one of the leading Kosovo Serb activists, Kosta Bulatović, the SPO found that their efforts at organisation were met with resistance. When the SPO announced its intention to hold a meeting in Kosovo Polje on 29 September 1990 a series of demonstrations were held by local Serbs urging that the SPO gathering be banned.[18]

The SPO increasingly sought to cultivate an image which identified it with the small towns and villages of the rural Šumadijan heartland. For a neo-traditional movement such as the SPO the

Šumadija was a historically attractive region containing centres associated with the royal dynasty, such as the Karadjordjević mausoleum at Topola, and with a long record of resistance to foreign occupiers stretching from the rebellions of the nineteenth century to the Second World War. During the December 1990 elections Drašković nominated the small Šumadijan town of Valjevo, with a population of 60,000, as his political 'capital'. In subsequent years he would frequently return there to celebrate Christmas or at moments of political or personal crisis. There was an element of irony in this relationship as the SPO were defeated in the 1990 elections in Valjevo, although one of their leaders, Milan Komnenić, was the local candidate. In subsequent elections Valjevo remained a Socialist stronghold.[19] Indeed despite the attempts by the SPO to nurture a rural image, the primary areas of support for the SPO were in urban areas, particularly metropolitan Belgrade.

Anti-communism and repudiation of the existing Communist order made up one of the key elements of the SPO belief system. At the First World Congress of the SPO Drašković said: 'The biggest obstacle to the realisation of our ideals...is neither the Ustaše flag in Croatia, nor revived Islamic passions in Bosnia and Raška, nor is it the double-headed eagle of Albania. The resurrection of Serbia is most ardently hampered by the Bolshevik and unfortunately ruling intellect in Serbia.'[20] It is indicative of the enduring reputation that Slobodan Milošević had created for himself as a *supra-political* figure that, despite the conscious anti-communism of the SPO gathering, Veselin Djuretić, as guest speaker, felt able to tell the conference: 'The SPO is the embodiment of that energy which was released in Kosovo in 1987 and the initiator of that energy is one man – Slobodan Milošević.' He called on Milošević 'to rise in the interests of Serbia, and the Serbian nation, and for the purpose of a fair political struggle, above the interests of the party to which he belongs.' Djuretić was contradicted by Drašković who stressed that the time for such *pre-political* sentiments had passed.[21]

Complementing the SPO's contemporary anti-communist stance was their historical desire to rehabilitate the memory of Draža Mihailović and the Četnik movement. On 13 May 1990 Vuk and Danica Drašković, and around 100 of their supporters sought to celebrate the anniversary of Mihailović's wartime arrival

at Ravna Gora. However, access to the area was blocked by a
cordon of riot police. Despite the failure of this attempt the incident
did establish a lasting tradition, among the SPO, of political pilgrimage
to the site of Ravna Gora.[22] The SPO identified strongly with
the religious values of the church, and articles by senior SPO
leaders, such as Vuk Drašković, Slobodan Rakitić and Milan
Komnenić, frequently featured in the religious press. The SPO
also championed causes valued by the Orthodox church such as
the introduction of religious education into schools.[23] Drašković
emphasised the spiritual links between the Serbs and other Orthodox
nations. In an interview with the Greek magazine *Diethnisi Epitheorisi,*
in June 1991, Drašković called for the spiritual unification of the
Balkans and said that he dreamed of a 'new Byzantine empire'
which would act as partner to Western Europe and reflect the
'close spiritual and cultural alliance of Greeks, Serbs, Bulgars,
Romanians and Russians'.[24]

The SPO's radical critique of the Titoist legacy ensured that
a considerable proportion of the SPO membership were young
people – observers of the SPO World Congress estimated that
they made up 70 per cent of the audience. By late 1990 the
SPO had between 15,000 and 25,000 members across Serbia.[25]

On 18 June 1990 Vojislav Šešelj founded the Serbian Četnik
Movement (SČP). Due to the open identification with the wartime
Četnik movement contained within this group's title the authorities,
in August 1990, refused to register it as a legal organisation. It
soon established a reputation for practising a militant and aggressive
brand of street politics. Šešelj was joined in this new organisation
by Aca Stefanović, formerly leader of the Valjevo based Liberal
Party which had been formed on 14 December 1989. Stefanović's
Liberal Party was an ideologically hybrid organisation. He himself
had written a book in praise of Draža Mihailović, but styled his
organisation as 'a party of the European left' and appeared to
enjoy notably good relations with the authorities.[26] On 15 May
1991 Stefanović was sentenced to fifty days in prison by a court
in Valjevo for destroying the bust of the Partisan hero Stevan
Filipović. The court condemned Stefanović for having 'insulted
the socialist and patriotic feelings of citizens and stirred up religious
and national hatred'. The sentence, however, was never put into
effect.[27] Stefanović was succeeded as head of the Liberal Party by
Predrag Vuletić, an engineer from Valjevo.

On 19 January 1990 two well-known Belgrade lawyers, Veljko Guberina and Milorad Stevanović, attempted to revive the pre-communist National Radical Party. Stevanović provided an organic link between the pre-communist party and its modern incarnation as he had been a member of the Radical Main Committee and President of its Students Club prior to its suppression by the Communists. In the first months of 1990 the NRS was one of the largest of the new opposition parties, with particularly impressive centres of strength in eastern Serbia. The party was, however, afflicted by a series of damaging splits with Stevanović leaving to found the Old Radical Party. While Guberina survived further revolts from within the party, the level of support for the NRS declined rapidly during the latter part of 1990. In the December elections the NRS failed to secure the election of a single representative.[28]

The Democratic Party (DS) Initiative Committee announced their intention to constitute themselves as a new political party at a press conference held on 12 December 1989. The first meeting of the DS was held on 3 February 1990. The DS sought, like the NRS, to revive the inter-war party of the same name. The party sought to present itself as having 'civic' and 'centrist' identity. Its initial statement of intentions issued in December 1989 reflected the prevailing atmosphere of tentative pluralisation: 'We found this party irrespective of the real prospect of the party's success in the near future in the firm conviction that this courageous action of ours will contribute to the speedy establishment of a democratic, multi-party system with an opposition.' It supported a mixed economy, with a strong role for the market, integration into European institutions, and the de-ideologisation of the state. On relations between the national groups in Yugoslavia the DS declared that 'the national problem is a problem of democracy' and 'instituting a pluralist democratic order...accompanied by constitutional and other guarantees of human security and freedom will by all means lead to a decrease in the existing ethnic conflicts.' The DS supported the idea of a federal Yugoslavia, the structure of which would be determined after Yugoslav-wide elections, and cultural and educational, but not territorial, autonomy for ethnic minorities within Serbia.[29]

Within this structure of civic policy, however, the DS was characterised by a number of heterogeneous groups and strands of opinion. Prominent among the founders of the DS were a number of key figures from the *Praxis* group including Dragoljub Mićunović, Ljubomir Tadić, and Zoran Djindjić. Djindjić, was born in 1952, the son of a JNA officer, at Bosanski Šamac in Bosnia, and studied philosophy at Belgrade University. In 1974 he had been arrested and imprisoned by the authorities after attempting to organise, in co-operation with students in universities in other republics, an independent students group within Belgrade University. After his release he undertook doctoral studies at Constance University in West Germany. While in Germany he was known to be close to the student anarchist movement. In 1979 he was one of the youngest participants at the *Praxis*-run Korčula summer school. In 1989, when the DS was founded, he was working at the Institute for Philosophical and Social Theory, was regarded as a close ally of Mićunović's, and as a noted 'liberal' on national issues.

Opposed in certain respects to the orientation of the *Praxis* group was an element within the DS whose analysis of the political scene stressed a need for the DS to play a stronger anti-communist role. This group included Kosta Čavoški, Vojislav Koštunica, and Nikola Milošević, an academic specialist in Serbian and Russian literature. The DS was also divided regarding the orientation of key individuals towards the national issue. Figures such as Slobodan Inić, a leading sociologist, and Vladimir Gligorov, the son of the future President of Macedonia, Kiro Gligorov, believed that national problems needed to be resolved within the framework of a common Yugoslav state. Also amongst the founders of the DS, however, were individuals of a 'national romantic' orientation, such as Gojko Djogo, who were to align themselves with the 'Great Serb' policy option. Djogo would later direct much of his political energy into promoting solidarity with the Serbs beyond the borders of Serbia through his role as the President of the Association of Serbs of Bosnia and Hercegovina. Continuity between the pre-war and the post-communist DS was provided by a group of its founding members. These included the highly respected author Borislav Pekić who had been imprisoned by the Communist authorities for his role as a DS student leader in the period immediately after the Second World War. Also among this group of DS veterans was Desimir Tošić, a pre-war DS student leader who subsequently lived in Paris and London and edited the Yugoslav dissident journal *Naša reč,* and Gradimir Cvetković.

The DS succeeded, in the first months of its existence, in attracting to it many of Serbia's cultural and academic elite. These included figures such as the writer and secretary of the Serbian PEN club, Miodrag Perišić, the theatre director, Vida Ognjenović, the film director, Aleksandar Saša Petrović, the Paris-based poet, Milovan Danoljić, and the classical scholar, Vladeta Janković.

The diverse 'conglomerate' or 'catch-all' nature of the DS meant that from its inception it was unstable and prone to splits. The first major defections from the DS came after the decision by the party's Main Committee on 15 September 1990 to invite Prince Tomislav Karadjordjević, uncle of Crown Prince Aleksandar, the heir to the throne, to act as their nominated candidate in the forthcoming presidential elections set for December 1990. This move had been initiated by Radoslav Stojanović, one of the founding members of the DS and a Belgrade University Professor of international law. The Main Committee justified their decision stating: 'Prince Karadjordjević as the republic's President, would contribute, more than anyone else, to the national reconciliation of Serbs and the overcoming of their schisms.'[30] Although Prince Tomislav ultimately declined the invitation to act as DS nominee this did not prevent the episode from creating dissension within the party's ranks with conflict between the 'traditionalists' and the 'rationalists' with their origins within the *Praxis* group. Slobodan Inić, a member of the DS Executive Committee, had long made plain his distrust of attempts to revive traditional Serbian institutions. Interviewed in December 1989, on the occasion of the foundation of the DS, Inić was questioned regarding the attitude of the DS towards the monarch, and said: 'I must admit we have not really thought about that. We are agreed that a monarchy is not necessary in a democracy.'[31] Inić greeted the invitation to Tomislav with dismay, and offered his resignation, saying that the prince did not have 'the reputation of a peacemaker' and that the Karadjordjević dynasty was associated with the 'rifts and conflicts of Yugoslavia's recent history'. Following this dispute Slobodan Inić and Vladimir Gligorov left the DS.[32]

The first DS National Assembly, held on 29 September 1990, saw further internal conflict when a faction within the party, including Nikola Milošević, Borislav Pekić, Kosta Čavoški and

Aleksandar Saša Petrović, attempted to have a stronger, more national, line adopted by the DS. This move, however, failed and the assembly confirmed Mićunović as party President with Vice-Presidents, Vojislav Koštunica and Desimir Tošić.

Leon Kojen, a specialist in literary theory had played a significant role in the discussions prior to the foundation of the DS. He had, however, withdrawn his support from the project before the party's launch. On 31 March Kojen, and a number of other intellectuals, formed the Democratic Forum which declared its three key aims to be the realisation of 'political democracy, social justice and national tolerance'.

Ante Marković became federal Prime Minister in March 1989, intent on instituting pan-Yugoslav economic reform. Marković, by origin a Croat from Bosnia-Hercegovina, continued to believe that his reforms were in line with a reformed brand of socialism, but he advocated the power of free market economics with an evangelical zeal. By March 1990, however, the League of Communists had disintegrated at a federal level. Marković, forced to look elsewhere for political support to counter-balance the growing power of nationalists in the republics, resolved to set up his own political party. The Alliance of Reform Forces of Yugoslavia (SRSJ) was formed at a rally of 100,000 people on Mount Kozara in Bosnia on 29 July 1990. On 17 October a Co-ordinating Committee was formed for a branch of the SRSJ in Serbia. The Co-ordinating Committee consisted of a number of prominent Yugoslav-orientated intellectuals including the architect and former Mayor of Belgrade, Bogdan Bogdanović, the economist, Ljubomir Maždar, and the Professor of social work and human rights activist, Vesna Pešić. The founding assembly of the SRSJ in Serbia was held on 3rd November 1990 with Vojin Dimitrijević heading the Main Committee.[33] Of similarly reformist nature was the Association for a Yugoslav Democratic Initiative (UJDI) which was formed in Zagreb on 3 February 1989, and had branches in all republics. Its Belgrade branch was headed by the organisation's Vice-President and former *Praxis* dissident, Nebojša Popov.[34]

The Serbian communists also sought to adapt themselves to the developing conditions of pluralism. On 16-17 July a Unification Congress was held at the Sava Centre in Belgrade which saw the fusion of the League of Communists of Serbia with the Socialist Alliance of Working People of Serbia to form the Socialist Party of Serbia (SPS). The SAWP had always been a Communist front organisation, but this merger allowed the SPS to gain control of its very considerable, estimated to be worth $160,000,000, material and financial assets.[35]

The congress confirmed Slobodan Milošević's leading role as President of the SPS. In the Presidential elections Milošević was opposed by Radmila Andjelković, but the result of this contest was never really in doubt.[36] A commentary by Milorad Vučelić, editor of *NIN* and loyal Milošević accolyte, written in anticipation of the congress, said: 'It is not possible to underestimate the role played in the formation of the Socialist Party by Slobodan Milošević who has been proposed as its leader. It is evident that Milošević does not want to, in the manner of Kučan in Slovenia, win the election simply as a personality, but rather he insists that the election battle should be entered with a properly formed social programme and political organisation whose undoubted merit and value, along with its great influence and support amongst the Serbian nation will be tested in the elections.'[37] Milošević himself was keen to emphasise that a new spirit infused the SPS: 'A party which from its birth is not ready to hear and take into consideration the opinions of those people who are well intentioned, well educated, and have material means, has no future. [...] it is necessary for us to liberate ourselves from some of our former political habits, such as a certain narrow mindedness and vengefulness, which was often present amongst the leadership of the communist and socialist movement, shown towards any opinion which is different from that held by the political establishment and its leaders.'[38]

This impression of new openness within the party was enhanced by the election to the SPS Main Committee of a number of Marxist former dissidents, such as the law professor Ratko Marković, the writer and SANU Vice-President Antonije Isaković, the economist Kosta Mihailović, and the *Praxis* philosopher Mihailo Marković. Marković had taught philosophy at Pennsylvania University in the United States, and as a theorist of 'non-party pluralism',[39] he became the chief ideologist of the SPS. Dobrica Ćosić also gave his blessing to the new party as a guest at the SPS founding congress. Alongside these intellectual dissidents on the SPS Main Committee were other new cadres who practised a more muscular brand of dissidence. These included men such as Mihalj Kertes, Nedeljko Šipovac, Radovan Pankov and Bogdan Kecman, whose skill in organising street demonstrations had played a critical role in bringing Milošević to power.[40] There were also attempts to revitalise the SPS at grass-roots level, co-opting some local dignatories as officials and potential candidates, who had not previously been involved in politics. The SPS marked its transition from communism to socialism symbolically by abandoning the five-pointed red star in favour of the red rose of European socialism.

Beneath these superficial changes in appearance there remained a fundamental continuity between the old LCS and the new SPS. The vast majority of people occupying positions of authority within the SPS were drawn from the ranks of the existing provincial officialdom of the LCS. Of the 135 members of the new SPS Main Committee, 111 were former officials of the LCS. Their world-view was characterised by a generalised belief in social leveling, a particular belief in administrative hierarchy, and an all-pervading confidence in the primacy of the Serbian 'national interest.' The SPS programme, written in October 1990, reflected this ideological continuity. While Tito, who was now considered anti-Serbian, ceased to figure in the iconography of the SPS, the other key elements of the Partisan myth remained intact. It was stated that the SPS sought to 'keep and develop the freedom loving traditions of the Struggle for National Liberation and the socialist revolution'. The failings of communism were attributed to 'bureaucratic deformations', and it was stated that the SPS 'will carry on all the progressive spiritual and social achievements of the workers movement, the development of socialism in the world, and the struggle of the poor and exploited classes and nations for freedom and justice, for a new more prosperous and human world.'[41]

On 17 June 1990 the League of Socialist Youth of Serbia transformed itself into a political party calling itself New Democracy-Movement for Serbia. In March 1993 the party's name was shortened to New Democracy. The New Democracy (ND) President was Dušan Mihailović, the head of the town government in Valjevo. Although the ND had been created from one of the fragments of the socialist state it sought, at this stage, to portray itself as an opposition party.

The League of Communists – Movement for Yugoslavia (SK-PJ) grew out of the desire of a group of senior serving and retired officers to preserve orthodox communism within a Yugoslav framework. The party enjoyed the backing of military figures such as the federal Defence Minister, Veljko Kadijević, the JNA Chief of Staff, Blagoje Adžić, and former Defence Minister Branko Mamula. A key role in the new party's organisation was taken by former general Stevan Mirković. Political input to this 'general's party' was provided by 'dogmatic' Communist officials and orthodox Marxist intellectuals such as the last editor of the LCS journal *Kommunist*, Minja Tomašević, and the academics, Dragomir Drašković and Mirjana Marković. By far the most important of these political figures was Mirjana Marković. As a Belgrade University lecturer in sociology, of provincial origins, Marković's rigid and uncomplicated interpretation of socialism was, during the 1980s, considered to be marginal to the ideological mainstream of the League of Communists. The fact that she was married to Slobodan Milošević, however, meant that by the end of that decade her beliefs had gained a new relevance, and any party to which she attached herself would have unrivalled access to the corridors of power in Serbia. In the short term, from 1990-1 the SK-PJ, played a specific role providing a link between the, still federally organised army, and the Serbian political establishment. The SK-PJ was officially founded on 19 November 1990, but its first congress was not held until 24 December that year.

A number of political parties representing ethnic minorities in specific regions of Serbia were formed during 1990. On 11 August 1990 the Party of Democratic Action (SDA) was founded in Novi Pazar by Sulejman Ugljanin, a former dentist and boxer, to represent Sandžak Muslims. The party bore the same name as its 'sister-party', to which it was affiliated, representing Muslims in Bosnia-Hercegovina. The December Union of Hungarians from Vojvodina was formed on 31 March 1990 by Andras Agoštan, a former trade union official. Other smaller ethnic parties included, among others, the Democratic Union of Croats in Vojvodina, the Democratic Union of Ruthenians, the Democratic Alliance of Bulgarians in Yugoslavia, the Democratic Political Party of Romanies in Yugoslavia, Movement of Vlachs and Romanians in Yugoslavia, and the Popular Independent Party of Vlachs.

A number of parties were formed seeking to represent Serbia's large agricultural constituency. On 20 May 1990 the National Peasants' Party was founded by Dragan Veselinov, a Professor of political science from Belgrade University. While apparently aimed at attracting elements of the agricultural population this small political party had a strongly academic and intellectual profile. Its main centre of local support was in the Vojvodinan town of Pančevo. On 26 October 1990 the Serbian Peasants' Union, headed by Milomir Babić from Kragujevac, transformed itself into the Party of the Serbian Peasant's Union. Its name was later changed to the Peasants Party of Serbia (SSS).

The period of 'neurotic pluralism'[42] through which Serbia found itself passing during 1990 saw the formation of many political groupings whose appeal was essentially local or regional including, for example, the Užice Movement, the Morava League, the Party of Bunjevci and Šokci, and the League for Pančevo – Party for Moderate Progress. Serbia even acquired its own 'joke' party in the shape of the Grand Rock n' Roll Party.

Notes

1. Dijana Vukomanović, 'The Creation Arising of Political Parties – A Chronological Review' in *Serbia – Between the Past and the Future*, Institute of Social Sciences (Belgrade), 1995 (a), p. 82.
2. Milan Andrejevich, 'Nationalist Movements in Yugoslavia', *Report on Eastern Europe*, 23 February 1990.
3. N. Todorović, 'Ulica je kriva za sve', *Naša borba*, 20-21 January 1996.
4. This term is used by Dijana Vukomanović, 'The Serbian National Interest and the Vicious Circle of Ethno-Nationalism' in *Nationalism and Minorities*, Institute of Social Sciences (Belgrade), 1995 (b), p. 70.
5. Tony Barber, 'Royalists Push Plan to Slice Up Yugoslavia', *Independent*, 16 July 1991.
6. 'Predlog programa stranke "Srpska narodna obnova" (SNO)' in Vuk Drašković (1990), p. 127.
7. Trivo Indjić, 'Interkulturalizam, nacija, i religija' in Božidar Jakšić (ed.), *Interkulturalnost*, Hobisport (Belgrade), 1995, p. 258.
8. Later, apparently embarrassed by his previous association with the increasingly extreme Mirko Jović, Drašković would attempt to write the period from January-March 1990 out of his political biography. In party publications the SPO therefore habitually, and incorrectly, dates the foundation of the movement from 6 January 1990. An example of this can be seen in 'Istina govori za nas', *Srpska reč*, 4 September 1997.
9. Miroslav Mikuljanac, 'Čovek koga ne valja imati za neprijatelja', *Velika Srbija*, September 1996.
10. 'Overthrowing Working Class Power' *South Slav Journal*, summer/autumn 1984; 'Zatvorski ciklus', *Vreme, 3 October 1994*.
11. Nenad Stefanović, *Pokrštavanje petokake*, Bigz (Belgrade), 1994, p. 84.
12. Tanja Simić, 'Šta je bog imao u planu' *NIN*, 10 June 1990.
13. Stefanović (1994), p. 85.

14. Vukomanović 1995 (a), p. 70.

15. Toma Džadžić, 'Svetski sabor SPO', *NIN*, 2 November 1990.

16. Vladimir Goati, 'Politički život Bosne i Hercegovine', Dušan Janjić and Paul Shoup (eds), *Bosna i Hercegovina izmedju rata i mira*, Institute of Social Studies (Belgrade), 1992, p. 56; Olivera Miletović, Aleksandar Stefanović and Ognjen Mihajlović, *Ko je ko u Republici Srpskoj*, Tamo daleko (Belgrade), 1995, pp. 55-6.

17. *Tanjug*, 31 October 1990 in *SWB EE/0909 B/16*, 28 October 1990.

18. *Belgrade Home Service*, 27 September 1990 in *SWB EE/0882 B/11*, September 1990.

19. Even in the local elections of November 1996 which saw widespread opposition victories Valjevo remained under the control of the SPS.

20. *Tanjug*, 28 October 1990 in *SWB EE/0909 B/16*, 3 October 1990.

21. *Tanjug*, 29 October 1990 in *SWB EE/0910 B/8*, 1 November 1990.

22. A detailed consideration of the importance of *Ravna Gora* for the SPO is given in Chapter 19 of *The Parties of 'War and Peace'*.

23. Radić (1996), p. 286; Nikola Miletich, 'The Serbian Orthodox Church Today', *Balkan Forum*, March 1997, p. 301.

24. *Tanjug*, 4 June 1991 in *SWB EE/1091 B/13*, 6 June 1991.

25. Džadžić, *NIN*, 2 November 1990; Nicholas. J. Miller, 'A Failed Transition –The Case of Serbia' in Karen Dawisha and Bruce Parrott (eds), *Politics, Power, and the Struggle for Democracy in South-East Europe*, Cambridge University Press, 1997, p. 156.

26. Stefanović (1994), p. 51.

27. *Tanjug*, 15 May 1991 in *SWB EE/1077 B/19*, 21 May 1991.

28. Stefanović (1994), pp. 23-49.

29. 'The Programme of the Democratic Party', *South Slav Journal*, autumn/winter 1989.

30. *Tanjug*, 16 September 1990 in *SWB EE/0873 B/8*, 19 September 1990.

31. Velizar Zečević, 'Novi zemljopis', *NIN*, 24 December 1989.

32. Milan Andrejevich, 'Milošević and the Serbian Opposition', *Report on Eastern Europe*, 19 October 1990; Slobodan Inić, 'Ispravitelji krive Drine', *Duga*, 21 June 1997.

33. *Tanjug*, 17 October 1990 in *SWB EE/0900 B/8*, 20 October 1990; and 3 November 1990 in *SWB EE/0914 B/15*, 6 November 1990.

34. Bojana Šušak, 'Alternativa rat' in Popov (1996), p. 532.

35. Milan Andrejevich, 'Milošević and the Socialist Party of Serbia', *Report on Eastern Europe*, 3 August 1990.

36. Radmila Andjelković became Vice-President of the SPS, but was removed after the Second SPS Congress on 23-24 October 1992. After leaving the SPS leadership she became President of the National Telecoms (PTT) Directorate.

37. Milorad Vučelić, 'Obnova levice', *NIN*, 17 June 1990.

38. Slobodan Milošević's speech is reprinted in 'Srbija i Evrosocijalizam', *NIN*, 20 July 1990.

39. Marković maintained that political parties were by nature 'bureaucratic', 'oligarchic' and 'authoritarian.' Non-party pluralism, with individuals organising through a multiplicity of civic initiatives and elected representatives

being responsible directly to the electorate, would, he suggested, be a system
which would transcend the formal constraints of party politics. Such ideas,
with their emphasis on the 'bureaucratic' nature of political parties, played
an important role in the rhetoric used by Milošević and his supporters
during the 'happening of the people'.

40. Bogdan Kecman failed to be re-elected to the SPS leadership at the October
1992 SPS Congress. He was subsequently Director of the Priština branch
of the Jugopetrol company.

41. Vukomanović, 1995(a), pp 85-6.

42. This phrase is used by Vladimire Goati, to describe the formation of a
multiplicity of small political parties which are themselves unstable and
prone to fragmentation, in 'Politički pluralizam u nas – stanje i perspektive'
in Vladimir Goati (ed.), *Smisao Jugoslovenskog pluralističkog šoka*, Književne
novine (Belgrade), 1989, pp. 10-13.

7. Electoral Politics and the Triumph of the Old Order (June–December 1990)

By mid-1990 the emergent opposition was making increasingly vociferous demands for the holding of multi-party elections followed by round-table talks between government and opposition in order to determine the shape of a new democratic constitution. The Serbian opposition were encouraged in pursuing this agenda by the fact that multi-party elections had already taken place in Slovenia (8 April) and Croatia (6-7 May). The government rejected these ideas pointing out that elections, under the old one party system, had been held in Serbia in December 1989. Seeking to strengthen their hand on this issue six Serbian opposition parties, the Democratic Party, Serbian Renewal Movement, National Radical Party, Democratic Forum, Liberal Party, and Serbian St Sava Party, formed the Associated Opposition of Serbia. This loose opposition association combined on 13 June to hold a rally in Belgrade attended, according to the opposition, by around 70,000 people. After the main rally a smaller demonstration took place outside the headquarters of the RTS protesting at the biased TV coverage of opposition activity. During subsequent clashes with the police a number of opposition supporters, including Borislav Pekić, were badly beaten. At the same time as the opposition were on the streets of Belgrade the authorities were also coming under pressure in the provinces. In Vojvodina the Solidarity organisation had played an important part in organising pro-Milošević meetings during the 'anti-bureaucratic revolution'. By 1990, however, despite the failure by elements in the leadership to transform the group into a political party in November 1989, this organisation was taking on an increasingly oppositional role. In June 1990 Solidarity organised meetings in Sremska Mitrovica attacking the Milošević loyalists in the local administration. Similar stirrings of local discontent were evident in Pančevo where local people threatened to march on Novi Sad and bring down the newly-installed administration headed by Milošević's henchmen, Nedeljko Šipovac and Radoman Božović. Underlying these manifestations of regional discontent were divisions between the 'old' inhabitants and the 'new' settlers in Vojvodina. Many of Milošević's supporters were drawn from among this latter group, and were scornfully labelled '*Kuferasi*' (carpetbaggers) by the longer-established elements of the population.[1]

The authorities responded to these pressures with political sleight of hand. Appearing at first to be ready to accede to opposition demands, the government then announced, on 25 June, that a referendum would be held on 1 and 2 July in order that the people should be able to decide whether the new constitution should be framed before or after the holding of multi-party elections. Milošević made it clear that the constitution he would implement would give priority to the 'national interest' and a 'unified Serbia', thereby confirming the political changes of 1987-9. A vote against the right of Milošević and his allies to shape the new constitution was therefore portrayed as a vote against the Serbian nation. Kosta Čavoški commented on the referendum: 'Slobodan Milošević and his party deliberately stirred up fears that the territorial integrity of Serbia was under threat and that only their constitutional project will be able to eliminate the permanent threat that Kosovo and Metohija would seccede from Serbia. Such deceitful propaganda seduced many citizens of Serbia who went to vote in the referendum in the strong belief they would decide whether Kosovo belonged to us or to the Albanians.'[2] With such national issues taking precedence in voters' minds the dangers for democracy of a constitution drawn up by the one-party assembly were neglected. Opposition calls to boycott the referendum were ignored, and the government gained 97 per cent approval for its right to formulate the constitution prior to elections. Only in Kosovo did large-scale abstentionism occur, with only 20 per cent of the electorate participating – a fact which could be attributed to a general Albanian alienation from the political system rather than any response to the appeals of the Serbian opposition. The result of the referendum demonstrated the continuing ability of the authorities to control the process of transition, and was a significant psychological blow to the opposition.

The new constitution defined Serbia as 'a democratic state...based on freedom, the rights of man and the citizen and the rule of law'. It further declared that Serbia was a 'sovereign, integral and unified state.' The constitution on the one hand granted strong powers to the President and on the other restricted the powers of parliament. This distribution of power was justified as necessary in order to avoid the political instability which, it was said, characterised classical parliamentary systems of government. However, it was widely suspected that the real reason for the strong presidential element in the constitution was Milošević's belief that his future election as President was assured and that he therefore needed to safeguard his position against control by the parliament which might, possibly, be opposition dominated.[3] As the new constitution was being debated in the Serbian assembly around 2,000 supporters of the SPO demonstrated outside angered by the repeated banning of their party magazine *Srpska reč* by the authorities. The new constitution was promulgated on 28 September, and on that same day multi-party elections were announced for 9 December 1990.[4]

The opposition parties began seeking concessions regarding the form that future elections would take shortly after the Serbian National Assembly, on 27 August, passed the law allowing the legal registration of political associations and paving the way for legal presidential and republican elections. The opposition expressed concern over the situation whereby under the newly-framed law electoral commissions would be composed of judges and state officials, who were considered likely to be sympathetic to the regime. The opposition also argued that the 500 signatures needed for a candidate to stand in elections would discriminate against new parties whose representatives were unfamiliar to the public.[9] Following the same line of argument the opposition parties also called for an extended three month long election campaign.[5]

On 12 September the parties of the Associated Opposition of Serbia held a rally attended by around 40,000 people in order to highlight their demands. An open letter to Slobodan Milošević, presented to the rally by Kosta Čavoški, called for a ninety-day election campaign, two hours of television air time to be allocated for the opposition during the election campaign, and for all parties to have representation on electoral bodies. It went on to renew the opposition's appeal for round-table talks: 'The only way leading to the first truly free multi-party elections in Serbia is to have a working agreement between the representatives of the government and the opposition presided over by you, as the nominal head of state, because we no longer have the intention of talking to second-rank politicians incapable of making a single independent move.'[6] The meeting did not pass without incident as towards the end of the rally Vojislav Šešelj and members of his Serbian Četnik Movement tried, unsuccessfully, to force their way onto the platform and hijack the meeting.

The government responded by granting some concessions to the opposition, including provision for opposition access to the television during the campaign and a reduction in the number of signatures needed for a candidate's nomination to one hundred, which were, on 28 September, incorporated into electoral law. The scheduled round-table talks, however, quickly broke down with the opposition questioning the government's commitment to the discussions. Vojislav Koštunica of the DS expressed the general dismay felt by the opposition: 'The authorities have no idea what the purpose of round-table negotiations is. The authorities simply see them as some kind of press conference at which they extol the virtues of what they have accomplished and dictate how things should be done. In most East European countries opposition groups had a say in the way the elections were organised; but in Serbia a few concessions rather than negotiations were preferred.'[7]

On 1 October the parties of the Associated Serbian Opposition held a meeting to repeat their demands. They were joined by a number of other political parties including the National Party, a Novi Sad based grouping led by Milan Paroški with a strong nationalist and anti-communist orientation, the Movement for the Protection of Human Rights, and the Old Radical Party. The meeting resolved that if their demands were not met fully by the authorities the opposition would boycott the election.[8]

The opposition, however, became increasingly divided on the issue. Vuk Drašković and the SPO argued strongly that the opposition should not participate in elections under conditions of inequality. A united boycott of the elections would, he argued, deny legitimacy to the new 'democratic' regime. On the other side Zoran Djindjić of the DS argued that the opposition could not ignore the opportunity that an election campaign would offer to 'record the illegal actions of the ruling Socialists and to inform the public of them.'[9] The relative merits of participation in or abstention from elections would, in subsequent years, be a recurring source of controversy amongst the Serbian opposition.

On 8 October the DS Main Committee decided that the party would participate in the 9 December elections. However, a number of leading figures in the DS, including Nikola Milošević, Kosta Čavoški, Aleksandar Petrović, Milan Božić (a Belgrade University professor of mathematics) and Vladeta Janković expressed their disatisfaction with this resolution which had been championed by Mićunović and Djindjić. On 9 October Veljko Guberina announced to a meeting in Kragujevac that the NRS would also take part in the elections.[10] On 11 October the SPO Executive issued a statement reaffirming its belief that a boycott was 'the only way to prevent the ruling party from repeating the fixed elections of 1945.' It expressed 'the hope that the leaders of the National Radical Party and the Democratic Party will re-consider their decision which can otherwise seriously jeopardise democracy in Serbia'.[11] The SPO position, however, became increasingly difficult to maintain. The 'boycott' tactic could only work if it was a unanimous action by opposition parties. A party which boycotted the election while other significant groups participated would risk being marginalised, both electorally, and in the eyes of the public.

Some degree of unity was restored when, on 25 October, a boycott was once again threatened by a group of fourteen opposition parties, including the DS and the SPO, if multi-party representation on election committees was not facilitated. Last minute concessions by the authorities on this issue finally allowed all the major opposition parties to announce, on 27 November, their participation in the poll. Only a handful of minor parties continued to favour the boycott. While a common position regarding the elections had eventually emerged the opportunity for conducting a 'long campaign', which had been favoured by the opposition, was effectively lost and the parties were instead faced with a 'last minute campaign'. The protracted wrangling over tactics and frequent policy U-turns had also laid bare the rivalries between the opposition leaders, and the fragility of the sources of agreement among the various groups.

Despite their problems the opposition groups entered the 9 December election campaign in a mood of optimism. In part this was due to the belief, which was encouraged by the collapse of communism in other countries, that socialism as a historically failed ideology would be rejected by the Serbian people. While Drašković was, prior to polling, willing to admit that Milošević would probably win the presidential elections he also thought it likely that his party, the SPO, would win a greater proportion of the vote than Milošević's SPS. In the event, however, the opposition parties were to be bitterly disappointed. Milošević swept to victory in the presidential election securing 65.34 per cent of the votes cast. His nearest rival, Vuk Drašković, gained 16.4 per cent of the vote. The only other candidate to secure a significant proportion of the vote was Ivan Djurić, the candidate of Ante Marković's Alliance of Reform Forces who gained 5.52 per cent of the vote. In the elections to the National Assembly the SPS won 46.1 per cent of the vote. Due to the way that the Serbian 'first-past-the-post' electoral system had been structured the SPS, with less than half of the vote, was able to secure 194 seats (77.6 per cent). The SPO gained 15.8 per cent of the vote which gave them nineteen seats (7.6 per cent). The Democratic Party with 7.4 per cent of the vote received seven seats (2.8 per cent). The Democratic Union of Vojvodina Hungarians – benefiting from the territorial concentration of their supporters – gained eight (3.2 per cent) seats with 2.6 per cent of the vote. While a number of smaller parties and independents did gain representatives in the assembly the election served to considerably narrow the political field. The forty-four political parties and association which contested the election were reduced to a relatively small number of 'relevant' parliamentary parties. The widespread abstentionism by Albanians, who made up some 12 per cent of the electorate, accounted for the relatively low general level of participation (71.5 per cent) in the poll.

The tone for Milošević's election campaign was set by his speech delivered in Pirot, in eastern Serbia, on 7 September. Milošević stated that: 'We cannot blame the Slovenes and the Croats for our huge economic difficulties, for our lack of work, or for false investments. Nor will we manage by searching through history, to find a culprit other than ourselves alone, or to open a single new workplace, or even less to create an efficient economy that will not reduce workers wages to a bare subsistence level, steal from the peasants, and humiliate scientists, teachers, or doctors by placing them in a material position not worthy of humankind.'[12]

This emphasis on 'positive' values such as economic development characterised the entire Milošević/SPS campaign. The nationalism, which had typified Milošević's rise to power, by contrast, played a distinctly subsidiary role. The nationalist speeches which were delivered tended to come from Milošević's intellectual supporters such as Mihailo Marković and Antonije Isaković rather than the SPS leader himself. Milošević rarely insulted opposition leaders preferring rather to ignore them as politically irrelevant. In a telling exception to this rule, however, Milošević speaking at an election rally in Bor, denounced the opposition as 'parties of madmen and false prophets.'[13] Radical and fiery nationalist rhetoric had also long been the trademark of Vuk Drašković, the SPO leader. On 9 September after one of Drašković's speeches in Novi Pazar police intervened to prevent clashes between his SPO supporters and local Muslims. Nevertheless, in the period following the SPO congress there was a detectable moderation in Drašković's statements, with an increasing willingness to engage in dialogue with those who might previously have been considered 'the enemies of Serbia'. These facts, combined with the essentially 'centrist' position taken by the DS, caused some observers to regard Serbian nationalism as a waning force.

One politician for whom nationalism remained of fundamental importance was, however, Vojislav Šešelj. Šešelj had, on 23 October 1990, been sentenced to forty-five days in prison for attempting to recruit volunteers to help the incipient Serbian revolt in Croatia.[14] His Serbian Četnik Movement, as an unregistered organisation, was prevented from taking part in the elections. Šešelj himself, however, was allowed leave from prison in order to submit his nomination papers as a presidential candidate. His presidential campaign may even have been helped by the degree of celebrity offered by his renewed imprisonment. His campaign was characterised by verbal attacks on opposition candidates, and particularly those of the SPO. When the votes were counted Šešelj had, to the surprise of some, garnered 96,277 votes. Somewhat incongruously for a politician who considered himself to be a fervent anti-communist, and who had taken to using the old royal military title of *vojvoda* (duke), Šešelj was the first Serbian politician to send his congratulations to Milošević on his presidential election victory.

A pro-government commentator explained the Socialist election

victory thus: 'In choosing the Serbian Socialist Party and its candidates, with its desire to continue, under stable conditions, the
processes of change which were begun three years ago, the Serbian
nation has articulated its legitimate will and orientation towards
the most rational national programme.'[15] In the immediate aftermath
of the election Vuk Drašković put a rather different interpretation
on events, declaring that Serbian voters in favouring the SPS had
voted for 'bondage, Bolshevism, the past, darkness and disgrace'.
The opposition parties also alleged that there had been widespread
abuse of election regulations by the SPS.

The reasons for the SPS triumph can be located in a number
of critical structural and institutional advantages that they enjoyed
over the opposition parties. The SPS had inherited from the LCS,
largely intact, a structure of branches and membership extending
across the whole country. At the time that the LCS transformed
itself into the SPS its membership was estimated at being 400,000
strong. The Law on Political Organisations, passed on 19 July
1990, had theoretically restricted political structures to 'territorial'
organisations abolishing the old LCS 'workplace' units. Prior to
the November elections, however, new 'workplace' SPS organisations were established in major factories. In Niš the decision to
set up these SPS workplace organisations in the city was taken
at a meeting held on 8 November 1990. Following the elections
a meeting on 31 January 1991 confirmed the existence of these
groups on a permanent basis in the major MIN and El Niš factories.[16]
This SPS presence in the factories served as an expression of the
party's dominance of economic as well as political life. The opposition parties, by contrast, had to create their new party local
and national structures from scratch, and over a relatively short
period of time. As a result, by the time polling took place on 9
December, many of the opposition parties, while aspiring to present
a national programme, had organisation and support limited to
only a few specific locations.

The opposition parties also faced severe financial problems which
seriously inhibited their capacity to effectively conduct their election
campaign. The purloining of the SAWP assets by the SPS had
not gone unnoticed by the opposition parties who periodically,
but with little effect, demanded their return. The SPS, however,
also enjoyed further logistical superiority over the opposition through

their total monopoly of power in local and central government, in the run up to and during the election campaign.

The greatest institutional advantage held by the SPS, however, was their almost total control over the electronic media. The opposition had, prior to the election campaign, won concessions regarding access to the media. The time allocated to the multitude of opposition groups, however, was of uniform length and did not distinguish between those with negligible support and those, such as the SPO and DS, who had a substantial following. By contrast support for the SPS permeated the entire news output of the RTS, the main Serbian TV network. Midway through the election campaign the new TV station, Studio B, began broadcasting, offering a more balanced news service. The broadcasting range of Studio B, however, did not reach beyond the greater Belgrade area leaving large parts of the inner Serbian hinterland, and particularly the rural areas, dependent on the state-controlled media.

During the election campaign even the army had been prepared to throw their support behind the SPS bid to retain power. Indirectly this was expressed through Stevan Mirković's statement that members of the SK-PJ should vote for the SPS in the election. More directly Veljko Kadijević made public statements during the election campaign warning Serbian voters of the danger that civil war might break out should the opposition be victorious.

Beyond the fact that the SPS controlled all the key features of the political landscape during the election period it must also be understood that their ideological message did have a powerful resonance with certain conservative sections of Serbian society. The SPS had been able to revise their image presenting themselves as following a policy of reform, but without the systematic change, and therefore disruptive upheaval, advocated by the opposition. The SPS election slogan told its supporters: 'With us there is no uncertainty'. For such people the popular and authoritative figure of Slobodan Milošević offered a powerful reassuring influence.

Among one key section of 'conservative' opinion, the rural/agricultural population, the SPS was able to combine this ideological formula with the promise of actual material gain. The SPS in November 1990 took measures to bolster its vote amongst the rural population by effecting the restitution of land confiscated from the peasantry by the authorities in 1946 and 1953. This sensitivity of the SPS to the needs of their rural constituency can be contrasted to the hostility of comparable parties in neighbouring countries, such as the Bulgarian Socialist Party, to policies of land restitution.[17] In general the Socialist voters, beyond the ranks of its senior leadership, could be characterised as those whose degree of poverty within the communist system was such that they feared any radical change would rob them of what little they had. This support group included not only Serbia's significant rural popula- tion, but also workers from heavy industry factories on the suburban fringes of large towns, low-level officials from the civil service, and old age pensioners. The Serbian working classes were the product of the processes of mass urbanisation and industrialisation which had been set in motion under communism. In this and subsequent elections they largely continued to give their support to the successor of the political party which was their progenitor. Political support patterns in Serbia not only showed a town/country division, but also a strong regional differentiation. The SPS vote was particularly strong in the poverty stricken areas of the south-east and was correspondingly weaker in the relatively more affluent north. In the far south of Serbia the Kosovo Serbs were a notably solid group of SPS supporters. Although few in number the Kosovo Serbs were consistently able, due to the Albanian policy of abstaining from Serbian elections, to deliver a considerable number of rep- resentatives to the SPS.

For the opposition parties the 1990 elections revealed a different pattern of support which, with some modification, would be repeated in subsequent elections. In contrast to that of the SPS opposition support was weaker in rural areas. In this respect there was some difference between the opposition parties with the SPO having a relatively greater level of rural support than the DS. Both of these parties, however, had their main centres of support within urban areas. In social terms opposition supporters were also generally younger and better educated than those supporting the SPS. They would frequently come from among the professional classes or from the burgeoning ranks of private businessmen. The opposition were also, in contrast to the SPS, strongest in northern and western Serbia. For such people the prospect of change was more likely to be a source of hope than fear. At the time of Serbia's first multi-party elections, however, this group remained a minority within the country's electorate.

Notes

1. Milan Andrejevich, 'Milošević and the Serbian Opposition', *Report on Eastern Europe: RFE/RL Research Report*, 19 October 1990.
2. Kosta Čavoški, 'Lex Milošević' in *Ustav kao jemstvo slobode*, Filip Višnjić (Belgrade), 1995, p. 134.
3. Slobodan Antonić, 'The Place and Role of Parliament' in Vladimir Goati (ed.), *Challenges of Parliamentarism*, Institute of Social Sciences (Belgrade), 1995, p. 28.
4. *Tanjug*, 21 September 1990 in *SWB EE/0878 B/10*, 25 September 1990.
5. Dragan Bujošević, 'Democracy, the Nation, and the Parties in Serbia', *East European Reporter*, autumn/winter 1990.
6. *Tanjug*, 12 September 1990 in *SWB EE/0869 B/11*, 14 September 1990.
7. Milan Andrejevich, *RFE/RL Research Report*, 19 October 1990.
8. Stefanović (1994), p. 118.
9. Dragan Bujošević, *East European Reporter*, autumn/winter 1990.
10. Stefanović (1994), p. 121.
11. *Tanjug*, 11 October 1990 in *SWB EE/0895 B/6*, 15 October 1990.
12. Milan Andrejevich, *RFE/RL Research Report*, 19 October 1990.
13. Zoran DJ Slavujević, 'Election Campaigns' in Goati (ed.), 1995, p. 178, n.19.
14. *Tanjug*, 24 October 1990 in *SWB EE/0906 B/6*.
15. Milorad Vuelić, 'Zašto su pobedili socijalisti', *NIN*, 14 November 1990.
16. Marija Obradović, 'Vladajuća stranka' in Popov (1996), p. 475.
17. *Tanjug*, 8 November 1990 in *SWB EE/0918 B/5*, 10 November 1990.

8. The Politics of Confrontation (January–July 1991)

The failure of the Serbian opposition to achieve an electoral break-through led to a period of introspection and realignment among the opposition parties. That faction of the Democratic Party which had favoured a boycott of the election blamed Mićunović for the catastrophic defeat which they had suffered. In their view the policy of participation, favoured by Mićunović and Djindić, had conferred political legitimacy on the Milošević regime whilst yielding little electoral reward in return. There was a strong correlation between the individuals who supported this position and those who had opposed Mićunović on the national issue during the DS congress of the previous September. On 22 January 1991 this group, including Kosta Čavoški, Nikola Milošević, Milan Božić and Vladan Vasiljević, split from the DS to form the Serbian Liberal Party (SLS). Zoran Djindjić took over the role of head of the DS Executive Committee which had been vacated by Kosta Čavoški. While the formation of the SLS saw the departure of key figures from the 'anti-communist/national' wing of the party this current continued to be represented by influential individuals such as Vojislav Koštunica and Borislav Pekić. Having removed themselves from the main body of the DS, and no longer having to accommodate the 'rationalist' beliefs of the *Praxis* group, the ,SLS took on an increasingly traditional ideological hue. On 16 October 1991 the SLS formally changed its policy position from one of republicanism to monarchism. On 21 October the SLS also played a key role in founding the Movement for Rebirth of the Constitutional Monarchy. Kosta Čavoški stated that the introduction of a constitutional monarchy in Serbia would mark a symbolic yet radical break with the past'.[1] While the formation of the SLS was marked by the departure from the DS of some of its founding members, they were not in the long term able to pose a serious challenge to their former party.

The National Radical Party was thrown into an even greater state of internal turmoil by their failure, under the leadership of Veljko Guberina, to gain any representatives in the Serbian parliament. A revolt against Guberina's leadership took shape under the leadership of Tomislav Nikolić, one of the NRS Vice-Presidents. Nikolić, an official with the Kragujevac town government, sought to merge his faction of the NRS with the Serbian Četnik Movement under the leadership of Vojislav Šešelj. Šešelj, however, faced opposition to the union of the two groups from within the SČP. This resistance was only overcome through the co-opting of Jovan Glamočanin, by Šešelj, into the SČP leadership. Glamočanin had enjoyed a short but chequered political career. Coming from Pančevo, of Bosnian origin, Glamočanin had in 1988 played a prominent role in the meetings of the 'anti-bureaucratic revolution' and was one of the founders of the Solidarity organisation. After a dispute with the other Solidarity leaders, however, Glamočanin left this organisation and joined, briefly, the small Belgrade based Democratic Freedom Party. In 1990 Glamočanin resumed his political travels and became a member of the recently founded SPS, before finally moving on to Šešelj's SČP. Despite these apparent political inconsistencies Glamočanin became an important ally of Vojislav Šešelj.[2] The union of the NRS and SČP resulted in the formation of the Serbian Radical Party (SRS) which held its founding meeting in Kragujevac on 23 February 1991. Having installed himself as President of the SRS it was observed that Šešelj's statements had taken on a tone which was increasingly sympathetic to the regime.

The analysis of the election by Vuk Drašković and the SPO emphasised the role of government domination of the media in their defeat. In February the SPO, supported by other opposition groups and most notably the DS, announced a protest rally to take place on 9 March 1991 calling for the liberalisation of the Serbian media. The fact that the meeting was banned by the authorities did not prevent 40,000 opposition supporters from gathering, on that day, in the Republic Square. As the meeting was in progress the demonstrators were attacked by riot police. Fierce and uncontrolled clashes between the police and demonstrators ensued during the course of which an eighteen-year-old student, Branivoje Milinović, was shot in the head by the police, and a fifty-four-year-old policeman, Nedeljko Kosović, was also killed.

Numerous other people were injured during the fighting.[3] In the late afternoon with the police having failed in their attempt to drive the demonstrators off the streets at the urging of Borisav Jović, the President of the Yugoslav collective Presidency and a Milošević loyalist, JNA tanks were deployed on the streets. The military intervention was followed by the arrest of Vuk Drašković, the SPO Vice-President, Jovan Marjanović, and the SPO branch Presidents from six provincial cities. The authorities also reacted by closing down the independent Studio B TV station, and the student radio station B-92. That evening, in a broadcast to the Serbian nation, Milošević said: 'Today in Serbia and in Belgrade that which is of greatest value for our land and nation came under attack – peace was threatened...the state organs of the republic will use all their constitutional authority to ensure that chaos and violence are not permitted to spread in Serbia.'

However, the army, unhappy with the role assigned to it by the regime, withdrew from the city centre on 10 March. The police were unable even after considerable violence to prevent a large group of students advancing into the city and occupying the Terazije. The numbers of students occupying the city centre was quickly swollen by the arrival of tens of thousands of other opposition supporters and citizens of Belgrade. At the height of the ten-day 'occupation' of the Terazije there were as many as 500,000 protesters gathered in the city centre. The students framed a number of demands which included the removal of key Milošević allies in the media, such as Dušan Mitević, and the sacking of Radmilo Bogdanović, the Minister of the Interior. They also called for the freeing of those arrested during the demonstrations, including Vuk Drašković, and the end to the state monopoly of the Serbian media. Meetings in support of the Belgrade protestors took place in major towns and cities across Serbia including Niš, Novi Sad and Kragujevac.

The state-controlled electronic media and the sympathetic press sought to rally support for the government from among the population by recalling memories of the Second World War, and utilising the 'Partisan' myth. According to the line taken by the state media the demonstrators were all rabid Četniks intent on destroying the achievements of socialism. These neo-Četniks, the state media maintained, like their Second World War predecessors, were collaborating with the enemies of Serbia. The pro-government weekly,

Intervju, noted: 'Flowers are laid and candles burn on the place where the two men died. The call of unity and togetherness is all the greater. These things are so much more precious because the HDZ regime is suddenly not unsympathetic to those lads who wear the cockade [traditional royalist/Četnik insignia], and for Mesić[4] Vuk is the only true democrat in Serbia. Saturday 9 March will remain a black day written in the history of Belgrade. The capital city has not seen so much furious hatred for a long time.'[5] The press also carried articles quoting Croatian Serbs who averred that they would be left at the mercy of Croatian nationalists if the SPO continued to 'stir up the people' against the Serbian government.[6] When, on 11 March, the SPS organised a counter-meeting at the Ušće, just outside the city centre, it was mainly attended by people, such as pensioners, war veterans, and officials, for whom the Partisan heritage still held some resonance. This meeting of around 30,000 was, however, dwarfed by the vast opposition host gathered on the Terazije.

The Ušće meeting also exposed a schism within the Serbian intellectual elite. In the period 1987-9 the academicians, Matija Bećković and Mihailo Marković, had supported Milošević in his push to end Kosovan autonomy. Now, however, they found themselves on different sides with Bećković backing the opposition while Marković addressed the counter-demonstrators at Ušće. He told them: 'Some unseen hand is here in Belgrade setting in motion the mechanisms for the break-up of Serbia. In that treacherous project all available forces are being used. There are leaders who in December announced that they, because they were not victorious in the elections, would come to power within three months by way of the streets. Those ninety days which Vuk Drašković gave himself have now expired. On the other hand there are, unfortunately, participating in this treacherous attempt to break up Serbia a number of young people, who perhaps naively, believe that this current destructive action will bring more freedom and democracy. For the first time in seventy years, in greater measure than at any time before now, all the parts of the Serbian nation have been united. We are fortunate to have at our head the most capable, honourable and courageous man since the time of King Peter the First – Slobodan Milošević.'[7]

At the Ušće meeting Milošević also received support from the leaders, of the Serbs outside Serbia, Radovan Karadžić, and Milan

Babić, the radical leader of the SDS from Croatia, and dentist, who in September 1990 had displaced his more moderate predecessor, Jovan Rašković. The backing given by these leaders to Milošević signalled a fundamental change in the relationship between Drašković, and the SPO, and the parties representing the Serbs outside Serbia. Before this date the relationship between the SPO and the two branches of the SDS had been an ambiguous mixture of ally and competitor. Afterwards, however, these political formations were to be irreversibly opposed.[8]

On the morning of 11 March at Dragoljub Mićunović's urging, Milošević agreed to meet a student delegation, but also declared that 'Drašković will get twenty years in jail because of the two lives that were lost.'[9] The meeting with the students took place that evening, and although Milošević was unwilling to accommodate their demands he was clearly shocked by his experience of direct confrontation with the young activists.

An atmosphere of extreme political tension pervaded Serbia. Behind the scenes the imposing of a Yugoslav-wide state of emergency was discussed, at Jović's request, by the federal Presidency and the military leadership. According to the journalist Miloš Vasić it was the most frightening time people in Belgrade could remember since the early 1950s and 'sensible people didn't sleep at home, political parties hid their membership lists and sensitive files, and the air could have been cut by a knife.'[10] On 10 March, in provincial Niš, the head of the local SPS, Mile Ilić, called a 'council of war' of all the 'left forces' in the city, including the SPS, SK-PJ, the local representatives in the national assembly, officials from the city government, local union officials, veterans' organisations, and youth groups. Those present at this meeting were charged with gathering information on opposition activists and sympathisers.[11] Ilić had been born in 1954 in the small village of Jovac, in the *opština* of Vladičin Han. His entire career had been spent as a political official, first of the LCS and then of the SPS. He was typical of the provincial cadres who rose to power with Milošević, and he was as determined to stay in power as his leader in Belgrade.[12]

Under increasing pressure, Milošević was apparently prepared to make concessions. On the evening of 12 March 1991 Drašković was released from prison. He went to the Terazije to address the demonstrators. He told the crowds gathered there: 'I have come straight from jail. For three days in prison I received no news. What I see here, therefore, is something new, and unknown to me, but something magnificient. For three days, not knowing what had happened, I waited for this. I could weep or fly with joy. I never felt greater pain than on 9 March when Serbian blood was shed on the streets of the capital, and two Serbian lives were cut short. We pay our respects to them this evening. Three days ago on the Republic Square we began the surge to freedom. Since that time, three days ago, it became the Square of Freedom. In our new holy democracy, on the Square of Freedom, we will raise a monument to our two brothers – for the policeman and the demonstrator – and we will inscribe upon it the words "Never Again" and sign it "Serbdom", so that this evil should be remembered so that it should not be repeated. Never again will a Serb dare to raise his hand against a Serb, never again will we allow this land to be led by senseless people, who are ready to send their children against their children, never again will a Serb dare to look on a Serb with hostility...Serbia after 9 March will not be the same as the Serbia which existed before 9 March...if some in Kosovo and Metohija and Croatia think that these events will weaken Serbdom then they are gravely mistaken. These events will create a free and democratic Serbia, and such a Serbia will be in a position to protect the rights of every Serb if he is threatened no matter where he is...Because of you my fortune today is too great. I have not come from prison to freedom, but rather I have come to conquer freedom.'[13]

Drašković's release was followed on 13 March by the dismissal of Dušan Mitević, and a number of other RTS officials, and the sacking of the Minister of the Interior, Radmilo Bogdanović. This former village school teacher from near the town of Jagodina had begun his police career following the fall of Alexandar Ranković, and his rise in the police ranks was paralleled by his increasing political influence within the LCS and the SPS. In spite of their formal departure from office both Radmilo Bogdanović and Dušan Mitević remained highly influential 'behind-the-scenes' political figures.[14]

Even as the demonstrations were still in progress Milošević was preparing a fundamental change of policy designed to safeguard his future position. He correctly reasoned that his tactical concessions would serve to defuse the immediate pressure from the

streets, but also sought to effect a strategic re-alignment which
would in the longer term distract attention from the internal
power structures in Serbia. Through 1987-90 Milošević's strategy
had been formulated within the framework of a federal Yugoslavia,
in which Serbia, under his control, would play the leading role.
From March 1991, however, Milošević became the enthusiastic
advocate and executor of 'Great Serb' ideas. This concept of the
creation of a territorial state, formed out of elements of Yugoslavia,
in which all Serbs would be able to live had formerly been the
preserve of Milošević's nationalist opponents. Vojislav Šešelj had
famously defined the borders of the new state as being bounded
in the west by the points of Karlobag, Karlovac and Virovitica.
Milošević's embrace of this new policy was signalled by his aggressive speech on 16 March to the mayors of the Serbian towns
who had been gathered in Belgrade. He told the assembled officials:
'If we don't know how to work, and do business, at least we
know how to fight.' On 25 March Milošević held secret talks
with Franjo Tudjman, the nationalist President of Croatia, at Karadjordjevo in northern Serbia. Both men agreed that Yugoslavia as
a unified state was finished, and while Milošević saw Greater
Serbia as a possible successor state Tudjman also dreamed of a
new Greater Croatia. While the two leaders could' agree on the
territorial division of Bosnia into Serbian and Croatian spheres of
influence, the status of the Serbs in Croatia, who had declared
independence on 15 March, would remain an obvious source of
disagreement. The radicalised policy pursued by Milošević involved increased political and military support to the Serbs in
Croatia. Milošević's intervention served to heighten the sense of
conflict between the Serbian population and the new Croatian
government. This cultivation of a crisis, which would swiftly lead
to war, acted to further distort the political processes within Serbia.
The 'national interest' was once again established as a primary,
defining, political value, and Milošević would once again be able
to portray himself as the leader of such a 'national crusade'.

The demonstrations of 9 March 1991 were the period, before
late 1996, when Milošević's government came under the greatest
popular pressure. Ultimately, however, they failed to seriously
shake his power. The reasons for this failure were to become a
matter of controversy in opposition circles. Some sections of the
opposition would later criticise Drašković for failing to take ad-

vantage of the demonstrators' initial success in controlling the streets and their 'critical mass' in terms of numbers, in order to have initiated a truly 'revolutionary situation'.

Others among the opposition, and in particular Vuk Drašković, would seek to incorporate the events of 9 March into modern opposition mythology as a symbol of resistance to the regime. There was in a sense something typically Serbian, and in line with the Kosovo tradition, in celebrating a heroic defeat. Writing later Vuk Drašković would explain the significance, to him, of 9 March. The wars in Croatia and Bosnia were not, he stated, wars in the interests of the Serbian people, but rather wars by the *nomenklatura* to retain power. This divergence between the state and its people was marked by the fact that the first people killed in the Yugoslav wars were Serbs slain in the Belgrade demonstrations. Drašković recalled: 'When I came to the Square of Freedom and saw the wild assaults of the police units, I understood that the regime was seeking blood and butchery. The entry of tanks onto the streets of Belgrade confirmed to me that Milošević and the generals had decided that 9 March would be the beginning of the war. The first dead and wounded fell in Belgrade, the first victims of aggression and uncontrolled violence were in our capital city.'[15]

On 27 March moves to form a Serbian National Council (SNC) were announced. The aim of the SNC was to provide an institutional framework within which political, eclesiastical and intellectual leaders would unite in the formulation of a national programme for the Serbs. The SNC it was declared would be the 'leading national institution which will represent the interests of all Serbs no matter where they live'.[16] The Initiative Committee of the SNC included intellectuals, such as Matija Bećković and Mihailo Marković, who had supported different sides during the recent demonstrations. Other leading intellectuals involved included Dobrica Ćosić, Jovan Rašković and Milorad Ekmečić, a respected historian from Sarajevo University who was close to the leadership of the Bosnian SDS. Both the SPS and the DS sent representatives to discussions on the formulation of an 'outline declaration on Serbian unity'.[17] Critics of the SNC, however, denounced it as a front for Milošević's new 'Great Serb' politics. According to Kosta Čavoški, of the SLS, Milošević had written: 'of Serbian nationalism only a few years ago as a serpent in the

bosom of the Serbian people, the Academy, and the Serbian Orthodox Church... when someone who was until recently a
national communist offers us a national programme it should be
seen as a lifejacket for himself rather than a true desire to create
a Serbian national programme.' The SPO also refused to take
part in the council's Initiative Committee. Milan Komnenić cited
as the reason for their non-participation the presence on the Initiative Committee of 'compromised individuals' such as Mihailo
Marković, on account of his role as chief ideologist of the SPS,
and Dobrica Ćosić, because of his well-known identification with
the Partisan tradition and antagonism towards the Četniks. Vuk
Drašković was even more dismissive of the concept declaring that
it was an 'umbrella to protect the regime' and 'the majority of
the members of the Initiative Committee are members or sympathisers of the SPS: Dobrica Ćosić, Brana Crnčević, Dušan Kanazir,
represent the SPS. It is clear who is the cook and where the
kitchen is – in Tolstoy Street [the street, in the Dedinje district,
where Milošević lived].'[18] The position taken by the SPO on
this issue did not, at this stage, mean that it had abandoned its
national position, but its strong oppositional position did mean
that it would be unwilling to be conscripted into any national
projects behind which the hand of Slobodan Milošević could
detected.

The SNC was a short-lived political experiment. Splits soon
developed between the 'left'-oriented Dobrica Ćosić and the royalist
Matija Bećković, who had proposed that Tomislav Karadjordjević
should be President of the SNC. By the summer of 1991 the
project had effectively collapsed. It was, however, an example of
the recurring desire to establish an institutional expression of Serbian
unity articulated through the nation's intellectual voice. The manner
in which the SNC foundered so swiftly only served to demonstrate
how fundamentally fractured Serbian opinion remained in reality.
A further attempt was made to gather Serbian 'opinion formers'
in one institution with the foundation of the Serbian Assembly
on 28 September 1991 under the presidency of Pavle Ivić. At its
founding congress the Serbian Assembly declared that its aim was
to 'realise and define the vital interests of the Serbian nation'.[19]

The divisions among the Serbian national political community
were dramatically displayed on 12 May after a ceremony to re-bury
the remains of the bishop and theologian Nikolaj Velimirović at

his birthplace in the Šumadijan village of Lelić. With Velimirović being a religious and national theorist whose memory was revered by Serbian traditionalist political figures, and who had died in exile in the United States, the ceremony should have been an occasion for a display of unity among those attending.[20] Instead, at a subsequent lunch in Valjevo, an altercation developed between Radomir Nešković, a member of the Bosnian SDS delegation headed by Radovan Karadžić, and Danica Drašković, in the course of which Drašković, known for her formidable personality and volatile temperament, smashed a wine bottle over her antagonist's head.

During the demonstrations of 9 March the Serbian opposition, under direct attack from the authorities, had achieved a degree of unity of purpose. In the aftermath of the March events, however, a situation of 'bi-lateral opposition' came into being, whereby the opposition parties were opposed to each other almost as fiercely as they were to the government. In April 1991 relations between the SPO and DS were soured by a series of critical and acrimonious exchanges in the party press. These tensions had been heightened by the widely-held perception that the DS had emerged from the March events with its reputation enhanced due to the role played by its leaders, Mićunović and Djindjić, during the critical days when Drašković had been in prison.[21]

When on 22 May a new opposition alliance, the United Serbian Democratic Opposition (USDO), was formed the DS remained aloof from this new alignment. The main components of the USDO alliance consisted of the SPO, SLS and New Democracy-Movement for Serbia. The Democratic Forum was also initially involved but later withdrew blaming 'insufficient pragmatism' on the part of the larger parties, and in particular the DS. The DS stated that while they were not opposed to co-operation with other political parties on 'concrete joint political goals' they saw no reason for a 'programmatic' coalition.[22] There was particular dislike of the fact that the idea of the USDO coalition had been framed by the SPO and the SLS. The DS, however, also opposed the formation of USDO on ideological as well as organisational grounds. A leading DS member, Radoslav Stojanović,[23] declared that the nationalist orientation of the USDO coalition was contrary to the 'civic' orientation of the DS. Such a nationalist strategy, he maintained, was not a political way forward for Serbia as it would leave the thirty per cent of the country's population from ethnic minorities in a 'political ghetto'. According to Stojanović, political parties need to be founded on 'political principles, that would make possible the integration of society into political and not ethnic communities. Members of the DS are citizens of Yugoslavia without regard to national membership and joining USDO would be a deviation from our programme and our binding statutes.' Vuk Drašković retorted sharply that he did not exclude ethnic minorities from the political organisations in which he was involved.[24]

The USDO alliance held its first rally on 9 June in the Republic Square in Belgrade. Unlike the 9 March demonstration it was not banned by the authorities, and went ahead without violent incident. The rally was, however, condemned by Vojislav Šešelj as 'an act of treason' which had, he suggested, been instigated by 'foreign intelligence services and Yugoslav Prime Minister Ante Marković'.[25] The organisers of the USDO alliance hit back at Šešelj, labelling his supporters as 'Red Četniks', and Šešelj himself as the Red Vojvoda. The use of these names drew attention to the irony of someone who portrayed himself as heir to the anti-communist Četnik tradition, and yet maintained an apparently close relationship to the neo-communist state. From the point of view of the SPO, it also differentiated their guardianship of the Četnik tradition from Šešelj's deviant claim to the same heritage.

The most important test of electoral opinion since the 9 December election arose with the death of Miodrag Bulatović, a writer who had played a prominent role in the 'happening of the people', the Socialist representative for the Belgrade industrial suburb of Rakovica. The opposition parties fielded some of their leading figures in this by-election with Jovan Marjanović, Vice-President of the SPO (USDO), standing along with Borislav Pekić (DS) and Vojislav Šešelj (SRS). The Socialist candidate by contrast was a relatively minor figure, Radoš Karaklajić. During the election campaign there were press reports, officially denied by the SPS, that the Socialists had decided to facilitate the election of Šešelj[26] − a view reinforced when state-controlled television chose to conduct an hour-long interview with him shortly before polling took place.[27] Observers also noted that on polling day known supporters of the SK-PJ were openly declaring their intention of voting for the SRS leader.[28] When on 30 June it was announced that Šešelj had been elected to parliament, defeating his Socialist and opposition rivals, it signalled the cementing of his alliance with the state establishment. The USDO opposition alliance, by contrast, fragmented and ceased to operate effectively during the summer of 1991.

Notes

1. 'Serbia's Complete Isolation': Kosta Čavoški interviewed in *East European Reporter*, May/June 1992.
2. Stefanović (1994), p. 54; Milivoje Glišić, 'Joghurt i Vlast', *NIN*, 9 February 1996; Zoran Spremo, 'Dvostruki aksl', *Vreme*, 17 October 1994.
3. A first-hand journalistic account of the events of 9 March 1991 can be found in Misha Glenny, *The Fall of Yugoslavia – The Third Balkan War*, Penguin (London), 1992, pp. 46-61.
4. The Croatian Democratic Union (HDZ) was founded on 17 June 1989 under the leadership of Franjo Tudjman. It won a decisive victory in the Croatian elections of April 1990. The HDZ was formed as a broad coalition incorporating different strands of Croatian political opinion. Its political tone was strongly nationalistic. Stipe Mesić was appointed as Prime Minister in the HDZ government before taking up the position as Croatia's representative in the Yugoslav presidency in August 1990. Mesić was due to become Yugoslav President on 15 May 1991 but his accession was blocked by the Serbian government until 1 July 1991. In April 1994 Mesić broke with Tudjman and the HDZ to become President of the Croatian Independent Democrats (HND).
5. Goran Košić, 'Crna slova i kalendaru Beograda', *Intervju*, 15 March 1991.
6. Marko Lopušina, 'Srbi se vraćaju kući', *Intervju*, 15 March 1991.
7. Marković's speech is reprinted in Vesna Mališić, 'Srbija na istoku', *Duga*, 16 March 1991.
8. Filip Švarm, 'Ljubav do groba', *Vreme*, 22 November 1993.
9. Ljubiša Stavrić and Violeta Maretić, 'Bio jedan 9. Mart', *NIN*, 10 March 1995.
10. Miloš Vasić, 'Yugoslavia and the Post-Yugoslav Armies' in David Dyker and Ivan Vejvoda (eds), *Yugoslavia and After – A Study in Fragmentation, Despair and Rebirth*, Longman (London), 1996, p. 126.
11. Marija Obradović, 'Vladajuća stranka' in Popov (1996), p. 477.
12. Milivoje Glišić, 'Ide Mile', *NIN*, 10 November 1995.
13. Milena Popović, *Junska dogadjanja '93*, Srpska reč (Belgrade), 1994, pp. 23-5.
14. Slavoljub Djukić, *On, ona, i mi*, B-92 (Belgrade), 1997, p. 102.
15. Vuk Drašković, 'Svi – 9 March 1991-1996', *NIN*, 8 March 1996.
16. Olivera Milosavljević, 'Zloupotreba autoriteta nauke' in Popov (1996), p. 326.
17. 'Da li je mati trudna?', Dragan Stavljanin, *NIN*, 12 April 1991.
18. Milan Nikolić, 'U vrtlogu deoba', *Intervju*, 26 April 1991.

19. Milosavljević (1996), p. 327.
20. Nada Novaković, 'Povratak zlatoustog vladike', *Intervju*, 26 April 1991.
21. Dragoljub Mićunović, 'Milošević nije Srbija', interviewed by Slobodan Reljić, *NIN*, 3 May 1991.
22. *Tanjug*, 22 May 1991 in *SWB EE/1081 B/10*, 25 May 1991, and 27 May 1991 in *SWB EE/1085 B/19*, 30 May 1991.
23. Radoslav Stojanović was among the group of DS members who left the party in July 1992 to join the DSS. He later became a leading member of the SPO.
24. Vesna Mališić, 'Fabrike heroja i izdajnika', *Duga*, 7 June 1991.
25. *Tanjug*, 6 June 1991 in *SWB EE/1094 B/15*, 10 June 1991.
26. *Tanjug*, 12 June 1991 in *SWB EE/1100 B/17*, 17 June 1991.
27. Ognjen Pribićević, *Vlast i opozicija u Srbiji*, B-92 (Belgrade), 1997, p. 54.
28. Nenad LJ Stefanović, 'Pretedent na vožda', *Vreme*, 28 December 1992.

9. Politics and the Gun: The Paramilitary Dimension in Serbian Politics (October 1990–December 1991)

In the period 1987-90 Slobodan Milošević and his followers seized control of the major institutions of public power. Beneath the surface, however, Milošević also gained control of another vital institution, the secret police. His supporters in the SPS and the police had by the end of 1990 begun to recruit individuals who would, unofficially, be willing to support the state, and Milošević's agenda, through the use of extra-political methods and physical force. During the war in Croatia in 1991, and later Bosnia, these groups and individuals would be deployed as paramilitary formations gaining notoriety as auxillaries to the regular military forces. The key state functionaries involved in recruiting such people were the Minister of the Interior, Radmilo Bogdanović, Mihalj Kertes, the head of the secret police, Jovica Stanišić, and his subordinates, Franko Simatović ('Frenki') and Radovan Stojičić ('Badža'). Stanišić, coming from a family of Montenegrin origin, had, like Kertes, been born in the Vojvodinan town of Bačka Palanka. After studying political science at Belgrade University he went on in 1974 to work for the Serbian State Security (SDB), and during the 'anti-bureaucratic revolution' was promoted from head of SDB operations in Belgrade to chief of the SDB in Serbia. Stojičić, originally from Sremska Kamenica in Vojvodina, began his career as a uniformed police officer in the Belgrade city police. He was later promoted into the police special forces rising to command the Internal Affairs Ministry's Special Purposes Unit. During Milošević's rise to power Stojičić's unit had been deployed in Kosovo taking measures to remove Albanian strikers who had been occupying the Stari Trg mine. Franko Simatović also rose rapidly through the ranks of the security-bureaucracy due to his intimate involvement with the workings of the 'shadow state' apparatus.

One of the first, and most significant, figures to become active in this paramilitary network was Željko Ražnatović or, as he was widely known, 'Arkan'. Ražnatović, whose father had been a high-ranking officer in the Yugoslav air force, was born in 1952 in Brežice in Slovenia. His career, however, took a more unorthodox path, and during the 1970s and '80s he gained an international reputation as an armed bank robber. In 1975 he was sentenced to fifteen years in prison by a court in Brussels. However, he escaped in July 1979 and resumed his criminal career. During that year he carried out three more armed raids on banks in Sweden and Holland. After being arrested in Amsterdam he was sentenced on 7 May 1980 to seven years in prison, only to escape once again a year later. The years 1981-2 saw Ražnatović engaged in further criminal activity being detained by, and escaping from, the authorities in West Germany and Sweden. It was widely believed that during this same period Ražnatović was also responsible for a series of attacks on émigrés carried out on behalf of the Yugoslav secret services.

Returning to Belgrade in 1986 Ražnatović began a new career as an ostensibly respectable patisserie owner. After September 1990 Ražnatović also established himself as a patron of the Red Star Belgrade football club, and in particular its fanatical supporters, organisation, the Delije (Warriors). The nationalist propensities of these football supporters had been displayed on 13 May 1990 when the Delije from Red Star clashed with the 'Bad Blue Boys' supporters of the Croatian club Dinamo at a match in Zagreb. The authorites, however, were concerned that nationalist politicians beyond their direct control, and in particular Šešelj's Serbian Četnik Movement, would gain support amongst this group. Ražnatović's role was to neutralise such influences, and channel them into directions which could be controlled by the state. Ražnatović's close links with the ruling elite were well known, and he was frequently seen in the company of senior government officials, such as Radmilo Bogdanović, at Red Star functions. When on 11 October 1990, at the monastery of Pokajnica, Ražnatović founded the Serbian Volunteer Guard (SDG) or, as they were also known, the Tigers, the nucleus of this paramilitary force came from within the ranks of the Delije.[1] Among the first recruits to the SDG was Nebojša Djordjević Šuca the leader of the Delije who, coming from a family which had migrated from the south to settle in the village of Resnik near Belgrade, had been Vice-President of Šešelj's SČM before defecting to Ražnatović's organisation.[2] Also among the senior figures in the newly-founded SDG was Mihailo Ulmek, a café-owner from Stara Pazova who had briefly been a member of the SPO.[3]

Ražnatović's first paramilitary activities, however, were not notable for their success. On 29 November 1990 he was arrested at Dvor on the Una by the Croatian authorities and charged with arms offences. While Ražnatović claimed that he and his armed companions had been in the area 'out of curiosity' it was suspected that his real purpose was to liaise with local Serbian insurgents. After being held in custody for six months Ražnatović was sentenced to twenty months in prison by a Zagreb court. However, he was allowed to return to Belgrade pending an appeal against his sentence. Once back in Serbia, Ražnatović unsurprisingly showed little inclination to return to Croatia to face justice. In spite of this initial failure the Serbian authorities did not lose faith in Ražnatović's abilities with Radmilo Bogdanović commenting during the 9 March demonstrations: 'If Arkan had been here then everything would have been different.'[4] After his release from prison Ražnatović and the SDG were deployed in eastern Slavonia where they were heavily engaged in the actions around Vukovar in the summer and autumn of 1991. During the first months of the war in Bosnia the SDG took part in the seizure of the towns of Zvornik and Bijeljina, and the expulsion of their Muslim populations. The SDG was estimated to have a permanent core of 200 well-armed fighters based at Erdut in eastern Slavonia which could be expanded during periods of heavy military activity.[5]

At the end of 1990 Mirko Jović was joined in the depleted SNO by Dragoslav Bokan, who became General Secretary of the party. Bokan, recently returned from America, regarded himself as an intellectual, and under his influence the activities of the SNO took on an even more extreme tone. He became the 'commander' of the SNO youth wing, the White Eagles, which took its name from the youth wing of Ljotić's inter-war *Zbor* movement. Bokan's ultra-nationalist ideological orientation was matched by his militant attitude to politics with his followers being responsible for a series of attacks on opponents.

The interest taken by the state in the SNO and its need for paramilitary allies gave the organisation a new lease of life. During the war in Croatia the SNO deployed volunteer forces, identifying themselves as fighters of Dušan the Mighty (*Dušan Silni*) or White Eagles, which were armed and controlled by the Serbian state security services. They lacked the size and formal independence which characterised Ražnatović's SDG, and were frequently integrated into the existing Croatian Serb territorial defence forces. Jović described the role of the SNO: 'The party was a service which enabled its members and sympathisers to go easily to the front. Those who had resolved to go would have have made their way in any case. We directed them to where Serbian villages were most under threat.'[6] In Bokan's view the role of the SNO was to direct the energies of the Serbian people towards the military struggle. In August 1991 he said: 'The place for young Serbian people to be is on the battlefront and not in cafés.'[7] The SNO volunteers were active in Slavonia throughout 1991 and were present around Borovo Selo in May 1991 during the first clashes between the Serbian militia and Croatian police and national guardsmen. On the night of 13 December the last act of the SNO volunteers before withdrawing from the west Slavonian village of Voćin was to massacre thirty-nine of the villagers.[8] The downfall of the SNO, however, came when they sought to back Milan Babić, the leader of the SDS in Croatia, in his resistance to the Milošević-supported Vance Plan for Croatia in December 1991. The Vance Plan, called for the withdrawal of JNA forces, and the deployment of UN peacekeeping forces. Babić regarded the withdrawal of the JNA as a betrayal of Serbian national interests saying: 'Today, as 600 years ago, there is a sector of the Serbian nation which rejects its Serbian identity, which adheres to hollow ideas, and will implement foreign plans to annihilate the Serbian nation...Serbs from the Morava river to whom we entrusted our destiny have sold us to the foreigners.'[9] The SNO defiance of Milošević on this issue led, predictably, to the withdrawal of state backing from the organisation. In the absence of such state patronage attempts by Mirko Jović, in January 1992, to re-establish himself as an independent actor on the political scene ended in failure, and the SNO retreated to the margins of Serbian political life.[10]

In the autumn of 1990 Vojislav Šešelj's attempts to organise volunteers to support the Serbian rebels in Knin had earned him another spell in prison. By the summer of 1991 such efforts, on his part, were enjoying official approval. Šešelj was, at that time reticient regarding his sources of support and his level of co-operation with the authorities. In later years, and under different political circumstances, however, he was more candid. According to Šešelj, speaking in 1994, the first detachment of SRS volunteers, consisting of fourteen fighters, arrived in Borovo Selo in April 1991 at the request of the commander of the local Serbian territorial defence forces, Vukašin Šoškočanin. Once there, the fighters were issued with firearms by the local Serbian militia who were acting with the approval of officials from the Serbian police. Šešelj claimed: 'Our first contact with the police was in the summer of 1991. Then we began to receive arms directly. The first man who we had such contacts with was Kertes. And during this time it was Kertes who was most in evidence. [...] Later, when the army entered the war, we co-operated with the army. The police did not have as many weapons as the army, and the army gave weapons to us. We were given buses and a barracks at Bubanj Potok, and we armed ourselves there, and seated on the buses we went to the front. Sometimes we sent volunteers by aeroplane to Udbina, or to Banja Luka airport. All these contacts functioned well.'[11] This level of paramilitary collaboration between the Radicals and the Socialists would persist from the time of the the first armed clashes in Croatia, through the outbreak of war in Bosnia, until the latter half of 1993. The relationship established between Šešelj and the Serbian state authorities in Belgrade was paralleled by similar agreements between Radical and Socialist officials in the provinces. According to Branislav Vakić, the leader of the SRS in Niš, in late 1992, 'When it was necessary to urgently send seventy people to Srebrenica, the buses were secured for us, at my request, by Mile Ilić, the President of the local SPS.'[12]

Formally Šešelj sought to differentiate between the paramilitary role, which was officially assigned to the Serbian Četnik Movement, and the political role of the SRS. In practice, however, the paramilitary and the political wings of Šešelj's organisation were strongly interconnected. Paramilitary service frequently held the key to political advancement within the ranks of the SRS. Branislav Vakić, a former boxer and taxi driver had, like Šešelj, briefly been a member of the SPO before being expelled for 'criminality' and 'extremism' at the begining of 1991. He then transferred his loyalties to the SRS, and after spending eight months on the front-line around Vukovar, as part of a Četnik unit, he was appointed as head of the Niš SRS. He would also, subsequently, head the SRS federal candidate lists for south-eastern Serbia.[13] Tomislav Nikolić, the SRS Vice-President, also served as a paramilitary Četnik volunteer first around Vukovar and later in Bosnia. In May 1992 he was promoted by Šešelj to the rank of *knez*, meaning head-man or leader, at a ceremony held on the Romanija mountain above Sarajevo.[14] Similarily for Ljubiša Petković, a former taxi-driver and NRS activist, political advancement within the SRS was facilitated by his role as commander of the SRS War Staff. In this role he co-ordinated the dispatch of volunteers to the front and acted as liaison with the SRS's backers in the Interior Ministry.[15] Milika Dačević, a hospital cook in Belgrade originally from the village of Odjak near Pljevlja in the Montenegrin Sandžak, was also propelled into a political career through his paramilitary involvement. Dačević fought as a volunteer around Vukovar, where his brother Luka was killed, and later in Bosnia, in the Goražde region. Returning to his native village he was to be returned as a SRS federal representative in the December 1992 elections.[16]

Individuals such as Dačević typified the way in which paramilitary volunteers came to enjoy an enhanced status beyond their normal, rather marginal, existence. A survey of fifty SRS volunteers carried out by the newspaper *Borba* at the end of 1991 characterised these individuals: 'Between twenty and thirty-five years of age, with a secondary education, employed, with at least one child, and one failed marriage, most of the volunteers had a rural background, but with permanent residence in one of the regional centres. Every fifth volunteer had had serious problems with the law (a suspended or actual prison sentence), and some went to the front-lines directly from prison. According to unverified sources, some of the prisoners who were about to finish their sentence were able to reduce it if they agreed to join the volunteers.'[17] These paramilitary groups included not only forces attached to significant political parties, such as the SRS, or independent military forma-tions, such as the SDG, but also small, unattached groups such as the Yellow Wasps led by the brothers Dušan and Vojin Vučković, the Serbian Falcons led by Siniša Vučinić, and the Četnik Avengers led by Milan Lukić. Milan Lukić, originally from the village of Rujište near Višegrad in Bosnia, after failing to continue his education beyond secondary level due to 'bad material conditions,' worked in Germany before returning to run a café in the town of Obrenovac outside Belgrade. His paramilitary unit essentially consisted of relatives, colleagues, and individuals recruited from the clientele of his café. In spite of this narrow support base Lukić had considerable pretensions regarding the status and role of his group. Training within the Četnik Avengers, he declared, would include not only instruction in military techniques but also lectures on 'Serbian war ethics, the history of the Četniks and the Komitas (guerrillas) in southern Serbia and other areas, and religious studies, including, above all the spiritual, philosophical, and political speeches and sermons of bishop Nikolaj Velimirović.' Lukić's Četnik Avengers were held to be responsible for a series of atrocities committed in his native town of Višegrad during the first months of the war in Bosnia.[18]

The role of the paramilitaries as auxillaries to the JNA in the war effort in Croatia was recognised in mid-July 1991 when a secret directive acknowledged the volunteers as members of the armed forces. Such recognition, even in this covert form, marked a major shift in the ideological orientation of the army from its Yugoslav and Communist position to one which accommodated groups dedicated to the Serbian nationalist cause. Volunteer units were fully integrated into the re-organised JNA forces which finally suceeded in taking the devastated town of Vukovar on 19 November. The status of the volunteers was officially and openly confirmed in an order issued by Branko Kostić, the Federal Yugoslav Vice-President on 10 December 1991.[19]

Vuk Drašković reacted to the inter-communal hostilities in Croatia, and the clashes between the JNA and the Slovenian National Guard following their declaration of independence on 25 June, by hardening his position on national issues, and temporarily abandoning the 'moderate' line which he had cultivated in the previous months. At the 9 June USDO rally his speech took on a strongly 'heroic' tone with a call for the formation of a Serbian National Guard to mirror those existing in Croatia and Slovenia, but which would be 'twice as large as all Croatia's armed forces put together.' He told the demonstration: 'The Serbian state must take it upon itself to defend the Serbian people in those parts of Croatia where they constitute a majority ...Serbia must punish those who threaten Serbs, demolish their homes, and force them to migrate, when Croatia is not doing so herself.'[20] On 30 June Drašković reiterated his message: 'The Yugoslav National Army has been defeated in Slovenia, and in a way all of us have been humiliated. The army that has been claiming to be one of the most prepared armies in Europe was defeated by an amateur gang bearing a lime tree leaf on their caps, by a gang that has never had armed forces or an army. Unfortunately it was mainly Serbian children that lost their lives, and our children are becoming Janša hostages [Janez Janša – Slovenian Defence Minister]. In this way the Serbian soldier has been humiliated. [...] We must set up a Serbian army quickly and then we will see whether the things that have been happening in Slovenia will happen again.'[21]

Drašković at first intended that Simo Dubajić, an SPO activist from Croatia, and Kosta Bulatović, from Kosovo, should be the leaders of this new Serbian Guard. With these two unable to take up the leadership Drašković turned to two other close associates, Djordje Božović, also known as 'Giška', and Branislav Matić or 'Beli'. Borivoje Borović, a senior SPO member, defined the relationship between the SPO and the Guard saying: 'The Serbian Guard was never part of the SPO, but its foundation was the idea of our party. The SPO proposed that Giška should be commander, but there were members of other parties in the Guard, mainly Radicals, but there were even several Socialists.'[22] Božović, who was to be the first commander of the Serbain Guard, had earned notoriety for his criminal activities in both Serbia and Western Europe. He had served a six-year prison sentence in Milan for his part in 'underworld' activities in Italy. During his time in Western Europe he was reported to have worked for the SDB carrying out covert operations against dissident émigrés. Subsequently, however, he developed anti-communist beliefs and an admiration for the Četnik tradition which caused him, by 1990, to declare his support for the SPO. He would later seek to rationalise his criminal activities as a form of anti-communist dissidence:[23] 'In the Serbian Guard only I had a criminal past...a man cannot change his past. In the Serbian Guard – and I will swear to this –there were no criminals. In all liberation and resistance movements across the world a place will always be found for patriotic "criminals".' [24]

Branislav Matić, who was to be Božović's deputy and one of

the Serbian Guard's main financial backers, had made his fortune as a Belgrade scrap metal dealer. However, like his friend and colleague Giška, he was believed to be close to 'underground' criminal circles in Serbia. During the 'anti-bureaucratic revolution' Matić had been an enthusiastic supporter of Slobodan Milošević – apparently believing that he had abandoned Communism – contributing considerable sums of money to his cause. Matić was, however, swiftly disillusioned with Milošević, and in 1990 he transferred his allegiance to Vuk Drašković.[25]

Before the formation of the Serbian Guard these individuals had played a key role in providing security for the SPO during the 9 March 1991 demonstrations. The personal contacts of these individuals among the 'hard men' of the Belgrade underworld meant that they were able to involve other individuals in this task who were otherwise not known for their political activism. One such individual was Aleksandar Knežević ('Knele'), a notorious young gangster. Knežević was to be murdered in October 1992 in Belgrade's Hyatt hotel in what was widely believed to be part of a gangland feud.[26] Milika Dačević was also present on 9 March, and was to be active in the Serbian Guard prior to his defection to the SRS.[27] Goran Vuković, another major figure in the Serbian 'underworld' was known, before his assasination in December 1994, to be close to senior figures within the SPO including Milan Komnenić and Borivoje Borović.[28]

With such individuals as Giška, Beli, Čeko, and Knele involved in maintaining security at the 9 March demonstrations it is perhaps not surprising that the police attacks on the demonstrators met with such a ferocious response. These contacts ensured that the SPO, in this early 'populist' phase, contained within its upper ranks an eclectic combination of poets and gangsters.[29]

Interviewed in November 1993 Danica Drašković fiercely denied that any valid comparison could be made between the Serbian Guard leaders, Djordje Božović and Branislav Matić, and other paramilitary leaders, such as Željko Ražnatović ('Arkan'): 'They were not the same type of people. [...] If they had remained alive Beli and Giška would never have used blood money to make political propaganda nor would they have constructed a house of blood.'[30] In spite of these denials similarities could be observed – in their underworld connections and their consequent celebrity status – between these individuals and other paramilitary leaders.[30] At the same time, however, a clear difference did exist between the Serbian Guard and rival groupings. While other paramilitary formations were drawn under the umbrella of the state, the Serbian Guard enjoyed the patronage of Vuk Drašković, a well-known anti-communist and opposition figure, and its commanders remained strongly antagonistic towards the authorities. Božović talked of his desire to 'deliver the final blow to communism with his bare hands', while Matić stated that his dream was to see the 'expulsion of Communism from Serbia'.[31]

The activities of the Serbian Guard were officially inaugurated on 6 July 1991. The Guard was described as the nucleus of a 'non-ideological, non-party, and all-party army of Serbia organised to defend the nation and democracy'. In his new role Božović styled himself as 'supreme commander of the Serbian Guard and temporary commander of the Serbian people until the king returns to the fatherland'.[32] While the formation and operation of the Serbian Guard was not actually prevented by the authorities, a constant level of pressure was exerted on it by the state. While the deeds of other paramilitary forces were glorified on the state-controlled media those of the Serbian Guard came under frequent attack. On 3 August Božović narrowly escaped, by jumping from a second floor window, after he was attacked by a gang in the restaurant of the Slavija hotel. On 4 August, after returning from reviewing newly-formed Serbian Guard units near the town of Takovo, Branislav Matić was cut down by automatic gunfire from unidentified assailants, outside his home in the Voždovac district of Belgrade. For the SPO there was no doubt that the hand of the authorities could be detected behind these attacks. A few days earlier, speaking in the Serbian parliament, Vojislav Šešelj had denounced the leaders of the Serbian Guard. Matić, the SPO declared was a 'victim of the red terror' and his killers were 'regime hired fascists'. Božović saw the two attacks as a demonstration of the regime's 'desire to prevent support for the Guard growing.'[33] Drašković paid tribute to Matić: 'He was the best man that I knew, I will write books about him.'[34]

In September when the Serbian Guard attempted to deploy in eastern Slavonia they were prevented from crossing the Danube by the Serbian police. The Guard was eventually allowed, with the help of transportation provided by the JNA, to take up positions around the town of Gospić in Lika. Branko Lainović ('Dugi'), at that time the Guard's deputy commander, would later complain that in Gospić the Serbian Guard had found themselves caught 'between two fires' fighting the Croatian National Guard while at the same time facing a constant 'blockade and obstruction' from the local Serbian territorial defence forces.[35] Members of the Serbian Guard even complained that their positions were accidentally or deliberately shelled by the JNA.[36] It was in this situation that on 14 September Božović was killed by a Croatian sniper's bullet. The atmosphere of hostility between the Guard and the state authorities gave rise to suggestions that there were 'mysterious' circumstances surrounding his death.[37]

Djordje Božović was mourned in Serbian nationalist circles as a fallen hero.[38] One article in the magazine *Duga* paid tribute to him: 'He departed with the victorious smile of someone who was convinced to the end...that he had given his life and his death for the new Serbia, even though many people would never be able to understand his final act of courage among the plum trees of Lika. [...] He died standing like a tree trunk, and even at that moment, hit by a sniper's bullet which struck and carried away a part of his heart, he lived longer than other people. [...] He longed for someone to write that Lika was his Kosovo and that the unconquered knight of the most renowned city brawls had migrated into an epic and forever settled in the heavenly kingdom of the Serbian warriors.'[39] Vuk Drašković, speaking at Božović's funeral was just as eloquent in his praise of the Serbian Guard declaring that it was 'an army with the soul of a maiden, the habits of a priest, and the heart of Obilić'.[40]

Božović's place as commander of the Serbian Guard was taken by Branko Lainović. Lainović was the owner of a popular nightclub in Novi Sad, who like Božović, was reputed to have been involved in organised crime in Western Europe, and had been deported from West Germany for this reason.[41] The relationship between Lainović and Drašković was characterised by rapidly developing personal and political tensions. The paramilitary commander found it particularily hard to reconcile himself with the policy of 'peace' which Drašković was following during the latter half of 1991. By December 1991 the split had become so profound that Lainović had broken off all formal links with Drašković. Lainović did, however, retain personal contacts with certain key figures within the SPO including Slobodan Rakitić and Zoran Horvan. However, he also developed links with individuals known to be close to the ruling establishment such as Brana Crnčević, the writer, SPS parliamentary representative and head of the organisation *Matica iseljenika*, dedicated to helping Serbs outside Serbia. These connections were apparently useful in helping the Serbian Guard, which now defined itself as a 'supra-political organisation', to obtain offices in central Belgrade.[42] In the spring and summer of 1992 Lainović's Guards were among the many Serbian paramilitary groups who were active in the first months of the war in Bosnia-Hercegovina. In September 1992 it was recorded that the Serbian Guard had 15,000 registered members with 600 being active on the Bosnia-Hercegovina battlefront.[43] Lainović's split with Drašković precipitated a fragmentation of the Serbian Guard organisation with one faction, led by Zvonko Osmalji´ cand favourably disposed towards the SPO, forming its own independent organisation. This faction continued to provide security at opposition gatherings backed by the SPO such as the Vidovdan Sabor of June 1992.[44] The Osmaljić wing of the Serbian Guard dissolved itself in the autumn of 1994. Osmaljić, however, continued to act as head of security for the SPO. In December 1991 a bomb exploded at Lainović's nightclub in Novi Sad in an apparent attempt to kill him, and, one year later, on 21 December 1992 Lainović was seriously wounded in another assasination attempt. It was, however, unclear whether the motive behind these attacks related to the political or the criminal activities in which Lainović was engaged.[45]

Notes

1. Vladimir Jovanović, 'Traži se zbog....', *Monitor*, 13 June 1997; Ivan Čolović 'Fudbal, huligani i rat' in Popov (ed.), 1996, pp. 435-44; Mirko Tomov Matović, 'Tigrovi – Srpska dobrovlački garda', *Srpsko jedinstvo*, July/August 1995.
2. Slobodan Ikonić, 'Šuca i Žuća', *NIN*, 18 October 1996.
3. Uroš Komlenović *et al.* 'Birtijaš i pukovnik', *Vreme*, 5 September 1994.
4. Tim Judah, *The Serbs – History, Myth and the Destruction of Yugoslavia*, Yale University Press (New Haven), 1997, p. 184; 'Wanted – *Arkan* ocima Si-En-Ena', CNN documentary transcibed by Dejan Anastesijević, *Vreme*, 31 May 1997; Uroš Komlenović, 'Ljudi za ova vremena', *NIN*, 20 September 1991.
5. Miloš Vašić, 'The Yugoslav Army and the Post-Yugoslav Armies' in David

Dyker and Ivan Vejoda, *Yugoslavia and After – A Study of Fragmentation, Despair and Rebirth*, Belgrade (1996), p. 134.

6. Branka Andjelković and Batić Bačević, 'Tigrovi odlaze?', *NIN*, 21 April 1995.
7. Filip Švarm and Dejan Anastasijević, 'Bokan –jedan karijera', *Vreme*, 19 October 1996.
8. 'Massacre at Vočin', *The Economist*, 21 December 1991.
9. *Tanjug*, 12 April 1992 in *SWB EE/4415 C/11*, 14 April 1992.
10. Radio Belgrade, 27 January 1992 in *SWB EE/2423 C/5*, 29 January 1992.
11. *Guja u nedrima*, Vojislav Šešelj interviewed by Mirjana Bobić-Mojsilović, Glas (1994), pp. 76-7.
12. Srboljub Bogdanović, 'Odlozeni nokaut', *NIN*, 10 March 1995.
13. Uroš Komlenović, 'Hronika najavljenog nokauta', *Vreme*, 7 June 1993.
14. Nenad LJ Stefanović, 'Lik i delo – Tomislav Nikolić', *Vreme*, 1 August 1994.
15. Stefanović (1994), pp. 66-71.
16. Vanja Bulić, 'Kako je dvojka postala trojka', *Duga*, 13 March 1993.
17. Maja Korać, 'Understanding Ethnic National Identity in Times of War and Social Change' in Robert Pynesent (ed.) *The Literature of Nationalism*, SSEES (London), 1996, p. 240.
18. Branislav Matić, 'Komandant bez dozvole za nošenje oružje', *Duga*, 21 November 1992; Ed Vulliamy, 'Butcher of the Drina', *The Guardian*, 11 March 1996.
19. Milos Vasić and Filip Švarm, 'Generalski "crni petak"', *Vreme*, 30 December 1995.
20. *Tanjug*, 9 June 1991 in *SWB EE/1095 B/16*, 11 June 1991.
21. Belgrade TV, 30 June 1991 in *SWB EE/1114 B/10*, 3 July 1991.
22. Alexandar Knežević and Vojislav Tufegžić, 'Kriminal koji je izmenio Srbiju', B-92 (Belgrade), 1995, p. 28.
23. Stojan Cerović, 'Obilići garavoga lica', *Vreme*, 23 September 1991.
24. Knežević and Tufegžić (1995), p. 13.
25. 'I dobrotvore ubijaju, zar ne?', *Srpska reč*, 19 August 1991.
26. Bogdan Ivanišević, 'Odlazak surovog zaštitnika', *NIN*, 6 November 1992.
27. 'Život za gusle', Milika 'Čeko' Dačević interviewed by Branka Andjelković and Batić Bačević, *NIN*, 21 April 1995.
28. Knežević and Tufegžić (1995), p. 72.
29. Vanja Bulić, 'Odsutni sa slike na trgu', *Duga*, 15 March 1997.
30. 'Ne moliti nego tući', Danica Drašković interviewed by Luka Mičeta, *NIN*, 12 November 1993.
31. Vojislav Tufegdžić, 'Majke Jugovića – Srbije', *Profil*, October/November 1995.
32. Branka Andjelković and Batić Bačević, 'Tigrovi odlaze?', *NIN*, 21 April 1995.
33. 'Izbegao sam odred likvidaciju', Djordje Božovic 'Giška' interviewed by Slavica Laúzić, *Srpska reč*, 19 August 1991.
34. Knežević and Tufegžić (1995), p. 12.
35. Uroš Komlenović, *NIN*, 20 September 1995.
36. Vladimir Paunović, 'Bože garde – istina o srpskim vitezovima', *Pogledi*, 31 January 1992.

37. 'Pobedjuju neinformisani', Aleksandar Jokanović interviewed by Vanja Bulić, *Duga*, 2 July 1993.
38. Vuk Drašković would continue to revere the memory of Giška and Beli long after the SPO had abandoned such paramilitary links. In his speech to the SPO congress in June 1997 he gave a 'roll of honour' in which the names of SPO members and opposition supporters, killed or injured in the recent, consciously pacific street protests were linked with the names of these paramilitary leaders. Drašković's speech is reprinted in Vuk Drašković, 'Piromani su i dalje pored benzina', *Srpska reč*, 10 July 1997.
39. Duška Jovanić, 'The Thief of Liberty – The Last Battle of the Commander of the Serbian Guard', *Duga*, 28 September 1991 (transl. Wendy Bracewell).
40. Dubravka Stojanović, 'Traumatični krug srpske opozicije' in Popov (ed.), 1996, p. 528.
41. Gordana Jovanović, 'Niko mu nista ne može', *Duga*, 21 November 1992.
42. Branko Andjelković, 'Kratki rafal u dugog', *NIN*, 1 January 1993.
43. Vojislav Tufegdžić and Andjelka Popović, 'Srpske jedinice pod jednom komandom', *Intervju*: 18 September 1992.
44. Miško Lazović, 'U Srbiji hajka na Srbe', *Stav*, 24 July 1992.
45. Ivan Radovanović, 'Godina opasnog življenja', *Vreme*, 4 January 1993.

10. Divisions and Alliances: The Serbian Opposition (July 1991–July 1992)

The progress of the fighting in Croatia prompted a wave of anti-war sentiment across Serbia. Instances of resistance to conscription were common not only in the capital and other larger cities, but also in the small towns of the Serbian interior. The forms that this resistance took ranged from individual acts of evasion to instances of collective mutiny. Perhaps the most serious of such cases was the refusal in March 1992 of 380 reservists from the town of Gornji Milanovac in the Šumadija, to return to their positions in western Slavonia. The demonstration later grew as relatives and other local people joined the protest.[1]

This condemnation of the war was echoed by Serbian opposition politicians. In a leaflet issued in late September 1991 Vuk Drašković urged Serbian troops conscripted into the JNA to 'pick up their guns and run' from the front-line. He added: 'The strategy of total and fatal war, which Serbia does not want, will leave it without prosperity, without allies and friends.' The SPO also condemned the attack by the JNA on Dubrovnik. A spokesman stated that it was not 'in the interest or the spirit of the Serbian people for scores of thousands of residents of the beseiged town to be exposed to hunger'. The DS also denounced the role of the Serbian government in the conflict. Desimir Tošić stated: 'We want to stop this shameless and senseless war immediately. People do not know what they are fighting for. I don't think the Serbian government really knows what it wants to achieve. Milošević is using the conflict to cling to power.'[2]

Among Serbian ultra-nationalists the fall of Vukovar in November 1991 was a cause for rejoicing. However, a very different note was struck by Drašković in an article, 'Take off your cap – and be silent', published on 28 November in the daily newspaper

Borba. He wrote: 'It is not possible for me to celebrate the victory at Vukovar, which is euphorically proclaimed in the war propaganda of an intoxicated Serbia. It is not possible, because I will not sin against the dead, against the thousands of dead, nor against the survivors of Vukovar who must endure eternal pain and misfortune. "You are damned for what you have done to us"–curse the Serb and Croat survivors of Vukovar. And when they do so two names are mentioned most often. No one amongst the victims is ignorant of where the epicentere of their suffering should be located. "Independent Croatia or death!" said Tudjman. "Federation or death" said Milošević, as if death was one stop on the route of their train. The inevitable result of such politics is what now remains of Vukovar. It is not and never will be Vukovar. It is the Hiroshima of Croatian and Serbian madness.'[3] During this period, however, Drašković's forthright condemnation of the 'offensive' actions of the state-backed JNA in Vukovar and other places in Croatia did not prevent him, on the basis of ideological differentiation, from supporting the involvement of the Četnik Serbian Guard in Croatia who he considered to be engaged in 'defensive' actions protecting the Serbian population.[4]

Milošević reacted angrily to Drašković's condemnation of war, promising his followers that he was ready to deal with such 'conservative forces' threatening Serbia from within. In consequence, at the end of January 1992 Drašković was once again threatened with prosecution for his part in organising the demonstrations of 9 March 1991. At the same time Branko Lainović, the commander of the anti-Drašković faction of the now fragmented Serbian Guard, claimed to have evidence that Vuk and Danica Drašković, along with Simo Dubajić, had been smuggling arms into Belgrade with the intention of staging a coup against the authorities. It was because of their activities, he claimed, that 'Belgrade is the most heavily armed town in Europe'. Lainović stated that he and the Serbian Guard were 'anti-communists and part of the opposition, but they will invest all their energy in fighting bolshevism among the Serbian opposition'. The ambiguous nature of this statement, and the fact that his claims were given prominent coverage by the state media suggests that they enjoyed official approval. These various attacks, however, did not deter the SPO from continuing their criticism of the war effort.[5] On 21 March the SPO responded to the refusal of the authorities to grant an amnesty to those who had deserted from the army or failed to heed their call-up by observing: 'There will be no amnesty for politicians and generals who caused this dirty, senseless, and for the Serbian people, fatal war...200,000 young men..will fight for their freedom and civil rights with all available means, including appeals to international legal institutions.'[6]

The declarations of independence by Slovenia and Croatia on 25 June 1991, the subsequent war, and the recognition of these republics independence by the European community on 15 January 1992 set in motion a process of reassessment amongst the Serbian opposition parties of their attitude towards the 'national question'. While in his first months on the political scene, in 1990, Drašković had been willing to talk and write of the possibility of realising a 'Great Serbian' territorial settlement by 1991 he saw the preservation of Yugoslavia as the only viable solution to the developing crisis. In March 1991 he explained: 'As a Serbian party, we want all Serbs to live in freedom, in democracy, and in one country, and that country cannot be other than Yugoslavia.'[7] In February 1992 Drašković proposed that Yugoslavia be replaced by a Yugoslav commonwealth. In this arrangement Serbia, Montenegro, Bosnia–Hercegovina and Macedonia would form a union of south Slav states which would form a looser economic or customs union with Croatia and Slovenia. This was known as the '4+2' solution to Yugoslavia's problems. Drašković welcomed the deployment of UN peacekeeping forces in Croatia as a vital pre-condition to the resolution of the Serbo-Croatian conflict, and supported, albeit with some reservations, the conditions of the Vance Plan. Drašković, however, lamented that the preservation of the pre-1991 state of Yugoslavia was now impossible, saying: 'The fate of the common state has been determined by the spiteful politics of Milošević's crew. This unfortunate situation was set in motion when primitives arrived in positions where they were able to determine our national destiny.'[8]

The DS was founded on the idea that Yugoslavia needed to be preserved as a federal state. On 26 May 1991 Dragoljub Mićunović called for new federal Yugoslav elections: 'Consent to federal elections in their own right means consent to Yugoslavia...it is high time that the responsible men of politics in the feuding Yugoslav republics resign and cede their jobs to those capable of negotiating.'[9] In August the Democratic Party organised a meeting in Sarajevo of parliamentarians from all the Yugoslav republics in an attempt to promote dialogue between the parties. The events of that year placed this 'Yugoslav' position under increasing strain. In the same month that Mićunović had called for an electoral re-affirmation of the federal identity the leading DS figures Mirko Petrović and Zoran Djindjić were talking in parliament of the need to 'determine the western borders of Serbdom'. Speaking in January 1992 Djindjić rejected the '4+2' arrangement or any other type of renewed Yugoslav federation: 'We do not think that it is wise to create a truncated Yugoslavia...that is simply one option from the political carousel which cannot be taken seriously. We do not intend to turn our backs on the Serbs outside Serbia. Serbia must provide the framework for a union of Serbian states.' A representative of the Croatian SDS in Serbia, Dragan Vranković, greeted Djindjić's statement: 'The Democratic Party has become pan-Serbian.'[10] The DS was also critical of the Vance Plan, and on the 17 January Mićunović met the leaders of the SDS, Milan Babić who was by that time in open confrontation with Milošević, and Radovan Karadžić who was still a firm Milošević ally, for talks in Belgrade. After the meeting he raised the question of the disarming of Serbian forces during the deployment of UN peacekeepers in Croatia: 'Why is it suspected that these formations shall not adhere to a peace agreement unlike other military formations in Croatia?', and concluded that the 'Serbian people's fears are logical that, if disarmed, they will fall easy prey to the Croatian extremists.'[11] In the event, however, the UN deployment in Serbian held areas of Croatia, or the Republic of Serbian Krajina (RSK), did not lead to the disarmament of local forces and the infrastructure of a new Serbian army was left behind by the departing JNA.

While the DS and the SPO differed on constitutional issues they were united in their opposition to the Milošević government. The opposition parties seized the opportunity offered by the end of the fighting in Croatia to launch a renewed offensive against the regime. On 9 February the DS presented its 'Proclamation of the Democratic Party to the Serbian Public'. This document declared: 'Today there can be no doubt that politically Serbia has suffered a crushing defeat – on the national, economic and social levels. The political leadership of Serbia must carry full responsibility for the fact that the Serbian nation and the citizens of Serbia have been left as the greatest losers in the break-up of Yugoslavia. [...] Those who have the greatest power must carry the greatest responsibility, and the Democratic Party demands that the President of the Republic of Serbia, Slobodan Milošević, submits his resignation. So that Serbia can set out on its way towards recovery and rebirth, the Democratic Party considers it necessary that elections are held without delay for a constitution forming assembly, which will put in place Serbia's future state order, and its national and state interests. We invite all free-thinking and patriotic citizens, of all political parties, institutions and associations from across Serbia, to place their signatures in support of these two demands.' The signature gathering drive for the DS petition was supported by the SPO, New Democracy, Serbian Liberal Party, National Peasants Party and the Reformists. The Reformist Party, led by Vesna Pešić, was the re-named Serbian section of the Alliance of Reform Forces. The same collection of parties agreed to co-operate in staging, on the initiative of the SPO, a rally in Belgrade on 9 March. By the time that the rally took place the petition had succeeded in gathering 320,000 signatures – ultimately this figure would rise to a total of 840,000 signatures. One wit called these events the 'happening of the signatures'.[12]

The run-up to 9 March saw attempts to mobilise both for and against the rally. Vesna Pešić, speaking on Studio B TV, said that the 'citizens need to free themselves from the fear which the regime has inspired.' Kosta Čavoški stressed that the rally would be an important step towards overthrowing Milošević who 'will not fall through parliament, but rather on the streets'.

The Socialists on the other hand condemned the proposed rally with Petar Škundrić, the SPS General Secretary, declaring 'For Serbia's enemies 9 March is a great day of joy, but for all Serbs it is a great misfortune.' Socialist officials also sought to suggest that Albanians would take advantage of Serbian divisions in order to subvert their control over the province of Kosovo. As in the previous year, Serbs from outside Serbia were brought in by the regime so as to express their concerns about the impending rally. Radovan Karadžić warned that the rally would mark 'a defeat for the Serbs'. The rally was condemned in similar terms by Gojko Djogo in his capacity as President of the Association of Serbs from Bosnia and Hercegovina, despite the fact that he was a founding member of the DS, one of the rally's main organisers.[13] Djogo was well known for his support for the Serbs beyond the Drina expressed in strong, and almost mystical terms. He had said on one occasion: 'Serbia is a metaphor for a utopia cherished for centuries by the sightless minstrel, to the strings of the fiddle, in the arms of the widow, Serbia is the mother. He who has a mother cannot fully understand that kind of love. People from Šumadija do not understand what Serbia is, what the Serbia of Dučić and Crnjanski is. They know what Ćosić's is, a small Serbia of the Morava.'[14]

On 9 March 50,000 opposition supporters attended the rally held outside St Sava's cathedral. The event was notable for the support offered to the opposition by the head of the Serbian Orthodox church, Patriarch Pavle. Originally from Slavonia, he had succeeded as head of the Orthodox church on the death of his predecessor German in December 1990. His pronouncements were, as was characteristic of Orthodox clerics, often couched in obscure language and peppered with biblical allusions. He was, however, regarded as a moderate voice at the head of the Serbian church. During the March 1991 demonstrations, convinced that Serbia was on the verge of civil war, he had addressed meetings on both the Terazije and the Ušće pleading for reconciliation between the contending sides. Before the 1992 rally the authorities had exerted considerable pressure in order to dissuade him from attending the rally. Speaking before the opposition audience outside the cathedral, he addressed himself to Slobodan Milošević and the Serbian government: 'To you all the shedding of blood and all the misfortune in the madness of this fraticidal war has not made plain the truth that out of such evil no good can come.'[15] Simultaneously, renewed student protests occurred on the Terazije.

The 9 March rally saw renewed calls for opposition unity, but these contrasted starkly with the obvious tensions within the opposition leadership. These opposition unity moves were, however, pushed energetically by a group of Serbian intellectuals. Some of these intellectuals, including Matija Bećković, Borislav Mihailović Mihiz and Predrag Palavestra, had also played prominent roles in the founding of the royalist Crown Council on 15 February. This group held meetings with Dragoljub Mićunović on 1 and 21 April, but was disappointed by his lack of enthusiasm for the formation of a new opposition alliance. A further round of meetings followed between the intellectual supporters of unity, and Vuk

Drašković who travelled to London to discuss the proposed new alliance with Crown Prince Alexander of Yugoslavia. Vuk Drašković also held talks on opposition unity with an element of the DS, consisting most notably of Vojislav Koštunica, Vladeta Janković and Mirko Petrović, who regarded the idea of a common opposition front more favourably than Mićunović. On 13 May Vuk Drašković, addressing SPO supporters at Ravna Gora, promised them that the end of May would see renewed demonstrations and the formation of a new coalition which would have three paramount aims: 'to overthrow communism, to overthrow communism, and to overthrow communism'.[16]

On 23 May the new coalition, the Democratic Movement of Serbia, DEPOS, held its first meeting. The alliance joined together the SPO, SLS, New Democracy – Movement for Serbia, and the Serbian Peasant's Party (SSS). Additionally it enjoyed the support of Koštunica's faction of the DS, which styled itself 'the Democrats for DEPOS'. DEPOS was, however, intended to be more than simply a political alliance, but was meant to be a broad coalition of interests and individuals for the democratic transformation of Serbia. The intellectuals who had been pivotal in the construction of the alliance were incorporated into the leadership of the alliance as a separate body. On the basis of this intellectual involvement one commentator compared DEPOS with the inter-war Serbian Cultural Club. Matija Bećković chaired the forty-seven man governing body of the alliance.

On 28 June DEPOS launched a series of demonstrations, known as the Vidovdan Sabor, which continued until 5 July. These DEPOS demonstrations ran parallel with anti-government student demonstrations which started on 4 June, and continued for the next forty days.[17] The support given by Koštunica's faction in the DS to DEPOS heightened the already existing tensions within the party. On 26 July, having been unable to bring the whole of the DS into DEPOS, the 'Democrats for DEPOS' broke with the DS and transformed themselves into the Democratic Party of Serbia (DSS).[18]

Mićunović and his allies within the DS, such as Zoran Djindjić and Desimir Tošić, cited a number of different reasons for their refusal to join DEPOS. At an organisational level Mićunović accused his opposition rivals of being overly concerned with the idea of 'grand alliances'. He stated: 'At the beginning one of their spokesmen stated that DEPOS would provide co-ordination while the parties would pull the coaches. However, that idea is wholly mistaken. We are not in a pre-political stage. We have parties which have created their own infrastructures and images, they have their own representatives, and they have no reason now to come under some form of tutorship. Political parties are voluntarily joined on the basis of belief. It would therefore be wholly illegitimate to collectively place people in another political organisation...it would also, I think, be like returning to some sort of "popular front" where all party differences are submerged within a body which makes binding decisions and inhibits the development of diverse political programmes.'[19] The 'DEPOS faction' within the DS replied to the charge that they were 'fixated on popular fronts' by pointing out that the extraordinary political situation which existed in Serbia, which Mirko Petrović at that time described as 'an authoritarian system which takes on an increasingly totalitarian form', justified the creation of extraordinary supra-party alliances and coalitons.[20]

Related differences existed regarding the tactics which the opposition should follow. The Mićunović faction of the DS favoured a policy of 'compromise' and opposition to the government through the existing institutions. They rejected the model of confrontation, demonstration, and the 'orientation towards the streets' which, they said, was favoured by other opposition groups. Vojislav Koštunica retorted that 'compromise is something which is the appropriate model for a stable democratic order' but could not apply in Serbia where the institutions were fashioned in order to preserve the dominant position of the ruling Socialists.[21]

Important differences in ideology and identity also alienated the Mićunović faction, with their 'rationalist/left' *Praxis* origins, from the DEPOS project. Later Mićunović would write: 'I was never against a unified opposition, but that unification must be principled. [...] When DEPOS was created in a form which directly incorporated intellectuals into the leadership without reference to the electors, and insisted on a strong monarchist orientation with the church acting as a powerful influence, we regarded this as narrowing its support base.' According to Mićunović the coalition had to go beyond the 'Draža-monarchy-church' model if it was to gather to it the votes of the majority of Serbian citizens.[22] Another DS founder and former *Praxis* intellectual, Ljubomir Tadić, also spoke scornfully of the neo-traditionalist image and the tactics of DEPOS: 'I was against it for principled reasons because the Serbian Renewal Movement and its satellite, the Liberal Party, made up of our former members, have in their programmes only two solutions, to which they hold to blindly – boycotts and permanent meetings...or with Vuk Drašković the magic number nine [referring to 9 March]. [...] Drašković is a good boy – as long as he does not involve himself in politics. But I believe that he has strayed into politics without understanding the thinking of those people who hold up three fingers [the traditional Serbian national sign]...or chant the slogan *"svi, svi, svi"* [a royalist/Četnik chant]'. He later added: 'I have called the Vidovdan Sabor a "fairground conceit" because it was a manifestation of the most traditional demagoguery. [...] They summoned one hundred thousand people and then after a few days Vladeta Janković asked the exhausted people in front of the parliament whether the meeting should be continued.'[23]

On the other side those people who supported DEPOS came broadly from among the members of the 'right' or 'traditional/anti-communist' wing of the DS, who had remained in the party after the departure of the SLS grouping. Koštunica acknowledged the differences which existed between the 'left' and 'right' wings of the DS saying that there were 'two programmes and two souls in one body and it was not possible for them to remain as one party'.[24] The most senior member of this latter group had been Borislav Pekić who died in May 1992, two months before the foundation of the DSS. He left behind him a political testament in which he sought to define the vexed question of the relationship between the concepts of 'nation' and 'democracy'. He noted: 'As democrats we cannot permit ourselves to become entangled in the artificial dilemma of choosing between the nation and democracy, because for democracy the nation is an unavoidable reality, for the nation democracy is its chosen aim.'[25] The youth wing of the DSS was named the Alliance of Democratic Youth of Serbia (SDOS) after the DS youth organisation in which Pekić had worked, and for which he had been imprisoned, in the aftermath of the Second World War.[26]

At the founding meeting of the DSS Vojislav Koštunica was elected as the new party's President. Koštunica was born in Belgrade in 1944, and came from a family of Šumadijan origin from the village of Koštunica near Gornji Milanovac. His father had been an officer in the pre-war royal army. In addition Koštunica, unlike many of the other opposition leaders, had never been a member of the Communist Party. These factors, as well as his reputation as an academic, endeared him to some of the 'neo-traditionalist' DEPOS intellectuals and leading figures in the church who one observer described as the 'Slavic party'.[27] Matija Bećković in particular gave his backing to Koštunica describing him as 'the personification of the new, young, educated, modern, handsome, and uncompromised Serbia'.[28] Bećković, whose personal and political relations with Drašković had frequently been hostile, regarded Koštunica as a potential leader of the newly-unified opposition. This situation was a significant background factor in the rivalry which would develop between Drašković, and the SPO, and Koštunica, and the DSS within DEPOS.

Koštunica succeeded in bringing with him into the DSS a significant proportion of the membership and branches of the DS. Particular regional centres of strength for the DSS were established in Belgrade, the Šumadija and western Serbia. The support base of the DSS was to remain characterised by broadly the same 'modern' social attitudes and origins to that of the DS.

Sociological surveys of party supporters suggest that the only significant area of divergence in the attitudes of the two parties' voters is in the relatively greater degree of religiosity and respect for religious institutions professed by members of the DSS.[29] The key differences, however, between the two groups should be located in their leadership image and identity rather than programmatic or social contrasts.

Shortly after the formation of DEPOS another opposition coalition, the Civic Alliance of Serbia (GSS), also appeared on the political scene. The GSS united four parties: The Reformists, the National Peasants Party, The League of Vojvodina Social Democrats led by Nenad Čanak, and the Republican Club. The Republican Club had been formed at the end of 1991 by a group within the UJDI who sought to take on a more overtly political identity in contrast to its established role as an intellectual and cultural forum. In many ways the GSS and DEPOS were ideological opposites. DEPOS was firmly rooted within the Serbian national tradition while the GSS had a strongly Yugoslavist orientation. The DEPOS parties had a strong anti-communist identity in contrast to the GSS, some of whose key constituent parties descended from genuinely reformist elements within the LCS. DEPOS also emerged as an avowedly royalist formation while this option was rejected by the GSS with Nebojša Popov of the Republican Club stating: 'The scarce elements of civil society are unlikely to develop in a monarchy; they would degenerate instead. There is the real danger of two coalitions the crown might forge: with the sword and with the altar, so to speak. Both coalitions have played a fatal role in the Serbian past and most probably would have disasterous effects today.'[30] The GSS programme declared: 'Its aims are to overcome nationalist and class collectivism and reform, political, social, cultural, scientific, artistic and other institutions in accord with its principles.'[31]

Notes

1. Radio Zagreb, 23 March 1992 in *SWB EE/1365 C/1/6*, 25 March 1992.
2. Yigal Chazan, 'Serbians Disown Milošević's War Against Croatia', *The Guardian*, 30 October 1991.
3. Vuk Drašković, 'Poskidati kape i – ćutati', *Borba*, 28 December 1991–1 January 1992.
4. A retrospective analysis of their support for the Serbian Guard is offered by the SPO in 'Istina govori za nas', *Srpska reč*, 4 September 1997.
5. *Tanjug*, 31 January 1992 in *SWB EE/1297 C/110*, 6 February 1992.
6. *Tanjug*, 21 March 1992 in *SWB EE/1337 C1/4*, 23 March 1992.
7. *Tanjug*, 26 May 1991 in *SWB EE/1084 B/14*, 29 May 1991.
8. 'Martovski zahtevi', *Vreme*, 9 March 1992.
9. Tanjug, 26 May 1991 in *SWB EE/1084 B/14*, 29 May 1991.
10. Milan Milošević, 'Dogadjanje potpis', *Vreme*, 17 February 1992; Dubravka Stojanović, 'Traumatični krug srpskih opozicije' in Popov (1996), p. 522.
11. *Tanjug*, 20 January 1992 in *SWB EE/1284 C1/2*, 22 January 1992.
12. Milan Milošević *Vreme*, 17 February 1992.
13. Milan Milošević, 'Jaka straža na Svetosavskom platou', *Vreme*, 9 March 1992.
14. Dušan Janjić 'Serbia Between Identity Crisis and the Challenge of Modernisation', in *Serbia – Between the Past and the Future*, Institute for Social Sciences (Belgrade), 1995, p. 21; 'Dučić' and 'Crnjanski' refers to the inter-war poet and writer Jovan Dučić and the novelist and poet Miloš Crnjanski.
15. Milan Milošević, 'Mart 92, Beograd', *Vreme*, 16 March 1992.
16. Milan Milošević, 'Ćorava kutija na srpskom sabor', *Vreme*, 4 May 1992.
17. Nebojša Popov, 'Univerzitet u ideološkom omotaču in Popov (ed.), 1996, pp. 358-64.
18. 'United for a Change', Vojislav Koštunica interviewed in *East European Reporter*, July/August 1992.

19. 'Nisam spasavao Miloševića', Dragoljub Mićunović interviewed by Milivoje Glišić, *NIN*, 6 November 1992.
20. 'Struje od osnivanja', Mirko Petrović interviewed by Dragan Čičić, *NIN*, 8 May 1992.
21. 'Kad jaganjci utihnu', Vojislav Koštunica interviewed by Bogdan Ivanišević, *NIN*, 3 April 1992.
22. 'Ispustili smo sudbinu iz ruku', Dragoljub Mićunović interviewed by Slobodan Savić, *Intervju*, 20 September 1996.
23. 'Zavrtanje i odvrtanje mozga', Ljudomir Tadić interviewed by Zdenka Aćin, *Duga*, 19 July 1992; 'Holbrukovanje po Srbiji još nije završeno', Ljubomir Tadić interviewed by Momčilo Djorgović and Dragan Belić, *Nedeljni telegraf*, 21 August 1996.
24. Dragoslav Grujić, 'Lik i delo – Vojislav Koštunica', *Vreme*, 10 August 1996.
25. Stefanović (1994), pp. 168-70.
26. *Zašto postojimo, šta želimo da postigemo, kako mislimo da to uradimo*, Democratic Party of Serbia (Belgrade), 1996, p. 44.
27. Milan Milošević, 'Veliki transfer', *Vreme*, 12 September 1994.
28. 'Snalazimo se da nestanemo', Matija Bećković interviewed by Nenad Stefanović, *Duga*, 21 November 1992.
29. For the social and political attitudes of DSS supporters and their differentiation, or lack of it, from supporters of the DS see Dragomir Pantić, 'Voters Value Orientations' in Vladimir Goati (ed.), *The Challenges of Parliamentarism – The Case of Serbia in the Early 1990s*, 1995, pp. 93-131; Ratko Nesković, 'Poverene gradjana jugoslavije u institucije i objašnjenje izborne pobede socijalista; *Gledišta*, January-April 1996, p. 100; Zagorka Golubović, Bora Kuzmanović and Mirjana Vasović, *Društveni karakter i društvene promene u svetlu nacional-nih sukoba*, Filip Višnjić (Belgrade), 1995, pp. 278-84.
30. 'Hope Springs Eternal', Nebojša Popov interviewed in *East European Reporter*, September/October 1992.
31. 'Letter of Intentions', Civic Alliance of Serbia (Belgrade), 1994.

11. Politics amid the Ruins: War and the New Yugoslav State (March–December 1992)

Throughout the spring of 1992 the political crisis in Bosnia had gathered pace threatening to overshadow events within Serbia. When on 2-3 March Serbian militants erected barricades, which were swiftly followed by the counter-barricades of their Muslim counterparts, on the streets of Sarajevo the SPO urged both Serbs and Muslims to 'take down the barricades which had been put up and return to normal life'.[1] This conciliatory tone was repeated by Vuk Drašković in his 'Appeal to the citizens of Bosnia and Hercegovina' published on the eve of the outbreak of full-scale war in Bosnia, in the SPO journal *Srpska reč* of 6 April 1992. It stated: 'In this hour of judgement when Bosnia and Hercegovina hovers between war and peace, between death and life, I support the revolt of all nations against chauvinist-fascist madness. [...] This is the last moment for the citizens of Bosnia and Hercegovina to rise above their background of religious, national or party loyalties and speak and embrace as people.'[2]

Such messages were, however, received with little enthusiasm by the hard-line forces which had become increasingly dominant on the Serbian political scene in Bosnia. The SDS having established itself as the primary Serbian national force, with the relegation of the Bosnian SPO to the political sidelines in the November 1990 elections, was able to effect a further homogenisation by drawing into its ranks activists such as Todor Dutina and Dragan Kalinić who had formely supported Ante Marković's Reformists. The remnants of Marković's Serbian Reformists continued to operate as 'independents' under the leadership of Milorad Dodik, a businessman from the town of Laktaši near Banja Luka. Following the declaration of independence by the Bosnian government on 3 March 1992, Radovan Karadžić and the SDS leadership announced on 27 March that the SDS-controlled territory, the self-proclaimed Serbian Autonomous Areas, had constituted themselves into an independent Serbian Republic (Republika Srpska).³

On 28 March 500 delegates, from Serbia and Bosnia, gathered in Sarajevo for the First Congress of Serbian Intellectuals. The ostensible purpose of the meeting was to seek a solution to the 'Yugoslav crisis'. The resolutions passed at the Congress, however, made clear their support for the policies being pursued by the SDS. At the same time as the SDS militants were gaining this open support from Serbian intellectuals they were also receiving covert but more tangible aid from agents of the Milošević government. The men who had been instrumental in the setting up and arming of paramilitary forces in Serbia also played key roles in distributing weapons to putative Serbian militias in Bosnia. Mihalj Kertes' role in this project was notorious, with one Serbian journalist writing of him: 'Wherever he travels he leaves a trail of weapons behind him.'⁴ On 6 April the independence of Bosnia–Hercegovina was recognised by the European Community and the United States. On 7 and 8 April the war reached Sarajevo, having been under way in the surrounding countryside since mid-March, when fierce fighting erupted between Serbian forces, aided by elements of the JNA, and those of the Bosnian government.

With international recognition of Bosnia's independence, moves were initiated to reconstitute Yugoslavia as a federation consisting only of Serbia and its remaining ally Montenegro. The new federal constitution was hatched during a conclave of the ruling Socialist elites of Serbia and Montenegro. The opposition, as had been the case during the framing of the Serbian constitution in 1990, were not consulted regarding the make-up of the new state. While generally approving of a federally-linked Serbia and Montenegro, it wanted the constitutional structure of the new state determined by an elected constitutional assembly. Afterwards the opposition would refer to the new constitution scornfully as the 'Žabljak constitution' after the mountain resort in Montengro where the Socialist *nomenklatura* had met in order to create the new state. From a different perspective the Serbian Radical Party objected to the new state on the grounds that as the Serbs and Montenegrins were one people they should be united in one centralised state.⁵

On 27 April 1992 the new Federal Republic of Yugoslavia (FRY) formally came into existence. In a conspicuous attempt to demonstrate the continuity between the 'second' and 'third' Yugoslavias the FRY was voted into existence by the federal chamber of the parliament of the old Socialist Federal Republic of Yugoslavia. Of the 220 delegates who would once have sat in the federal chamber only seventy-three were present to vote this decision into effect. The new constitution ensured that while the state would be headed by a federal President and Prime Minister, the essential power would remain firmly in the hands of the Presidents of the republics, and in particular with Slobodan Milošević as President of Serbia. The first federal elections followed soon afterwards being set for 31 May. The main opposition parties announced that they would boycott this hurriedly-organised poll. As a result only 56 per cent of the electorate voted, and a further 12 per cent of the votes cast were declared invalid. Unsurprisingly, in these circumstances, the SPS won an easy electoral victory securing 43 per cent of the votes cast. Less predictable, however, was the startling success of the SRS who gained 30 per cent of the vote. At the time this was explained as an anomaly caused by the opposition boycott. In addition the Democratic Community of Vojvodina Hungarians gained 3 per cent of the vote, and other parties accounted for a further 12 per cent of the votes cast.

After the FRY came into being on 27 April the JNA began to withdraw from Bosnia. Before this, however, the JNA in Bosnia had been undergoing a process of military 'domestication'. This involved the transferring to Bosnia-Hercegovina of Serbian military personnel who were originally natives of the republic. After the JNA's departure this group, numbering some 80,000 military personnel, would remain behind to form the backbone of a new Bosnian Serb army. The departure of the JNA from Bosnia was followed by a wide-ranging purge of its senior ranks. On 8 May thirty-eight generals were removed from office. General Blagoje Adžić, the acting Defence Minister and army Chief-of-Staff resigned in protest. He was replaced by his deputy, General Života Panić. Also among those removed was General Milutin Kukanjac, the commander of the JNA in the Sarajevo military district, who, because of his unwillingness to commit his. forces in Sarajevo to support Karadžić and the SDS militias, was held by many nationalists to be responsible for the Serbian failure to take the Bosnian capital in the first weeks of the war. One of the victims of the purge said: 'This is a coup within the army. It was masterminded by

Milošević'.[6] On 19 May the JNA formally ceased to exist, being renamed as the Yugoslav Army (VJ). The Bosnian Serb army was also formally constituted as the Army of the Serbian Republic (VRS). The command of the VRS was taken by Ratko Mladić, a Serb originally from Kalinovik in Bosnia who had formerly been commander of the JNA garrison in Knin. Strong and enduring links persisted between the command structures of the VJ and the VRS.

By the spring of 1992 Milošević was coming under increasing pressure on a number of different fronts. On 30 May, in response to the involvement of the Serbian government in the war in Bosnia, the United Nations Security Council had introduced economic sanctions against the FRY. In addition Milošević was facing renewed mobilisation from the opposition, and rifts were even appearing with the ranks of the SPS. On 25 June a faction within the SPS led by Čedomir Mirković, seeking to present a more reformist agenda, split off to form the Social Democratic Party. The defection of the Mirković faction occurred in the context of a period of general turbulence within the SPS which culminated at its Second Congress on 23-24 October. During the Congress Milošević reasserted his personal control over the SPS and sought to change the party by means of promoting a number of younger cadres. While the image of these new leaders, such as Goran Perčević and Ivica Dačić, was superficially more 'modern' their ideological/political attitudes showed little sign of change. One notable new arrival in the front ranks of the SPS, however, was Nebojša Čović, a formerly little-known official with a technocratic background, who distinguished himself from other SPS cadres by his directness in communicating with the public and the media.

At a national level Milošević sought to widen his support base while never seriously contemplating relinquishing or sharing any real power. To this end Milošević invited Dobrica Ćosić to become the first President of the new Yugoslav state. Ćosić was formally elected to this position by the federal assembly on 15 June. Milošević reasoned that Ćosić's reputation would grant a degree of prestige to the novel federal structures. Milan Panić, an American business-man of Serbian origin, was also invited to take on the post of federal Prime Minister. Panić had been born in Belgrade in 1929 and joined the Partisans at the age of fourteen. In 1956 he defected to the Netherlands while representing Yugoslavia in a cycling competition, and in 1963 became a naturalised citizen of the United States, where he built up the highly profitable firm ICN Pharmaceuticals, based at Costa Mesa in California. Panić forged strong links between ICN and the Yugoslav pharmaceuticals company, Galenika, but when elected federal Prime Minister on 14 July he had not been to Serbia for thirty-five years. Milošević apparently calculated that Panić would project a moderate image for the government at home and abroad while being easy to control politically.

With his heavily-accented English and, after his many years in American, halting Serbian, Panić appeared to some observers a strange and eccentric new actor on the Serbian political stage. However, he soon proved that he had a mind of his own. On 20 July, only a few days after his appointment, he travelled in a UN-provided aircraft to the beseiged city of Sarajevo to demonstrate his dedication to the cause of peace. After a meeting with the Bosnian President Alija Izetbegović, he made a thinly-veiled criticism of Slobodan Milošević, condemning 'cheap politicians who have played on nationalism and created a civil war'.[7] In appointing ministers to the federal government Ćosić and Panić had accepted many individuals who were senior members of the SPS and Milošević loyalists. In late July, however, Panić removed the key Milošević henchman, Mihalj Kertes, from his position as deputy federal Minister of the Interior. The new federal government also agreed in early August, as a concession to the opposition, to hold federal, republican and presidential elections before 31 December 1992.

The tensions between Milošević and Panić came into the open at the International Peace Conference organised in London on 27-28 August. Panić sought to assert his authority and demonstrate to Milošević that, as Yugoslav premier, he was the senior representative of Serbian interests at the conference. At one point he ostentatiously and bluntly told Milošević to 'shut up'.[8]

Milošević's counter-attack against Panić came shortly after their return from the peace conference. On 4 September, at Milošević's instigation, the Serbian Radical Party representatives in the federal parliament moved a motion of no-confidence in Panić's premiership, and he was only saved by the intervention on his side of the federal deputies from Montenegro. International diplomats, who had initially tended to regard Panić as a stooge for Milošević, now saw him as a serious factor in the achieving of peace in the former Yugoslavia. On 22 September the United Nations ruled that, despite Panić's arguments to the contrary, the FRY should not be allowed to inherit the seat in the UN General Assembly formerly occupied by the SFRY. The five permanent members of the Security Council, however, urged Panić to submit a new application on behalf of the FRY once he had been able to provide firm evidence of the Yugoslav government's on-going commitment to the peace process.

The rivalry between Milošević and Panić intensified during the autumn. Despite the purges he had carried out in May, Milošević still harboured fears that the army was a dangerous centre of potentially independent and Yugoslavist sentiment. These concerns were heightened when, during October, Panić held a series of meetings with Života Panić, the head of the federal army. On 19 October a force of Serbian policemen seized control of the federal Interior Ministry building. The raid locked the federal Minister of the Interior, Pavle Bulatović, out of his own ministry and was carried out while both Panić and Ćosić were absent from Belgrade. Considerable speculation surrounded the exact purpose of this incursion into the federal government buildings. The fact that the marauding force of Serbian policemen was headed by Mihalj Kertes led to suggestions that its aim was to remove files and documents which might link the Serbian authorities to paramilitary groups active in Croatia and Bosnia. Although the policemen subsequently withdrew from the federal ministry, the episode served to emphasise how powerless Panić was in the face of the armed coercive force which Milošević was capable of mobilising. The federal police force was only 1,000-strong compared to the 40,000-strong paramilitary force which Milošević had at his command. The federal army, which Panić had tried to court, was too demoralised and ideologically confused to be able to offer any significant support to the beleaguered Yugoslav premier.[9]

On 3 November Vuk Drašković called on Dobrica Ćosić to take a decisive role in resolving the political crisis in Serbia: 'Together with the democratic opposition Ćosić can save this country and thereby have a decisive influence on ending the war in Bosnia-Hercegovina. Milošević only wants to stay in power. He must be stopped at any cost and by any means.'[10] Drašković made it clear that the political way forward lay through the holding of democratic elections, but stressed that the SPO and DEPOS had not yet decided whether the conditions would be appropriate for their participation in the elections which were now set for 20 December. Dobrica Ćosić had emerged as an ally of Milan Panić in his confrontation with Milošević, and, like Panić, he had come to be regarded by Western diplomats as a serious negotiator. The Serbian press carried reports that Ćosić was preparing to make an electoral challenge to Milošević for the Presidency of Serbia. But in public Ćosić, elderly and in poor health, refused to commit himself to the electoral contest or to support any specific political alignment.

Milošević and his allies had continued to exert pressure on Milan Panić with another vote of no-confidence being moved against him on 4 November. Again Panić was able to survive with the support of the Montenegrin deputies in the federal parliament. In the face of these attacks Panić sought to take a pro-active role in encouraging a common opposition position regarding the approaching elections. On 11 November at a meeting attended by representatives of DEPOS, the DS, the GSS and the Social Democratic Party it was decided that a new electoral alliance known as the Democratic Coalition (DEKO) should be formed in order to co-ordinate opposition activities. This development was initially greeted with enthusiasm by some opposition parties with Čedomir Mirković declaring that it was 'a crucial date in the creation of democracy'.[11]

Such optimism regarding the potential of DEKO, however, would prove to be premature. The alliance fell apart after only a few days, foundering on the continuing rivalry between the DS and the SPO. These differences surfaced when on 13 November the DS announced its independent decision to participate in the elections without consultation with the other opposition parties. On 16 November, during further talks hosted by Milan Panić, it was decided that there would be no common opposition list of candidates, but rather that two lists should be formed centred on the DS and DEPOS.[12] On 17 November the DEPOS council finally confirmed that they would be taking part in the elections. The debate on whether to participate in the elections revealed sharp divisions within DEPOS. The decision to enter the elections was supported by the SPO, ND, and by members of the intellectual section of DEPOS. Opposition to this move was headed by the

DSS and the SLS with the support of Matija Bećković.[13] Despite their opposition to involvement in the election, the DSS ultimately did place candidates on the DEPOS list for the republican elections, but not for those at federal level. The SLS, however, chose to boycott the elections in their entirety. At the same time Drašković declared that he was ready to put himself forward as a candidate for the republican presidency.[14]

Panić, dismayed by the failure to construct a viable opposition alliance, described the opposition as 'poorly organised' and 'more against the system than in favour of something'.[15] Vesna Pešić summed up the situation: 'The events which have recently taken place among the opposition are best understood as part of our mentality and are therefore repeated again and again. People have difficulty communicating and concentrating on the essential facts of our situation. Our political life is contradictory. In all the former communist states power was changed by means of an opposition "front". In Serbia we also need change but the parties cannot bring themselves to unify against the old regime.' Drašković, however, was dismissive of the shortlived DEKO combination: 'A united opposition exists and that is DEPOS'.[16]

Dobrica Ćosić had also been unwilling to work with any opposition coalition which included DEPOS. Zoran Djindjić recognised the fact that, regarding DEPOS, Dobrica Ćosić 'would not want to be identified as the leader of a movement or coalition of parties in which there are people who wear the cockade, people who propagandise for the Ravna Gora movement, and where there will be parties with a clear monarchist orientation.'[17] Djindjić, however, expressed the hope that the two elements of the 'federal tandem' might divide with Ćosić giving his backing to the DS-led list, and Panić working with DEPOS. On 20 November, however, Ćosić officially declared that he would remain aloof in the coming electoral struggle. He gave as his reason for staying above the fray 'my desire to be the President of all the citizens of Serbia and Montenegro without separating them into parties'.[18]

As the elections approached Milošević's supporters within the federal government began to withdraw their support from Panić in a co-ordinated attempt to undermine his position. On 26 November the federal Minister for Foreign Affairs, Vladislav Jovanović, resigned – followed on 28 November by Radmila Milentijević, Minister without Portfolio in the federal government, who denounced

Panić for engaging in 'activities which did not coincide with the interests of the Serbian people'. On 29 November Nikola Šainović resigned from the position of federal Economics Minister and he was joined the next day by Oskar Kovač, the federal Deputy Prime Minister. According to Kovač, Panić had been 'introducing foreigners and the interests of foreign powers into government policies'. Milan Panić described the resignations as 'a transparent attempt by Milošević to undermine a government of reconciliation and hope in a frenzied effort to stay in power at all costs'.[19]

These Milošević loyalists were replaced by individuals drawn from among the ranks of the opposition. The position of Foreign Minister was taken by Ilija Djukić, a senior member of the DS who had served as SFRY ambassador to China, the Soviet Union, and Bulgaria. Ljubomir Maždar, a former member of Ante Marković's Reformists, became the Economics Minister. Miodrag Perišić of the DS was appointed as federal Information Minister. Tibor Varadi, a Vojvodina Reformist, was given the position of federal Minister for Human Rights.

The changing composition of the Panić government did not spread harmony in the opposition ranks. Ćosić's natural political orientation was towards the socialist/left. By the end of 1992, however, his quarrels with Milošević and his supporters had caused him to look elsewhere for political allies. Ćosić's links with the *Praxis* group had always been strong, and his chief political adviser Svetozar Stojanović had been a *Praxis* luminary. It was therefore natural that he, along with Panić whose life in America divorced him from the traditions and symbolism of Serbian nationalism, would seek to recruit new government ministers from among the 'rationalist' wing of the opposition, consisting of such groups as Mićunović's DS and Čedomir Mirković's Social Democrats. Some of the opposition figures associated with DEPOS were increasingly uneasy about what they saw as their exclusion from the government. Zoran Cvijić of the SLS Executive Committee accused Ćosić of 'practically creating his own party'.[20] Further disquiet was expressed by Slobodan Rakitić of the SPO when interviewed in early December: 'Ćosić is certainly oriented towards the left...his closest collaborators are mainly *Praxis* members. Prime Minister Panić has declared that he is a member of the [American] Democratic Party. It is symptomatic that he has declared that he is on the left wing of that party. Here such a statement has specific political connotations. It means that Panić has given his support to the forces of the left in Serbia. It is even possible that he is further to the left than Dragoljub Mićunović's Democratic Party. It must be said, however, that to support a left-wing party is not the same here as it is in America.'[21] Other, more neutral, observers criticised Ćosić for pursuing his own ideological inclinations rather than acting to unite the disparate opposition parties.

On 30 November Milan Panić, after a last minute signature gathering campaign conducted by Belgrade University students, submitted his registration papers as a candidate for the presidency of Serbia. Panić stated that he was standing because 'Under Milošević we have become isolated internationally and have become the victim of crippling sanctions. [...] War rages out of control, and yet Milošević has done nothing.'[22] The Serbian Electoral Commission headed by Časlav Ignjatović, however, declared that Panić's candidature was invalid. The commission claimed that Panić had not been resident in Serbia for the period of a year which was required of all presidential candidates. Panić expressed contempt at the Electoral Commission's objections: 'I have been the Prime Minister of the Federal Republic of Yugoslavia since 1992. How is it possible that a Prime Minister of Yugoslavia does not fulfill the requirements to run for the Serbian Presidency. It is insane.'[23] Observers noted that this residence requirement had only been introduced in November 1992 – when the conflict between Panić and Milošević was at its height and the prospect of a Panić presidential challenge had become a real possibility. Panić appealed against the decision of the electoral commission to the Serbian constitutional court – which was also chaired by Časlav Ignjatović. He backed his appeal with documentary proof that he had signed a lease for a property in Belgrade as early June 1991. On 5 December, under pressure from the opposition parties who threatened to boycott the election if Panić was not allowed to run, the constitutional court overruled the decision of the electoral commission. On 6 December, however, the political tussle continued when the electoral commission again refused to accept Panić's candidacy, only to be overruled by the constitutional court once again on 9 December. This judgement finally removed the obstacles to Panić's candidacy, and on 10 December Vuk Drašković withdrew his nomination to leave the field clear for Panić to challenge Milošević.

Notes

1. Milan Milošević, 'Jaka straža na Svetosavskom platou', *Vreme*, 9 March 1992.
2. 'Apel gradjanima Bosne i Hercegovine', *Srpska reč*, 6 April 1992.
3. R. Ninčić, 'Prokleta avlija', *Vreme*, 9 March 1992.
4. Robert Fisk, 'Writing on the Wall for Belgrade', *Independent*, 17 October 1992.
5. Vladimir Goati, 'Peculiarities of the Serbian Political Scene' in *Challenges of Parliamentarism – The Case of Serbia in the early 1990s*, Institute for Social Sciences (Belgrade), 1995, pp. 13-14.
6. Ian Traynor, 'Belgrade Sacks Generals in Military Purge', *Guardian*, 9 May 1993.
7. Steve Crawshaw, 'Panić for Peace, Double-Glazing or Eternal Life', *Independent*, 21 July 1992.
8. Laura Silber and Allan Little, *The Death of Yugoslavia*, Penguin (London), 1995, p. 287.
9. Ian Traynor, 'Police Loyal to Milošević Hold Ministry', *Guardian*, 20 October 1992; Marcus Tanner, 'Panić Demands End to Takeover', *Independent*, 21 October 1992.
10. *Tanjug*, 5 November 1992 in *SWB EE/1530 C1/3*, 5 November 1992.
11. Milan Milošević, 'Pobednička kombinacija', *Vreme*, 16 November 1992.
12. *Tanjug*, 16 November 1992 in *SWB EE/1541 C1/4*, 18 November 1992.
13. Stefanović (1994), pp. 309-11.
14. *Tanjug*, 16 November 1992 in *SWB EE/1541 C1/4*, 18 November 1992.
15. *Tanjug*, 2 November 1992 in *SWB EE/1544 C1/8*, 21 November 1992.
16. Bogdan Ivanišević, 'Trčanje za strelom', *NIN*, 27 November 1992.
17. 'Slom tutorske države', Zoran Djindjić interviewed by Vesna Mališić, *Duga*, 21 November 1992.
18. *Tanjug*, 21 November 1992 in *EE/1546 C1/3*, 24 November 1992.
19. Milan Andrejevich, 'What Future for Serbia', *RFE/RL Research Report*, 18 December 1992.
20. *Tanjug*, 25 November 1992 in *SWB EE/1549 C1/12*, 27 November 1992.
21. 'Dosta nam je revolucija', Slobodan Rakitić interviewed by Luka Mičeta, *NIN*, 4 December 1992.
22. Yigal Chazan, 'Panić Challenges Milošević for the Serbian Presidency', *Guardian*, 2 December 1992.
23. Yigal Chazan, 'Panić Barred from Presidential Race', *Guardian*, 4 December 1992.

12. Winter in Serbia: Elections and their Aftermath (December 1992– January 1993)

Milan Panić fought a characteristically active and energetic election campaign. He carried the election struggle out of opposition areas, in Belgrade and the north, and into areas which were considered bastions of support for Milošević. When he visited the town of Niš, officials of the Socialist local government refused to meet him and suggested that he come back in January 1993 when they would have more time to see him. Despite this snub, 10,000 of the city's inhabitants turned out to hear him speak at a rally held nearby. In his final election meeting held in Belgrade 100,000 people attended the rally and heard him condemn Milošević for 'building a Chinese wall around Serbia'.[1]

The key message of the Panić campaign was the imperative need for sanctions to be removed and for Serbia to re-integrate itself into the world community. In the preceeding months Panić had pursued a vigorous programme of personal diplomacy meeting some 100 world leaders in thirty cities. His message stressed that the cause of peace in Bosnia-Hercegovina and his own struggle with Milošević were 'inextricably linked': 'If Europe is unable to distinguish between those Bosnian and Serbian leaders who pursue their interests by force of arms and those of us who are seeking to direct Yugoslavia on the path of peace and democracy, then we are all doomed to endless conflict and tragedy in the Balkans.'[2] But despite his efforts sanctions had, on 17 November, been tightened rather than eased with the United Nations approval of a proposed naval blockade of the Adriatic and the Danube. Senior SPS officials did not disguise their belief that this move was a rebuff for Milan Panić and would strengthen Milošević's position. Mihailo Marković commented: 'Whatever we do, we are punished. This gives people reason to think that Milošević was right because

Panić only got a tightening of sanctions. They will cling to the present leadership and be even more obstinate. It will help Milošević win the elections.'[3] Panić pleaded in vain for sanctions to be suspended for a trial period of 60 days – to be reimposed if the elections were not judged to have taken place under free and democratic conditions – so that he would be able to demonstrate to Serbian voters some tangible reason for placing their faith in his candidacy.

The election message put forward by DEPOS was considerably more moderate than that presented by the SPO in the 1990 election. DEPOS talked of the need to offer 'the hand of reconciliation': 'We seek solutions, and not culprits'.[4] Some within DEPOS, however, saw the West's failure to offer them significant support as an implicit indication of support for the existing leadership of Slobodan Milošević. About this situation Matija Bećković said: 'I feel like "Čiča" Draža [Mihailović] when he heard over Radio London that Tito had become the commander of the royal army. The West is again supporting tyranny is Serbia.'[5]

In contrast to the relative moderation of DEPOS the Socialist campaign had undergone a fundamental radicalisation since 1990. Their propaganda presented to voters a Manichean vision of Serbian political life as divided between 'patriots' (Socialists and their Radical Party allies) and 'traitors' (the opposition). Within such a world-view international isolation became a state of virtue rather than a national disaster. The Socialist campaign slogans proclaimed: 'Serbia is not for Sale.' Milošević wound up his election campaign in the Kosovo region, his old stamping-ground, where such raw and emotional messages of defiance found their deepest resonance.

In their election campaign Milošević and the SPS enjoyed all the institutional advantages, in terms of control of the media, local government organisations, and the police, which had previously played a critical role in securing their victory in the 1990 election. Panić described Milošević as having the 'power to intimidate the voters in every village and town beyond the reach of Belgrade's opposition voices'.[6] Opposition observers were granted the right to observe voting taking place, but neither they nor those from international organisations were allowed to observe the counting of votes. This task was in the hands of the Socialist-controlled electoral commissions. Opposition activists who had volunteered to act as observers of the polling process reported being threatened with dismissal by the Socialist mangers of the state-run enterprises where they worked.

During these elections, however, Milošević enjoyed a number of new advantages over his opponents. Since the outbreak of the wars in Croatia and Bosnia, Serbia had seen the arrival of large numbers of refugees fleeing from the war zones. Milošević and the SPS hierarchy calculated that these people, radicalised by their experiences, would provide a receptive constituency for his brand of nationalist politics. For this reason 231,707 refugees in the FRY were included on the electoral lists. On the other hand some 120,000 voters who had left Yugoslavia during the war years, many to avoid conscription into the army, were left off the voting lists. These emigrants could to a large degree be counted on to be opposition supporters. Many of those opposition supporters who had boycotted the 30 May federal elections also found themselves removed from the electoral roll. Observers estimated that the number of exclusions accounted for around 5 per cent of the electorate.[7]

In spite of Milošević's built-in advantages, polls conducted in the run-up to the election appeared to indicate that Milan Panić was leading in the election race, and exit polls carried out on the day showed the two rivals to be running neck-and-neck. The final results, however, once more confirmed Milošević and his party as the victors in the political battle. In the elections for President of Serbia Milošević gained 53.24 per cent of the votes cast (37.12 per cent of the electorate) against 32.11 per cent of the votes (22.38 per cent of the electorate) for Panić. Other more marginal candidates also contested the election, including Dragan Vasiljković, the paramilitary commander better known as 'Kapetan Dragan', who gained 1.86 per cent of the vote (1.29 per cent of the electorate) and Milan Paroški, leader of the National Party, who gained 3.13 per cent of the vote (2.18 per cent of the electorate).

In the elections for the republican parliament the SPS secured 28.1 per cent of the vote, giving them 101 representatives (40 per cent of the seats). They were followed by the SRS with 22.6 per cent of the vote and seventy-three representatives (29.2 per cent of the seats). The DEPOS coalition won 16.9 per cent of the vote electing fifty representatives to the parliament (20 per cent of the seats). The Democratic Community of Vojvodina

Hungarians won 3 per cent of the vote and secured nine representatives (3.6 per cent of seats). In terms of the number of seats won the DS came fifth in the poll with 4.2 per cent of the vote and six representatives (2.4 per cent of the seats). The ultra-nationalist paramilitary commander Željko Ražnatović ('Arkan') and a group of associated candidates (categorised officially as a 'group of citizens') gained only 0.3 per cent of the vote consisting of a total 17,352 votes. Due to the fact that he restricted his campaigning efforts to the Kosovo region, where due to the Albanian boycott of the election a small number of Serbian voters were able to return a relatively large number of representatives, he was, however, able to gain five parliamentary representatives. Representation in the parliament was also gained by the Peasants Party of Serbia (three seats), the coalition of the Democratic Party of Vojvodina and the Reform Democratic Party of Vojvodina (two seats), and the Democratic Reform Party of Muslims (one seat).

In the federal parliament this pattern of dominance by the SPS and the SRS was repeated. The SPS gained forty-seven seats, the SRS thirty-four, DEPOS twenty, the DS five, the Democratic Party of Socialists of Montenegro five, the National Party (Montenegrin) four, and Vojvodina regional representatives three.

Local elections also took place in parallel with those on the republican and federal level. Multi-party local elections had previously taken place in December 1990 and May 1992, but in the latter instance they, like the federal elections, had been boycotted by the opposition parties. The dominance of the SPS was even more pronounced with their accumulation of a total of 59.4 per cent of the elected councillors. DEPOS came second securing 10.9 per cent of the elected representatives while the DS gained 2 per cent. Despite the relative lack of success of the Serbian opposition in these municipal elections, it was noted that at local level, and particularly in Vojvodina, the opposition parties displayed a capacity for co-operation which was often not manifest by their national leadership. At a local level the SRS did far worse than they did nationally, securing only 8 per cent of the vote. Their national vision of a 'Great Serb' state was not seen to be relevant to the more pragmatic and mundane concerns of local government. The fall in the vote for the SRS in the local elections was paralleled by an increase in the number of votes at local level for both the

SPS and the opposition parties compared to their national totals. At local level the SPS gained 300,000 votes more than at national level while the opposition parties gained some 100,000 votes more than in the national poll. There were, however, pockets of local SRS support in the Drina valley with the SRS gaining control of the town of Mali Zvornik. The high level of support for the Radicals in the Drina valley can be explained by this region's close political/cultural contacts with their kinsfolk on the Bosnian side of the riverbank. In this context it is significant that the elections took place during a period of fierce fighting in the Bratunac-Srebrenica region with movement of refugees across the Drina into Serbia.[8]

The opposition parties not only suffered a general defeat in the local elections, but also failed to achieve gains in areas which they considered to be their strongholds, such as the city of Belgrade. In the elections for the Belgrade city assembly the SPS secured 48 per cent of the elected councillors, DEPOS 29.4 per cent, DS 9.8 per cent, SRS 7.8 per cent, Independents 3.1 per cent. In Belgrade the opposition not only had the greatest concentration of the activists, but were also, through independent TV and radio stations, able to some extent to circumvent the Socialist dominance of the state media. The results of the first round of elections held on 20 December appeared to show DEPOS posed to take the largest number of seats in the city assembly. In the second round of voting on 3 January, however, there was a low turn-out of 29 per cent, and the opposition vote collapsed, apparently due to the extreme demoralisation of the opposition supporters following their defeat in the presidential and republican elections. The various opposition alignments did, however, succeed in securing a number of local victories in the central *opštinas* of Belgrade consisting of Stari Grad, Vračar, Savski Venac, Zvezdara and Voždovac. The Socialist vote was particularly strong in the outer regions of the city such as New Belgrade, Barajevo, Rakovica, and Obrenovac. Even in the central districts opposition control would remain fragile, depending on continued co-operation between the various opposition parties. The opposition politicians in these local government *opštinas* also complained that they faced systematic attempts by the Socialist government to deprive them of necessary economic resources.[9]

The elections of December 1992 were for the opposition a

crushing defeat. The opposition leaders, almost certainly correctly, drew attention to the degree of manipulation which had characterised the election campaign and the counting of votes. Vuk Drašković described the elections as being 'rigged to the last degree'. The international observers sent to monitor the elections admitted that the elections were 'seriously flawed'.[10] Such considerations could not, however, disguise the scale of the electoral reverse suffered by the opposition. The DS despite the degree of patronage they had enjoyed from Dobrica Ćosić, and the involvement of some of their high-ranking members in the federal government, had gained only six representatives in the republican parliament. This figure was less than the seven gained in December 1990 and only one seat more than had been gained by the followers of the paramilitary warlord Arkan. The inability of Dobrica Ćosić, despite his prestige as a dissident, to influence politics on a practical level was underlined by the fact that in his home village of Drenova the Socialists gained some 67 per cent of the vote.[11] DEPOS performed better than the DS, but they too had to face the humiliation of being forced into third place by the SRS who had hitherto been a marginal group in terms of representation within the Serbian parliament.

Notes

1. Marcus Tanner, 'Panić Exhorts Voters to Choose Peace Over War', *Independent*, 18 December 1992.
2. Ian Traynor, 'Panić Seeks Support to Beat Rival and Avoid "Balkans War"?', *Guardian*, 6 November 1992.
3. Tim Judah, Dessa Trevisan and James Bone, 'Blockade Boosts Serb Defiance and Poll Hopes for Milošević, *The Times*, 18 November 1992.
4. Zoran DJ Slavujević 'Election Campaigns' in Vladimir Goati (ed.), *The Challenges of Parliamentarism – The Case of Serbia in the Early Nineties*, Institute of Social Sciences (Belgrade), 1995, p. 171.
5. Stefanović (1994), p. 291.
6. Ian Traynor, *Guardian*, 6 November 1992.
7. Milan Milošević, 'Stvarno i moguće', *Vreme*, 28 December 1992.
8. Milan Jovanović, 'Election of Councillors in Municipal and City Assemblies in December 1992 in the FR Yugoslavia', *Yugoslav Survey*, 3 (1993).
9. Kosta Čavoski, 'Opštinska vlast bez novca', in Filip Višnjić (ed.) *Ustav kao jemstvo slobode* (Belgrade), 1995, pp. 173-8.
10. Tim Judah and Dessa Trevisan, 'Defiant Panić Urges World to Snub Milošević', *The Times*, 23 December 1992.
11. Milan Milošević, *Vreme*, 28 December 1992.

13. The Red and the Black: The Socialist–Radical Alliance (1992–93)

The dramatic rise in the SRS vote shocked Serbian and world opinion. As the second largest party in the Serbian parliament the support of the SRS was vital for the SPS to maintain its government in power. Vojislav Šešelj had become the 'kingmaker' of Serbian politics. Opposition politicians and commentators were quick to dismiss the significance of the rise of the SRS. According to Dragan Veselinov, 'The fantastic success of Šešelj's extremists is artificial. This party does not have a sufficiently powerful organisation on the ground which could explain its alleged electoral success. Its cadres are primitive, and often drawn from disreputable elements and local trash. It is a civilian military-police organisation.'[1] Vuk Drašković, noting the sympathetic coverage that the SRS had received in the state-controlled media, scornfully labelled the SRS 'a television party'.[2] Slobodan Antonić, a political scientist from the Institute for Political Studies, also recognised the role of a state-directed political agenda in securing a niche for the SRS. He stated: 'Public opinion in Serbia as a whole is in a kind of schizophrenic state, torn between the stereotypes of propaganda and everyday experience. Citizens are faced with the clear failures of one policy – that is one party or person – but because of efficient propaganda they recoil from the main competing parties and their leaders. That's why they turn to the one party – the SRS, which presents itself as an opposition but which is not demonised by the key media – or else retreat into passivity confused and disappointed.'[3]

The level of co-operation which existed between the SRS and the SPS in 1992-3 was at first sight contradictory in view of the fact that the SRS was a party which sought to portray itself as drawing on a 'rightist' Ravna Gora tradition while the SPS was a 'leftist' communist successor party. The SRS was later to portray its alliance during this period as a 'marriage of convenience' based on the temporary agreement of the SRS and the SPS on a number of key issues of national policy.

According to Tomislav Nikolić the SPS, in the aftermath of the 1992 election, sought to tempt the SRS into a formal coalition: 'We were offered two-fifths of the ministerial places, flats, houses, and office space. Vojislav Šešelj replied to the President of Serbia saying: "We are not a party which it is possible to buy. We will support the President of Serbia, Slobodan Milošević, as long as he acts as a true nationalist and a patriot. We will not, however, become part of the Socialist government into which the corrupt and the criminal have been brought."'[4]

In reality the informal coalition benefitted both parties allowing the SRS to maintain its semi-independent 'oppositional' status while the Serbian government was able to avoid the international opprobrium which would have followed from a formal alliance with the SRS. According to Vladimir Goati, 'By firmly siding with the ruling party the SRS became an *alter ego* of the Socialist Party in the consciousness of the voters, its idealised version, devoid of deficiencies resulting from the exercise of power.'[5] It was also notable that the SRS appeared to draw its supporters from broadly the same social strata as the SPS. The following of the SRS was particularly strong among the older, industrial workers living on the outskirts of the main cities. Srboljub Branković also noted the existence of a 'left' element in the social and economic orientation of the SRS: 'The political profile of the newly formed Serbian Radical Party was an eclectic combination of elements of the extreme right (ultra-nationalism) and the extreme left (social radicalism – a desire to equalise salaries and pensions, identification, in terms of class, with those lower down the social scale).'[6]

The leaders of the SPS had gone out of their way to indicate their support for Vojislav Šešelj and the SRS. In March 1992 Slobodan Milošević famously observed that of all the opposition leaders 'I value Šešelj the most...since he is consistent in expressing his political views.' Mihailo Marković similarly praised Šešelj for his 'understanding of the position and interests of Serbia'.[7] Some Socialists, such as the newly-elected Mayor of Belgrade, Nebojša Čović, did appear to be nervous about the newly-acquired power of the SRS, but such voices of dissent were at this time muted and in a distinct minority.[8]

Perhaps even more striking was the praise which Šešelj received from the leaders of the orthodox communist SK-PJ. Goran Latinović, the President of the Republican Committee of the SK-PJ, observed in the summer of 1993: 'International encirclement has pushed the SPS and the SRS into one patriotic block. Amongst the members of these two parties there are no differences in attitudes and aspirations. Patriotism forms the basis of their alliance. The other parties did not feel that patriotism was at this time the most essential factor and therefore they lost the election...Šešelj's ideas have a great deal in common with the ideas of communists. He is close to us. In the SK-PJ we think that all the pre-requisites are in place for the formation of a Radical Left. The conclusion of this war will see the ending of the idea that it will be possible to introduce neo-liberal capitalism into this territory which desires to transform the Yugoslav nation into white slaves of the European Community and the USA.' According to Latinović, this new Radical Left would be an umbrella group including young political activists drawn from 'the membership of the SPS, the SRS, SK-PJ and other sympathisers from small parties of a pro-worker and communist orientation'.[9] Stevan Mirković recorded later that he had at one point suggested to Mirjana Marković that the SK-PJ should condemn the ultra-nationalist line being taken by the SRS. Revealingly Marković had replied: 'It is not necessary to attack Šešelj. At the moment we only need to attack Vuk Drašković.'[10]

This association between the SRS and their 'left'-oriented allies in the SPS brought about key changes in the way that the SRS sought to present itself. Less emphasis was put on 'traditional' aspects of Serbian nationalism, and stress was instead placed on the way in which the party identified itself as a 'modern' nationalist party. Interviewed in January 1993, in the wake of his election triumph, Šešelj had sought to define the position of the SRS on the Serbian political scene saying: 'On the far-left there are the various communist parties who have practically no influence. The SPS is a party of the moderate left, the Democrats are a party of the centre. We are the moderate right and DEPOS are the extreme right.' Šešelj justified this unusual categorisation: 'We favour only parliamentary forms of struggle while DEPOS favours other forms of political struggle which are characteristic of the extreme right. We are for a republic and they are for a monarchy. We take more account of social politics. Our party is against the intervention of the church in politics although we are believers, but they believe that the church should have a role in politics, even in some sort of theocratic shape, such as was the case when they suggested that there should be a government of national unity in which the Patriarch would play a role.'[11]

By late 1992-early 1993 Šešelj would claim that he had 'never been a monarchist' and that his refusal to join the SNO in January 1990 had been prompted by objections to the royalist elements of its programme.[12] It was well known, however, that in the early stages of his political career he adhered to all the traditional elements of the 'nationalist opposition discourse' of which royalism was a key aspect.[13] Šešelj's departure from the monarchist line was demonstrated in February 1992 when in a bizarre episode he and an SRS delegation visited Spain, apparently with the aim of offering the Serbian crown to a self-styled 'Prince' Alexis of Anjou who also described himself as Alexei II Romanov Dolgorukov Nemanjić, and a claimant to the thrones of Russia, Ukraine, Greece and latterly Serbia. These contacts between the SRS leader and such an obvious charlatan prompted predictable denunciation from the representatives of the Karadjordjević dynasty.[14] Šešelj's actions were widely seen as a deliberate attempt to discredit royalism as a political option. During 1992 the royalist symbolism and iconography which had previously adorned SRS literature and publications were removed. For disillusioned royalists within the SRS it was clear that these moves were made by Šešelj to ingratiate himself with the Socialist authorities before the elections of December 1992.[15] In the longer term, however, the discarding of royalism meant that within the belief system of the SRS there would be no alternative focus of loyalty besides the leader himself, Vojislav Šešelj. For ultra-nationalists such as Šešelj the Serbian monarchy had also become an increasingly inconvenient symbol of authority, and point of deference, due to the relatively moderate position on national issues taken by the heir to the Serbian throne, Crown Prince Aleksandar Karadjordjević.

The period of collaboration between the SRS and the Socialists in 1992-3 also saw an attempt to redefine the meaning of the term Četnik – seeking to modify its traditional and anti-communist essence. Nikola Poplašen, the head of the SRS in Bosnia-

Hercegovina and a former lecturer in political science from Sarajevo University, wrote: 'Četnikdom has been presented from the side of the Communist regime...in a completely negative light. The model for photographs, films and stories regarding the Četniks are the films of Veljko Bulajić in which the Četnik is presented with a long mass of hair, a large beard, a knife in his teeth, completely uneducated and of rural origin, and without any ideology with the exception of a desire for revenge against those who are not of a Serbian monarchist orientation. The Četniks, however, must be understood primarily as a Serbian defensive and liberation movement. [...] Our conception of nationalism is of an ordered and modern Četnik movement, and we understand that the Četnik movement today is not only not identical with that which existed before 1941, but is also completely different from the Četnik organisation which existed between 1941 and 1945. When I say that it is completely different, above all I mean that the Četniks are not a movement which is opposed to, or needs to be opposed to, any other part or element of the Serbian nation. The Serbian nation as a whole, without regard to where they live today, must dedicate itself to realising its strategic interests including the final definition of the borders of the Serbian state, the creation of which is a necessity, and we regard the Četniks as an elite unit whose aim is the realisation of these aims.'[16]

The rift with the SPS, which would develop after 1993, meant that the SRS no longer had to accommodate itself ideologically to the beliefs of its Socialist allies. In this context Draža Mihailović, the anti-communist warlord, could once more became an acceptable political icon with his portrait being displayed prominently at SRS rallies. Mihailović, however, remained a figure of comparatively minor significance for the ultra-nationalists of the SRS in contrast to the liberal nationalists of the SPO for whom he acted as the defining 'master symbol' of their movement. The SRS journal *Velika Srbija*, for instance, carried an account of how a group of SRS Četniks, from the Old Serbia unit, led by the head of the SRS in Niš, Branislav Vakić, had gathered on Mount Tresibaba in southern Serbia on 13 May 1996 to celebrate the anniversary of the start of the 'third Serbian uprising' in 1941. It was said that 'The thirteenth of May is a great day in the history of Serbian resistance to all those, from 1941 until the present day, who are not Serbian and who have sought to annihilate

Serbdom. It was the day when Draža Mihailović came with his Četniks to Ravna Gora from where he led the resistance of all Serbian lands against those who for centuries have sought to expel and drive out the Serbs.'[17] The commemoration of Draža Mihailović's memory was therefore an acceptable event for the SRS leadership and its official publications, but it is notable that the gathering was a relatively small-scale meeting taking place under the patronage of the regional rather than national leadership.

The accommodation between the SRS and the SPS in 1992-3 also served to alienate some individuals from the anti-communist/ Četnik tradition who had formerly given him their backing. Momčilo Djujić had commanded the Knin-based Četnik units during the Second World War and by the early 1990s, when he was living in California, he was the oldest surviving leader of the wartime Četniks. In August 1990 a facsimile of a letter from Djujić was published in *Velika Srbija* in which he recognised Šešelj as his successor as *Četnik Vojvoda* (duke). By 1993, however, Šešelj's rapproachement with the SPS had left Djujić bitter and angry with his protégé. He condemned: 'Vojislav Šešelj who, by openly siding with the Socialist Party of Serbia, who are Communists who have only changed their name, has sullied the name of Četnikdom and Serbian nationalism with which he sought in the beginning to disguise himself.'[18]

In 1995 Vojislav Šešelj, looking back over recent years, sought to portray his political career as following a consistent political course: 'My political course has remained irreproachably clear. I began in 1981 an open revolt against the Communist regime, and I have persisted with that to this day. With me there have been no deviations or U-turns.'[19] This interpretation of events, however, conveniently ignored the period of 1992-3 when a state of informal but effective coalition existed between the Radicals and the Socialists.

Notes

1. Dragan Veselinov, 'Opasna pobeda', *Vreme*, 28 December 1992.
2. 'Smrt Fašizmu?', Vuk Drašković interviewed by Dragan Bujošević, *NIN*, 15 October 1993.
3. Slobodan Antonić, 'Fighting For the Truth', *East European Reporter*, July/ August 1993.

4. Tomislav Nikolić, 'Od disidenta do srpskog vodje', *Velika Srbija*, September 1996.

5. Vladimir Goati, 'Serbian Parties and the Party System' in *Serbia – Between the Past and the Future*, Institute of Social Sciences (Belgrade), 1995, p. 78.

6. Srboljub Branković quoted in Vladimir Goati, 'Osnove podele u partijskom sistemu Savezne republike Jugoslavije (SRJ)' in Dragomir Pantić *et al.* (eds), *Socijalni konflicti u zemljama tranzicije*, Institute of Social Sciences (Belgrade), 1996, p. 166.

7. Milos Vasić and Filip Švarm, 'Četnički votergejt', *Vreme*, 15 November 1993.

8. Milan Milošević, 'Stvarno i moguće', *Vreme*, 28 December 1992.

9. Vesna Mališić, 'Šešelj je najeveći komunist', *Duga*, 2 July 1993.

10. Slavoljub Djukić, *On, ona, mi*, B-92 (Belgrade), 1997, p. 153.

11. 'Disciplina uspeha', Vojislav Šešelj interviewed by Dragan Čičić, *NIN*, 1 January 1993.

12. 'Po meri režima', Vojislav Šešelj interviewed by Toma Džadžić, *NIN*, 22 October 1993.

13. Miroslav Mikuljanac and Veselin Simonović, 'Srećni zajedno', *NIN*, 24 December 1993.

14. *Tanjug*, 12 February 1992 in *SWB EE/1305 C1/6*, 15 February 1996.

15. Aleksandar Cvetković, 'U odbrani časnog imena i dela Nikole Pašića', *Srpska reč*, 25 December 1997.

16. 'Samoosvešćenje Srba od manje važnosti', Nikola Poplašen interviewed by Zoran Marković, *Duga*, 2 July 1993.

17. Radoman Mladjenović, 'Četnici na tresibabi', *Velika Srbija*, 15 June 1996.

18. 'Šešelj je moje razočaranje', Momčilo Djujić interviewed by Milo Gligorijević, *NIN*, 14 May 1993.

19. 'Branili smo muslimane od arkana', Vojislav Šešelj interviewed by Ljilja Jorgovanović, *Srpska reč*, 11 September 1995.

14. A House Divided (December 1992–May 1993)

On 7 January 1993 the head of the Serbian church, Patriarch Pavle, in the course of his Christmas message to Orthodox believers, told them: 'We are filled with shame, brothers and sisters, because we are less ready than ever in our history to welcome the holy visitor. Our region is poisoned with gunpowder, the smell of blood, and the cries of undiscovered and unburied bones on the battlefields. There is not enough of the black cloth needed for mourning.' He called on the faithful to repent and forgive: 'For if we the adults cannot do it, thousands of war orphans, who in their souls already feel a lack of brotherly love among the older generation, will begin to cry in despair.'[1] In spite of this seasonal message of peace and reconciliation the new year in Serbia, and in the former Yugoslavia, would be one of renewed political conflict and division. Following Milan Panić's election defeat his enemies had moved swiftly against him. On 29 December 1992 a no-confidence motion was passed, on the initiative of the Serbian Radical Party, by both houses of the federal government in the federal premier and his government. The Montenegrin deputies who had helped Panić to survive the two previous attempts to unseat him now abandoned the Prime Minister in the wake of his electoral failure stating that his decision to run for the position of Serbian President was incompatable with his continuing role as Yugoslav Prime Minister. While, according to the constitution, Panić had the right to stay in his post until a new government had been formed the federal parliament voted that he should be immediately replaced by his deputy the Montenegrin, Radoje Kontić. Panić condemned the move against him, saying: 'Instead of being the protector of lawfulness and constitutionality parliament has turned into a place where the constitution is violated.'[2] Despite the unconstitutionality of Panić's displacement Dobrica Ćosić indicated that he would accept Kontić as the new Yugoslav premier.

Kontić's federal government, formed and approved by the federal assembly on 2 March, was perhaps most notable for the reappointment of Vladislav Jovanović to the position of Foreign Minister from which he had resigned at the end of November 1992. A statement issued by the SPO spoke scornfully of the new government saying that it was elected by the 'diktat and intransigence of Slobodan Milošević' adding: 'We can expect even greater international isolation with further national and state disgrace with a minister like the old-new Vladislav Jovanović who brought about our expulsion from the international community. Instead of a government of experts...or of national salvation, we got a puppet government serving Slobodan Milošević, a communofascist, and a government of organised crime.' Koštunica, speaking for the DSS, declared Kontić's new government to be the 'worst cabinet that has appeared on our political scene lately'.[3]

Before leaving office Milan Panić urged Dobrica Ćosić to remain in his post as President of Yugoslavia. However, Ćosić's position soon came under concerted pressure from the Radicals. Vojislav Šešelj repeatedly called on him to resign, accusing him of secretly plotting with the Croatian President Franjo Tudjman to betray Serbian national interests. It became clear that Ćosić was Šešelj's next intended political victim.

The removal of Panić and the attacks on Ćosić were only the first moves in the attempt by the SPS and the SRS to consolidate their influence at all levels of Serbian society. At a press conference held on 6 January, Šešelj ominously promised: 'Wherever we are in power or participate in power purges will follow.'[4] He demanded that the number of people employed by RTS should be reduced by 30 per cent, and that individuals who had shown 'lack of discipline' or support for opposition political parties should be removed. Following Šešelj's pronouncements RTS announced a programme of 'rationalisation measures' with 1,500 employees being placed on compulsory leave. It was observed that those chosen to be placed on the list for 'leave' tended to be members of independent rather than the official Socialist-controlled unions. Large numbers of police were used to prevent these employees by force from coming to work.[5]

The independent media were also subject to harassment. On 19 December 1992 two trucks carrying equipment destined for TV Studio B, and donated by the International Media Fund, were intercepted and stolen shortly after they entered Serbia from Hungary. On 13 January 1993 another attempt was made to deliver a transmitter to Studio B. This new attempt was successful despite a further attack near the Hungarian border by a group of armed men.

This purge of 'unreliable' elements extended beyond the media into the fields of industry, academia and culture. In the town of Kula, for instance, Djordje Romada, the director of the Istra metalworking firm, was forced to resign by the firm's management committee. According to Romada this decision was made due to 'government pressure to remove a successful but unsuitable director'. The SPS also managed to place their own appointees in key positions within the administration of Belgrade University. Imposition of political control over this institution of higher education was considered particularly important in view of the role which had been played in the opposition demonstrations by academics and students from Belgrade University. The Socialists were also able to take the key positions of authority in public institutions such as the National Theatre, the National Library, the Institute for Protection of Cultural Monuments and the Museum of Contemporary Art.[6]

On 28 January, on the initiative of the SRS, changes were instituted in the Serbian parliament whereby those delegates would be elected to the Chamber of Republics of the federal parliament who gained the greatest number of votes from lists presented by each party. This system replaced the previous mechanism where candidates were chosen on the basis of proportional representation. The opposition objected that this change would simply lead to the federal parliament coming under the total domination of the Socialists and the Radicals. In response to this move, and the wave of Socialist-directed purges, the DEPOS deputies in the Serbian parliament staged a walk-out from the parliament on 28 January. The DS similarily condemned the move as 'one of the biggest legal scandals'. On 2 February Vojislav Koštunica stated: 'Under the conditions which we are now facing, DEPOS has no business in the parliament. We will therefore not participate in its work, but we will not return our mandates which we do not owe to this parliament or this majority.'[7] The DS followed DEPOS in boycotting the work of parliament. The opposition withdrawal from parliament left the Radicals and the Socialists in undisputed control of the Serbian parliament. Relations between the Socialists and their ultra-nationalist allies appeared harmonious. On 18 February Šešelj called for the adoption of 'crisis measures' to cope with the effects of economic sanctions including equalisation of wages and a programme of public works. Mihailo Marković of the SPS, while condemning the SPO as a 'right-wing and irrational party' praised the SRS for its 'left-wing social package'.[8] On 18 March the SPS announced in the Serbian parliament that they were commencing a campaign against 'economic crime and corruption'. To demonstrate the government's seriousness in pursuing this policy, a serving and a former minister, Savo Vlajković and Velimir Mihajlović, were accused, in what became known as the 'ministers affair', of involvement in the illicit smuggling of petrol. However, the Serbian premier Radoman Božović, who was regarded as the key figure in the state-sanctioned petrol smuggling business, retained his position as a privileged member of the Socialist political-economic elite. The SRS was keen to support this populist crusade, with Tomislav Nikolić mourning the fact that 'while some Serbs, proud that the whole world fears them, go hungry, others travel in their stolen Mercedes.' The opposition, however, was sceptical of this move with Koštunica noting: 'This regime could not exist without criminals – and yet at the same time they produce a struggle against them.'[9] While the politics of Serbia had fallen under the sway of the Socialists and the Radicals, with their combination of chauvinism and social demagoguery, international moves were under way to bring about a peace settlement across the former Yugoslavia. The Vance–Owen Peace Plan (VOPP) was first presented to the participants in the conflict at a meeting of the International Conference on the Former Yugoslavia in Geneva on 2 January 1993.[10] The plan's co-authors, David Owen and Cyrus Vance, sought to maintain Bosnia-Hercegovina as a formally united state within its internationally recognised frontiers. However, this state would be highly decentralised, being divided into ten provinces. The armed forces of the three national groups would withdraw to within their designed provinces. The province containing the city of Sarajevo would be a demilitarised zone. The degree of autonomy given to the provinces created a situation which was far removed from the unitary state which the Sarajevo government had hoped to create at the start of the war. A number of elements in the plan, however, ensured that it was considered even less acceptable by the Bosnian Serbs. The Bosnian Serbs at that time had under their control around 70 per cent of the territory of Bosnia-Hercegovina. The peace plan would have meant them giving up around 40 per cent of the territory they controlled. Under the plan the designated Serbian provinces were divided in such a way that there was no territorial continuity between the provinces therefore calling into question the future existence of the Republika Srpska. Most important, however, the plan would, if agreed to, have cut off the Serbian held territories in Bosnia from Serbia itself. The northern Bosnian Posavina corridor connection to Serbia would, under the peace plan, fall within a Croatian designated province.[11] In spite of these facts Milošević had by late April been persuaded to lend his support to the VOPP. His decision to comply with the terms of the plan was based on a number of important considerations. He now appeared convinced that priority needed to be given to escaping from the increasingly severe regime of UN economic sanctions. Further sanctions against the FRY, which would freeze Yugoslavia's foreign assets and prevent transhipment of goods through Serbia and Montenegro, were threatened if the peace plan was not accepted. Milošević also apparently believed that some of the elements of the VOPP which were, in Serbian eyes, most contentious would be practically unenforcable. On 24 April Milošević had secured from David Owen clarification on these issues. A UN-patrolled corridor through the Posavina province would be provided maintaining the link between Bosnian Serb and Serbian territory. Constitutional guarantees would be provided that the Bosnian state would be run on the basis of tripartite consensus giving each national community a veto over decisions which were felt to be contrary to their interests. It was further provided that the territory relinquished by the Bosnian Serbs would be patrolled by UN forces and not by Bosnian government or Croatian forces. Milošević therefore concluded that a *de facto* Serbian mini-state could be brought into being in spite of the VOPP's paper committment to maintaining the integrity of the Bosnian state. For Bosnian Serb politicians such as Radovan Karadžić, however, such a leap of faith entailed an unacceptable element of risk.

Having committed himself to the VOPP Milošević dispatched the Yugoslav Foreign Minister, Vladislav Jovanović, in order to convince the Bosnian Serb assembly, meeting in the Bosnian border town of Bijeljina, that they should approve the VOPP. Jovanović's appeals, however, fell on deaf ears and the assembly rejected the VOPP. It further announced that this decision would be put to the people in a referendum to be held on 15-16 May. The resolution of the Bosnian Serb assembly triggered, on 27 April, the imposition of the new and more stringent UN sanctions package. Undeterred by this rebuff, however, Owen and Vance scheduled a meeting, hosted by the Greek premier Konstantin Mitsotaksis, to take place in Athens on 1 and 2 May. At this meeting the Bosnian Serb representatives Radovan Karadžić and Nikola Koljević were pressurised by the triumvirate of Slobodan Milošević, Dobrica Ćosić and Momir Bulatović into giving their assent to the peace plan. Karadžić, however, would only place his signature on the VOPP documents on condition that his decision was referred back to the Bosnian Serb Assembly for ratification. The Bosnian Serb assembly met in their mountain capital at Pale near Sarajevo on 8 May. A powerful delegation consisting of Milošević, Ćosić, Bulatović and Konstantin Mitsotakis set out from Belgrade for the Republika Srpska in an attempt to convince the assembly of the need to accept the VOPP. While the Bosnian Serb assembly was flattered by the international attention it was receiving, the gathering was in no mood for compromise. A succession of hardline delegates, including Momčilo Krajišnik and Biljana Plavšić, denounced the plan while Karadžić, back among his followers, expressed only lukewarm support for it. Perhaps the most decisive intervention came from General Ratko Mladić who, arriving late in the evening, delivered an impassioned forty-five minute speech which spelt out to the delegates the full extent of the territorial losses which the Bosnian Serbs would face if the plan were accepted. The assembly voted once again to reject the Vance-Owen peace plan. Milošević, enraged by the assembly's decision, returned to Belgrade. Milošević made a number of further attempts to exert pressure on the defiant Bosnian Serbs. A temporary blockade was imposed on the river Drina preventing the passage of supplies, with the exception of food and medicines, into Bosnian Serb territory. Senior members of the Bosnian Serb leadership were prevented from entering Serbia. Milošević also called a pan-Serb assembly for 14 May, consisting of the 'five parliaments' of Serbia, Montenegro, the Federal Republic of Yugoslavia, the Republika Srpska and the Republic of Serbian Krajina, in order to give support to his demand that the VOPP should be approved. While predictably the pan-Serb assembly, meeting in Belgrade, gave its support to Milošević, this had little effect on the Bosnian Serb referendum which overwhelmingly rejected the VOPP. In the face of these setbacks and lacking international, and particularly American, support the Vance-Owen plan foundered. Attitudes taken to the VOPP among the differing Serbian political parties, however, came to represent a major and enduring point of political division on the Serbian political scene.

The opposition, having decided that nothing significant could be achieved by attending the Socialist-Radical dominated parliament, were faced with the challenge of creating a viable extra-parliamentary strategy. Vojislav Koštunica proposed the formation of a 'movement for civic resistance' modelled on the example of Solidarity in Poland. Critics of this idea pointed to the differences between the situation in Poland and that existing in Serbia where there was no comparable independent trade union organisation and where, as the recent election results suggested, a large section of the population did not, appear to equate their dire economic position with the failure of the government.[12] On 9 March Vuk Drašković, at a gathering of SPO supporters, laid a wreath at the monument of Prince Mihailo to commemorate those killed in the 1991 demonstrations. However, there was no repetition of the mass demonstrations which had taken place in 1991 and 1992. On 25 March the DEPOS leaders, Vuk Drašković, Vojislav Koštunica, Dušan Mihailović and Matija Bećković met Patriarch Pavle who appealed to them to resume parliamentary work. By mid-April serious divisions had arisen within the DEPOS ranks regarding future opposition strategy. In a decision taken independently of its coalition colleagues the SPO resolved on 15 April to return to parliament. New Democracy also indicated that it was ready to return to parliament. The other DEPOS parties, however, were deeply critical of the SPO move. Nikola Milošević of the SLS declared that the 'lack of a credible programme of extra-parliamentary work is not sufficient reason for returning to parliament.' Mirko Petrović confirmed that the DSS intended to continue their boycott of the 'fake parliament'.[13]

This schism over strategy among the parliamentary parties of the DEPOS coalition was paralleled by disatisfaction amongst the 'non-parliamentary intellectuals' within the alliance. At the end of April the six parliamentary representatives of this grouping declared that they would not only refuse to be involved in the work of parliament, but would also be withdrawing from politics altogether and returning their mandates. According to Ljubomir Simović, they were 'withdrawing completely from parliament because it is a place where only issues of secondary importance are discussed'. Unimpressed by this gesture Ivan Kovačević, a spokesman for the SPO and Belgrade University Professor of anthropology, said 'Thank you and have a good journey' to the 'intellectuals'.[14] The mandates of the departing intellectuals were distributed among the remaining DEPOS representatives. It appeared that DEPOS, which had been formed amidst such high hopes a year earlier, had foundered due to the incompatible aims of its constituent parts, and the deeply hostile post-election political environment in which the coalition was forced to operate. On 30 April an independent observer of the political scene passed judgement on the coalition, saying 'DEPOS is dead now. The date of its burial will be announced later.'[15]

The divisions amongst the DEPOS parties on 'strategic' issues were further heightened by their disagreements over national questions, and in particular their attitude towards the Vance-Owen peace plan. The SPO had since the end of 1991 developed an increasing strong orientation towards 'peace', and had shown itself ready to give a sympathetic reception to international peace proposals. When, however, Drašković felt Serbian interests to be directly under threat, he and the SPO would take up a more militant position. On 22 January the Croatian army launched an assault on Croatian Serb positions around the strategic Maslenica bridge. This attack was fiercely condemned by Drašković: 'If the international community does not fulfill its obligations, then it is clear that the aggression of the Croatian state and the Croatian army must be answered with a counter-attack by the Serbian state and its army.'[16] As the Vance-Owen plan unfolded, however, Drašković indicated that in order to achieve peace he was willing to lend his support to the plan 'without regard to all its failings'. The SPO leadership stressed the responsibility of the Milošević government for the failure of the Bosnian Serbs to accept the plan. The inability of the Serbian government to convince the Bijeljina assembly, of 25 April, to accept the VOPP was blamed on the fact that the Serbian government intervention came too late, and before this too little had been done to convince the Bosnian Serbs of the case for adopting the VOPP. When the Pale assembly of 8 May again threw out the VOPP Drašković condemned this as a 'catastrophe', but made it clear that he did not believe the Bosnian Serbs should bear the sole burden of responsibility for this deed. He said: 'Slobodan Milošević's policies pursued over a period of six years won at Pale. What was created over the past six years could not be undone in six days.'[17] He went on to call for the resignation of Slobodan Milošević and Dobrica Ćosić.

The DSS, however, took the opposite position. In Koštunica's opinion the plan would have left the Bosnian Serbs in an unacceptably vulnerable position, and that their rejection of the plan was a rational decision. The sudden conversion of Milošević and the SPS to acceptance of the peace plan, which they had previously opposed, followed by intense pressure on the Bosnian Serb leadership was, in his opinion, a 'typical communist mode of action'.[18] The decision by the DSS to reject the VOPP marked a major turning point in its attitude to national issues from a position where the interests of the Serbs of Serbia [*Srbijanci*] were of primary importance to one where solidarity with the communities of Serbs outside Serbia became a key theme. Both the DSS and the SPO, although with different perspectives on the VOPP, refused to take part in the pan-Serb meeting of five parliaments regarding it as an attempt by the SPS to share the blame for the failure of their 'national policy'.

Drašković's decision to support the VOPP also brought to the boil simmering tensions within the SPO. A faction, led by the Vice-President, Slobodan Rakitić, and former Vice-President Mladen Markov, within the movement regarded this decision as symptomatic of the SPO's abandonment of its original 'national' identity. Rakitić had previously expressed his disatisfaction at the direction that the SPO was taking saying: 'We always criticise our own side during this war. We are constantly pointing out our errors, errors which originate with the Serbian side, and yet we close our eyes towards many serious things, towards crimes which are committed against the Serbian nation in Croatia and Bosnia-Hercegovina. We do not speak of them.'[19] The conflict between Drašković and this rebel faction culminated at a meeting of the SPO Main Committee on 30 April.

The SPO dissidents also sharply attacked Drašković's leadership style. Mladen Markov, a writer who had been a long-standing critic of the SPO leader from within the movement, believed that as a 'movement' the SPO should provide the freedom for intellectuals such as himself to express their views without having to observe the formal discipline of a political party. He made it clear that he was sceptical of Drašković's abilities: 'As a man Drašković is more of a lamb than a wolf.'[20] For his part Drašković condemned individuals among the opposition who did not 'understand the fundamental difference between being a dissident, and working as part of an "opposition" and organising a political party'.[21] In the debates over whether DEPOS should participate in the 1992 elections Markov was one of the few SPO representatives to vote against entering the election contest. During the 30 April meeting Markov attacked the SPO leader in colourful terms describing how 'President Drašković rides on his white horse while his coat-tails flutter in the wind in a romantic delerium, such as is only found in those passing through puberty, well read in the literature which is dear to small boys and uncontrolled populist politicians.'[22] The role of Danica Drašković in the SPO also came under attack. Danica Drašković's family came originally from Kolašin in Montenegro. Her father had been active in the Četnik movement during the Second World War. Danica Drašković studied law at Belgrade University and, like Vuk, had taken part in the 1968 student protests.[23] She made it clear that she regarded herself as 'a politician by vocation' and was regarded as a powerful figure within the SPO. Some individuals within the movement resented this apparent influence describing her, in a reference to Tito's wife, as 'the new Jovanka Broz'.[24] Danica Drašković's political position had been confirmed when, at the SPO World Convention held on 6-7 March, she topped the poll in elections for the SPO Main Committee. Known to favour the more moderate national policy course over the movement's original radical line she had talked openly of how she would 'attempt to re-educate the SPO'. The fears of the 'old guard' within the SPO were apparently confirmed by Danica Drašković's remarks during an appearance on Studio B TV on 11 April. During a debate with a representative of the SPS she was pressed to say why Vuk Drašković, in view of his Hercegovinan roots, had not volunteered to fight with the Bosnian Serb army. She replied that he was in fact born in Serbia, not in Bosnia, and then warming to her theme she exclaimed:

'When Vuk Drašković went to war what would he be defending, his hearth? It was not under attack. The Serbs in Gacko were never attacked. Vuk Drašković if he went there would have to have gone to defend the Muslims in Gacko from the Serbs. The Muslims were killed there, driven out, and deprived of their homes. Of the forty-nine per cent of Gacko's population who were Muslims not one remained'.[25] At the 30 April meeting Danica Drašković repeated these statements, despite fierce criticism of her position. Her comments were of particular significance as she singled out for condemnation the paramilitary forces of the Serbian Guard, an organisation previously linked to the SPO.

A final ingredient was added to this conflict within the SPO by differences of opinion between Slobodan Rakitić and Vuk Drašković over the strategy that the movement should pursue. Drašković had called for a renewal of the Vidovdan Sabor with a new wave of street demonstrations to start on 28 June. Rakitić argued that the movement's interests were best served by concentrating on parliamentary struggle, and he was scornful of the so-called 'scheduled revolution'.[26]

After an acrimonious session of the SPO Main Committee Vuk Drašković emerged as the victor from this power struggle. Slobodan Rakitić submitted his resignation as Vice-President declaring that the SPO was no longer the party that he had originally joined. Rakitić, however, remained a powerful political figure as head of the DEPOS representatives group in the federal parliament. In spite of the failure of the rebel faction in their attempt to remove Drašković, serious divisions would continue to exist within the SPO. With Drašković's decision to support the Vance-Owen peace plan having been one of the major factors in this internal schism the decision of the Western powers to drop the VOPP was regarded by the SPO leader with considerable dismay.

The DS also, despite reservations, accepted the necessity of the VOPP. Dragoljub Mićunović after the Bosnian Serb rejection of the plan called on the UN to ignore the decision of the assembly and deploy peacekeeping forces. The Serbs in Serbia, he said, 'would now become the hostages of the Bosnian Serbs'. Ratomir Tanić of the GSS also mourned the passing of the Vance-Owen peace plan. The Bosnian Serb leadership, he said, 'had shown massive irresponsibility when the decision in question was one on which life and death depended'.[27]

The move by Slobodan Milošević to accept the terms of the VOPP exposed the fragility of his post-election alliance with the SRS. Šešelj's ideological approach to nationalism could not accommodate itself to the pragmatic solutions favoured by Milošević. Maja Gojković , a lawyer from Novi Sad and SRS Vice-President, would later comment that her greatest political error had been to ever believe 'that a communist was able to become a nationalist'.[28] For Vojislav Šešelj the Vance-Owen plan was 'a time bomb planted under Serbdom'. By contrast Željko Ražnatović, always essentially obedient to the Milošević line, urged support for the Vance-Owen peace plan and condemned those who opposed it as 'a false patriot'.[29]

By the spring of 1993 the Serbian opposition was fragmented and preoccupied with mutual recrimination. In an article published in *NIN* on 21 May Vuk Drašković made a wide-ranging attack on the rest of the Serbian opposition, accusing it of indecision, lack of direction and suffering from the 'illness of SPO-phobia'. He said: 'The gentlemen from DEPOS do not want to take part in elections, but at the same time want to take part in elections. They do not want to be involved in parliament but at the same time want to be involved in parliament. They will not go out into the streets, but at the same time demand a radical relationship with government. It is not possible to solve that riddle. If some of them will say clearly what they want then I will join them. But they only do not want what the SPO does want. That is true of the whole of the Serbian opposition.'[30] Some elements within the Serbian opposition, however, saw hope for themselves in the gap which was opening between the SPS and the SRS over the Vance-Owen peace plan. It was reasoned that, with the SRS becoming a potentially unreliable source of support, Milošević would have to open up channels of communication with the opposition. However, Vesna Pešić of the GSS remained sceptical, observing: 'I do not believe that Milošević will now seek any sort of talks or agreement with the opposition. His psychology is such that it is simply not possible. He is not communicative, he does not practice dialogue, but rather demands obedience. I do not believe that it can be any other way.'[31] The events of June 1993 were to demonstrate the correctness of her analysis.

Notes

1. *Tanjug*, 7 January 1993 in *SWB EE/1582 C1/4*, 9 January 1993.
2. Serbian Radio, 30 December 1992 in *SWB EE/1576 C1/2*, 1 January 1993.
3. *Tanjug*, 3 March 1993 in *SWB EE/1629 C1/10*, 5 March 1993; ibid., in *SWB EE/1629 C1/11*, 5 March 1993.
4. Srecko Mihailović, 'The Parliamentary Elections of 1990, 1992, and 1993' in Vladimir Goati (ed.) 1996, p. 64 n. 17.
5. Mark Thompson, *Forging War – The Media in Serbia, Croatia, and Bosnia-Hercegovina*, Article 19 (London), 1994, pp. 92-3.
6. 'Čistke su usledile', *NIN*, 5 February 1993.
7. Dragan Bujošević, 'Opozicija je zatvorila vrata', *NIN*, 5 February 1993.
8. *Tanjug*, 18 February 1993 in *SWB EE/1618 C1/10*, 20 February 1993.
9. 'Drž'te Agoštana!', Milan Milošević, *Vreme*, 22 March 1993.
10. David Owen has given an extensive and detailed personal perspective on these negotiations in *Balkan Odyssey*, Indigo (1996), pp. 94-197.
11. An authoritative/journalistic account of this period is given in Laura Silber and Alan Little, *The Death of Yugoslavia*, Penguin (London), 1995, pp. 306-22.
12. Dragan Bujošević, 'Strah od ćutanja', *NIN*, 12 March 1993.
13. Milan Milošević, 'Vaskrs Vidovdana na Djurdjevdan', *Vreme*, 19 April 1993.
14. Vladimir Jovanović, 'Memorandumski vlažni barut', *Monitor*, 30 April 1993.
15. Bogdan Tiranić, 'Dimni signal jednog neuspeha', *NIN*, 30 April 1993.
16. Serbian Radio, 28 January 1993 in *SWB EE/1600 C1/6*, 30 January 1993.
17. *Tanjug*, 6 May 1993 in *SWB EE/1679 C1/15*, 8 May 1993.
18. Milan Milošević, 'Kockari i kibiceri', *Vreme*, 10 May 1993.
19. 'Farsa sa tužnim krajem', Slobodan Rakitić interviewed by Zdenka Aćin, *Duga*, 23 May 1992.
20. 'Pomodno uterivanje boga', Mladen Markov interviewed by Dušica Milanović, *Intervju*, 26 April 1991.
21. 'Vreme za 'muški potez', Vuk Drašković interviewed by Dragan Bujošević, *NIN*, 9 April 1993.
22. Milena Popović, *Junska dogadjanja* Srpska reč (Belgrade), 1994, p. 37.
23. Nenad LJ Stefanović, 'Danin gambit', *Vreme*, 1 June 1993.
24. Vladimir Jovanović, *Monitor*, 30 April 1993.
25. 'Revolucija koja teče' (transcribed by Olivera Kovačević), *NIN*, 16 April 1993.
26. Popović (1994), p. 39.
27. Milan Milošević, *Vreme*, 10 May 1993.
28. 'Maja Gojković: 20 Plus 20', Maja Gojković interviewed in *Argument*, 31 September 1996; 'Tempirana bomba pod srbijom', Vojislav Šešelj interviewed by Ivan Radovanović, *Vreme*, 10 May 1993.
29. *Tanjug*, 4 May 1993 in *SWB EE/1681 C/1*, 6 May 1993.
30. Vuk Drašković, 'Bolest zvana SPO-fobija', *NIN*, 21 May 1993.
31. Dragan Bujošević, 'Vreme čekanja', *NIN*, 14 May 1993.

15. The June Days

Milošević had seen his political course thwarted in his attempt to get the Bosnian Serbs to adopt the Vance-Owen peace plan. In the aftermath of this reverse he sought to consolidate his power within Serbia. Ironically, however, the objects of his attentions were to be those individuals within Serbia who had supported the Vance-Owen plan, and he would carry out this attack in alliance with Vojislav Šešelj a vehement opponent of the plan.

On 31 May the SRS moved a motion of no-confidence in Dobrica Ćosić in the federal parliament. The SRS believed that Dobrica Ćosić with his willingness to see a negotiated solution to the Yugoslav conflict had betrayed Serbian national interests. The motion was, however, also supported by the SPS representatives who accused Ćosić of plotting to carry out a military coup against the Milošević government. The only evidence cited for this was a meeting which Ćosić had held with the VJ officers including the Chief of the General Staff, Života Panić, at a military base in Belgrade on 27 May. The idea that Ćosić was involved in a conspiracy with the military was widely disbelieved. Dragoljub Mićunović commented: 'I do not believe that he would embark on such an adventure. He is not a putschist.'[1] Even Šešelj seemed unconvinced by this story. The real reason for the assault on Ćosić appeared to be that with his failure, for all his nationalist prestige, to exert proper influence over the Bosnian Serbs he had in Milošević's eyes outlived his usefulness.

Vuk Drašković reacted with little sympathy to Ćosić's predicament. He observed at a news conference on 1 June: 'Dobrica Ćosić has become the victim of those he created. In the federal parliament a fierce struggle of the most primitive kind has taken place within one family.'[2] In the late afternoon of that same day Mihajlo Marković, a SPO deputy from Kragujevac, was assaulted and knocked unconscious, in the chamber of the federal parliament, by Branislav Vakić, a SRS representative. Marković had won a degree of renown for his speeches attacking the SRS, and had particularly enraged Šešelj when in a previous sitting of parliament he had read out a poem in praise of Tito composed by the SRS leader in his days as a communist. In return Šešelj had denounced Marković as a 'psychiatric case'. Observers noted, however, that Vakić seemed to be acting on a prearranged signal from the Socialist representative, Radovan Radović.[3]

As news of the attack on Marković spread that evening, around 5,000 opposition demonstrators gathered outside the federal parliament. This impromptu rally was peaceful until, at around ten o'clock, heavily armed units of police special forces arrived. Shortly afterwards the police attacked the demonstrators firing tear-gas, making baton charges and using their firearms. The opposition supporters replied by hurling stones at the police. During the clashes twelve policemen and sixteen demonstrators were injured. One policeman, Milorad Nikolić, was shot and later died. The authorities blamed his death on the actions of one of the demonstrators, but the SPO were to claim that his assailant had in fact been a member of the SRS, acting on behalf of the state in order to incriminate the opposition.[4]

Following the fighting Drašković sought to disperse the demonstrators, telling them that they should reassemble the next morning to hold another peaceful protest. Vuk and Danica Drašković, along with a number of the movement's officials withdrew to the SPO headquarters in central Belgrade. At around 1 a.m. that morning the SPO offices were raided by police special forces. Vuk and Danica Drašković were severely beaten and arrested.

The official version portrayed these violent events as an attempt by the opposition to seize power by force. On 3 June the SPS issued a statement saying: 'The SPS Main Committee condemns in the strongest terms the violence on the streets of Belgrade and the criminal killing of an employee of the Ministry of the Interior. The leadership of the Serbian Renewal Movement has declared war on the government and have called for conflict. After all their political defeats and debacles in democratic elections the SPO has again returned to the streets and to violence.'[5] On that same day the Serbian public prosecutor's office called on the Serbian Constitutional Court to ban the SPO. This was justified on the grounds that the SPO had apparently called for the overthrow of the state on a number of occasions, including the 9 March 1991 demonstrations and the Vidovdan Sabor of 1992. Dragan Veselinov described the move against the SPO as 'an attempt to restore one-party rule and ensure that there is no challenge to the military-police dictatorship of Slobodan Milošević and the fascist Vojislav Šešelj'.[6] The Serbian government had praised the 'energetic, efficient and dignified conduct' of the police on the night of 1 June.[7]

International opinion began to rally in support of Drašković. On 4 June the Greek premier Konstantin Mitsotakis sought to intervene on Drašković's behalf, urging that he should be released and warning Milošević: 'This event risks changing the positive impression which has been created in the international community.'[8] The French President, François Mitterrand, also demanded that Drašković be released 'in the name of democracy and human rights'. This did little to moderate the stance of the authorities who announced that Vuk and Danica would be held for a further thirty days while investigations were carried out into whether charges should be brought against them for 'violating the constitutional system', an offence which carried a penalty of ten years in prison. Drašković was also alleged to have assaulted a policeman while trying to enter the parliament building. This offence of assaulting an authorised official carried a potential penalty of fifteen years in jail.

Those people who were able to visit Drašković in prison, including Vojislav Koštunica, Patriarch Pavle and his lawyers, voiced increasing concern regarding his deteriorating state of health due to the injuries he had received during his arrest. The authorities, however, maintained their hard line with Margit Savović, the federal Minister for Human Rights and National Minorities, commenting on 10 June: 'Those who seek to beat policemen must expect to be beaten themselves.'[9]

The opposition parties had begun to mobilise in support of the imprisoned leader with intellectuals organising a series of protest evening and signatures being gathered for a petition demanding Drašković's release. On 19 June an opposition protest rally attended by around 5,000 people was held, despite being officially banned, but the demonstrators were prevented by a heavy police presence from marching on the Central Prison where Drašković was being held. A particularily strong role was played in the organising of this rally, and other activities, calling for Drašković's release by the GSS led by Vesna Pešić and the SLS headed by Kosta Čavoški and Nikola Milošević.

On 16 June the British Prime Minister, John Major, joined the chorus of international opinion calling for Drašković to be freed; David Owen had also raised the issue of his imprisonment in talks with Milošević.[10] In spite of these interventions there were many within the opposition for whom the inpunity of Milošević's actions towards his internal opponents was directly connected with the degree of credibility he had been afforded by the West as a negotiating partner. Mihaljo Marković of the SPO commented: 'Europe and the US have given Milošević the green light, and that will have a big impact on us inside Serbia. Lord Owen has pronounced him a peace-maker and a factor of stability in the Balkans. He naively thinks that Milošević will calm down the war for him. He has never understood that the man who set Yugoslavia on fire will never put the fire out, that the lifeblood of the Serbian government is war.'[11]

On 27 June a further rally was held in Belgrade to mark the first anniversary of the foundation of DEPOS. Academician Predrag Palavestra speaking at the rally noted that while 'during the first year of its existence DEPOS might not have fulfilled all the expectations, it certainly stirred the lethargic conscience of the people.'[12] Other opposition politicians were to express optimism in the light of the renewed wave of activism. Slobodan Rakitić spoke of how 'the opposition is united once again with one aim. We will gain that, and democracy as well.'[13] Even when they were under direct attack from the forces of the state the opposition parties continued to jostle for position and act our their personal rivalries. At a rally held on 4 July the leaders of the DS and DSS were notable by their absence.[14] Leading figures within the DS attributed the active role taken by the extra-parliamentary parties, the GSS and the SLS, in the protests to their desire to make political capital and gain publicity for themselves, and suggested that Vojislav Koštunica would attempt to use Drašković's detention to assert his position within DEPOS.[15]

On 28 June Drašković sent a message from prison in which he nominated Slobodan Rakitić as leader of the SPO while he was in prison. This offer was made in spite of Rakitić's earlier resignation and might be seen as an attempt to overcome the divisions within the SPO which had inhibited its response to the crisis. Having made provision for the continued leadership of the SPO Drašković announced that he was ready to embark on a hunger strike which, unless he was released, would continue until his death. When the news of Drašković's move reached his supporters a group of SPO representatives and movement leaders announced their intention of occupying space beneath the monument to Prince Mihailo in Republic Square while conducting their own hunger-strike. On 3 July, the SPO leadership, fearing that in his weakened condition his life would soon be in danger, called on Drašković to call off his hunger-strike. Their appeal was reinforced when on 5 July Patriarch Pavle visited Drašković and also requested him to cease refusing food.

The authorities reacted with some irritation to the opposition's new hunger-striking tactics. On 3 July a group of hunger-strikers from the pro-Drašković Iron Brigade faction of the Serbian Guard, who had travelled to Belgrade from Niš, were arrested and deported back to their home-town. This action was followed on 5 July by a large force of police removing all the hunger-strikers from Republic Square except for those who as elected representatives could claim immunity.

The ratchet of international pressure was further heightened when on 5 July Danielle Mitterrand, wife of the French President, arrived in Belgrade as an official representative of the charity France-Libertés in an attempt to influence the Milošević government. As well as visiting Vuk Drašković in prison, Mme Mitterrand also held talks with Milošević. The Serbian President, seeking to maintain the fiction of judicial independence, emphasised that Drašković's fate was a matter not for him but for the Serbian courts. These sentiments were echoed by the Socialist spokesman, Ivica Dačić, who sought to reject the suggestion that the SPO leader's imprisonment was a human rights issue stating: 'Drašković's case is one of punishment for an act of violence and it does not mean that we intend to punish those who have different opinions.'[16]

Further international representations were made on Drašković's behalf by the Russian and American governments, and individuals who included Simon Weisenthal, head of the Jewish Documentation Centre in Vienna, and the financier and philanphropist George Soros. On 9 July Milošević sought to retreat from the crisis which he had created by signing an act of pardon for Vuk and Danica Drašković which released them from prison. This apparent act of clemency by the Serbian President was carried out with typical ambiguity: although the charges of attempting to overthrow the state were dropped, those for assaulting the policeman would remain hanging over the SPO leader for several months to come. Danica Drašković commented on her release: 'The government has capitulated to pressure from the world and this land.' She was adamant that she and her husband owed no gratitude to the Serbian President for their release, saying: 'He is really only trying to pardon himself for the things he has done to us. He realises he has overstepped the mark and the risk of my husband starving himself to death was simply something he could not take.'[17] She did, however, acknowledge their debt to Danielle Mitterrand by laying a wreath at the memorial in Belgrade to the French war dead.

The release of Vuk Drašković from prison was a victory of sorts for the opposition. Slobodan Milošević had failed to remove from the political scene a key opponent and his party, and the undemocratic nature of his rule in Serbia had once again been exposed to international view. At another level, however, the attack on Drašković served as a demonstration of the ability of the Serbian police to crush any threat to Milošević's rule. With Milošević never entirely trusting the army, he had sought to cultivate the police as an alternative source of coercive power on which he could rely. By 1993 the Serbian police were a heavily militarised, well-trained and well-armed 'praetorian guard' some 80,000 strong. Many of the police recruits were drawn from among Serbs from Bosnia and Croatia or came from rural areas of the Serbian interior, and had little sympathy for the urban 'intellectual' politics of the Serbian opposition. In Belgrade there were 25,000 policemen – which in proportion to the population made it the most heavily policed capital in Europe – of whom 15,000 came from outside Serbia itself.[18] It was also notable that throughout Drašković's detention, despite the energetic efforts of some opposition leaders and members, the numbers taking part in demonstrations were relatively modest. In part this was un-doubtedly the consequence of disillusionment with the opposition parties with their frequent disputes and tendency towards frag-mentation. More important, however, was the fact that the economic crisis which was engulfing Serbia during 1993 was producing a politically-disoriented public, consumed by the day-to-day problems of existence.

Notes

1. Ivan Radovanović, 'Puč, a ne puč', *Vreme*, 7 June 1993.
2. Popović (1994), p. 61.
3. Uroš Komlenović, 'Hronika najavljenog nokauta', *Vreme*, 7 June 1993.
4. Miloš Vasić, 'Opasne igre', *Vreme*, 21 June 1993.
5. 'Saopštenje glavnog odbora sociajalističke partije srbije', *Vreme*, 14 June 1993.
6. Dragan Veselinov, 'Obnova jednopartizma', *Borba*, 5-6 June 1993.
7. 'Iz saopštenje savezne vlade', *Vreme*, 14 June 1993.
8. *Tanjug*, 4 June 1993 in *SWB EE/1708 C1/3*, 7 June 1993.
9. Popović (1994), p. 384.
10. Owen (1996), pp. 198-9.
11. Marcus Tanner, 'Serbia Subtly Stifles Democracy', *Independent*, 24 June 1993.
12. Radio Belgrade, 27 June in *SWB EE/1726 C1/7*, 29 June 1993.
13. Ivan Radovanović, 'Ko se boji Vuka još', *Vreme*, 5 July 1993.
14. Milan Milošević, 'Pravo pod topuzom', *Vreme*, 19 July 1993.
15. Popović (1994), p. 230.
16. Ibid., p. 439.
17. 'Drašković Wife Says Resistance Will Go On', *The Times*, 15 July 1993.
18. James Lyon, 'Yugoslavia's Hyperinflation 1993-1994 – A Social History', *East European Politics and Societies*, spring 1996, p. 326.

16. Economy and Society in Crisis (1992–93)

At the start of the 1990s the Serbian economy was diagnosed as being characterised by serious overall weaknesses including low rates of capital formation, a relatively low level of technological development, a burdensome system of social administration, high tax-rates and a lack of either a rational system of resource allocation or a labour market. Under-use of economic potential could be identified in key sectors of the economy including agriculture, branches of heavy industry, electricity generation, transportation, and small businesses. The political crisis which unfolded in Serbia in the late 1980s and early 1990s occurred against a background of dramatic economic failure.[1]

The imposition of a progressively more severe programme of international sanctions served to heighten the negative trends within the Serbian economy. Sanctions were first imposed on 30 May 1992. On 16 November of the same year the UN authorised a naval blockade of Serbia and Montenegro in order to enforce fuel sanctions. On 26 April 1993 sanctions were further extended in order to freeze Yugoslav assets held abroad and prevent the transhipment of goods through the FRY. The sanctions regime had an immediate effect on the Serbian industrial sector which prior to the crisis had maintained a relatively high degree of integration with Western markets. The Kragujevac based Zastava car manufacturing giant, for instance, saw its longstanding links with the Italian company Fiat severed. The large state-owned firms suffered most from the blockade since they tended to lack the flexibility to adapt to the new adverse conditions. Other smaller firms, frequently privately owned, sought to change by pursuing policies of diversification and import substitution. In the provincial town of Jagodina the large state-run cable-maker, Fabrike kablova Jagodina, had, by mid-1933, been reduced to operating at 30 per cent capacity. The smaller privately-owned Feman company, which also made cable but had widened its production range to include machine-tools and electronic goods, was working at full capacity. The owner, Miodrag Nikolić, was also a member of the Main Committee of the DS.[2] The director of Fabrike kablova Jagodina, Jovan Simović, was a prominent local Socialist supporter and stood as SPS candidate in the federal elections of November 1996. The large Elektronska Industrija firm in Niš, which normally produced telephones and televisions, also sought to follow the path of diversification by branching out to produce goods such as computers and video games. Nevertheless, by the end of 1993 its workforce had fallen from 7,000 to only 1,500.[3] Overall unemployment in Serbia rose from 20 per cent before the imposition of sanctions to over 50 per cent afterwards. Only 10 per cent of factories were working normally. Other companies sought to evade sanctions by exporting goods through 'sister-companies' registered in neighbouring countries.

Sanctions, however, were only one factor in the grim economic situation which developed in Serbia from 1992-3. A heavy burden was placed on the economy by the cost of subsidising the 'mini-states' of the Republika Srpska Krajina and the Republika Srpska. The VRS was also dependent on Serbia for critical logistical support in the form of fuel, raw materials and ammunition. The war also brought a heavy influx of refugees into Serbia whose support created further financial strains. According to UNHCR figures in May 1993 there were 540,000 refugees in Serbia. In Belgrade alone there were some 170,000 refugees. Most of the refugees were Serbs from Croatia and Bosnia, but there were also numbers of Croats, Muslims and other nationalities.[4] The financial commitment needed to accommodate such a migrant population was to some extent reduced by the fact that the majority of refugees were given shelter by friends and relatives.

The Serbian state and economy also continued to operate within an ideological framework of unreformed socialism with a bloated bureaucracy supervising an obsolescent state-run industrial sector. Milošević, and the SPS, were disinclined to institute any serious attempt at reform as any diminution of state control over the social and economic apparatus would also diminish his personal and political power. With the ruling elite antipathetic to reform of the economy and unable to borrow money internationally, as Tito had done, they sought to finance the state structures by the incontinent printing of money. This unrestrained issuing of money helped to set in motion a massive hyper-inflationary spiral which started in February 1992 and ran until 1 October 1993. At the end of this period the National Bank of Yugoslavia sought to control inflation by lopping off six noughts from the dinar. The 10 billion dinar note was converted overnight into the 10,000 dinar note. However, this massive adjustment failed to have the desired effect and inflation accelerated again. At the end of November a new 50 million dinar note was issued. By that time inflation was running at 18.7 per cent a day, 21,190 per cent a month and 286 billion per cent a year. This meant that Serbia had achieved the dubious distinction of exceeding the inflation rate of Weimar Germany in the early 1920s.[5]

This economic collapse and rampant inflation had fundamental effects on Serbian society. The middle and professional classes – who should have formed the social backbone of the opposition – were pauperised by the hyper-inflationary processes. Many such educated and skilled individuals were driven to emigrate, creating a powerful 'brain drain' in Serbia. At the same time, the public infrastructure began to collapse with many state-owned factories and public buildings simply closing as the authorities no longer had the capacity to heat them in the winter months. The desperate state of Serbia's public institutions was graphically illustrated at the Belgrade zoo where visitors were required to pay not in money, which was worthless, but in food for the animals. Only those individuals with close associations with the ruling elite were insulated from the destructive economic pressures which had been unleashed.

At a state and individual level Serbia developed a number of survival mechanisms to cope with the economic situation. The inherent strength of the Serbian agricultural sector meant that while Serbian industry might crumble, its government at least had a reliable source of food. Speaking at a country fair in May 1994 Milošević told his audience: 'There is no computer that can calculate how much our farmers can produce. We will be a well-fed country from this war.'[6] In December 1993 Mihailo Marković of the SPS was even willing to contemplate the 'transition to a natural economy',[7] with barter playing an increasing role as money ceased to have meaningful value. City-dwellers could also rely on relatives in the countryside to supply them with basic agricultural produce. By the winter of 1993/4, however, the relationship between the town and countryside had broken down. Farmers refused to sell their crops and produce in exchange for worthless dinars. Basic foodstuffs such as milk vanished from the shelves of Belgrade shops. In the countryside farmers slaughtered their livestock rather than sending them to market.[8] On both sides of this rural/urban divide there were many who did not blame the government or the President for this crisis. In the towns food shortages were blamed by some on the laziness or vindictiveness of the peasantry. In the rural areas blame for the lack of basic materials such as petrol and fertiliser was often aimed at a general class of urban bureaucrats, who were held responsible for exploiting the peasantry, rather than specifically at the government.[9] In the last grim months of 1993 many citizens of Belgrade became dependent on hand-outs from soup kitchens run by charities affiliated to opposition political parties, such a Spona (link) run by the SPO. Other opposition political parties also had charitable organisations attached to them, such as Luča (light) of the DSS.

The large number of Serbs working abroad meant that there was a steady flow of hard currency back into the country providing an element of financial stability in the economic anarchy. During this period, while the dinar was the official currency, many transactions were conducted in German marks. The greater concentration of German marks in the north of Serbia and the Belgrade area caused the dinar to devalue rapidly and inflation to soar in southern areas such as Vranje. This differential inflation served further to emphasise Serbia's north/south divide.[10]

A number of private banks also appeared, offering Serbian citizens exceedingly favourable rates of interest (10-15 per cent a month) on hard currency deposits. These banks were able to utilise the need of the population for cash and their distrust of the state banks in order to secure a strong flow of investments. The largest of these private banks were Jugoskandic run by Jezdimir Vasiljević ('Gazda Jezda') and Dafiment run by Dafina Milanović. Jezdimir Vasiljević was a flamboyant character, originally from the village of Topolovik near Veliko Gradište in eastern Serbia, who was variously said to have begun his career working in a rubber factory, as a cinema operator and as a stockbroker. He was rumoured to have travelled widely across the world working, it was said, in America, Canada, Australia, Sri Lanka and Singapore. At the beginning of 1990 Vasiljević founded the Jugoskandic firm based in Požarevac, which at first specialised in the marketing of televisions, video recorders and cars. In January 1991 it began its banking activities, although it was not formally registered as Jugoskandic Bank until March 1992. The burgeoning banking business provided an umbrella for other profitable sidelines including trading in petrol and cigarettes. Vasiljević sought to maintain a high social and public profile – for example, in the autumn of 1992 he sponsored a visit to Serbia by the renowned and controversial chess-player Bobby Fisher.[11] He also took steps to carve out a political role for himself, running as a candidate in the December 1992 presidential elections and securing 61,729 votes. He enjoyed the closest possible links with the ruling political and financial elite. At the height of Jugoskandic's financial fortunes he was able to boast that he had money invested in more than 100 Serbian firms. During the 1992 local elections Vasiljević had shown his support for the SPS by contributing some 200,000 marks to its election campaign in Belgrade. He also maintained strong links with the SRS and with Željko Ražnatović 'Arkan'. He was believed to be a major financial backer of Serbian paramilitary groups, contributing some 7 million marks to buying guns and equipment for the volunteers.[12] However, Vasiljević's business empire was to be shortlived. The Jugoskandic bank was organised on a 'pyramid' principle and as such its lifespan was bound to be limited. On 12 March it collapsed and Vasiljević fled to Israel and later to Ecuador. The last act in Jugoskandic's history was played out when on 15 March masked gunmen broke into its offices in the Vračar district of Belgrade and stole $2 million, accounting for most of its remaining reserve of cash. The bank's numerous ordinary investors lost their savings.

The Dafiment bank operated on an even grander scale than Jugoskandic. Dafina Milanović, who was born in 1947 in the village of Skobalj near Smederevo, had been accused on a number of occasions during 1986-9, while working as chief book-keeper for a major Serbian public company, of abusing her position for financial gain. Her capacity for providing plausible excuses, claiming on one occasion that the money she had gained by fraudulent means had been spent on 'medicine for her brother who worked in the Smederevo ironworks', had not prevented her from being sentenced during this period to spend fourteen months and thirteen days in prison. The Dafiment bank was founded on 9 October 1991, only three months after Milanović had once again received a sentence of six months in prison, suspended for two years, for financial corruption.[13]

Observers suggested that the Dafiment bank had from the start served a *para-state* function. Milanović like Vasiljević, had cultivated close links with the ruling party. The investments held by her bank were concentrated in southern Serbia, the electoral heartland of the SPS, with 100 million marks being invested in the Simpo furniture company in Vranje. In the period before the December 1992 elections Milanović made a major contribution of 7 billion dinars to the depleted state pension funds, thereby helping to secure the support of older voters for the SPS.[14] Milanović sought to portray her activities in a philanthropic light: 'I'm feeding the people and preserving social peace', she proclaimed.[15] Milanović, however, was also believed to have been involved in the channeling of money to paramilitary formations. She was a major financial donor to the Kapetan Dragan Fund set up to provide financial aid to former paramilitary volunteers. She was known to have invested with Željko Ražnatović in a 'business centre' and petrol station near Arkan's base at Erdut in eastern Slavonia. This 'joint venture' between Milanović and Arkan was, of course, a tran-shipment point for smuggled petrol.

Shortly after the collapse of Jugoskandic bank, Dafiment also began to falter as investors panicked and sought to withdraw their deposits. Attempts were made by Milanović on 30 March to stop the outflow of funds from the bank by placing limits on the amounts of money which could be withdrawn and instituting sharp cuts in the level of interest offered to investors. This coincided with the attempts by the authorities to prevent hard currency leaving Serbia with large quantities being seized by customs officials at the Hungarian border. The attempts to shore up the position of Dafiment, however, ultimately failed and its investors were left disappointed and impoverished. It was widely believed, however, that state officials and senior supporters of the SPS had been allowed to withdraw their deposits before the bank finally closed. Despite the massive failure of her financial experiment, Milanović was able to go into comfortable retirement in the elite Dedinje quarter of Belgrade.

Sanctions-breaking operations became a major aspect of Serbian economic and social life. These ranged from major state-sponsored operations, frequently carried out by businessmen or paramilitary leaders friendly to the regime, to the entrepreneurial efforts of individuals. Countries on Serbia's borders were at first relatively willing to participate in the implementation of the sanctions blockade regarding the international effort as a step towards integration into European institutions. Even Romania, whose President – the former communist, Ion Iliescu – enjoyed good relations with the ideologically compatible Slobodan Milošević, was praised in June 1993 by the British Foreign Secretary, Douglas Hurd, for the level of co-operation it had shown in enforcing sanctions.[16] These countries, however, became increasingly dissatisfied with the failure of the West to supply compensation for the disruption of their trade with the Federal Republic of Yugoslavia. The International Monetary Fund estimated that the embargo on Serbia and Montenegro cost Bulgaria $1.1 billion in 1993 and a further $700 million in the first half of 1994. The Bulgarian Deputy Foreign Minister put the figure for the same period at $3.6 billion.[17] As a consequence of these discontents the embargo began to show increasing signs of decay towards the end of 1993 and the first half of 1994. As a consequence sanctions-breaking projects saw further growth in scale and sophistication.

At some points on Serbia's borders 'boom towns' grew up based on the profits of sanctions-busting. The small Romanian villages of Moldova Veche and Pescari suddenly grew rich from transporting petrol across the Danube into Serbia. The villagers from these places jealously guarded this trade from any outsiders who attempted to move in on their business. The militant reputation of these fishermen-smugglers ensured that the Sanctions Assistance Monitors of the West European Union also avoided their most notorious haunts.[18] Albanian villages near Lake Shkoder also saw a sudden transformation of their fortunes when, particularly during the later period of the blockade, they became a major transhipment point for fuel from Greece and Italy into Montenegro and onwards to Serbia.[19] At Kalotino on the Bulgarian border Sanctions Assistance Monitors recorded constant attempts to smuggle goods into Serbia ranging from individuals crossing from Bulgaria to Serbia to sell petrol carried in Coca-Cola bottles or emptied from their motorcycle tanks, to one attempt to bring in the engine for a MiG-29 aircraft concealed within a cargo of soap powder. In

September 1992 at the southern Bulgarian border town of Petrich it was estimated that 1,000 tonnes of petrol-based products were passing through the town each day. It had become, in the words of an official, 'one huge petrol station'.[20]

The Republic of Macedonia had, before the introduction of sanctions, conducted 70 per cent of its trade with Serbia and Montenegro. In these circumstances, and bearing in mind Macedonia's economic weakness, the complete cessation of this trade with the FRY was widely considered to be impossible. The strong links between the political-bureaucratic establishments in Skopje and Belgrade also facilitated the continuation of economic links between the two countries.[21] The Macedonian dependence on trade with Serbia was further strengthened after February 1994 when Greece imposed its own economic blockade on Macedonia. Macedonia offered to Serbia a convenient and porous southern frontier and in September 1993 it was estimated that $2.8 billion in goods had been imported to Serbia through Macedonia in the previous six months. The import-export relationship was partly one of agricultural barter with, in early 1994, vegetables being exported from Macedonia to Serbia in exchange for Serbian seed-corn. At another level Serbian front companies and agents based in Skopje played a critical role in the organisation of imports of oil and steel. As was the case with other countries who shared borders with Serbia the crossing points were manned by the Macedonian Sanctions Assistance Mission of the Conference for Security and Co-operation in Europe. The twenty-eight-man monitoring team, however, observed the border by day while the sanctions-busting trucks bound for Serbia crossed the border by night. In the middle of 1993 one observer at a border point near Skopje estimated that 150–200 trucks crossed each way every night. The scale of sanctions violations in Macedonia was well known to the United Nations and other international agencies, but it was calculated that any punitive action against the Macedonian government would jeopardise the fragile political and ethnic peace in the country and therefore be counter-productive.[22]

Nicosia, the capital of Cyprus, also became an important base for Serbian companies organising trade deals between the FRY and other countries. There was speculation that the Serbian companies controlled by the government, helped by the favourable Cypriot laws on banking secrecy, were involved in the buying of essential goods including industrial, machinery, trucks and oil. It was also suspected that the companies and banks in Cyprus provided a means by which members of the state elite, including businessmen and party officials, were also to channel money out of the state and into private accounts.[23]

In 1993 Yugoslav foreign trade was at 20 per cent of its pre-sanctions level.[24] This represented a dramatic fall in the export levels of the FRY. Nevertheless the figures showed that a significant proportion of foreign trade had survived despite the fact that it was theoretically illegal. The criminalisation of foreign trade, however, meant that the handling and transportation of vital resources were placed in the hands of a new class of sanctions-busting 'businessmen', war profiteers and gangsters with intimate links to the inner circles of government. The sanctions regime in Serbia cemented the triangular inter-linked relationship between political power, business and criminality. The triumphant role attained by this group marked a further degeneration in the social and economic life of Serbia.

In this atmosphere of international isolation and extreme material insecurity, artists and writers rose to prominence in whose work there was a powerful stress on themes of mysticism and irrationality. This group was epitomised by Milić od Mačve (Milić Stanković) a talented surrealist whose work revolved around the depiction of mythic and historical themes. This artist's public pronouncements showed a world-view which mixed ultra-nationalist politics with elements of occultism. At one point he told the public that the apocalypse was approaching and the world would soon witness a series of tectonic catastrophes from which only the Serbs would survive by retreating into their mountain fastnesses, while on another occasion he announced his intention of helping to organise a crusade of Orthodox peoples, which he suggested would be led by General Ratko Mladić, to capture Istanbul and refound the Byzantine empire. In the same vein the Belgrade writer Radomir Smiljanić proposed in December 1993 that a giant white cross should be erected on the Kalemegdan to affirm Serbia's adherence to the Orthodox faith. Milić of Mačve founded an organisation called New Byzantium and Smiljanić set up a similar group called White Rose to act as vehicles for their ideas. These groups worked together during 1993 attempting to organise a blockade of the Danube to prevent international traffic gaining access to the waterway, and staging demonstrations outside the US and German embassies.[25] This fundamentalist outlook was shared by popular writers such as Momo Kapor, originally from Sarajevo, whose commentaries on political events and the war in Bosnia appeared in the pages of *Duga* and other journals. Writing in the journal *Pogledi* in early 1992, Kapor recalled a journey he had made from urban Belgrade to the Hercegovinan mountains. In the small town of Trebinje he hears a soldier singing folksongs accompanied by the traditional Serbian stringed instrument, the *gusle*, and realises that the cosmopolitanism of the city is worthless when compared to the 'forgotten essence' which this national culture represents: 'When I think back over the last year and its most important events I will put in first place hearing the voice of that young fighter, the sound of whose *gusle* travels across the dark centuries uniting him with his ancestors who played on the same instruments, and the defiant bursts of gunfire into the sky which accompanied that sound.'[26] Such 'blood and soil' sentiments were echoed by Dragoš Kalajić whose articles dwelt on the threat to Serbia, and the Orthodox world, from the 'new world order'.[27] These writers and artists were regarded by many people as being self-publicising eccentrics and their political importance was marginal, but the prominence that their opinions were given added to the feverish and confused miasma of nationalism prevailing during the period.

At a lower cultural level the phenomenon of 'Turbo-folk' also rose in popularity during this period. Turbo-folk consisted of an incongruous mixture of synthesised pop music and traditional Serbian folk. Its female singers such as Svetlana 'Ceca' Veličković, Dragana Mirković, 'Lepa Brena' (Fahreta Jahić), Vesna Zmijanac, and Simonida Stanković, attracted a large following with their brash glamour and uninhibited hedonism. However, Turbo-folk was not universally admired and was regarded with disdain by many educated young people, who preferred European and American rock, as the music of the uncultured and migrants to the city from the countryside. In the case of Svetlana Veličković this characterisation was literally correct since she had come originally from the small south Serbian village Žitoradje and moved to Belgrade to pursue her career as a folk star. There were strong links between the turbo-folk singers and nationalist politics. Svetlana Veličković had shown her political sympathies when during the war in Croatia she had appeared near the front-line in combat fatigues. Vesna

Zmijanac was known to be close to the Socialist establishment, and particularily to Milorad Vučelić, helping to secure her favourable coverage on the state TV network. The lyrics of Simonida Stanković's songs praised the deeds of Arkan's fighters in Bosnia. As befitted the daughter of Milić od Mačve she sought to articulate her own political/social agenda by calling on Serbs to return to their peasant roots in order to escape the control of foreign multi-nationals. In her view the Serbs were like 'modern Mohicans defending their land'.[28] A touch of the bizarre was added to her stage performances by the fact that she frequently appeared on stage wearing a wreath of garlic, apparently to protect her from the 'vampires so often present in our political life today'. Unlike Svetlana Veličković, however, she was not a 'country girl made good' but the daughter of an intellectual who had developed her garlic-wearing habit while playing in a rock band in Paris. Her penchant for garlic should therefore be seen as an attempt to create some 'exotic' eastern ethnic chic in a Western cosmopolitian urban environment rather than as a genuine echo of Serbian peasant folkways. Sonja Karadžić, the daughter of the Bosnian Serb leader, also sought briefly – and unsuccessfully – to forge a career for herself on the turbo-folk scene. One of her first songs condemned the 'degenerate, materialistic' Serbs of Belgrade who, she said, owed everything to the Bosnian Serbs.[29] One Serbian observer described turbo-folk as 'the sound of the war and everything that the war has brought to this country. It represents everything that has happened to this country over the last few years.'[30]

It is nevertheless a curious fact that despite their strident Serbian nationalism, the turbo-folk singers attracted a substantial following in neighbouring countries including Romania, where Lepa Brena played to large audiences in the early 1990s, and Bulgaria. In 1992 the Bulgarian nationalist intellectual Nikolai Tontiev wrote lamenting the fact that 'the problem with Bulgaria today is that Lepa Brena is more popular than Raina Kabaivanska a leading Bulgarian opera singer.'[31] These countries, however, not only shared broad cultural similarities with Serbia, but also had undergone the same processes of rapid urbanisation, and were subject to comparable contemporary uncertainties. Even more remarkable, however, was the fact that throughout the war Serbian turbo-folk singers continued to have their admirers both in Croatia and among Bosnian Muslims.[32]

Notes

1. Danilo Šuković, 'The Economic Crisis and the Necessity of Changing the Economic System' in Dušan Janjić (ed.), *Serbia – Between the Past and the Future*, Institute of Social Sciences (Belgrade), 1995, pp. 59-61.
2. 'Business in Serbia – Crumbling', *Economist*, 14 August 1993.
3. James Lyon (1996), p. 321.
4. 'The former Yugoslavia: Refugees and War Resisters', *RFE/RL Research Report*, 24 June 1994.
5. Michael Montgomery, 'Serbia's Inflated Dinar Set to Burst', *Daily Telegraph*, 26 November 1993.
6. Michael Montgomery, 'Diet of Optimism Helps Serbs to Stomach Sanctions', *Daily Telegraph*, 30 May 1994.
7. 'Milošević's Weimar Republic', *Economist*, 11 December 1993.
8. Dusko Doder; 'Fistfulls of Dinars Replaced by Gold', *European*, 24 July-4 August 1994.
9. An illustration of this could be seen in a placard held by a farmer at a demonstration in April 1995 which depicted two peasants yoked to a plough which was being pushed by a figure dressed in a suit who is clearly meant to be a government official. This photograph is contained in Vesna Kostić, 'Okretni specijalisti', *NIN*, 7 April 1995.
10. Lyon (1996), p. 312.
11. Mladjan Dinkić, *Ekonomija destrukcije – velika pljačka naroda*, Stubove kulture (Belgrade), 1996, pp. 161-74.
12. Milan Milošević et al., 'Jezda otišao dafinitivno', *Vreme*, 15 March 1993.
13. Dinkić (1996), pp. 197-8.
14. Milan Milošević et al., *Vreme*, 15 March 1993.
15. Yigal Chazan, 'End of the Line for Belgrade's Flashy Financial Matriarch', *Guardian*, 16 April 1993.
16. Annika Savill, 'Romania Boycott Praised by Hurd', *Independent*, 3 June 1993. The relationship between Milošević and Iliescu is examined in Tom Gallagher, *Romania After Ceausecu – The Politics of Intolerance*, Edinburgh University Press, 1995, pp. 133-5.
17. Mark Milner, 'Sanctions Cost a Bomb as Sofia feels the Pinch', *Guardian*, 18 August 1994.
18. Julius Strauss, 'Romanians Grow Rich Fuelling Bosnia War', *Daily Telegraph*, 29 March 1995.
19. Raymond Bonner, 'Albania's Lakeside Smugglers Help Fuel Serbian War Machine', *Guardian*, 4 April 1995.
20. Nikola Antonov, 'Greeks Help Serbs Beat Oil Embargo', *Guardian*, 6 September 1992.
21. James Pettifer, 'Macedonia – Still the Apple of Discord', *World Today*, March 1995.
22. Yigal Chazan, 'Macedonia Tightens Sanctions compliance on Serbian Border', *Guardian*, 7 September 1993; Yigal Chazan, 'Impoverished Macedonia Flouts Sanctions on Serbs', *Guardian*, 2 July 1994; Andrew Tarnowski, 'Night Brings Out Sanctions Busters', *The Times*, 14 July 1993.

23. Ian Traynor, 'Serbia Busts the UN Blockade', *Guardian*, 12 September 1992.
24. Yigal Chazan, *Guardian*, 2 July 1994.
25. Milič od Mačve, 'Puška i tapija', *NIN*, 7 July 1993.
26. Momo Kapor, 'Predeo spružen mržnjom', *Pogledi*, 17 January 1992.
27. An example of this can be seen in Dragoš Kalajić, 'Pravoslavni svih zemalja', *Duga*, 26 March 1993.
28. Simonida Stanković interviewed on Euro-File, BBC Radio 4, 3 July 1993.
29. Milan Milošević and Dragoslav Grujić, 'Sve srpske deobe', *Vreme*, 23 May 1994.
30. Robert Block, 'Ethnic Cleansing's Balladeers get their Marching Orders', *Independent*, 25 March 1994.
31. Nikolai Tontiev, The Bulgarian as Jew', *East European Reporter*, March/April 1992.
32. Milivoj Djilas, 'Nešto za plakanje', *NIN*, 20 September 1996.

17. A 'Quarrel Among Brothers': The Radical–Socialist Split (July–November 1993)

While the SPS had been ready to co-operate in their joint operations against Drašković and Ćosić, the political differences between the two parties, which had first emerged over the Vance-Owen peace plan, were becoming progressively more apparent. Speaking on 3 June Šešelj was cautious in his attitude to Milošević: 'We are his political opponents and we have always claimed this. But we have also stressed that we admire Milošević as a Serbian patriot and a man who is doing everything in his power to contribute to the well being of his own people and solve their problems.'[1] He was also reluctant to give his support to the Socialist-sponsored attempt to have the SPO banned: 'The fact that some members of the party's leadership and some members of the party have committed criminal acts and crimes in the street does not mean that the entire party should be banned.'[2]

On 18 June a group of twenty-one opposition deputies moved a motion of no-confidence in Nikola Šainović's government. The Radicals intervened to save the government, but expressed their 'reservations' about this move indicating that if the Socialists had not produced substantial improvements in their government's policy by 15 September then the SRS would withdraw their support. This call for overall improvements in government policy was combined with a series of specific demands. On 1 July the SRS announced that their approval of the government's budget proposals would be conditional on abolition of the three republican ministries for Foreign Affairs, Foreign Economic Relations, and Defence, which the Radicals considered to duplicate the functions of federal ministries. They also called for finance to be withdrawn from a number of social organisations normally funded from the republican budget.[3] A week later, on 8 July, the Radicals sought to raise the stakes by demanding the removal of a number of senior VJ officers including the Chief of the General Staff, Života Panić. On 26 August Panić and forty-two other generals were replaced in a major purge of the army's ranks. He was replaced by Momčilo Perišić who had served in eastern Hercegovina, around Mostar, in the first months of the war in Bosnia, and was an old comrade of the VRS commander, Ratko Mladić.[4]

On 7 July Šešelj was able to reflect on the position the SRS held balanced between government and opposition: 'These times are very difficult. The Serbian Radical Party is in a particularly difficult position. You know we are in a situation where neither the republican or the federal authorities would be able to function without our support and help. This is a heavy burden because we could bring a government down at any time, we could prevent laws being passed, we could, in fact, cause chaos in the country.'[5] The formation by the SRS, on 3 September, of a 'shadow cabinet' headed by Tomislav Nikolić formally marked the transition in their relationship with the SPS from 'coalition partner' to formal 'opposition.'[6]

The taking on by the SRS of this oppositional position inevitably saw a marked increase in tension between the SRS and the SPS. Tomislav Nikolić would later recall: 'Relations between the state and our [paramilitary] volunteers saw a drastic change after May 1993. Then great problems began with the medical care of our wounded, with permision for paid leave, and soon with the paying of funeral costs to the families of the fallen.'[7] In late 1992 and early 1993 Branislav Vakić and his Četnik volunteers had been deployed in the eastern Bosnian Srebrenica-Bratunac region, operating out of Bajina Bašta, they had co-operated with the Red Beret Interior Ministry Forces, headed by Franko Simatović 'Frenki', Jovica Stanišić's deputy. The co-operative relationship between Vakić and the Interior Ministry officials was clearly close, and when SRS-SPS relations broke down attempts were made to persude Vakić to leave the SRS. Vakić, however, remained loyal to Šešelj.[8] On 10 September a military revolt broke out in the Serbian-controlled northern Bosnian town of Banja Luka. The 'September 93' revolt, which appeared to enjoy considerable support from the local civilian population, was ostensibly directed against corrupt local politicians and war profiteers. It was also an expression of the regional tensions between Banja Luka and the

Bosnian Serb leadership in Pale, near Sarajevo. One member of the rebel Crisis Committee summed this situation up by saying: 'Banja Luka is a European town while Pale is a village with a television station.'[9] One of the actions of these military insurrectionists, however, was to arrest SRS officials in the town. Šešelj interpreted the Banja Luka revolt as a conspiracy undertaken by members of SK-PJ within the Bosnian Serb army with the intention of undermining the position of their nationalist political leadership headed by Radovan Karadžić. According to Šešelj this revolt was ultimately directed by Slobodan Milošević from Belgrade and was a dress rehearsal for a similar coup which was aimed at the SRS in Serbia.[10]

The political rivalry between the SRS and the SPS came to a head on 20 September when the Radicals, seeking to make good the threat they had issued in June, proposed a vote of no-confidence in the government. The SRS stated: 'The Serbian government, regardless of what measures it is taking at present, does not deserve our confidence and therefore it has to go.'[11] Immediately before the vote of no-confidence a bitter war of words broke out between the SRS and the SPS in which the 'allies turned enemies' traded accusations and counter-accusations. On 28 September the Main Committee of the SPS delivered a blistering attack on Šešelj and the SRS: 'Šešelj's policy is at the opposite pole from the policy of the SPS, as well as at the opposite pole from the interests of the Serbian people and the interests of all the citizens of Serbia. In his political conduct Vojislav Šešelj demonstrates an extremely primitive chauvinism. [...] The society that he advocates is a foolish combination of feudal autarchy and war communism. [...] In a most dishonest way, in the pure pursuit of power, Šešelj's party charges the SPS and the government with responsibility for economic and social problems that are an obvious consequence of the war imposed on the Serbian people and the unjust sanctions against our country. The SPS will do its best to establish and publically expose Šešelj's participation and his own contribution to the forming of paramilitary groups on the territory of the Republic of the Serbian Krajina and the Republika Srpska, the crimes which they have committed against the Serbian population – be it Croat, Muslim, or Serb – as well as the criminal activity which Šešelj and his associates have participated in. We care about Bosnia-Hercegovina, the Republika Srpska and the Serbian people outside Serbia, but that is no reason for a politico from Sarajevo, such as Šešelj, to preach to Serbia. The SPS is against violence and primitivism, and therefore it is against Šešelj's policy because he is the embodiment of violence and primitivism who must be stopped. It is no accident that, now that peace is before us, Šešelj wants to destabilise Serbia. Šešelj is afraid of peace because such people can surface only during a crisis and a war. The future of Serbia is not dictatorship and fascism, but democracy and prosperity. All democratic political forces and all honest people in Serbia should join in the struggle against the evil personified by Šešelj.'[12] This wide-ranging attack was notable for the ferocity with which the SPS condemned the 'primitivism' of the 'fascist' Radicals, in contrast to their previous attempts to domesticate the SRS as 'honorary leftists', and the way in which Šešelj was denounced for his Bosnian Serb origins in contradiction to the 'Great Serbian' ideology. This had previously been a main pillar of SPS policy, and assumed that all Serbs were components of one national community. Šešelj was keen to rebut the Socialist attack on him, telling an interviewer on 1 October: 'I am a Sarajevo politico. This is clear from the fact that I was convicted in Sarajevo for promoting the idea of a multi-party system while the older members of the SPS were persecuting free-thinkers and the younger ones were playing marbles.'[13]

Following his release from prison, Vuk Drašković spent a month in Greece. According to Drašković, 'I was isolated at my own wish on the island of Limnos. I visited the holy mountain of Athos and came back.' He combined this religious pilgrimage with a political meeting, holding talks with the Greek premier Konstantin Mitsotakis. At the end of September Vuk and Danica Drašković, in an effort to raise the opposition's political profile, visited London at the invitation of the British Foreign Office. Drašković was keen to emphasise the difference in approach to the national question between himself and the Serbian President. Drašković told British reporters: 'I am an advocate of greater Serbia now in the same way that I was three years ago. There are two ways of approaching a greater Serbia: first the way of the Socialist party, hatred, disaster. This leads to the smallest Serbia in history, the most powerless Serbia in history.' He went on to emphasise the material difficulties faced by the opposition in Serbia: 'I want concrete support. The Serbian Renewal Movement is the biggest opposition group in Serbia, and the only property we have is one car. If we could under such circumstances get – as we got in the last election – 1.2 million votes, only 100,000 less than Milošević's party who have faxes and control the television, then we must be the eighth wonder of the world. Let's see the Conservatives or the Labour Party do that! Can you imagine that?'[14]

Drašković made his first public appearance in Serbia on 7 October at a meeting of around 10,000 people in Valjevo. He restated his condemnation of the Serbian government, which had said: 'All that is necessary for us to achieve a great and historic victory would be that all Serbs should live in one state.' But he said that in reality there had been no victory and Serbia had suffered the 'greatest defeat since the time of Karadjordje'. Nevertheless the SPO resolved that they, and the representatives of New Democracy, would not take part' in the forthcoming vote of no-confidence which was, they said, a 'quarrel among brothers'.[15] Drašković called instead for the formation of a transitional government of national unity, headed by an apolitical figure, which would prepare the way for the holding of new elections. Vojislav Koštunica, however, announced that the DSS would back the SRS no-confidence motion. The DSS leader said that the government's: 'irresponsible policies threaten the existence of the entire nation. We cannot allow it to continue any longer.'[16] The DS also saw the no-confidence motion as an opportunity to overturn the SPS government and signalled their willingness to support the no-confidence motion. With the abstention of the SPO and ND being widely regarded as a vital factor for the survival of the Šainović government it came as no surprise therefore when on 6 October the District Prosecutor's Office in Belgrade announced that the outstanding charges against Vuk Drašković for assaulting a policeman were finally to be dropped. Vladimir Gajić of the SPO commented: 'Politically this trial was the last thing that the government needed.'[17]

The no-confidence debate began on 7 October with Tomislav Nikolić leading the attack for the SRS. He recalled the way in which the SRS had backed the Serbian government in resisting the earlier SPO initiated motion of no- confidence: 'We attempted to save this government so that it should have time to begin serious work. [...]: It is completely clear that those measures have yielded no results, that the people of Serbia have become split into a large number of citizens who are struggling to survive, and a small number of those for whom the hungry ones will soon work in the former state factories. [...] Now it is completely obvious that this Serbian government does not enjoy trust and cannot be allowed to lead Serbia.' Nikolić also asserted that the Socialist acceptance of the Vance-Owen peace plan 'supported by part of DEPOS and the Democrats' was the 'first great defeat for the SPS' and reminded them that 'it is not possible to be a patriot if you are supported by those [in the opposition] whom you have labelled as traitors.' He was also scornful of the sudden turn-about in the Socialist attitude to the SRS' pointing out that during the period of Radical support for the SPS 'you in the Socialist Party of Serbia hailed us as partiots, as a "constructive" opposition, as those who sought office through the ballot box but did not threaten the national interest. That was not so long ago, and we have not changed. We are still a constructive opposition, we seek office by parliamentary means.'

The SRS Vice-President concluded by calling on the opposition to support the motion of no-confidence: 'If you have a conscience, you whom the people have chosen to work on their behalf, who oppose the government, and one hopes do not act in opposition to the people, who have sought to bring down the government from the streets, must make use of this democratic, parliamentary opportunity to remove this government that you do not want. There is no need to organise daily acts of madness in Belgrade, there is no need to break glass, there is no need to be cold, there is no need to fight with the police, it is not necessary for anyone to be killed. Simply raise your hands and you will ensure that for many years to come socialism will be banished from Serbia.'

Zoran Andjelković replied for the Socialists to the SRS attacks: 'The Radicals accuse us of being bad patriots. Once again they want to give lectures to us on patriotism. Beating their breasts they proclaim their patriotic virtues as if patriotism depends on the noises made in their speeches. The Socialists uncompromisingly defend and protect their land and their nation, but also foster respect towards the interests of other nations. [...] Our patriotism is principled and humanistic, but not vengeful. [...] Šešelj's Radicals have shown themselves by their deeds to be chauvinistic in their habits, which is an evil thing for the Serbian people and their interests. They are chauvinist-patriots, and a chauvinist, who hates other nations, is not able to bring any good to his own nation.'

While the SRS and the SPS exchanged accusations across the floor of the Serbian parliament the SPO-ND representatives maintained their position of neutrality. Milan Miković, the leader of the DEPOS group within the parliament, stated: 'Our position is moral and politically principled. We will not stretch out our hands to intervene in what is really a squabble within one party or faction.' Only Mladen Markov dissented from this position, insisting that in order to remain true to the original principles of DEPOS as a 'democratic Serbian opposition with a clear national programme' he was compelled to cast his vote against the Šainović government. When on 8 October the SPO-ND deputies staged a walk-out, Markov continued to participate in the debate.[18]

On 12 October, however, a woman, Nadežda Bulatović, was seriously beaten by the police in an incident which occurred while she was queuing to buy flour. DEPOS raised the incident in parliament, linking it to a number of recent murders of prominent businessmen, and demanded the resignation of the Interior Minister, Zoran Sokolović. The minister apologised for the incident, but refused to resign, prompting the DEPOS representatives to indicate, on 15 October, that they were now ready to support the SRS motion of no-confidence. However, the debate was suspended on 18 October when parliament went into recess and the vote was not scheduled to take place till 25 October. Faced by the prospect of imminent defeat at the hands of this array of opposition parties, and the prospect that the victorious groups might go on to use their parliamentary position to break the Socialist monopoly on the media, Milošević moved on 20 October to dissolve the parliament and outflank the opposition by calling new parliamentary elections in Serbia.

The poll was scheduled for the earliest date possible, 19 December, in order to capitalise to the fullest extent on the ruling party's institutional advantages over the opposition parties. The advent of the elections found the opposition once more in a state of disarray. Vojislav Koštunica had throughout the autumn been indicating that he believed it would not be possible to revive DEPOS as an active electoral force. On 28 October he gave his final indication that he would not participate in a reconstituted DEPOS stating that the policy differences between themselves and the SPO were now too great for the presentation of any meaningful common platform and that: 'For us, DEPOS is simply an episode in the past.'[19] The DSS resolved to enter the election without national coalition partners although it declared itself willing to contemplate regional alliances with groups such as Milomir Babić's Serbian Peasant's Party in the Šumadija. The DSS was undoubtedly encouraged to take this independent course by the predictions of prominent backers, such as Matija Bećković that they were set to replace the SRS as the second largest party in the Serbian parliament.[20] In spite of the adverse conditions the SPO leadership continued to stress the importance of opposition unity. Milan Komnenić put their case: 'If we go forward divided, then we will lose together.' He stressed that the main disputes between the SPO and the DSS were arguments between the two parties leaderships and did not reflect broad differences at the level of membership.[21] The Serbian Liberal Party, like the DSS, signalled that it would withdraw from DEPOS and also announced that it would boycott the elections, which it regarded as an electoral device being used by Milošević to consolidate his personal power. One influential member of the SLS, Milan Božić, however, favouring participation in the election, chose to remain with DEPOS and would later join the SPO acting as a key adviser to Vuk Drašković.[22] With an accord with the DSS being obviously unsustainable the SPO, determined to preserve the DEPOS name and the memory of unity which it still embodied, began looking elsewhere for coalition partners.[23] On 15 November it was announced that the SPO and ND would be joined by the GSS in a reformulated DEPOS. The GSS had, since the 1992 elections, seen two of its component elements, the National Peasants Party of Dragan Veselinov and the League of Vojvodina Social Democrats led by Nenad Čanak, leave in order to continue their political activities independent of the alliance. Cooperation between the leadership of the GSS and the SPO, united by their opposition to the war and their approval of the international peace proposals, had been growing throughout 1993. The official declaration of their alliance under the DEPOS banner, however, was widely seen as marking the end point of Vuk Drašković's long journey from his original position of national radicalism to a civic-national position.[24] During the pre-election campaign Drašković was dismissive of his former allies in the DSS and their policy of solidarity with the Bosnian Serbs: 'I cannot understand how Mr Koštunica, who is from [the village of] Koštunica, in the heart of Serbia, near to Ravna Gora, was able to raise his hand together with a man [Šešelj] who has publically declared that the *Srbijanci* are Serbs of the second order, made up of worn out national material, who need to be revitalised and re-educated by the real Serbs from across the Drina.'[25]

The Democratic Party also approached the election campaign in a state of severe internal convulsion. An increasingly severe rift had opened up between the incumbent DS President, Dragoljub Mićunović, and his deputy and former ally, the head of the DS Executive Committee, Zoran Djindjić. At a meeting on 30 October Zoran Djindjić gained the support of the DS Main Committee for the adoption of his proposed platform for the election campaign rather than that put forward by Mićunović. Djindjić stressed the need to address the actual economic and social problems facing the population of Serbia rather than engaging in anti-communist sloganising. Djindjić sought to combine this social agenda with an increasingly hard line attitude to national issues. Djindjić defined his position: 'Wherever possible the Serbian people has had and does have the right to have its own state, that the states which are in the process of being created should be defended, should be helped, that one should strive to create one unified state and that it is necessary – both in Serbia and in Yugoslavia – to create mechanisms and conditions for us to become stronger and richer and for this state of ours to be able...to defend what has been attained and to ensure international recognition of everything which now represents the real state of affairs.'[26] Mićunović while formally remaining President of the party was forced to take a back seat in the forthcoming election campaign.

On 25 November Milan Panić arrived in Serbia and held an intensive series of meetings with the aim of encouraging some form of renewed unity among the fragmented opposition forces. His efforts, however, bore little fruit. Drašković appeared keen to form some sort of wider opposition alliance, but Mićunović, while he personally favoured co-operation, did not now command the loyalty of the DS. Zoran Djindjić, who was now effectively the DS leader, and Vojislav Koštunica both resisted these attempts to be drawn into such a new opposition alignment.[27]

The dissolution of parliament and the approach of the election campaign saw an intensification of the state-directed attacks on the SRS. The newspaper *Borba* carried a report from a correspondent, Mirko Jovičević, working with the Yugoslav Army, which accused the SRS paramilitary volunteers of committing numerous atrocities in the first months of the war in Bosnia including 'murders, rapes, stabbing, and playing football with chopped off heads'.[28] At the same time *Politika* published a commentary, on 10 November, which observed: 'The story of Vojislav Šešelj is best compared to the trail of a comet: it flew by in an instant, fully ablaze, then plunged into the darkness from where it had come.'[29] On 11 and 12 November the authorities arrested two groups of seventeen and ten SRS activists in Vojvodina and southern Serbia. The Radicals were held responsible for criminal activities and a series of attacks on members of national minorities and opposition political parties. Among those arrested were Milenko Petrić, the SRS Vice-President in Šid, and Branislav Vakić, the leader of the Radicals from Niš. The lawless activities of these SRS members who had been detained had long been known about, and, while the SRS and SPS were in alliance, tolerated by the authorities. Šešelj sought to hit back accusing Milošević of being the 'greatest mafioso in Serbia' and said that 'without his support Dafina and Jezda would never have been able to plunder the people.' Šešelj suggested that he would be happy to go to Geneva or the Hague to answer for any war crimes that he was accused of having committed, but he would not go without Milošević. Šešelj also sought to purge the SRS of those that he considered to be disloyal publically 'unmasking' one of his key paramilitary operatives, Ljubiša Petković, as a police spy. Šešelj, however, also sought to avoid confrontation between the SRS and the authorities banning his members from carrying firearms without specific permission from the party leadership.[30]

Milošević also appeared to be attempting to undermine Šešelj's ultra-nationalist support base by promoting Željko Ražnatović, Arkan, as a 'loyal' nationalist alternative. On 2 November Ražnatović formed the Serbian Unity Party (SSJ). The preparations which preceded this formal launch of the party led some observers to suggest that Ražnatović had received prior warning of the imminent dissolution of parliament. Ražnatović's campaign was conspicuously well funded in sharp contrast to the poverty of the other non-Socialist parties.[31] His meetings were a cross between political rallies and rock concerts with support being offered by a wide range of turbo-folk singers. The singer Ceca addressed one meeting: 'You can be as happy as me – just join the Serbian Unity Party.'[32] While the state media abused Šešelj it provided sympathetic coverage of Arkan's ultra-nationalist activities. In one TV confrontation Arkan accused Šešelj of growing fat by spending the war feasting on roast lamb while Šešelj retaliated by suggesting that Arkan's bank account had grown fat from plunder taken during the war.[33] Serbia therefore entered another round of elections at the end of 1993 with these former allies settling political scores while the fragmented opposition were unable to capitalise on the social and economic chaos in order to achieve electoral victory.

Notes

1. Serbian Radio, 3 June 1993 in *SWB EE/1707 C1/2*, 5 June 1993.
2. Serbian Radio, 14 June 1993 in *SWB EE/1714 C/15* 14 June 1993; Roksanda Ninčić, 'Strepnja s jaknim razlogom', *Vreme*, 14 June 1993.
3. Serbian Radio, 1 July 1993 in *EE/1731 C1/7*, 3 July 1993.
4. Serbian Radio, 8 July 1993 in *SWB EE/1737 C1/8*, 10 July 1993.
5. Serbian TV, 7 June 1993 in *SWB EE/1736 C1/10*, 9 June 1993.
6. *Tanjug*, 3 September 1993 in *SWB EE/1786 C/4*, 6 September 1993.
7. Branka Andjelković and Batić Bačević, 'Tigrovi odlaze?', *NIN*, 21 April 1995.
8. Julian Borger, 'The President's Secret Henchmen', *Guardian*, 3 February 1997.
9. Uroš Komlenović, 'Svaki dan utorak', *Vreme*, 20 September 1993.
10. Serbian Radio, 16 September 1993 in *SWB EE/1797 C/1*, 18 September 1991.
11. *Tanjug*, 20 September 1993 in *SWB EE/1800 C/1*, 22 September 1993.
12. Serbian Radio, 28 September 1993 in *SWB EE/1808 C/2*, 1 October 1993.
13. *Borba*, 1 October 1993 in *SWB EE/1810 C/4*, 4 October 1993.
14. Annika Savill, 'Drašković Back in the Fray for Greater Serbia', *Independent*, 23 September 1993.
15. 'Promena kursa', Dragan Todorović, *Vreme*, 11 October 1993.
16. Serbian Radio, 8 October 1993 in *SWB EE/1817 C/3*, 12 October 1993.
17. *Tanjug*, 6 October 1993 in *SWB EE/1814 C/5*, 8 October 1993.
18. The debate's proceedings were collected and published by the SRS who evidently seemed, at the time, to regard it as their 'finest hour', in Tomislav Nikolić, 'Kad padne vlada, Milošević pada', Glas (Belgrade), 1994, pp. 13-27, 36-7, 47-8.
19. Serbian TV, 28 October 1993 in *SWB EE/1833 C/3*, 30 October 1993.

20. Stan Markotich, 'Serbia Prepares for Elections', *RFE/RL Research Report*, 10 December 1993.
21. Ivan Radovanović, 'Iznenadjeni i uvredjeni', *Vreme*, 1 November 1993.
22. Srboljub Bogdanović, 'Eci, peci, pec', *NIN*, 19 November 1993.
23. Stefanović (1994), p. 171.
24. Milan Milošević, 'Levica u desnici', *Vreme*, 22 November 1993.
25. 'Smrt fašizmu!', Vuk Drašković interviewed by Dragan Bujošević, *NIN*, 15 October 1993.
26. Serbian TV, 30 October 1993 in *EE/1834 C/5*, 1 November 1993.
27. Ivan Radovanović *Vreme*, 'Ko je tata opozicije', 29 November 1993.
28. Louise Branson, 'Serb Unity Cracks in Election Free-For-All', *Sunday Times*, 19 December 1993.
29. Stan Markotich, *RFE/RL Research Report*, 10 December 1993.
30. Miloš Vasić and Filip Švarm, 'Četnički Votergejt', *Vreme*, 15 November 1993.
31. Milos Vašić, 'The December Vote – Slobodan and Arkan's Flying Circus', *War Report*, December 1993.
32. Tim Judah, 'Guerilla Chief Swaps Tank For Election Battle Bus', *The Times*, 30 November 1993.
33. Tim Judah, 'Bargaining Ahead as Serbia Heads for Coalition After Poll', *The Times*, 20 December 1993.

18. Continuity and Reform: The Political Landscape (December 1993–July 1994)

The results of the 19 December elections showed that considerable changes had been effected in the Serbian political landscape. The Socialists gained 36.7 per cent of the vote gaining 123 seats (49.2 per cent). This represented a qualified victory for the SPS who had gained twenty-two more seats than they had done in December 1992. Nevertheless they were left three seats short of commanding an overall parliamentary majority. The SRS had been cut down to size, gaining only 13.8 per cent of the vote and thirty-nine seats (15.6 per cent), and it was further weakened when at the start of 1994 a group of its members broke away to join the National Radical Party. It had, however, retained a solid core of support and the reports of its political death had turned out to be much exaggerated. The SRS would later present the December 1993 election as a victory for itself in which they 'saved the Serbian Radical Party and lost nothing'.[1] The SSJ, which opinion polls before the election had shown to be gaining as much as 15 per cent of the vote, ultimately secured less than 2 per cent of the vote, a total of 41,299, and failed to secure a single seat in parliament. One commentator observed that Arkan had been unsuccessful in advancing his political career because 'he had sufficient money but lacked the vocabulary'.[2] He scored marginally more than the neo-communist United Left who gained 34,307 votes.[3]

From the democratic opposition parties the DSS, who had placed the strongest accent on national themes in their campaign, gained 5.1 per cent of the vote and seven seats (2.8 per cent). While Koštunica was widely respected for his personal and intellectual integrity this standing had not been translated into votes and seats gained by the DSS. DEPOS gained 16.6 per cent of the vote and forty-five seats (18 per cent). The DEPOS result saw a reduction in the number of seats won compared to their 1992 total – a fact largely accounted for by the departure of the DSS from this coalition – but they did emerge from the 1993 election as the second largest political grouping. Nevertheless in the aftermath of the elections serious divisions once more emerged within the main DEPOS grouping, the SPO. Vuk Drašković and Slobodan Rakitić had been temporarily reconciled during the political crisis in the summer of 1993. During the autumn, however, tensions had once again emerged particularily regarding their different attitudes to the Geneva peace plan.[4] On 12 January 1994 Rakitić and ten other representatives of DEPOS in the federal parliament announced that they were leaving the SPO and would act as an autonomous group within the parliament. The rebel deputies accused Vuk Drašković of behaving in an undemocratic way and 'the introduction of absolutism in the party similar to the absolutism of the Communist Party at the time of Josip Broz' and of turning the SPO 'from a democratic and national party into an undemocratic and quasi-national party which pursues views easily dropped to support personal promotions'.[5] The SPO swiftly expelled this group of deputies and sought the return of their mandates so that places could be filled by new SPO nominees. The schismatic deputies resisted this move pointing out that they had not been elected as representatives of the SPO but rather from the DEPOS coalition, as it existed in December 1992. For tactical reasons the Socialists and Radicals in the federal parliament chose to support the arguments of Rakitić's group who continued to operate in parliament under the DEPOS name. On 28 January 1995 Rakitić and his faction formed the Assembly National Party (SNS). Rakitić regarded the SNS as the inheritor and preserver of the traditions associated with the original political programme of the SPO which had been forsaken by Drašković in favour of an 'anational' brand of politics. Speaking in early 1996 Rakitić put forward the idea that his views remained representative of the SPO's provincial membership many of whom, he suggested, were unaware of the drastic policy shifts undertaken by the leadership in Belgrade: 'It appears that the greatest gainer from the media blockade has been Vuk Drašković because many even of the membership of the SPO are not informed of the politics and positions of their leadership. Many members of the SPO today think that nothing has changed in the orientation of this party since 1991 when the SPO was the most serious national and democratic party in Serbia. It must be said that the civic orientation cannot be an anational orientation. The opposition of the civic and national positions is artificial and reflects the confusion in our political situation. Each citizen must have a state, and the state is created by the nation.'[6] Tensions also occurred within the GSS with Ljubiša Rajić one of the editors of the journal *Republika*, quitting his post; he gave as his reasons disquiet at the new closeness of the GSS to the SPO, an apparent weakening of its connections with minority groups within Serbia, and the ascendancy of 'liberal', as opposed to 'social democratic', attitudes to economic and social questions.[7]

The elections saw the DS making a significant electoral break-through gaining 11.6 per cent of the vote and twenty-nine seats. The success of the campaign confirmed Djindjić in his position as the leading figure in the DS, with his admirers within the party referring to him as the 'Serbian Kennedy'.[8] The assumption of leadership within the DS by Zoran Djindjić was accompanied by a change of personal/political image. With his hair worn in a pony-tail he had previously cultivated an image as a radical academic sociologist, but he now took to appearing short-haired and soberly suited. During the campaign he had declared himself and the DS ready to to take part in a post-election coalition, and did not rule out the possibility of working with the Socialists. The authorities had reacted positively to Djindjić's pragmatic at-titude giving the DS relatively favourable coverage on the state-controlled media. At the DS assembly held on 29 January Dragoljub Mićunović was removed from office after losing a vote of confidence in his presidency. Djindjić was duly elected as President of the party in his place. In protest at the removal of Mićunović a number of longstanding and senior DS members had by March resigned from their positions within the party. In July Mićunović together with Desimir Tošić, Vida Ognjenović, Bora Kuzmanović, and Velimir Simonović, founded the Democratic Centre (DC). The DC saw itself as a non–party rallying point for the civic ideas which had originally inspired the formation of the DS. They opposed what they saw as the 'populist' course being taken by Djindjić and accused him of attempting to transform the DS into a 'leadership party' centred around his own personality. According to Mićunović the DC was founded and it 'began to gather together people for whom democracy was not simply a phrase but rather an orientation'.[9]

In the immediate aftermath of the elections no one party was capable of forming a government and some form of coalition government was a necessity. Vojislav Koštunica proposed that a government should be formed through a grand coalition of opposition parties including the DSS, DS, DEPOS, SRS, and DZVM.[10] A government based on this unlikely combination, however, proved impractical and the initiative passed back to Slobodan Milošević and the SPS. Milošević began to hold a round of talks with the opposition leaders Zoran Djindjić, Vuk Drašković and Andras Agoštan of the DZVM with the aim of forming a government of 'national unity'. After meeting Milošević on 21 January Drašković described their talks as having been 'frank and dynamic' and said that he found the Serbian President, who he was meeting for the first time, to be a 'congenial and witty man'.[11] The talks, taking place on the same day, between Milošević and Zoran Djindjić took place in a similarily positive and cordial atmosphere with Djindjić stressing the need for the formation of a technocratic non-party government headed by a 'man of consensus'.[12] Tomislav Nikolić, representing the SRS, was also invited to talks with Milošević, but the Radical Vice-President declined the invitation: 'I have nothing to discuss with Slobodan Milošević as long as the state television is imposing a ban on the SRS.'[13] Ultimately, however, neither Drašković nor Djindjić were suitable partners for a coalition government with the Socialists as the parties which they headed were too powerful to be easily accomodated into the framework of a Milošević-controlled government.

Instead the Socialists were able to obtain a parliamentary majority by, on 23 February, detaching New Democracy (ND), with six representatives in parliament, from the DEPOS coalition. Dušan Mihailović, the ND leader, emphasised that his decision to enter the government was based on a belief that the situation in Serbia could be more effectively 'changed from the inside than from the outside by participating and dealing with responsibilities instead of criticising and watching from a safe distance'.[14] The 'pragmatic' politics of the ND were contrasted with the 'ideological' politics of their former coalition partners in DEPOS. The ND, however, would be generously rewarded by the Socialists, both in terms of access to political office, gaining four ministerial portfolios and material resources, and for their willingness to follow a co-operative course. The ND, as a partner in government, attracted various individuals from the 'left' of Serbian politics who had formerly taken an opposition position. Čedomir Mirković's Social Democratic Party, which had split off from the SPS, effectively came back under the SPS umberella when it merged with the ND in mid-1994. Ratomir Tanić, one of the founding members and Vice-President of the Civic Alliance, defected on 5 September to the ND. He praised the social democratic orientation of his new party as well as its capacity to place practical politics above rhetoric. Žarko Jokanović, who had played a prominent role as student leader in the 9 March 1991 anti-Milošević demonstrations, served as ND Vice-President during the period of the new SPS-ND government. A number of private businessmen were also attracted into the ND camp including Rodoljub, the brother of Vuk, Drašković, who ran the successful VIK food proccessing firm based in Vršac in Vojvodina.

The Socialists sought to strengthen the 'multi-party' nature of the new government by bringing into its ranks two senior defectors from the DS, Slobodan Radulović and Radoje Djukić. Both of these individuals were leading businessmen with Djukić, who was appointed Minister for Enterprise, being the director of the Djukić Trikotaza firm and Radulović, who became one of the new government's Deputy Prime Ministers, was the head of the C – Marketing group. Mirko Marjanović was nominated as Prime Minister in the post-election government. Marjanović, born in 1937, came originally from Knin in Croatia and though known as a loyal SPS cadre had held no major political office before his appointment as Serbian premier.[15] In his new cabinet particular stress was given to the business qualifications of its members with Marjanović describing it as a 'cabinet of economists'. At one level this technocratic/business emphasis was clearly meant to contrast with the nationalism which had characterised the SPS in the period 1991-3, and provide the political framework for economic reform.[16] At another level, however, it further confirmed the dominance within the highest reaches of the Serbian government of a group of individuals for whom there existed an interdependent relationship between the holding of political office and their highly profitable array of business interests. Typical of this Socialist plutocracy of *nomenklatura* businessmen were the two individuals, both named Dragan Tomić, who were appointed to serve in Marjanović's cabinet. The first of these politicians had been the general of director of Jugo Petrol since 1990 and had also acted as the leader of the SPS parliamentary group. Tomić had been presented with a gold 'Obilić' medal by Željko Ražnatović in gratitude for his supplying petrol to the Serbian Volunteer Guard. On 1 February Tomić was elected to the position of President of the Serbian parliament. The second of these Socialist politicians was head of the Simpo furniture firm based in Vranje in southern Serbia. In March he was appointed to the new government as Minister Without Portfolio with special responsibility for helping to co-ordinate economic reform. Marjanović himself, while serving as Prime Minister, also worked as General Director of the powerful Progresgas trading company.

On 19 January 1994 Dragoslav Avramović, the seventy-four-year-old new head of the National Bank of Yugoslavia and a former World Bank economist, announced a major programme of fiscal stabilisation. From 24 January the old inflated dinar would be phased out and replaced by a new (super) dinar. A limited number of these new dinars would be printed, to the value of $200 million, and this new currency issue would be backed by the bank's hard currency reserves. The value of the new dinar would be pegged, at a rate of 1:1, to the value of the German mark. Avramović's strategy soon yielded results with a dramatic reduction in the rate of inflation from 310 million per cent in January to a reported rate of 1 per cent. At the same time significant rises in production, 12 per cent in February and 22 per cent in March, were reported by the authorities. These apparent increases in production were achieved in spite of the straightjacket of the international sanctions regime, and when questioned about their significance Avramović remarked optimistically: 'Sanctions? – we wriggled out.'[17] A renewed sense of public confidence was further enhanced by the release of hoarded supplies into the shops. Many outside observers and opposition politicians, however, were sceptical as to how viable Avramović's strategy would prove in the long term. Milan Komnenić predicted that 'this economic programme will soon collapse', and suggested that Avramović was acting 'more like a loudspeaker for the SPS and less as a creator of that programme'. For Vojislav Koštunica the obviously close co-operation between the head of the National Bank and the Serbian President 'provoked suspicion in the whole of the Avramović programme'. Zoran Djindjić complained about the limited scope of Avramović's measures and its failure to address key problems such as privatization.[18] Among the general population, however, he was widely revered for bringing to an end the wild and demoralising bout of hyper-inflation, and in a short time he gained an almost mythical status in their eyes. He was also lionised by the official media and the state institutions which helped to cultivate the septuagenarian's star status. In dealing with the farmers Avramović took drastic measures to restore their confidence in the state. On 18 June the National Bank of Yugoslavia announced that it would issue a limited number of 22-carat gold coins whose value would be linked to the price of gold on the international market. They would be used, the NBJ stated, to buy 1.8 million tonnes of the 3.5 million tonne harvest. Avramović himself made it clear that he regarded his stabilisation programme as a temporary measure preparing the way for further reform once sanctions had been lifted. In spite of its relatively modest objectives Avramović's fiscal reforms did provide a broad measure of financial stability with the dinar maintaining its parity with the German mark for six months after it was fixed at this rate. While subsequently the dinar did slip in value there was no return to the hyper-inflationary chaos which had characterised the Serbian financial affairs in 1993.

This concentration on economic reform occurred in a context where the position of the Bosnian Serb political and military forces was coming under increasing pressure. On 17 February, in response to the threat of NATO air strikes, Bosnian Serb military forces had withdrawn, or placed under United Nations supervision, their heavy weaponary which had been concentrated around Sarajevo. More ominous for their strategic position was the fact that, under diplomatic pressure from the United States, the Bosnian Croats and Muslims had agreed to end the bitter conflict which had divided them since the spring of 1993. The American-backed agreement, signed in Washington on 2 March, persuaded the Croatian government of Franjo Tudjman apparently to abandon the idea of created a Croatian mini-state (Herceg-Bosna) in favour of a cantonised common federal state with the Bosnian Muslims. However, it would become clear that Franjo Tudjman had not abandoned his expansionist ambitions in Bosnia-Hercegovina.

Nevertheless in the short term the agreement did facilitate the concentration of Bosnian government, Bosnian Croat and considerable numbers of regular Croatian forces against the common Serbian enemy. The Bosnian Serb military forces, having retreated around Sarajevo and in central Bosnia, moved rapidly to compensate for this by attacking, from 7-23 April, the Muslim stronghold of Goražde in eastern Bosnia. The Bosnian Serb assault ultimately, in the face of limited NATO air strikes and strong international pressure, failed to take the town of Goražde. In May and June an initially successful Bosnian government offensive in the central Bosnian Doboj-Ozren region faltered before Serbian firepower. During this period of heavy military activity there was continuing evidence of commitment by the Yugoslav military authorities to supporting, in terms of logistics and personnel, the VRS war effort. There was also evidence that despite the change in rhetorical tone on the part of the Socialist authorities there was a continuing ideological commitment to the idea of a Great Serbian territorial arrangement. On 22-23 April the Second Congress of Serbian Intellectuals was held in Belgrade, bringing together 1,400 academics and intellectuals from Serbia, Montenegro and the Serbian populations of Croatia and Bosnia. While the conference was ostensibly apolitical in content one of its chief organisers the Socialist elder, Mihailo Marković, made it clear that their discussions took place in a context where 'the first and most important principle of national politics must be the complete union of all ethnic Serbs.'[19] Marković went on: 'The Serbian people must resolve the shape of their state and common life when the Serbs of the Republika Srpska and the Republic of Serbian Krajina have definitively defended their right to self-determination.'[20] Vuk Drašković, however, made a speech to the conference which was notable for the way in which it used all the most potent and cherished symbols of the Serbian historical tradition to denounce the nationalist intellectuals. Drašković, in his characteristic 'national romantic' style, suggested that the 'real' or 'authentic' Serbia should be sought among the Serbian peasantry rather than amongst the urban intellectuals gathered at the conference.[21] He asked his audience: 'Were you gentlemen aware at that first "Sarajevo Congress" what furrow you were ploughing, how much your "patriotism" was going to cost us and where it would lead us? If you did, you are monsters who – lured by miserable wages and prospects of personal glory, and bloody glory at that – have pushed our nation into the greatest tragedy in its history. If you are now beginning to realise what you did then, get out of the furrow and help us. And you could help us most if you said nothing. So we won't have Jasenovac or Saint Sava or Jadovno or the Nemanjicis or Njegoš or Obilić permeating through your brains and mouths. The Serbs do not need you to tell them who they are and who they were before you came. And where they were slaughtered and who slaughtered them. [...] There can be no erasure from the memory of the great crime committed against the Serbs, but neither was there ever a shred of a collective frenzy and desire for revenge. Every peasant on Mount Kozara knew that he was the victor, just like the one on the hill overlooking Jerusalem without any blame. Every schoolchild in Hercegovina knew that Ustaše crimes and criminals and all similar crimes and criminals are inscribed in the book of shame and defeat, a book which is eternal and immortal. No Serb name was written in this book until this war. Our national name was inscribed in a different book, the one which is kept by the Lamb and which has seven seals of God, according to the Revelation of John. I regret to say that the Serb name has now also been inscribed into the book of shame. The spiritual degenerates of our nation have become is leaders. The same people who forbade the rememberance of the Korić limestone pit and the Jasenovac knife who had never before entered a church and who screamed with froth on their lips that they were communists not Serbs now led the Serbs into the struggle for "Serb national interests". Revenge became their battle cry and the preservation of power or ascension to power, pillage or bloody personal glory their only interest. [...] Our future is in Serbia's past. That is where our signposts are. Let us go to the Šumadija and every farmer will tell us what we must do. The farmer has experience. He was the one to create renew and expand that state. The Serb communists and their spiritual brothers – many of them sitting in this hall – have disgraced the farmer's state, honour and reputation. Go to Šumadija and Pomoravlje, gentlemen. That's where you should seek advice.'[22]

In the spring of 1994 tentative moves were made by the opposition to once again create a united front against the Socialist government in which curiously the prime movers were Vuk Drašković and Vojislav Šešelj. On 20 May the leaders of the SPO and the

SRS held a joint news conference in which they shook hands and pledged themselves to common action against Milošević. This was followed on 23 May by a meeting of representatives of the SPO, SRS, DS, and DSS in order to strengthen the basis for concerted opposition action against the regime. The Drašković-Šešelj rapprochement continued following an incident on 22 July when clashes between SRS representatives and the police had broken out on the floor of the Serbian parliament. Šešelj portrayed this brawl as part of the continuing attempt by the government to victimise and intimidate the SRS. Drašković had agreed with this analysis and suggested that the opposition jointly boycott the parliament in protest at the police incursion. Djindjić, however, rejected this suggestion: 'It would be irresponsible for us to abandon the legislature...and go out into the sea where Vojislav Šešelj and from time to time Vuk Drašković splash around.' However, such a reconciliation between Drašković and Šešelj, inevitably proved short-lived since there was a fundamental and unbridgeable division between their attitudes to the national question, and their only basis for united action lay in a common feeling of animosity towards Milošević. The events which would take shape in Bosnia and Hercegovina in July-August 1994 would serve further to radicalise and polarise the political scene in Serbia.[23]

Notes

1. Nikolić (1994), p. 4.
2. Milan Milošević, 'Moć srpskih radikala', *Vreme*, 30 January 1995.
3. 'Arkan ispred levice', *Vreme*, 27 December 1993.
4. Serbian Radio, 24 August 1993 in *SWB EE/1778 C/11*, 27 August 1993.
5. *Tanjug*, 10 January 1994 in *SWB EE/1894 C/4*, 13 January 1994; and 12 January 1994 in *SWB EE/1897 C/3*, 17 January 1994.
6. 'Uvek je neko do sada iz opozicije pomogao režimu da bezbrižno vlada i donosi zakone', Slobodan Rakitić interviewed by Sredoje Simić, *Argument*, 19 April 1996.
7. Milan Milošević, 'Veliki transfer', *Vreme*, 12 September 1994.
8. Milan Milošević, 'Izborni bluz', *Vreme* 27 December 1993.
9. ' "Razredni" se naljutio', Dragoljub Mićunović interviewed by Sandra Petrušić, *Srpska reč*, 1 January 1996.
10. S. Ristcć, 'Koštunica: Opozicija može da formira vladu', *Politika*, 22 December 1993.
11. *Tanjug*, 21 January 1994 in *SWB EE/1903 C/3*, 24 January 1994.
12. *Tanjug*, 21 January 1994 in *SWB EE/1903 C/2*, 24 January 1994.

13. *Tanjug*, 21 January 1994 in *SWB EE/1903 C/3*, 24 January 1994.

14. 'New Democracy – The Most Serious Political Offer of the Center in Serbia for the Beginning of 21st Century', speech of Dušan Mihailović of the Sixth Electoral Convention of New Democracy on 9 December 1995, distributed by New Democracy (Belgrade), 1996.

15. Stan Markotich, 'Serbia's New Government', *RFE/RL Research Report*, 29 April 1994.

16. *Tanjug*, 14 March 1994 in *SWB EE/1947 C/5*, 16 March 1994.

17. 'Serbia – Gurgles in the Pipeline', *Economist*, 7 May 1994.

18. 'Nikad ne poslušaj ženu', Marijana Mirosavljević, *NIN*, 4 October 1996.

19. Stan Markotich, 'Serbian Intellectuals Promote Concept of 'Greater Serbia', *RFE/RL Research Report*, 10 June 1994.

20. 'Srpska "umetnost"', Mihailo Marković interviewed in *NIN*, 6 May 1994.

21. This is an example of the way in which the symbolic form of Drašković's rhetoric remained constant despite the change in its political content.

22. 'Vuk Drašković's Speech at the Second Congress of Serbian Intellectuals in the Sava Center, 22 April 1994', Serbian Renewal Movement (Belgrade), 1997.

23. Stan Markotich, 'Opposition Parties Attempt Unity – Again', *Transition*, 9 June 1995.

19. The Belgrade–Pale Schism (July–August 1994)

While Milošević still aimed to achieve territorial gains in Bosnia-Hercegovina he had, by the spring of 1994, come to regard the maximal demands of the Bosnian Serb political and military leadership as an obstacle to Serbia's economic and political reintegration into the international community. Attacks on the Bosnian Serb leaders which began to appear in the state-controlled Belgrade media were widely regarded as an attempt to undermine their credibility in the eyes of the Serbian population. At the beginning of March a retired JNA officer and former editor of the journal *Narodne Armije*, Gajo Petković, writing in the pages on *NIN* launched a bitter personal attack on Mladić which apparently enjoyed official sanction. Petković accused Mladić of being 'carried away by rage and brutality' and stated that he bore 'the undoubted responsibility for the crimes of the members of the army'. An infuriated Mladić had phoned Petković in Belgrade from the mountain fastness of Pale threatening him with retribution. Later in that same month Ana Mladić, the general's daughter, a twenty-three-year-old medical student at Belgrade University, committed suicide by shooting herself with a revolver. According to family friends she had been deeply depressed following the attacks on her father in the press. The Bosnian Serb journal *Javnost* portrayed her as a young patriot destroyed by the poisonous urban cosmopolitanism of Belgrade, and asked: 'Was it possible for Ana Mladić to tolerate all those "peacemakers" and similar trash in the Serb capital Belgrade? She was surrounded by them day and night, as a student in Belgrade. Her young healthy spirit and honourable patriotism, and the "Serbian milk" which she fed upon, found it difficult to bear all that which destroyed, undermined and slandered the battle of our and her brethren in the Serbian land west of the watery arteries of the Serbian cause: the Drava, Danube, Drina and Sava rivers.'[1] However these attacks and his daughter's suicide did nothing to restrain Mladić, and his relentless pursuit of the attack on Goražde in April served to antagonise Milošević further. In May the magzine *Duga* carried an interview with Dafina Milanović in which she claimed that a number of prominent people had received financial gifts from her Dafiment bank before its collapse. These suggestions were not inherently improbable, but it was notable that those named were all well-known nationalist critics of Milošević, including Radovan Karadžić and his family who were said to have carried away their money 'in large sacks'.[2] It was widely believed that this was another example of a state-sponsored attack on a rival of Milošević. These covert actions, however, merely set the scene for the wider conflict which was to come.

As the tensions between the Milošević government in Belgrade and the Bosnian Serb leadership in Pale grew, so Radovan Karadžić sought to put ideological/symbolic distance between himself and the Serbian President. During the demonstrations of March 1991 Karadžić, as an ally of Milošević, had urged the Serbian people to unite and reject divisions into Četnik-Royalist and partisan/communist camps in favour of national unity. By early 1994, however, Karadžić could be observed, to Milošević's fury, attending international negotiations at Geneva sporting the royalist cockade.[3] In this newly found reverence for the Četnik tradition Karadžić was joining other members of the SDS leadership who had ostentatiously displayed their royalist sympathies. Biljana Plavšić, who was known for her strong anti-communist views, had, for instance, been a pilgrim to Ravna Gora and the Karadjordjević mausoleum at Topola in the Šumadija.[4] While Radovan Karadžić was to remain flexible in the way that he used political symbolism, sometimes rhetorically invoking the memory of Partisan exploits during the Second World War, his flirtation with the symbolism of Ravna Gora during late 1993 and early 1994 signalled his desire to define himself as an oppositional figure against Milošević and his government in Belgrade.[5]

In April of that year the United States, Russia, Britain, France and Germany had formed a diplomatic working party, known as the Contact Group, dedicated to the formulation of another peace plan for Bosnia-Hercegovina. The final draft of the Contact Group peace plan was unveiled on 7 July in Geneva, when the belligerent parties were given until 19 July to respond to it. The Bosnian government reluctantly signalled its support for the plan while Milošević also made it clear that he favoured its acceptance. However, strong objections were raised by the Bosnian Serbs: the plan, while theoretically maintaining Bosnia-Hercegovina as a unitary state effectively partitioned the republic between the Serbs and the Muslim-Croat Federation, and the Bosnian Serbs would receive 49 per cent of the territory compared to 51 per cent allocated to the Muslim-Croat Federation. In view of the fact that they, at that point, held some 70 per cent of the territory of Bosnia-Hercegovina this sacrifice was considered too heavy to be readily acceptable. The plan also distributed the proportion of the land allocated to the Bosnian Serbs in such a way that it would be rendered indefensible in any future war. Additionally the Bosnian Serbs were convinced that the plan denied them sufficient access to natural and industrial resources.

When on 18 July the Bosnian Serb assembly met to discuss the peace plan attitudes amongst the delegates had hardened against the Contact group proposals. The delegates were joined in their deliberations, held in a disused factory building in Pale, by Prince Tomislav Karadjordjević, but General Ratko Mladić was notably absent. Milošević, apparently unwilling to see a repeat of the humiliation he had suffered in Pale the previous May, also chose to stay away. Messages of support for the hard line being championed by the Bosnian Serb leadership were sent to the Pale meeting by nationalist politicians within Serbia. The Serbian Orthodox church also sent an appeal to the assembly, warning: 'An unjust peace is the foundation of new wars.' When Vuk Drašković's message to the gathering, advocating acceptance of the peace plan, was read out it was met by derisive jeers from the audience.[6] The determination of the Bosnian Serb politicians to resist incorporation into a Bosnian state and instead seek union with Serbia was demonstrated by the words of *Miomčilo* Krajišnik, the Speaker of the Bosnian Serb parliament, who told his fellow politicians: 'There will be one people, one faith, one alphabet, and one state. We have to have one aim, one hope, faith in God and our right – all this will be Serbia.'[7] Karadžić warned that if the plan was rejected the Bosnian Serbs should be prepared for a military attack by 'the whole of NATO'.[8]

The Bosnian Serb representatives finally resolved, by eighty-one votes to five, to accept the peace plan, but only as the basis for renewed negotiations. The Contact Group made it clear that they regarded such an equivocal response as effectively an outright rejection of their proposals. On 3 August the Bosnian Serb assembly once again refused to give unqualified support to the peace plan. On 4 August Milošević, anxious to avoid sanctions on Serbia being tightened yet further and furious at the intransigence of the Bosnian Serbs, imposed his own sanctions on the Republika Srpska. The movement of all goods over the Drina, apart from food, clothing and medicine was prohibited. In the first days of the blockade even telephone links were cut. While a similar blockade of the Bosnian Serb territory had temporarily been instituted in May 1993, following their rejection of the Vance-Owen peace plan, there was a widespread understanding that on this occasion the schism between Belgrade and Pale would be more fundamental and long lasting. In a demonstration of his willingness to co-operate with the Contact Group Milošević even allowed the effectiveness of his blockade to be inspected by a team of international monitors. While the 135-strong team, who arrived in Serbia in mid-September, were able to deploy at the main crossing points into Bosnia they were, however, too few in number to guarantee that supplies were not being covertly transported across other points along the 375-mile-long frontier. On 5 October the United Nations Security Council, in response to reports from the international monitors that the embargo on the Bosnian Serbs was being thoroughly enforced, voted to ease sanctions on the Federal Republic of Yugoslavia allowing international flights to resume to and from Belgrade airport, and the restoration of sporting, educational and cultural links with the rest of the world.

Following the imposition of the blockade a bitter war of words broke out between the rival leaderships as they battled for the hearts and minds of Serbs on both sides of the Drina. On 4 August Milošević issued a statement in which he attacked 'the mad political ambitions and greed of the [Bosnian Serb] leadership... [which includes] war profiteers...and people whose conscience is not clear [and] who are afraid of peace, in the event of which all their wrong doings would come to light'.[9] Specific allegations, against the Bosnian Serb leadership, of corruption also began to appear in the pro-government media in Belgrade. Radovan Karadžić and Momčilo Krajišnik were accused of having accumulated £6 million from the sale of cars plundered from a volkswagen plant near Sarajevo. Bosnian Serb officials were also alleged to have made fortunes by selling appropriated humanitarian aid.[10] Immediately prior to the Bosnian Serb referendum Zoran Lilić, the Yugoslav Federal President, joined in the chorus of denunciation emanating from official circles in Belgrade. Lilić was widely regarded as a politically weak 'man of straw' but his statements were considered to reflect the thinking of the more powerful Serbian President. His statements, in an interview carried in *Politika*, broke new ground in that they accused the Bosnian Serb political leaders of being responsible for the killing of civillians in Bosnia-Hercegovina. Lilić said: 'It is difficult even to mention how many times they went back on their word, how many times they promised they would not bomb Sarajevo and continued the agony of civillians in that city.'[11] Lilić also made a barely disguised attempt to capitalise on the regional discontents of the northern Bosnian region of Banja Luka by accusing the Pale-based leadership of behaving 'like a stepmother' towards the city. This attempt to incite regional strife did not immediately bear fruit and when Karadžić went on 21 August to Banja Luka (a place he had been careful to avoid since the military revolt of September 1993) to address a rally, he was greeted by a crowd of 15,000 supporters.[12]

The authorities in Belgrade also sought to detach the military commander of the VRS, Ratko Mladić, from the political leadership. Tensions had existed between Karadžić and Mladić since the start of the war arising, in part, out of the fact that the VRS, having been created out of the remains of the JNA, developed as an institution independent of, and competing with, the political leaders. Ideological factors may also have coloured the conflicts between the military and political hierarchies. Mladić's political character had been formed within the ranks of the JNA where acceptance of the Titoist/Partisan heritage was assumed. During his time as commander of the JNA forces in Knin Mladić had been involved in a confrontation with Serbian paramilitary volunteers in which he ordered them to remove the Četnik cockade which he told them was in his eyes as bad as the Croatian *Šahovnica* [the traditional Croatian heraldic symbol – used by nationalists during the Second World War and the contemporary period]. Observers of Mladić's antagonism towards the Četnik tradition recalled that members of Mladić's family had narrowly escaped death at the hands of Četnik forces in intra-Serb fighting during the Second

World War. Nevertheless for Mladić, as with Karadžić, the use of such symbolism was essentially pragmatic, and Mladić's institutional or familial affinities with the Partisan tradition did not prevent him from replacing the Titoist caps worn by officers in the VRS with headgear modelled on that worn by the Serbian royal army. Perhaps as important in explaining the military-political conflict, however, was Mladić's personal and sometimes publicly expressed contempt for the character of the Bosnian Serb politicians whom he regarded as a corrupt group of war profiteers.[31]

In spite of these personal rivalries and simmering animosities both Karadžić and Mladić were united in their belief that the Contact Group plan was unacceptable to the Serbian people in Bosnia. It was rumoured that when Mladić heard that the Serbian government in Belgrade was preparing to impose a blockade on the Bosnian Serbs he furiously declared that he was ready to lead his tanks across the river in a march on Belgrade. It was speculated that other elements in the VJ under Momčilo Perišić would be prepared to back his 'rejectionist' position. The Serbian government, however, appeared ready to adopt a conciliatory attitude towards Mladić, and sources close to Milošević made clear their belief that 'Mladić knows that his future lies with Belgrade and not with Pale.' It was also believed that Mladić and Milošević had held a secret meeting during which the Serbian President offered Mladić a senior position in the Yugoslav army if he would agree to abandon the Bosnian Serb forces. However, when Karadžić and Mladić both visited the village of Sokolac on 17 August to help with the gathering in of the harvest, it was taken as a sign that Mladić had finally decided that his loyalties should remain located on the western side of the river Drina. His decision did not, however, mean that his close contacts with the Belgrade government were severed. Indeed he remained in contact with his old comrades in the VJ and through them with the other institutions and agencies of the regime. The persistence of this link with the Milošević government allowed Mladić and the VRS to continue to call on aid from the FRY at moments of extreme military pressure. In October-November Bosnian government forces, aided by Croat military units, began co-ordinated military offensives in the north, around the town of Bihać, and in the south which resulted in considerable territorial losses for the Bosnian Serbs. In the subsequent Bosnian Serb counter-offensive there was evidence that the VRS forces had been bolstered by the arrival of new supplies of fuel and additional manpower from Serbia. Such a move was, of course, in line with Milošević's policy which sought to effect the political subordination of the Bosnian Serb leadership rather than the military destruction of the Republika Srpska.[14]

Faced by these attempts by the Milošević government to subvert his leadership Radovan Karadžić sought to strengthen his position within the Republika Srpska. On 6 August orders were issued for the mobilisation of the population into compulsory labour units. It was declared that all people of working age 'must be subject to compulsory work regardless of their religion and nationality, on the basis of equality, and without any form of discrimination'.[15] Moves were also made to remove from positions of power those whose loyalties were considered doubtful. One of the first to suffer the consequences of this purge was Mića Stanišić, the Minister of the Interior of the Republika Srpska and a relative of Jovica Stanišić, the head of the Serbian secret police. The Typhoon intelligence unit, consisting of officers co-opted from the army and placed at Karadžić's service at the start of the war, based in Banja Luka was disbanded by the Bosnian Serb leader who clearly now believed that its old links with the Belgrade establishment made it unreliable.[16] There were persistent rumours that Milošević planned to remove Karadžić by means of a coup engineered by his security forces. Bosnian Serb members of the assembly suspected of sympathising with the Belgrade line were condemned by the Pale leadership as 'traitors and enemies'.[17] In view of Milošević's hostility the Bosnian Serb leaders ceased to talk about the immediate unification of the Republika Srpska with Serbia. Instead their political plans revolved around the consolidation of their territory in co-operation with the RSK into a new republic of Western Serbia. As winter approached and the Bosnian Serbs continued to defy the will of their former mentor in Belgrade it had become clear that Karadžić would be a far harder figure to bring to heel than Milošević had at first believed.

Relations between the Serbs from Serbia (*Srbijanci*) and the Serbs outside Serbia had always been complex. At one level there was a fundamental and enduring core belief that the two groups constituted one national community. In a radicalised political form this belief formed the basis of the 'Great' Serbian programme of

territorial unification of Serbian populated lands. The mutual identification of the *Srbijanci* with the populations from outside Serbia
had been further reinforced by the large-scale migration of Bosnian
and Croatian Serb populations into Serbia, and by the influence
of Bosnian and Croatian Serbs in key positions of power both
within the government and the opposition. At another more sub-
dued level there was a persistent popular belief, rarely openly
acknowledged in political discourse, that there were strong differences in character and interests between the *Srbijanci* and those
Serbs from outside Serbia. This 'narrow' Serbianism was an amplifica-
tion of the political regionalism which was a potent factor within
Serbia itself. Milošević relied on this 'narrow Serbian' sentiment,
coupled with a general weariness with the war and international
isolation, in order to secure a degree of public support for his
efforts to pressurise the Bosnian Serbs into accepting the Contact
Group peace plan. Nevertheless initial public opinion poll soundings
in Serbia showed the majority of the population to be opposed
to the blockade of the Drina.

Significant groups of opinion formers were ready to throw
their moral support behind the Bosnian Serb cause. The Serbian
Orthodox church was among the first to speak out against the
Drina blockade. One bishop publicly cursed Milošević, saying.
'Damned be the hand that is putting up walls between us and
our brothers in distress.' He condemned the Serbian President
for taking action against our 'crucified brethren'.[18] Elements of
the nationalist intellectual establishment were also ready to express
their solidarity with the Bosnian Serbs. For some national intellectuals the Bosnian highlands, and the struggle of its Serbian
population, exercised a 'romantic' attraction when compared to
the mundanity of urban Belgrade. The historian, Radovan Samardžić,
who was himself originally from Bosnia, typified these sentiments:
'The Serbs have the right to carry through to its conclusion their
centuries old aspiration and the centuries old struggle for national
unification. I must add that it is in a way painful to me that in
recent times the centre of Serbian spirituality and national resistance
has moved from Belgrade and Serbia, which has gradually lost
its soul, to the Republika Srpska and the 'Republic of Serbian
Krajina.'[19] This intellectual idealisation of the Bosnian Serb struggle
continued after the Belgrade-Pale schism with Serbian academics
and writers from Serbia making regular visits to the Bosnia to

express their solidarity with the Republika Srpska. On 13 March, for instance, a party of prominent Serbian intellectuals and literary figures, including Dobrica Ćosić, Ljubomir Tadić and Slobodan Rakitić, journeyed to Višegrad ostensibly to celebrate the work of the writer and Nobel laureate Ivo Andrić. The meeting, however, had clear political implications and was attended by an array of senior figures from the Bosnian Serb political leadership. Ljudomir Tadić described the meeting as an 'intellectual call for the unification of the Serbian nation'.[20]

Political opinion within Serbia was divided over what attitude to take towards the split between Belgrade and Pale. The decision of the Serbian government to break off relations with the Bosnian Serbs was debated in an extraordinary session of the Serbian parliament held on 27 August. Acceptance of the peace plan was championed by the SPS and their allies in New Democracy. Radovan Pankov of the SPS argued: 'It is not possible to gain from continued war, but it is possible to lose much' and emphasised that the peace plan would give official recognition to the borders of the Republika Srpska. His party colleague and SPS parliamentary group leader, Milorad Vučelić, stated that the peace plan had to be accepted and the leadership of the RS would recognise this fact when in the coming months they were still faced by sanctions. He further criticised the 'senseless ambition' and 'dictatorial mania' of the Pale leadership. The only people who would support them from within Serbia he said were those who saw their 'only chance of power in continued war and destruction'. New Democracy called for the acceptance of the peace plan, but argued that the possibility remained for its revision and adjustment. These government parties were joined in their support of the Contact Group plan by the SPO and the GSS from the opposition side of Serbia's political divide. Vuk Drašković while urging acceptance of the peace plan criticised those amongst the Serbian government who 'had earlier been advocates of war, but now presented themselves as peacemakers.' Vesna Pešić, of the GSS, likewise called for acceptance of the plan as 'the best peace which will be offered'.

The other opposition parties, however, came down firmly against the peace plan as it had been presented by the international community. Tomislav Nikolić of the SRS said: 'We only know that the peace plan is a terrible decision forced on us by the international community.' Vojislav Koštunica said on behalf of the DSS that the Contact Group plan would offer no solution to the situation in Bosnia-Hercegovina and lead to 'war rather than peace' because it saw Bosnia as one state recognised within its international borders in which the federal units would have regional rather than republican status, and in which there was no provision for a confederal relationship between the RS and the FRY. Koštunica also criticised the Serbian government for creating an 'iron curtain on the Drina and waging a cold war against the Serbian nation in the RS'. The DS suggested that rather than setting up barriers between the FRY and the RS the Serbian government should be concentrating its efforts on creating economic and political confederal links between the two Serbian territories.[21]

This division between those parties who accepted the terms of the peace plan proposed by the international community and those who regarded it as a betrayal of Serbian national interests was to remain the key line of division in Serbian politics between the autumn of 1994 and 1995.

Notes

1. 'Politika samoubistva', Nenad LJ Stefanović, *Vreme*, 11 April 1994.
2. Yigal Chazan 'Belgrade Implicates Karadžić in Bank's Fall', *Guardian*, 3 May 1994.
3. Stefanović (1994), p. 75.
4. Dragan Todorović, 'Pet godina osvajanja Ravne gore', *Vreme*, 23 May 1994; and 'Izmedju krune i petokrake', *Vreme*, 18 July 1994.
5. For a view of Karadžić as neo-Četnik leader see Owen (1995), pp. 325-6.
6. Tim Judah, 'Serbs Warned They Face War to the Death', *The Times*, 19 July 1994.
7. Ian Traynor, 'Bosnian Serbs Expected to Reject Peace Plan', *Guardian*, 19 July 1994.
8. Tim Judah, *The Times*, 19 July 1994.
9. Patrick Moore, 'Serbian Leader Cuts Support for Proxy Warriors', *RFE/RL Research Brief*, 5 August 1994.
10. Donald Macintyre, 'Milošević Risks All For Redemption', *Independent*, 7 August 1994.
11. 'Belgrade Accuses Karadžić of War Crimes', Louise Branson, *Sunday Times*, 21 August 1994.
12. Dejan Anastasejević, 'Kosidbe u zoru i u podne', *Vreme*, 29 August 1994.
13. Nenad LJ Stefanović, 'Znate li gde je vaše sklonište', *Vreme*, 24 May 1993.
14. 'Belgrade 'aided Bihać Attack', AP Report, *Independent*, 2 December 1994.

15. Emma Daly, 'Karadžić Mobilises Serbs Into Work Units', *Independent*, 7 August 1994.
16. 'Fear and Loathing Beyond the Pale', *The Economist*, 12 November 1994.
17. Yigal Chazan, 'Karadžić Ready to Rejoin Peace Talks', *Guardian*, 8 December 1994.
18. 'Serbian Bishops Condemn Blockade', *European*, 19-25 October 1994.
19. 'Ljudi i Vreme', *Vreme*, 17 May 1993.
20. Nenad LJ Stenaović, 'Andrić medju Srbima', *Vreme*, 20 March 1995.
21. 'Nastavak rata je žločin protiv naroda' and 'Vanredno zasedanje skupštine Srbije', *Politika*, 27 August 1994.

20. Parties of 'War and Peace' (1994–95)

In the period 1994-5 the SPO was the foremost advocate among the opposition parties of acceptance of the internationally-brokered peace deal. In his characteristic 'national romantic' political and rhetorical style Drašković consistently presented the achievment of peace as an ethical and moral imperative. In early September 1994 he wrote appealing to the Contact Group to help the 'parties of peace' within Serbia by easing international sanctions: 'If the forces of peace are defeated here, then perhaps tomorrow might not Russia too be in danger? Karadžić and Zhirinovsky are two sides of the same coin. [...] I do not support President Milošević nor do I appeal to you to support him. I support peace and nothing more. [...] The fact that President Milošević has accepted many of the positions of my party is, for me, a valid fact. It is necessary to defend peace and help the cause of peace. No one should dare to beat anyone, not even the President of Serbia, for their dedication to peace.'[1] The SPO only took on a more national and militant line in circumstances where it perceived Serbian interests to be directly under threat or treated in an unjust fashion. Even in such cases, however, the SPO did not depart from its overall position that the Contact Group peace plan must be accepted by the Bosnian Serbs. On 11 October, for instance, Milan Komnenić reacted to an incident several days earlier when a number of Serbian soldiers and female nurses had been killed in a raid by Bosnian government commandos through the demilitarised zone on Mt Igman near Sarajevo. Komnenić stated that the Bosnian Serb failure to accept the Contact Group plan 'provided Muslim killers, although inadvertently, with cover for crimes like the one on Mount Igman'. He further added that the Serbian refusal to sign the peace plan was treated by the Bosnian Muslim leadership as a pretext for the 'Arabisation' of Bosnia.[2] Similarly on 22

November 1994, following NATO air attacks on Serbian positions within the RSK during fighting around the Bihać pocket, the SPO stated: 'In connection with the NATO air attack on Udbina airport, we most strongly condemn all those who support the spreading of the war, be it countries that openly side with the Muslim-Croat alliance or the political and military extremists in the Republika Srpska and the Republic of Serbian Krajina whose aim is to drag Serbia and Montenegro into the conflict at all costs. At this dangerous point in time wise decisions and reactions are needed. The SPO believes that the acceptance of the Contact Group plan is the only reasonable response that will prevent the spreading of the war and a tragedy of great magnitude. So long as the Pale leadership rejects the peace plan, the international community will label the Serbs the main culprits for the continuation of the war, even when the offensives are started by the Muslims or Croats.'[3]

The orientation of the SPO towards the cause of 'peace' in Bosnia-Hercegovina was paralleled by attempts to forge links with parties representing ethnic minorities within Serbia such as the Sandžak Muslim SDA. These efforts were to some extent reciprocated, with Rasim Ljajić of the SDA stating that 'in the current political market the SPO represents the most acceptable political alternative'. He, however, continued to express reservations as to whether the SPO 'membership on the ground had followed its evolution towards the civic path'.[4] The SPO was also willing to maintain contact with groups, such as Nenad Čanak's League of Vojvodina Social Democrats, whose views on regional autonomy made them unacceptable to more nationally orientated Serbian parties. While SPO representatives were strongly critical of the Bosnian Serb political leadership Danica Drašković was willing to praise the work of the Serbian Civic Council, which represented Serbs loyal to the Bosnian government, describing it as the 'only legitimate representative of the Serbs' in Bosnia.[5] On economic issues the SPO portrayed itself as strongly aligned with the free market with Drašković advocating reforms 'on the model carried out by [Vaclav] Klaus in the Czech Republic' with the implementation of a programme of 'full privatisation'.[6]

In spite of this 'modernisation' of the SPO there remained a strong historicist and neo-traditional element in the SPO identity. The importance of the personality cult of Draža Mihailović had if anything grown in significance within the SPO as Drašković shifted from his 'radical' nationalist to 'civic' position. Drašković's ideological journey did, however, spark conflict between the SPO and those parties who, having retained a nationalist orientation, sought to contest the right of the SPO to utilise Mihailović and the site of Ravna Gora as a symbolic resource. On 13 May 1991 two rival Četnik celebrations took place, one hosted by the SPO in Belgrade and the other organised by Šešelj at Ravna Gora.[7] In 1992, however, the SPO was effectively able to establish symbolic dominance over the site of Ravna Gora with the erection of a monument to General Mihailović on the mountain summit. The statue of Mihailović was unveiled at a meeting of some 30,000 people, with Orthodox bishops present who blessed the meeting and consecrated the statue. Drašković described the event as 'a Serbian resurrection' and said to the meeting: 'You are here again General Mihailović, on Ravna Gora, and again you are with us, and we are with you. The report we bring to you today is of our defeat and our misfortune. The Serbian nation is experiencing the same fate as it did half a century ago when you came to Ravna Gora, shaking the dust from our banners, showing us the way to salvation, healing the wings of our nation.' Drašković emphasised the degree of political continuity which existed between the SPO and the Četnik movement, saying: 'The Serbian resistance movement began on Ravna Gora in 1941 and was continued in 1990 as the SPO.'[8]

Drašković's critics, however, disputed the legitimacy of his claim to celebrate Mihailović's memory. In May 1993 Mirko Jović attacked the SPO: 'The SPO have no right to raise a monument to General Mihailović, a monument to a man who in 1941 said 'I do not recognise this capitulation – that word does not exist in the Serbian language" when in May 1993 Drašković publicly called for the signing of the Vance-Owen "peace plan" – in other words capitulation.'[9] During the celebrations of the centenary of Draža Mihailović's birth, held on the 13th of that same month, clashes occurred between members of the SPO and a group of SNO supporters headed by Mirko Jović who had arrived to lay a wreath at the Mihailović monument.[10] In the December 1993 elections Vojislav Mihailović, the grandson of General Mihailović, was elected as SPO representative in the Kragujevac area, establishing a living/familial link between the current political activity of the SPO and the wartime Četnik leader.[11] The changing nature of Drašković's political position manifested itself in the way he sought to present General Mihailović as a figure who was ready not simply to champion Serbian rights but also to respect the rights of other nationalities. Speaking in the spring of 1994 Drašković told his audience: 'Not even in the Second World War, when the Sava carried our slaughtered fighters, did anyone in Serbia attack his Croat neighbours. General Mihailović himself issued a newspaper for Muslims from the free Serbian mountains.'[12] In 1995 the annual, SPO-sponsored 13 May Ravna Gora celebrations were combined with ceremonies to mark the fiftieth anniversary of the end of the Second War. While the event took place with all the usual neo-traditionalist Četnik trappings of insignia, songs and dress, attempts were also made to give the event an 'international' flavour with Serbia's role as a pro-allied nation being emphasised, and the Serbian tricolour displayed on the central podium alongside those of the other allied powers.[13] A few days earlier, on 8 May, a rival gathering was held by Vojislav Koštunica (DSS), Nikola Milošević (SLS) and Slobodan Rakitić at the nearby village of Ba, which had been the site of the Četnik Saint Sava political congress in 1944.[14]

In the autumn of 1994 Drašković's latest novel, *Noć generala* (Night of the General), was published, taking as its subject matter the last days of General Mihailović before his execution in 1946. The book carried the dedication to 'the Ravna Gorans – killed, wounded, imprisoned, scattered across the whole world. Their crucifixion.'[15] The May 1996 celebrations on Ravna Gora were marked by an addition to the 'ritual landscape' on the mountain top when, supported by the *Spona* charity, work was started on the building of a church dedicated to the souls of the Ravna Gorans 'and all the fallen Serbian warriors from the time of Kosovo until today'.[16] In August 1996 Aleksandar Čotrić again affirmed the centrality of the myth of Ravna Gora to the SPO when he wrote in the pages of *Srpska reč* : 'In the hearts of all Serbian patriots, no matter where they live, the memory of Draža has not faded in the fifty years from his martyr's death.'[17] Čotrić, a journalist with the Novi Sad based newspaper *Svet*, was the co-author with Radovan Kalabić in 1996 of *Spomenik Draži* (A Memorial to Draža), a collection of essays dedicated to the memory of the Četnik leader.[18] Drašković, however, was keen to disassociate

Draža Mihailović and the wartime Četnik movement from those contemporary ultra-nationalist paramilitary volunteers who described themselves as Četniks. In Drašković's view the atrocities commited by these groups would have been alien to Mihailović for whom 'a soldier's honour was a sacred thing'.[19] Drašković also rejected the accusations made by his nationalist rivals that he had betrayed the Četnik tradition through his advocacy of peace. Indeed he responded by accusing his opponents of adopting ideas external to the Serbian tradition, condemning them as 'those contemporary usurpers of the right, who prattle of the Orthodox superman, who are the spiritual creators and advocates of ethnic cleansing and undisguised Nazism... they are made up of an illegitimate mixture of homegrown national hysteria and an extreme European project where the nation is seen as a family and identified with blood and soil.'[20]

The neo-traditionalism of the SPO was also manifest in its continued incorporation and reverence for religious symbols and festivals. This religious element in the SPO identity persisted in spite of the disputes which occurred between Drašković and some of the nationalist hardliners within the Orthodox church. Vuk and Danica Drašković were prominent participants in the ceremony held at Lilić in May 1996 when a monastery was dedicated to the memory of Nikolaj Velimirović. The *Srpska reč* publishing house, of which Danica Drašković was the director, also published editions of Velimirović's collected sermons and lectures. The SPO continued to maintain a strongly royalist identity, believing that the Karadjordjević dynasty should return to Serbia and rule as part of a constitutional monarchy.[21]

The role of Ravna Gora and other neo-traditional elements in the SPO identity served a number of different purposes for the various groups which made up the movement's support base. For elderly Četnik veterans celebration of the Ravna Gora tradition offered a final vindication and rehabilitation not only of Draža Mihailović's memory but also of their own individual pasts which had been officially stigmatised during the years of communist rule. The Ravna Goran tradition also gave to young activists a ready made and potent set of symbols in direct opposition to the communist symbols which had been embedded in Socialist state ritual. By celebrating the arrival of Mihailović at Ravna Gora on 13 May 1941 the SPO's anti-communist supporters were challenging that element of the Partisan myth which declared that resistance to the Nazi occupier in Serbia had been initiated by Tito's forces on 7 July of that same year. As a symbol of party identity, closely identified with the movement's leader, Ravna Gora acted as a powerful factor in defining and maintaining the SPO's internal cohesion. This sense of ritual solidarity was heightened by the fact that the Ravna Gora celebrations brought activists together in a rural setting far removed from the urban milieu in which many of them would normally conduct their political activity.[22] While such symbolism appeared relevant to party activists it was, however, more doubtful how far such historicism, with its potentially divisive emphasis on memories of past conflicts and battles gone by, was able to reach out to less politically committed members of the Serbian public and the electorate. Indeed to some observers the incongruous mixture of modern and neo-traditional themes within the movement struck an awkwardly anachronistic tone. The continued emphasis of the SPO on 'political symbolism' suggested that it remained in essence a 'movement' directed towards the political/spiritual regeneration of Serbia which had not fully effected the transition to being a programmatically based political party.

The support by the SPO for the Contact Group peace plan placed them in the uncomfortable position of being on the same side of the key political divide as the SPS. The disatisfaction which arose amongst some activists, who believed that the SPO policy of 'peace' involved an abandonment of their ethnic kindred in Bosnia, was compounded by the perception that such a position involved collaboration with the regime. This perception was heightened by the relatively favourable coverage which the SPO and its leadership began to receive in state-controlled media. In the view of these members the natural position for an anti-communist movement was in opposition to the Socialist government. It was observed by some that Drašković's leadership style lacked the vigour which had characterised it prior to his spell in prison.[23] In the autumn of 1994 a number of defections of prominent members from the movement occurred prompted by these issues, and a more general sense of disquiet over the internal organisation and direction of the SPO. Those departing from the movement during that period included Vladimir Gajić, the SPO general Secretary, Mihaljo Marković, the movement Vice-President, Pavle Aksentijević, a member of the Main Committee, Dragan Miličić, one of the movement's main financial backers, and Branko Vasiljević, the President of the Belgrade Committee of the SPO. Vasiljević gave as his reasons for leaving the SPO the movement's having 'abandoned its national identity under which sign it was founded' and the fact that 'the wave of the SPO had broken on the rock of the regime'.[24] At the same time there were clashes between the SPO leadership at the centre and some of their local committees in Palilula, Smederevska Palanka, and Požarevac which led to the SPO national representative for Požarevac, Dragan Djurčija, resigning his parliamentary mandate.[25] Marković, Vasiljević, Gajić and Miličić all migrated to the ranks of the Democratic Party. In parallel with the movement of these activists there was a drift away of support from the movement among the public, and while the SPO remained as one of the significant forces in Serbian politics it did suffer a relative decline in fortunes from the position it had enjoyed from 1990-3 as the primary opposition grouping. While the SPO suffered these losses of party activists its alliance with the GSS remained solid despite unease amongst some of the latter's membership regarding their linkage with the SPO with its national roots and traditions.

In the period August 1994-5 the SRS, DSS and DS were united in their opposition to acceptance of the Contact Group peace plan and the economic and political blockade of the Bosnian Serbs. The connection between these three parties was (apart from a shortlived agreement on local co-operation signed on 13 February 1995) informal and focussed on this 'national' issue of policy.[26] In other senses these parties were distinguished by key aspects of policy and identity. A hostile observer of these parties, the government supporting leader of New Democracy, Dušan Mihailović, described them as the 'war lobby' of which 'Šešelj is the striking fist, Koštunica is the intellectual part, and Djindjić is the profiteering part.'[27]

In the immediate aftermath of the Belgrade-Pale schism the Milošević government appeared to regard the SRS as their main political enemies and accordingly concentrated the coercive force of the state against Šešelj's party. At the same time, however, the desire by the Serbian state to harass the SRS was undoubtedly aided by Šešelj's own penchant for 'bad behaviour' or political exhibitionism. On 16 September Šešelj voiced his firm opposition

to the blockade of the Drina and, in particular, to the deployment
of foreign monitors on the frontier between Serbia and the Republika
Srpska: 'No controllers can be effective on the Drina river, in
the heart of Serbia, because we will find ways of evading every
control and, if need be, we will drink the river Drina dry.'[28]
Three days later the authorities acted against Šešelj passing an
eight-month sentence on him suspended for three years for his
part in a violent incident which had occurred in the federal parliament on 18 May that year. Several other SRS deputies also
received suspended sentences at the same time. Šešelj responded
to his suspended sentence with characteristic defiance saying that
he was ready to: 'commit another thousand such crimes because
the honest individual's place under Slobodan Milošević's regime
is in prison.'[29] Šešelj was soon to test the will of the authorities
when on 27 September an altercation ocurred during which he
spat on the federal Prime Minister, Radoman Božović. The
authorities responded swiftly depriving him of his parliamentary
immunity and on 29 September arrested him early in the morning
while he was driving in the district of Batajnica. He was subsequently
sentenced to thirty days in prison to be served in addition to the
suspended sentence which had previously been passed on him.
During the period of Šešelj's imprisonment the SRS, temporarily
headed by Tomislav Nikolić, embarked on a programme of
'grassroots' activism with some 100 meetings being held calling
for Šešelj's release from prison.[30]

In early October, however, the SRS suffered a new blow
when a group of seven deputies in the federal parliament led by
Jovan Glamočanin broke away from the SRS. Glamočanin justified
his action, saying: 'We are not setting up a new party – we are
disassociating ourselves from Šešelj.'[31] It was, however, widely
suspected that Glamočanin's action had been instigated by the
Serbian government. The break-away group of Radical deputies
stated that they wished to make a 'constructive contribution to
the work of the federal parliament'.[32] On 27 January 1995, two
days before Šešelj's release from prison, Glamočanin formed his
parliamentary dissidents into the Serbian Radical Party-Nikola Pašić
(SRS-NP). The actions of the Glamočanin faction would in future
show them to be acting as loyal supporters of the Milošević government.

In spite of these setbacks Šešelj emerged from prison on 29

January 1995 prepared for renewed confrontation with the Socialist authorities, saying to his waiting supporters: 'Slobodan Milošević is the greatest criminal and traitor.'[33] Šešelj was swiftly able to resume his agitation against the regime. In April he addressed a rally of around 4,000 people in the town of Loznica before leading his followers in a march across the river Drina into Bosnia where they were greeted with gifts of bread, salt and brandy, the traditional signs of greeting. He told his followers: 'We have crossed the proud river Drina which flows through the heart of Serbia. Only one people lives on both sides of the river – the proud, bold, dignified and heroic Serb people.'[34] The series of SRS meetings held in the spring and summer of that year was scheduled to culminate in a rally held in Belgrade on 17 June. With international negotiations at a delicate stage, however, the Serbian authorities remained highly sensitive too such ultra-nationalist political activity. On 3 June when Šešelj addressed a small SRS gathering of around 100 people in the town of Gnjilane in Kosovo a violent incident occurred, apparently provoked by the police, in which shots were fired. This resulted in the arrest of Vojislav Šešelj, Tomislav Nikolić and the SRS national representatives Ranko Babić and Milorad Jevrić. Šešelj was sentenced to a further two months in jail and by the time he was released, fundamental changes would be underway in the national politics of Serbia and the former Yugoslavia.[35]

While Šešelj and the SRS were at the receiving end during 1994-5 of harassment from the state authorities in Serbia, the SRS was also cultivating new friends and allies on the international scene. Close relations were established between it and and Vladimir Zhirinovsky's Russian Liberal Democratic Party (LDP). One observer commented that both these ultra-nationalist leaders showed patterns of behaviour which were not 'psychiatric but rather manipulative' and were created 'by similar mechanisms with the help of the military-police complex and the energies of national frustration'.[36]

Zhirinovsky visited Serbia on a number of occasions to express his support for the SRS directly. During a visit in January 1994 he said to a rally: 'This is the start of the Slav world. You defend the Slav world. Now the time has come for Russia to at last rise and defend the Serbs. We will punish all your enemies. Remember we have had enough of being afraid. Today it is they who fear us in London, Paris, Bonn, Washington and Tel Aviv.'[37]

In October 1995 Zhirinovsky was once again in Serbia touring the country addressing a series of meetings at Novi Sad, Šabac, and Zvornik. In September 1996 the SRS and LDP leaders planned to campaign together in the Republika Srpska, but their planned visit was halted when Serbian police stopped them from entering Bosnia at the Sremska Rača crossing point.

At a lower level the SRS and the LDP regularily exchanged visiting delegations to each other's conferences and meetings. The 'Fourth Fatherland Congress' on 22 May 1996 was attended by a group of LDP officials headed by the party's General Secretary, Leontiy Arkhipov, who stated that the alliance of the two parties was 'functioning excellently'.[38] The SRS also forged links in Western Europe with the French ultra-nationalists of Jean-Marie Le Pen's National Front (FN). In May 1996 Dominique Chaboche led a party of FN delegates on a visit to the SRS in Belgrade. This was followed in January 1997 when Le Pen himself visited the Serbian capital to hold talks with the SRS leader.[39]

It is instructive to contrast the hostile relations between the Socialist government and the ultra-nationalist SRS and the positive relations which existed between the authorities, in spite of their adoption of a 'peace policy,' and the hard-line nationalist paramilitary leader and aspiring politician, Željko Ražnatović (Arkan). On 19 February 1995 Ražnatović married the the turbo-folk singer Ceca who had supported him in his unsuccessful December 1993 election campaign. The wedding ceremony had been lavishly conducted amidst much pomp and pseudo-traditional trappings. Arkan wore the uniform of a First World War officer of the Serbian army, while Ceca was compared by a writer in the magazine *Duga* to the 'Kosovo Maiden' who according to legend had tended the wounds of the Serbian heroes in the aftermath of the medieval battle of Kosovo. The favourable coverage given to the wedding ceremony by the Serbian state-controlled media indicated that Arkan, the paramilitary commander, was still considered an acceptable personality, enjoying celebrity status, for official Belgrade.

In the division over the Contact Group peace plan and the Belgrade-Pale schism Zoran Djindjić placed the DS firmly on the side of the Bosnian Serb leadership. Djindjić speaking in October 1994 restated his belief that the 'the aim of the Muslim side is to create a unified Bosnia' and that 'the war will not end until the international community clearly says that Bosnia-Hercegovina will be divided into two confederal parts.'[40] In December 1994, in the wake of the NATO air attacks on Bosnian Serb positions around Bihać, Djindjić travelled to the Bosnian Serb headquarters at Pale. He defined his mission as 'providing good offices for the leadership of the Republika Srpska, so its people can retain their fate in their own hands.'[41]

Djindjić, however, characteristically sought to present the path which he had taken as a 'rational' response to political circumstances eschewing the emotional or 'romantic' symbolism widely favoured in Serbian nationalist discourse. In August 1995 Djindjić defined his attitude to the 'national question': 'The placing of the greatest part of the Serbian people under the same state roof was a logical aim of national politics at a time when the state in which the whole people was provided for had ceased to exist.'[42] The self-conscious 'modernity' and 'rationality' of Djindjić's approach to politics was used by him as a key factor in staking his claim to the 'centre' ground of Serbian politics, and dismissing the 'archaic' politics of the SPO and its leader. In March 1995 Djindjić observed: 'The DS is a party of the centre and our position regarding the solution to the crisis in Bosnia or the Krajina cannot be sufficient reason to classify us as hardline nationalists. The SPO say that they are a party of the centre, but they are founded on the Ravna Gora tradition and are advocates of the monarchy. That is their problem. It is not ours.'[43]

Djindjić was also keen to stress the willingness of the DS to compromise and give priority to 'issues' over the 'ideological' stance apparently favoured by other opposition parties. Djindjić described this situation: 'We never agreed with the division into black and white. First there was the division into the communists and anti-communists, with the opposition identifying themselves with the latter. At that time we did not want to wear the cockade [Četnik/royalist insignia] and for that we counted the cost. With the creation of DEPOS there arose a division between government and opposition, but we did not want to go into the fold and bleat like sheep: '*svi, svi, svi*' [a traditional opposition/Ravna Gora chant]. It is not true that all that the government does is bad, and all that the opposition does is good. They are not all Saddam Hussein nor are we all Saint Sava. They are not all devils, nor are we all angels.'[44]

The nationalist stance taken by this essentially urban and middle class party was dubbed by some observers as 'salon nationalism'.[45]

There was also some scepticism regarding the depth of Djindjić's dedication to the nationalist cause. One interpretation saw his support for the Bosnian Serbs as a 'pragmatic' move whereby Djindjić, believing that the opposition forces within Serbia were not sufficiently strong as to seriously threaten Milošević, sought to draw on the strength of the Bosnian Serbs and the appeal of their cause in order to achieve this aim.

Alongside this identity as a 'national' party Djindjić also sought to cultivate an image for the DS as a technocratic party capable of dealing with the economic problems faced by the Serbian population. The DS had run in the December 1993 election under the slogan 'honesty' and had sought in its rhetoric and publicity to contrast this value with the corruption of the regime. Addressing a rally in Niš on 13 December 1993 Djindjić told his supporters: 'In the last fifty years we have tried everything...and you see how far we have come. The only thing we have not tried, one simple thing, is honest government.'[46]

During 1994-5 Djindjić made a number of attacks on the 'incestuous' relationship between the political role of Socialist politicians and their business affairs, and was particularly critical of Dragan Tomić accusing him of having used his position to gain credit for his Simpo firm, Dušan Matković, the head of Smederevo Ironworks, and the Bogoljub Karić of the 'Karić Brothers' business conglomerate.[47] However, he made it clear that the sickness afflicting Serbian economic life went beyond the deeds of such individuals but was rather embedded in the environment where no clear dividing line was drawn between economic and political interests. The image of the DS as a party of technocratic/economic orientation was strengthened by the role played as DS Vice-President by Miroljub Labus, a leading academic economist.

During 1994 DS parliamentary representatives sponsored, albeit unsuccessfully, a series of bills addressing economic issues such as privatisation, anti-trust legislation, and monitoring of the financial interests of state officials. The DS developed links with parties outside Serbia who shared their belief in reforms based on economic liberalism with particularly strong contacts being maintained with Russia's Democratic Choice headed by the economist and former adviser to President Yeltsin, Yegor Gaidar. The technocratic image and values promoted by the DS made it an attractive political home for private businessmen ensuring that it was relatively well financed compared to other opposition parties.

During this period the DS sought to build on the degree of electoral success which they had enjoyed in the December 1993 election by strengthening their party structures in the provinces. This process was accompanied by the promotion of younger activists within the party structures. The DS claimed that during 1994 10,000 new members were recruited and fifty municipal committees were founded. By the end of 1995 the DS membership figures officially stood at 41,000. The DS was also expanding into areas of Serbia where they had not previously maintained a presence. By April 1997 the DS stated that they had established fifteen local committees in the Kosovo region.[48]

The DSS saw itself as distinguished from the other 'democratic' political parties by its 'consistent' and unwavering solidarity, since the division over the Vance-Owen peace plan, with the Serbs across the Drina. Koštunica defined the differing opposition attitudes to the 'national question' and compared them to the position taken by the DSS: 'One position is to take an unstable and calculating attitude. That is the position taken by the Democratic Party. The other position is "anational" and in a sense "anti-national". That is the position of the Civic Alliance of Serbia. We see the same position with the Serbian Renewal Movement, only accompanied by an interest in nationalism in its most archaic and caricatured form. We do not need such mythology, nor do we need a simplified and discredited past, but rather a modern solution to the Serbian national question as it exists at the end of the twentieth and the dawn of the new century.'[49] He was dismissive of any political attempt to divide the Serbian national community: 'There exists in our current political and public life an unusual, quasi-national position. In this position it is only possible to be a Serb in a fragment of territory, and the division of Serbdom is just. For our "patriots" of this type American patriotism can stretch out as far as Vietnam, the Soviets to Afghanistan, the British to the Malvinas Islands, the French to New Caledonia, but the Serbs can only go as far as the Drina, and not one step further. This understanding is imposed from outside, supported by the government and part of the so-called opposition, and depends on the old, irrational myth that Serbia across the Drina is a separate entity or part of "Great Serbia", and Serbia up to the Drina, with the possibility that in the north and the south it would be shortened by a head and a foot, is a just and sufficient Serbia. Surely from the moment that Yugoslavia disappeared Serbia was one indivisible territory on both sides of the Drina, and the Serbs both here and there are one and the same nation. Whatever foreign and domestic "peace-lovers" think or say peace is only possible once this natural fact is acknowledged rather than rejected.'[50] For Koštunica the primary place given to the national question was the inevitable consequence of the circumstances prevailing during the breakdown of Yugoslavia.

He explained: 'When five or six years ago we tried to save Yugoslavia, we pointed to all the consequences of its violent breakdown, and it followed from this that democracy was our founding idea. Then when the state broke down it became necessary to think in a different way. It is a fact that a man is naturally a member both of his family and his nation. There are people for whom membership of this latter category means nothing. I understand that position, but I am one of those people who is not indifferent to national feeling.'[51] The DSS forged strong links with the Serbian Democratic Party in Bosnia. As the leader of the DSS Koštunica was presented as being 'consistent' not only in his pursuit of the 'national' line, but also in his refusal to compromise with the regime. This was contrasted with the willingness of Drašković and Djindjić to engage in negotiations with Milošević regarding the formation of a coalition government after the December 1993 elections. The DSS also accused the SPO of collaborating with the regime in the running of local councils such as Stari Grad and Savski Venac.[52] The DSS by contrast saw themselves as pursuing a policy of 'pure anti-communism'.[53] This image of political 'honesty' could be set alongside Koštunica's reputation for personal probity which was believed to be manifest in his following of a modest lifestyle.[54] Such personal factors could be of particular importance in Serbia where it was always suspected that the political classes used their office in order to profit financially. In their attitude towards domestic political issues the DSS maintained an image of social and economic liberalism. This was paralleled by the social identity of its supporters.

The public retreat by the Socialist government from support for the Bosnian Serbs did not mean that there had been any moderation in its internal policies. Indeed the Belgrade–Pale schism was followed by a renewed campaign of harassment by the Serbian government directed against the independent media. The daily newspaper *Borba* (The Struggle) had originally been the journal of the Yugoslav Communist Party. In 1990 under legislation passed by the then Yugoslav Prime Minister, however, it had converted itself into a joint-stock company and thereby established its independence. In November 1994, however, the Yugoslav authorities decided to take legal action against *Borba* claiming that it had been incorrectly incorporated four years previously. The court ruled in favour of the authorities declaring that *Borba* in effect had no legal basis for its existence.

On 26 December a new edition of *Borba* was launched with the financial backing of the authorities and with its content under the firm ideological control of the SPS. On 19 January 1995 a group of *Borba* journalists, including the former editor Gordana Logar, announced the formation of a new independent daily newspaper, *Naša borba* (Our Struggle). This new journal was initially prevented from publishing by the authorities on the ground that there was a shortage of newsprint – an occurrence widely believed to have been manufactured by the Serbian government to prevent the newspaper getting off the ground. *Naša borba* did, however, gain financial support from a number of international journalistic organisations and its first edition finally went on sale on 1 February. In spite of this state-directed obstruction *Naša borba* went on to become one of the key sources of independent and reliable political information in Serbia while the financial state of the Socialist-backed *Borba* became ever more parlous.[55]

It had been a longstanding aim of the Milošević government to create a loyal and subservient media within Serbia, but the reasons for the timing of its attack on *Borba's* independence remained obscure. It was, however, speculated that Milošević was seeking to stamp out those independent media institutions who might otherwise be in a position to expose his continued covert involvement in the politics of the Republika Srpska. In another, and quite different, sphere the Minister for Culture, Nada Popović-Perišić, sought to designate 1994–5 as a 'Year of Culture' apparently with the intention of countering the popularity of turbo-folk music. Some observers saw this as an attempt to move away from this form of popular culture which had enjoyed such a symbiotic relationship with the nationalist 'war culture' of the early 1990s.[56]

The period after the Belgrade-Pale schism also saw a revival in the conspicuous celebration by the Socialists and the state authorities of Partisan holidays. In particular the 7 July 'Day of the Uprising' was marked by the opening of public buildings or other symbols of Serbia's 'progress' under Socialist rule. On 7 July 1995 Milošević opened Serbia's first underground stations at Vuk Spomenik in Belgrade. Milošević told a crowd of several thousand: 'The fact that our country has realised such a project at a time when it was under complete international blockade and unprecedented pressure from the outside proves that [nothing] could prevent Belgrade getting this most beautiful and most modern underground station in Europe. [...] I am certain that all this and all these projects being realised throughout Serbia...show a picture of a future, modern, developed, democratic, prosperous Serbia as it will undoubtedly be very soon.'[57] On 7 July 1996 Milošević again emphasised the theme of Serbia's modernisation when he opened a satellite station near the village of Ivanjica in central Serbia. He told the gathering that the satellite signified Serbia's 'continuing rapid development and movement forward in terms of our connections with surrounding countries and the outside world'.[58] The use of Partisan festivals by the Belgrade Socialist elite was in direct contrast to the fashionability of Četnik symbolism among the Pale leadership. The utilisation of these rituals was clearly meant to signal their ideological differentiation from the Bosnian Serbs with whom they had previously been united in the pursuit of a common national crusade.

This period was to witness the inception of a fundamental shift in the balance of forces on the 'left' of Serbian politics. In mid-1993 the League of Communists-Movement for Yugoslavia had seen a power struggle within its ranks in which the remnants of its original military faction were removed by a civilian grouping headed by Mirjana Marković, Goran Latinović and Zoran Todorović ('Kundak'). When the SK-PJ ran in the December 1993 elections, under the United Left banner, however, it failed to gather a significant number of votes in spite of a well funded campaign and generous coverage of their activities in the state-controlled media. Even Mirjana Marković running in Smederevo failed to make any electoral headway. This failure was followed by moves on the part of the SK-PJ to relaunch their organisation under a new name. On 24 and 25 March 1995 the Yugoslav

United Left (JUL) held its first congress at the Sava Centre in Belgrade. In theory JUL was a broad left-wing coalition made up of twenty-one constituent parties. In practice, however, some of those groups were merely elements of the SK-PJ without any independent existence (League of Communists-Movement for Yugos-lavia in Serbia, League of Communists-Movement for Yugoslavia in Montenegro, Youth League of the Movement for Yugoslavia, Yugoslav Revolutionary Youth); ones whose support did not ex-tend beyond a single town or local region (The Moravan League from Jagodina, the Party of Multi-Party Socialism from Kruševac); or small bodies representing ethnic minorities (the Democratic Party of Roma, the Social Democratic Party of the Roma).[59]

The illusion of inclusiveness was heightened by the appointment of Ljubiša Ristić, a well-known theatre director, as President of JUL. Ristić, however, was widely regarded merely as a figurehead while real power within JUL resided with Mirjana Marković who headed the Executive Committee. Ristić had been born in 1947 the son of a high-ranking Partisan officer from Kosovo. He had played an active role in the student demonstrations in 1968, and withdrew from the League of Communists in 1972. In 1985 he had been appointed as Director of the National Theatre in Sub-otica,[60] and in this role enjoyed a reputation for staging *avant garde* productions. In 1988 he had faced an attempt to remove him as head of the theatre by local Hungarians who objected to the way he had sought to dissolve the Hungarian sections within the theatre. In a lengthy panegyric to Ristić in his book *A Paper House*, the British writer Mark Thompson condemned his Hun-garian opponents as narrow-minded provincials ('multi-national provincialism is still provincialism') incapable of understanding his sophisticated cosmopolitanism. Ristić is quoted as saying: 'To be a Yugoslav is not to claim a nationality, it is a statement about one's position in the world and history. [...] There is something else very specific to Yugoslavia. Taboos were attacked in the theatre first. Anyone who wants to turn the theatre into an in-strument of national revival or of a political party will usually be rejected.'[61] Ristić survived this attack on his position through the intervention of Radoman Božović, the then SPS Prime Minister of Vojvodina. Božović had been brought to power in 1988 through his role in overthrowing the provincial elite during the anti-bureaucratic revolution in Vojvodina. For such 'new men' in the

Socialist Vojvodina leadership Ristić's tussle with the local Hungarians could be seen as the cultural counterpart to their own political struggle with 'regional particularism'. Ristić's sense of artistic innovation was, however, ultimately defined by the limits of his Socialist ideology. As JUL grew in power after 1995 he was to use his political influence in an attempt to make ideological conformity a criteria for advancement within theatrical and cultural circles in Serbia.

It was soon to become clear that JUL was intended to be more than simply a coalition of fragmentary and marginal left-wing parties. Instead Slobodan Milošević and Mirjana Marković saw JUL as an alternative source of reliable socialist cadres who, unlike those from the ranks of the SPS, would not be compromised in the eyes of the world and disillusioned Socialist voters by their association with the Milošević government's period of nationalism. Superficial external observers of JUL's creation might be ready to conclude that this new organisation was a reformed Communist party of the type which had come into being in Poland and Hungary.[62] One Socialist official, Milisav Milenković, greeted the formation of JUL: 'The SPS and JUL form a strong political front which is necessary in order to conduct a defence against the abundance of retrograde ideas.' Ristić reacted to such gestures of support, saying: 'JUL is a confederation of different parties and associations. We welcome the support from the group, which is dominant, within the SPS, which supports peace.'[63] Observers were swift to comment that JUL was capable of acting as a 'reserve echelon' for the SPS. In fact its intended task was to supersede the SPS, a fact which would become increasingly clear as senior members of JUL began to fill the positions of power and influence within the state and para-state apparatus.

The JUL leaders made statements which were apparently forthright in their rejection of nationalist politics. Ristić defined JUL as 'a movement of citizens of the FRY oriented towards peace and the Yugoslav way of life'. Mirjana Marković declared in mid-1995 that JUL was 'opposed to the terrible, primitive, Četnik, nationalism at work in Bosnia and personified by Radovan Karadžić', and condemned 'each grotesque attack by the Serbian army in Bosnia on some mountain village with ten Muslim houses in it, which makes no contribution to the struggle of the Serbian people, but brings the twelve million citizens of the FRY to the brink of war'.[64] These apparently clear statements should not, however, be viewed as an unconditional disavowal of the policies associated with the prosecution of the war in Bosnia-Hercegovina. A number of senior figures within the VRS had been recruited as, and remained, members of the SK-PJ. The SK-PJ policy document *Platform for the Resolution of the Crisis in Bosnia-Hercegovina*, adopted at a meeting of the party on 4 March 1995, stated: 'Aiding the Serbs in Bosnia from the Federal Republic of Yugoslavia, which should have been in the function of a struggle against neo-imperialism and neo-fascism grew increasingly uncontrolled and unselective...Instead of a broad front for protection against fascism there developed a narrow nationalist movement. [...] It is an illusion to expect that the present nationalisms and the exclusive territorial consciousness are conducive to resolving the national issue. This cannot be done without new social and class forces as developments so far have confirmed. The war in Bosnia has resulted in a defeat for the "heroic" and spiteful mentality.' The document went on to argue that union between the Federal Republic of Yugoslavia and the Republika Srpska was not, at that time, possible because in the latter territory 'all connections with the people's liberation struggle and its traditions have been broken and Četniks are held in high esteem.' It also condemns the privileged position within the Republika Srpska given to the Orthodox church and the alleged devotion of the Bosnian Serb leadership to 'market liberalism.'[65] The SK-PJ in this statement of their national policy did not therefore object to the reality of intervention on behalf of the Bosnian Serbs, but merely rejected the ideological orientation of the Bosnian Serb leadership with their deviation from the progressive 'left' path and their embracing of reactionary 'right' tendencies. In their 'leftism' JUL and its leadership also showed a fundamental fear and rejection of the West and its values. Mirjana Marković had written in her *Duga* column in December 1994: 'For four years the colonisation process has been underway in Eastern Europe under cover of the New World Order, under cover of its demo-cratisation, under cover of introducing a market economy. [...] It won't be long before we know who took part in financing some parties and some media in Eastern Europe. But that iden-tification will run parallel to the identification of those who were financed, who were paid to to turn their countries into colonies. It is still, and will remain so for a long time, the most shameful act an individual can do towards his country. [...] Most traitors in history have tried to present their treason as activities in some higher interest – national or even global...and most luckily and naturally did not manage that. These extended party and journalists' arms of the new modern conquistadors in Eastern Europe won't succeed either.'[66] Furthermore Marković believed that Western-style democracy was anachronistic while she and the forces involved in JUL were in the vanguard of the search for more popular and effective forms of representation. Marković stated: 'The era of parliamentary democracy is expiring and it is imperative to find a new form of political organisation that is more democratic than the parliamentary systems of the bourgeois societies.'[67] The anti-Western orientation of JUL and its contempt for 'primitive' Četnickdom were combined by Ljubiša Ristić in his statement in September 1995 that the interests of the United States, and the 'New World Order,' were being promoted in Bosnia-Hercegovina by its 'two agents', the Bosnian Serb leader Radovan Karadžić and the Bosnian Prime Minister Haris Silajdžić.[68] While Western societies were despised by JUL, it held up Communist China as an example of successful development for Serbia to emulate. There was also a sense in which Marković, even when in the process of denouncing nationalism, would betray the chauvinistic attitudes which formed part of her small-town provincial upbringing. Typical of this were her statements when before the split between the SRS and the SPS in 1993 she began to denounce Šešelj via her column in *Duga*. Šešelj she said was 'neither a man nor a Serb, being a Turk in the most primitive historic form.'[69] Marković's regular columns in *Duga* displayed a similar inchoate mixture of Marxist ideology, romanticism and prejudice.

In the strategic thinking of Marković and Milošević the 'anti-nationalism' of JUL would not only restore the credibility of the regime in the eyes of the international opinion, but would also allow the regime to gather support, amongst the ethnic minorities who made up thirty-five per cent of Serbia's population. It was reasoned that if support for the SPS waned amongst Serbs then members of minority groups, for whom the SPS was irrevocably tainted with nationalism might be persuaded to cast their votes for an apparently 'non-nationalist' party of the 'left'. The sympathy of JUL for ethnic minorities was displayed in June 1995 when its officials in Valjevo intervened to save Nezir Omerović, a local

Muslim forester with relatives in Bosnia, whose removal had been demanded by the local Serbian population.[70] In particular, however, JUL sought to establish itself in the Sandžak region as an alternative to both the SPS and the SDA. The role of JUL, as Zuhra Mumdžić, the head of the JUL council, proclaimed, was 'affirmation of inter- ethnic tolerance in Sandžak and...resisting both Muslim and Serbian nationalism'. In the spring of 1996 JUL even launched an initiative to establish its own TV station to broadcast to the Novi Pazar area in competition with the satellite, Bosnian and Croatian programmes favoured by many local Muslims. On 25 March 1996 it was announced that Ferid Hamidović, a Sandžak Muslim member of JUL and the SK-PJ, had been appointed as Serbian Deputy Minister of the Environment. Gorica Gajević, the SPS General Secretary, also with political origins in the Sandžak region, had served as President of the Raška court. She enjoyed close political relations with the JUL leadership in the area and, being herself married to a Hungarian, typified the new emphasis on 'multi-culturalism' fashionable on the Serbian 'left'.[71]

The political and economic rhetoric of Mirjana Marković was classically Marxist in her deep hostility to private enterprise and the market. In October 1995 she warned: 'If the Yugoslav left does not in the time to come seriously involve itself in the life of our society its existence will be threatened by a primitive, predatory, South American type of capitalism. This fear arises from the existence of two dangerous ideas, that of the total and absolute privatisation of all that is socially valuable and that of the unlimited importation of foreign capital.'[72] In practical political terms, however, the strategy pursued by Marković and JUL was not to abolish the the Serbian private sector but rather to assert their political control over it. The immediate political circle surrounding Marković, and through her Milošević, consisted of a clique of ultra-rich plutocrats whose business careers had been forged through the development of client-patron relationships with the state bureaucracy. Zoran Todorović 'Kundak', one of JUL's key supporters and a leading 'red businessman' was reputed to be amongst the richest men in Serbia.[73] Nenad Djordjević had been a member of the SK-PJ and was one of JUL's founders. He had worked as an official of the secret police (SDB) before becoming a lecturer at the Interior Ministry training school. In 1991 he was able through his political connections to become the head of the Belgrade Trade Centre conglomerate. He was also able to purchase, at a bargain price, the Velika Plana furniture company. Subsequently his financial empire expanded rapidly and was valued in mid-1995 at $40 million. Perhaps the most important figure in the charmed circle surrounding Mira Marković, however, was Bogoljub Karić who, with his brothers Sreten, Zoran and Dragan, headed the Braća Karić group of companies. Karić originally came from the town of Peć in Kosovo, and was the youngest in his family. The Karić brothers began their careers working as musicians playing folk music at weddings; Bogoljub worked as the manager of their band. Working alongside them at this time was the the folk-singer Zorica Brunclik who, like the Karić brothers, was to become rich, successful and a prominent supporter of JUL. Bogoljub Karić went on to found his own business manufacturing tools from the family workshop. Showing acute business acumen and an ability to manipulate the development subsidies which flowed down to Kosovo from the federal government, the Karić business expanded rapidly. Bogoljub's fortunes flourished in parallel with those of his political ally Slobodan Milošević. In 1990 he founded his own bank, the Karić Bank, which became the centre of an interconnected web of companies based in Serbia and beyond. The brothers' business empire had substantial bases in Russia and the United States, and by 1995 it had its own TV station, BK TV, and its own university, Karić Brothers University.[74] Like other prominent business allies of the regime, Karić acted during 1992 as a channel through which money was directed towards the coffers of the SRS. Vojislav Šešelj would later attest that Karić had contributed 30,000 marks to the SRS 1992 election campaign.[75] The closeness of the Karić group to the regime was underlined by the fact that they undertook the translation and publishing of Mira Marković's collected diary columns and articles. At a lower level JUL let it be known that private businesses needed to lend their financial support to JUL if they were to enjoy the political patronage necessary to operate in Serbia's bureaucratised economic environment. This strategy served to enrich JUL's already full coffers and at the same time draw private businessmen away from the opposition camp and in this way impoverishing the opponents of the regime.[76] The collecting of business support by JUL also created tension within the ranks of the government itself where New Democracy, who had previously presented itself as a business-orientated party with access to the corridors of power, now found itself competing with an alternative, and more powerful rival.

For Mirjana Marković, while her beliefs were defined by the tenets of theoretical Marxism her ultimate political purpose was the pursuit of power. The desire to placate his wife's wish to exert influence through her own political party may, in addition to any strategic consideration, be considered a significant motivating factor in Milošević's decision to allow JUL to operate as an 'alternative' party of the 'left'. Marković was also believed to have the ability to determine who was appointed to the key Yugoslav diplomatic and ambassadorial posts. JUL had its own radio station, Košava, whose editor-in-chief was Marković's daughter, Marija Milošević. Such was Marković's reputation as an omnipotent figure presiding over the Serbian state and all its workings that she was satirised in the song 'Baba Jula' (Granny JUL) by Bora Djordjević of the rock band Riblja čorba (Fish Soup).[77] Her enemies among the opposition called her 'the Red Witch' or else likened her to Elena Ceauşescu, the wife of the former Romanian dictator.[78]

However, the strategy formulated by Marković and Milošević, of which JUL formed the spearhead, was to prove fatally flawed. While JUL sought to create a façade of modernity for itself, attracting a number of prominent personalities from the world of entertainment and sport to its banner, it remained obvious to both domestic and international opinion that it was a thoroughly unreformed movement which had taken shape around a fossilised brand of Marxist ideology. For all its power at the centre and its financial wealth JUL could also never realistically hope to replace the SPS, with its powerful structure of branches and its mass membership, in the provinces. As with Arkan's SSJ, the case of JUL demonstrated that it took more than copious amounts of money and a sympathetic media to create a genuine political party with strong popular support. The fact that it aspired to this aim, however, would be a source of tension between the SPS and JUL. Conflict within the ruling coalition would become a factor in towns across Serbia. In attracting ethnic minority support JUL was also largely a failure; as a party so openly and explicitly attached to the regime it had little serious hope, for all its powers of regional and national patronage, of challenging the influence of the national parties such as the Sandžak SDA. The Serbian population also found it hard to reconcile the ferociously Marxist and anti-capitalist rhetoric emanating from the JUL leaders with their legendary accumulated wealth. Ordinary Serbs came to regard the ideological position taken by JUL towards business and personal wealth as deeply hypocritical and this further contributed to its increasing unpopularity. Later events were to prove that by creating JUL at his wife's behest, Milošević had ensured that political disaster would await him in the future.

Notes

1. 'Vuk Drašković: "Podržavam mir"', *Vreme*, 17 October 1994.
2. *Tanjug*, 11 October 1994 in *SWB EE/2125 C/31*, 13 October 1994.
3. *Borba*, 22 November 1994 in *SWB EE/2161 C/21*, 24 November 1994.
4. 'Ljudi bez rodjendana', Rasim Ljajić interviewed by Mila Manojlović, *Duga*, 13 April 1996.
5. 'Nije strašno da budemo poraženi', Danica Drašković interviewed by Vera Didanovic, *Naša borba*, 2-3 September 1995.
6. Vuk Drašković, 'Raskid sa komunizmom', *NIN*, 7 April 1995.
7. *Tanjug*, 13 May 1991 in *SWB EE/1074 B/12*, 17 May 1991.
8. Dragan Todorović, 'Pet godina osvajanja Ravne gore', *Vreme*, 23 May 1994; Nenad Stefanović, 'Vratio se Čiča', *Duga*, 23 May 1992.
9. Mirko Jović, 'Fašizma nema', *NIN*, 28 May 1993.
10. Serbian Radio 13 May in *SWB EE/1690 C/1*, 19 May 1993.
11. Srboljub Bogdanović, 'Eci, peci, pec....', *NIN*, 19 November 1993.
12. 'Speech by Vuk Drašković at the Second Congress of Serb Intellectuals in the Sava Centre' 22 April 1994, Serbian Renewal Movement (Belgrade), 1997.
13. Batić Bačević, 'Mirenje sa sudbinom', *NIN*, 19 May 1995.
14. Dragan Todorović, 'Poraženi i u sećanju', *Vreme*, 22 May 1995.
15. Vuk Drašković, *Noć generala*, Srpska reč (Belgrade), 1995.
16. Dragan Todorović, 'Jeremija sa Ravne gore', *Vreme*, 18 May 1996.
17. Radovan Kalabić and Aleksandar Čotrić, 'Krst Vinstona Čerčila', *Srpska reč*, 12 August 1996.
18. Radovan Kalabić and Aleksandar Čotrić, *Spomenik Draži, Srpska reč* (Belgrade), 1996.
19. Branislav Boškov; 'Došla moda partizana', *Oslobodjene*, 20 April 1995.
20. Vuk Drašković, 'Glupost jaše Srbijom', *NIN*, 17 November 1995.
21. The Serbian Renewal Movement programme, adopted on 7 March 1993 at the SPO Second World Congress in Belgrade, states: 'Our aim is to end half a century of dictatorship and arbitary rule and enable Serbia's citizens to choose the form of their state in a free referendum supervised by all political parties. Whatever the result of the referendum, we will return to Aleksandar Karadjordjević and all members of the Karadjordjević and Petrović dynasties their Serbian citizenship and all confiscated property and guarantee them freedom in their homeland. The SPO considers that all forms of

monarchy are outdated apart from those in which the monarchy acts as a passive, non-party roof for active parliamentary democracy.' Quoted from Documentary Appendix in Vladimir Goati (ed.), *Challenges of Parliamentarism – The Case of Serbia in the 1990s*, Institute of Social Science (Belgrade), 1995, p. 285.

22. Nenad Stefanović, 'Fina regulacija iracionalnog', *Duga*, 19 July 1997.
23. Slavoljub Djukić, *On, ona, i mi, B-92* (Belgrade), 1997, p. 188.
24. 'Odlazak apostola SPO-a', Branko Vasiljević interviewed by Luka Mičeta, *NIN*, 10 February 1995.
25. Z. Simić, 'Nove ili stare nesuglasice u srpskom pokretu obnove', *Politika*, 2 September 1994.
26. Ivan Radovanović, 'Vuk samotnjak', *Vreme*, 20 February 1995.
27. 'Rat i demokratija ne idu zajedno', Dušan Mihailović interviewed by Bahri Cani, *Naša borba*, 6 September 1995.
28. *Borba*, 16 September 1994 in *SWB EE/2106 C/1*, 21 September 1994.
29. *Tanjug*, 19 September 1994 in *SWB EE/2106 C/1*, 21 September 1994.
30. Milan Milošević, 'Moć srpskih radikala', *Vreme*, 30 January 1995.
31. *Tanjug*, 7 October 1994 in *SWB EE/2123 C/3*, 11 October 1994.
32. Vojislav Vignjević, 'Pašićevi u službi socijalista?', *Borba*, 6 December 1994.
33. Richard Schneider, 'interview with Vojislav Šešelj', *South Slav Journal* (6, 3-4).
34. 'Hardline Nationalists March to End Bosnia's Blockade', *Balkan News International*, 23 April 1995.
35. Petar Ignja, 'Uloga državnog neprijatelja', *NIN*, 9 June 1995.
36. Milan MIlošević, 'Radikalna rez', *Vreme*, 12 June 1995.
37. Ian Traynor, 'Serbian Day Out for Wild Bear', *Guardian*, 31 January 1994.
38. *Tanjug*, 22 May 1996 in *SWB EE/2619 A/7*, 23 May 1996.
39. Sandra Jokanović, 'Delegacije Liberalno-demokratske partije Rusije i Nacionalnog fronta Francuske u Srbiji', *Velika Srbija*, 15 June 1996; Julian Borger, 'Le Pen Finds Nationalist Unity Lies in Common Hatreds', *Guardian*, 22 January 1997.
40. Serbian Radio, 17 October 1994 in *SWB EE/2130 C/2*, 19 October 1994.
41. *SRNA*, 12 December 1994 in *SWB EE/2178 C/5*, 14 December 1994.
42. Zoran Djindjić, 'Srbi, danas i sutra', *Vreme*, 14 August 1995.
43. Batić Bačević, 'Lideri u klinču', *NIN*, 3 March 1995.
44. 'Mi nismo andjeli', Zoran Djindjić interviewed by Dragan Bujošević, *NIN*, 21 April 1995.
45. The term 'salon nationalism' is used in particular in the analysis of the Serbian political scene by Milan Milošević in *Vreme*.
46. Serbian TV, 13 December 1993 in *SWB EE/1904 C/2*, 25 December 1993.
47. Ivan Radovanović, 'Kompanija protiv preduzeća', *Vreme*, 6 March 1995.
48. Nenad Stefanoviic, 'Red, rad i disciplina kičme', *Duga*, 12 April 1997. The figures for membership are given by the DS in *Profile of the Democratic Party* (Belgrade), 1996.
49. 'Protiv sejanja magle', Vojislav Koštunica interviewed by M. Gligorijević, *NIN*, 21 March 1997.
50. Vojislav Koštunica, 'Protiv despotije', *NIN*, 28 June 1995.

51. 'Sudbonosna godina', Vojislav Koštunica interviewed by Nenad LJ Stefanović, *Vreme*, 17 February 1996.
52. This point was made by Mirko Petrović, Vice-President of DSS, in an interview with the author, 7 December 1996.
53. This phrase was used in personal communication with the author by an official of the DSS in the Belgrade area
54. Nenad Stefanović, 'Gledajući gore ka dedinju', *Duga*, 17 August 1996.
55. Stan Markotich, 'Milošević's Renewed Attack on the Independent Media', *Transition*, 15 March 1995.
56. Tim Judah, 'Serb Offensive on Disco Folk', *The Times*, 19 June 1994.
57. Stan Markotich 'Milošević Backtracks', *Transition*, 11 August 1995,
58. Dragan Todorović, 'U prilike po priliku', *Vreme*, 13 July 1996.
59. The full list of JUL constituent parties is given in Nenad Stefanović, 'Sneg u julu', *BNA Tiker* (Belgrade), 1996, p. 166.
60. Dejan Anastasejević, 'Ljubiša Ristić – Lik i delo', *Vreme*, 3 April 1995.
61. Mark Thompson, *A Paper House – The Ending of Yugoslavia*, Radius (London), 1992, p. 249.
62. Jonathan Steele, 'The Oracular Mrs Milošević Enjoys a Larger-than-Wife Role', *Guardian*, 14 July 1995.
63. Nenad LJ Stefanović, 'Turbo-JUL, *Vreme*, 3 April 1995.
64. Nenad LJ Stefanović, 'Porodična radionica', *Vreme*, 31 July 1995.
65. *Platform for the Resolution of the Crisis in the Former Yugoslav Republic of Bosnia-Herzegovina*, SK-PJ (Belgrade), 1995.
66. This quote was reproduced as part of the SPO press release, *Extract from Mirjana Marković Column in Duga* (Belgrade), December 1994.
67. 'Serbia', *East European Newsletter*, 7 July 1995.
68. 'Karadžić je Američki čovek', Ljubiša Ristić interviewed by Ksenija Janković, *Srpska reč*, 11 September 1995.
69. Nenad LJ Stefanović, 'Ličnosti iz dnevnika Mirjane Marković', *Vreme*, 10 October 1994.
70. Dragan Todorović, 'Šumska priča', *Vreme*, 3 July 1995.
71. *Naša borba*, 25 March 1996 in *SWB/EE2574 A/11*, 30 March 1996.
72. Zoran Jelčić, 'Preobražaj tranzicije', *Vreme*, 16 October 1995.
73. Roksanda Ninčić, 'Poslovi u četiri oka', *Vreme*, 8 February 1997.
74. Djukić (1996), pp. 173-4.
75. 'Nisam socijalistički vojvoda', Vojislav Šešelj interviewed by Tamara Nikčević, *Gradjanin*, 5-6 April 1997.
76. Ognjen Pribičević, 'Serbia's Strongman uses Dayton to Tighten his Grip on Power at Home', *Transition*, 13 December 1996.
77. The song 'Baba Jula' is included on the album *Treći Srpski ustanak* by Riblja Čorba.
78. The apellation 'Red Witch' was often applied to Mirjana Marković in the pages of *Srpska reč*.

21. The Twilight of Greater Serbia – Intervention and Settlement (August–November 1995)

The fighting in Bosnia-Hercegovina in the autumn and winter of 1994 ended in a negotiated truce which came into effect on 1 January 1995, being formally strengthened on 11 January, and was set to last for four months. The year had ended well for the Bosnian Serbs with their forces, fighting in alliance with Muslim forces loyal to the regional power-broker Fikret Abdić, retaking the northern town of Velika Kladuša. Nevertheless individuals the Bosnian Serb camp were increasingly aware that the balance of forces within Bosnia-Hercegovina was shifting against them. The danger to the Bosnian Serb position was underlined when on 20 March Bosnian government forces launched a co-ordinated offensive against Serbian positions around Mount Vlašić and the Majevica hills.

These events further heightened tensions among the Bosnian Serb leaders. Ratko Mladić in particular apparently became convinced that the proportional division of Bosnia-Hercegovina, if not the actual maps, offered in the Contact Group plan should form the basis of a peace settlement. The divisions came out into the open at the meeting of the parliament of the Republika Srpska held on 15-17 April. The civilian representatives accused the military commanders of failing to achieve their military objectives. Mladić hit back, denouncing the politicians for undermining the chain of command and appropriating economic resources which were vital for the war effort. The split between Belgrade and Pale, Mladić declared, was the 'greatest tragedy for the Serbian nation'. It was known that before the meeting of the assembly he and several members of his staff had, on 6 April, visited Belgrade where Karadžić and his fellow-politicians were considered to be *persona non grata*.[1] On 1 May the Croatian army moved against the western Slavonian portion of the RSK. The Milošević government, however, proved unwilling to intervene to defend this region. Paramilitary volunteers from Šešelj's SRS were prevented from reaching the area by the Serbian authorities. The defences of the west Slavonian pocket collapsed swiftly leading to the exodus of most of its 15,000 inhabitants into the Republika Srpska.

Within Bosnia itself the military situation remained a fiercely contested stalemate. In late May the Bosnian Serbs responded to NATO air strikes by taking soldiers of the UN peacekeeping force hostage. The fact that they were only released after the intervention of Jovica Stanišić, the head of the Serbian secret police, who travelled from Belgrade to Pale on the orders of the Serbian President served to reinforce Milošević's image in Western diplomatic circles as an ally in the pursuit of peace. On 15 and 16 June Bosnian government forces in Sarajevo attempted to break out of the city and through the Serbian lines on the surrounding hills. However, their offensive foundered and they sustained heavy casualties during the bitter fighting. On 28 June, shortly after his troops had repelled the Bosnian government assault, Mladić celebrated *Vidovdan* in the town of Bijeljina. Speaking to his fighters, he recalled the circumstances of the battle of Kosovo and affirmed his continuing sense of personal mission. He said that on the day of the battle 'Prince Lazar took communion with his army and submitted himself to the heavenly kingdom, defending his fatherland, faith, freedom and the honour of the Serbian nation. We must understand the essense of that sacrifice so that we can draw from it a historical lesson. The fact that we have today created a victorious army has ensured that Lazar's sacrifice has passed beyond the realms of simple myth.'[2] At the same gathering Mladić was eager to identify himself with the people and the army speaking scornfully of the influence enjoyed by 'highly rated advisers' and other 'marginal persons'. He also criticised paramilitary leaders 'who concerned themselves with running around to jewellery stores, banks and well-supplied supermarkets. There is not a single hill that they kept or liberated. On the other hand our soldiers and officers in the army lead modest lives.'[3] One observer has described Mladić's psychological state during this period as being 'on a perpetual high'.[4]

On 6 July Bosnian Serb forces began an attack on the eastern Bosnian Muslim enclave of Srebrenica. Mladić and the Bosnian

Serb military had long wished to eliminate this pocket of Muslim-controlled territory which acted as a base for Muslim raiders, tied down Bosnian Serb forces, and disrupted Bosnian Serb attempts to form a continuous territory. The attack, however, would not have taken place without it being sanctioned by Milošević and his government in Belgrade. Following the fall of Srebrenica, an estimated several thousand of the captured Muslim men were executed and the women and children were expelled from the enclave.[5] The fall of Srebrenica was followed by the reduction of the nearby Žepa enclave. The taking of Žepa was celebrated by the VRS who declared: 'There is a fact that the Muslim people find unbelievable and difficult to accept, which nevertheless is a cruel and unavoidable reality, with which they must reconcile themselves – Žepa's famed reputation for invincibility is over. Legend tells how over all the centuries since the arrival of the Turkish army, because of the inaccessible natural terrain, the dangerous high mountains and ravines, and because it is inhabited by the most extreme and bloodthirsty descendants of the worst part of the Serbian nation, not one soldier of any army has ever set foot in Žepa. Never – until today.'[6] As the VRS proclaimed their victory among the eastern enclaves, however, disaster was about to overtake the Serbs in the west.

At the end of July regular Croatian forces launched an offensive in western Bosnia, taking the towns of Grahovo and Glamoč. In the immediate aftermath of the Croatian action tensions rose in the RSK, which feared that it was about to be encircled by hostile forces, and on 31 July Ratko Mladić and Patriarch Pavle travelled to Knin to give assurances of military and ecclesiastical solidarity to the Krajina Serbs.[7] On 4 August, however, the Croatian army attacked the RSK, and the Serbian defences crumpled before the sustained Croatian assault. By the summer of 1995 the military odds were stacked against the army of the RSK, which with 50,000 men was outnumbered by the Croatian forces by a ratio of 2:1, outgunned and suffering from serious morale problems. Nevertheless the speed of the Croatian advance, with the military operation largely completed within ninety-six hours, shocked Serbian opinion. The only section of the Krajina left under Serb control was eastern Slavonia. In this case Milošević had not only failed to offer support to the beleaguered Serbs of the RSK, but had also apparently ordered that the Krajina army should withdraw rather than offer sustained resistance to the Croats. For the Serbs the bitterness of defeat would be mixed with anger at this betrayal.

As the army of the RSK pulled back from their positions they were followed by around 165,000 refugees, almost the entire Serbian population of the Krajina. The refugees, harried by the Croatian army and civilian mobs as they fled, sought refuge in Serbia itself, where they were human evidence of the failure of Milošević's policies which could not be concealed from the country's population even by the state-controlled media. The Serbian government responded by seeking to disperse the refugees across the country, and were particularily keen to prevent them from concentrating in the capital. A sense that the Serbs were undergoing a national catastrophe of apocalyptic proportions informed public discourse during the late summer of 1995. Vladan Batić, the DSS Vice-President, denounced Milošević: 'After six centuries Vuk Branković, for the first time, can sleep peacefully in his grave. A bigger traitor has now appeared and his name is Slobodan Milošević.' In less mythic but equally direct terms the 50,000 fans at a 'Red Star Belgrade' match also showed their feelings when they chanted 'Slobo – You have betrayed the Krajina'.[8] Matija Bećković spoke of the flight of the Serbs from Krajina: 'this event has been so great that it is not possible for our minds to comprehend it. For us it is not possible even to reach the foot of this event nor yet to arrive at its summit and survey the whole. Such an event as has befallen the Serbs of Krajina has never before occurred in the history of the whole world. I do not know if such an exodus even occurred in biblical times, nor do I believe such a thing could possibly be imagined.'[9] In spite of the vehemence of such sentiments, which were shared albeit in less dramatic form by many individuals across Serbia, the demonstrations which took place in protest were limited in size. On 7 August the Serbian police intervened to break up a meeting of around 2,000 people led by leaders of non-parliamentary nationalist groupings, including Mirko Jović (SNO) and Milan Paroški (NS), after windows in the American and German embassies were smashed.[10]

In the Republika Srpska Radovan Karadžić took advantage of the fall of the Krajina to attempt to remove Ratko Mladić from his position as head of the General Staff of the VRS. Mladić refused to accept this decision declaring it 'unconstitutional and illegal'. He swiftly secured the support of the military commanders meeting in Banja Luka who signed a letter of protest addressed to the Bosnian Serb assembly meeting at Jahorina. The letter condemned Karadžić's action as 'a mistaken decision, made in the most difficult moment we have faced so far, which will have unforeseeable and negative consequences for our nation, our struggle, and our army. [...] Today, above all, we need the unity of all Serbs and not conflict and division. Every man is needed and particularily such a man as General Mladić whose qualities are known to the whole world as well as to his enemies.'[11] The concentration of the military leaders in Banja Luka and the civilians in Pale brought into focus both the military and regional discontents in the Republika Srpska. The Belgrade government quickly sought to back Mladić with television broadcasts describing him as 'a man of peace...who is ready to sign the Contact group peace plan', while Karadžić and the politicians were attacked as 'war-mongers from Pale'.[12] Karadžić, in spite of enjoying the support of members of the assembly, was forced to backdown before Mladić, who as well as having the backing of the military was revered by the populace of the Republika Srpska. He declared that he had 'decided to stop all announced changes in the army' as a gesture 'in the name of Serb unity and victory'. Mladić, for his part, apparently rejected Milošević's request that he launch a coup against the political leadership. While the two branches of the Bosnian Serb power structure were superficially reconciled fundamental divisions between the military and the politicians remained beneath the surface.[13]

The collapse of the Serbian forces in the Krajina had made the position of the Serbs in the RS even more acute. Before August 1995 the VRS had already been suffering from a profound manpower shortage, which only became more serious when the defeat of the RSK caused them to inherit a new frontier with Croatia. These difficulties led to the emergence of a more pragmatic response by the RS politicians to the latest American peace proposal. This favourable attitude was also prompted by the indications that the new peace plan would recognise, in some form, the division of Bosnia-Hercegovina into two parts, the Muslim-Croat Federa-tion and the Republika Srpska. On 27 August Ratko Mladić, Momčilo Krajišnik and Radovan Karadžić met Milošević in Belgrade and agreed that in future negotiations Milošević should act as the leader of a joint Serbian-RS negotiating team. This decision was endorsed by the Bosnian Serb assembly during a marathon session which lasted from 5.00 p.m. on 28 August until 5.00 a.m. the next day. On 30 August the text of this agreement was published by the Serbian government bearing the signatures of Slobodan Milošević, Momir Bulatović and Zoran Lilić as Presidents of Serbia, Montenegro and Yugoslavia. The political leadership of the RS were represented by Radovan Karadžić, Nikola Koljević, Biljana Plavšić, Momčilo Krajišnik, Aleksa Buha and the Prime Minister of the RS, Dušan Kozić. Ratko Mladić signed for the VRS and Momčilo Perišić for the VJ. The signatures of Patriarch Pavle and bishop Irinej Bulović lent moral and spiritual approval to this declaration of 'Serbian unity'.[14]

On 28 August, however, a mortar shell exploded over Sarajevo's main market place killing thirty-seven people and wounding over eighty-five. Following this incident, on 30 August, NATO aircraft launched waves of airstrikes on Bosnian Serb military targets. The bombing campaign lasted till 14 September when Ratko Mladić agreed to the withdrawal of heavy weapons from around Sarajevo. The air raids had caused particularily heavy damage to the communications systems and logistical resources of the Bosnian Serbs. The effect of the air attacks was manifest during September in the rapid advances made by the Muslim-Croat Federation forces, backed by elements of the regular Croat army, in western Bosnia. Before an agreed ceasefire came into force on 10 October the Serbian-held towns of Donji Vakuf, Jajce, Sanski Most and Mrkonjić Grad had fallen to Federation forces. Observers suggested that the scale of these losses might be accounted for by a selective and deliberate military withdrawal, sanctioned by the Serbian government, in order to bring the land held by Serbian forces into line with the proportional divisions set out in the Contact Group plan.[15] It was noted that while some areas were given up with relatively little resistance the Serbs appeared ready to defend other key positions at Doboj-Ozren, Brčko and Banja Luka.[16] The Croatian journalist Jelena Lovrić, taking into account the obvious tensions between the supposedly allied Mulsims and Croats, saw in the events of the autumn of 1995 the realisation, albeit in a limited form, of the desire of Tudjman and Milošević for the territorial aggrandisement of their states.[17] Such diplomatic and military manouverings, however, produced a new wave of refugees fleeing west.

During the period of the NATO bombing Zoran Djindjić and

the DS backed the defiant stand taken by General Mladić towards the NATO airstrikes: 'If the Serbs withdraw from around Sarajevo, then the 40,000 Muslim soldiers based around Sarajevo will appear on some other front producing a drastic change in the balance of forces.'[18] On 8 September the DS organised a several hundred-strong demonstration outside the American Cultural Centre in central Belgrade. The demonstrators carried placards bearing slogans written in English such as 'NATO go home' and 'Yesterday Vietnam, today Bosnia, tomorrow Russia'.[19] A fiercer and more concerted attack on the conduct of the Milošević government came from the SRS. In the pages of *Velika Srbija* Tomislav Nikolić denounced the Serbian President in mythic terms: 'The Serbian nation remembers Vuk Branković as the greatest traitor in their history. Apart from the folk-songs there is no reliable evidence that Vuk Branković was a traitor or that he was the chief commander of the Serbian army at the battle of Kosovo. You, Mr Milošević, *are* the greatest traitor in history. You *are* the commander of the Serbian armies, your generals lead all the Serbian armies. All that has happened to us happened under your command and the blame for it must fall on your head, or on the head of your wife. [...] You are a foreign body and a force of great evil in the Serbian organism, and such foreign bodies must be expelled. Your death will be a great relief for the Serbian nation. And if you have not been reading this letter carefully I will repeat it one more time: You are the greatest traitor in Serbian history – you are damned.'[20]

On 21 September the SRS held a rally outside the federal parliament to voice their anger at the failure of the Serbian regime to intervene on behalf of the Bosnian and Croatian Serbs. Šešelj addressed a crowd of around 15,000 telling them that Milošević was to blame for the sufferings of the Serbian people and should resign. Šešelj also demanded that the blockade on the RS be lifted and that help should be sent by Serbia to their 'Western brothers'. According to the SRS leader, 'the only place for the Radicals is in prison or in power.'[21] It was notable, however, that the Radicals made efforts to avoid confrontation with the police at the rally. The SPO continued to support acceptance of the Contact Group plan and urged the VRS to comply with the NATO demands for withdrawal of heavy weapons from around Sarajevo. Milan Božić speaking for the SPO, however, made clear that it regarded the Muslim-Croat advances in western Bosnia as

a direct threat to Serbian interests, and an attack on Banja Luka
by the Federation forces would mean that 'Yugoslavia would be
seriously involved in the fighting in that region.'[22] While Milošević
ostentatiously refused to intervene directly in the fighting in western
Bosnia the appearance of Arkan's Serbian Volunteer Guard in
northern Bosnia in late August suggested that the Serbian President
was attempting to exert influence indirectly through his paramilitary
agents. Members of the SDG who were deployed in northern
Bosnia portrayed themselves as having played a critical role in
the defence of Serbian territory and in that way had 'avenged
the honour of the Serbian nation' and proved their worth as the
'nucleus of an operative and professional Serbian army'.[23]

Other accounts of the activities of the SDG were less com-
plimentary. Their role, in reality, appeared to be one of maintaining
internal security for the Republika Srpska regime amongst fleeing
and demoralised refugees.[24] Officers in the VRS complained that
Arkan's paramilitary volunteers had plundered and maltreated
refugees. At one point during an altercation Ražnatović struck a
VRS officer and was promptly disarmed and arrested.[25] On 22
September on hearing of Arkan's arrival in Banja Luka Mladić
had furiously demanded that Ražnatović remove himself and the
SDG from the territory of the Republika Srpska within forty-eight
hours. The SDG, however, remained in Bosnia, apparently at the
invitation of the Interior Ministry of the RS.[26] Ražnatović participated in the Bosnian Serb assembly, held on 16 October, although it was unclear who he was meant to be representing.[27]
Radovan Karadžić had used the deliberations of the assembly to
attempt, once again, to assert his control over the military. The
assembly resolved to remove the Prime Minister of the RS, Dušan
Kozić, who was widely considered to be a political figurehead,
and five VRS generals who were regarded as close confidants of
Ratko Mladić. On 17 October the military high command of
the VRS indicated that they would ignore the decision of the
political leadership describing it as 'unconstitutional and unlawful'.
The events of September/October cast an interesting light on
both the internal politics of the RS, and the role of intervention
from Serbia itself by the Milošević government. They demonstrate
that there was no permanent division in loyalties between those
aligned with Belgrade and those with the Pale leadership. While
Mladić had from August 1994-5 been seen as aligned with the

Belgrade government against the Republika Srpska political leadership, during September/October he was willing to engage in a political struggle with Arkan the paramilitary leader who was acting as an agent of the Milošević regime. At the same time the RS Interior Ministry and secret police, whose powers Karadžić had enhanced in order to safeguard his position against a possible coup attempt directed from Belgrade, was to show itself willing to co-operate with Ražnatović and his followers. Ražnatović and an SDG delegation were the honoured guests of the Bosnian Serb leadership at a meeting of SDS activists on 23 October in the town of Bijeljina.[28] The politics of the RS, and of Serbia, would continue to take the form of a kaleidoscopic landscape of shifting loyalties and interests.

Throughout this period of political/military crisis the SPO had continued to develop its apparent rapprochement with the Milošević government. Drašković spoke in increasingly favourable terms of what he perceived to be the changed politics of the Serbian President. In one interview he observed that: 'If you compare Milošević before May 1993 with the Milošević of today you will see two different men. Today Milošević's speeches include whole passages from the programme of the SPO – 'We do not defend Serbia in Knin, but rather defend Knin in Serbia. To us life is the greatest national interest; peace and not war, the cradle and not the grave, wealth and not poverty, co-operation with the world and not the prison of the world.'[29] The impression of cordial relations between the SPO and SPS was reinforced by a series of meetings which took place between the leaders of these parties. On 11 July a meeting was held, hosted by Dušan Mitević, between Vuk and Danica Drašković, ND leader Dušan Mihailović and the influential government supporting businessman, Bogoljub Karić.[30] In mid-August Drašković met Milošević apparently in order to discuss the newly-issued SPO 'Programme of National and State Rebirth'. This policy document consisted of a twelve-point plan for Serbia's future including a programme of privatisation and 'Europeanisation' of the economy, professionalisation of the army, de-politicisation of the police, and freeing of the media.[31] There was, however, widespread scepticism among other political groupings over whether Milošević had met Drašković simply to discuss the finer points of policy. Speculation became rife that the SPO was about to enter the Milošević government and its political rivals took to referring to the SPO as the 'coalition partner' of the SPS. By the end of September the Serbian popular press was even naming the candidates for office from the SPO and the ministerial portfolio's which, they said, would imminently be taken by them.[32] The SPO fiercely denied that a coalition agreement was under discussion with Danica Drašković stating that such an alliance would be a repudiation of the SPO's ideological/symbolic heritage. She said: 'There has been no talk of entering the government. For us to enter the government and celebrate the 7 July would be a defeat for our politics.'[33] Vuk Drašković himself was equally dismissive of such speculations as mere 'café talk'.[34] In spite of the common ground shared temporarily by the SPO and the SPS regarding their attitudes to the Contact Group peace plan, the fundamental differences between these parties, at the level of ideology and identity, would have precluded any more permanent or formal co-operation between them. The willingness of Milošević to listen to Vuk Drašković's political views and concerns during this period most probably arose from his desire to compromise the SPO leader in the eyes of the other opposition groupings, and the Serbian electorate. Drašković would later attest that he finally realised that there was no basis for a constructive relationship with the SPS government when, in late November, Zoran Lilić returned from China and hailed its social and economic achievments, a position which contrasted strongly with Drašković's stated desire to pursue a Europeanist agenda.

This apparent flirtation between Drašković and Milošević, however, was merely a distraction in comparison to the rise of JUL on the Serbian political scene, and its increasingly open attempts to displace key SPS personnel. In late 1994 Zoran Čičak, an official of the SK-PJ had launched an attack on the SPS leaders, Mihailo Marković, Milorad Vučelić and Borisav Jović, describing them as 'the greatest warmongers in the Serbian government'.[35] These named individuals protested vociferously at this attack from within the left camp and Čičak was duly expelled from the leadership of the SK-PJ. It was later to become apparent that Čičak had prematurely revealed the strategy being formulated by the Milošević-Mirjana Marković axis. All three of these individuals would fall from power between August and November 1995. This 'changing of the guard' within the ranks of the ruling elite began on 15 August with the removal of the Yugoslav Foreign Minister, Vladisav

Jovanović, and his replacement by Milan Milutinović. Jovanović was said to have been unhappy at the passive stance taken by the Yugoslav government regarding the fate of the Krajina. On 31 August Milorad Vučelić, the head of RTS and the leader of the Socialist parliamentary group was replaced by Dragoljub Milanović. One journalistic observer commented caustically on this change: 'Of the two evils Vučelić was the lesser...at least he read books.'[36] Mihailo Marković had also been increasingly dissatisfied with the course that the Serbian government had taken in regard to the Croatian and Bosnian Serbs. During August and September Marković had offered Milošević some increasingly outspoken 'comradely criticism' of his attitude towards the 'national question': 'For those who desire peace at any price, capitulation is something which can be easily accepted.'[37] Unfortunately for Marković, however, his advice was rejected and he was summarily deprived of his position within the SPS at a meeting of the party's Main Committee on 28 November. Mihailo Marković was also well known to be one of the leading opponent's within the SPS of Mirjana Marković and her followers from JUL. He observed of JUL that: 'There are amongst its leaders sincere leftists and honest individuals, but many of them are simply mafiosi and war profiteers.'[38] Another casualty of the 28 November purge was Borisav Jović, the SPS Vice-President in 1992-5 and former member of the pre-1992 Yugoslav Presidency. The ostensible reason for his removal was the exception taken by Milošević to the revelations contained within Jović's memoir, *Poslednji dani SFRJ* (The Last Days of the SFRY). Having been pushed out of the circles of power Jović was ready to make clear his opposition to the dominant position that JUL was gaining: 'It has now come so far that JUL receives more space on radio and television than our party does! I am also opposed to JUL because that left-wing party is headed by the wife of the Republic's President, and that is a fact which is difficult for our people to understand or to bear. [...] Our people find it difficult to accept that two members of the same family should head two parties. And not only two parties – because of their personal power and ambitions we have here the makings of a dynasty.'[39] In his disquiet at the role of JUL, Jović's statements were simply the tip of an iceberg of discontent existing within the SPS. The individuals who were ousted during this period were all people who had been intimately connected with the rise to power of Slobodan Milošević. Mihailo Marković had since the founding of the SPS acted as the party's main ideologist giving articulation to its mixture of nationalism and socialism. Milorad Vučelić, as head of RTS, had managed the Serbian media during Milošević's 1991-2 nationalist phase, and had ensured that it remained a key instrument of social control for the SPS. During the same period Jović, as a member of the SFRY presidency, had acted as a faithful executor of Milošević's policy in the diplomatic moves which had led to the dissolution of the old Yugoslavia. Their displacement signalled Milošević's determination to cut himself off from his political roots.

Other senior members of the SPS 'old guard' also fell victim to this autumn purge. Živorad Minović, the editor of *Politika*, was replaced on 5 October by Hadži Dragan Antić, a close associate of the political/commercial clique surrounding Mirjana Marković. Radovan Pankov, head of the SPS in Vojvodina, and Slobodan Jovanović, head of the state news agency *Tanjug*, were also ousted on 28 November.

These domestic political manouvres took place alongside international diplomatic moves to achieve a peace settlement in the former Yugoslavia. The first significant breakthrough in the peace process came on 8 September during negotiations in Geneva. This agreement involved the recognition of a number of negotiating principles including: the recognition of Bosnia-Hercegovina within its international borders, the division of the country into two 'entities', the Muslim-Croat Federation and the Republika Srpska, and a 51:49 per cent territorial division between these two units. The political reaction within Serbia to this agreement was mixed. The Main Committee of the SPS issued a statement which hailed the agreement as representing 'a victory for the principled and persistent peace policy pursued by Slobodan Milošević'. Drašković welcomed the news from Geneva suggesting that it marked 'the ending of a time of death and the dawning of a time of peace'. Vesna Pešić stated that the Geneva agreement marked the 'acceptance of the existence of Bosnia-Hercegovina as an independent state and the abandonment of all territorial pretensions towards Bosnia-Hercegovina' with the Serbian entity 'probably enjoying some independence within Bosnia-Hercegovina'. The leaders of the DSS and the DS were, however, more cautious about the agreement with Koštunica stressing that 'many difficult territorial and constitutional questions remained to be resolved' while Zoran Djindjić observed: 'It [the agreement] mentions the Republika Srpska which indicates a readiness to recognise its existence as a legal entity, satisfying the just demand of the Serbs in the former Bosnia-Hercegovina to live in their own state within the union of Bosnia-Hercegovina.'[40] On 26 September the Foreign Ministers of Yugoslavia, Croatia and Bosnia-Hercegovina met for a new round of talks in New York hosted by the US Assistant Secretary of State, Richard Holbrooke. The subsequent declaration sought to set out the basic constitutional principles for the operation of a future post-war Bosnia-Hercegovina. The negotiations reconvened at the American airbase at Dayton on 1st November. Milošević, as had been agreed prior to the NATO intervention, headed a joint FRY/Republika Srpska negotiating team. While Milošević was in Dayton his responsibilities as President of Serbia were temporarily left in the hands of the President of the Serbian parliament, Dragan Tomić. Figures within the Serbian opposition were quick to comment on the incongruity of Milošević taking on the mantle of a 'peacemaker'. Zoran Djindjić remarked: 'The irony of our situation is that the loudest cries for peace come precisely from the most bitter opponents of democracy. Peace has become the oath of those who are dedicated to creating a personal monopoly of power, those who are turning the media into personal propaganda services, those who are at the same time violating even the most elementary human rights which they profess to accept. The regime in Serbia cannot secure a normal and lasting peace because such a peace can be secured only by a regime which practises reconciliation and compromise, a regime which creates mechanisms for the fulfillment of the above objectives. The mechanisms for reaching compromise are the mechanisms of a democratic state: delegation of power, an independent legal system, independent media. Peace is the straw at which Milošević is clutching, hoping that, with the help of this straw he will manage to save his undemocratic regime.'[41] The Dayton peace agreement was concluded on 21 November, and was officially signed in Paris on 14 December. The agreement, as had been expected, confirmed the existence of a Bosnian state where a weak central authority held sway over two territorial units, the Muslim-Croat Federation and the Republika Srpska. The Bosnian Serb leadership, however, were horrified by the agreed territorial division which granted full control over Sarajevo to the Muslim-Croat Federation.

The Dayton agreement contained clauses providing for the return of refugees to their former homes. Its most immediate result, however, was to prompt a new exodus of refugees from the Serbian held suburbs of Sarajevo which were due to be handed over to Bosnian government control. Some international diplomats initially expressed the hope that the Serbian population would remain in the suburbs and demonstrate the viability of a multicultural Sarajevo. The logic and circumstances of the war, however, had demonstrated such beliefs to be misplaced, and made the flight of a majority of the Serb population inevitable. Their departure, however, was hastened both by the manipulations of the Bosnian Serb political leaders, and the hardline attitude of the Muslim representatives of the Bosnian government. The Serbs from the Sarajevo suburbs made, ultimately futile, attempts to mobilise against this provision of the Dayton accords. One rally of 7,000 people held in the Ilidža suburb was addressed by seventeen-year-old Vanja Vujadin, who told the demonstrators: 'The ground is full of our blood. [...] The graves are a source of power for new generations.'[42] As the refugees left the suburbs, some exhumed their dead relatives to take their remains with them. Houses and flats in the suburbs went up in flames, burned either by their departing inhabitants or by gangs of arsonists who roamed the area. Ljubiša Lazić, a Serb from the Grbavica suburb, expressed the despairing sense of betrayal felt towards Slobodan Milošević when he reproached him as follows: 'Do you remember the time when the people chanted your name Slobo, Slobodo [freedom]? Do you remember it, our leader? We were those people who dedicated our lives to your idea – all the Serbs in a single state. You have since renounced and betrayed everything to do with Cyril, Christ and St Sava...with your right hand you destroyed our soul and strangled us. Leader, you have the power. Tell us how we can put out the candles and open up the graves. Our Sarajevo was not bought, it was born with us...if we lose Sarajevo then we are all lost. We do not believe this is you, leader, but some confused civilian. You are not the man whose picture we kept like an icon.'[43] Throughout the winter of 1995 and the early spring of 1996 Serbian refugees streamed out of the suburbs in anticipation of their hand-over to the Muslim-Croat Federation.

Many of the new refugees were settled in areas such as Srebrenica and Brčko where the politicians of the Republika Srpska wished to establish their ethnic/demographic dominance while others swelled the ranks of the dispossessed within Serbia itself.

The Dayton agreement also specified that individuals indicted as war criminals by the Hague War Crimes Tribunal should take no part in post-Dayton political life in Bosnia-Hercegovina in that way theoretically excluding their political and military leaders, Radovan Karadžić and Ratko Mladić. The ownership of the strategic town of Brčko, which linked the Republika Srpska to Serbia as well as joining the northern and southern halves of the Serbian entity, was to be decided by international arbitration. On 22 November, as part of the terms of the Dayton agreement, sanctions on the Federal Republic of Yugoslavia were suspended. They would be formally lifted after 'free and fair' elections had been held in Bosnia-Hercegovina.

When the terms of the Dayton agreement were announced in Serbia Zoran Lilić declared that this agreement 'means the beginning of a new era in the Balkans'. Mile Ilić, the loyal SPS *apparatchik* from Niš, suggested that Milošević should be nominated for the Nobel peace prize. New Democracy praised the 'tolerance and political wisdom' which the Serbian delegation had showed at Dayton. Vojislav Šešelj fulminated against the agreement and suggested that new 'betrayals' awaited the Serbian people at the hands of their government. 'Next in line', he warned 'are the Republika Srpska, Montenegro, Kosovo, Sandžak and Vojvodina.' For Vojislav Koštunica Dayton was a 'peace with little justice'. Zoran Djindjić responded to the news from Dayton by observing: 'There is no particular reason for euphoria or triumphalism because a difficult period of renewal in the lands of the former Bosnia-Hercegovina lies ahead of us, as well as the task of building of democratic institutions in Serbia and Yugoslavia.'[44] Of the major opposition forces only the SPO and the GSS welcomed the Dayton agreement, with Vuk Drašković declaring 'We are happy with the signing of the peace agreement in Paris and we pay tribute to those who have contributed to the halting of the madness of war. [...] I would also like the signing of peace in Bosnia and Croatia to be a lesson to us here in Serbia. We should sign up to peace here too. We should end half a century of war hatred, we should stop hatred in general, and we should put a stop to ideological divisions.'[45]

As 1995 drew to a close Milošević had every reason to be pleased with the course politics had taken. The international community had accepted him, albeit reluctantly as a guarantor of peace in the Balkans and a pillar of the Dayton agreement. Milošević could now present himself to the Serbian people as a man who had brought Serbia peace, relief from the sanctions regime, and acceptance back into the international community. His grip on the state institutions and the party apparatus appeared to be unchallenged. In the last months of 1995 he had for instance continued to tighten the state system of control over the media. In early September the local Socialist authorities in Kragujevac had sought to take over the independent weekly journal *Svetlost*. This magazine, like *Naša borba* the previous year was forced to reconstitute itself as a new publication *Nezavisna svetlost* (Independent Svetlost).[46] While discontent at the role of JUL was germinating at the grassroots level within the SPS no one within the SPS hierarchy was willing openly to defy Milosević or had reason to do so.

The forces ranged against Milošević were weak and divided. A significant section of the opposition had acted in alliance with the leadership of the SDS in Bosnia-Hercegovina. The Bosnian Serbs, however, had been defeated on the battlefield and humiliated at the negotiating table. Vuk Drašković and the SPO had eschewed this course, but the fact that he had travelled down the same political path as the regime had left him tainted in the eyes of many opposition supporters. Nevertheless the fundamental weakness of the Serbian economy, and the inability of the Milošević government to address this problem would form an increasing source of popular discontent in post-Dayton Serbia. The task of the Serbian opposition would be to provide an effective and coherent focus for such discontents.

Notes

1. Filip Švarm, 'Civilno-vojni igrokaz', *Vreme*, 24 April 1995.
2. 'Vreme i ljudi', *Vreme*, 10 July 1995.
3. Robert Block, 'Serbs Idolise Bosnia's Bloodstained Warlord', *Independent*, 30 June 1995.

4. Jan Willem Honig and Norbert Both, *Srebrenica – The Record of a War Crime*, Penguin (London), 1996, p. 179.
5. The exact numbers killed in the aftermath of the fall of Srebrenica remain unclear. This issue is discussed in Hong and Both (1996), pp. 64-6.
6. Goran Maunaga, 'Konačna demilitarizacija', *Srpska vojska*, 25 August 1995.
7. Robert Block, 'Men of God and Guns Come Down to Knin', *Independent*, 1 August 1995.
8. Laura Silber, 'Serbs Turn on their Big Daddy', *Observer*, 13 August 1995.
9. 'Vreme i Ijudi', *Vreme*, 26 September 1995.
10. Uroš Komlenović, 'Nedelja', *Vreme*, 14 August 1995.
11. 'Jači smo jer je prvada na našoj strani', *Srpska vojska*, 25 August 1995.
12. Miloš Vašić, 'Presednik ili general', *Vreme*, 14 August 1995.
13. Emma Daly, 'Karadžić Bows to General Over Control of the Army', *Independent*, 12 August 1995.
14. Ivan Radovanović *et al.*, 'Savez jednog', *Vreme*, 4 September 1995.
15. Mirko Klarin, 'Misterija vojnog kolapsa bosanskih Srba', *Naša borba*, 19 September 1995.
16. Xavier Bougarel, 'Bosnia-Hercegovina – State and Communitarianism', in David Dyker and Ivan Vejvoda (eds) *Yugoslavia and After – A Study of Fragmentation, Despair and Rebirth*, Longman (London) 1996, p. 113.
17. Jelena Lovrić, 'Preraspodela' Bosne – začetak velike Hrvatske i velike Srbije', *Naša borba* 19 September 1995.
18. 'U Vašingtonu je ključ rata i mira', Zoran Djindjić interviewed by Vojislava Vignjević, *Naša borba*, 2-3 September 1995.
19. 'Protest zbog NATO bombardovanja', *Naša borba*, 9-10 September 1995.
20. Tomislav Nikolić, 'Otvoreno pismo komunističkom diktatoru Slobodanu Miloševiću', *Velika Srbija*, September 1995.
21. 'Šešelj – Povratićemo sve srpske teritorije', *Naša borba*, 22 September 1995.
22. Vera Didanović, 'Pad Banjaluke uvukao bi Jugoslaviju u rat', *Naša borba*, 19 September 1995.
23. Rade Dušanović, 'Garda odbranila Prijedor', *Pogledi*, 25 December 1995.
24. Milan Milutinović, 'Ko je pozvao Arkana', *NIN*, 28 February 1997.
25. Dejan Anastasijević, 'Tigrovska posla', *Vreme*, 16 October 1995.
26. Milutinović, *NIN*, 28 February 1997.
27. Julian Borger, 'Serbs Crowd Infamous Prison Camp', *Guardian*, 17 October 1995.
28. Dragan Todorović, 'Haški handicap', *Vreme*, 30 October 1995.
29. 'Guraću na svaka vrata', Vuk Drašković interviewed by Perica Vučinić, *Vreme*, 21 August 1995.
30. Djukić (1997), pp. 193-4.
31. 'Kao jesenja kiša', Vuk Drašković interviewed by Petar Ignja, *NIN*, 1 September 1995.
32. 'Kako će se formirati nova srpska vlada', *Telegraf*, 20 September 1995.
33. Danica Draúsković interviewed in *Naša borba*, 2-3 September 1995.
34. Dragan Bujošević, 'Ikona i sekira', *NIN*, 13 October 1995.
35. Pribićević, *Transition*, 13 December 1996.
36. Dragoljub Petrović, 'Lomljenje tvrdog krila – čovek na liniji', *Naša borba*,

37. 'Kritikovao sam Miloševića', Mihailo Marković interviewed by Vladan Dinić, *Telegraf*, 13 September 1995.
38. 'Ljudi i vreme', *Vreme*, 23 October 1995.
39. 'JUL je velika greška', Borisav Jović interviewed in *Republika* (Ljubljana), reprinted in *Vreme*, 29 July 1996.
40. The reactions of the political leaders to the Geneva agreement are given in *Naša borba*, 9-10 September 1995.
41. Zoran Djindjić, 'Rat, mir, demokratija', *Demokratija*, October/November 1995.
42. Patrick Bishop, 'Serbs Vow Never to Accept the Muslim "Devil",' *Daily Telegraph*, 30 December 1995.
43. SRNA, 7 December 1995 in *SWB EE/2482 A/1*, 9 December 1995.
44. Milan Milošević, 'Skidanje madjije', *Vreme*, 27 November 1995.
45. Serbian Radio, 14 December 1995 in *SWB EE/2488 A/11*, 16 December 1995.
46. Uroš Komlenović, 'Svetlost u mraku', *Vreme*, 11 September 1995.

22. Serbia After Dayton – The Illusion of Change (November 1995–March 1996)

The SPS was keen to emphasise that it had embraced the new political age which, it was said, had dawned with the signing of the Dayton agreement. In December 1995 it was announced that in March 1996 the SPS would hold its Third Party Congress at which the new party programme entitled 'Serbia 2000 – A Step into the New Century' would be presented to the domestic and international public. The SPS Vice-Chairman, Goran Perčević, looked forward optimistically: [The SPS] as a modern left-wing party definitely has the strength and cadre to respond to all challenges and lead Serbia and Yugoslavia into the next century.'[1] Socialist officials also appeared to be competing with each other to give the highest estimate of the rate at which SPS membership was growing. On 24 January 1996 Uroš Šuvaković, a member of the SPS Main Committee and General Secretary of the Young Socialists, told *Politika* that in the previous two months the SPS had recruited 12,000 new members. This was followed on 26 January by Nikola Šainović, the SPS Vice-President and a member of the Co-ordinating Committee for the Third Party Congress, stating in the same journal that 30,000 new members had joined the SPS.[2] The prospects for the SPS seemed to get better and better by the day.

The Serbian opposition by contrast entered the post-Dayton era in a mood of introspection as it went through a series of realignments in search of a viable way to oppose the SPS. In late October and early November there had been a number of defections from the ranks of the DSS to the DS including Tihomir Milošević, a member of the DSS Main Committee, Miodrag Stanisavljević, head of the area committee in Peć, and several senior members from Leskovac. According to Miodrag Stanisavljević he had

returned to the DS from the DSS because, under Djindjić's leadership, the party had broadened its appeal and had ceased to be an
'elitist' or 'Belgrade' party. Following these arrivals senior figures
within the DS, including Slobodan Gavrilović, the DS Vice-
President from Užice, and Miodrag Perišić, launched an initiative
for the reunification of the DS and the DSS. This move was,
however, decisively rejected by the Main Committee of DSS.
The DSS indicated that while it considered that policy differences
prevented any union between the two groups, it was willing to
discuss further co-operation between the parties. Djindjić responded
positively to this statement, suggesting: 'For us successful co-operation
with the DSS is more important than having half of their members
defect to us.'[3]

The DS itself was afflicted by internal dissension. On 2 December
Dragoljub Mićunović and Velimir Simonović were expelled from
it after being accused of 'party indiscipline' and 'damaging the
reputation of the party'. Mićunović described his exclusion as a
clear attempt 'to amputate the peacemaking part of the party',[4]
and on 22 February 1996 he reconstituted his Democratic Centre
faction into an independent political party. Among those who
left the DS in order to join Mićunović in the DC was Desimir
Tošić who commented that: 'I have nothing in common with
today's Democrats. Of the party of 1989/90-4 only the name
now remains.'[5]

On 3 December 1995, the day after Mićunović was removed,
it was announced that a new Democratic Alliance (DA) was being
formed which would unite the DS, DSS, SLS and SNS. The DA
was formally constituted as a coalition on 25 December. Its founding
declaration described it as 'a bloc of democratic and patriotic
parties' and set out among its aims 'the setting up of a democratic
order of freedom, the rule of law, genuine party pluralism, sound
parliamentarism, responsible government and efficacious opposition'
and 'the reintegration of our people and state into Europe in a
manner which does not impair our sovereignty, equality, and
independence'. The DA also pledged itself to 'unceasing care for
the entire Serb people and for our fellow countrymen on the
other side of the rivers Danube and Drina in particular'.[6]

On 18 December it was announced that the National Party
(NS) led by Milan Paroški was merging with the DS.[7] This decision
proved highly controversial; while by late 1995 Paroški's organisa-

tion was largely dormant politically, it had in the early 1990s enjoyed a reputation for active and militant nationalism. When asked why someone with Paroški's nationalist credentials had been welcomed into the ranks of the DS, Djindjić sought to rationalise his decision: 'He remains in the memory of the people not for all his talk of the monarchy but rather as a fighter against the abuses of Radoman Božović. On our political scene there exists a deficit of popular tribunes, who will fight against such abuses. It is now a vital necessity for us to work with all those in whom the people have faith.'[8]

The formation of the DA and the merger of the NS with the Democratic Party appeared to confirm Djindjé's party on the 'national democratic' course pursued from the autumn of 1994 into 1995. However, there were, also signs that the DS during this period was seeking to bring to prominence the social/economic aspects in the party identity with a consequent relative downplaying, but not abandonment, of the national element. Djindjić remarked: 'Since 1988 the Serbian national question has been an issue on the political scene. When the party was created that theme was number one, and the next five places were empty. With the coming of peace it will fall into third place, and in the first two will be found "quality of life" [economic and social questions] and "entry into Europe" (whether we remain with the Byzantine variant of Socialism or finally accept European standards). The political tradition in Serbia shows that since 1850 there has never existed any political party which has been silent on the national question.' Djindjić also sought to distinguish his position adopted during the period of the Belgrade-Pale schism from that maintained by other nationalists: 'We never made any suggestions regarding borders, nor did we speak of "sacred territory". Of the ten motions that we moved in parliament only one proposed a confederation with the Republika Srpska while the others dealt with pensions, privatisations, interest rates....'[9] Djindjić also continued to assert that the DS was the primary political force in the Serbian civic 'centre'. In an interview given in February 1996 Djindjić sought to define the Serbian political scene in the following terms: 'In Serbia there exist three political positions. One is the Socialist administrative way which brings into each person's life a small dose of social corruption. That is the position taken by the SPS and its competitor JUL. The other tradition is that of national populism of which there is a radical tradition in Serbia. It is an anti-European, anti-development and provincial mentality. The followers of this course have little discipline or organisation they do not know about expenditure and their only aim is to have a little, bread, potatoes and meat. The SPO began in that position and they voluntarily left it, and then later Šešelj settled in the same place. The third position is one of development and modernisation, what some call the civic position. This position favours structural change and the DS occupied it at a relatively early stage. The Liberal Party and the DSS which split off from us have not found a fourth position. And neither has Vuk.'[10] The DS was active at this time in seeking to cultivate international contacts as part of its own effort to achieve Serbian reintegration into 'Europe'. In late January 1996 a DS delegation visited Strasbourg to discuss future Yugoslav relations with the Council of Europe. According to Djindjić the representatives that the DS had met all 'expressed an interest in Yugoslavia's return to the European family'.[11]

In mid-December 1995 Djindjić made it clear during a visit to Kragujevac that while he and the DS still offered their support to the people of the Republika Srpska, he was distancing himself politically from the Bosnian Serb leadership. He had not, he said, met Karadžić and Krajišnik since the previous January and had found them 'completely cut off from reality'. He was, however, ready to see the breakdown in the political divisions which had characterised the Serbian political scene in the preceding period. In particular he offered the 'hand of reconciliation' to the leader of the SPO. Vuk Drašković reciprocated these sentiments when shortly afterwards he spoke in the same location. 'The war is over and there is no more division between war and anti-war lobbies.' In the post-war period, he said, it was necessary for 'all parties and civic associations who are dedicated to the idea of democratic change to unite in one front for the salvation of Serbia from those who want to revive the communist corpse and create a Balkan Cuba or [North] Korea.'[12] After a meeting held in Belgrade, in the same month, to discuss the post-Dayton political situation Drašković announced that the SPO would organise a rally on 9 March 1996 in order to commemorate the demonstrations which took place five years earlier. He also repeated his call for the formation of an anti-government electoral alliance under the slogan 'One List – No Communists'.[13]

The first concrete manifestation of the new spirit of opposition co-operation came when on 26 December all the opposition parliamentary parties (SPO, SRS, DS, DSS, DZVM, GSS) decided to boycott the Serbian parliament and hold their own 'parallel parliament' in protest at the government's decision to suspend TV coverage of the parliament's proceedings. The opposition parties sought to emphasise their common need to defend parliament from the encroachments of the government. The attempt, on 1 February 1996, by the 'parallel parliament' to adopt two documents entitled 'The Violation of Human Rights in Serbia' and 'The Democratic Transformation of Serbia' was, however, disrupted when the Vice-President of the Serbian parliament, Miroslav Zdravković, banned the opposition deputies from holding their meetings within the parliament building. The opposition leaders were forced to give an improvised press conference on the steps of the parliament building.[14] In spite of the obvious policy differences between the parties involved in the 'parallel parliament', Vuk Drašković saw such a 'grand coalition' as a means by which the SPS could be defeated. He justified such an arrangement, whereby forces as diverse as the SRS and the Vojvodina Hungarians would be united under the same banner, saying: 'In the face of storms and blizzards the wolf, the bear, the fox, and the hare will be found gathered together in the same cave.'[15] Drašković was even apparently willing to make overtures towards New Democracy as a future member of such an inclusive coalition. Speaking in Valjevo on 6 January, Drašković replied to one of his supporters who suggested that New Democracy were 'traitors and thieves' by observing that the SPO and ND had similar programmes, and that Dušan Mihailović 'without having any bad intentions had unsuccessfully attempted to change the government from within.'[16]

Strong personal animosities, however, continued to divide the Serbian opposition and make any such broad-based co-operation difficult to sustain. Šešelj, for instance, talked of his readiness to work with the major Serbian parliamentary parties, the SPO, DS, and DSS. His deputy, Tomislav Nikolić, however, frequently made clear his detestation of Drašković and the SPO in terms which would realistically preclude any effective collaboration. The unreconstructed ultra-nationalist Nikolić Drašković was reviled not simply for his opposition to the war but also because as someone who had once followed a populist nationalist path his adoption of an anti-war stance was considered to be a form of apostasy. In late 1995 Nikolić said: 'Vuk Drašković would now be happy to deny that he had written some of his books. I believe that he would love it if he had never written "The Knife" because that book talks of how we cannot live with the Muslims because they came on the Orthodox Christmas, fell on the village and slaughtered the infants in the cradle. But when Vuk thought people were afraid of the war in Bosnia he said "Bosnia must be united" or his wife, who is the ideologue of the party, said: "If my brother in Grbavica [a Sarajevo suburb] bombards Sarajevo then I would approve of NATO bombing my brother." I know that there is something morally wrong in this.' This was a theme which Nikolić would return to when in the spring of 1996 he told an interviewer: 'I feel particularly bitter towards the SPO because I know that in 1991 it drew into its ranks many honourable Serbian patriots, because their programme was one of a Serbian nationalist party, and the writings and declarations of their President were absolutely dedicated to the defence of the Serbian national interest. And as well as all that he formed the Serbian Guard, raised volunteers from across Serbia, and sent them into battle.'[17]

The most venerable of Serbian institutions, the Orthodox church, was also rocked by internal disputes in the aftermath of the Dayton agreement. Hardline bishops within it believed that because Patriarch Pavle had put his name to the document recognising Milošević as the leader of the FRY-Bosnian Serb delegation at the peace negotations he had therefore given his blessing to what they saw as the betrayal of Bosnian Serb interests. The attacks on the Patriarch were spearheaded by Bishop Atanasije of Zahumlje-Hercegovina who commanded the loyalty of ten other bishops. It was rumoured that Pavle would resign in the face of these assaults or else that the bishops would tender their resignations as a sign of protest at the direction church policy was taking under Pavle's leadership. These internal convulsions culminated in a behind closed doors meeting of the church assembly held on 21 December 1995. The Patriarch survived these attacks on his leadership, but his subsequent statements attacking the Dayton agreement were seen as attempts to placate the militant elements within the church.[18] Other Orthodox clerics, however, were willing to make unambiguous statements in support of the Dayton agreement. Bishop Hrizostom who administered the area of north-west Bosnia centred on Banja Luka stated after the signing of the peace treaty: 'This is the moment that we decide whether we will be the beggars of this world or whether we will return to our homes as the international accords and conventions foresee. They [The Bosnian Serb leaders] are cheating you when they tell you that they have solved our problems by giving us burned and looted homes that belong to others, who are also refugees just as we are.'[19]

Even while the opposition was seeking to adapt to the new circumstances the authorities moved to place further restrictions on the freedom of independent media. On 15 February the state authorities, following the same procedure which had been used in the attempt to stifle *Borba* in December 1994, declared that independent TV Studio B had been incorrectly privatised and should be returned to social ownership under the control of the SPS dominated Belgrade city assembly. A new management board was appointed headed by Ljubiša Milić, a leading Socialist official. The imposition of Socialist control over Studio B effectively closed down the last TV channel which had been willing to give space to opposition opinions. The Socialist takeover of Studio B was accompanied by the sacking of twenty of the station's journalists. It was announced that under the new management there would be a switch in emphasis from news and current affairs to entertainment and sport. On 16 February several hundred Studio B employees and opposition supporters demonstrated against the takeover. The leaders of the SPO, DS, DSS, GSS and the National party of Montenegro also held a joint press conference. Vuk Drašković asked: 'Do the agreements in Dayton and Paris give Slobodan Milošević the freedom to do whatever he likes in Serbia?'[20] Vojislav Koštunica was also critical of the attitude of the international community, saying: 'The position of the West has changed since 1989. Then they insisted on respect for human rights, a democratic society, and the creation of equal conditions for the organisation of political parties. In the meantime the USSR has ceased to exist and in the former Yugoslavia the war began. I think that their criteria have now been lowered and have contracted to just one formal position – a democracy exists where there is more than one party and where elections take place. In this present phase Milošević is necessary to them and they will not ask anything more from him, but it is possible that in a subsequent phase he will become superfluous to them.'[21] A number of Western intellectuals and independent organisations, including the International Federation of Journalists, and Reporters Sans Frontières, did rally to the support of Studio B, issuing statements sharply critical of the Milošević regime. The reactions of Western governments, who actually had the power to influence the policy of the Serbian authorities, were, however, muted. The EU commissioner Hans van den Broek demanded that 'measures be taken to preserve the independence of Studio B', but no concrete steps were taken to back up these sentiments. On 13 March after meeting Milošević the US Assistant Secretary of State John Kornblum was quoted in *Naša borba* as saying: 'I told Milošević there are some areas where democracy in Serbia is not as complete as it should be. Freedom of the press is one of them.' He went on: 'We do believe that nothing more will be banned here.' An observer commented that this was indeed correct in the sense that 'as far as the electronic media is concerned there's nothing left to ban.'[22] The Studio B episode demonstrated Milošević's willingness to violate with impunity basic democratic procedures, the apparent inability of the opposition to mobilise their supporters in any great numbers to oppose these moves, and the unwillingness of the West to undermine Milošević, who was accepted as a 'man they could do business with'.

Notes

1. Serbian TV, 1 December 1995 in *SWB EE/2478 A/15*, 5 December 1995.
2. N. Kovačević, 'Koliko nas je?', *Naša borba*, 29 January 1996.
3. Srboljub Bogdanović, 'Neuspeo flert', *NIN*, 17 November 1995; Nenad LJ Stefanovic, 'Radna grupa za Koštunicu', Vreme, 20 November 1995; Miodrag Stanisavljevic, 'Zbrka oko ujedinjenja', *Vreme*, 4 December 1995.
4. Stan Markotich, 'For the Serbian Opposition the Possibility of Peace Brings Little Unity', *Transition*, 12 January 1996.
5. 'Mi stranaka više nemamo', Desimir Tošić interviewed by Milan Milošević, *Vreme*, 23 March 1996.
6. The founding declaration of the Democratic Alliance was carried in the *South Slav Journal* (spring 1996).
7. 'Zajedno DS i NS', *Večernje novosti*, 18 December 1995.
8. 'Srbija je velika tajna', Zoran Djindjić interviewed by Nenad LJ Stefanović, *Vreme*, 13 January 1996.
9. Dragan Bujošević, 'Druga Srbija', *NIN*, 27 October 1995.

10. Djindjić, *Vreme*, 13 January 1996.
11. Mirko Klarin, 'Evropa čeka 'povratak' Jugoslavije', *Naša borba*, 27–28 January 1996.
12. Z. Radovanović, 'Nova stranačka mapa', *Naša borba*, 20 December 1995.
13. Ivan Radovanović, 'Vuk, medved, lisica, i zec', *Vreme*, 25 December 1995.
14. Batić Bačević, 'Trojedina opozicija', *NIN*, 9 February 1996.
15. 'Jedna lista – poraz komunista !', Vuk Drašković interviewed in *Srpska reč*,
16. Dragan Todorović, 'Heroj ulice', *Vreme*, 13 January 1996.
17. 'V. Drašković i Z. Djindjić se prosto utrkuju ko će se zapadu više svideti kao Slobin naslednik', Tomislav Nikolić interviewed by Olja Mamuzić, *Argument*, 29 December 1995; 'Stvarimo koalicijou sa V. Koštunicom, koja će u većini mesta da pobedi Miloševića i Vukov blok', Tomislav Nikolić interviewed by Sredoje Simić, *Argument*, 31 May 1996.
18. Milan Milošević, 'Zeleni jed', *Vreme*, 25 December 1995.
19. Stan Markotich, 'Serbian Orthodox Church Regains a Limited Political Role', *Transition*, 5 April 1996.
20. Danica Vučenić, 'Pulling the Plug on Studio B', *War Report*, March/April 1996.
21. Batić Bačević, 'SOS kanali', *NIN*, 23 February 1996.
22. Ognjen Pribičević, *Transition*, 13 December 1996.

23. The Formation of Zajedno (March–November 1996)

The Third SPS Congress held in Belgrade's Sava Centre on 2 March was intended as a demonstration, both for the Serbian people and international community, of the ruling party's self-confident domination of political life. With the help of modern presentational techniques the SPS sought to mark themselves out as a 'party of the contemporary left'. Some foreign observers, however, were not impressed by the proceedings which they witnessed. Hans Timmermann, a representative of the German Social Democrats who had attended the Congress, commented: 'On the one hand the Congress was excellently organised, and projected, in the style of a multi-media presentation, an optimistic perspective of the future orientation of "Serbia 2000". On the other hand the technically perfect staging was in conspicuous contrast with the traditionalist, pseudo-monolithic character of the Congress. There was no real discussion, criticism or even controversy. There was no debate regarding the causes, responsibility, or consequences of the events of the recent past. The picture of the future remained strangely unreal and abstract in comparison with the murderous past and the grey present.'[1] The Congress also provided Milošević with the opportunity for a new bout of 'cadre change' with the party being cleansed of those who were now considered unsuitable. Such purges served only to strengthen the already firmly entrenched position of JUL in relation to the SPS. A Serbian journalist observed: 'The last step towards what one Serbian politician has called the transformation of the Socialist Party of Serbia into a sort of "socialist alliance" was made in the Sava Centre on 2 March. By changing two-thirds of his own party's leadership, Slobodan Milošević has in fact demonstrated how insignificant that party is. It turned out that the only task of the well trained Socialists, who at his whistle came running to the Third SPS Congress, was to proclaim him

the great leader almost by acclamation. In return they were distributed pieces of meat and beer which they drank straight from
the bottle.'[2] One of the most prominent casualties of the reorganisation was the SPS Vice-President, Goran Perčević. In contrast
to those SPS veterans who had been the previous victims of this
on-going transformation of the party's personnel Perčević was a
youthful figure in his early thirties. Like these Socialist elders,
however, his political career was bound up with the creation and
rise of the SPS under Slobodan Milošević. He had been the
founder and first President of the party's Young Socialist organisation. During this same period Dušanka Djogo, his successor as
head of the Young Socialists, was also moved from her senior
position within the party.

On the same day that the Socialists were holding their carefully
choreographed gathering in Belgrade the SPO, DS, and GSS held
a joint opposition rally in the town of Kragujevac. The choice
of Kragujevac as the location for the launching of this new opposition alignment was significant as there was a strong local tradition of co-operation between the various opposition parties dating
back to the first phase of pluralisation in the early 1990s. In
January 1996, the Kragujevac SPO, DS, and DSS had formally
concluded their own agreement on a local alliance even while
the national leaders of these parties were still manoeuvring and
contemplating the prospects of opposition unity.[3] The rally was
attended by around 15,000 people with Zoran Djindjić telling
them that the time had come for the 'expulsion of the vampires
from Serbia' and Vesna Pešić talking of how the meeting signalled
not the start of a pre-election campaign but rather of a 'war for
the liberation of Serbia'.[4]

A week later the same three political parties came together at
the scheduled rally on 9 March in Belgrade. The meeting was
notable for the fact that it pointed to a developing co-operation
between the SPO and the DS, two of the largest political forces
on the opposition scene, who had in the past studiously avoided
any formal alliance. While Vuk Drašković had long called for
the holding of an anniversary meeting on 9 March Zoran Djindjić
had only a few months earlier spoken of his scepticism regarding
the wisdom of celebrating events which had been marked by
defeat for the opposition forces. The organisers of the rally, in
their rhetoric and the symbolism they used, placed a strong emphasis

on the 'European' and pro-Western orientation of the Serbian opposition forces involved. This was meant to contrast sharply with the 'Eastern' orientation of the regime with their stated admiration of the communist government of China. The demonstration was proclaimed to be 'an assembly of the European Serbs in opposition to the congress of the Chinese Serbs'.[5] The leaders of the political parties spoke under the banner of the European Union. Drašković addressed Slobodan Milošević assuring him: 'You have not destroyed the seed of rebellion, the seed of that Serbia which will explode in order to achieve the goals of 9 March 1991.'[6]

The Novi Sad-based newspaper *Svet* commented on the contrast between such 'internationalism' and the nationalist roots of some opposition figures, and in particular Vuk Drašković. It stated: 'Around Vuk Drašković not many remained of those who were with him in the front rank on 9 March 1991. There was no Giška, Beli, Goran Vuković, Kostadin Dimić or any of their accomplices. Nor could the banners under which they stood then be seen now. The ideas which inspired them to take part in the first 9 March were not present on this occasion. It would be difficult for Giška, Beli and Kole to have stood under the blue banner of the European Union with Vuk Drašković, Vesna Pešić, and Zoran Djindjić, and lamented their fate. They believed in Vuk Drašković as he once was without Pešić or Djindjić. In place of the blue banner with the twelve stars the fighters of the Serbian Guard preferred the black Četnik banner with the skull and crossed bones under which was written 'Liberty or death – with faith in God, for the King and the Fatherland'.[7]

Other writers noted, in the context of the 'international' tone of the meeting, the continuing complexity of the constituency to which the opposition leaders were seeking to appeal. Commentators in the magazine *NIN* described the marriage of the 'old' and 'new' Serbia which could be detected within the ranks of the opposition supporters where it was possible 'to see students, members of the middle class, small businessmen, intellectuals, but also Ravna Gorans and villagers with pictures of the Karadjordjevićs. The union between the traditional Serbia, with *šajkača* [peasant headgear] and peasant trousers, and the modern civic Serbia was reflected in the periodic deviations from the dramaturgy of the protest.[...] In the middle of a speech about the values of the

democratic, civic state and its integration into Europe the crowd
spontaneously began to chant the inappropriate slogan "Fuck you,
Slobo, you betrayed the Krajina".[8]

The Belgrade rally was attended by some 30,000 opposition
supporters. It was reported that a series of administrative measures
were taken by the authorities in order to prevent people attending
the gathering. In Pančevo opposition parties were evicted from
their offices after they had announced an organised trip to the
rally, in Novi Sad the police were reported to be monitoring the
identities of those travelling to Belgrade for the rally, in Belgrade
itself state run factories suddenly, and suspiciously, announced
that they needed to open over the weekend in order to handle
emergency export orders.[9] The organisers determined that the
Belgrade meeting should be only the first event in a series of
rallies taking place across the provinces. An opposition rally at
Niš, held on 30 March, was followed by a similar event in Novi
Sad on 22 April. In Novi Sad the opposition demonstrators were
met by a heavy concentration of riot police and a hostile organised
SPS counter-demonstration. During the demonstration scuffles occurred between the two gatherings, and one SPO representative,
Miroslav Negrojević, was beaten by the police.[10] While the opposition leaders continued to tour Serbia the relationship between
the SPO, DS and GSS remained, at this stage, an informal alignment
referred to variously as the '9th March Coalition' or the 'The
Partnership for Peaceful Change'.

The other main 'democratic' force in Serbia, the DSS, remained
aloof from the 9 March gathering and the subsequent meetings.
Vojislav Koštunica, the DSS President maintained that the parties
involved in these events were, by seeking to concentrate on reform
within Serbia, neglecting the fate of Serbs outside of Serbia itself:
'March just like February, will pass marked by a wave of refugees
from Sarajevo. Sarajevo comes after western Slavonia, Serb Krajina,
western Bosnia, forgotten Mostar, and before eastern Slavonia,
accompanied by indifference not only from the regime, but also
from the international community, which is even worse. One
cannot organise a big rally to pass over it or hush it up. The
impression is one of avoiding circumstances as they are and the
regime as it is.'[11] Other DSS leaders, such as Mirko Petrović,
expressed disquiet at the prominent display of foreign flags at the
rally and the concentration on the affinity of Serbs with international

institutions. It was stressed that while that while the DSS leadership did not oppose foreign contacts it was felt that too short a time had elapsed since the bombing of the Bosnian Serbs by NATO forces for such uncritical admiration of the West to be a viable political option. In their view the original demonstration of 9 March 1991 had been launched in order to demand 'national' and 'democratic' rights whereas the 9 March 1996 demonstration was interested only in the 'democratic' aspects of the equation. There was also a degree of scepticism, on the basis of their previous experience in the DEPOS coalition, as to whether any coalition involving Vuk Drašković would prove durable. The fact that Djindjić had transfered his political loyalties from the Democratic Alliance, in which he had been a joint actor with the DSS, to the new DS-SPO-GSS alignment was a cause of some irritation to the DSS.[12]

Other political groupings were also scornful of the prospects for this new alignment. Kosta Čavoški described the situation: 'It is an alliance which is wholly unnatural. For a good two years Zoran Djindjić's party has followed a path of democratic and healthy national politics. It has upheld the interests of the Serbian nation and the Serbian people across the Drina and the Danube. For taking that position he was criticised by Slobodan Milošević who did not remain faithful to the Serbian national interest, and indeed betrayed those interests. And then for some unexplained reason Djindjić enters an alliance with Vuk Drašković who follows an anational course, and also with Vesna Pešić.'[13] For Čavoški, representing the Serbian Liberal Party, his resentment at the way that Djindjić had crossed the ideological confrontation lines established during the period 1994/5 was combined with practical political considerations. The SLS, like the DSS, had been allied with Djindjić and the Democratic Party in the DA. Djindjić's withdrawal signalled the effective collapse of this grouping and the SLS, unlike the DSS, lacked the political capacity to gain parliamentary representation as an independent force without powerful allies. From a more 'civic/centrist' position, but with the same political logic Dragoljub Mićunović also criticised the DS-SPO-GSS axis. Mićunović had hoped to frame some sort of alliance with the SPO and GSS, but this had been rendered impossible when these two parties began to work with Djindjić, Mićunović's protégé-turned-rival. From within the Serbian government Dušan

Mihailović of New Democracy sought to sow discord among the allies by describing the coalition as 'an unnatural political marriage' and suggesting that 'it cannot be possible for those who wept over the fate of Srebrenica to act with those who worked to bring it about.'[14]

The decision by Vesna Pešić to lead the GSS into this alliance, however, caused a serious schism to develop within its ranks. A group within the GSS headed by the party's Vice-President and parliamentary representative, Žarko Korać, and the President of the party's Executive Committee, Miljenko Dereta raised strong objections towards their working with the DS who they considered to be unacceptably nationalist in their political outlook. Dereta would observe: 'We were not ready to overlook the fact that the DS supported the "warmongering" politics of the Bosnian Serbs. I think in politics one must bear the responsibility for your political decisions.'[15] Pešić was dismissive of the attacks made on her leadership by this faction and by another party Vice-President, Steven Lilić, who accused her of collaborating with 'nationalists' and acting with political expediency. She replied that these attacks came from the same man who half a year ago 'accused our party of being moralists and dissidents who had no sense of pragmatism'.[16] On 20 May Korać's faction of the GSS formally split off from the party to form its own grouping, the Social Democratic Union (SDU). According to Korać the Social Democratic Union would be a party of the 'left-centre' which would 'understand the Left in the way it is understood in Western Europe today'. He stated: 'The European Left took over and accepted the principles of classical liberalism – the notions such as the civil state, pluralism, parliamentarism and human rights while simultaneously retaining the liberal economic structure'.[17] The already diverse state of Serbian political life in this way found itself the richer for the presence of one more political party.

The regime responded to the formation of the new coalition by launching a series of attacks on the alliance leaders. In the aftermath of the 9 March rally Vuk Drašković had written an open letter to the Foreign Ministers of Britain, France, Germany, Russia and the United States in which he detailed the woeful state of democracy in Serbia: 'The Serbian President, Slobodan Milošević, has increased the terror campaign against the Serbian democratic opposition particularly after Dayton and Paris; he has

banned the last independent electronic media; he has prevented
privatisation in the economy; he is nationalising by force the
existing private property; has increased the police system of repression, mobilised the members of the democratic opposition for
military exercises, forced thousands of people into his party....'
The letter went on to assure the Western leaders that 'the Al
Capones of the Balkans can never turn into Mahatma Gandhis'
and called on them to support 'democratic Serbia'.[18] The state-
controlled media reacted to the Drašković letter with a co-ordinated
barrage of accusations which included the suggestion that Drašković
had called for the Western powers to intervene militarily in Serbia.
Typical of this coverage was the attack made by the commentator,
Steven Zec, in the pages of *Borba*, who equated Drašković with
Vuk Branković, the mythic archetype of infidelity to the Serbian
national cause. He wrote: 'From the point of view of the internal
political scene it is unlikely that Mr Drašković will find anyone
apart from his wife and adviser [Danica Drašković has been calling
for foreign military intervention publicly for a long time in the
paper that she runs] who would justify his attempts to use foreign
political or military power, therefore illegal means, to achieve
power in Serbia. Between the two Vuks [Branković and Drašković]
no open collaborator ever had mass support from the Serbian
people. Seen from the outside, Mr Drašković appears terribly
naive to believe that he will endear himself to any foreign service
by describing his opposition vision of political developments here.
The naivety of the SPO leader is all the greater since he hopes
in vain – no country will give open support of any kind (political,
financial, military) at the behest of an opposition politician.'[19]
The state media was also sharply critical of the German *chargé
d'affaires*, Gerhard Schroembgens, who had attended the 9 March
demonstration as an observer.

The moves directed by the government against Zoran Djindjić,
however, went further than such state-sanctioned name-calling.
On 14 May charges were brought against Djindjić accusing him
of 'damaging the reputation of the Republic of Serbia'. The charges
related to an advertisement placed by the DS in the journal *Telegraf*
on 24 January 1996, in which the Serbian Prime Minister Mirko
Marjanović was accused of abusing his position within the government in order to buy up cheap wheat from bankrupt farmers in
Vojvodina. The wheat was then allegedly sold on the international

market making massive profits for Marjanović. Djindjić took full responsibility for the contents of the advertisement and made it clear that he considered the action to be part of a state-directed vendetta against the opposition, saying 'This is not a legal but a political conflict.' The whole affair, he said, was a reflection of the 'magic triangle of corruption' which existed in Serbia and was based on a 'systematic abuse of power that has been cultivated to perfection'. Charges were also brought against Dragoljub Bjelić, editor of the *Telegraf,* for allowing the advertisement to be published.[20] On 1 July, immediately before the start of Djindjić's trial, the sixty-two parliamentary representatives of the DS, the SPO and GSS collectively put their names to a declaration expressing their solidarity with the DS leader and repeating the allegations he had made against Mirko Marjanović.[21] In spite of the fact that Djindjić was able to present a considerable amount of evidence in support of his allegations against Marjanović he was ultimately found guilty of the charges made against him and sentenced in September to four months in prison suspended for two years. The authorities clearly intended this judgement to be another demonstration of the way in which they exerted political control over the key institutions of power and how this authority could be directed against opposition figures who attempted to defy them. While it was considered inappropriate for the Serbian government to be seen to be imprisoning one of the key opposition leaders in the run-up to the autumn federal elections the imposition of a suspended sentence, however, allowed the authorities to maintain a threat hanging over the DS leader which would have the potential to be utilised at some point in the future. Indeed in October 1996 a Belgrade lawyer, Svetozvar Vujačić, did raise the possibility of bringing new criminal charges against the DS leader with his offence on this occasion apparently having been to have, during a rally at Vranje on 10 October, described Slobodan Milošević as 'a sick person who needs to be sent to hospital'.[22] However, Djindjić after receiving his sentence was unrepentant and pledged that the DS would continue to draw attention to cases of business coruption by government ministers, with particular reference to the C – Marketing group headed by former DS functionary and serving government minister, Slobodan Radulović.[23]

The SRS observed the conflict between the government and opposition from the sidelines. As an 'opposition' party Šešelj had been keen to assure the supporters that the SRS would soon be in a position to take power. In March, at a rally in the Bosnian border town of Bijeljina, he told them: 'In the spring of 1993, in this very place, I promised you that we would overthrow Dobrica Ćosić because he had betrayed the Serbian national interest.[...] I promise you today we will overthrow Milošević too!'[24] Gradually, however, as the SPO-DS-GSS coalition began to appear as an increasingly durable actor on the political stage Šešelj shifted to the opposition as a focus for his political abuse. In May Šešelj would say: 'We are not willing to form an alliance with the SPO, a party of the NATO pact. We like power; however, we prefer dignity, honesty and honour. The Djindjić–Drašković alliance will be short lived and afterwards other possibilities will appear on the opposition scene'.[25] Later Šešelj would go further accusing Djindjić of being an agent of the German government and Drašković of the American. As the year progressed it appeared that Šešelj was inching back towards the position of informal co-operation which had existed between him and Milošević in the period 1992-3.

Despite the suspension of international sanctions, the signing of the Dayton agreement had brought little relief for the general Serbian population from the processes of economic decay which afflicted their country. The southern industrial town of Niš had traditionally enjoyed a reputation as a political stronghold of the SPS. It was often referred to as 'Red Niš'. In the local city assembly fifty-six out of the seventy representatives' places were filled by Socialists. Mile Ilić, the leader of the local Socialists, had through his control over the local media developed a minor personality cult which set him up as a provincial imitation of his leader, Slobodan Milošević, in Belgrade.[26] Interviewed in the spring of 1996 Ilić sought to extol the virtues and benefits which SPS rule had brought to Niš, stating that under the newly-approved development plan 'Niš would be the centre of southern Serbia, one of the centres of Balkan integration, and containing, as the second city in Serbia should, all the essentials of a modern European centre.'[27] Beneath this Socialist rhetoric of development the reality of life in Niš was one of deepening economic and social devastation. The degree of discontent felt by the population of Niš was reflected in the fact that when in March the SPO, DS and GSS, with their coalition appearing for the first time with the title Zajedno

(Together), held a meeting, over 10,000 people attended despite considerable hostility and obstruction from the local authorities.[28] On 24 April workers in the Angropromet factory came out on strike protesting over the fact that they had not been paid for several months. On 8 May employees at the El and MIN electronics firms and other enterprises, with a similar set of grievances, also joined the protest. As these industrial workers demonstrated on the streets Mile Ilić was strangely absent from the city having apparently left for Belgrade for 'consultations'.[29] The Socialist authorities sought to portray the popular protests as the work of *provocateurs* from opposition parties. While opposition supporters were indeed present among the protestors activists from the SPO and the DS denied that they had any 'control' over the strikers declaring instead that the strike represented 'a march of the hungry on the city of the Socialists'. Indeed some of the strikers were eager to proclaim their traditional loyalty to the SPS with one placard declaring: 'We want to be with the SPS, but the SPS does not want to be with us.'[30] While the Serbian government was, by the end of May, able to find the financial resources needed to meet the demands of the striking workers it could offer no long-term solution to Serbia's problems. The events in Niš also demonstrated the way in which economic hardship was slowly eroding the previously solid support for the SPS among its 'core' constituency of industrial workers. Following the example of the Niš workers industrial unrest spread across Serbia during the spring of 1996. On 13 May metalworkers from Rakovica in Belgrade came out on strike, followed by textile workers in Leskovac on 17 May and health workers in Vojvodina on 20 May, and on 3 June the three manufacturing firms which employed the majority of workers in the town of Kraljevo also took industrial action.[31] At the end of August another major industrial dispute began in the Kragujevac 'Red Banner' arms manufacturing firm. During this dispute a number of workers went on 'hunger strike' to draw attention to their plight. When it was reported that the police were preparing to intervene to end the strike, one of the union leaders remarked darkly that the authorities had to understand that 'we do not make yoghurt here.'[32]

Dragoslav Avramović, the man who had been charged with solving Serbia's economic problems, had come to the country at the end of 1993 as a loyal supporter of Slobodan Milošević. Indeed such was his political 'suitability' in the eyes of the regime that when in early 1995 Mirjana Marković was casting around for a 'figurehead' President for her new party the position was first offered to Avramović before finally being given to Ljubiša Ristić.[33] However, Avramović considered that his programme of financial stabilisation instituted at the start of 1994 was only the first stage of a wider policy of economic reform (Programme 2) which would be put into effect after sanctions had been suspended. The key elements of the Programme included a devaluation of the dinar so that it would stand at 3.3 dinars to the mark and the official rate would once again achieve parity with the black market rate. The devaluation would be carried out within an overall framework of continued monetary stringency and financial control. This would be accompanied by measures for import/export liberalisation and a programme of large-scale privatisation. Avramović reasoned that foreign capital was vital if there was to be an effective revival of the Yugoslav economy. Such investment would only become available if it could be demonstrated that reform of Yugoslavia's ill-defined law on property was implemented. A programme of privatisation was also considered a necessity if Yugoslavia was to achieve re-integration into international financial institutions including the International Monetary Fund. While the Yugoslav government was formally ready to declare its adherence to market principles Avramović found himself facing increasingly fierce opposition to his reform proposals from within the ranks of the Serbian government, and particularly from supporters of JUL. In December 1995 Ljubiša Ristić attacked Avramović's programme: 'If the workers, peasants and intellectuals are to protect the wealth of our nation we cannot permit ourselves to be transformed into a semi-colonised state by unrestrained foreign capital and ideologically blind fanatics.'[34] While individuals such as Ristić condemned Avramović using the language of social demagoguery it was widely appreciated that any real economic reform, which introduced a degree of transparency into economic life, would act to undercut the power base of the financial oligarchy who held the positions of power within JUL. By the end of 1995 Avramović was in a somewhat contradictory position for a Milošević appointee whereby the only people he could rely on to support his proposals for radical reform came from among the ranks of the opposition parties. The official media, which had once helped to cultivate his formidable reputation with the Serbian public became increasingly hostile.[35]

In early 1996 tensions between the Avramović and the government were heightened as he, in order to prevent a return to hyper-inflation, prevented the government from funding expansionary budgets by printing money. A rift also emerged between Avramović and his colleagues within the Serbian government over their approach to negotiations with the International Monetary Fund. At the end of March negotiations with the IMF broke down after the Yugoslav government insisted that any agreement on membership should involve a recognition of the 'continuity' between the FRY and the old SFRY. There were political and financial motivations behind this negotiating position. In political terms the acknowledgement of Yugoslav 'continuity' would confer a form of political legitimacy on the FRY while at the same time designating the other former Yugoslav republics as secessionist 'successor' states. Financially, it was clearly hoped that recognition of its 'continuity' with the old state would give the FRY the right to the assets of the SFRY. Avramović had by contrast taken a pragmatic and realistic position being ready to accept the terms set by the IMF, including the acceptance of 'successor' status for FRY. For Avramović Serbia's re-entry to the international community was of primary importance. When on 23 April Avramović was removed as chief negotiator with the IMF for the FRY it was an unmistakable sign that his days in office were numbered. Although Avramović had been deserted by his colleagues within the administration he continued to enjoy the trust of the ordinary people. On 10 May when Avramović attended a conference of economists in Niš he was met by a group of strikers one of whom bore a placard inscribed with the simple message 'Avram –Do not print money'.[36] In Belgrade, on 13 May, Avramović took his message to the people and addressing a meeting of metalworkers from Rakovica explained to them the necessity of economic reform in Yugoslavia. On 15 May a motion to oust Avramović from his position as head of the National Bank of Yugoslavia was formally moved in the federal parliament. The SPO, DS and GSS deputies promptly rallied to support Avramović, but they were unable to prevent his dismissal. During the debate of censure Avramović made an impassioned defence of his position and roundly denounced his accusers. In particular he made a withering attack on the Minister for Agriculture, Ivko Djonović, who he described as 'a trader who blackmails peasants to hand over their produce almost for free then sells it to people at astronomical prices.'[37] After the motion of censure had been passed by 74 votes to 33, Avramović was moved to reflect on his fate: 'I never betrayed those whose interests are closest to my heart – the workers and the peasants, and I saved the authorities too because I came to this job at a time when the sky fell in.'[38]

In purely political terms the demise of Avramović was yet another demonstration of Milošević's ability to dispose of subordinates who had outlived their usefulness. In economic terms, however, it was a major self-inflicted wound by which the Yugoslav government chose to sacrifice any credibility which they might have had with the international economic institutions. When New Democracy had in 1994 entered the Serbian government it had given one of the chief reasons for this move as a desire to give practical support to Avramović in the implementation of his reform programme. New Democracy, however, had remained passive while their Socialist allies moved to overthrow him. Only Rodoljub Drašković raised his voice in defence of Avramović protesting that: 'New Democracy has from the start stood by the Avramović programme. It is part of New Democracy's basic political orientation. If Avramović falls then New Democracy will have no business being in the government or in parliament.'[39] When, following Avramović's departure, Drašković resigned from his position as Vice-President of New Democracy his former ND colleague, Ratomir Tanić, was dismissive of his objections suggesting that Drašković 'does not understand the difference between the Avramović we supported and the new Avramović who calls people out on to the streets'.[40] Ultimately New Democracy gained too much from its proximity to the centre of political power, and was too feeble in its own right, for it to be able to act as anything other than a political client of the ruling party. However, the dismissal of Avramović was only one of a number of measures taken by Milošević to bolster his position in anticipation of the autumn federal elections. At the end of April a new federal election law had been framed. The law, which divided Serbia into twenty-seven electoral units, was widely seen as being specifically designed to help the ruling parties in Serbia and Montenegro gain an absolute electoral majority over the opposition. According to the testimony of Darko Milošević, a businessman, a former military intelligence operative, and bodyguard to Jovan Glamočanin, the support of the SRS-NP for the passing of the electoral law and removal of Avramović was purchased with gifts to Glamočanin of a flat, a luxury car and 50,000 German marks.[41] On 27 March the Serbian government underwent another 'reshuffle'. In this rearranging of the cadres one of the most significant new recruits to the government ranks was Aleksandar Tijanić, the new Minister of Information. Tijanić had been a respected journalist who was previously regarded as having 'liberal' sympathies. Although he had not, during the period of multi-party politics, been a member of any political party he had supported the March 1991 demonstrations. He was also known to have been close to Mićunović, and had acted as an informal adviser to Zoran Djindjić and the DS during the December 1993 election campaign.[42] In 1994, however, he had became the director and editor-in-chief of BK TV, and in this position he came within the political orbit of Mirjana Marković and JUL. In his new ministerial position Tijanić, in spite of his past 'opposition' associations, soon distinguished himself by his hardline and intolerant attitude towards the independent media.

When in August it was confirmed that the federal elections were to be held on 3 November, with local elections taking place at the same time, the imperative to place the SPO-DS-GSS coalition on a formal basis became all the more urgent. In spite of the apparently close co-operation between these three parties during the spring and early summer sources of friction continued to exist within the coalition, and specifically between the SPO and the DS. While there was little significant divergence in policy between the SPO and the DS at the level of domestic policy differences of emphasis persisted regarding relations with the Republika Srpska. On 19 July, commenting on the withdrawal – under international pressure – of Radovan Karadžić from public and political life, Ivan Kovačević , as spokesman for the SPO, said that the decision was 'good for the Serbs in Bosnia-Hercegovina and for the Serb Democratic Party. The forthcoming elections in Bosnia would otherwise not have democratic and free, and they would not have been fair if the SDS could not participate.' On earlier occasions the SPO had urged 'maximum co-operation with the Hague tribunal' on war crimes.[43] The DS also welcomed the departure of Radovan Karadžić from the leadership of the SDS with Zoran Djindjić stating that with his resignation 'an important obstacle, which has hitherto hampered the integration of the Republika Srpska into international processes, has been removed.' But on 21 June Slobodan Vuksanović, speaking for the DS, had supported Karaožić's candidacy in the Bosnia–Hercegovina declaring: 'President Karadžić has so far shown sufficient responsibility to the people he leads, and has always placed their interests above his own.'[44] The DS had also begun to build up a network of branches within the Republika Srpska claiming by the beginning of 1996 to have set up some eighteen local committees in this territory. The main causes of friction between the DS and the SPO, however, related not to differences in national policy, but rather to the competition between the two parties with had not ceased even when they were joined within the same coalition. These tensions came to a head in late August when, during negotiations over the agreement of a common candidates list, the SPO objected to the inclusion of a number of leading members of the DS. These included Milan Paroški, and a number of individuals who had defected from the SPO to join the DS including Mihaljo Marković, Vladimir Gajić, and Dragoslav Miličić. The DS reacted angrily to what they regarded as an attack on their 'sovereignty' as a political party. The dispute between the two parties became so bitter that, in spite of attempts by the GSS to act as an intermediary and conciliator, the 'coalition' which had been nurtured through the spring and summer of that year came close to unravelling. Finally, however, Djindjić agreed that these named individuals would not be included on the DS candidates list, and this concession opened the way for the conclusion of a coalition agreement.[45]

On 2 September the Zajedno coalition formally came into existence. The agreement signed by Drašković, Djindjić and Pešić specified that the seats won by the coalition would be divided in proportion to the number of votes gained in the December 1993 elections with 54 per cent going to the SPO, 5 per cent to the GSS, and 41 per cent to the DS. The fact that Djindjić agreed to an allocation of seats which reflected the balance of power between the parties which existed several years before was seen as another manifestation of his 'pragmatic' attitude towards the coalition arrangements. The agreement also left the door open for the DSS to join stating that should this happen seats would be divided with the SPO and GSS taking half and the DS and

DSS together the other half.[46] Having completed the difficult task of constructing the Zajedno coalition the party leaders sought to recruit Dragoslav Avramović, calculating that his popular prestige and reputation would add weight to their alliance. Avramović agreed to lend his name to their cause on condition that their alliance was widened to include the DSS. Zoran Djindjić, and the DS, favoured this proposal for the broadening of the coalition regarding the DSS as a potential counter-weight to the influence of the SPO within Zajedno. Equally the SPO regarded the idea with deep hostility.

The DSS itself had long been antagonistic to any suggestion that they should place themselves within the framework of this opposition 'front'. In June when Zoran Djindjić, Vesna Pešić, and Milan Komnenić had visited the DSS conference the SPO and GSS representatives had encountered heckling from individuals within the audience shouting 'out traitors' and 'go to Pale'.[47] During July and August an increasingly acrimonious exchange of accusations developed between the leaders of the DSS and the SPO. Vojislav Koštunica made it clear that he regarded Vuk Drašković and the SPO as 'an unsuitable coalition partner' and asked: 'Where is the integrity in a man who is the author of flattering statements about Josip Broz and Slobodan Milošević, and shameful essays about Draža Mihailović, a man who when he felt it to be necessary collaborated with the Socialists and in place of the declaration that we should "live like the rest of the world" only wanted to be in power?'[48] Danica Drašković struck back with a blistering attack on Koštunica and his family background and that of his wife.[49] Such an exchange of insults was, of course, an unfavourable basis for the formation of an effective coalition arrangement. On 8 September the DSS Main Committee once again rejected the proposal that they should join the Zajedno coalition. Koštunica described Zajedno as a 'power-loving and opportunistic combination'.[50] Co-operation with the alliance was, however, favoured by a number of influential DSS members including Vladan Batić and Dragoljub Popović. A number of provincial branches also supported co-operation with Zajedno. Avramović remained determined to secure the compliance of the DSS leadership. In on-going negotiations he threatened to withdraw from the Zajedno project and publically announce that the DSS were responsible for his resignation unless they led their party into the coalition. The DSS leadership, believing that such an event would destroy their credibility with the Serbian public, finally and reluctantly, gave their assent to participation in the Zajedno coalition. According to Vladeta Janković, 'He [Avramović] was regarded by the public as an angel from heaven, as a saviour...he told us that the DSS would be crucified. We found ourselves in a position from which we could not gain any advantage.'[51] On 28 September it was officially announced that a widened coalition would contest the federal elections led by Avramović who, in the event of a Zajedno victory would be their candidate for federal Prime Minister. The new expanded Zajedno also included the Association of Free and Independent Trade Syndicates of Serbia, an organisation of independent trade unionists which had been founded on 2 July of that year under the leadership of Dragan Milovanović. The relationship between Avramović and this trade union organisation, which was particularly strong amongst the Rakovica metalworkers, had been forged during his last days in office when, under pressure from the authorities, he had sought to take his message out to the workers. Milovanović commented on the support offered by his trade unionists to Zajedno: 'We joined Zajedno because there is a clear division in this country between those who support democracy, economic recovery, and a return to civilization, and, on the other side, local feudal overlords, men of power, war profiteers, and *latifundists* of the South American type. We chose which side to be on.'[52] Dragoljub Mićunović and the Democratic Centre was also included within the final Zajedno agreement with it being determined that the DC would receive one representative place in the new federal parliament. This reformulated coalition was referred to itself as 'Zajedno – the coalition of peasants, workers, and democrats' and included all the non-government political forces with the exception of Vojislav Šešelj's ultra-nationalist SRS.[53] It was opposed by a 'left' coalition of governing parties consisting of the SPS, JUL, and New Democracy. Opinion polls conducted in early October showed Avramović to be considered to be the most popular political personality by 43 per cent of people compared to 29 per cent who expressed support for Slobodan Milošević.[54] The leaders of the Zajedno parties had every reason to expect that his presence on their ticket would give the coalition a degree of supra-political appeal allowing them to reach out to normally uncommitted Serbian voters.

The optimistic atmosphere in the Zajedno ranks did not, however, last for long. On 7 October Avramović had made his first election appearance addressing a rally in the provincial town of Jagodina. The political scene in Jagodina was distinguished by the close co-operation which existed between the SPS-JUL and Dragan Marković, a prominent businessman and local leader of Arkan's Serbian Unity Party.[55] Avramović's message to the 12,000-strong rally had been sober and pragmatic stating that economic recovery in Serbia would only be possible if there was substantial economic investment from the United States and the European Union countries. In order for this investment to become available it would be necessary, he said, for Western 'principles of behaviour' to be accepted as part of Serbian economic life. Avramović promised that as Prime Minister he would institute a programme of 'privatisation, liberalisation and democratistion' which would unfold over the following four years.[56] Only two days later, however, while Djindjić, Drašković and Pešić were visiting Brussels and Koštunica was in Pale, Avramović sent a message to the DS headquarters which told the Zajedno leadership: 'With sincere regret I must inform you that because of a deterioration in the state of my health over the last week I am not able to lead the Zajedno coalition.'[57] Avramović's statement that he was withdrawing for 'health reasons' and due to 'high blood pressure' was widely disbelieved. It seemed improbable that, while his health was indeed known to be fragile, he would withdraw completely from the coalition after having put so much energy into moulding it after his own image. Rumours were rife that pressure had been put on him by the authorities or by Western diplomats who wanted to maintain the political *status quo* in Serbia. The exact reasons for Avramović's abrupt departure from the political scene, however, remained unclear. While Avramović's departure was indeed a bitter blow to Zajedno's hopes it did not, as some might have expected, lead to the dissolution of the coalition. Instead the Zajedno leaders fought a vigorous campaign holding meetings across the country in a vain attempt to compensate for Zajedno's almost total exclusion from the electronic media.

The election did not pass without violent incident. On 17 October, Milovan Brkić, a journalist with the magazine *Srpska reč* and Zajedno candidate in the local elections was detained and severely beaten in the street by a group of policemen. The incident followed the publication of an article by Brkić in which he had alleged that members of the police had been participating in the drugs trade. A complaint made to Alesandar Tijanić, the Minister for Information, about the assault on Brkić brought the reply that he had often wanted to 'beat him up myself'.[58] On 29 October police special forces were used to expel striking transport workers from the premises of the Belgrade City Transport Company. Dragoljub Stošić, the chairman of the bus drivers union and Zajedno local election candidate was arrested. Events such as these, although not typical, set the tone for a bitterly contested campaign.[59] On 25 October the leaders of the Zajedno coalition complained that in places across Serbia their representatives were being systematically excluded from participation in the local election committees which were being kept under exclusive control of representatives of the SPS. The situation was particularly difficult in Niš where Mile Ilić was said, by the opposition, to be openly boasting that he had been instructed by Slobodan Milošević to 'steal votes' in the forthcoming elections. In this town leaders of the SPO, DS, DSS, and SRS went on hunger-strike in protest at the fact that they had been denied representatives at the 200 polling stations opened for the local elections. During the election campaign Mile Ilić had hired security guards from the Serbian Kick-Boxing Association. The Chairman of this Association was Borislav Pelević who was also Vice-President of Željko Ražnatović Arkan's Serbian Unity Party and a prominent figure in the Serbian Volunteer Guard. These security guards were accused of attempting to intimidate and threaten opposition supporters and officials. Even JUL, who were contesting the local elections in Niš independent of the SPS, complained angrily about the abuses of electoral procedure being sanctioned by the ruling party in the city.[60] The Zajedno leaders were scornful of international observers who declared the elections to have been 'free and fair'. According to the opposition, the international observers had arrived so late and in such small numbers that 'it would have been better if they had not come.'[61] All the international observers left Yugoslavia after polling had taken place for the federal elections on 3 November, and before the conclusion of the local election campaign, whose second round of voting was due to take place on 17 November. The sense of rancour felt by some opposition politicians against the West was heightened by the apparent willingness of Western diplomats during the campaign to appear on official visits alongside leading members of the ruling 'left' coalition. Most notable was the occasion when the American ambassador, Richard Miles, visited the giant Smederevo iron works in the company of SPS potentate, Dušan Matković. Film of this visit was broadcast on the main state TV channel between two election broadcasts for the SPS and JUL.[62]

The results of the federal elections appeared to confirm once again the dominance of the SPS, and the political failure of the Zajedno coalition. The left coalition (SPS-JUL-ND) secured 1,847,610 votes and gained sixty-four seats in the federal parliament. As a participant in the 'left' coalition the federal elections allowed JUL to become a parliamentary party for the first time in spite of its negligible popular support. By contrast Zajedno gained 969,198 votes and twenty-two seats. For the Zajedno parties this was a particularly dispiriting result as it represented a 'loss' of almost 400,000 votes compared to the collective totals of those parties who had stood independently in 1993 and formed part of the Zajedno coalition in 1996 (DEPOS: 715, 564, DS: 497,582, DSS: 218,056). The SRS, however, won an unexpectedly high total of 779,126 votes gaining sixteen seats. Some observers accounted for the reduction in the opposition vote by suggesting that a broad alliance of parties, along the lines of Zajedno, alienated as many opposition supporters as it attracted such were the publicly known conflicts of personality and policy between the various parties involved. In support of this they pointed to the large number of abstentions and spoilt ballot papers. The DSS in particular argued that their decision to join Zajedno had been a mistake suggesting that the vote gained by the SRS had been artifically high because there had been no 'moderate' nationalist alternative, positioned between Zajedno and the SRS, such as themselves, for electors to vote for. The DSS, however, had been a late, and reluctant, arrival within the Zajedno camp, and the key question remained how far the 'core' of the Zajedno coalition (SPO, DS, GSS) would be able to withstand the disappointment of their first electoral test.

Notes

1. Hans Timmermann, 'Saradnja bez iluzija'; *Vreme*, 6 April 1996.
2. *Naša borba*, 4 March 1996 in *SWB EE/2554 A/11*, 7 March 1996.

3. 'Zajednička lista SPO, DS, DSS', *Naša borba*, 29 January 1996.
4. Dragan Todorović, 'Isterivanje vampira', *Vreme*, 9 March 1996.
5. Milan Milošević, 'Mane i obmane', *Vreme*, 16 March 1996.
6. FoNet, 9 March 1996 in *SWB EE/2537 A/11*, 11 March 1996.
7. Predrag Popović, 'Vesna Pešić pod četničkom, četnici pod zastavom Evropske unije', *Svet*, 18 March 1996.
8. Batić Bačević, Violeta Marčetić and Ivana Janković, 'Od Evrope do Ravne gore', *NIN*, 15 March 1996.
9. *Naša borba*, 8 March 1996 in *SWB EE/2537 A/11*, 11 March 1996.
10. Milan Milošević, 'Kordon za 21. vek', *Vreme*, 27 April 1996.
11. *Naša borba*, 5 March 1996 in *SWB EE/2554 A/11*, 7 March 1996.
12. This account of the DSS attitude to the coalition is based on interviews with Mirko Petrović, Vice-President DSS (7 December 1996) and Vladeta Janković, Vice-President DSS (9 April 1997).
13. 'Ulaskom u koaliciju sa Draškovićem i V. Pešić, Zoran Djindjić je razbio Demokratsku alijansu', Kosta Čavoski interviewed by Sredoje Simić, *Argument*, 14 June 1996.
14. 'Rugova nije terorista', Dušan Mihajlović interviewed by Marko Lopušina, *Intervju*, 23 August 1996.
15. 'Što se partnerstva tiče računamo na saradnju sa D. Mićunovićem, N. Čankom, R. Ljajićem, reformistima...'., Miljenko Dereta interviewed by Mila Manojlović, *Argument*, 14 June 1996.
16. 'Gradjanski rat i mir', Vesna Pešić interviewed by Nenad LJ Stefanović, *Vreme*, 2 March 1996.
17. *Tanjug*, 20 May 1996 in *SWB EE/2618 A/12*, 22 May 1996.
18. Nenad LJ Stefanović, 'Lov na Vuka I pudlice', *Vreme*, 30 March 1996.
19. *Borba*, 26 March 1996 in *SWB EE/2572 A/11*, 28 March 1996.
20. *Naša borba*, 2 April 1996 in *SWB EE/2578 A/9*, 4 April 1996; Gradiša Katić; 'Marjanović protiv Djindjića'; *Nedeljni telegraf*, 24 April 1996.
21. 'Gospodine Marjanoviću, ne otimajte narodu hleb!', *Vreme*, 1 July 1996.
22. *Beta*, 15 October 1996 in *SWB EE/2745 A/6*, 17 October 1996.
23. 'Uoči izbora lansiraćemo nove afere: sa cementom, veštačkim, djubrivom, 'Dafimentom' i 'C Marketom', Zoran Djindjić interviewed by Predrag Popović, *Svet*, 30 September 1996.
24. *Naša borba*, 25 March 1996 in *SWB EE/2571 A/8*, 27 March 1996.
25. *Naša borba*, 3 May 1996 in *SWB EE/2604 A/18*, 6 May 1996.
26. Zorica Miladinović, 'Skromnosti, ime ti je – Mile', *Naša borba*, 20 December 1996.
27. 'Radi se i gradi a Nišava mirno teče', Mile Ilić interviewed by Jovanka Matić, *Duga*, 27 April 1996.
28. Milica Kuburović, 'Ume Mile', *NIN*, 5 April 1996.
29. Nenad LJ Stefanović, 'Kupovina siromtinje', *Vreme*, 18 May 1996.
30. Zorica Miladinović, 'Štrajk u Nišu: Prodavci hleba i mleka traže hleb za sebe', *Nedeljni telegraf*, 1 May 1996.
31. *Tanjug*, 28 May 1996 in *SWB EE/2625 A/10*, 30 May 1996.
32. Miloš Vasić, 'Oružari na ulici', *Vreme*, 31 August 1996.
33. Djukić (1997), p. 261.
34. Dinkić (1996), p. 296.

35. Nenad LJ Stefanović, 'Rok upotrebe', *Vreme*, 20 April 1996.
36. Srboljub Bogdanović and Batić Bačević, 'Otkude Niš!', *NIN*, 17 May 1996.
37. Philip Švarm, 'Killing the Messenger', *War Report*, June 1996.
38. *SRNA*, 16 May 1996 in *SWB EE/2615 A/19*, 18 May 1996.
39. 'Što dalje od brata', Rodoljub Drašković interviewed by Gordana Jovanović, *Intervju*, 17 May 1996.
40. 'Rastakanje Srbije i slom poretka', Ratomir Tanić interviewed by Nenad Stefanović, *Duga*, 20 July 1996.
41. Djukić (1997), p. 187.
42. 'Od nečega mora da se živi', Aleksandar Tijanić interviewed by Igor Mekina and Svetlana Vasović, *Intervju*, 26 July 1996.
43. *Beta*, 19 July 1996 in *SWB EE/2344 A/11*, 21 July 1996; *Tanjug*, 2 April 1996 in *SWB EE/2579 A/10*, 4 April 1996.
44. *Tanjug*, 5 July 1996 in *SWB EE/2569 A/13*, 8 July 1996; *SRNA*, 21 June in *SWB EE/2646 A/12*, 24 June 1996.
45. Milan Milošević, 'Zajedno, i obrnuto', *Vreme*, 31 August 1996.
46. 'Sporazumo koaliciji Zajedno', *Vreme*, 7 September 1996.
47. Predrag Popović, 'Čekajući kojem će se carstvu Koštunica privoleti', *Svet*, 24 June 1996.
48. Dragoslav Grujić, 'Povratak cicvarića', *Vreme*, 3 August 1996.
49. Danica Drašković, 'Šumadinac iz Nevesinja', *Srpska reč*, 29 July 1996. This article accused Koštunica, among other things, of having his family origins in Hercegovina rather then the Šumadija. While this form of attack would appear somewhat strange, considering that both Vuk and Danica Drašković themselves have origins outside Serbia, it should be seen in the context of the rivalry between the SPO and the DSS both of whom had sought to develop centres of support in the Šumadija.
50. 'DSS ide odvojeno jer je Zajedno heterogena, vlastoljubiva i opportunistička, koalicija', Vojislav Koštunica interviewed by Radmila Stanković, *Nedeljni telegraf*, 11 September 1996.
51. Vladeta Janković, DSS Vice-President, interviewed by the author, 9 April 1997, and in 'Poslednjim raskolom DSS se oslobodila svih štetnih elemenata', *Demokratska stranka Srbije vesti*, March 1997.
52. Uroš Komlenović, 'Protiv latifundista', *Vreme*, 5 October 1996.
53. The final Zajedno agreement on division of mandates is reprinted in Sandra Petrušić, 'Bez starca nema udarca', *Srpska reč*, 3 October 1996.
54. Milan Milošević, 'Budjenje nade', *Vreme*, 5 October 1996.
55. Nenad Stefanović, 'Ne može nam niko nista jači smo od sudbine', *Duga*, 15 February 1997.
56. Srdjan Radulović and Radmila Stanković, 'Avramović opominje stranačke lidere', *Nedeljni telegraf*, 9 October 1996.
57. The text of Avramović's letter is reprinted in *Vreme*, 12 October 1996.
58. *Beta*, 22 October 1996 in *SWB EE/1834 C/5*, 1 November 1996.
59. *Beta*, 29 October 1996 in *SWB EE/2756 A/8*, 30 October 1996.
60. *Beta*, 27 October 1996 in *SWB EE/2755 A/6*, 29 October 1996, *Beta*, 3 November 1996 in *SWB EE/2761 A/8*, 5 November 1996.
61. *Tanjug*, 3 November 1996 in *SWB EE/2761 A/8*, 5 November 1996.
62. Stevan Nikšić, 'Gvozdena naklonost', *NIN*, 18 October 1996.

24. The 'Happening of the Citizens' (November 1996–February 1997)

The gloom in the ranks of the opposition following the 3 November poll was to some extent relieved by hopeful results in the first round of the local elections. In the local elections the Zajedno coalition consisted of its original members, the SPO, DS and GSS, with the DSS contesting the elections independently. In a small number of places, including Kragujevac, Smederevo, Čačak, and Pančevo, the DSS fought the local elections as part of the Zajedno coalition. The conditions for the local elections were generally considered to be more favourable to the opposition, allowing the expression of their concentrations of support in urban areas, than the federal elections in which the proportional system allowed urban areas to be 'swamped' by surrounding rural, Socialist-supporting hinterlands. The preliminary results were nevertheless surprising, showing Zajedno candidates to be in the lead in fourteen of the most significant towns across Serbia including Belgrade, Kragujevac, Niš, Čačak, Novi Sad, Kraljevo, Pirot and Užice. These results were a major factor in allowing the Zajedno to maintain its cohesion. On 7 November Milan Paunović, Vice-President of the GSS, stated: 'The opposition should now stop whining about the inadequate electoral conditions and should concentrate on the second round of elections so as to win as many votes in as many municipalities and towns as possible. We pointed out and fought against the inadequate electoral conditions, but that's history now.'[1] When the votes were counted on 17 November, the Zajedno victories were confirmed. However, the election commission in Belgrade refused to give official recognition to this result citing reports of irregularities apparently received from polling stations across the city. On 18 November the Zajedno alliance held a victory rally in Belgrade's Republic Square. Zoran Djindjić, who was introduced to the audience as the 'new Mayor of Belgrade,' said to the crowd: 'Serbia's friends will be able to say that Serbia is neither Cuba nor Korea.' Drašković declared: 'We won with both our hands and feet bound. They [the authorities] have to congratulate us on our victory.'[2]

On the following day opposition supporters took to the streets in Niš in protest at attempts by the local election commission to falsify the election results. Drašković travelled down to Niš to tell a rally of 35,000 opposition supporters: 'In these elections in Niš the citizens of this town and the democratic dreams of half a century have been victorious. I beg you to defend with all means our Niš, and our and your victory in it.'[3] In other towns such as Užiće, Pirot, and Jagodina, attempts by the authorities to annul the opposition victories prompted similar popular protests. As the opposition protests continued the Zajedno leaders sought to present their case to the diplomatic community holding meetings with a number of Western ambassadors protesting at the attempts to annul the election results in the majority of places where Zajedno had defeated the Socialists. At the same time, however, a less 'diplomatic' impression was made when comments made by Danica Drašković, in a private conversation at a Zajedno rally, were picked up and broadcast on the RTS news. She was heard to say: 'It is a shame that there is no Apis in Serbia today or any such terrorism to respond to the physical and spiritual terrorism of the state.'[4] This statement was later to form a key argument in the attempts by the authorities to brand Zajedno as a 'terrorist' organisation. Following this incident Danica Drašković claimed that she was abducted by unidentified members of the state security service who sought to intimidate her into persuading her husband to cease organising the demonstrations and abandoning his alliance with Djindjić.

On 22 November a Student Protest Committee was formed both to pursue their own demands, including the removal of the unpopular rector of Belgrade University, SPS nominee, Dragutin Veličković, and to support the Zajedno call for the recognition of their local election victories. On 24 November it was announced that the victories of thirty-three Zajedno candidates in the Belgrade area had been annulled, and that a third round of elections would be held, on 27 November, to decide the results in these seats. In a separate judgement the city election commission in Niš officially awarded victory in the town to the SPS. The Zajedno parties swiftly rejected any suggestion that they would participate in the proposed third election round in Belgrade, Niš or the other towns where elections were being annulled. The opposition call to boycott the third round of elections appeared to have been heeded by a large section of the population and turn-out in the Belgrade area was recorded at less than 20 per cent. When Slobodan Milošević was filmed by Serbian TV casting his ballot, the only other person voting in the polling station was his son Marko. According to a Western journalist who observed the polling, only six other people had voted in the previous two hours. While very few people were in the polling stations, increasingly large numbers were coming out on to the streets. The demonstrations quickly took on a regular and familiar pattern. The protesters would gather in the early afternoon outside the headquarters of the DS on the Terazije before setting out on a 'walk' around central Belgrade, whistling and chanting anti-government slogans as they passed major state buildings and institutions. On 27 November some demonstrators pelted the headquarters of RTS, *Politika* and Radio Belgrade with eggs and stones, smashing many of the windows on their lower floors. The demonstrators had vented their anger on these buildings, because they represented the key institutions of the Serbian state-controlled media which had refused to give any coverage to the daily demonstrations. The Zajedno leaders, however, were aware that such damage to property would only help the Socialists and undermine their own cause. It was made clear to their supporters that while it was acceptable to throw eggs at government buildings there should be no more stone-throwing. This appeal was heeded, but the continuing barrage of eggs aimed at the state institutions led to the demonstrations being given the title of the 'Egg Revolution' in conscious imitation of the 'Yoghurt Revolution' which had helped to bring Milošević to power in Vojvodina in 1988. Vuk Drašković told one rally that Milošević had 'come in on yoghurt and will go out on eggs'.[5] This decision, at an early stage, by the opposition leaders to use egg-throwing as a symbolic form of peaceful protest while eschewing real violence set the tone for the on-going demonstrations. It became common for the demonstrators to use the Red Star Belgrade football chant 'Get ready, Go, All attack!' in their daily acts of protest. These ritual chants borrowed from the football terraces acted as a substitute for any form of real violence. The 'attacks' mentioned in the chant would frequently take the form of increasingly inventive jokes such as the 'bombarding' of the RTS building with paper aeroplanes. Young women protestors carried bunches of flowers in order to emphasise their pacific intent. The non-violent nature of the demonstrations and the fact that the protestors seemed to be competing with each other to produce the most witty slogans on their placards combined to give their daily 'walks' the flavour of a carnival. The fact that the demonstrators took to carrying the flags of foreign countries, alongside some more traditional Serbian, royalist and Četnik banners, also gave these occasions a strangely 'post-modern' atmosphere. This 'internationalism' was in line with the desire of the Zajedno leaders, which had been evident 'since the 9 March rally, to emphasise to the outside world their pro-Western orientation. But it also reflected the genuine belief of ordinary demonstrators that Serbia needed to 'return to Europe', and that political and economic life should be governed by European standards and practices.

The history of opposition activity in Serbia since 1990 had in some senses been a chronicle of street demonstrations, but the protests which began in November 1996 were broader and would be more sustained than any which had taken place before. Events in the capital were mirrored by those taking place in the provinces. On 27 November, the eighth day of the protests, when 200,000 demonstrated in Belgrade, at the same time 20,000 people were on the streets in Niš, 15,000 in Kragujevac, and 5,000 in Kraljevo. Similar numbers of people were taking part in protests in other places across Serbia and while the demonstrations remained a largely urban phenomenon there were signs that they were involving a growing number of people from relatively small settlements. Demonstrations were also recorded in places such as Valjevo and Leskovac where the Socialists had emerged victorious. On 4 December representatives of the Zajedno coalition in Valjevo unveiled a 'black book' of election abuses carried out by the SPS, and from 7 December several thousand-strong daily demonstrations, in solidarity with the Belgrade protestors, began in the town.[6] The demonstrations were also inclusive in that they involved people of all ages from students, who took part in their own independent demonstrations as well as those organised by Zajedno, to pensioners. The Zajedno leaders were keen to distinguish themselves from other demonstrations of 'popular power' in recent Yugoslav history. Ilija Djukić stated: 'The massive protests of citizens directed against the equally massive falsification of their votes on 17 November are an expression of a new quality in the political life of Serbia. This is not a "movement of the masses" or a "mass movement", and it should never be called that. Nor is it an organised populist "happening of the people". The time for such events has past. This is a mass protest of citizens against the theft of their votes in the recent elections. This is a protest of citizen-voters against the falsification of their free elections.'[7] While the decision of the authorities to annul the Zajedno victories in the elections was the immediate cause of the demonstrations it was clear that many citizens were taking to the streets as a protest against the general political and economic failure of the government, and the all-pervading corruption of the regime. Members of political parties who had not formed part of the Zajedno coalition in the local elections also took part in the demonstrations, and the banners of the DSS, SNS, Democratic Centre and SDU could be seen among the crowds. More important, as the demonstrations continued they began to attract numerous individuals who owed their allegiance to no particular party. While the non-violent spirit of the demonstrations quickly impressed the Western journalists who were arriving in Belgrade in increasing numbers it was deeply frustrating for the authorities who wanted nothing better than a confrontation which would give them the excuse they needed to restore order.

There was a strong feeling among the demonstrators that power was inexorably slipping away from the Socialist authorities. In Niš it was noted that Mile Ilić, sensing that his local power bastion was crumbling, had rapidly disappeared from view. Ilić's chief opponent in the Niš area was Zoran Živković, a young private businessman and national Vice-President of the DS. At the end of November Živković was asked by journalists whether he had any idea where Ilić was. He replied: 'For me personally, and I believe for most of those who are involved in this common enterprise, the whereabouts of Mile Ilić and his collaborators are of no interest. I have no desire to see him and it feels pleasant when I do not have to see him. For those who want to see him I advise that they look in the cellars, the pantries and the stores.'[8] When on 4 December Ilić resigned as leader of the Niš Socialists, apparently after the intervention of Nikola Šainović, he was widely seen as being the scapegoat for the deeper failures of SPS rule.

In Belgrade the SPS Mayor, Nebojša Čović, had also become strangely elusive. Cornered by a journalist on 11 December, Čović refused to make any comment on the on-going demonstrations.[9] Local Socialist officials in the provinces had begun to rationalise their electoral defeat by blaming the unpopularity of their erstwhile allies in JUL. Dobrivoje Budimirović the leader of the SPS from Svilajnac in central Serbia stated that the worst defeats suffered by the SPS had taken place in areas where their relationship with JUL had been closest because 'when the SPS disowned some people because of their dubious morals and other qualities they found their way magically into the ranks of JUL and in this election the greatest hostility towards the SPS came from those former members of the SPS who are now in JUL.'[10] Radovan Radović, the SPS representative from Trstenik in the Šumadija, was moved by the SPS defeat at the hands of Zajedno and the subsequent demonstrations to reflect that: 'I do not believe that it is necessary to have any party other than the Socialists. We have seen what happened to that party [JUL] which was created a month ago in different offices. I am generally not concerned about what happens to JUL. I know, however, that the SPS would have fared better if it had not been allied with JUL.'[11] In the Sandžak, where there had also been bitter feuds between the SPS and JUL, the local elections showed that the bid by JUL to attract ethnic minority support had foundered with the 'left' candidates being routed at the polls by the local Muslim SDA. These battles between the cadres of the SPS and JUL were to grow in bitterness as the pressure exerted from the streets became more intense.[12]

The Serbian government appeared to have been taken by surprise by the scale and strength of the popular demonstrations. Their first reaction was to attempt to ignore the demonstrations in the apparent hope that they would simply run out of energy once it became clear that their demands were not going to be satisfied immediately. The authorities saw the bitterly cold winter weather as an important ally in their battle of wills with the demonstrators. It was also calculated that by maintaining a total 'media blockade' the authorities would be able to insulate the core areas of Socialist support in the countryside from the subversive events taking place in urban Serbia. As a result the news on Serbian state-controlled media assumed a particularly bizarre aspect during the first days of the crisis. The news would be dominated by a series of items which emphasised Yugoslavia's 'progress' and 'co-operation' with other countries and detailed the meetings which had taken place between Serbian ministers and visiting foreign delegations. On 29 November, for instance, the main news consisted of items dealing with the visit of a delegation of Russian businessmen, a meeting between representatives of the Yugoslav and Bulgarian military, and the successful and peaceful progress of the third round of elections. Political dissension in other countries was also a favourite theme in the state-controlled media. It was possible to hear or read detailed analyses of transport strikes in France or political divisions within the British government, but there was no mention of the political crisis convulsing Serbia itself.

After over a week of protests, however, the authorities had apparently decided that the failure to react to the demonstrations was making them appear increasingly ridiculous. On 1 December Dragan Tomić launched a strong denunciation of the Zajedno and student demonstrators branding them as 'destroyers and violent individuals with all the characteristics of pro-fascist groups and ideologies'. He went on to say that 'the worst thing about all this is the way that they manipulate children. We have had the opportunity to see that take place in Kosovo, and also in history in the period when Hitler came to power.'[13] This attack was accompanied by a statement from the Serbian police that unauthorised gatherings on the streets of Belgrade would no longer be tolerated. The students and opposition were, however, undeterred by these attempts to label them as 'fascists'. The Initiative Committee of the Student Protest promptly issued this statement: 'Last night Dragan Tomić, the President of the Serbian parliament claimed that "the students are manipulated children". It is wonderful that you are so worried about us, Mr Tomić, but where were you when those of our own age, on the orders of the regime, went to their deaths around Vukovar and on other battlefields. While you shed our blood you did not worry at all about our tender years. We are not children Mr (or if you like Comrade) Tomić. We are voters, with all the rights of citizens in this community, who with all legal and moral responsibility, go out onto the streets each day to ask that you show "serious adult responsibility" and honour the laws which you yourself have proposed. You are a child because you do not have sufficient seriousness as to honour the laws which you yourself have created. Last night you threatened us saying that you will no longer tolerate the mass occupation of the cities of Serbia. We are not afraid. The government claims that we are a handful of manipulated students and *provocateurs*. What serious government would place in readiness a repressive apparatus of 100,000 policemen to deal with such a paltry group of young rebels. This threat certainly does not move us.'[14] One student protester could be seen at demonstrations carrying a slogan which made a mocking reference to Tomić's words: 'I have an under-aged, retarded, impressionable, seduced, manipulated pro-fascist temperament.'[15] The Zajedno demonstrators were similarily unimpressed by Tomić's statement and on 2 December 80,000 people came out onto the streets in spite of the heavy snowfalls during the day. Vuk Drašković told the demonstrators: 'None other than the President of Serbia's parliament has called our capital "a capital of fascism". This is the city which in 1941 had the heart and the courage to go out on to the streets and say of fascism "better the grave than slavery".'[16] The pro-government parties, however, continued to present the demonstrations as a re-play of the Second World War struggles with the protesters playing the role of the forces of 'reaction'. Ljubiša Ristić warned in apocalyptic tones that if the opposition were allowed to win 'we will have a Četnik Belgrade, the left will be placed in a position of anti-fascist struggle, and we will take up that challenge.'[17] This critique of the demonstrations was taken up by Mira Marković, who on 2 December had returned from a trip to India where she had been promoting her latest book, in her column in *Duga* when she accused the opposition of wanting to initiate a civil war in Serbia. She wrote: 'In Bosnia the war is over, but it should not be continued in Serbia, it should be finished in the whole of the Balkans. I do not know really whether this summons to war, this call for violence is simply the product of sick minds or whether it is a question of a planned strategy whereby the war in the territory of the former Yugoslavia will not be allowed to finish. In any case violence, that type of violence which is most widespread and most difficult to stop and claims the greatest number of victims, is knocking on our door. The door should not be opened to violence by those who would pay the greatest price –young people.'[18]

With Serbian TV having abandoned its policy of ignoring the

demonstrations it launched a concerted attempt to discredit the protestors. In the undertaking of this media offensive the Serbian state TV bosses employed tactics which involved acts of petty subterfuge. News reports would frequently quote selectively from foreign, and particularily Western, press articles to give the impression that the international media opposed the demonstrations, or alternatively they would quote from foreign papers sympathetic to the Socialist regime, such as the newspaper *Duma* affiliated to the Bulgarian Socialist Party. On 7 December RTS news carried an item which purported to be a series of interviews with ordinary members of the public in which they were asked to give their views of the recent street protests. All but one of the interviewees, who were uniformly hostile to the protests, appeared to be older people who had been questioned in rural or suburban contexts. The exception was a young woman who, when apparently asked her opinion of the opposition rallies, replied: 'That really can't be tolerated any more.' The young woman, a supporter of the opposition, later made a statement to the Student Protest Committee in which she attested that her reply had been given when she was asked by reporters, who did not identify themselves as being from RTS, what she thought of the 'media blockade'.[19] An organisation calling itself the Independent Student Movement also made an appearance calling for 'depoliticisation of the faculties' and for students to return to their studies. This 'movement' claimed to have widespread support amongst students, but was widely considered to be a 'phantom' organisation with no real existence beyond the range of the RTS cameras, which gave the group extensive coverage.[20]

For all its efforts at presenting a monolithic SPS–centred view of the world behind the scenes all was not well within the state media establishment. On 5 December Aleksandar Tijanić resigned from his position as Information Minister. Reports suggested that Tijanić's 'journalist's stomach' could no longer tolerate the line he was required to take in the state media, and the systematic pressure which was being exerted on the independent media.[21] In a further sign of dissension within the state establishment the BK news reports ceased to follow the party line, and began to give broadly impartial coverage to the demonstrations. The shift in the position of the BK· TV was followed by the decision of students at the Braća Karić University to support the demonstrations which had been initiated by the Belgrade University students. Taken together both these events reflected the changing loyalties of Bogoljub Karić, and his desire to break free from his alliance with Milošević, who he apparently regarded as a politically spent force, and establish himself as an independent actor on the political scene. The independent Belgrade radio station B-92 also came under attack from the authorities, and on 3 December its broadcasts were suspended without explanation. On 5 December, after considerable international pressure, the radio station was once again able to start broadcasting. The official explanation given by Dragoljub Milanović, the head of RTS, in a letter to the Director of B-92, for the two-day interruption in the station's programmes was that water had entered the coaxial antenna cable. While B-92 was able to remain on the air, the local station Radio BUM 93 serving the Požarevac area was effectively closed down by state pressure. During the demonstrations the opposition sought new ways to communicate with the public. On 8 December the opposition parties sought to 'break the media blockade' by setting up a television outside the headquarters of the DS which broadcast a compilation of unedited foreign TV coverage of the demonstrations. This period also witnessed the conversion of *Demokratija*, the journal of the DS, from a magazine characterised by worthy articles on political/economic theory and primarily designed for internal party consumption, to a popular daily newspaper. *Demokratija* in its new form was specifically designed to address the events taking place across Serbia, and it noted in an editorial on 1 December: 'It is evident that, unfortunately, in the conditions in which we live it is not possible for our citizens to be uninterested in politics. We are a boulevard newspaper – we write above all about what is happening on the streets'. Other independent newspapers also reported a dramatic rise in their sales during this period.[22]

During the initial period of the demonstrations, in November and early December, there was no attempt by the police to stop the demonstrators gathering and walking along their chosen route through the city. It was well known, however, that police special forces were deployed in government buildings along the route of the march and people went out to demonstrate in the daily knowledge that a violent police intervention might be imminent. The belief that the use of force was being contemplated within the inner circles of the ruling party was heightened by the bellicose pronouncements emanating from senior figures in the SPS and JUL. Observers of the Serbian political scene pointed to the 'tradition' in post-communist Serbia of confrontations between the demonstrators and the police being resolved by violent means. One academic noted, in an article written in early December: 'In American theory which deals with the transition from an authoritarian regime to democracy, the most important factor is the readiness of certain individuals from within the existing regime to come to an agreement with individuals from the elite which is coming to power. While this is most desirable [in Serbia] it is also the least likely outcome. Will we face a new Bucharest here?'[23] While the predicted mass confrontation between the opposition and the police did not materialise there was a constant stream of incidents whereby individual opposition supporters were arrested by the police, and frequently beaten or mistreated, as they were leaving the rallies. The most notable of these incidents occurred on 5 December following the Zajedno rally and walk. On this occasion, as well as the customary speeches from the Zajedno leaders, the crowd had been entertained by the antics of a full-sized puppet of Slobodan Milošević dressed in a convict's uniform. The puppet had been operated by Dejan Bulatović, a twenty-one-year-old member of the SPO from Šid. After the rally Bulatović was arrested by the police and savagely beaten and abused during his detention. He was later sentenced to twenty-five days in prison for 'obstructing the traffic'. Following his sentence, however, he remained defiant saying: 'I was not afraid. I am a Serb, and I will not bend. I will continue with the struggle.'[24] The 14 December issue of the magazine *Vreme* carried on its front cover a picture of Bulatović with his Milošević puppet ironically underlined by Milošević's words uttered in Kosovo in 1987: 'No one should dare to beat you.'

In addition to commanding the energetic support of numerous ordinary citizens the demonstrations were endorsed by a wide range of figures from Serbian cultural, intellectual, and public life. Over the years a growing range of individuals, with differing or even conflicting interests, had become deeply alienated by the rule of Slobodan Milošević, and for all of them the demonstrations provided an opportunity to strike back at him. On 23 November Dobrica Ćosić addressed one of the Zajedno rallies in Belgrade in support of their demand for recognition of the local election results. Ćosić said afterwards: 'I do not agree with the political positions of many people from the coalition Zajedno, with their programme and their conduct. But we are in agreement regarding the battle for democratic rights and for the democratic transformation of this country.'[25] On 28 November thirty members of the Serbian Academy of Arts and Sciences signed an appeal supporting the demands of the students and opposition demonstrators. The appeal called on the students to 'persist until the end in your protest against the most shameless lawlessness known to the contemporary world'.[26] The appeal was signed by amongst others Ljubomir Simović, Matija Bećković, Predrag Palavestra and Nikola Milošević. The Association of Serbian Writers, the President of which was Slobodan Rakitić, also publically expressed its support for the demonstrations. Rakitić in his support for the protests was prepared to put aside his long-standing differences with Drašković: 'It [the election] was an expression of the conscious desire for political change. It was a vote against the existing regime, against the existing government, against the existing political system. It is not so relevant who is on the other side. This time the Zajedno coalition of three political parties is on the other side, that is the political situation, but the most important fact is that this time the majority of citizens voted against the existing political position.'[27] From a 'liberal' perspective the Belgrade Circle issued a declaration which stated: 'In these extraordinary circumstances the Belgrade Circle asks its friends and allies from abroad to support the civic option in Serbia to which the students and Professors of Belgrade University have dedicated themselves.'[28] Dragoslav Avramović also made a brief reappearance on the political scene when on 6 December he appeared amongst the crowd at a Zajedno demonstration. Among the many other people to lend their support to the popular movement were the film director Emir Kusturica, the playwright Dušan Kovačević, and the actor Rade Šerbedžija.

Patriarch Pavle had at first been mindful of his role as spiritual leader of all the Serbs, and reluctant to give unequivocal support to the demonstrators. When on 7 December the protesting students had asked the Patriarch to give them his blessing he had declined, saying that in such difficult times it would be unwise for the church to be seen taking sides in a political dispute. In an earlier public declaration on 27 November, he called on all Serbian political leaders in the government and opposition to 'maintain just forms of democratic conduct and accept the freely expressed will of the people'.[29] From London the heir to the Serbian throne, Prince Alexander, also offered his moral support to the demonstrators. In Montenegro the opposition coalition, Narodna Sloga (National Unity), led jointly by Novak Kilibarda and Slavko Perović, launched a series of rallies in solidarity with the Zajedno opposition and against their own government, which they described as the 'twin brother' of the regime in Serbia.[30] From the Bosnian Serbs Biljana Plavšić, the newly-elected President of the Republika Srpska, said: 'Protesting students are always a sign that freedom and democracy are in danger.' She added: 'I hope that Serbia will emerge from these tempestuous days as a strong national state comparable to other states in Europe.'[31] More remarkable, however, was the message of support addressed to the Serbian people sent by Adem Demaci, the veteran Albanian activist from Kosovo on 5 December, who suggested in his letter that despite all the political upheavals and tensions of recent years underlying ties had remained between the Serbian and Albanian peoples. He wrote: 'And we were right to love you, Serbian people, because today the healthy land of Serbia has shed its dank, narrow, provincial spirit and a new, broad, light, freedom-loving, European spirit has been born.'[32] The Sandžak Muslim SDA leader, Rasim Ljajić also aligned himself with the Zajedno movement describing the protests as 'the last chance to carry out change.[...] If the opposition does not succeed this time, there will be a return to one-party rule.'[33]

In this trial of strength between the government and the opposition a third player in the game was provided by the international community. The international community initially appeared to be taken aback by the strong public reaction to the attempt by the Milošević government to annul the elections. Milošević's grip on the levers of power within Serbia had been assumed to be secure. Gradually, however, the international institutions and media focused on the events unfolding in Belgrade. On 29 November the Organisation for Security and Co-operation in Europe (OSCE) expressed its 'exceptional concern' at the annulment of the elections, saying that it would be willing to provide help in the verification of the election results if this was sought. At the same time the Council of Europe condemned the refusal to honour the election results. This declaration was followed on 30 November by a demand from the United States government that Milošević should recognise the results of the local elections. However, Milošević was not entirely without friends in the international community. On 3 December pressure from the Russian government had resulted in the revision of a proposed statement by the OSCE critical of the Milošević government. The original text contained the statement: 'The OSCE believes that democracy, an independent media, and free and honest elections in Yugoslavia are of vital significance to the stability of the Balkans.' The amended version of the document, however, simply stated that the OSCE would work to 'accelerate the process of democratisation, urge a free media and secure free and honest elections'.[34] The United States and the European Union, however, continued their criticism of the Milošević government and their pressure on it. At the London peace implementation conference on Bosnia the British Foreign Secretary, Malcolm Rifkind, stated that the Yugoslav Foreign Minister, Milan Milutinović, had not succeeded in dealing with the concerns of the majority of delegates regarding the latest abuse of human rights by the Milošević regime. The American Deputy Secretary of State, Strobe Talbott, did however extract from Milutinović the assurance that force would not be used against the demonstrators. Indeed while Milošević had at this stage showed no sign of conceding to international demands to recognise the election results many observers believed that fear of the international community's reaction was the chief factor in restraining the regime from attempting to use violence to crush the demonstrations. On 9 December Milošević received Kati Marton, the wife of Richard Holbrooke, representing the New York Committee for the Protection of Journalists. Marton had written out a declaration, which she presented to Milošević, stating: 'In our conversation today Slobodan Milošević and Kati Marton reiterated our support for a free press in the Federal Republic of Yugoslavia, and the right to publish and broadcast without censorship.'[35] Milošević crossed out the last two words before putting his name to the paper.

While Western governments sought to maintain a steady level of pressure on the Milošević government, they were faced with a dilemma as to what further moves they could take to back up their diplomatic protests. Senior European Union officials made it clear that Yugoslavia's path to further integration with European political and economic institutions would be blocked as long as the local elections issue remained unresolved. Carl Bildt, the High

Representative of the International Peace Conference, said that the Serbian government 'must understand that Europe and democracy are synonymous' and that any attempt to draw closer to the EU would be dependent on 'full respect for international democratic standards'.[36] However, the EU was reluctant to make any steps which involved the re-imposition of economic sanctions on Yugoslavia which they believed would be counter-productive. This position was supported by the Serbian opposition parties who stressed that it would primarily be the urban middle classes who would suffer under sanctions – they were a section of Serbian society from which a large proportion of the demonstrators were drawn. The Socialist hierarchy and the ruling elite by contrast would be sufficiently wealthy to insulate themselves against the negative effects of the embargo. The 'core' SPS support group in the countryside could also, at a basic level, protect themselves from the effects of sanctions through their access to agricultural produce. The opposition were also acutely aware that a renewed programme of sanctions would enable the SPS to portray Serbia's misfortunes as being the product of intervention by hostile foreign powers aided by a treacherous opposition 'fifth column'. The opposition had been active in impressing this view on the diplomatic community in Belgrade. Vesna Pešić said: 'I think that pressure must be placed directly on Milošević and measures should not be threatened which would once again place innocent people in a hopeless situation. In all our conversations with foreign diplomats and politicians we insist that this is true...I think that they have clearly understood our message: We do not want sanctions because they will not help to bring down this regime.'[37] The opposition pursued a policy of 'parallel diplomacy', seeking to take their case to the international community, and on 11 December Miodrag Perišić and Miroljub Labus visited Washington to meet members of the American administration and argue that sanctions, if they were applied, should be 'selective' targeting the assets held abroad by senior members of the Serbian government and their families. These measures, they suggested, would be similar in form to those already applied to international narcotics criminals.[38]

In addition to the declarations of support from Western powers the opposition demonstrators also received messages of solidarity from other political parties in Eastern Europe including Russia's Democratic Choice and the Magyar Democratic Forum from

Hungary. From Romania the mayor of Timişoara, the town where
in December 1989 the uprising against Nicolae Ceauşescu began,
and the Organisation of Timişoara Revolutionaries sent this message
to the Zajedno coalition: 'We who six years ago on the streets
of Timişoara opened the door to democracy in the whole of
Romania are all in our hearts with our Serbian brothers who on
the streets of Belgrade, by peaceful means, are fighting for truth
and freedom. The sun which illuminated Timişoara in December
1989 now in December 1996 drives away the fog of the last
communist dictatorship in Europe. God is with you.'[39] The links
between the Zajedno parties and the Bulgarian Union of Democratic
Forces (SDS) were of particular significance. The SDS signalled
their support for the Zajedno coalition soon after the demonstrations
in Serbia began. On 28 December the Bulgarian Prime Minister
Zhan Videnov resigned and his ruling Bulgarian Socialist Party
(BSP) attempted to form a new government in the midst of an
economic meltdown. Determined to prevent the selection of a
new BSP government the SDS decided to launch a series of
anti-government demonstrations. Senior figures within the SDS
leadership met Zajedno leaders in Belgrade to discuss tactics. When
the Bulgarian demonstrations began in Sofia after 10 January they,
in spite of one serious violent incident at their start, closely followed
the example of peaceful protest established in Belgrade. Ordinary
Bulgarians were ready to acknowledge the similarity between these
two expressions of popular protest. One demonstrator remarked:
'When we saw our neighbours go out and do something we
decided to do it too. We've taken courage from the Serbs.'[40]
Zoran Djindjić remarked: 'In Bulgaria the whistle salesmen are
making a mint as the Bulgarian opposition have taken up our
model.' The Serbian Socialists and their propaganda machine, however, sought to portray both the Serbian and Bulgarian demonstrations
as part of a common conspiracy masterminded by a powerful but
unnamed foreign centre.[41]

   The opposition leaders during the first weeks of the protests
had been generally pleased with the stream of declarations of
support they had been receiving from Western governments, and
the favourable media attention which had focussed on their movement. On 12 December, however, the Italian Foreign Minister,
Lamberto Dini, had meetings in Belgrade with representatives of
both the opposition and the government. Following these meetings

Dini declared that the opposition demands for the recognition of the elections were 'unrealistic' and that the opposition should seek instead to engage in dialogue with the government. The Zajedno representatives declared themselves to be 'discontented and surprised' by Dini's suggestions. They affirmed that they would only take part in talks with the government after their victory in the 17 November elections had been acknowledged.

The Serbian government appeared to take Dini's declaration as marking the limit of Western willingness to support Zajedno and the street protestors.[42] Apparently encouraged by this Milošević sought to regain the political and diplomatic initiative. On 13 December he wrote a letter to the American Secretary of State, Warren Christopher, in which he invited the OSCE to send a delegation to Serbia so that the international community could understand the true nature of the situation regarding the local elections. The opposition reacted with great scepticism to this new development suspecting that it heralded an attempt by Milošević to dupe world opinion. Vuk Drašković remarked: 'We have proved to the world public that our election victory has been stolen from us. After all this Milošević has invited a legal commission to come and talk to him and to representatives of the local authorities. This means that the thieves are inviting foreign judges to listen only to thieves.'[43] The OSCE swiftly announced that they were ready to send a mission to Belgrade headed by the former Spanish Prime Minister, Felipe Gonzales.

The demonstrations by supporters of the Zajedno coalition, and other opposition groups, had dominated the political agenda during the early weeks of December. The SRS had, however, emerged from the federal elections as a powerful political force gaining 17.8 per cent of the vote. In the local elections the SRS had gained control of Zemun, a northern suburb of Belgrade, with the Radicals in the local assembly taking thirty-three representatives places to the fourteen held by Zajedno, and six by the Socialists, with one place taken by the DSS and JUL. In contrast to the situation in areas where Zajedno had been victorious this result was not challenged by the authorities. Šešelj was duly elected as the mayor of Zemun. Šešelj continued to suggest officially that he, and the SRS, occupied a neutral position between the government and opposition. He observed: 'There is political distance between us and the regime in Serbia, the regime of Slobodan

Milošević and the Socialist Party of Serbia, and we will do all in our power to overthrow the regime, however, on the other hand we do not agree with many of the acts of the Zajedno coalition, in particular we are against all acts of violence, and the destruction of state and social property. We believe that the regime must be overthrown but using civilised and democratic methods.'[44] Nevertheless it was widely accepted, particularly in the light of the favourable coverage given to the SRS by the state TV during the period of the protests, that Zemun was now the power-base of an ally of the Serbian President. In Niš at the end of November the SRS took steps to purge its organisation of a large group of members who had been accused of being Zajedno sympathisers.

In anticipation of the OSCE delegation's visit to Belgrade the SPS sought to mobilise their members and supporters in a series of rallies to rival those of the Zajedno coalition. These meetings were to demonstrate to the international community that a 'silent majority' of Serbs remained loyal to Milošević. The first meeting was on 17 December in Majdanpek. The next day further meetings in support of the government were held at Vranje, Kosovska Mitrovica and Sremska Mitrovica. On 21 December pro-Milošević gatherings took place in Kragujevac and Pirot. It was planned that this series of rallies would culminate in a 'Meeting for Serbia', organised by the SPS and JUL, in Belgrade on 24 December. A leading role in organising this gathering was taken by Mihalj Kertes, the SPS veteran of street politics, and Gorica Gajević. With the SPS counter-meeting set to take place on the Terazije, where the Zajedno demonstrators gathered each afternoon, the rally was a recipe for disorder. The opposition saw the SPS counter-rally as a deliberate attempt to provoke a major confrontation in the city during the visit to Belgrade by the OSCE delegation. New Democracy, anxious that this event would aggravate the already tense political situation, refused to help their partners in government with the preparations for the rally. Patriarch Pavle also appealed to the SPS and Zajedno to call off their parallel meetings. The authorities apparently believed that when the in-evitable clashes broke out between the massed supporters of govern-ment and opposition this would provide the perfect justification for police intervention.

The 'counter-meeting' did not, however, go as the authorities had planned. The organisers had boasted that they would swamp the Zajedno demonstration by mobilising 500,000 SPS supporters from across the Serbian provinces. The authorities had requisitioned 10,000 buses to ferry the government supporters into Belgrade where they were provided with food and drink before the rally began. In spite of these careful preparations, however, they were only able to bring around 60,000 supporters into the city. Many of these demonstrators, fed on a diet of state-controlled media propaganda, came to Belgrade from the countryside convinced that they were 'defending Serbia' from a 'handful of hooligans and *provocateurs*'. The barrage of accusations and propaganda aimed at the opposition in the preceding weeks had served to stigmatise them in the eyes of these provincial supporters of the government, and prepare the way for violent confrontation. The largest number of these counter-demonstrators came from the SPS strongholds of southern and eastern Serbia, and Kosovo. They were shocked therefore to find themselves outnumbered by the 300,000 strong column of Zajedno supporters.

When Milošević appeared before the pro-government crowd, surrounded by his closest followers and henchmen, he was observably angered by the small size of the gathering. In the background the characteristic chants and whistles of the much larger Zajedno crowd could be heard. The state media, however, dutifully reported that half a million people had assembled to hear Milošević. The short speech Milošević delivered to his followers had, in its rhetoric and form, all the appearances of being a relic dredged up from the days of the 'anti-bureaucratic revolution'. He told them: 'Many powerful forces outside of our land do not want to see the existence of a strong Serbia. Therefore they are attempting with the help of a "fifth column" which has been formed here to destabilise our land and weaken us. We surely cannot allow that. It is said that life is difficult. Of course life is difficult, sanctions made our life difficult, but we have shown that we were able to overcome that, and that we are able to live, and build our land, so that everything is better and better, and we have protected our economy, and developed as a modern, rich, and well integrated society in Europe and the world. What are the aims of all these demonstrations? first it is to retard our economic development, and secondly to weaken us so as to threaten the integrity of Yugoslavia and Serbia. But Serbia will not be divided.'[45] During the speech his loyal supporters began to chant 'Slobo we love you'. He replied to his admirers telling them 'I love you'. This sentence was extracted from Milošević's speech by the radio station B-92, and played repeatedly during B-92 news coverage. Among the Zajedno demonstrators badges bearing the same ironical message also proliferated.

During and after the 'counter-meeting' clashes occurred when SPS demonstrators attacked supporters of Zajedno. The initial attacks by the SPS were followed by a large-scale intervention by police special forces against the Zajedno protestors. A number of Socialists were carrying guns and opened fire on their opponents. One Zajedno supporter, Ivica Lazović, an SPO member, was shot in the head and critically injured. The incident was filmed by members of the international media, and a member of the SPS from Vrbas in Vojvodina was subsequently arrested. In another incident a Zajedno protester, Predrag Starčević, was so badly beaten by supporters of the SPS that he died the next day. A total of fifty-eight people were hospitalised as a result of the fighting. In spite of the ferocity of these clashes, however, the day had witnessed a series of skirmishes rather than the full-scale battle which might have been expected. The limited number of SPS supporters who had arrived in Belgrade appeared to have dissuaded some of them from taking on the larger numbers of Zajedno protestors. The situation in Belgrade might have been very different had the anticipated number of government supporters arrived in the city. Reports also suggested that some units of the police had been unwilling to intervene when fighting broke out between the SPS and Zajedno even where the struggle looked as though it was turning against the government supporters.[46] The events of 24 December misfired for Milošević in the sense that they had been recorded by the international and domestic media who were ready to clearly lay the blame for the violence at the door of Milošević and his government. During the clashes riot police had unsuccessfully attempted to drive reporters and journalists away from the scene of the fighting.

The diplomatic community was similarily unimpressed by this manoeuvre on the part of the regime. Strobe Talbott, speaking for the US State Department, commented: 'Rather than making a goodwill gesture to resolve the political crisis, the Serbian authorities have flagrantly and provocatively chosen to heighten tensions by bringing thousands of people into Belgrade to confront the peaceful demonstrators.' He added that the United States 'holds the Serbian government and its President responsible for the violent action of the demonstrators'. Even the Russian government, normally supportive of the Milošević regime, issued a statement which warned: 'Any force, any action, bearing a heavy risk of confrontation must be ruled out.'[47]

On 25 December *Demokratija* published an editorial comment on the previous day's events: 'The President of Serbia has finally succeeded in assembling his followers and those of the opposition in one place. He did that with just one aim – that they would fight against each other and that Serbia, which has just been freed from the danger of war, should be pushed into civil war. For days he prepared for this campaign against the capital. To defend Serbia from foreign banners, and everything which comes from the outside world (apart from that which he invites). He provided them with transport, placards, and pictures of their beloved President (all the same so that no one should be jealous because the President loves them all) and brought them to the Terazije confusing it with Ušće. He forgot to tell them that this is not the Belgrade of 1988 which believed that Milošević would bring it prosperity and take it into Europe. He forgot to tell them that there were people waiting here who were not able to ignore what had happened in Bosnia, Serbian Krajina, Kosovo and Serbia itself...people who knowing what has happened could not give their votes this time to a party to which Slobodan Milošević belongs and leads. The President of Serbia walked through the streets crossing the cordons of police. He appealed to the people. Of the two groups which had come out onto the streets he chose the smaller. He chose a fragment of the people, but did not choose the others. Because "when those who attempt to destabilise us succeed Serbia will be worth nothing." He opened his heart to them and said "I love you". Nothing more and nothing less. But he did not love the others. Because they wanted to live normal lives, they wanted to work, to teach, to travel, to think with their heads. They did not want to be leaders. Nor to be led. For them these things would be enough.'[48]

The events of 24 December marked a hardening in the attitude of the authorities towards the protesters. The next day the police issued a statement which declared that the demonstrators would no longer be permitted to hold their daily walks through the city which, it was said, were blocking the traffic and causing suffering to other citizens and businesses. While the Zajedno demonstrators continued to hold their rallies in the Republic square heavy deployments of riot police prevented them from moving beyond this area. Plain clothes squads of anti-terrorist police were active on the streets after rallies in search of opposition supporters to attack. Milošević had apparently closed his ears to the entreaties of the international community. A request by Richard Miles, the American ambassador, for a meeting with Milošević in order to convey the concerns of the US government was refused.

The OSCE mission had from the start indicated its seriousness of intent when it had demanded, as a condition of going to Belgrade, that it should be able to meet whoever it wanted and see whatever evidence they considered necessary. In addition to Felipe Gonzalez, the high-powered OSCE delegation also drew on the services of the veteran American diplomat, Max Kampelman. Having invited the OSCE to Belgrade the Serbian government proved unable to present a coherent case for their decision to annul the elections. The Zajedno coalition's legal team, headed by Vojin Dimitrijević, was able to present ample documentary evidence to support its claim that they had won the elections in the contested councils. On 27 December the OSCE delegation ruled that the Zajedno coalition had indeed been victorious in Pirot, Kraljevo, Užice, Smederevska Palanka, Vršac, Niš, Soko Banja, Kragujevac, Pančevo, Jagodina, Lapovo, Šabac, Zrenjanin and eight districts of Belgrade, as well as the Belgrade City assembly. Gonzalez further commented that these election results had been annulled by the Serbian courts on the basis of arguments 'that no democratic country could have accepted'. He observed: 'There exists an extraordinary opportunity for the Federal Republic of Yugoslavia to solve this concrete problem, to initiate real democracy in the country, and to reintegrate itself into the international community.'[49] The Zajedno demonstrators gathered in central Belgrade greeted the news that the OSCE had backed their position with jubilation. The authorities, however, responded cautiously, with Milan Milutinović saying that the OSCE report was 'constructive and balanced' but suggested that in some places they had 'confused different issues'. It was by now obvious that by inviting the OSCE to Belgrade Milošević had caused himself to suffer a major self-inflicted wound. The Zajedno call for recognition of their electoral gains had ceased to be simply the demand of one contending

Serbian faction and now enjoyed the official endorsement of one of the leading international political institutions.

While the weight of international opprobrium being borne by the Milošević regime grew heavier, there were also signs that the regime's edifice of power was fragmenting from within. In the early weeks of the demonstrations when the columns of protestors passed army barracks in the city it was common to see soldiers and military personnel inside the buildings waving or signalling their support for the demonstrators. It was widely believed by the demonstrators that the army, being largely made up of conscripts, would be unwilling to use force against the protesters. The army, however, officially made no intervention, on either side in the crisis. At the end of December, however, a private radio station in Niš broadcast the contents of a letter written by officers from a number of army units based near Niš, including the elite 63rd Parachute Brigade, expressing their support for the Zajedno demonstrators. Under pressure to prove the authenticity of this statement the Zajedno leaders produced a copy of the letter which was read to a rally in Belgrade on 29 December. The letter said: 'We are fully committed to one policy only, which is Serbia, and if necessary we will place ourselves at the head of the Serb people to attain the final victory and truth. We pilots, gunners, men and officers of the Serb people greet our people. We are firmly with the people.'[50] At Milošević's urging the army Chief-of-Staff issued a declaration aimed at clarifying the position of the army. Perišić asserted that the army would 'continue to carry out its constitutional tasks faithfully and will not deviate from its established social status and constitutional role'. This statement, which neither explicitly condemned the opposition nor supported the government, was not the unambiguous gesture of support which Milošević had been seeking. On 6 January 1997 Perišić agreed to meet the leaders of the student protest movement. The meeting lasted for one and a half hours, and according to an official statement, 'General Perišić during the talks emphasised the constitutional role and tasks of the Yugoslav Army, with particular attention being paid to the resolution of the current problems through legal institutions, in the manner of all democratic countries, so that the Federal Republic of Yugoslavia can swiftly be admitted to international institutions on the basis of equality.' One of the student leaders, Čedomir Jovanović, summed up the meeting more succinctly:

'Perišić said that we were on the same side. Both of us wanted to see the constitution respected.'[51] These indications of army discontent raised the possibility that in the event of there occurring a major confrontation between government and opposition the authorities might not have a monopoly on armed force.

The next blow to the authorities was important in moral and spiritual rather than than purely political terms. On 2 January the assembly of the Serbian Orthodox church met in an emergency session to discuss the political crisis. The church condemned the 'Communist, godless and satanic' regime for the 'falsification of the people's votes, the elimination of political and religious freedom, and particularly the beating and killing of people on the streets of Belgrade'. It declared that: 'He [Milošević] has already set us against the whole world and now he wants to pit us against each other and trigger bloodshed in order to preserve his power.'[52]

The Zajedno leaders faced with the hardline being taken by the government sought new ways in which to defy and frustrate the authorities. On the night of 31 December Zajedno held a meeting in the Republic Square which was part political meeting and part giant New Year's Eve party. The opposition also encouraged their supporters to make as much noise as possible each evening, with the banging of pots and pans and the blowing of horns, in order to 'drown out the lies' of the main evening TV news. On 5 January a new tactic was deployed with opposition supporters driving their cars very slowly through the centre of Belgrade or pretending that they had broken down. As the traffic ground to a halt an opposition protest march would quickly form around the gridlocked traffic. The police, whose professed reason for banning demonstrations was to help the free movement of traffic, were forced to look on in baffled impotence. On 6 January 500,000 people came out on to the streets of Belgrade to support Zajedno and to celebrate the Orthodox Christmas Eve. They were led in procession, unopposed by the police, to the St Sava cathedral by Patriarch Pavle. The Zajedno rallies also incorporated novelties in order to maintain the interest of the participants. On one day the demonstrators would be encouraged to bring their pet animals with them, on another people would dress up in uniforms or fancy dress to mock the ranks of uniformed police they confronted. At one protest sheep were brought to the demonstration and, in order to represent socialist voters, were festooned with placards bearing such slogans as 'We support the SPS' and 'The whole world is against us'. Faced with such frivolity one provincial police commander was heard to complain that when he sent his personnel to the capital to police the demonstrations, they returned ideologically polluted by the subversive cosmopolitanism of Belgrade. From 8 January the students began to maintain a twenty-four-hour vigil confronting the police 'eye-to-eye'. This tactic, pursued peacefully, forced the authorities to keep the riot police on the streets permanently. Having been prevented from taking their usual afternoon walking route through the city centre by the riot police, Zajedno began to take a new form of action. Instead of meeting in one place and marching as a single column they designated over twenty different gathering places across the city from which groups of citizens were able to set out on different routes shouting, banging their pots and pans and whistling as they went. During mid to late January the organisers estimated that between 100,000 and 130,000 people were participating in these walks each evening.[53] While the police had found it relatively easy to block a single 'walk' following a predetermined route these multiple 'walks' snaking their way noisily across the city served utterly to confound them.

On 31 December, while the opposition were gathering on the streets and squares to greet the arrival of the New Year, Slobodan Milošević made his New Year address to the nation. He promised the people: 'The coming year will be a year of reforms – major ownership and structural changes which should make possible an affirmation of all motivating elements in a market economy.' His only reference to the political crisis was indirect: 'I think we can justly say that we have used this year well, having in mind the...internal obstructions we have experienced, especially in the past few months.'[54] The Yugoslav government appeared to be maintaining its hardline attitude, and on 3 January it rejected the findings of the OSCE with Milutinović informing them that Serbia's political crisis would be resolved 'within the framework of its institutional system'. Milošević was, however, also looking for ways out of the impasse which would not involve total surrender. He therefore began to offer a series of concessions which he hoped would deflect the attentions of the international community and sap the resolve of the opposition. On 8 January the Serbian government formally acknowledged the opposition victory in Niš.

The new Mayor of Niš was Zoran Živković, of the DS, and the presidency of the city assembly went to Zvonimir Budić, a local doctor and leader of the SPO. Earlier in the week a similar recognition had been made of the Zajedno gains in Vršac and Lapovo. While Milošević was willing to relinquish these provincial towns he remained determined to hold on to Belgrade. Nebojša Čović, who was still officially Mayor of Belgrade, was by the middle of January making clear his increasing unhappiness with Milošević's refusal to give ground to the opposition. On 14 January both Nebojša Čović and Mile Ilić were expelled from the SPS. With the opposition taking power in Niš and with its former overlord cast out, members of the SPS in the town began to break ranks. The officials in the provinces felt betrayed by their party leaders in the capital. Branislav Todorović, the owner of a large bakery in the town and reputedly one of the richest men in Niš as well as being a key member of the local SPS, came forward with an account of how the SPS had organised ballot rigging in the local and federal elections: 'The party betrayed its people...the people in Niš were only the executors and all the orders came from Belgrade. Of course, the people who obeyed blindly will have to answer for that but if it had not been for Šainović and Gajević everything would have been regular.' According to his testimony, Nikola Šainović had phoned the Niš Socialists on the day of the election and 'just kept repeating that Niš must not fall into the hands of the opposition'. He said that party members in Niš had been sent between 15,000 and 20,000 fake ballots in order to effect a Socialist victory.[55] The scale of the opposition victory in the local elections was further emphasised by the fact that they had prevailed in spite of such ballot-rigging activities.

On 14 January the Belgrade city election commission, normally subservient to the regime, declared that Zajedno had been the victors in the city. The government, however, appeared no more ready to take notice of this decision than it had been to respond to other calls to respect the 17 November results. On 18 January the SPS formally challenged the decision of the city election commission. The objections raised by the SPS were seen as a tactical move designed to entangle the opposition in a prolonged legal battle while their demonstrations on the streets lost impetus. Dušan Mihailović, the leader of New Democracy, claimed that the decision

by the Belgrade election commission had been taken at his suggestion, and attempted to put some political distance between
himself and the SPS. He told the daily newspaper *Blic* that ND
had 'no obligations' towards the SPS, and that it was 'an independent
party' which 'does not need to be close to other political
organisations'.[56] Rumours abounded that splits had developed at
the highest levels within the ruling elite. It was reported that
Mirjana Marković, who advocated the determined use of force
against the opposition, was locked in conflict with Jovica Stanišić,
the head of the secret police who argued for restraint. At the
same time a power-struggle had erupted between Stanišić and
Radovan Stojičić ('Badža'), who commanded the police, over
control of the Ministry of the Interior.

In Kragujevac the opposition victory had not been challenged
by the authorities, and in December a new town government
headed by Veroljub Stevanović, the leader of the local SPO, as
mayor and Borivoje Radić of the DS as President of the town
government, had taken office. The Serbian government, however,
were unwilling to relinquish control over the local Kragujevac
TV station (RTK) the management of which was normally nominated
by the local authorities. In their eyes RTK was a vital strategic
asset able to broadcast not only to the town itself, but also to a
large swathe of the central Serbian countryside. An attempt was
therefore made to bring RTK under the control of the state TV
network RTS. When on 22 January the newly-appointed Director
of RTK, Vidosav Stevanović, attempted to enter the TV building
he found that it had been occupied by heavily-armed special
police sent from Belgrade at the request of the head of RTS,
Dragoljub Milanović. A crowd of several thousand angry protesters
swiftly gathered outside the building. The intervention of the
local Zajedno political leaders helped to dissuade the demonstrators
from entering the building by force. Instead they decided to stage
a new peaceful protest by blocking the main roads around
Kragujevac the next afternoon. During the next day's protest,
however, the police intervened to break the blockade placed on
the road near the village of Batočina. In the ensuing action fifty
opposition supporters, including Zoran Simonović, a SPO representative in the federal Parliament, were injured by police batons.
Similar road-blocking tactics were used near Kraljevo, where clashes
also occurred with the police, and in the Niš area. On 24 December

a compromise deal was worked out between the head of RTS and the Zajedno leadership whereby Vidosav Stevanović would take over as head of RTK on the condition that for the duration of the crisis it broadcast only light entertainment and not news programmes. In the long term this agreement marked a clear retreat by the authorities with a breach being opened in the 'media blockade'. It was also a demonstration of the inability of the state to use coercive force effectively to 'resolve' the political problems they were facing.[57]

By the end of January, after two and a half months of street protests, there had been a relative decline in the number of people taking part in the demonstrations in Belgrade. A persistent and determined hardcore of demonstrators, however, ensured that there was no let up for the Serbian government from the domestic and international pressure they had been facing. On 27 January the police withdrew from the streets in order to allow Patriarch Pavle to lead a church procession as part of the celebrations of Saint Sava's Day. Over 100,000 people turned out to join the procession, and show their support for the opposition protests. The Patriarch told them: 'Today, eyes are watching us from the sky and ground and are telling us to endure on the holy and righteous road.'[58] Statements from individuals close to Milošević suggested that some attempt to find a comprehensive solution to the crisis was under consideration. On 30 January Zoran Lilić said: 'The results of the elections should be recognised...everywhere the opposition won by the will of the people.'[59] It was widely assumed that Lilić's words reflected Milošević's desire to prepare the way for recognition of the election results. The comments by Milošević's close associate, Dušan Mitević, that the post-election crisis was a consequence of 'stupidity' on the part of certain individuals in government was also taken as an indication that acceptance of the opposition victory would be followed by a search for scapegoats among the ranks of the SPS. Such hints of compromise were, however, in sharp contrast to the continuing hard line being taken on the streets where small-scale clashes between police and citizens were a daily occurrence.

On the evening of 2 February a number of different groups of Zajedno supporters sought to converge on the Republic square from different parts of the city. One column of several thousand demonstrators, led by Vuk Drasković, found that their way from

New Belgrade to the old town was blocked at the Branko Bridge by a cordon of heavily-armed riot police. Two other columns of Zajedno supporters, headed by Zoran Djindjić and Vesna Pešić, had been approaching the Republic Square when they heard that Drašković's group were trapped on the New Belgrade side of the river Sava. They promptly diverted their march towards the Branko Bridge in order to help their blockaded fellow-citizens. Vuk Drašković, interviewed by Radio B-92, also called on the citizens of Belgrade to gather at the bridge. With the arrival of these reinforcements there were, on both sides of the river, around 20,000 demonstrators facing the police who were armed with riot batons, water cannon, and automatic rifles. In this new location the Zajedno leaders began to hold an inpromtu rally. At around 11.30, however, the situation changed rapidly when the police suddenly moved forward to clear demonstrators from the streets. Supported by water-cannon the police clubbed anyone who got in their way. Scattered attempts by the demonstrators to put up resistance soon faltered. Vesna Pešić was amongst the Zajedno supporters injured as the police advanced. The police attacks on people who were, or appeared to be, opposition supporters continued across the city and throughout the night. In a move which particularily outraged academic opinion riot police even entered the philosophy faculty of Belgrade University to hunt for student activists. A total of eighty demonstrators were injured during the night's events.[60]

The opposition leaders saw the police action as part of carefully planned and co-ordinated attack. They pointed to the fact that the police had been strangely absent from the centre of Belgrade that evening, and had instead taken the unusual step of concentrating at a point on the edge of the city where it was known that the opposition were going to pass. Responsibility for the decision to use force was widely ascribed to Mirjana Marković. Opposition leaders, in the immediate aftermath of the attack, believed that it might herald the start of a general security clampdown. They drew attention to reports that police reinforcements had recently been brought into Belgrade from Kosovo. The feared clampdown, however, did not materialise and the next day the opposition were again able to hold a 60,000-strong rally in central Belgrade. Around 30,000 Zajedno supporters also walked unopposed over the Branko Bridge which had been the scene of violence on the previous night. The opposition leaders confessed themselves to be baffled by the inconsistent policy being pursued by the Serbian government. Under the pressure of the previous night's events, Drašković had at one point exclaimed: 'There can be no more Gandhi-style resistance to this violence.' He added that during the next day's demonstrations 'all participants must take with them something they can use to defend themselves.'[61] This apparent call for an abandonment of the strategy of non-violence was embarrassing for the other opposition leaders. Interviewed the next day by the BBC, Miodrag Perišić sought to explain away Drašković's statement as 'a joke'. Drašković subsequently affirmed that he continued to believe in a policy of peaceful resistance describing his previous statement as an 'emotional response' and saying: 'Last night the police not only failed to break the Gandhi-style way of resistance, rather their brutality will encourage even greater peaceful mass resistance to violence.'[62] The incident, however, underlined the continuing tensions over strategy and personality which underlay the Zajedno alliance. As with the events of 24 December, the action on 2–3 February served to attract further international condemnation for the regime and support for the opposition. On 3 February the French Foreign Minister, Hervé de Charette, invited the Zajedno leaders to come to France for talks. A similar invitation was extended shortly afterwards by the British Foreign Secretary, Malcolm Rifkind.

On 4 February Slobodan Milošević wrote a letter to Mirko Marjanović in which he urged the Prime Minister to frame a law which would recognise the Zajedno victories as recommended by the OSCE. Strangely, for a leader who formally professed to follow democratic practice, Milošević gave as his reason for the recognition of these victories a desire to appease international opinion rather than any wish to respect the will of the voters. His letter declared: 'I would like to stress that the interests of the state in promoting our country's good relations with the OSCE and the international community far outweigh the importance of any number of council seats in a handful of towns.'[63] The recognition of the election victories would, it was suggested, require extraordinary legislation or as it was termed a *Lex Specialis*. Milošević's decision to write to Marjanović was apparently taken after a final meeting with his security chiefs, Jovica Stanišić and Radovan Stojičić.

The Zajedno leaders were cautious in their response to the Milošević letter. The opposition, and the OSCE, saw the legal device of the *Lex Specialis* as a way in which Milošević even in defeat was still trying to emphasise that he was in control of events. A meeting of legal theorists from Belgrade University declared the *Lex Specialis* was 'unconstitutional' and was simply meant to convey the message that for Milošević *'L'état c'est moi'*.[64] Ultimately, however, it was impossible for Milošević to disguise the fact that the recognition of the election results was a massive, and unprecedented, political reverse. It was announced that the Zajedno demonstrations would continue until the new town governments in the opposition-controlled areas had been fully constituted. On 11 February the *Lex Specialis* was passed through parliament recognising the opposition gains in all the areas that they claimed except for New Belgrade and Mladenovac. In the Belgrade city assembly it was confirmed that Zajedno had been the victors gaining sixty-seven seats, SPS-JUL-ND gained twenty-four seats, the SRS seventeen, and the DSS two. The Zajedno strength later rose to sixty-eight when one of the DSS representatives, Aleksandra Joksimović, defected to the DS. On 15 December the Zajedno coalition announced that it was holding its last protest meeting. A meeting to celebrate the formation of the new city government, with Zoran Djindjić as Mayor would, however, be held on 21 February. The students pledged that they would continue their demonstrations until their demand for the resignation of the rector, Dragutin Veličković, was satisfied. With the departure of Veličković on 7 March the way was finally cleared for the students to resume their studies.

On 21 February 150,000 people turned out to celebrate Zajedno's assumption of power in Belgrade. The first act of the new city government that evening was to remove the five-pointed communist star which had stood above the city assembly building for the previous fifty years. The state media fulminated angrily against the coalition. The main Serbian TV news told its viewers: 'The symbol which has testified for five decades to the freedom-loving nature of these people and their rejection of foreign tutelage and occupation has been removed from Belgrade. This an act which insults every patriot; the new authorities in Belgrade are trying to remove swiftly with one move the evidence that the people fought under these symbols – which fervid Djindjić and his supporters are now removing – against the German fascist evil and occupation during the most difficult period, and paid the price in an enormous number of killed and executed.[...] By destroying the most sacred traces of the peace-loving nature of his people, has Djindjić not started to erase the dark patches from the past of those whom he is frequently visiting in Bonn for consultations, and whose flag he has been carrying through the streets of Belgrade for months?'[65] The vehemence of this declaration and its strongly nationalist tone were indicative both of the authorities' bitterness in defeat and the strategy which they would employ in the battle to regain ground from the opposition.

Notes

1. *Beta*, 7 November 1996 in *SWB EE/2765 A/10*, 10 November 1996.
2. *Beta*, 18 November 1996 in *SWB EE/2774 A/11*, 20 November 1996.
3. Zoran Kosanović, 'Bezočna Kradja', *Vreme*, 23 November 1996.
4. *Demokratija – Dani bunta* (Demokratija Supplement), Belgrade, (1997), p. 3.
5. B. Lazukić, 'Ovo je treći srpski ustanak', *Demokratija*, 1 December 1996.
6. 'Crna knjijga o izbornim kradjama', *Naša borba*, 4 December 1996; 'Solidarnost sa demonstrantima I studentima', *Naša borba*, 7-8 December 1996.
7. Ilija Djukić, 'Početak kraja srpskog režima', *Naša borba*, 3 December 1996.
8. 'Osmi dan', Zoran Živković interviewed by Petar Ignja, *NIN*, 29 November 1996.
9. 'Čović 'bez komentara', *Naša borba*, 11 December 1996.
10. 'Iz Beograda u Svilajnac dolazili su visoki funkcioneri vlade i ministri da ruše mene I socijaliste Žešće nego što je to radila koalicija "Zajedno"', Dobrivoje Budimirović ('Bidža') interviewed by Vladan Dinić, *Svedok*, 3 December 1996.
11. 'Neću da se Živciram zbog ovog naroda', Radovan ('Raka') Radović interviewed by Violeta Marčetić, *NIN*, 29 November 1996.
12. *Beta*, 8 November 1996 in *SWB EE/2766 A/11*, 11 November 1996.
13. 'Tomić: Manipulacija decom', *Demokratija*, 3 December 1996.
14. 'Studenti: Nismo izmanipulisana deca', *Demokratija*, 3 December 1996.
15. '*Buka u modi*' Student Protest '96 (Belgrade), 1997.
16. A. Bogdanović and DJ. Todorović, 'Prestonica nije fašistička', *Demokratija*, 3 December 1996.
17. Ljubiša Ristić, 'Reči upozorenja', *NIN*, 29 November 1996.
18. Mirjana Marković, 'Priča sa Beogradskih ulica', *Duga*, 21 December 1996-3 January 1997.
19. '*Buka u modi*' Student Protest '96 (Belgrade), 1997.
20. 'Nezavisni studentski pokret traži nesmetanu nastavu', *Demokratija*, 12 December 1996.

21. 'Tijanić podneo ostavku, ostavku usvojena pre tri dana?', *Dnevni telegraf*, 5 December 1996.
22. 'Bili smo s vama', editorial in *Demokratija*, 1 December 1996.
23. Ognjen Pribičević, 'Milošević će srušiti demonstranti', *Naša borba*, 5 December 1996.
24. Violeta Marčetić, 'Treniranje državnog terora', *NIN*, 13 December 1996.
25. Srdjan Radulović, 'Ne slažem se sa mnogim ljudima iz koalicije Zajedno, ali pozivam Miloševića da poštuje zakone Srbije', *Nedeljni telegraf*, 20 November 1996.
26. 'Apel akademika studentima', *Demokratija*, 29th November 1996.
27. 'Narod glasao protiv vlasti', Slobodan Rakitić interviewed by A. Bogdanović, *Demokratija*, 7 December 1996.
28. 'Javno podržite gradjansku opciju Srbiji', *Naša borba*, 5 December 1996.
29. Tatjana D Nikolić, 'Rečima oblačimo misli, reči su simboli', *Demokratija*, 12 December 1996.
30. 'Pritisak na Crnogorsku vlast', *Naša borba*, 2 December 1996.
31. 'Biljana Plavšić podržala proteste u Srbiji', *Naša borba*, 12 December 1996.
32. Adem Demaci, 'Srpski narode, ne pokolebaj se', *Naša borba*, 6 December 1996.
33. Lidija Destanović, 'Opozicija će sigurno uspeti', *Demokratija*, 6 December 1996.
34. Branko Stošić, 'Moskva ne odobrava demonstracije jer ih i kod kuće – Ne voli', *Naša borba*, 5 December 1996.
35. 'Predsednik Srbije dobro informisan', *Naša borba*, 9 December 1996.
36. Mirko Klarin, 'Kinkel i Bilt protiv obnavljanja sankcija', *Naša borba*, 7-8 December 1996.
37. 'Mi nećemo sankcije', Vesna Pešić interviewed by Violeta Marčetić, *NIN*, 13 December 1996.
38. Slobodan Pavlović, 'Traži se zamrzavanje inostrane imovine Miloševića i dvadesetak vladajućih porodica', *Naša borba*, 12 December 1996.
39. 'Podrška temišvarskih revolucionara', *Demokratija*, 6 December 1996.
40. Tim Judah, 'Bulgarians Follow the Serb Line', *Sunday Telegraph*, 1 January 1997.
41. 'Serbian Television Explains Sofia Demonstrations', *Transition*, 21 February 1997.
42. *Tanjug*, 13 December 1996 in *EE/2796 A/13*, 16 December 1996.
43. Serbian TV, 13 December 1996 in *SWB EE/2796 A/13*, 16 December 1996.
44. 'Šešelj posmenjivao sve koje je mogao', Vojislav Šešelj interviewed by Vladimir Sudar, *Demokratija*, 3 December 1996.
45. Slobodan Milošević, 'I ja vas volim', *NIN*, 27 December 1996.
46. Julian Borger, 'Marchers Defy Milošević Crackdown', *Guardian*, 30 December 1996.
47. Julius Strauss, 'Milošević Blamed after Serbia Riots', *Daily Telegraph*, 26 December 1996.
48. 'SAO Terazije', *Demokratija*, 25 December 1996.
49. Julian Borger, 'Report Damns Serb Poll Fix', *Guardian*, 28 December 1996.

50. Julius Strauss, 'Army Plays Down Serbia Coup Threat', *Daily Telegraph*, 31 December 1996.
51. Dejan Anastasejević, 'Modro I zeleno', *Vreme*, 11 January 1997.
52. Anthony Lloyd, 'Church Attack on Milošević Bolsters Serb Protestors', *The Times*, 3 January 1997.
53. Dragoslav Grujić, 'Beogradski korzo', *Vreme*, 25 January 1997.
54. Judith Ingram and Jovan Kovačević, 'Milošević Offers No Hope to Protesters', *Independent*, 1 January 1997.
55. 'Niškim socijalistima podeljeno pred izbore izmedju 15 I 20 hiljada lažnih glasačkih listića', Branko Todorović interviewed by Aleksandar Djuričić, *Nedeljni telegraf*, 22 January 1997.
56. *Beta*, 15 January 1997 in *SWB EE/2819 A/6*, 17 January 1997.
57. Dejan Anastasijević, 'Pečat pendreka', *Vreme*, 1st February 1997.
58. Milan Milošević, 'Prelazak preko albanija', *Vreme*, 1 February 1997.
59. Andrew Gumbel, 'Milošević Set to Concede Defeat in Elections', *Independent*, 10th January 1997.
60. Milan Milošević, 'Prva pobeda opozicije', *Vreme*, 8 February 1997; N. Kovačević *et al.* 'Vodenim topovima i palicama na narod', *Naša borba*, 3 February 1997.
61. Tom Walker, 'Night of Fear as Relentless Police go on the Attack', *The Times*, 4 February 1997.
62. A. Bogdanović, 'Još masovniji Gandijevski otpor', *Demokratija*, 4 February 1997.
63. 'Miloševića predlaže donošenje zakona o priznavanju rezultata izbora', *Naša borba*, 5 December 1997.
64. *Demokratija – dani bunta*, p. 40.
65. Serbian TV, 22 February 1997 in *SWB EE/2851 A/13*, 24 February 1997.

25. The Time of Uncertainty (February–July 1997)

In their struggle with the government the Zajedno leaders had honed their strategy of peaceful resistance and civil protest to perfection. The recognition of victory, however, presented them with new challenges. Even before they had formally taken power, splits had appeared in their ranks over the division of office. The suggestion by the SPO that Danica Drašković should take the position of President of the city government was vetoed by the the other coalition parties. Vuk Drašković observed bitterly: 'She had every quality on her side except for one, that she was my wife.'[1] It was felt that the holding of power by an opposition leader and his wife would create a negative symmetry between themselves and the Milošević-Marković partnership. Vesna Pešić commented on the objections to Danica Drašković's candidature: 'This is natural. It is not because they have something against her personally, but rather because they will not permit there to be any nepotism. I think the people are deeply offended by that. If the SPO need to fill that place in the town parliament, they have many people who could do that job, why should they choose Vuk's wife? People are disappointed by such a nepotistic idea. I have said this openly to Vuk Drašković, because we are friends and I can say that to him.'[2] Following this decision the SPO nominated Spasoje Krunić as president of the city government. Differences between the coalition forces also appeared as they turned their attention to wider issues such as Serbia's future constitutional order.

On 4 March the SPO announced that they were founding a Committee for the Renewal of the Monarchy. The SPO had a longstanding and well-known commitment to the monarchist idea, but the other opposition parties were less keen on this concept. It was feared that while a belief in the monarchy was a powerful symbolic motivating force for some opposition activists, it was not the type of issue which would enable the opposition to reach out to previously uncommitted voters or disillusioned Socialists. Djindjić noted: 'I have travelled around this country as a politician for the last five years, and not more than a handful of people called to have the king back.'[3] The role of political symbolism was also emphasised by an incident on 13 March when the monument to Draža Mihailović at Ravna Gora was pulled down. Vuk Drašković responded by blaming JUL for this act of vandalism, and declaring that Mihailović's statue would be raised once again on 13 May. He went on: 'Soon Užiće Street in Belgrade will bear the name of General Mihailović, and a statue to that national hero and martyr will be raised in Belgrade.'[4] This apparent desire to replace the political symbolism associated with one political faction, such as that of the communist past, with a different but equally politically charged iconography such as that of Mihailović and the Četnik past was not in accordance with the desire of other strands of thought within the opposition to de-politicise public and civic space. Responsibility for the destruction of Mihailović's monument was claimed by the SRS parliamentary representative, Aca Stefanović.[5] The *Vreme* commentator, Stojan Cerović, described Drašković's renewed emphasis on the Ravna Gora heritage as a political 'return to the forest'.[6]

The first session of the new Belgrade City Assembly was boycotted by the SPS and Radical deputies. Surveying Belgrade's parlous finances Djindjić told the opposition representatives: 'Discipline and efficiency must make up for lack of funds. The city council members must be trained and have an efficient attitude which will allow us to achieve results measured in kilometres and square metres, not theory.'[7] The new city government moved swiftly to appoint a new management team, headed by Milan Božić, for Studio B TV. Under this new management many of the journalists who had been dismissed after the February 1995 takeover were invited to return to their old jobs. Studio B quickly shed the conformism it had adopted under SPS control. Its new spirit was exemplified by the presenter reading the evening news sitting behind a table shaped like a giant whistle, the symbol of the street protests. It was announced that the week of 6-13 April would be marked by a concerted effort to improve Belgrade's appearance with Djindjić declaring that they would make Belgrade the 'cleanest city in the Balkans'. Priority was also placed on the upgrading of the city's rundown transport system. Across Serbia other new city governments found themselves caught in a struggle between the financial needs of their towns, their acute lack of resources, and the outright hostility of the central government which sought to deny vital finance to those areas controlled by the opposition.

The Zajedno leaders found themselves, in the aftermath of the demonstrations, enjoying far greater international credibility than the Serbian opposition had done before. Western governments had begun to examine the political alternatives to Milošević's authoritarian brand of rule. Between February and April the Zajedno leaders met senior government ministers in France, Britain, Spain, Germany, Denmark, Sweden and the United States. At a rally held on 9 March the Zajedno leaders widened their demands calling on the government to engage in a programme of 'round table' discussions with the opposition in order to frame a new policy of political and economic reform. They also renewed their calls for the liberalisation of the media. On 25 March the Zajedno leadership formally set out their programme for economic and social change. Serbia, they declared, should aim to secure admission to the European Union by 2005.[8] These ambitions, however, were to founder on the internal divisions which were becoming increasingly evident within the alliance.

On 20 February the three Zajedno parties signed an agreement dealing with the nomination of candidates in the forthcoming Presidential and Republican elections. It was agreed that the SPO should nominate the Presidential candidate, the DS the candidate for Prime Minister, and the GSS the candidate for the President of the government. This was taken by the SPO as being an acknowledgment that Vuk Drašković would be the Zajedno Presidential candidate. Djindjić, however, was known to be deeply unhappy with this idea. These reservations regarding Drašković's candidature were also held by other observers of the political scene. Their analysis recognised that while Drašković commanded a high degree of loyalty from his supporters he lacked the ability to reach out to voters outside the range of his own party's support base. In a multi-party system with an even larger 'party' of un-committed voters such a narrow support base was fatal for a Presidential candidate. It was calculated that if the Zajedno candidate failed to gather sufficient votes the opposition might be faced with the 'nightmare scenario' of a Presidential second round in which opposition supporters would be faced by a choice between voting for Vojislav Šešelj or a Socialist candidate backed by Slobodan Milošević.[9] Djindjić favoured a solution whereby all of the Zajedno leaders should stand aloof from the Presidential election and a 'non-party' independent, or 'Serbian Havel', should be chosen as their candidate instead. However, it was unclear who that candidate would be. Among those whose names were mentioned in the media as potential 'independent' Presidential candidates were the former federal Premier, Milan Panić, and the businessman and former Milošević confidant, Bogoljub Karić. Karić was keen to play down his formerly intimate relations with Milošević, and sought to establish himself on the 'centre ground' of politics between the 'radicalism of the left and right'.[10] Karić, however, continued to be regarded with suspicion by the opposition who saw him as a potential rival rather than as an ally in their struggle with the government. SPO representatives observed that the opposition had previously relied on such 'independent' candidates, whose origins lay within the Socialist establishment. In the view of Aleksandra Janković, a member of the SPO Main Committee, 'We have always had their people. Panić at the start was one of *their* people as were Ćosić and Avramović...I do not think that it is a good idea for their favourites to become our favourites.'[11] The time had come, it was maintained, for the opposition to rely on its own leaders for their appeal to the people and not to put their faith in *supra-political* personalities. This issue was brought into focus when on 31 March Veroljub Stevanović, the SPO Mayor of Kragujevac nominated Drašković as Presidential candidate. According to Stevanović, 'Vuk is a symbol of 9 March, the Vidovdan Sabor, the demonstrations of June 1993, and the three month long revolt at the end of last and the beginning of this year.'[12]

While the DS on 4 April appeared to confirm that they would support Drašković's candidature Djindjić remained obviously cool towards the idea. He suggested that it was too early for opposition political parties to be nominating candidates, and they should be turning their attention instead to securing fair conditions for participation in the elections. The unwillingness of the DS to give their unequivocal support to Drašković's candidature led to an increasingly bitter series of exchanges between the coalition 'partners'.

On 16 April a formal agreement was signed between the coalition parties in the hope that the 'crisis of trust' could be put behind them. However, tensions between Drašković and Djindjić, continued to exist, barely concealed beneath this display of unity. A key factor in the ongoing confrontation between the two leaders was Drašković's awareness that the DS had been growing, during and after the demonstrations, in terms both of its numerical strength and the international reputation of its leader. The desire to break the deadlock between the two leaders, which had come to characterise relations within the coalition, partly accounted for Djindjić's efforts in early May to widen the basis of the Zajedno coalition to draw in other political groups, and non-party individuals who had given their support to the demonstrations. Djindjić termed this coalition proposal the Democratic Initiative and suggested that it should operate as a loose 'asymmetrical' alliance centred around the SPO-DS-GSS core. This proposal for an expanded coalition was, however, flatly rejected by Drašković.

By the summer of 1997 a complete breakdown of communications between the SPO on one side and the DS-GSS on the other had developed. It was, of course, a matter of dispute between the parties as to who was responsible for the collapse of Zajedno. Vesna Pešić stated: 'It is my belief that the SPO broke up the coalition...the whole of their strategy was based on a desire to block the DS.' She went on to explain that during the winter demonstrations 'a civic movement was created and a new programmatic profile was drawn up, and many people joined who were not aligned with any party. When those people arrived, many of whom had formerly been abstentionists, it was not clear to whom they would give their loyalties. At that moment the SPO began to think that they were losing out in this combination, and that someone else was becoming popular. It was then that they took the decision that it was necessary to break up Zajedno. Then the SPO energetically came out with, without any consultation, a completely separate programme which insisted that their identity should be dominant, and that effectively resulted in the destruction of the coalition.'[13]

A somewhat different interpretation of events was given by Milan Paunović, who resigned as GSS Vice-President on 1 July: 'Immediately after the demonstrations, in which the coalition was victorious, things began to be said such as that it was not the right moment to name a presidential candidate, that it was not the right moment to talk about Ravna Gora or to speak of the monarchy, because these things would be rejected by a section of the electorate. This talk originated with the Democratic Party, probably because they believed such statements would be damaging to their party. My party came to the same decision, in which I did not participate, and supported the Democratic Party. It formally supported the agreement which had been signed, in reality it acted in such a way as to bring down Zajedno's presidential candidate.'[14] The final breakup of Zajedno was signalled on 28 June when Drašković told the SPO's Third Congress that it was possible for the movement to achieve victory for the 'new Serbia' on its own without help from its former coalition partners.[15] The collapse of Zajedno after this prolonged period of internecine strife came as a bitter disappointment to many ordinary Serbs who had during the winter protests invested much hope and energy in the success of the coalition.

During the street protests the DSS had expressed its moral support for the protest movement, and DSS members had been active on the streets in the daily demonstrations. The party leadership had, however, refrained from active participation or addressing the meetings which were taking place across the country. This attitude arose partly from conflicts over organisation between the DSS and Zajedno, but was also a product of Koštunica's continued desire to present the DSS as ideologically separate from Zajedno. In December 1996 Koštunica had spelt out this position: 'We agree with the Zajedno coalition that the most important aim is democracy. We, however, place priority on solving the questions of the federal state, Kosovo, Vojvodina, Sandžak, the Republika Srpska, the issue of national identity, while Djindjić, Drašković and Pešić place priority on social and economic questions. For them it is more important how much money Mirko Marjanović has stolen than why two centuries of our national history have been stolen from us. If we followed such a political course then it would end in national defeat.'[16] This policy of political 'separatism', however, drew a considerable degree of criticism from elements of the DSS who believed that it would result in the party being 'marginalised' and 'demobilised'. They argued that the DSS should co-operate with the Zajedno alliance. This dissent over party strategy was particularily strong in provincial towns where there was a tradition of co-operation with other opposition groups. The leaders of the revolt in the provinces included Gvozden Jovanović from Kragujevac, Predrag Stojanović from Kraljevo, and Dušan Drinjaković from Čačak. Among the DSS leadership these dissidents were supported by Vladan Batić, the DSS Vice-President and a lawyer from the town of Obrenovac, who declared that Koštunica's position presented 'an artificial division between the democratic and the national. We have gone too far to be detained by nationalism or quasi-nationalism. It is not possible to create a strong national state, if it is not first democratic.'[17] Other individuals, such as Dragoljub Popović, called for the DSS to return to its roots: 'The Democratic Party of Serbia was created around the idea of a united opposition and democracy. It was for that reason that we broke away from the Democratic Party. A party which arose out of the idea of opposition unity must participate in attempts which are made to form a united opposition.'[18] After a meeting held by the DSS rebels in Kragujevac on 12 April this wing of the party split off to form a new Christian Democratic Party of Serbia (DHSS). It was Batić's misfortune that by the time he had formed the Christian Democratic Party the Zajedno alliance, with which he had hoped to ally himself, was already falling apart.

During the spring of 1997 Milošević was engaged in an attempt to revitalise the battered structures of the Serbian government and the SPS. On 11 February the Serbian government had been reshuffled and Radmila Milentijević was appointed as the new Serbian Minister for Information. Milentijević, a professor of history who had emigrated from Yugoslavia to America in 1953, was well-known for her hardline nationalist views, and in the early 1990s had been an energetic lobbyist on Milošević's behalf in the United States. She had also represented his interests in the federal government of Milan Panić in which she had served briefly as Minister without Portfolio. Her appointment showed Milošević to be searching for 'new' ministers from amongst those who had previously held office during his government's most militant period of nationalism. The opposition saw her arrival as signalling a rejection by the government of any form of compromise on the key issue of liberalisation of the media. Milentijević's primary task as the Minister for Information was to frame a new law governing public information. This legislative move was widely seen as seeking to give a 'reformist' gloss to the Milošević government, for the consumption of Western governments, while maintaining effective state control over the main media institutions. The hardline attitude towards the media taken under Milentijević was manifest in the attempts by the authorities to put financial pressure on BK TV following its departure from the 'party line'. Harassment of the independent media continued throughout the spring and summer of 1997. In June *Naša borba* found itself subject to financially crippling and apparently arbitrary demands for 'unpaid' tax after a visitation by the financial police. Between December 1996 and July 1997 fifty-five local radio and TV stations were closed down with technical infringements of the broadcasting regulations being cited as justification for this purge.[19]

Leading members of the SPS considered to be from the party's 'nationalist' wing, who had been pushed aside during the rise of JUL in late 1995/early 1996, also found their way back into the inner circles of the SPS hierarchy. On 24 April at a meeting of the SPS Main Committee the three Vice-Presidents of the SPS were replaced by new functionaries. The most prominent of these appointees was Milorad Vučelić. It was said of Vučelić that 'in 1995 Mira [Marković] threw him out of the door, but now he has climbed back through the window.'[20] Also among the new Vice-Presidents was Dušan Matković, an old-style SPS regional-industrial overlord who ran the giant Smederevo ironworks. Smederevo was one of the urban centres where the SPS had managed to cling on to to power in the local elections. Opposition politicians in the town attributed this directly to the dominance of the state-owned and SPS-controlled Smederevo ironworks over the economic life and political loyalties of a large section of the town's inhabitants. They estimated that with 10,000 workers employed in the factory a total of 40,000 people were effectively dependent on it for their daily existence.[21] The large number of the town's inhabitants who were migrants from Kosovo was also regarded as a significant factor in maintaining Smederevo as a SPS fiefdom.[22] Gorica Gajević, who had been associated with the JUL experiment of 1995/6 and whose departure had been widely rumoured during the previous months, retained her position as General Secretary of the SPS, but it was understood that many of her previously-held responsibilities would be taken over by Vučelić. Goran Perčević, another casualty of the previous year's 'bloodletting' within the SPS, also returned as one of the SPS Deputy-Chairmen. Perčević's former colleague in the Young Socialists, Dušanka Djogo, made her reappearance as spokesman for the Belgrade SPS. The re-organised Socialists sought to define their role: 'In our conditions today linked and complex left-wing and democratic forces have the primary objective of preserving the state and reconstructing the country. Their primary role thus has an explicitly patriotic character. So in our current circumstances the alliance of left-wing and democratic forces is, above all, an alliance of patriotic forces. To this end it should thoroughly mobilise society towards the notions of unity and the country's reconstruction.'[23]

The reorganisation of the SPS extended beyond their national leadership and into the provinces. The street demonstrations had dealt a heavy blow to the SPS local and regional organisations. In Čačak, in central Serbia, the efficient structures of the opposition parties and their tradition of local co-operation had enabled them to inflict a decisive defeat on the Socialists.[24] The SPS only succeeded in gaining eight out of the seventy seats in the local town assembly. The new Zajedno (SPO) Mayor of Čačak, Velimir Ilić, commented: 'The SPS no longer exists in this town – its committee is dissolved, its President has been replaced..the Čačak SPS has been placed under the control of the Gornja Milanovac committee.'[25] The Socialist loss of power also brought revelations regarding their misappropriation of funds whilst in office. It was reported that in Čačak money allocated for refugees in the area had been diverted to the Republika Srpska and used to fund the Socialist campaign in Banja Luka during the Bosnian election of September 1996.[26] In Niš the SPS had, before November 1996, controlled a formidable 18,000-strong local organisation. During the protests, however, over 5,000 of these members left the party. A number of senior SPS officials also found themselves facing criminal charges. Two members of the city election commission and SPS officials were charged with falsifying the election results while another two SPS officials, Miroslav Dimitrijević and Vojislav Mitić, were charged with taking over a million dinars from the civic budget in order to fund the SPS local election campaign.[27] The SPS in Niš, however, sought to reorganise themselves stating on 2 March that it had elected a new leadership and taken measures to deal with the 'negative legacy of the past.' The Niš Socialists also announced that, having lost control over the local media, they had the resources to found their own local newspaper and TV station. A similar process of cadre change and renewal took place among the defeated Socialists of Kragujevac. In this town the first issue of their newly-founded local newspaper, bearing the title 'Left Information Daily – LID', informed its readers that the new Zajedno local government had carried out 'genocide against Socialists' and the 'rape of democracy'. It went on to accuse the Zajedno officials of 'the violation of respectable individuals by the mass removal of directors of committees and directors of firms, the abuse of statutes, and the calling on the unemployed to commit criminal acts'.[28] In the early summer of 1997 Milošević began, after his long absence from public view during the winter of 1996/7, to visit the provinces in an attempt to bolster the SPS in anticipation of the forthcoming republican elections. On 22 May he met factory workers and local party functionaries at Arandjelovac in the Šumadija while on 25 June he was in Priština seeking to assure the local Serbian population that he would not give up even 'one foot of territory' in Kosovo.[29]

In spite of Milošević's attempts to shore up the edifice of the regime, there were increasing signs that dangerous tensions existed among the ranks of the political-economic elite. On 20 February a businessman, Vladan Kovačević ('Tref'), was killed in a mafia-style 'execution'. Kovačević was a close personal friend and business partner of Slobodan Milošević's son, Marko. Kovačević had sponsored Marko's early attempt to forge a career as a racing driver and they had subsequently collaborated in running the black market cigarette trade based in Niš. On the night of 10 April Radovan Stojičić ('Badža'), the Minister for the Police, was eating with his son and a senior customs official in a Belgrade restaurant when he was killed by a masked gunman who shot him repeatedly with an automatic rifle. The event sent shock-waves through the ranks of the political elite and across Serbian society. The parties of the ruling coalition, however, appeared to be unsure as to whom they should blame for the killing. The SPS stated that it was an act of 'organised criminality' while JUL characterised it as 'political terrorism'. Stojičić's funeral, held on 12 April, was attended by all the most powerful figures in Serbian political and public life. Slobodan Milošević was there himself along with his daughter Marija and son Marko. Stojičić as well as being in charge of the security arrangements for the Milošević family, had been a close personal friend of Marko Milošević. Of the Milošević family only Mirjana Marković did not attend the funeral. Milorad Vučelić also appeared among the prominent figures gathered around the Serbian President at the funeral. Present in the crowd of mourners was the former paramilitary warlord and underworld boss, Željko Ražnjatović ('Arkan'), his wife Ceca, and his body-guards.[30] Vlajko Stojiljković was appointed as the new Serbian Minister for the Police. Stojiljković, originally from Milošević's home-town of Požarevac, had formerly been the head of the Serbian Economic Chamber in which position he had distinguished himself by his unrelenting opposition to economic reform. The opposition greeted Stolijković's appointment with scorn and sug-gested that Milošević had now been forced to fall back on barely-known functionaries drawn from the 'Požarevac clan'. His arrival was also regarded with dismay within the Interior Ministry, which was reported to be in 'total disarrary' after a number of senior officials resigned on hearing of his appointment.[31] Although the Serbian police were able to deploy formidable resources in their hunt for Stojičić's killer they proved unable to apprehend anyone for the crime.

In his role as the mayor of Zemun, Vojislav Šešelj, while continuing to follow the SRS ultra-nationalist agenda, sought to project a 'pragmatic' image. The pages of the local journal *Zemunske novine* were filled with articles dealing with his efforts to improve the local public infra-structure.[32] Observers began to regard Šešelj's amalgam of social radicalism, energetic local government and ultra-nationalism as an increasingly dangerous force.[33] An analysis of the situation in *Naša borba* concluded: 'He [Šešelj] retains his extreme nationalism but he does not empathise it, giving priority to the realities of society. While the Zajedno coalition is trying its best to win over the church, students, intellectuals, actors and lawyers, the Radicals' leader is talking to the impoverished, the uneducated and semi-literate masses, particularily the workers, and is trying to win over farmers and refugees by using demagoguery that can sound ridiculous and even anachronistic to his political opponents, but finds its mark where it counts, where power is won.'[34] Vesna Pešić evaluated the dangerous, complicating factor which Šešelj and the SRS added to the political scene: 'I think that Šešelj is a force of evil in Serbia, but his popularity is growing. He has become necessary to the SPS once again, they want to construct some sort of 'patriotic front' in which there is a place marked out for Šešelj. They are never officially in a coalition, but instead make some sort of secret or silent coalition in which there are two reactionary currents of isolationism and conservatism. These types of "left" and "right" always come together in the end when a democratic force appears which they must work together in order to crush.'[35] Although the Socialists appeared to be cultivating the Radicals to draw support away from the opposition, it was soon clear that the SRS was gaining ground among those alienated by the public squabbling of the Zajedno parties and the manifest failures of the Socialist government.

With the apparent blessing of the Serbian government Šešelj was able to act as if he was above the law. On 2 July Šešelj installed Ognjen Mijoković, the editor of *Zemunske novine*, and his family in a flat which was empty while its tewants, the Barbalic family who were ethnic Croats, were away on holiday.[36] This move was interpreted as a populist anti-Croat measure designed to secure support from the substantial number of impoverished and politically alienated Serbian war refugees in the area. The Barbalićs successfully challenged their eviction in the Belgrade courts, but the police appeared unwilling to reinstate them in their property. On 17 July a debate took place on BK Television between Šešelj and Nikola Barović, the Barbalićs' lawyer. The televised confrontation rapidly degenerated into an exchange of personal abuse, and the broadcast had to be cut short. Following the programme Barović was assaulted and severely beaten by Šešelj's bodyguard, Petar Panić, while the SRS leader looked on. This act of political violence prompted a wave of condemnation from opposition political parties. Only the Socialists seemed unconcerned by Šešelj's actions, with the SPS representative Radovan Radović saying: 'The lawyer acted very provocatively towards Šešelj, they are both to blame.' Dragan Tomić and the Serbian Justice Minister, Arandjel Markićević, answered journalists' questions by claiming that they knew nothing of the incident.[37] Opposition supporters and Zemun residents responded by staging a series of demonstrations outside the Zemun town hall and on the street opposite the Barbalić's flat. Miodrag Perišić stated: 'We are concentrating on tying Šešelj to Milošević because the one is the bastard son of the other, following his instructions transparently and explicitly.'[38] On 4 May the Central Fatherland Administration of the SRS unanimously nominated Šešelj as their candidate in the forthcoming Presidential elections.[39]

In the aftermath of his recognition of the local election results Milošević sought to bolster his weakened position by strengthening his emphasis on national issues and stressing the need for links with the Serbs beyond the Drina. On 28 February an 'Agreement on Special Relations' was signed between the Federal Republic of Yugoslavia and the Republika Srpska. The agreement was signed by Zoran Lilić for the FRY and by Momčilo Krajišnik for the RS. Milošević insisted that the agreement, which concentrated on the strengthening of economic and cultural links between the FRY and RS, was fully in line with the terms of the Dayton agreement. It was widely seen by the opposition, however, as a deliberate attempt by Milošević to court nationalist opinion by stressing his promotion of solidarity with the Bosnian Serbs. The Serbian opposition were scornful of the agreement with Slobodan Vuksanović of the DS, dismissing it as 'an act of self-publicity on the part of the leadership of the FRY and Serbia which will be of no essential benefit to the citizens of the Republika Srpska in their difficult economic and material position.' Vuk Drašković commented: 'This agreement is signed by the people who are responsible for the fact there are no longer any Serbs in Sarajevo, Mostar, Zenica, Drvar and many other places where Serbian people have lived for centuries.'[40] The agreement was also strongly opposed from within the RS where Biljana Plavšić denounced it as being 'unconstitutional'. Plavšić and Milošević had long been known for their mutual antipathy, and she regarded this agreement as a 'lifebelt' for Milošević.[41] Ranged against her was a section of the SDS, the ruling party of the Republika Srpska, led by Krajišnik, and from behind the scenes by Radovan Karadžić. The Krajišnik-Karadžić faction represented a powerful coalition of business and 'police-mafia' interests within the Republika Srpska. During this period reports appeared in the Western media, citing sources from within the government of the RS, which asserted that Krajišnik and Karadžić operated a business partnership in the RS and had become millionaires through control of the petrol, cigarette and construction material monopolies. Plavšić, who was a convinced Serbian nationalist, believed that the future of the Republika Srpska was endangered by the continuing role being taken in its affairs by Krajišnik and Karadžić. Plavšić accounted for Krajišnik's support for the agreement by observing: 'It is probable that Milošević has certain mechanisms by which he is able to hold such people under his control, but I am not one of those people.'[42] It was reported that Radovan Karadžić had, in exchange for his co-operation, been offered an assurance by Milošević that he would not be arrested as a war criminal and sent to The Hague. Carl Bildt, the international community's High Representative in Bosnia, declared that the 'Agreement on Special Relations', which had been agreed without reference to the Muslim-Croat Federation, was in violation of the Dayton agreement.

The power struggle among the leadership of the Republika Srpska drew in actors from Serbia itself. On 20 March Momčilo Krajišnik met Vojislav Šešelj in Zvornik in order to enlist his help in the struggle with Plavšić. Following this meeting Šešelj launched a series of attacks on Plavšić calling repeatedly for her resignation.[43] On 3 April Šešelj said of Plavšić that 'it would be best if she withdrew from politics to live a peaceful pensioner's life, because she has absolutely no political capability.' Šešelj was now acting as Milošević's 'hatchet man' in the Republika Srpska, in the same way as he had done in 1992-3 when the Radicals had spearheaded Milošević's attempt to displace Milan Panić and Dobrica Ćosić. Plavšić similarly sought the support of parties within Serbia. On 23 April Zoran Djindjić commented on the situation in the Republika Srpska and praised Plavšić's efforts to fight corruption and 'gradually return financial decisions to legal institutions which will progressive normalise life'. She was, he said, 'a more sincere nationalist than many of those who used to beat their breasts to prove what great nationalists they were, but are now engaged in attacking her.'[44] Plavšić, however, appeared increasingly isolated within the ruling elite of the Republika Srpska. The FRY-RS agreement was finally passed bearing the signature of the RS Vice-President, Dragoljub Mirjanić.

The political crisis in the Republika Srpska reached a new level of intensity when, while Plavšić was away on a three-day visit to London, the RS Interior Minister Dragan Kijač moved on 30 June to disband a Banja Luka-based anti-terrorist police unit commanded by Major Dragan Lukač. Lukač had been entrusted by Plavšić with investigating the activities of the Centreks and Selekt-Impeks companies under the political control of Momčilo Krajišnik and Radovan Karadžić. Plavšić reacted to these events by suspending Kijać, and cutting short her stay in London in order to return to the Republika Srpska. On arriving at Belgrade airport, however, Plavšić was detained by Serbian police who questioned her for a hour and a half before escorting her to Republika Srpska's border. The actions of the Serbian police were a clear attempt by Milošević to intimidate Plavšić, and exposed the extent to which the Belgrade government was involved in the power struggles of the Republika Srpska. Plavšić was handed over to Bosnian Serb police, who were theoretically under her command, who detained her overnight. On being released the next day she was escorted to Banja Luka by NATO (SFOR) peacekeeping forces which also took steps to secure the presidential building in Banja Luka against attack by pro-Karadžić forces.[45] Safely ensconced in her Banja Luka stronghold Plavšić defiantly announced that she would invoke her powers as President of the RS and dissolve the Republika Srpska parliament. New elections would, she declared, be held on 1 September. In spite of this declaration the parliament met on 4 July. The parliament, which was boycotted by opposition deputies, was, however, unable to muster the two-thirds majority which was constitutionally necessary to set in motion the popular referendum by which a President of the RS could be removed from office. The assembly, meeting in Pale, nevertheless voted to deprive Plavšić of her presidential powers and called on her to resign. She ignored this move, which she regarded as 'unconstitutional', and also, perhaps wisely in view of her recent experiences, rejected an invitation made by Milošević that she and Momčilo Krajišnik should come to Belgrade where he would act as a 'neutral mediator' between the two sides.[46]

Having broken with her former colleagues in the SDS, who expelled her from the party on 20 July, Plavšić sought to mobilise public opinion in the Republika Srpska. Starting on 4 July in Banja Luka a series of meetings were organised across the north of the Republika Srpska in support of the embattled President. On 5 July a 30,000-strong crowd gathered in Banja Luka to hear Plavšić tell them: 'You are all that I have left. But you are the strongest, the most honourable, I feel the greatest obligation towards you. How can I feel any obligation to such people [the Karadžić faction of the SDS in Pale]. [...] You tested them and you can see for yourselves. I cannot understand certain people who are afraid of saying what they think, even at the cost of their life. Is their life more precious than their honour and dignity? [...] Be strict, be energetic, turn your heads away from me when I make a mistake. That will be the most difficult thing for me.'[47] Further meetings followed in Prijedor, Doboj, Derventa, Modriča and Bijeljina. The demonstrations were consciously modelled on those which had taken place earlier that year in Serbia. In Banja Luka on 4 July there were, for instance, separate student demonstrations, and in Bijeljina on 9 July demonstrators, encouraged by the local political leader Ljubiša Savić, threw eggs at the television building.[48]

The meetings were organised by a coalition of opposition political parties who termed themselves the United Serb Front.[49] The presence among the parties in the coalition of the Socialist Party of the Republika Srpska, an offshoot of the Serbian SPS, however, suggested that the Socialist regime in Belgrade was following a form of 'twin-track' strategy in the Republika Srpska. While the Serbian security apparatus, headed by Jovica Stanišić, maintained links with the Krajišnik-Karadžić camp, the political structures of the SPS, directed by Nikola Šainović, were willing to allow their Bosnian sister-party to co-operate with the Plavšić supporters. In this way Milošević apparently hoped that while he was giving his backing to Krajišnik-Karadžić, links would not entirely be broken with the Plavšić camp should she turn out to be the victor in the power struggle.[50]

It was with good reason therefore that Radovan Karadžić appeared distinctly unsure of the reliability of his allies within the Milošević government. On 10 July British SAS special forces launched an operation to detain two war crimes suspects in the northern town of Prijedor. One of them was successfully arrested but the other, Simo Drljača, the former police chief in Prijedor, was killed while resisting arrest. The immediate and visible effect of the action on the Plavšić-Karadžić power struggle was to rally popular support around Karadžić. Although Plavšić felt compelled publicly to condemn the NATO operation, she was notably absent from Drljača's funeral which took place on 13 July in Banja Luka. Drljača, however, had been a key supporter of Karadžić in northern Bosnia, and his death was a sharp reminder to Karadžić of his own vulnerability. Karadžić reacted by purging his bodyguard of a number of individuals who were considered unreliable. They had apparently been working clandestinely for Slobodan Milošević, and had received instructions that should NATO attempt to arrest

Karadžić they should kill him rather than allow him to be sent to The Hague, where his testimony would no doubt be embarrassing to Milošević. Karadžić reportedly also took personal control of the contingency plans for his departure from Bosnia, which had previously been formulated in co-operation with Jovica Stanišić and the Serbian SDB.[51]

By the end of July the struggle appeared to have developed into an inconclusive stalemate. Plavšić had been cast out of her party and lacked the backing of key elements in the police and the media. She did, however, enjoy the support of a considerable proportion of the ordinary people in the Republika Srpska and of the international community who saw in her 'pragmatic' nationalism a willingness to take seriously the provisions of the Dayton agreement. The political re-alignments in the RS also resulted in changing attitudes among political parties in Serbia. During the war in Bosnia there had been little love lost between the SPO and Biljana Plavšić, but on 8 July the SPO spokesman Ivan Kovačević stated: 'Today to support Biljana Plavšić means to support our nation and our homeland' and added that 'those people who celebrate the 7 July [the Socialists], a black and deadly day for the Serbs which marked the beginning of civil war among our people, have decided to provoke a war amongst the Serbs in the Republika Srpska...the centre of the cancer which is eating up the RS is to be found in Belgrade.' The Belgrade City Assembly also announced on 2 July that it would be sending a delegation to Banja Luka to express solidarity with its citizens in their support for the President of the RS.[52]

While the power struggle in the Republika Srpska was unfolding, Milošević was also taking steps to assert political control over Montenegro. During the winter demonstrations the Montenegrin Prime Minister, Milo Djukanović, had defied Milošević calling for the opposition election victories to be recognised and had, in an interview in February 1997, described Milošević as an 'obsolescent politician'.[53] In addition to expressing such sentiments Djukanović had been following an economic line which involved an increasing degree of autonomy from the regime in Belgrade. He had most notably proposed the introduction of a new Montengrin currency, known as the *perper*, in order to protect his country's finances from the danger of renewed hyper-inflation within the Yugoslav system. In Milošević's view the removal of

Djukanović and his key supporters from within the Montenegrin political-business elite had become a necessity. On 24 March, at a meeting of the Executive Committee of the Montenegrin Democratic Party of Socialists (DPS), in a move initiated by Momir Bulatović, Djukanović was forced to resign as Deputy Chairman of the party. The vote was carried by sixty-five votes to seven with twenty abstentions. Djukanović was also instructed to sack his Deputy Finance Minister, Slavko Drljević, his Security Chief, Vukašin Maras, Culture Minister, Goran Rakoce, and the head of the Montenegrin Trade office in Washington. In Belgrade the Serbian Prime Minister, Mirko Marjanović, declared that Djukanović had been 'defeated' and therefore could not remain as Montenegrin Prime Minister. Djukanović, however, determinedly refused to relinquish power. While he had lost his tussle for power with Bulatović among the upper ranks of the DPS he retained significant support amongst key sections of the ruling establishment, including business managers and the police. For his part Bulatović could rely on the backing of the Montenegrin media, and the regime in Belgrade. Djukanović could also count on the support of a significant proportion of the Montenegrin public with a particularily strong power base in his home town of Nikšić. The Montenegrin opposition, at one level, regarded the Djukanović-Bulatović clash as an internal affair between two members of the Socialist establishment. At another level, however, they were willing to back Djukanović as the more forward-looking of the two contenders. One student involved in demonstrations in Podgorica in support of the Montenegrin Prime Minister justified his presence by saying: 'In reality this is more an act of resistance against Milošević than in favour of Djukanović, because we know the way he has acted this year. We are forced to choose between two evils, and Djukanović is undoubtedly the lesser.'[54] The Serbian opposition were similarily ambivalent in their attitude towards Djukanović regarding his role as a technocrat and reformer positively, but remaining suspicious of his past role as a protégé of Milošević and the 'separatist' aspects of the policies he was pursuing in Montenegro.

Milošević, however, had more pragmatic and immediate reasons for wanting to exert his personal control over Montenegro. Under the Serbian constitution an individual was only allowed to occupy the position of President for two terms. Milošević had been elected as President for the first time in 1990, and re-elected for his second term in 1992. New presidential elections were due in the autumn of 1997, and for Milošević the idea of relinquishing power was unthinkable. Before the demonstrations of autumn 1996 Milošević may well have contemplated running for a third tern as President of Serbia regardless of the constitutional restrictions. After the political convulsions of the winter of 1996/7 it was obvious to Milošević that such an abuse of the constitution would court disaster. The other means by which Milošević could remain in power, and still act within the bounds of the constitution, was to move from being President of Serbia to being President of Yugoslavia. In order to make such a jump from republican to federal level, however, it would be necessary to secure the compliance of the governing elite in Montenegro. Milošević launched his attack on Djukanović apparently believing that the Montenegrin Premier would not be willing to offer him the support necessary to become President of the FRY. When it became increasingly clear that Djukanović was set to survive the assault on his position Milošević appeared to back away from his attempt to become President of the Federal Republic of Yugoslavia. On 29 April Ratko Marković, the Vice-President of the Serbian government and Professor of constitutional law, suggested that Milošević might run for a third term as President of Serbia. He justified this on the dubious grounds that while the constitution specified that no individual could be President for more than two terms, Milošević's first term had lasted for only two years and therefore should not be counted as a full term. The opposition were predictably unimpressed by such constitutional manoeuvres. Zoran Djindjić commented: 'If President Milošević had any international credibility or reputation he would not consider standing for a third term which is a blatant abuse of the constitution.'[55]

On 5 June a group of high-ranking officials from the SPS visited Montenegro to meet senior figures from the Democratic Party of Socialists headed by Momir Bulatović. This meeting of Socialist functionaries from the two republics resolved that Slobodan Milošević should be their candidate of President of Yugoslavia, and that the constitution should be changed so that the Yugoslav President would be directly elected by popular vote rather than, as was then the case, through the votes of the representatives in the assembly. Senior pro-Djukanović figures within the Montenegrin government, however, voiced opposition to such measures believing that the direct election of the President would result in the subordination of Montenegro, whose population was 644,000, to Serbia with its almost 10 million inhabitants. Svetozar Marović, the Montenegrin parliamentary speaker, stated: 'Montenegro believes in an open, democratic and federal Yugoslavia, and will not agree to any changes in the constitution that would be to the detriment of Montenegro's people and equality.'[56] Within Serbia opposition reaction to the proposed changes were mixed. Slobodan Vuksanović, the DS spokesman, said: 'It is strange that as we approach the end of the twentieth century the constitution of Serbia and Montenegro is being used in an attempt to save one individual's political career which has entered its twilight and is now really beyond salvation.'[57] These sentiments were broadly echoed by the representatives of the other opposition parties with the exception of the SPO. Drašković said that he was not opposed to the changes in the constitution as the direct election of the President would be 'more democratic.'[58] On 23 June at a meeting of the DPS Main Committee Milošević's candidacy for federal Presidency was endorsed with fifty-one in favour, thirty-one against, and ten abstentions. The Main Committee, however, also unanimously rejected any suggestion that the constitution should be changed. The Montenegrins were willing to let Milošević occupy the Presidency in its existing 'ceremonial' form, but were clearly unwilling to allow him to effect the transition to a Presidency with 'executive' powers.

Fearful of the increasing divisions within the Montenegrin DPS Milošević moved quickly to secure his elevation to the Yugoslav Presidency. On 15 July Milošević was elected by a vote of the federal parliament. In the Chamber of Citizens, the lower house of the federal parliament, the vote was carried with eighty-eight votes in favour and ten against, with the Chamber of Republics, the upper house, voting twenty-nine in favour and two against. Only the parties of the Serbian 'left' coalition (SPS-JUL-ND), the Montenegrin DPS, and the SRS voted. The Zajedno deputies maintained their boycott of the federal assembly which had been in place since the November 1996 elections. Although the Montenegrin DPS had, as had previously been agreed, given their support to Milošević there were expressions of disquiet by senior DPS officials over the fact that they had been given little notice of the vote's timing. The precipitate way in which Milošević was hurried into the Yugoslav Presidency served to heighten the existing tensions between the Serbian and Montenegrin political establishments. Milošević was sworn in as Yugoslav President on 23 July. In his inaugural speech in the federal parliament he promised to bring 'peace, progress, and prosperity' to Yugoslavia, and attacked the independent media who accused him of being under foreign 'financial, political, and moral influence'. A group of 300 SPS supporters had been brought to chant and cheer their support for Milošević. They were, however, outnumbered by several thousand student demonstrators who turned out to show their opposition to the new Yugoslav President. The opposition protesters were kept away from the parliament building by a large deployment of riot police. However, the police were unable to prevent around 1,000 demonstrators entering a park adjacent to the parliament. As Milošević left the building his car was bombarded by shoes and other missiles thrown by the demonstrators over the heads of the riot police. The shoes were meant to symbolise those who had been compelled to emigrate during the years of his rule.

Notes

1. Adam Bogdanović, 'Kandidovanje za predsednika gradske vlade pravo SPO', *Demokratija*, 18 February 1997.
2. Vesna Pešić quoted in 'Ljudi i vreme', *Vreme*, 22 February 1997.
3. Christopher Lockwood, 'Opposition in Serbia Backed by Rifkind', *Daily Telegraph*, 27 February 1997.
4. Blagica Stojanović, 'Sa kundaka prešli na bonsek, *Srpska reč*, 20 March 1997.
5. Nenad Stefanović, 'Testera sa dve ručke', *Duga*, 29 March 1997.
6. Stojan Cerović, 'Povratak u šumu', *Naša borba*, 19 May 1997.
7. *Beta*, 21 February 1997 in *SWB EE/2581 A/12*, 24 February 1997.
8. *Naša borba*, 'Vlast pozvana na dijalog', 10 March 1997; J. Kosanić, 'Cilj –Ulazak u EU do 2005 godine', *Naša borba*, 26 March 1997.
9. A political scenario along these lines was outlined by Vladimir Goati, interviewed by the author on 7 April 1997.
10. '21 vek je sutra', Bogoljub Karić interviewed by Dragoljub Žarković, *Vreme*, 8 March 1997.
11. 'Nema me u medijima ne mogu da stignem da red od Rade Milentijević', Aleksandra Janković interviewed by Brankica Treskavica, *Svedok*, 8 April 1997.
12. 'Vuka Drašković za Predsednike Srbije', *Dnevni telegraf*, 30 March 1997.

13. 'SPO razbio *Zajedno'*, Vesna Pešić interviewed by Vesna Vujić, *Naša borba*, 2 July 1997.
14. 'Svi dobri, samo Vuk nije valjao', Milan Paunović interviewed by Aleksandar Cvetković, *Srpska reč*, 10 July 1997.
15. 'Sloga i snaga', *Srpska reč*, 10 July 1997.
16. 'Demokratija se ne uvozi!', Vojislav Koštunica interviewed by Donko Rakočević, *Istok*, January 1997.
17. 'Stranka se može spasiti', Vladan Batić interviewed by Tomo Kuzmanović, *Duga*, 1 March 1997.
18. 'Nove deobe demokrata', Dragoljub Popović interviewed by Milomir Ilić, *Intervju*, 17 January 1997.
19. 'Nezakonito nametanje ogromnih materijalnih obaveza *Našoj borbi'*, *Naša borba*, 16 June 1997; Aleksandar Ćirić, 'Frekventno zavodjenje reda', *Vreme*, 26 July 1997.
20. Nenad LJ Stefanović, 'Komuna starih asova', *Vreme*, 3 May 1997.
21. 'Komunisti su podmićivali birače', Milorad Klašnja interviewed by Rajko Novaković, *Pogledi*, 24 December 1996 to 12 January 1997.
22. Although the Socialists held on to power in Smederevo, the opposition increased its strength in the *opština* from 11 to 27 representatives.
23. *Tanjug*, 24 April 1997 in *SWB EE/2903 A/10*, 26 April 1997
24. Jaćim Milunović, 'Ponos bez gordosti', *Glasnik*, 20 March 1997.
25. 'Rapušten opštinski odbor SPS?', *Naša borba*, 28 February 1997; Jovanka Nikolić, 'Republike sankcije', *Nezavisna svetlost*, 27 March 1997.
26. 'Opština Čačak izbegličkim parama finansirala predizbornu kampanju socialista u Banjaluci', *Dnevni telegraf*, 4 April 1997.
27. 'Tužilac započlinje istraga o falsifikovanju izbora', *Naša borba*, 31 March 1997; 'Aktivi SPS u niškim preduzećima', *Naša borba*, 30 March 1997; 'Mislim da SPS u Nišu više i ne postoji', Zoran Živković interviewed by Ivana Stanojević, *Nedeljni telegraf*, 26 February 1997; Tanjug, 2 March 1997 in *SWB EE/2858 A/7*, 4 March 1997.
28. 'Lokalni vlast vrši genocid and socijalistima', *Dnevni telegraf*, 8 April 1997.
29. Zoran Stoljiković, 'Baci kosku, pa podeli', *Vreme*, 12 July 1997.
30. Miloš Vasić and Uroš Komlenović, 'Država i mafija', *Vreme*, 19 April 1997.
31. N. Todorović, 'Ko je taj Vlajko?', *Naša borba*, 16 April 1997; *Beta*, 17 April 1997 in *SWB EE/2897 A/8*, 19 April 1997.
32. An example of this can be seen in Žana Živaljević, 'Bez radnog vremena', *Zemunske novine*, 20 March 1997.
33. Miloš Vasić, ' "New Deal" Dr Šešelj', *Vreme*, 17 May 1997.
34. *Naša borba*, 26-27 April 1997 in *SWB EE/2911 A/6*, 6 May 1997.
35. 'Milošević ne može da smjenjuje po Crnoj Gori', Vesna Pešić interviewed by Šeki Radončić, *Monitor*, 2 May 1997.
36. Vesna Mališić, 'Stanovati ili Ietovati', *Duga*, 19 July 1997.
37. 'Opšta osuda', *Dnevni telegraf*, 18 July 1997.
38. Andrew Gumbel, 'Evicted for Going For a Walk', *Independent on Sunday*, 27 July 1997.
39. *Tanjug*, 4 May 1997 in SWB 2910 A/11, 5 May 1997.
40. Liljana Kovačević, 'Doprinos miru ili politička manipulacija', *Naša borba*, 3 March 1997.

41. Plavšić had famously demonstrated her contempt for Milošević when, on 8 May 1993, the Serbian President arrived in Pale in his attempt to persuade the Bosnian Serbs to accept the Vance-Owen peace plan. Milošević approached Plavšić with his hand extended, and she turned away refusing to shake his hand. Milošević had neither forgiven nor forgotten this snub.

42. 'Milošević ume da drži neke ljude u šaci', Biljana Plavšić interviewed by Vesna Kešelj, *Demokratija*, 27 March 1997.

43. 'Tajni politički susreti – Šešelj, Krajišnik u Zvornik- Djindjić, Plavšić u Bijeljini', *Argument*, 31 March 1997.

44. 'Plavšićka apsolutno nesposobno za politika', *Dnevni telegraf*, 4 April 1997; 'Djindjić podržao Biljanu Plavšić', *Naša borba*, 23 April 1997.

45. Tanja Topić, 'Jedna mračna afera', *Vreme*, 5 July 1997.

46. 'Milošević pozvao Plavšićevu i Krajišnika u Beograd', *Naša borba*, 9 July 1997.

47. Radio B-92, 5 July 1997 in *EE/2964 A/10*, 7 July 1997.

48. Ljubiša Savić, a former social worker, had during the war in Bosnia commanded the Bijeljina-based paramilitary unit, the Panthers, and fought under the *nom de guerre* of 'Major Mauzer'. With the end of the war Savić left the SDS and was elected to the RS assembly on the list of the Democratic Patriotic Bloc headed by Predrag Radić, the Mayor of Banja Luka. He was later the leader of the Democratic Party of the Republika Srpska.

49. *Beta*, 4 July 1997 in *SWB EE/2964 A/10*, 7 July 1997.

50. 'Direckitive stižu iz Beorgrada', *Naša borba*, 7 July 1997.

51. Julius Strauss, 'SAS Gun Battle Puts Karadžić Under Siege', *Daily Telegraph*, 11 July 1997; *Beta*, 8 July 1997 in *SWB EE/2966 A/9*, 9 July 1997.

52. 'Biljani Plavšić se sprema sudbina Milana Babića', *Naša borba*, 9 July 1997; *Beta*, 2 July 1997 in *SWB EE/2962 A/10*, 4 July 1997.

53. 'Milošević je prevazidjen političar', Milo Djukanović interviewed by Velizar Brajović, *Vreme*, 22 February 1997.

54. Aleksandar Djurić, 'Milo i Momir – Zatišje pred buru', *Nedeljni telegraf*, 2 April 1997.

55. 'Milošević može ponovo de se kandiduje!', *Naša borba*, 30 April-1 May 1997.

56. *Tanjug*, 6 June 1997 in *SWB EE/2940 A/13*, 9 June 1997.

57. Slobodan Vuksanović, 'Spasavanje karijere zalasku', *Nedeljni telegraf*, 11 June 1997.

58. *Beta*, 6 June 1997 in *SWB EE/2940 A/8*, 9 June 1997.

26. Electoral Deadlock – Round One (August–October 1997)

Having installed himself as President of Yugoslavia, Milošević moved quickly to strengthen his position. Zoran Sokolović was moved from being Serbian Minister of the Interior to occupy the same position at federal level. Sokolović, a former provincial director of an agricultural co-operative, had risen under the tutelage of Ivan Stambolić to become Secretary of the Serbian Communist Party. Since the late 1980s he had been one of Milošević's most loyal acolytes. In November Jovica Stanišić was appointed as Milošević's National Security Advisor. Throughout Milošević's time as President of Serbia Stanišić had acted as a trusted henchman charged with the carrying out of the most delicate and important tasks. In November 1995 Stanišić had accompanied Milošević to the Dayton negotiations. Officially he had been listed as attending in his capacity as 'Aide to the Serbian Foreign Ministry'. This description, however, was clearly fictitious since the Serbian Foreign Ministry no longer existed having been abolished in 1993.[1] In his new role as National Security Advisor Stanišić would continue to act as Milošević's political 'right hand'.

Slobodan Milošević had promised that 1997 would be a year of economic reform and privatisation. In order to realise this aim Milošević appointed a number of individuals who were supporters of economic 'reform' and 'liberalisation' to positions within the Yugoslav and Serbian governments. The key representatives of this 'reformist' current were Milan Beko, the Serbian Privatisation Minister, and Danko Djunić, Vice-President of the federal government. Djunić who had gained his position within the federal government in March 1997 was an academic economist who had formerly headed the Belgrade Institute of Economics. He maintained strong contacts with Western business through his role as a partner with the accountants Deloitte and Touche in Belgrade. The first significant achievement by the 'reformists' came in June with the sale of a 49 per cent share in the Serbian state telecoms company (PTT) to the Italian telecoms operator Stet and the Greek company OTE for DM 1.6 billion. It soon became clear, however, that a rift existed between the reformers such as Djunić who wanted to use the money gained from privatisation in order to rebuild Yugoslavia's crumbling infrastructure, and the SPS-JUL hierarchy who wanted use the money to reduce the backlog of unpaid pensions and wages. In July Djunić stated that 'the cake called "social product" is not large enough to feed all the hungry mouths. The worst thing that we could do at this point is to spend the money which we have gained from the telecoms sale.'[2] However, Djunić was unable to prevent the privatisation revenues from being used in an attempt to 'buy' the votes of state employees and pensioners. Much of the money disbursed in this way was used to buy imported goods serving to further widen Yugoslavia's trade deficit. Danica Popović, a Belgrade University economist, commented wryly: 'It turns out that Italian and Greek money invested in the PTT went back to Italian shoemakers and Greek hoteliers. Calming down social unrest cost us approximately DM 1.3 billion.'[3] Djunić had also, as part of his reform package, sought to negotiate with the London Club of creditor banks the rescheduling of Yugoslavia's debts. In June Djunić boldly proposed that 80 per cent of Yugoslavia's commercial debt should be written off. During the lengthy negotiations Djunić argued that such radical concessions were necessary if the London Club were to stand a reasonable chance of getting any of their money back.[4] The ending of these negotiations without agreement on 23 October was a significant blow to Djunić's credibility.[5] By the end of the year Djunić appeared increasingly isolated within the federal government bureaucracy and his imminent removal from office was widely rumoured.

Milošević's vacation of the Serbian Presidency precipitated the holding of new elections for this position. The Serbian presidential and parliamentary elections were fixed to take place on 21 September. The Serbian Socialists and their allies in JUL and New Democracy chose Zoran Lilić as their candidate for President. With Lilić having served as President of the FRY in 1993-7 his adoption as candidate for the Serbian Presidency represented a simple exchange of political offices between himself and Milošević. Lilić had a background in business and had formerly been director of the Rakovica metalworking factory. In 1990 he had been elected as an SPS member of parliament and from 1992-3 served as the leader of the SPS parliamentary group. As President of the FRY Lilić was a feeble figure and had always remained subservient to Milošević. Although he was officially head of the Yugoslav state he was frequently excluded from international peace negotiations where his presence was considered to be of little relevance to their outcome.[6] There was considerable speculation over why Milošević had promoted as candidate an individual with as little political credibility as Lilić rather than a more politically competent figure such as Milorad Vučelić. Milošević apparently believed that it was better that a politically malleable individual should occupy the Serbian presidency rather than a more capable and ambitious figure who might be tempted to use this office's formidable institutional powers to chart an independent course. It was hoped that the strength of the Socialist political machinery would compensate for Lilić's lack of charisma. Milošević's analysis of the political situation was undoubtedly influenced by the events which had been unfolding in the Republika Srpska. In the RS Radovan Karadžić had been forced to relinquish a powerful presidency, which had been designed by himself for himself, and had subsequently found himself in confrontation with his successor, formerly his loyal nominee. Milošević did not wish to see this scenario repeated within Serbia itself.[7]

The differing responses of the opposition parties to the announcement of new elections was symptomatic of the general fragmentation which now characterised the opposition political scene. On 24 May the DSS and the GSS drew up an agreement whereby it was stated that they would not take part in the elections unless a series of conditions, in line with the suggestions made by Felipe Gonzales for the OSCE the previous winter, were met. The agreement was also singed by a number of other opposition groups including the Democratic Party, the SLS, and the SNS.[8] When the date of the elections was announced in August these political parties saw no reason to depart from their earlier position. Djindjić stated: 'The DS will not haggle over the electoral conditions, because last winter we promised the citizens that we would not participate in the elections if fair rules of the game were not determined beforehand.'[9] In Djindjić's view the DS had by deciding to boycott the elections made a hard but necessary choice: 'It is always more difficult to boycott elections than to participate in them. In the last ten years no political leader has offered to resign because of poor election results. I would have no need to be afraid that bad election results would weaken my position, I would always be able to find a justification in the adverse [electoral] conditions. It is a more difficult act to go into the wilderness and declare that we will not participate in the elections.'[10] The GSS condemned the conditions under which the elections had been called as 'irregular' while the DSS described them as 'illegitimate'.[11]

Vuk Drašković and the SPO, however, had been notably absent from the opposition agreement on election conditions. Milošević invited Drašković, on 3 August, to hold talks with him at his presidential residence in Belgrade. During these talks Milošević offered to 'liberalise' the state media and invite international observers from the OSCE to oversee the elections in return for Drašković's participation in the polls. Drašković was clearly flattered by the fact that, as he saw it, Milošević's invitation implicitly recognised his status as 'leader of the opposition'. He said: 'At this mini round-table between the chief of the Socialist Party of Serbia and the leader of the democratic opposition honest election conditions were agreed. I know there will be some attacks on me when they [the other opposition parties] hear that I have been recognised as leader of the democratic opposition, but it is a fact.'[12] The other opposition parties predictably rejected Drašković's claim to act as 'leader of the opposition'. They also condemned his decision to take part in the elections which they said would merely lend credibility to the flawed election process while there would be no guarantee that Milošević would honour the promises that he had made to Drašković.

Following his meeting with Milošević Drašković went to the headquarters of RTS, the building on which the demonstrators had vented their anger during the winter demonstrations, in order to appear on state-controlled television. Drašković told the interviewer: 'This time I have come without eggs.' Drašković went on to criticise his former colleagues in the opposition telling the audience that 'Vain [opposition] leaders will have to explain to voters why they refuse to run in the elections when they agreed to run in last year's federal elections under the same, if not worse, conditions.'[13]

In the run-up to the September elections it had become clear that a new and fundamental fissure had opened up in the Serbian political landscape. This division saw the political parties divided not simply along the lines of government/opposition but also between 'participating' and 'boycotting' forces. It appeared that the SPO and the DS had undergone a reversal of positions in terms of the historic attitudes of their parties towards political strategy and their relationship with the state. At its foundation the SPO had followed a radical ideological path whose rejection of the legitimacy of state institutions led them to look favourably on extra-parliamentary actions such as street demonstrations. The DS, and in particular that faction with which Djindjić was associated, had by contrast been dedicated to a 'gradualist' strategy of working through the existing institutions. By 1997, however, Drašković was arguing for the pursuit of an electoral and parliamentary strategy while Djindjić had placed himself at the head of an 'anti-election' boycott campaign.

Djindjić's decision to boycott the election met with criticism from both the 'left' and 'right'. An editorial in the pro-Socialist newspaper *Borba* accused Djindjić of calling for a boycott in order to avoid 'taking part in an election where the real strength of his party could be measured.'[14] In similar terms Ivan Kovačević of the SPO condemned the boycotting parties for 'deserting the battlefield for no reason'.[15] Djindjić explained the fact that these diverse groups were united in their attacks on him by observing: 'They have a common style, a common patriarchal mentality, they are parties organised along populist lines with inviolable leaders. They are anti-modern and anti-democratic parties.[...] For them I do not represent a competing party, but rather a completely different vision of politics. In terms of the degree of hatred shown towards me there is no great difference between *Zemunske novine*, JUL and *Srpska reč*. They find it easy, after exchanging harsh words, to sit down together to eat and make agreements. They are all part of the same family.'[16] Boris Tadić, a DS parliamentary representative, sought to explain the conflict between the SPO and the DS as a clash of political cultures. During the winter demonstrations, he said, 'the citizens saw only the outer wall of the coalition they did not see how things were functioning on the inside. The SPO and the DS and the SPO have a different approach to politics in terms of the way that they work, their organisation and their political aims and ideology. The Serbian

Renewal Movement is an anti-parliamentary organisation which expends its energies on heraldic projects. They occupy themselves with the symbols on flags, coats-of-arms and names...while for us the key thing is to achieve reform. At one point [after the winter protests] we entertained the hope that we would be able to remove Slobodan Milošević and carry out fundamental reform. We were, however, unable to fulfill the demands which the citizens were making because Vuk Drašković insisted that he should at all costs stand by his symbols of Četnikdom and the monarchy.'[17]

There were occasions during the pre-election period when the tensions between the DS and the SPO were manifest in physical confrontations between the parties' rival groups of supporters. On 15 August a DS 'anti-election' rally held in Kraljevo and addressed by Zoran Djindjić was disrupted by a group of SPO supporters throwing eggs and various missiles.[18] A number of incidents also took place in Belgrade between SPO postering teams putting up election publicity and DS members putting up their 'anti-election' posters urging voters to boycott the elections. Dragoslav Božović, the DS head of security, responded to these events by stating that the DS had enough members who were 'politically tolerant but loyal to the party' and ready to provide the 'physical help' needed to protect their meetings.[19] On 4 September Božović held a meeting with his opposite number from the SPO, Zvonko Osmajlić, at which it was agreed that the two parties should call a halt to the 'poster war' and 'co-operate' during the remainder of the election campaign.[20] While these incidents between the two former coalition parties were, in themselves, of minor importance they were symptomatic of the unstable and potentially dangerous political atmosphere prevailing in Serbia during the pre-election campaign.

In the poll which took place on 21 September Zoran Lilić secured 35.9 per cent of the vote as 'left coalition' Presidential candidate. In the parliamentary elections the 'left coalition' gained 110 seats. Although Lilić had emerged as the leading candidate in the Presidential race and the 'left coalition' was the largest parliamentary grouping these results were nevertheless disappointing for Milošević and the SPS. The fact that Lilić had failed to get 51 per cent or more of the vote meant that he would have to go take part in a second run-off round of elections. The 'left coalition' with only 110 seats would no longer be able to command an overall majority in parliament. The relative lack of success of the 'left coalition' can be accounted for by a combination of a still weakened SPS political organisation and profile, and a lacklustre candidate. During the campaign the Socialists had sought to compensate for Lilić's lack of appeal to the voters by clearly stressing his association with Milošević. The Socialists ensured that posters of Milošević were always put up directly alongside those of Lilić. In this way it was apparently hoped that Lilić would be able to appropriate a portion of Milošević's political charisma. Lilić's attempts at campaigning in the Serbian interior also ran into trouble. On 15 September violent clashes occurred in Kragujevac between riot police and supporters of the opposition who had turned up to heckle at a meeting addressed by Lilić.[21]

Vuk Drašković gained 22 per cent of the vote, and the SPO gained forty-five parliamentary seats. This result was better than some analysts had predicted and could in this sense be considered a 'success'.[22] In the period before the election, however, Drašković had been confidently predicting that he would be elected as Serbian President, and the SPO would gain a majority in parliament, without the help of the other opposition parties. At a rally held in Kraljevo on 16 September Drašković told his supporters that when he was elected as Serbian President he would behave towards all Serbian citizens 'like a good master of the house towards the members of his household'.[23] The fact that Drašković had come third in the Presidential race and was excluded from the run-off contest should therefore, by the criteria that Drašković set for himself in his rhetoric and campaign promises, be considered to be a disappointing failure. It is notable that Drašković did not succeed in making an electoral breakthrough at a time when rival 'democratic' parties were boycotting the elections and the SPO might have been expected to attract at least some of their voters who did not want to observe the boycott.

The 'boycotting' group of parties, however, also had little reason to claim that their tactics had been successful. The aim of the 'boycotting' bloc had been to deny the legitimacy of the election. They hoped that the turn-out would fall below 50 per cent and the election would be declared invalid. In the event, however, at 57.47 per cent the turn-out was comfortably above the 50 per cent mark. The lowest voter turn-outs were recorded in parts of central Belgrade such as Palilula (48.8 per cent) and Voždovac (53.6 per cent) and Vojvodina including Subotica (54.4 per cent) and Pančevo (55.5 per cent). In addition to the 'boycott' organised by the Serbian opposition parties the Albanians in Kosovo also, once again, boycotted the election. In Priština only 13.6 per cent and in Peć 18 per cent of voters went to the polls.[24]

With Vojislav Šešelj gaining 28.6 per cent of the vote in the presidential contest and the SRS gaining eighty-two parliamentary seats the Radicals might legitimately be considered to be the real 'victors' in the election. The Socialists were obviously shocked by the advances that the Radicals had made. They had undoubtedly intended to build up the SRS as a 'third force' in Serbian politics they, however, seemed unprepared for the scale of the Radical gains. Western diplomats were also alarmed at the success of the ultra-nationalist Vojislav Šešelj with his unrelenting opposition to the Dayton agreement. The high level of support for Šešelj, however, should not simply be seen as an expression by a large section of the Serbian electorate of their continued support for ultra-nationalist policies or a desire to create a territorial 'Great Serbia.' During the winter protests of 1996 the Zajedno alliance had managed to seriously wound the Socialist government. Zajedno itself, however, had proved too internally weak and incohesive to be able to capitalise on its successes. It was Šešelj who took the opportunity to exploit the damage which Zajedno had done to the credibility of the Milošević regime. Both before and during the election campaign Šešelj had been able to project an image of strength and confidence, showing himself to be firmly in control of his party.

On 19 September he had stated that he would resign if he failed to reach the second round of the presidential elections, but that he added could not happen 'even in a dream'.[25] The 'democratic' opposition parties had frequently, and accurately, sought to portray Šešelj as maintaining a relationship of tacit co-operation with the Socialists. The Radicals, however, vehemently denied that any such ambivalence existed in their attitude towards Socialists. During the election campaign Maja Gojković summed up the SRS position: 'Our aim is definitely that Slobodan Milošević should leave the political scene in Serbia and Yugoslavia, and that his party should be removed from power. My key political aim is to see communism pushed out of our current political scene and confined to history, and that after thirty-four years under the communists and with them for the next thirty-four years life should "as long as we remain" be lived like the rest of the normal world.'[26] At least a part of the 'opposition' electorate appeared to be ready to take the Radicals at their word. With such oppositional and anti-communist rhetoric being combined with structures and policies which resembled those of the Socialists the Radicals were able to put out a powerful, if contradictory, message which was capable of appealing to voters of the 'left' and 'right'.[27] Analysis of the votes gained by the SRS showed them to be picking up supporters both in areas of western Serbia, such as Kragujevac, which were traditional strongholds of the opposition and in parts of southern Serbia, such as Vranje and Leskovac, where the Socialists had long been considered to be the dominant force.[28] Although Šešelj had come second in the presidential race the strength of his vote meant that he would go through into the second round of the election with considerably more momentum than the Socialist candidate could muster.

In the aftermath of the elections Vuk Drašković had attempted to put a position 'spin' on the results. During a press conference on 22 September when Drašković was asked whether he intended to resign as leader of the SPO he replied indignantly: 'Why should somebody who has achieved the best individual and party results ever now consider resignation? I continue to be at the head of democratic Serbia, because there is nobody else apart from us. [...] We have demonstrated that we are a convincing leading democratic force in Serbia despite the tricks, plots and traps by all sides.'[29] However, Drašković was clearly furious with his former opposition colleagues whose call for a boycott of the election he held to be responsible for his poor result in the presidential poll. On 30 September the representatives of the SPO moved a motion at an extraordinary session of the Belgrade city assembly to remove Zoran Djindjić from his position as Mayor of Belgrade. The motion was supported by the Socialist and Radical representatives. Representatives of the DS, GSS and DSS did not attend the session of the assembly which they maintained had been improperly called. During the same session of the assembly the SPO also co-operated with Radicals and the Socialists in order to replace the management board of Studio B. The SPO stated that this purge of Studio B was justified because the TV station had given overly favourable coverage to the 'boycotting' parties during the election campaign. Following these moves a change was noted in the news output of Studio B with the activities of the SPO being heavily covered while those of the other opposition parties were neglected.

On the evening of 30 September 15,000 people gathered to protest at the measures which had been taken that day in the city assembly. Those attending the rally heard speeches by Vesna Pešić and Zoran Djindjić before it was proposed that they should set out on a 'walk' through the city just as they had done during the period of the winter protests. As the column of demonstrators began to make their way through the centre of Belgrade they were ambushed by large numbers of riot police who were waiting in the surrounding streets. Zoran Djindjić was among those beaten by the police, but he escaped more serious injury when his bodyguards pulled him clear of the melée. On 1 October when demonstrators once again tried to gather in the city centre the police responded with a similar degree of violence. A rally on 4 October called to protest at the earlier violence and attended by around 5,000 people passed off without incident. This rally was addressed by a number of public personalities and intellectuals including journalists who had resigned or been sacked from Studio B. The singer Aleksandra Kovač gave a *cri de coeur* which expressed the sentiments of many young urbanites when she told the meeting that she was there not to support Djindjić or even because of Studio B but rather because she was 'sick and tired of the whole lot of them, sick and tired of their lies, because many of her contemporaries had left the city, and because they had turned Belgrade into a village'.[30]

The SPO had justified their move to oust Djindjić by stating that he had abused his office by using his position as mayor of Belgrade in order to promote the anti-election 'boycott' campaign. Drašković's pronouncements on these events, however, appeared to be confused and contradictory. Interviewed by the BBC, he stated that he had acted against Djindjić because the leader of the DS was a 'nationalist' who was conspiring with Radovan Karadžić against the Dayton agreement.[31] Interviewed in the Serbian press Drašković, however, took a different line suggesting that Zoran Djindjić was plotting with Albanian separatists against Serbian national interests, and drew attention to the 'strange coincidence' that the demonstrations organised by Zoran Djindjić and Vesna Pešić should occur at the same time as demonstrations organised by Kosovo Albanians.[32] At one press conference, however, Drašković was more candid about his motives. When a journalist asked him whether the move against Djindjić was an act of 'personal revenge' he replied: 'Of course. He betrayed the coalition. I created him and now I have eliminated him. I have done nothing wrong.'[33] For Drašković to be implicated, even indirectly, in an episode where force was used by the police against demonstrators was particularly damaging for someone whose political image had on previous occasions, such as 9 March 1991 and 1 June 1993, been centred on the idea of his being the victim of state-directed violence. Although Drašković tried to dissociate himself from the police violence which took place on the nights of 30 September and 1 October his role in these events served to severely undermine his credibility among the inhabitants of Belgrade.

Šešelj and the SRS approached the second round of Presidential elections, set for 5 October, in an upbeat mood. The Socialists by contrast appeared increasingly confused and unsure of how to deal with the developing situation. On 5 October, before casting his vote, Šešelj told journalists that his victory in the election would 'rule out the possibility of Serbia ever kneeling before any Western power'.[34] When the votes were counted Socialist fears regarding the result proved to be justified. Šešelj gained 49.98 per cent of the vote wheras Zoran Lilić trailed with 46.99 per cent. Before the election Vuk Drašković had stated that he could not advise his supporters to vote for either Šešelj or Lilić and therefore urged voters to boycott the second round of elections.[35] However, he was no doubt aware that he had now been forced to fall in line with the position held by his opposition rivals all along, and thus made this call for a boycott with little enthusiasm. The results of the election indicated that a significant proportion of those who voted for Drašković in the first round of the elections gave their votes to Šešelj in the second round. Although Šešelj had 'won' the election the poll was ruled invalid because only 49 per cent of the electorate had turned out to vote. The failure of the poll meant that yet another round of elections would have to be held in the hope that this would produce a more conclusive result. Officials from the SRS protested that the authorities had manipulated the turn-out figures in order to deprive Šešelj of his victory. Šešelj, however, appeared ready to reconcile himself calmly with the fact that he would have to contest a new round of elections. His followers sought to console their leader by presenting him with a cake in the shape of the 'Great Serbian' state which the SRS was pledged to create.

The parliamentary elections had produced three rival blocs of representatives none of which could command an overall majority and all of which were divided by fierce mutual antagonisms. In this situation, although there were lengthy contacts and negotiations on all sides, it proved impossible to form a viable government. Relations within the 'left coalition' were particularly fraught. The 110 representatives won by the 'left coalition' had been divided so that the SPS received eighty-six representatives, JUL nineteen and New Democracy five. All the elements of the coalition expressed barely-concealed dissatisfaction with the number of representatives they received as part of this arrangement. Members of the SPS were known to believe that JUL was an essentially 'parasitic' organization and that too many seats had been conceded to this organization.[36] For its part JUL was reported to have blamed Šešelj's success on the political incompetence of the SPS hierarchy and to have suggested that their leadership role should have been recognized with the allocation of 'at least thirty-four seats'.[37] New Democracy were deeply unhappy with the five seats they had received, observing that this was even less than they had gained when they had fought the election in 1993 as part of DEPOS.[38]

It was amid this atmosphere of internecine strife and jostling for position that the 'left' political elite was rocked by another high-level murder. On the morning of 24 October Zoran Todorović ('Kundak'), the General Secretary of JUL and director of the Beopetrol oil company, was shot dead by an unidentified gunman as he was arriving for work at his offices in New Belgrade; he was hit several times and died immediately, and his bodyguard was also seriously wounded. The thirty-eight-year-old Todorović had been a close friend and confidant of Mirjana Marković, and as part of the charmed circle surrounding the Milošević family he had seen his business and political career progress rapidly. Slobodan Milošević attended his funeral and was seen to weep openly for his murdered friend and political colleague. As with the other similar murders earlier in the year, the police were unable to catch the killer of this powerful member of Serbia's political elite.[39]

In the aftermath of the elections there were increasing signs of dissatisfaction amongst provincial branches of the SPO, and in particular some of those in the Šumadija, with the leadership decisions being taken by Vuk Drašković. These branches were particularly disturbed by the way in which the Belgrade SPO had acted in concert with the Socialists and Radicals in order to displace Djindjić and the fact that by maintaining ongoing contacts with the SPS hierarchy the SPO leadership appeared ready to contemplate the possibility of forming a coalition government with the Socialists.[40] The provincial dissidents blamed many of the SPO's problems on the fact that Drašković was overly reliant for advice on a clique of Belgrade-based intellectuals including Milan Božić, Ivan Kovačević and Aleksandar Čotrić. They had been particularly enraged by one statement in which Milan Božić reportedly referred to the critics of the SPO leadership from inner Serbia as 'provincials and spiritually sick individuals who do not understand high politics'.[41] The sense of disquiet felt by many SPO activists coalesced around Velimir Ilić, the Mayor of Čačak. Ilić, who was himself a private businessman, having been appointed Mayor of Čačak after the opposition local election victories had sought to build on what he saw as the town's local tradition of entrepreneurship. Ilić attributed the present-day density of private firms in Čačak to the fact that during the Second World War the area had been known for its strong Četnik sympathies and had therefore received little state-directed industrial development aid in the post-war period. The population had as a result been forced to fall back on their own initiative and resources.[42] In the September elections Čačak had been one of the few towns where the SPO had topped the poll. Ilić was also a leading light in the Association of Free Towns and Opštinas, an organization set up after the opposition local election victories of in order to encourage co-operation between the various areas where Zajedno had been victorious in addressing common problems of civic government. On 27 October during a meeting of the Association of Free Towns and Opštinas which took place in the Vojvodinan town of Kikinda, Zoran Mićović, Vice-President of the Arilje town government and a member of the DS, suggested that the association should nominate its own candidate for the next round of presidential elections. Although Mićović did not specifically name him, it was known that Ilić had been mentioned as a possible candidate by a number of figures within the association.[43] Drašković reacted to this by removing Ilić from his position as Vice-President of the SPO, stating that he had 'grossly violated' the movement's statues.[44] Ilić reacted angrily to his dismissal, saying: 'I headed the [candidates'] list in Čačak and won the most convincing victory in the whole of Serbia. [...] He [Drašković] can only have me removed where he and his"gentlemen" make the decisions. That is not the case in Čačak. The people of Čačak know who I am and what I am, and now they know who Vuk is.'[45] The SPO accused Ilić of working to undermine the SPO leadership out of 'personal ambition'. Veroljub Stevanović, the SPO Mayor of Kragujevac sought to deny that there was any significant discontent among the movement's members in the Šumadija and dismissed any signs of revolt as the 'work of the SDB and the DS'.[46] On 8 December, at a meeting in Mladenovac, Velimir Ilić and a group of other SPO members announced that they were leaving the movement in order to form a new political party which was to be called SPO-Zajedno.[47] Among those members who co-operated with Ilić in setting up SPO-Zajedno were the former SPO Vice-President's, Jovan Marjanović and Ilija Radulović.

Radulović, a former judge and latterly a lawyer based in Šabac in central Serbia, was a long-standing friend of Vuk Drašković. Drašković had even used Radulović's work as a judge as the basis for his novel *Sudija* (The Judge) which was published in 1981. Radulović had also collaborated closely with Drašković in his attempt during the early 1990s to push the SPO from a 'radical nationalist' to a 'centre-right' position. Now, however, Radulović condemned Drašković: 'Vuk was and still is an authentic Bolshevik. His thought structure is exclusive and autocratic. [...] In that party for the last seven years no one has been able to engage him in dialogue.'[48] Velimir Ilić proposed that the SPO-Zajedno grouping should play a leading role in forging a new 'anti-regime bloc.' The SPO-Zajedno constituent assembly held on 22 December was attended by a number of representives from other political parties including Zoran Djindjić (DS), Vesna Pešić (GSS), Nikola Milošević (SLS), and Vladan Batić (DHSS).[49]

Notes

1. Roksanda Ninčić, 'Čovek od karijere', *Vreme*, 22 November 1997.
2. "Najveća greška" ako bi se potrošio novac od prodaje telekomunikacija', *Naša borba*, 2 July 1997.

3. Guy Dinmore, 'Prospects are Still Bleak Despite Signs of Recovery', *Financial Times*, 27 January 1998.
4. Matej Vipotnik, 'Belgrade Firm Over Write-Off Proposal', *Financial Times*, 8 August 1997.
5. 'Fijasko pregovora SRJ i Londonskog kluba', *Naša borba*, 24 October 1997.
6. Pribićević (1997), p. 79.
7. Nenad LJ Stefanović, 'Serbia's Caesar Enters an Age of Uncertainty', *Transitions*, September 1997.
8. 'Stranački dogovor o minimumu izbornih uslova?', *Naša borba*, 28 May 1997.
9. *Beta*, 3 August 1997 in *SWB EE/2989 A/10*, 5 August 1997.
10. 'Jedino osovina Plavšić, Djindjić, Djukanović može da sruši S. Miloševića', Zoran Djindjić interviewed by Ratko Dimitrović and Zoran Preradović, *Argument*, 15 September 1997.
11. *Beta*, 31 July 1997 in *SWB EE/2987 A/9*, 2 August 1997; Radio B-92, 3 August 1997 in *SWB EE/2989 A/10*, 5 August 1992.
12. 'Sa megdana ne bežimo', Vuk Drašković interviewed by Dragan Jovanović, *NIN*, 8 August 1997.
13. *Tanjug*, 4 August 1997 in *SWB EE/2989 A/10*, 5 August 1997.
14. Dragica Lukić, 'Djindjićev autogol', *Borba*, 12 August 1997.
15. Ivan Kovačević interviewed by Jasmina Spasić, 'Nije isključena koalicija levice i SPO', *Nedeljni telegraf*, 17 September 1997.
16. 'Vuk Drašković je općinjen, Dušan Mihailović kurir SPS, a Zoran Lilić pogrešio državu', Zoran Djindjić interviewed by Momčilo Djorgović, *Nedeljni telegraf*, 17 September 1997.
17. Svetlana Djurdjević-Lukić, 'Pukovnik ili pokojnik', *NIN*, 19 August 1997.
18. 'Jeste li i vi ostavili jaja?', *Dnevni telegraf*, 15 August 1997.
19. Jasmina Spasić and Vojislava Crnjanski, 'Centrala SPO naredila opštinskim odborima da aktiviraju svoje jurišnike', *Nedeljni telegraf*, 20 August 1997.
20. *Beta*, 4 September 1997 in *SWB EE 3017 A/5*, 6 September 1997.
21. *Radio B-92*, 15 September 1997 in *SWB EE/3026 A/13*,
22. Ognjen Pribićević interviewed in *NIN* on 29 August drew attention to opinion poll data which showed only 6.4 per cent of respondents saying they would vote for Drašković.
23. *Tanjug*, 17 September 1997 in *SWB EE/3027 A/7*, 18 September 1997.
24. Milan Milošević, 'Nekako nakrivo', *Vreme*, 27 September 1997.
25. *Dnevni telegraf*, 19 September in *SWB EE/3029 A/8*, 20 September 1997.
26. 'Nikola Barović je imao mnogo sreće što nije naleteo na moju pesnicu ja bih ga premlatila i izgledao bi još gore', Maja Gojković interviewed by Branko Milenković, *Argument*, 25 August 1997.
27. The nature of the Serbian Radical Party's constituency and its political appeal is discussed in Chapters 13 and 20.
28. Aleksandra Ranković and Predrag Vujić, 'Šešelj pobjednik stolica prazna', *Monitor*, 10 October 1997.
29. *Beta*, 22 September 1997 in *SWB EE/3032 A/12*, 24 October 1997.
30. *Beta*, 4 October 1997 in *SWB EE/3042 A/12*, 6 October 1997.
31. Vuk Drašković interviewed on News Day, BBC World Service, 1 October 1997.

32. Nenad LJ Stefanović, 'Kurs nemilosrdne demokratije', *Vreme*, 2 October 1997.
33. Milan Milošević, 'Odoše jaja', *Vreme*, 11 October 1997.
34. *Beta*, 5 October 1997 in *SWB EE/3043 A/2*, 7 October 1997.
35. *Beta*, 27 September 1997 in *SWB EE/3036 A/12*, 29 September 1997.
36. J. Kosanić, 'Nezadovljno članstvo sve tri stranke', *Naša borba*, 25-26 October 1997.
37. *Argument*, 6 October 1997 in *SWB EE/3045 A/10*, 7 October 1997.
38. 'Dušan Mihajlović nije podneo neopozivu ostavku', *Naša borba*, 25-26 October 1997.
39. D. Petrović, 'Ubijen generalni sekretar JUL Zoran Todorović *Kundak*', *Naša borba*, 25-26 October 1997.
40. Dragan Todorović, 'Čačanski glas', *Vreme*, 25 October 1997.
41. 'Neko nam stalno zabada trn u zdravu nogu', Velimir Ilić interviewed by Blagica Stojanović, *Srpska reč*, 16 October 1997.
42. 'Samo nade tračak', Velimir Ilić interviewed by Nenad Stefanović, *Duga*, 30 August 1997.
43. 'Slobodni gradovi hoće na izbore Veroljub Stevanović koči kandidaturu', *Dnevni telegraf*, 27 October 1997.
44. *Beta*, 30 October 1997 in *SWB EE/3065 A/5*, 1 November 1997.
45. 'Ne mogu me isključiti iz – Čačka', *Naša borba*, 1-2 November 1997.
46. *Tanjug*, 22 December 1997 in *SWB EE/3110 A/7*, 24 December 1997.

27. Milošević's Crumbling Hegemony – Power Struggles in the Republika Srpska and Montenegro

While this struggle to break the electoral and political deadlock was taking place a different drama was being played out across the Drina in the Republika Srpska. It was a drama in which actors from Serbia would play important roles and the results would have consequences within Serbia itself. The power struggle between Plavšić and Karadžić entered a new phase with the international community increasingly throwing its weight behind the Plavšić faction. From the start of this internecine conflict the SFOR forces had been ready to provide passive support to Plavšić helping to secure her personal safety against attack by pro- Karadžić forces. Now, however, they began to provide her with more active support. Initially the international community were wary of associating themselves too closely with Plavšić's cause on account of her well-known role as part of the Bosnian Serb wartime leadership. However, there was also a realisation that if the Dayton agreement was to have any chance of success they would need to find people within the Serbian leadership who would be willing to follow a more 'moderate' and 'co-operative' path. During early 1996 the international agencies in Bosnia had sought to promote the Banja Luka-based Prime Minister of the RS, Rajko Kasagić, as a suitable 'moderate' with whom they could 'do business'. Kasagić's attempts at following an independent line were, however, brought to a swift end in May of that year when he was summarily excluded from office on the orders of Radovan Karadžić. For the international community Biljana Plavšić came to be seen as their last chance of finding a Bosnian Serb politician who would be ready to abandon the entrenched nationalist positions occupied during the war and who would also have sufficient strength to survive in the hostile political landscape of the Republika Srpska.

Plavšić sought to cultivate the support of the international community with some skill surrounding herself with a circle of Western-educated advisers. The mitigated nationalist line being followed by Biljana Plavšić was reflected in the public statements of this group. Ana Mitrović, a young graduate of the Fletcher School of Law and Diplomacy in Boston who was working as an adviser to Biljana Plavšić, said: 'I believe that we should become part of Europe, that economic barriers should be removed, that people should be able to travel freely, that there should be one single market, but there must always be borders inside which people are able to feel secure. [...] It is time for us to end our isolation and rejoin the international community...but it is very important that the Republika Srpska exists within Bosnia-Hercegovina. [...] It is possible to accept that other people live in your land, but you will know that it is your land and not that of those with another culture and customs.'[1]

In an attempt to resolve the dispute between the Pale SDS leadership and Biljana Plavšić over whether she had acted within her rights when she dissolved the Bosnian Serb parliament the matter was referred to the constitutional court of the Republika Srpska. The OSCE took their own legal advice which concluded that Plavšić had acted legitimately when she had dissolved the parliament. It soon became clear, however, that legal considerations would not be uppermost in the deliberations of the Republika Srpska's judges. Before the judgment was delivered the President of the constitutional court, Gaso Mijanović, had declared that their decision would take into account the 'economic, social, and political consequences of the President's decision'.[2] It came as little surprise therefore when on 15 August the court announced that by seven votes to four it had voted to declare Plavšić's actions 'unconstitutional'.[3] The Pale faction expressed satisfaction with the court's declaration with Gojko Kličković, the Prime Minister of the Republika Srpska, stating that the ruling was 'a step forward and a solution which had a calming effect. Finally we shall have to understand that there are no irreplaceable individuals or protected institutions'. On 17 August, however, it was revealed that one of the judges from the constitutional court, Jovan Rosić, was in hospital in Banja Luka, having reportedly been severely beaten by unidentified attackers while staying in a hotel in Pale. On 21 August Rosić addressed a press conference in Banja Luka relating how his assailants had placed guns to his head and told him: 'you will not vote for the decision by that whore from Banja Luka.' He was told that if he did not follow their instructions he would be 'liquidated'.[5] Milorad Dodik, the leader of the Party of Independent Social Democrats of the Republika Srpska and a key ally of Plavšić's, said that the President of the Republika Srpska was under no obligation to accept a judgment which had been obtained using such coercive methods.

On 8 August SFOR and International Police representatives had informed the Bosnian Serb authorities that anti-terrorist and police special forces in the Republika Srpska would henceforth be classified as military forces and would therefore come under the control of SFOR. This decision was meant to exert further pressure on Radovan Karadžić, who relied on these police special forces to act as his bodyguards. Significantly, however, it was decided that the anti-terrorist unit headed by Dragan Lukač could continue to provide security for Biljana Plavšić.[6] On 17 August Lukač and his anti-terrorist unit occupied the main police building in Banja Luka. It was stated that they were carrying out this operation because they had evidence that the building was being used by pro-Karadžić police to intercept the phone and fax communications being made by the RS President and two constitutional court judges resident in the town. A confrontation quickly developed between Lukač's men and pro-Karadžić loyalists who arrived from other police stations across the city. At this point SFOR troops intervened ostensibly to separate the two sides. The SFOR troops, however, occupied the building and continued the search which had been begun by Lukač's unit. During the course of the next week SFOR carried out searches of five more police stations in the Banja Luka area uncovering large stockpiles of weaponary. Following the take-over of these police stations a new pro-Plavšić leadership was appointed to control the police. The conflict within the police spread to the area around Banja Luka with, on 22 August, the two Serbian factions exchanging fire when pro-Plavšić police took over the police station at Prnjavor.

Plavšić was also able to gain control of other key institutions of power. The electronic media had been a critical tool in the hands of the SDS hardliners in their struggle with Plavšić and her followers. Their broadcasts had over the previous months, sought to systmatically vilify the President of the RS. In the wake of the SFOR moves to take over the police stations in Banja Luka the Bosnian Serb media had launched another offensive against Plavšić and her Western allies. On 20 August the Bosnian Serb TV presenter, Duško Oljača, informed viewers: 'History reminds us that Benito Mussolini used to address people from Roman balconies just like Biljana Plavšić did yesterday. Events that brought the RS and the Serbian nation to the edge of the abyss did not start last night from the balcony of the Banski Dvori [the presidential residence] but with violations of the constitution, demagogy, manipulation and usurpation.'[7] The SFOR troops were described as 'occupying forces' and a film of them was shown intercut with archive footage of Nazi soldiers from the Second World War. On 24 August, however, the Radio and TV journalists based in Banja Luka transferred their loyalties to the Plavšić camp. The employees told their general manager: 'You have told too many lies and we do not believe you any more.'[8] Their secession meant that separate TV services began operating from the Pale and Banja Luka stations. This represented a crucial breach in the walls of the 'media blockade' which had helped to sustain SDS power among the Bosnian Serbs.

While both factions could rely on the loyalty of different elements within the police the loyalties of the VRS remained in doubt. On 26 August two-thirds of the army leadership attended a meeting called by Plavšić in Banja Luka. Among those present who pledged their support to the President were the leaders of the main military units in northern Bosnia, General Momir Talić of the 1st Krajina Corps and General Novica Simić of the Bijeljina Corps. A notable absentee was the VRS Chief of Staff, Pero Čolić, who had served in the war as a middle-ranking officer based in north-western Bosnia. In November 1996, however, he had been appointed by Biljana Plavšić to take Ratko Mladić's place as head of the VRS. Although Čolić owed his rapid advance within the army to Plavšić, he had recently been critical of her actions to which, in a leaked letter, he had referred as being 'unconstitutional'.[9] Čolić, however, swiftly reconsidered his position and on 3 September he travelled to Banja Luka where he met Plavšić and acknowledged her as 'supreme commander' of the VRS.[10] Čolić's indecision and vacillation during this period can be explained by the fact that having recently risen from the ranks he lacked the authority and power-base necessary to sustain a firm and independent line. The final decision of the VRS to stay effectively neutral in the conflict, however, can be compared to the similar line followed by the VJ in the Federal Republic of Yugoslavia who in the period 1996-8 chose to stay out of potentially violent political conflicts.[11]

On 11 August Biljana Plavšić announced that she intended to found a new political party. She stated that the political mission of this party would be to defend 'the Serbian national state, and protect the Serbian national interests in this territory, but these interests cannot be protected without democratisation.'[12] The news of this initiative set in motion a series of high-level defections from the Banja Luka SDS. On 15 August Ostoja Knežević resigned as President of the Banja Luka SDS. He was followed on 16 August by Branislav Lolić, the Deputy Chairman of the Banja Luka organisation and a number of other city officials.[13] On 25 August Dragoljub Mirjanić, the Vice-President of the RS deserted the Krajišnik-Karadžić faction apparently alienated by the 'primitive and unprofessional' methods used by his former colleagues.[14] The former Prime Minister of the Republika Srpska, Rajko Kasagić, also pledged his support to the new party, saying: 'Biljana and I have been slandered in the same way by the Pale government, and we both worked on an honest project, the project of creating a legal state.'[15] Plavšić's party, the Serbian National Alliance, held its first meeting on 28 August with Plavšić as President and Ostoja Knežević as Vice-President. Knežević stressed the continuity between the the Serbian National Alliance and the SDS in terms of ideology and policy: 'The SDS has a good programme and there isn't much difference between the two. The crucial difference is that we are determined to fulfill what we say in our programme.'[16] Sceptical observers dubbed the Serbian National Alliance the 'new SDS'. Plavšić, however, was ready to emphasise that the Serbian National Alliance would not be exclusive in its national policy. She told the party's founding congress: 'On this occasion I wish to stress our goal is not a 100 per cent ethnically pure Republika Srpska. Anyone who is ready to adopt the values of a country, respect its laws and institutions and defend it if need be is welcome here.'[17] The Serbian National Alliance soon began to gather supporters from across northern Bosnia. In Bijeljina a significant proportion of the Main Committee of the SDS came over to the Serbian National Alliance. In Zvornik the local Serbian National Alliance committee was founded by a number of former VRS officers and soldiers. An attempt by the SDS to prevent the Serbian National Alliance operating in the town was anticipated but in the event the Pale faction, perhaps wisely, decided not to interfere with this group.[19] Some of the opposition parties who had provided Plavšić with initial support were, however, critical of her decision to found her own party. Milorad Dodik insisted that Plavšić should have remained above party politics appealing to the people as a *supra-political* personality. It was argued that since she had gathered her following on the basis of a campaign against SDS corruption it would undermine her credibility if she was seen to be organising a party whose key figures were largely made up of SDS defectors. However, it was doubtful whether Plavšić would have had a realistic chance of success in taking on the still powerful SDS establishment with only the support of the fragmented opposition parties. In order to break the hold of the SDS on the loyalties of the Bosnian Serbs it was necessary for her to appropriate a section of their membership and their political hierarchy.[19] The foundation of the Serbian National Alliance took place too late for it to participate in the local elections in Bosnia-Hercegovina scheduled for 13-14 September but it was set to be a major contender in the elections for the Republika Srpska national assembly proposed by Plavšić.

Western diplomats sought to exert pressure on Slobodan Milošević urging him to interven in the conflict on Plavšić's side. Publically Milošević maintained that the power struggle was an internal matter for the Republika Srpska and that Serbia and the FRY were obliged to maintain a policy of 'neutrality'. On 27 August it appeared that Milošević was ready to change his position when SFOR officials received a request from his office for his plane to be allowed to land at Banja Luka airport. However, this anticipated intervention by the President of Yugoslavia, failed to materialise. In reality, beneath his surface rhetoric, Milošević continued to support and direct the efforts to overthrow Plavšić, and he was rumoured to be increasingly impatient with the failure of Krajišnik and Karadžić to displace her and they in turn were distrustful of their former mentor in Belgrade.[20]

On 1 September American SFOR troops cordoned off the television transmitter at Udrigovo near Bijeljina. Pro-Karadžić Serbs had apparently been planning to destroy the transmitter rather than let it fall into the hands of followers of Biljana Plavšić. That evening the SFOR soldiers came under attack from a crowd of around 300 people throwing stones and other missiles. The SFOR forces responded by firing tear gas at the crowd. The next day, after a face-saving 'agreement' had been drawn up, the SFOR troops withdrew from around the transmitter effectively handing it over to Karadžić's supporters. In Brčko police loyal to Plavšić had attempted to take over the local police station. The pro-Karadžić authorities in response summoned people out onto the streets to protest by sounding air raid sirens. Calls were broadcast over the radio for the Serbian people to show their 'national rage' against the 'occupiers'. Around 1,000 people went on the rampage attacking United Nations property, the international police and SFOR soldiers. SFOR helicopters dropped tear-gas on the crowd from the air while soldiers fired shots over the rioters' heads. After two soldiers were injured in the confrontation, a tactical withdrawal was made from Brčko by SFOR. Similar violent incidents also took place in Doboj and Zvornik.[21] These retreats represented a major blow to the prestige of the international community and a psychological victory for the pro-Pale faction.

Many of the Serbs in Brčko were refugees who had been settled in the area having originally come from areas in the Muslim-Croat Federation such as the suburbs of Sarajevo. Their recent experiences combined with the uncertain status of Brčko under the Dayton agreement made these people a volatile and easily manipulated group. Furthermore they tended to see themselves as 'victims' of the Dayton agreement and for this reason identified their fate with that of Radovan Karadžić who had been consistently presented by Bosnian Serb radio and TV as a 'martyr' persecuted by the international community. During the riots in Brčko the crowds had chanted 'Bastards, leave us in our homes' at the SFOR soldiers, reflecting the fears of an element of the populace that any international intervention would be a prelude to the separation of Brčko from the Republika Srpska. However, there was evidence that the Brčko riots were the product of external intervention. In a subsequent news conference Biljana Plavšić blamed the violence on infiltrators from across the Serbian border, saying: 'To take such irresponsible action there, driving in criminals from Yugoslavia...and then put women and children up front as shields is insane and amoral for a normal man.' Robert Farrand, the US diplomat who had been appointed as Brčko's international supervisor, was more reticient regarding the origin of those external elements involved in the riots: 'When I say outsiders, I'm not only talking about persons from outside Brčko, I'm talking outside Bosnia-Hercegovina.' When he was asked whether these individuals came from the FRY, he told the journalists to 'draw your own conclusions'. According to SFOR sources, however, up to 250 operatives from the Serbian Ministry of the Interior had been active in the towns of eastern Bosnia during the riots.[22]

Following these events the SDS announced that they intended to hold a major rally in Banja Luka on 8 September in the run up to the local elections. The SDS spokesman in Banja Luka Mira Mladjenović estimated that 10,000 SDS supporters would attend the rally from across the Republika Srpska.[23] The authorities in Banja Luka maintained that they had information from sources in Pale that armed members of the pro-Karadžić police special forces intended to infiltrate the town using the demonstration as a cover in order to initiate a *coup* against Plavšić. The fact that Franko Simatović, one of Milošević's covert operations coordinators from the Serbian Ministry of the Interior, had been sighted in Banja Luka in the week before the 'demonstration' tended to confirm the belief that Milošević had given his backing to the *coup* attempt. Milošević had apparently concluded that the recent reverses suffered by SFOR showed them to lack the will to continue their support for Plavšić in the face of the determined use of violence. The Banja Luka police therefore decided to ban the meeting on the technicality that they had not received sufficient notice for the calling of a meeting. The OSCE initially raised objections to this ban telling the pro-Plavšić authorities that it was 'undemocratic' to ban meetings held by their opponents. This ruling however, was, countermanded by Jacques Klein, the deputy to the International High Representative, who approved the ban on 'security' grounds. The SDS, however, declared that the rally would go ahead in spite of the moves to prohibit it. Momčilo Krajišnik arrived in Banja Luka on the morning of 8 September accompanied by the RS Prime Minister and Pale-backed Interior Minister, Dragan Kijač. The Orthodox church helped to mediate and arrange a meeting between Krajišnik and Plavšić. The two leaders arrived at the meeting each backed by a retinue of armed policemen. The meeting ended without agreement, and Krajišnik and his followers retired to the Hotel Bosna directly opposite the presidential residence. The large number of supporters who Krajišnik had anticipated would be coming to Banja Luka during the day did not turn up, but this was because the local Banja Luka police had been given authorisation by SFOR to set up road-blocks on the routes around Banja Luka to prevent the demonstrators getting through. The local police were backed by British and Czech SFOR troops from the Banja Luka area as well as Dutch reinforcements who had been drafted in from Muslim-Croat Federation territory to cope with the situation. During that day and the following night the combined police and SFOR cordon around Banja Luka turned back seventy buses and 130 cars carrying demonstrators. The identities of those turned back were checked against lists of known pro-Karadžić special policemen. Large quantities of arms were found in the buses and cars. The operation did not pass without incident, and late in the evening two policemen were shot, with one being seriously wounded, while trying to search vehicles on their way to Banja Luka. During the night local police also thwarted an attempt by Karadžić's men to storm the television transmitter on Mount Kozara.

As a result the SDS rally scheduled for 6.00 p.m. was attended only by a few hundred supporters from the Banja Luka area. The speakers at the rally were heckled throughout by a rival crowd of Plavšić supporters. Their chants of 'Thieves, thieves' and 'Back to the forest' showed the way in which they characterised the supporters of the Pale leadership as rural 'invaders' of of their town. One participant in the pro-Plavšić gathering recalled: 'Krajišnik and Kličković began to use tired old phrases in the style of "You are the heroes of this war", "You are legendary", "You are honourable Serbs"...but I did not think such recognition was necessary. For me what is necessary is that we have a peaceful and democratic Republika Srpska, that my town of Banja Luka should not suffer from poverty. For me what is necessary is that thievery and injustice should end and that people should be able to live a normal life. During the speeches I noticed that Krajišnik and Kličković were very frightened. Kličković in particular. At each noise or chant they trembled. They were as white as chalk.'[24]

Following the failure of the rally Krajišnik and the other SDS leaders rather than leaving Banja Luka chose to withdraw again to the Hotel Bosna apparently in the hope that their other supporters would be able to penetrate the security cordon which had been placed around Banja Luka. Krajišnik and his entourage of advisors and bodyguards, however, soon found themselves beseiged inside the hotel by a crowd of around 1,500 Plavšić supporters angered by reports that armed Karadžić supporters had been trying to enter the town. The Pale officials inside the hotel appeared increasingly concerned by the situation in which they found themselves. Kličković was heard to mutter forlornly: 'There must be something wrong here when there are so many angry people outside.'[25] Jacques Klein negotiated the evacuation of around eighty of Krajišnik's men from the hotel in SFOR armoured personnel carriers. Krajišnik, however, refused to accompany them stating that he would only leave in his official car. He maintained this position in spite of the fact that Klein had persuaded the Yugoslav Foreign Minister, Milan Milutinović, to phone Krajišnik in an attempt to cajole him into leaving under SFOR protection. In the end Krajišnik and the hardcore of his supporters succeeded in reaching their cars and leaving Banja Luka although their departure was accompanied by a shower of eggs from the townspeople gathered outside the hotel.[26]

The humiliation of the SDS leadership on the streets of Banja Luka was paralleled by setbacks for the party at the polls. In the local elections of 13 and 14 September the SDS maintained its position as the primary political force in the Republika Srpska being the only party with representation in all its municipalities. In the north and west of the RS, however, the SDS found their support-base being eaten into by the opposition parties who had supported Plavšić in the previous months. In Banja Luka the SDS vote collapsed with the party gaining only seven representatives on the seventy-seat city council. The largest groups of representatives on the council were won by the Socialist Party of the RS and the Serb Party of Posavina and Krajina who both won twelve seats. Both of these parties had backed the RS President in the ongoing intra-Serb feud.[27] Milovan Regoda, a leading SDS official in Banja Luka, sought to explain the SDS debacle in the city as an unfortunate, but inevitable, consequence of the process of post-communist 'transition' stating that: 'Before and during the war we had a party which was also a "national movement"...that was the Serbian Democratic Party. We hope that, following the logic of what happened to Solidarity in Poland, it will be able to return to power. I strongly believe that the Serbian Democratic Party will once again take the leading role in the post-Dayton process of democratisation in this territory.'[28] The SDS, however, also lost votes to the Serbian Radical Party. The Bosnian Radicals had undoubtedly benefited from the upswing in the support for the SRS across the Drina in Serbia. In Bosnia, as in Serbia, the Radicals had also been able to gather votes by positioning themselves between two contending political forces and appealing to the voters using a number of different messages. The SRS deployed anti-corruption rhetoric similar in tone to that used by Plavšić alongside a nationalism even more hardline than that practiced by the SDS. This enabled them to pick up votes from people who were critical of the failings of the SDS, but remained suspicious of Plavšić's relationship with the Western powers. The reputation of the SRS among a section of the voters in eastern Bosnia had been further strengthened by the prominent role played by SRS activists in the anti-SFOR demonstrations in August. Co-operation between the SRS and the SDS became increasingly close as the rift between Milošević and the Pale leadership widened.

Milošević had by now concluded that Krajišnik and Karadžić were unlikely to succeed in overthrowing Plavšić. He therefore decided to change his strategy abandoning the Pale leaders and seeking instead to cultivate contacts within the Plavšić camp. In particular he was determined to see that the SPRS should play a pivotal role in the affairs of the Republika Srpska should events be concluded in Plavšić's favour. In this way Milošević believed that he could retain influence within the RS without coming into open confrontation with the international community. On 24 September Milošević acted as mediator during a five-hour meeting in Belgrade between Biljana Plavšić and Momčilo Krajišnik. The meeting was also attended by Jovica Stanišić and Pedrag Ćeranić, the Plavšić-supporting Head of State Security from Banja Luka. It concluded in an agreement whereby elections for the Republika Srpska parliament would go ahead on 15 November. Plavšić conceded that there should also be Presidential elections to be held on 7 December. It was agreed that the OSCE should supervise the elections. The parliamentary elections were later to be postponed until 23 November while the Presidential elections were delayed indefinitely. Agreement was also reached on the reintegration of the Bosnian Serb TV network with the rival Pale and Banja Luka factions having access to TV coverage on alternate days. Plavšić was willing to accept this agreement which essentially recognised the legitimacy of her decision to call new elections. She had accepted the role played by Milošević in the framing of this agreement as necessary in order to weaken the forces ranged against her. However, few people doubted that, in spite of the diplomatic language they were now using, the two leaders continued to regard each other with bitter and enduring emnity. Krajišnik had for his part consented to the agreement because the failure of the 'confrontational' strategy left him with little option but reluctantly to embrace the 'electoral' path.[29]

The signing of the agreement between the rival factions meant that the level of physical confrontation between the two sides abated. The leaders of the two Bosnian Serb factions, however, continued to conduct a bitter war of words. Speaking in late September Krajišnik sought to present his willingness to accept the agreement as an act of traditional 'heroic' virtue: 'We are serious people, we represent the people. I could not look the people in the eye and say that I had agreed to hold elections but revoked the decision because I am hungry for power. No, our people, who are an epic and honourable people, would not forgive us.' He went on to criticise Plavšić for exploiting regional sentiment which, he maintained, would disrupt the 'nation-building' efforts of the Bosnian Serb people: 'Regionalism throughout history served as a defence mechanism against the state, which was always a foreign state, and these regionalisms were so strong that they were a perfect defence against anyone wanting to impose authority, and this was the state. Throughout history, during Turkish rule, under Austia-Hungary, in the old Kingdom and even in the former system – we never had time to mature as a nation, so certain regions developed a very high degree of regional identity – Hercegovina, Romanija, Semberija – but the most pronounced regionalism developed in Krajina. [...] Somebody has rekindled this regionalism in Krajina, so now you have tremendous resistance against this state. Because of traditional resistance to the state they think they must now expose all the shortcomings of this state as well. [...] Well, it is either a state or it is not, it is either based on coercion or on authority. So now we have a serious situation because of this interference by international factors. We must view this very objectively and we must emerge from the crisis through elections.'[30] Plavšić replied to such attacks in equally vehement terms, saying of Krajišnik: 'He has placed himself at the centre of everything. He is a capricious individual who wants to make himself the lord of this land. That is his nature. The aims of his party [SDS] are identified with the aims of the nation and it is presented as the only force capable of solving the problems of the Serbian people in the Republika Srpska. I know that there are people in that party who must be silent or repeat the position dictated by two men – Karadžić and Krajišnik.'[31]

In the period before the RS elections the international community took an increasingly firm line with the Pale-controlled Bosnian Serb TV. On 1 October SFOR troops seized control of four Bosnian Serb TV transmitters. The immediate cause of this military intervention was the decision by Bosnian Serb TV to censor coverage of a news conference by the Hague Tribunal Prosecutor, Louise Arbour. The occupations were, however, also a reflection of the long-standing frustration felt by the international community at the refusal of the official Bosnian Serb TV to moderate their broadcasting output. The SDS controllers of Bosnian Serb TV in Pale had never disguised the fact that they considered their TV coverage to be a manifestation of their nationalist mission. In the words of Miroslav Toholj, the Bosnian Serb TV director, 'Who will answer to the dead and those still alive if the state disappears?'[32] The international community's High Representative, Carlos Westendorp, informed the Pale Serbs that SFOR would relinquish control over the transmitters once senior SDS functionaries had been removed from management positions in Bosnian Serb TV. The pro-Krajišnik Serbs, however, rejected these demands as 'unrealistic' with the station's editor declaring: 'The international community plans to impose a protectorate over SRT [Bosnian Serb TV] and in that way extinguish it, which is something we cannot accept as human beings, as professionals, and as Serbs.'[33] On 16 October Pale TV resumed broadcasting using hidden 'pirate' transmitters. Two days later SFOR troops, having located the source of these broadcasts, seized control of another transmitter near the Bosnian Serb military stronghold of Han Pijesak. Before leaving the station, however, the Bosnian Serbs removed vital components from the transmitter in order to make it inoperable. SFOR sought to prevent any further 'pirate' broadcasts being made by using aircraft to jam the frequencies normally used by the Pale-based Bosnian Serb TV service. With Pale TV no longer functioning, Banja Luka TV moved to fill the gap and, with the support of SFOR, began broadcasting to eastern Bosnia.[34] The SDS leadership complained bitterly that the broadcasts coming from Banja Luka favoured Biljana Plavšić. Outside observers concluded that while there may have been an element of truth in this statement the coverage offered by the Banja Luka-based TV to opponents of the RS President was considerably fairer than the vilification which the political enemies of the SDS had found themselves subjected to on Pale-controlled TV.[35] The representatives of the international community in Bosnia were, however, reluctant to see SFOR troops remaining in control of the transmitters during the pre-election period and strenuous efforts were made to secure a compromise with the authorities in Pale. The SDS, however, obstinately refused to make the concessions necessary to faciliate the return of the transmitters. It came to be suspected that the SDS were willing to allow the military occupation of the media outlets to continue as this would, they believed, strengthen their claim to be persecuted 'victims' of the international community while at the same time allowing them to portray Plavšić as a 'traitor' collaborating with the international community.

Milošević used the struggle over the media to put further political distance between himself and Krajišnik, suggesting on 26 October in an interview with the *New York Times* that if Krajišnik continued to follow his course of 'non-cooperation' it might become necessary for the High Representative in Bosnia to remove him from his position as Serbian representative in the Presidency of Bosnia-Hercegovina. Milošević's statement was widely seen by opposition politicians as an attempt to ingratiate himself with the international community. Nebojša Čović, who after his expulsion from the SPS had founded a new political party called the Democratic Alternative, stated: 'If "our leader" after his defeat on the domestic scene wants to gain points with the West by betraying one side in this unfortunate struggle in the RS, that will be a loss for the whole Serbian nation.'[36] However Milošević's statement was greeted cautiously by the DS, with Zoran Djindjić stating: 'I welcome this decision... only if it refers to the political concept of Pale symbolised by Krajišnik, and not if it is only another in his series of personnel reshuffles. [...] Momčilo Krajišnik and the Pale leadership are leading the Republika Srpska into isolation and further disintegration...a reaction from Belgrade was bound to come sooner or later, and it is good that Milošević has opted for one of his famous political U-turns.' Djindjič expressed the hope that following the Republika Srpska elections an alliance could be constructed between the Serbian National Alliance and the 'constructive forces within the Serb Democratic Party headed by Aleksa Buha'.[37] According to Djindjić the DS formed part of a 'reformist triangle' with the Serbian National Alliance in the Republika Srpska and Djukanović's supporters in Montenegro. Djindjić stated that the DS would send teams of activists to the Republika Srpska to help the Serbian National Alliance conduct their election campaign and that he would attend the final Serbian National Alliance rally which was set to take place in Banja Luka.[38]

Vuk Drašković also continued to make statements in support of Biljana Plavšić but was clearly suspicious of the close links which had developed between the DS and the Serbian National Alliance remarking: 'The RS President has the wrong allies.'[39] Vojislav Šešelj for his part maintained an unamibiguously hostile attitude towards Plavšić accusing her of 'breaking up the Republika Srpska' and committing 'high treason against the Serbian people'.[40]

The results of the 23 November elections did not, however, offer an immediate way out of the political deadlock which had developed in the RS. The SDS once again emerged from the elections as the largest political grouping in the assembly with an enduring hold on the loyalties of a significant section of the Bosnian Serb population. The twenty-four seats (32.8 per cent of the vote) gained by the SDS, however, represented a considerable reduction on the forty-five (54.9 per cent) which they had gained a year earlier in the September 1996 elections. By contrast the Serbian Radical Party increased its representation from six (7.3 per cent) in 1996 to fifteen (19.3 per cent) in the 1997 elections. The thirty-nine seats which these two hardline nationalist parties could muster between them fell short of the forty-three needed to command a majority in the national assembly.

The Serbian National Alliance gained fifteen seats and 19.8 per cent of the vote. Although some of Plavšić's supporters may have believed that they could secure a greater proportion of the vote this total nevertheless represented a considerable achievement for a party which had only existed for three months. Significantly 'opposition' parties whose political profile might broadly be considered to be of the 'anti-communist/right,' such as the Serbian Party of Krajina and Posavina led by Predrag Lazarević (1.17 per cent) and the Democratic Patriotic Party led by Predrag Radić (0.75 per cent), failed to make significant political headway. Their supporters would appear to have transferred their loyalties to the Serbian National Alliance which had emerged as the strongest anti-Pale political force, and whose leader was known for her traditionalist and anti-communist beliefs.[41] By contrast those opposition parties on the 'left' of the political spectrum did manage to gain representation with the Socialist Party of the Republika Srpska winning nine seats (12.2 per cent) and the Independent Social Democrats led by Milorad Dodik winning two seats (3.3 per cent). The pro-Plavšić vote was, predictably concentrated around her north-west Bosnian stronghold in Banja Luka. Interestingly, however, Plavšić's party also emerged as victor in the town of Prijedor. In July Prijedor had been the scene of anti-SFOR demonstrations following the death of Simo Drljača and the arrest of another suspect, Milan Kovačević. The heightened tensions surrounding these events combined with Prijedor's wartime reputation for militant nationalism might have suggested that the town would vote solidly for the SDS in the elections. During the election campaign the SDS sought to strengthen its electoral appeal by invoking Milan Kovačević's name with one SDS speaker saying at an election rally: 'They didn't succeed in destroying him. He's still here in our hearts and that's why it's as if he is still a candidate here.'[42] The fact that this message failed to find electoral resonance with the town's population may in part be accounted for by the fact that Plavšić had taken a number of steps aimed at strengthening her support, including the holding of a number of meetings in the town and the appointment of Marko Pavić, a former Mayor of Prijedor, as the new Interior Minister of the RS. In a broader sense, however, the rapid collapse of SDS support in the town was illustrative of the 'personal' nature of power both in the RS and in Serbia itself. With power essentially resting on a web of personal patronage and contacts rather than on institutions, the removal of a single central individual, such as Drljača, could result in the collapse of the whole political edifice. The dominant role played by a single individual in the political life of a small north Bosnian town was paralleled at a higher level by the role which Radovan Karadžić had played as the central figure in the RS, and that which Slobodan Milošević continued to seek to perform within Serbia and its surrounding territories.

An additional factor was added to the political equation by the fact that eighteen seats within the RS assembly had been won by parties based within the Muslim-Croat Federation. These consisted of sixteen seats from the SDA-dominated Coalition for a Unified and Democratic Bosnia and two from the Social Democratic Party. The election of these representatives was facilitated by the provision in the election rules for absentee voting by displaced persons who had previously lived within the RS. The bloc of Muslim representatives clearly had the potential to play a pivotal role in the formation of a new RS government. The formation of an alliance between Muslim deputies and any of the major Serbian parties would require a significant abandonment of nationalist taboos on the latter's part.

On 27 December the first attempt to form a new government was initiated. Biljana Plavšić nominated Mladen Ivanić as the Prime Minister-designate. Ivanić, a lecturer in economics at Banja Luka University, had run against Krajišnik in the 1996 contest as the candidate of a number of 'moderate' Serbian political parties for the Serbian position on the Bosnian collective Presidency.[43] Ivanić proposed that the new RS government should be one of 'national unity' being constituted half out of representatives of all the Serbian political parties and half out of non-party 'technocrats' and 'experts'. The SDS and the Radicals were dismissive of this proposal with Aleksa Buha describing it contemptuously as a 'silly' concept.[44] These parties still appeared at this stage to hope that representatives from the SPRS might, with Milošević's approval, be willing to give them the support necessary to enable them to form a new government.[45] The Serbian National Alliance angrily condemned the SDS-SRS attempts to block the formation of a government, and Milorad Dodik, the leader of the Independent Social Democrats, said: 'If the National Assembly of the Republika Srpska will not choose a new government then the Prime Minister and his cabinet will be named by the High Representative of the International Community in Bosnia-Hercegovina. [...] Apart from that the refusal of the SDS and the SRS to support the candidature of Mladen Ivanić risks the RS losing Brčko, because the position of the international community is that it cannot possibly belong to us if we are not able to choose a democratic government.'[46]

Following the failure of his 'political/technocratic' concept of government to gain support in the first session of the national assembly Ivanić had asked Plavšić to choose a new Prime Ministerial candidate. Plavšić, however, insisted that Ivanić should try once again to form a government which would 'offer a real chance of stabilising the political scene'.[47] When the Bosnian Serb national assembly reconvened on 12 January Ivanić sought to appeal to the SDS-SRS representatives using consciously nationalist rhetoric: 'The Serbs west of the river Drina are a small nation and history shows that its future has always been shaped somewhere else, so it has been up to us to adapt our interests to those of the world, which we can do today as well. Let us consolidate what we have in order to gain the right to decide what will happen to us. If we establish that we have equal rights in Bosnia-Hercegovina as other nations, then there is no reason to change our position. If we are denied equal rights, let us develop our own state, consolidate it, and fight for the right to join our mother country once and for all, but we cannot do this today. The world has spoken. It is demanded that we remain part of a loose Dayton Bosnia-Hercegovina and are given a chance to survive. Our future depends on our wisdom and unity...Dayton Bosnia-Hercegovina is possible but only as a union of equal nations, namely as the union of the Republika Srpska and the Federation. Any and all efforts to jeopardize the equality of the Serb people will not be tolerated by the new government.'[48] However, Ivanić's efforts at presenting a strong national line carried little credibility with the SDS-SRS representatives, who once again refused to accept even a modified version of Ivanić's proposal. Following the meeting Milošević summoned the leaders of the various political groupings to Belgrade for talks. Although Plavšić described this meeting as 'constructive', even Milošević's considerable influence did not succeed in producing consensus among the contending factions.[49] On 16 January Ivanić finally withdrew from the attempts to put together a government in the RS. The pro-Milošević SPRS criticised the failure of the SDS-SRS to support Ivanić, stating that 'the historic opportunity for all the parliamentary parties to elect jointly a democratic government has been missed.'[50]

When the national assembly resumed its work on 17 January Plavšić nominated Milorad Dodik as the new candidate for Prime Minister. It was by now clear that his candidacy was, with the support of the Muslim deputies, poised to achieve success. Shortly before midnight and while the choice of a new Prime Minister was still being debated, the Speaker of the Assembly, Dragan Kalinić (SDS), announced that the session was adjourned for seven days. After the SDS-SRS deputies had walked out of the assembly, however, the remaining representatives resolved to continue the session and duly elected Dodik Prime Minister of the Republika Srpska. Plavšić described his election as the start of a period of 'renewal' and 'regeneration' for the RS, telling him: 'You were elected RS Prime Minister on *Krstovdan* [an Orthodox church holiday], a very important day for the Serbian Orthodox population. That is a happy day and we can say that the government has been baptised. That is how I see it. There is a lot of symbolism in that...I am afraid that, ever since 1990, there has hardly been a period when anything was comfortable or easy for the Serb people, but this is a very difficult, as well as a very challenging period for a young capable man, a patriot.'[51] Dodik defined his mission in terms which were more 'pragmatic' and 'rationalist', saying that he would 'begin the process of renewal and development, provide solutions to the many social problems in the RS, and definitively and energetically oppose all forms of criminality, par-ticularily that which takes the form of state corruption.'[52] Dodik pledged that his new government would adhere to the terms of the Dayton agreement, facilitate the return of refugees to their former homes and break the link between church and state which had been established in the RS. One of the first acts of the new government was to officially move the capital of the RS from Pale to Banja Luka.

The SDS-SRS were taken by surprise by this turn of events. Gojko Kličković was bemused when he received a phone call from Dodik on 18 January informing him that he had been replaced as Prime Minister of the RS.[53] On that same day SFOR forces had taken up positions around government buildings in the RS in order to 'secure a peaceful transition from the old government to the new'.[54] Aleksa Buha for the SDS condemned these develop-ments as 'some kind of coup'.[55]

For the international community Dodik's election represented a long-awaited political breakthrough. Financial aid was quickly promised to help bolster the position of the new government. A week after Dodik's election the European Union agreed to supply the Republika Srpska with an Ecu 6 million aid package (£4 million). These funds would be used to pay the salary arrears of government employees and members of the police. Dodik also submitted further requests for financial aid totalling £18 million to the High Representative in Bosnia-Hercegovina. In mid-February Dodik visited the United States, meeting Madeleine Albright who described him as 'a breath of fresh air' and pledged £2.9 million of immediate aid. On 25 February the British government announced its first non-emergency aid of £1 million, along with a further £1.1 million to support refugee resettlement, to the government of the Republika Srpska.[56] In a further gesture of support for Dodik's government the British Foreign Secretary, Robin Cook, addressed a session of the Republika Srpska's assembly on 4 March telling them: 'The government of Mr Dodik did more in its first two weeks to improve the lives of the people than its predecessor did in two years.'[57] The highly positive Western assessment of the new government was understandably centred on Dodik's willingness to adhere to the terms of the Dayton agreement. Observers from within Serbia, however, tended also to see the formation of the new government as a further development in the ongoing contest for influence between Slobodan Milošević and Biljana Plavšić. A commentator in the journal *NIN* saw the new government as essentially a 'victory' for Milošević in which he had regained some of the ground lost earlier in the year when he had pursued his unsuccessful alliance with the Pale faction. He said: 'It is not only that the Independent Social Democrats from Laktaši [Dodik's home town] and the new Premier Milorad Dodik have a longer record of co-operation with Milošević than with President Plavšić, but also that the Socialist Party of the Republika Srpska has succeeded in gaining more representatives in in this government than they have representatives in the parliament. [...] At the same time as the election was greeted by the [British] Foreign Office and Klaus Kinkel it was also welcomed by Radoje Kontić and Mirko Marjanović.'[58] During the period of the intra-Serb power-struggle (1997-8) Dodik had played down his previous contact with Milošević, characterising them as being formed on a 'pragmatic' basis in the period 1994-5 when the only political option available had been a choice between Milošević and acceptance of the international peace plan and the rejectionist policy favoured by Karadžić and his allies. Dodik remarked: 'In

1994 Milošević supported the Contact Group peace plan which held a position similar to that of a group of RS deputies including myself. We felt that it was very important to support and co-operate with all those who wanted to bring about peace in the region. Since then we've hardly had any contact with Milošević.'[59] In May 1996, however, Dodik's Independent Social Democrats had signed a co-operation agreement with the Belgrade-based New Democracy party which formed part of the ruling 'left alliance' in Serbia.[60]

The international organisations involved in Bosnia were, of course, aware of Dodik's wartime links with Milošević, but could also legitimately point to the fact that he had followed a 'reformist' and 'progressive' path since 1987 when he became mayor of Laktaši, had been elected in 1990 as a member of the Bosnian parliament representing Ante Marković's Alliance of Reform Forces, and had remained in clandestine contact during the war with his old party colleagues such as Sejfudin Tokić, the Vice-President of the Union of Bosnian Social Democrats based in Tuzla.[61] These 'multi-ethnic' and 'non-nationalist' aspects were seen as the dominant elements in his political profile. His contacts with Milošević were considered to play a subsidiary role which was nevertheless useful in securing the Yugoslav President's acceptance of the change in government in the Republika Srpska.

Other figures within the new government, however, had even stronger links with the Serbian regime. The RS Defence Minister, Manolja Milovanović, had commanded VRS forces in western Bosnia during the war, and in November 1996 he was forced to retire as part off Plavšić's attempts to purge the old JNA cadres from the VRS. In retirement, however, he had remained in close contact with key figures within the Serbian political and military establishment including Slobodan Milošević and Momčilo Perišić. It was these connections with the Serbian regime which secured for Milovanović his entry into the RS government. Milovanović underlined the 'unreconstructed' nature of his views when he stated in the Belgrade newspaper *Svedok* that he regarded Ratko Mladić as a 'hero' and assured the interviewer: 'General Mladić is safe...whoever is looking for him cannot get him.'[62] Ratko Mladić had by that time left the VRS military base at Han Pijesak, where he had previously had his headquarters, and was believed to have taken refuge in Serbia.[63] The existence of people such as Milovanović and other pro-Milošević elements within the new government posed a problem for the West representing an element of instability in an already fragile coalition. However, it was believed that such elements were worth accommodating while they made possible the existence of a government whose overall policy direction was dictated by Dodik's technocratic reformism and Plavšić's pragmatic nationalism. It was calculated that as the connections of the Plavšić-Dodik government with the West grew stronger, Milošević's already weakened power within the Republika Srpska would diminish still further. It was believed that while Milošević may have made short-term gains by maintaining a foothold within the RS, in the longer term the influence exerted by the economically and politically weakened Serbian government would be eclipsed by that of the international community.

During this period Montenegro also witnessed an increasingly bitter struggle between rival factions of the Montenegrin Democratic Party of Socialists. This conflict had taken shape during the first half of 1997 as a competition between the supporters of the President, Momir Bulatović, and the Prime Minister, Milo Djukanović, for control of the party structures and the institutions of power. With the announcement that Presidential elections were to be held on 5 October the battle for power shifted to the electoral arena with both of the factional leaders entering the race for this office. Although Bulatović and Djukanović were long-standing associates, having both been leaders of the clique of young communists who seized power in 1989, and close friends, they chose during the elections to portray themselves in dramatically different ways. Bulatović sought to identify himself with the ordinary members of the DPS and the middle-and lower-ranking members of the party *nomenklatura*. His campaign rhetoric drew not only on left-wing and socialist imagery, but also on the symbols and traditions of Serbian nationalism. He defined himself in opposition to Djukanović, whom he portrayed as a ruthless capitalist *nouveau riche* who was conspiring to separate the Montenegrin people from their 'Serbian brothers'. In contrast to Bulatović's strategy of 'national puritanism' Djukanović sought to build up his image as a 'moderniser' and a 'technocrat' who could make use of his international contacts to solve Montenegro's problems.[64] While Bulatović's message found particular resonance among rural voters and industrial workers, Djukanović's support was strongest among young, educated and urban electors. While the two candidates presented different images to the electorate, in reality they had much in common since during the 1990s they had both used their political position to carve out influential and lucrative niches for themselves in Montenegro's patronage-based and corruption-ridden economic system.

During the campaign Djukanović pursued a multi-stranded strategy. At one level he sought to counter the allegations aimed at him by the Bulatović/Milošević camp, which suggested that he harboured secessionist ambitions. Adverts were placed in the independent Belgrade press which stressed that Djukanović was seeking to create 'a secure, rich, open, free and upright Montenegro within an internationally recognised Yugoslavia'.[65] Djukanović pledged that if elected he would implement the programme of free market economic reform which had been set out by the 'Group of 17' Serbian and Montenegrin economists. In addition, Djukanović maintained contacts with the DS leader, Zoran Djindjić, and also sought to cultivate the support of Novak Kilibarda, the leader of the anti-communist and pro-Serbian National Party. In this way Djukanović portrayed himself not as the leader of a Montenegrin 'separatist' faction, but rather as the focus of a pan-Yugoslav reform movement. This rapprochement with Djukanović and his 'reformists' precipitated divisions within the opposition National Party, with a breakaway faction headed by Božidar Bojović refusing to co-operate on account of his perceived 'separatism'.

While pursuing this 'Yugoslav' line Djukanović also made gestures towards Montenegrin nationalist opinion, emphasising the need to maintain Montenegrin equality and national integrity within the Yugoslav federation. A journalist who interviewed Djukanović in his office noted that a biography of King Nikola, the last Montenegrin monarch, was displayed prominently and symbolically on his desk.[66] Djukanović attempted to forge an alliance with the Albanian minority, concentrated around the towns of Ulcinje and Tuza, and the Muslims in the area around Plav. As part of this pact the Albanians and Muslims were promised, as part of an overall package of electoral reform in Montenegro, representation in parliament corresponding proportionally to their level of electoral support.

In his campaign Bulatović portrayed Djukanović's international contacts, his 'separatism' and his overtures to ethnic minorities as all being part of a plan to betray Yugoslav and Serbian interests.

In this way Bulatović fell back on the tried and tested formula of securing votes by polarising the electorate and turning the election into a contest between 'patriots' and 'traitors'. Bulatović pursued this nationalist strategy with most vigour in areas of northern Montenegro where the greatest affinity with Serbia was felt. Milošević and the government in Belgrade sought to supply considerable financial and material support to Bulatović. It was also believed that the policy being pursued by Bulatović was controlled and directed from Belgrade. The months before the election in Montenegro had seen a steady build-up in tension between the authorities in Belgrade and those in Podgorica. On the border between the two republics Serbian customs officials began to conduct an informal blockade of Montenegro, obstructing the passage of goods into the republic. Jets from the Yugoslav air force also took to flying frequent training runs over Podgorica, and there was open speculation that a victory by Djukanović might prompt an attempt by the Yugoslav Army to intervene in Montenegrin politics.[67]

Among ordinary Montenegrins the schism which had opened up within the political establishment caused considerable confusion and alarm. Some individuals were attracted by the economic opportunities which Djukanović appeared to offer while at the same time remaining suspicious of the uncertainties which this conflict with Belgrade was bringing into public life. In certain families the conflict between supporters of Djukanović and Bulatović took the form of an internal split between the younger and older generations.

In the first round of voting on 5 October Bulatović took the lead with 147,609 votes to Djukanović's 145,337. The turn-out in the election was 67 per cent. It seemed that Djukanović's 'modern' and 'glamorous' campaigning style had been surpassed by Bulatović's more basic form of campaigning which relied on the support of grassroots cadres. Although the elections were declared by the OSCE to have been broadly 'free and fair' both sides accused each other of attempted electoral fraud. With the two candidates running virtually neck-and-neck a new round of elections was called for 19 October. The two weeks between the rounds of voting saw desperate efforts by both sides to consolidate their vote. The Djukanović campaign in particular sought to compensate for their apparent failings by organising a house-to-house campaign in order to maximise their vote in the 19 October round.[68] As the vote approached angry accusations were exchanged between the two parties. On 14 October the Montenegrin media carried a report that Bulatović had received a substantial injection of cash in order to fund the new campaign: this sum of DM 3 million had reportedly been handed to Bulatović by JUL officials of Montenegrin origin.[69] On the same day the Montenegrin Interior Minister, Fillip Vujanović, said in a TV interview that vehicles belonging to the Serbian Interior Ministry had been identified at a Bulatović rally. This, he said, was proof that Bulatović's campaign had been 'well planned by the Belgrade circle of strategists for political agitation'.[70] The indications were that in the run-up to polling day the political temperature in Montenegro was rising to a dangerously high level.

On 21 October, after two days of waiting, the Montenegrin Election Commission announced the result of the second ballot. Djukanović emerged as the victor with 174,745 votes to the 169,257 gained by Bulatović. Djukanović's supporters rejoiced at the news with the liberal journal *Monitor* describing it as 'the morning of Montenegrin hope'.[71] Bulatović and his followers, however, reacted with predictable fury declaring that Djukanović's victory had been won by electoral fraud. Bulatović called on his followers to hold protest meetings in an attempt to reverse the result by extra-parliamentary means. In calling for these protests Bulatović was clearly following the precedent set by the Serbian opposition during the winter 1996/7 street protests. However, the 'civility' which had characterised the Serbian demonstrations was totally absent in the Bulatović-organised and Milošević-backed protests in Montenegro. The atmosphere at these rallies was militant and potentially violent, with some of the protesters carrying firearms. The slogans chanted by the demonstrators were strongly nationalistic, denouncing 'Milo the Turk' and chanting 'We will defeat the Turks'. Radovan Vuković, a close aide of Bulatović, highlighted his perception that the Montenegrin demonstrations drew not on ideas of peaceful and non-violent protest but rather on traditional Montenegrin concepts of honour and heroic virtue: 'The people's rallies in Montenegro will not go on for months. Everything will be sorted out in a week at the most. The Montenegrins will not rattle pans and blow whistles. They will behave as they have done in the past.'[72] According to one observer, the strongly provocative statements heard repeatedly at Bulatović rallies were a clear indication that 'Bulatović, in reality, is not interested in justice but rather in revenge.'[73] Djukanović for his part condemned Bulatović's attempts to 'defend his power and conquer through informal Cossack-like rallies, to which, in addition to bringing his deceived supporters, they are also bringing well known illusionists, people who do not think but react, travelling herads of evil and merchants of misfortune.'[74] To put pressure on the Montenegrin authorities Bulatović's followers attempted to march on the state TV station in Podgorica and organised a blockade of the main road between Belgrade and the Montenegrin capital. It was also suggested that anti-Serbian graffiti which proliferated in some towns with Muslim populations was the work of Bulatović's supporters who were intent on stirring up hostility between Montenegrins and the local Muslim minority. Although the tone of these rallies was angry and defiant they were also relatively poorly attended with rarely more than 10,000 present. It was Bulatović's inability to bring sufficient numbers of demonstrators out on to the streets, coupled with the determination of the Montenegrin authorities to stand firm in the face of this challenge to their authority, which ultimately prevented these demonstrations from plunging Montenegro into a period of violent civil and political unrest.

In the aftermath of the elections the pro-state media in Serbia gave strong support to Bulatović, and his allegations that the election had been 'stolen'. *Politika* informed its readers that the 'second round of the elections had descended into farce' and that 'Djukanović's victory was secured by the Muslims and Albanians who are celebrating this morning on the streets of Podgorica.' Radio Belgrade stated that Djukanović's election was a victory for 'Muslims, Albanians and Montenegrin Ustaša separatists'.[75] This condemnation of Djukanović's victory was echoed by officials of the ruling parties with Tatjana Lenard, a spokesman for JUL: 'The election manipulation in Montenegro represents a falsification of the will of the people. [...] It is not surprising that the separatists in Kosovo should say that Djukanović's election was an "excellent choice" because his attempts to break up the country will create the conditions for the realisation of a Kosovo Republic.' The position taken by the 'left coalition' parties was also followed by the SRS with Vojislav Šešelj stating that the election result should be annulled because of the 'abuse of laws, machinations and falsifications'.

Milo Djukanović, he said, was a candidate supported by the followers of 'Alija Izetbegović, the leader of the Kosovo Albanians Ibrahim Rugova, and Catholic elements from the coast'.[76] The Democratic Party condemned the media campaign being waged against Djukanović saying that 'the campaign launched after the defeat of the candidate backed in Montenegro by Slobodan Milošević resembles the Serbian Radio-TV campaign before the war in former Yugoslavia. The state media as a whole are calling for lynching and chauvinism. [...] With the help of its servile media, the Belgrade regime is trying to annul the election results for the second time this year, although this almost caused a civil war in Serbia last year.'[77]

The official transfer of power between Bulatović and Djukanović was set to take place on 15 January 1998 when the new President was due to be inaugurated in a ceremony held in the old Montenegrin royal capital of Cetinje. Bulatović and his backers in the Serbian government decided to make a last bid to prevent Djukanović from assuming office. It was announced that Bulatović and his supporters would be holding another demonstration on the evening of 14 January. Bulatović boasted that on this occasion he would bring 100,000 supporters out on to the streets in a mass show of strength. It was apparently planned that this public demonstration should provide the cover for a *coup* attempt against Djukanović. This scenario had significant similarities to the attempt on 8 September 1997 by supporters of the SDS to use the rally in Banja Luka as a springboard for an attempt to overthrow the Bosnian Serb President, and with the situation on 24 December 1996 when the Serbian authorities tried to use the conflict between rival political rallies in Belgrade to provoke a political crisis in Serbia. All three of these examples were situations where the agencies of the Serbian 'shadow state' had attempted to consciously manufacture violence for political ends. In all of these cases the Serbian state authorities exploited long-standing rural/urban and provincial/metropolitan social tensions and divisions. During the December 1996 demonstrations the authorities had sought to raise political tensions by bringing into the capital supporters from the provincial interior of Serbia. The events in the Republika Srpska had involved the 'invasion,' as it was perceived, of urban Banja Luka by demonstrators who identified themselves with the rural power centre in Pale. In a similar way Djukanović's supporters from Podgorica characterised Bulatović's faction as consisting of 'illiterate peasants' who could not adjust themselves to the new realities of the modern world.[78] It was also, however, indicative of the waning strength of these formerly all-powerful state security agencies that all of these attempts to forment unrest ended in failure.

In the event Bulatović wildly overestimated the number of those who would attend the rally; only 8,000 of his supporters turned up for the protest.[79] The placards and banners carried by the demonstrators showed that Bulatović's followers had embraced a confused mixture of ideological traditions and symbols. Portraits of Bulatović, Milošević and Radovan Karadžić were held aloft alongside banners bearing the images of Lenin and Draža Mihailović. It seemed that the only thing uniting this disparate group of people was nationalism and contempt for Djukanović.

Although the numbers of those attending the meeting were relatively low the demonstrators had come to the rally heavily armed and ready for violence. Bulatović proposed that his followers should march on the offices of the Montenegrin government with the intention of trying to occupy them. He apparently believed that he could rely on the support of 80 per cent of the ordinary members of the police force, and that his supporters would therefore face little resistance from the police who had been deployed around the government offices. Bulatović, however, had miscalculated once again and the police stood firm in the face of his marchers. As fighting broke out the protesters threw stones, Molotov cocktails and hand-grenades at the police lines. Shots were also fired by demonstrators carrying automatic rifles. The Montenegrin police withstood this sustained assault with remarkable restraint. They replied to the use of live ammunition and explosives by using only tear-gas, water-cannon and stun-grenades. This disparity in the levels of force used by the two sides was reflected in the casualties sustained on that night when over fifty people were injured of whom forty-four were police. While these violent events were taking place on the streets of Podgorica the Yugoslav Army had remained neutral. At one point during the fighting the demonstrators had stopped outside the army barracks chanting and calling on the army to give them arms. The gates of the barracks, however, remained firmly shut against Bulatović's rioting supporters.[80]

As the police covered the centre of the city in a cloud of tear-gas Bulatović's followers dispersed and the violence died down. In defiance of the facts the Serbian and federal Yugoslav authorities condemned the police for 'brutality' and 'excessive' use of force. In a bizarre interpretation of events Belgrade Radio even carried a report in which it was claimed that the police were in fact Italians sent by the Western powers to support Djukanović. The evidence offered for this unlikely contention was a statement by one of Bulatović's senior aides that he had heard a policeman giving an instruction to one of his subordinates using the word *pronto*. The international community, however, was in no doubt as to who was really responsible for the violence on the streets of Podgorica. Robert Gelbard, the US envoy in the Balkans, delivered a sharp rebuke to Milošević: 'The American government is deeply concerned and the international community deeply offended by the absolutely outrageous behaviour by outgoing President Bulatović in inciting these riots.' He maintained that Milošević was 'responsible for supporting these demonstrations and for not restraining his colleague.'[81]

In spite of the previous night's violence Djukanović was sworn in on 15 January as had been planned. His inauguration was attended by ambassadors from fifty-seven states. Montenegro under Djukanović was now apparently considered a significant factor on the diplomatic scene rather than simply a tame adjunct of the the Serbian regime. Bulatović had not only failed to reverse the result of the election but also now faced the possibility of being charged for his role in organising the 14 January violence.[82] The political struggle for Montenegro's future was set to be renewed during the early parliamentary elections which Djukanović had agreed to hold on 31 May. On 21 March Bulatović transformed his rebel wing of the Democratic Party of Socialists into a new political party, the Socialist National Party, in order to back him in his continuing struggle against Djukanović.[83] However, by the spring of 1998 the new President's position within the country was looking increasingly secure. As President of Montenegro Djukanović acted as a powerful and vocal critic of Milošević's policies from within the Federal Republic of Yugoslavia.

Notes

1. 'Lice s Flečera', Ana Mitrović interviewed by Ljiljana Smajlović, *Vreme*, 26 July 1997.
2. Igor Gajić 'Mutual Dismissals', *War Report*, August 1997.
3. Tanja Topić, 'Buba u uhu', *Vreme*, 23 August 1997.
4. *SRNA*, 16 August 1997 in *SWB EE/2887 A/2*, 18 August 1997.
5. Karen Coleman, 'Judge Tells of Beating by Karadžić Thugs', *Guardian*, 23 August 1997.
6. Colin Soloway, 'Karadžić Militia is Put Under NATO Control', *Daily Telegraph*, 8 August 1997.
7. Aleksandra Scepanović and Marina Bowder, 'In the News, Pale Style', *War Report*, September 1997.
8. 'Plavšić Breaks Hardliners TV Monopoly', Jovan Kovačević, *Guardian*, 25 August 1997.
9. Tanja Topić, 'Jedna raja, a dva gospodara', *Vreme*, 30 August 1997.
10. Jonathan Steele, 'Senior General Supports Plavšić', *Guardian*, 4 September 1997.
11. The conduct of the military during the 1996/7 demonstrations is examined in Chapter 24.
12. Lidija Kujundžić, 'Bitka za glasače', *NIN*, 15 August 1997.
13. *SRNA*, 16 August 1997 in *SWB EE/3000 A/2*, 18 August 1997.
14. Colin Soloway, 'Support for Karadžić Crumbles', *Daily Telegraph*, 26 August 1997.
15. 'Bivši premijer RS Kasagić u Plavšićinoj stranci', *Nedeljni telegraf*, 20 August 1997.
16. 'Ostoja Knežević – Changing Sides', *War Report*, October 1997.
17. 'Mob Attacks Peacekeepers', Dan De Luce, *Guardian*, 29 August 1997.
18. Jelena Stamenković, 'Plavšićeva očekuje 30 posto glasova kako SDS i Radikali ne bi mogli formirati vladu', *Slobodna Bosna*, 16 November 1997.
19. Tanja Topić, 'The Eldorado of Democracy', *War Report*, October 1997.
20. Tom Walker, 'Yugoslav Leader Plans to Rein in Plavšić', *The Times*, 28 August 1997.
21. Askold Krushelnycky, 'Violent Clashes May Wreck Bosnia Elections', *European*, 4 September 1997.
22. Tom Walker, 'Radio Incites Serbs to Attack NATO Force', *The Times*, 29 August 1997; Colin Soloway, 'Milošević Sent Serb Forces to Help Karadžić', *Daily Telegraph*, 2 Septem ber 1997; Jovan Kovačević, 'Plavšić Blames Yugoslav Infiltrators for Town Riot', *Guardian*, 1 September 1997.
23. Tanja Topić, 'Banjalučka drama', *Vreme*, 13 September 1997.
24. Željko Pećanac, 'Braća Krajišnik spremaju moju Iikvidaciju', *Nezavisne novine*, 24 September 1997.
25. Igor Gajić and Tihomir Loza, '*Republika Srpska* – Beyond the Pale', *War Report*, October 1997.
26. Askold Krushelnycky, 'Holed up at the Hotel Bosna', *European*, 11 September 1997.
27. Tanja Topić, Vlast na čekanju', *Vreme*, 15 November 1997.

28. 'SDS će stati na čelo procesa demokratizacije', Milovan Regoda interviewed by Andjelko Anušić, *Glas Srpski*, 1 November 1997.
29. 'Kompromis', *Vreme*, 27 September 1997; Lidija Kujundžić, 'Kralj, dama, pub...', *NIN*, 30 October 1997.
30. Bosnian Serb TV (Pale), 25 September 1997 in *SWB EE/3036 A/7*, 29 September 1997.
31. 'Udar na državu', Biljana Plavšić interviewed by Lidija Kujundžić, *NIN*, 20 November 1997.
32. Scepanović and Bowder, *War Report*, September 1997.
33. Lidija Kujundžić, 'Kad gora zazeleni', *NIN*, 23 October 1997.
34. RFE/RL Newsline (Bosnia Report), 17 and 20 October 1997.
35. The positive changes in the Banja Luka-based Bosnian Serb TV could be readily observed in its coverage of the crisis in Kosovo in March 1998. Reports on this area were provided by correspondents from the independent Belgrade radio station B-92. In Serbia itself, however, the state authorities had sought to harass and marginalise B-92 and other independent media sources.
36. D. Novaković and O. Zekić, 'Iznudjena smena Krajišnka kupovina poena na Zapadu!', *Dnevni telegraf*, 27 October 1997.
37. *Dnevni telegraf*, 26 October 1997 in *SWB EE/3062 A/7*, 29 October 1997.
38. D. Novaković, 'DS pomaže Plavšićevu, izvoz preko Crne Gore', *Dnevni telegraf*, 27 September 1997.
39. *Beta*, 25 September 1997 in *SWB EE/3030 A/11*, 27 September 1997.
40. *Beta*, 21 August 1997 in *SWB EE/3005 A/13*, 23 August 1997.
41. Andjelko Anušić, 'Pobednik stize u zavezanoj Evropskoj vreći', *Argument*, 1 December 1997.
42. Jonathan Steele, 'Fear of War Crimes Indictments Shakes Karadžić's Voter Base', *Guardian*, 12 September 1997.
43. Paul Shoup, 'The Elections in Bosnia-Herzegovina – The End of an Illusion', *Problems of Post-Communism*, January/February 1997, pp. 3-15.
44. *SRNA*, 30 December 1997 in *SWB EE/3113 A/2*, 31 December 1997.
45. Igor Gajić, 'Minority Politics in the RS', *War Report*, December 1997-January 1998.
46. 'Ako skupština RS ne izabere vladu premijerai ministere imenovaće Vestendorp', *Dnevni telegraf*, 12 January 1998.
47. 'Sporan koncept pomirenja', Mladen Ivanić interviewed in *NIN*, 22 January 1998.
48. Bosnian Serb TV (Banja Luka), 12 January 1998 in *SWB EE/3125 A/4*, 15 January 1998.
49. *Demokratija*, 13 January 1998 in *SWB EE/3124 A/3*, 15 January 1998.
50. *SRNA*, 19 January 1998 in *SWB EE/3129 A/4*, 20 January 1998.
51. Bosnian Serb TV, 18 January 1998 in *EE/3129 A/3*, 20 January 1998.
52. 'Borba protiv državnog kiminala', Milorad Dodik interviewed by Tanja Topić, *Vreme*, 24 January 1998.
53. Srdjan Rosić, 'Kalinić je obavijestio rukovodstvo SDS-a da mu je Plavšićeva obećala da će poništiti izbor Milorada Dodik!?' *Slobodna Bosna*, 22 January 1998.
54. *SRNA*, 18 January 1998 in *SWB EE/3129 A/1*, 20 January 1998.

55. Ibid.
56. Lionel Barber and David Buchan, 'New Bosnian Serb Leader Wins EU Aid', *Financial Times*, 27 January 1998; 'Short Sends Aid to Moderate Bosnian Serbs', *Guardian*, 26 February 1998.
57. 'Bosnia – A New Hope', Speech of the British Foreign Secretary, Robin Cook, to National Assembly of the Republika Srpska, 4 March 1998, Foreign Office (London).
58. Slobodan Reljić, 'Januar preokreta?', *NIN*, 29 January 1998.
59. 'Milorad Dodik – Opposition Strategy', *War Report*, October 1997.
60. *Tanjug*, 20 May 1996 in *SWB EE/2618 A/12*, 22 May 1996,
61. 'New RS Prime Minister in Most Significant Development since Dayton', International Crisis Group (Sarajevo), 20 January 1998.
62. 'Milovanovića vratili Milošević i general Perišić', *Argument*, 9 February 1998.
63. David Buchan, 'Washington Plans to Reward Milošević', *Financial Times*, 23 February 1998.
64. Zeljko Ivanović, 'Reform as Expediency', *Transitions*, March 1998.
65. 'Nikad sami, uvijek svoji!', Djukanović campaign advertisement carried in *Vreme*, 13 September 1997.
66. Tim Judah, 'Montenegro Pledges to Destroy Milošević', *Sunday Telegraph*, 27 September 1997.
67. Miloš Vasić and Filip Švarm, 'Puč koji traje', *Vreme*, 23 August 1997.
68. 'Montenegro', *Eastern Europe – Political Briefing*, 6 October 1997.
69. *Montena-fax*, 14 October 1997 in *SWB EE/3414 A/14*, 16 October 1997.
70. *Gradjanin*, 14 October 1997 in *SWB EE/3414 A/14*, 16 October 1997.
71. Draško Djunranović, 'Jutro crnogorske nade', *Monitor*, 24 October 1997.
72. *Dnevni telegraf*, 20 December in *SWB EE/3110 A/7*, 24 December 1997.
73. Šeki Radončić, 'Čeka se varnica', *Monitor*, 24 October 1997.
74. Beta, 30 December 1997 in *SWB EE/3114 A/9*, 1 January 1998.
75. Zoran Radulović, 'Balvani, sila, bahatosti', *Monitor*, 24 October 1997.
76. 'Reagovanja na rezulte izbora i situaciju u crnoj gori', *Dnevni telegraf*, 22 October 1997.
77. Radio B-92, 23 October 1997 in *SWB EE/3059 A/6*, 25 October 1997.
78. Karen Coleman, 'Ousted President's Men Fight to the End', *Guardian*, 15 January 1998.
79. Šeki Radončić, 'Povratak na mjesto zločina', *Monitor*, 16 January 1998.
80. Luka Mičeta, 'Demonstracije i inauguracija', *NIN*, 15th January 1998.
81. Tom Walker, 'Rebuke to US Adds to Milošević's Woes', *The Times*, 16 January 1998.
82. 'Bulatović pod istragom', *Vreme*, 14 February 1998.
83. Velizar Brajović, 'Voli On i njih', *Vreme*, 28 March 1998.

28. Electoral Deadlock – Round Two (November 1997–February 1998)

The Serbian authorities moved quickly to initiate a new round of elections which were set to take place on 7 December. The hapless Zoran Lilić was replaced as the candidate of the 'left coalition' by Milan Milutinović. Milutinović, who was at that time the Yugoslav Foreign Minister, had previously been the Yugoslav ambassador in Greece. For thirty years he had served as a loyal Communist, and later Socialist, cadre and in the 1970s played a prominent role in the attempts to remove the *Praxis* dissidents from their positions at Belgrade University. He was also a close friend of Slobodan Milošević with whom he had had studied law at Belgrade University. Immediately after his failure in the first round of elections Vuk Drašković had declared that he would be ready to contest the elections once again: 'The electoral situation in Serbia is clear, many people are frightened by the rise of extremism, and the communists have no chance because their support is falling steadily, in December I will be victorious.'[1] Vojislav Šešelj was also confident of success, though with a greater degree of justification. He said that his main opponent in the forthcoming election would be Milutinović and denounced Drašković, who he said would 'participate in these elections as a loser' with a campaign based on 'pure folklore' and whose role would only be to 'hamper the candidate of the SRS'.[2] The 'boycotting' parties were divided over how to react to the new elections. The DS and the GSS appeared during late October to be casting around for a suitable candidate whom they could back in the presidential race. A number of names were mooted including Slobodan Vučetić, a judge from the Serbian constitutional court, Ivan Stambolić, and Dragoslav Avramović. Vojislav Koštunica, however, was scornful of such last-minute attempts to find an opposition candidate. According to Koštunica, finding a presidential candidate without first securing fair election conditions was 'neither possible nor desirable. [...] Even if a common candidate succeeded in winning the forthcoming presidential election his hands would be tied because he would not have the support of any major party in parliament.'[3] Ultimately no new presidential candidate was found and the major parties of the 'boycotting' bloc continued to urge voters to abstain in the forthcoming elections. Vuk Obradović from the recently founded Social Democratic Party and Dragoljub Mićunović from the Democratic Centre also chose to contest the elections, but neither had the political strength to exert a significant influence on the electoral contest.[4]

While Milutinović was attempting to rally support for the SPS in the Serbian countryside Drašković and Šešelj engaged in a pre-election exchange of insults in which each sought to dispute the other's national credentials. Speaking at a rally in Jagodina on 22 November Drašković told his audience that in 1988 'Šešelj did not know how to make the sign of the cross and he was taught to do so by myself and Milan Komnenić at the Ljubostinje monastery.'[5] Later Drašković went further and disputed not only Šešelj's adherence to the neo-traditionalist aspects of the nationalist creed but also sought to question whether he was of Serbian origin, reviving the old rumour that the SRS leader was in fact of Croatian descent. Drašković observed: 'When we are speaking of the Serbian presidency we must know what the origins of all the candidates are. This is particularily important in the case of Mr Šešelj who insists in the name of Serbdom that the Serbs are what they never have in fact been. [...] Mr Šešelj has insisted on ethnic cleansing. Is that part of the Serbian tradition? This is why we must examine his origin, his tradition, so that we see in the name of whose tradition he speaks.'[6] Šešelj retorted angrily that he was of Serbian origin and a follower of Serbian traditions, adding: 'I was christened in Zavala monastery as soon as I was born. You should ask Drašković when he was christened. My father was never a communist, he was a religious man. [...] Vuk Drašković was born in the middle of November, but his father lied and said he was born on 29 November so that on all official documents he was shown as having been born on the day of the Republic. [...] I was christened at the Zavala monastery where my father taught in the school before the Second World War and kept the monastery's sheep. That monastery was built in the time of Milutin Nemanjić in the Middle ages.'[7] It was indicative of the nature of Serbian political discourse that so much time and energy were spent by these political leaders in proving the legitimacy (and the illegitimacy of their opponents' case) of their personal attachment, to the symbols of the national tradition, rather than entering into substantive debate of any sort over issues of policy. Šešelj's inability to respond effectively to these persistent attacks served to lessen the momentum of his hitherto self-confident campaign.[8]

The results of the elections on 7 December saw Milutinović taking the lead with 43.7 per cent of the vote. Vojislav Šešelj had fallen behind with 32.19 per cent. Šešelj, however, still had some cause to be optimistic as with the voter turn-out standing at only 52.75 per cent it was reasonable for him to expect that this total would fall in the run-off between him and Milutinović invalidating the election result once again. Drašković's vote slumped to only 15.42 per cent, a result which he explained as being due to a 'disappointment syndrome' among the voters. Drašković urged his supporters to boycott the election run-off.[9]

On 21 December Milan Milutinović emerged victorious from the Presidential election run-off gaining 58.6 per cent of the vote to the 38.14 per cent gained by Šešelj. The vote was declared valid with 50.9 per cent of the electorate voting. The Radicals complained that the Socialists had won the election through massive fraud and 'theft' of votes. Their complaints focused in particular on the situation in Kosovo where in many polling stations the number of votes cast exceeded the number of Serbs registered to vote at that station by a large margin. The Albanian leadership had once again called for a boycott of the poll and there was no sign that sufficient numbers of Albanians had chosen to defy their instructions as to account for the presence of these 'phantom' voters at the polls. Unsurprisingly this ghostly army of electors had voted almost uniformly for Milan Milutinović. At a polling station in Klina in Kosovo SRS election observers were attacked by a group of SPS supporters who were reportedly accompanied by the police. In Peć and Orahovac in western Kosovo a number of SRS deputies and councilors were arrested by the police while they were attempting to observe the polling taking place.[10] Independent observers tended to agree that the 'left coaltion' had been able to achieve its 'victory' at least in part through extensive electoral fraud. The international community, however, was not ready to raise too many objections to these events knowing that the alternative to a victory by Milutinović and the Socialist 'old order' would be the election of Šešelj whose reputation for wild nationalism and opposition to the Dayton agreement was well known. The fact that Milošević and his henchmen had been forced to rely, for the second year running, on blatant manipulation of the elections served to underline the increasing fragility of his support within the country.

The Radicals threatened to boycott the work of parliament in protest at the election fraud which had characterised the elections, but they failed to gain the support of the SPO for such a policy of 'obstruction', with Aleksandar Čotric remarking: 'Why should we interfere in the affairs of the Radical Party? They did not lift a little finger to help us when we protested over the "theft" of the local elections results.'[11] The degree of rancour between the SPS and the SRS created by the final round of election results appeared at this stage to rule out co-operation between the two parties in the formation of a new government, at least for the time being. Attention therefore came to be focused on the possibility of an alliance emerging between the SPO and the SPS. Drašković was apparently encouraged by the fact that although he had come out of the elections as a 'loser' he now found himself holding the balance of power in the parliament with the votes of the SPO being vital for the formation of a new government. For this reason Drašković felt able to demand a high price for his involvement in a new Serbian government. In negotiations which took place during January 1998 Drašković was reportedly demanding that the SPO should be given the positions of Prime Minister and President of the Government, ten ministerial places, and a proportion of the ambassadorial positions.[12] Drašković was also encouraged to take such a 'maximal' position by the knowledge that, while entering into such an alliance with the Socialists would make a considerable amount of material patronage available to him, it would also involve a threat to the political identity of the SPO. There would be an evident problem in justifying to his supporters why he as someone who had long cultivated such a Četnik, royalist and neo-traditionalist image had gone into alliance with the Socialists who were inheritors of the communist/Partisan tradition. Ultimately, however, the temptations of power overode such ideological considerations and the negotiations between the

SPO and the SPS continued throughout January and early February. During meetings between Drašković and Milutinović on 21 January and 16 February agreement was reached on a 'programme of national and state renewal' to be carried out by the new SPS-SPO government of 'national unity'. According to Drašković this programme would commit the new government to a 'pro-European reform' line, but few observers believed that such pledges on paper would mean that the government would make any attempt to overcome the political-economic vested interests which dominated Serbian public life. Following the 16 February meeting Drašković expressed the belief that agreement on the 'division of power and responsibility' along the lines proposed by the SPO would be reached over the next few days,[13] but the Socialist negotiators were aware that although the SPO were theoretically the 'kingmakers' in the Serbian parliament their only alternative to co-operation with the Socialists was to press for new elections to break the parliamentary deadlock. However, the SPO had no appetite for new elections, which they would enter tainted in the eyes of opposition voters by their association with the Socialists. This knowledge combined with a strong personal contempt felt by Milošević towards Drašković prompted the SPS to take a hard line in negotiations with the SPO. Milošević was reported to have told his officials to 'give him [Drašković] only crumbs, ministries of no importance. He will be satisfied with that.'[14]

When on 19 February Milan Milutinović announced that he had nominated Mirko Marjanović as the new Prime Minister, Drašković declared himself surprised by this unilateral decision saying that, considering the distribution of offices already agreed, it would be 'normal that the office of Prime Minister should be taken by the SPO'.[15] For other political parties, however, the appointment of Marjanović was less unexpected, with Zoran Djindjić describing it as heralding the arrival of 'yet another anti-reform incompetent government, guided by the principle of personal interests'.[16] The Sandžak Muslim leader, Rasim Ljajić, scornfully suggested that in a democratic country, Marjanović on the basis of his previous record, 'would not even qualify for the post of chief of a local fire brigade'.[17] Any disappointment the SPO may have felt at failing to secure the position of Prime Minister in the proposed government did not, however, stop them from continuing to hold talks with the Socialists over division of the remaining offices. Tomislav Nikolić of the SRS professed to be above such political deal making and contemptuously described the two sides as 'haggling like gypsies'. On 25 February 3,000 pensioners gathered outside the federal parliament to protest at the failure of the government to help them cope with the increasingly difficult economic and material conditions. In previous years it would have been natural for SPO leaders to have sought to place themselves at the head of such manifestations of popular anti-government street protest. On this occasion, however, when Milan Komnenić emerged from the parliament building to express his support for the pensioners' demands, the demonstrators reacted angrily, hurling abuse at the SPO leader and chanting 'Vuk thief'. In the face of this reaction Komnenić withdrew inside the parliament building.[18] This incident can be seen as a symbolic turning-point in the fortunes of the SPOs with the party which had originally defined itself as a movement for systematic change from below now becoming increasingly associated in the minds of the populace with its attempt to bargain its way into the institutions of power. By the end of February, in spite of the prolonged and inconclusive negotiations, the eventual entry of the SPO into the new government was widely seen as an accepted political fact.[19]

While these negotiations continued signs appeared indicating that the 'left coalition' was in a state of barely concealed ferment. Aleksandar Vulin resigned as Vice-President of JUL, stating that he had 'ideological' objections to the proposed coalition with the SPO: 'It is not possible for left-wingers who believe in the republic to enter into a coalition with SPO who are dedicated to the monarchy'.[20] Another Vice-President of JUL, Nenad Djordjević, was also removed from the political scene at this time although his departure was prompted by material concerns rather than such issues of principle and symbolism. On 19 February Djordjević was arrested while driving through Belgrade on his way to a meeting JUL's Main Committee. He was charged with having embezzled $10 million during the period before his removal on 5 November, when he was Director of the Health Insurance Fund,[21] but unusually for someone facing such serious charges, he was subsequently released from prison. It was speculated that Djordjević had been able to obtain his release by calling on help from his old contacts in the SDB. His reprieve was short-lived and on 22 February he was arrested once again. Significantly the main government-supporting newspaper, *Politika*, chose to report the incident without mentioning Djordjević's brief period out of prison.[22] On 15 February Smiljko Kostić, general director of the Niš cigarette manufacturing company DIN, was arrested while driving to Montenegro, and accused of defrauding his company of $10 million. It was rumoured that his arrest had really been prompted by a clash with Marko Milošević and his links with Montenegrin business interests close to Milo Djukanović. Others saw Kostić's ousting as a measure taken by the authorities in order to remove an obstacle to its 'cut-price' privatisation along the lines of the earlier sale of the PTT telecoms company. Zoran Živković, the Mayor of Niš (DS), stated: 'The arrest of Smiljka Kostić is a purely political act. He was unable to do anything without the knowledge of Slobodan Milošević. What Kostić was doing has been talked about for years. The police knew all about this.'[23]

In spite of the contradictions evident in the position of the SPO and the confusion prevalent amongst the ranks of the 'left coalition' the other opposition parties found it hard to take advantage of this situation. Their decision to boycott the elections meant that the DS, DSS, and GSS had now become extra-parliamentary political parties. Officials of the Democratic Party, however, suggested that having no representatives in a parliament which rarely met and had no real power should not be seen as a great disadvantage. In an attempt to formulate an extra-parliamentary strategy the DS announced that it would be drawing up a new 'Manifesto for Serbia' outlining their policy aims, forming a 'shadow' government, and launching an extended membership drive with the intention of raising the DS membership to 70,000 by June 1998.[24] However, Djindjić's attempts at overhauling the party structures met with resistance from a group of members who accused him of following a policy of 'centralisation' and seeking to 'concentrate all power in his own hands.' Prominent in this group were Slobodan Gavrilović, the DS Vice-President, and Miodrag Nikolić from Jagodina. One of the DS dissidents, Miroslav Prokopijević, criticised Djindjić for taking unilateral decisions on a range of policy issues including the transformation of the journal *Demokatija* into a daily newspaper and the moves to support Biljana Plavšić and Milo Djukanović. Djindjić, he said, had been seeking to 'privatise' the party.[25] However, Djindjić defended his actions: 'I do not understand what they mean when they talk about "privatisation". It is possible to talk about "privatisation" when a party is transformed into family property where friends, relatives and in-laws are given places in the hierarchy and the policies of the party are based on the wishes of the family. In accordance with this, the property of the party is treated as the family's property. There is not one member of my family in the DS, nor have I placed my friends in positions of power.[26] [...] I want us to be the dominant political force whose concept of social reform spreads its energies throughout the land. Without a strong organisation, however, our ideas might be taken over tommorrow by someone else and no one will know that their source was the DS.'[27]

Vojislav Koštunica was also sceptical of Djindjić's proclaimed plans for the expansion of the DS: 'Zoran Djindjić's plan resembles one of those communist plans for production which were never achieved. We will have nothing to do with such things. The strength of a party should be assessed in terms not of how many members it has but whether it functions well and has the right ideas.'[28] The DS and the DSS were, however, united in the hope that the SPS-SPO attempts at coalition building would ultimately fail and a new election would be called. In such elections it was believed that they would pick up votes from disaffected and alienated former supporters of the SPO.[29]

Vesna Pešić shared the other opposition leaders' disdain for Drašković's attempt to join the government: 'The SPO has no more political ideas, all that is left is a scrabble after power, to satisfy his family and clan with material privileges. In this way the number of Milošević's followers will be increased by the addition of one more rich family.' But she also looked forward to a time when political life had passed through the present 'sombre period' and a 'completely new relationship exists between citizens and politics, politicians and the state'.[30]

Notes

1. M. Manojlović, 'U decembru sigurno pobedjujem', *Dnevni telegraf*, 26 September 1997.
2. 'Šešelj za predsednika kampanja bez mitinga', *Dnevni telegraf*, 30 September 1997.
3. 'Kandidat opozicije bez Šansi', *Naša borba*, 25 October 1997.

4. In March 1998 Obradović's Social Democratic Party and Mićunović's Democratic Centre announced their intention of forming a single party of the 'social democratic centre'.

5. *Tanjug*, 23 November 1997 in *SWB EE/3085 A/9*, 25 November 1997.

6. 'Sveti Georgije ubiva aždahu', Vuk Drašković interviewed by Ilija Rapaić, *Duga*, 5 December 1997.

7. 'Vuk Drašković se ponaša kao pas koga ubace u ring da neprestano ometa protivnika', Vojislav Šešelj interviewed by Goran Radović, *Argument*, 1 December 1997.

8. Slobodan Reljić, 'Demagogue in Waiting', *Transitions*, March 1998.

9. Serbian Radio, 8 December 1997 in *SWB EE/3098 A/8*, 10 December 1997.

10. Roksanda Ninčić, 'Radikalna kradja', *Vreme*, 3 January 1988; *Beta*, 20 December 1997 in *SWB EE/3109 A/9*, 23 December 1997; and *B-92*, 21 December 1997 in *SWB EE/3109 A/9*, 23 December 1997.

11. 'Policija će izbaciti radikale, ako budu ometali zakletvu', *Dnevni telegraf*, 29 December 1997.

12. Nenad LJ Stefanović, 'Hranjenje Vuka', *Vreme*, 31 January 1998.

13. *Tanjug*, 16 February 1998 in *SWB EE/3149 A/6*, 18 February 1998.

14. Zoran Miljatović, 'Kod Vuka olovka, kod Dane gumica', *Nedeljni telegraf*, 18 February 1998.

15. *Tanjug*, 19 February 1988 in *SWB EE/3157 A/8*, 21 February 1998.

16. *Beta*, 19 February 1998 in *SWB EE/3157 A/8*, 21 February 1998.

17. Ibid.

18. Nenad LJ Stefanović, 'Šefe, šta da radim', *Vreme*, 28 February 1998.

19. Jasmina Spasić, 'Vukovo otkrovenje, razočaranje, isključenje', *Nedeljni telegraf*, 11 March 1998.

20. Sandra Petrušić, 'O dvoglavim orlovima', *NIN*, 19 February 1998.

21. Branka Kaljević, 'Virus na levici', *Vreme*, 4 December 1997.

22. Zoran B. Nikolić, 'Levo, levo, pa u aps', *Vreme*, 28 February 1998.

23. Milica R. Zorić and Perica Gunjić, 'Uspon i pad najbogatijeg jugoslovenskog direktora', *Nedeljni telegraf*, 18 February 1998.

24. 'Djindjić: Jovicu Stanišića i mene nemoguće je vrbovati', Zoran Djindjić interviewed by Dragan Novaković, *Dnevni telegraf*, 31 December 1997.

25. Miroslav Prokopijević, 'Zašto propada Demokratska stranka?', *Vreme*, 21 February 1998.

26. 'Nema štofa za cepanje', Zoran Djindjić interviewed by Nened LJ Stefanović, *Vreme*, 7 March 1998.

27. 'U DS-u se stalno nešto dešava i ključa, ali to je zdrav politički život', Zoran Djindjić interviewed by Goran Radović, *Argument*, 2 February 1998.

28. 'Posle crnogorskih parlamentarnih izbora Djukanović će se izduvati kao balon', Vojislav Koštunica interviewed by Svetlana Palić, *Dnevni telegraf*, 12 January 1998.

29. Roksanda Ninčić, 'Treći čovek', *Vreme*, 7 March 1998.

30. 'Rata neće biti', Vesna Pešić interviewed by Dragan Jovanović, *NIN*, 5 March 1998.

29. Full Circle: Conflict in Kosovo and the Radicals in Government (March–April 1998)

The inter-party manoeuvrings and negotiations were overshadowed when in late February fighting broke out in Kosovo between the Serbian security forces and Albanian insurgents. The potential for large-scale violence in Kosovo had been increasing since the conclusion of the Dayton agreement at the end of 1995. The strategy pursued since 1990 by the Democratic League of Kosovo (LDK), headed by Ibrahim Rugova, was centred on the idea that if the Albanian population effectively withdrew from the Serbian state, relying on their own parallel institutions, then in time the international community would recognise their right to secede from Yugoslavia. Some Albanian political activists in Kosovo convinced themselves that the Dayton negotiations, with the heavy involvement of the international community in the affairs of the former Yugoslavia, would provide the ideal opportunity for international intervention. The international community, however, was in reality unwilling to make those already formidably complex negotiations even more difficult by bringing in issues which were external to the conflict in Bosnia. For some Albanians the perception that their cause had been sidelined led them to express increasing disillusionment with the policies espoused by Rugova and the LDK and to call for more radical means to be used in pursuit of their struggle for independence. On 21 April 1996 an Albanian student, Armend Daci, was killed in a shooting incident in a suburb of Priština. Daci's killer was Zlatko Jovanović, a Serbian refugee, who had apparently believed that the student was attempting to steal his car. Subsequently 10,000 Albanians, angered by the lack of interest shown by the police in the case, held a peaceful demonstration at the scene of the shooting. On the evening of 22 April a group of Serbian refugees from the Krajina were

drinking in a café in the town of Dečani when a gunman opened
fire on them with an automatic rifle. Three Serbs were killed
and one other was seriously wounded. Shortly afterwards two
policemen were also wounded when they were attacked by gunmen
in the town of Peć. On the same night another policeman was
killed in an attack in Štimlje, and on the road between Kosovo
Mitrovica and Peć one policeman was killed and another wounded.
Some initial reactions to this wave of attacks saw them as being
part of a militant Albanian reaction to the earlier killing in Priština.[1]
Other observers questioned whether such a well co-ordinated
series of shootings could be attributed to 'spontaneous' action by
vengeful Albanians. When a group called the Kosovo Liberation
Army (UČK) claimed responsibility for these attacks this seemed
to confirm they were part of a strategy being pursued by an
armed Albanian faction. The mainstream Albanian political leadership in Kosovo, however, sought to cast doubt on the idea that
these killings were the work of Albanians using 'terrorist' methods.
According to Ibrahim Rugova they were more likely to be 'a
provocation whose origins can be found in Serbian extremist circles'.[2]
It came to be widely believed that the UČK was in fact a creation
of the Serbian state and its agencies. While it was perhaps not
surprising that such a belief should take root among the Albanian
population, who were fundamentally alienated from the Serbian
state and its institutions, it was more remarkable, and indicative,
that such ideas should find an echo with key Serbian 'opinion-
formers' in Kosovo. In January 1997, for instance, when the Serb
rector of Priština University, Radovoje Papović, was injured in
a bomb attack, for which the UČK reportedly claimed responsibility,
the Serbian Orthodox bishop of Raška-Prizen, Artemije, publicly
emphasised that it remained 'unclear' who was behind the bombing
and he suggested that the 'regime' could have been the true
initiator of the attack.[3] In reality, however, the confused and
contradictory statements which emanated from the authorities following the initial attacks as well as the reluctance of the state-
controlled media to cover these events were symptomatic of official
disarray rather than complicity.[4]

The start of the UČK attacks served to heighten the fears of
the Kosovo Serb population who not only felt threatened by the
armed Albanian insurgents but also suspected that Milošević
and the government in Belgrade were ready to betray them and

to allow them to suffer the fate which had previously befallen the Krajina Serbs. These anxieties were expressed by a number of Kosovo Serb activists and public figures who, calling themselves the Serbian Resistance Movement, organised a petition in May calling on Milošević to visit Kosovo in order to 'resolve the Kosovo and Metohija question'. The Serbian Resistance Movement stated: 'We want to participate in the defensive struggle for Serbian national and state interests, but using exclusively political methods.'[5] The Serbian Resistance Movement held a rally on 22 June, and the writer Aco Rakočević addressed it saying to the assembled Kosovo Serbs: 'One often hears that Kosovo-Metohija should be the third Yugoslav republic, that it should be handed to the Šiptars [Albanians] or, at best, divided between Serbia and Albania. This is why the Serbs and Montenegrins want to know whether in Dayton or somewhere else something was decided which we were unaware of. [...] Even cattle would, if they could, ask the owner whether they were going to be sold or slaughtered.' The Serbs of Kosovo, he said, would refuse 'to be cattle peacefully led to the slaughter without knowing what awaits them'.[6] Among those who gathered under the banner of the Serbian Resistance Movement were a number of individuals who had played pivotal roles in the pro-Milošević Kosovo Serb nationalist movement during the late 1980s such as Momčilo Trajković, Kosta Bulatović, and Miroslav Šolević. All these figures, however, had now turned firmly against the regime. Momčilo Trajković, the President of the Serbian Resistance Movement, stated: 'Kosovo and Metohija helped Milošević and the Socialist Party of Serbia to achieve and preserve their power...[now] the regime wants to turn the people against Kosovo and is seeking to create a situation in which the public will find it easy to accept some future act which will free Serbia from the burden which is called Kosovo.' The Serbian Resistance Movement professed itself ready to engage in talks with the Albanians because 'without compromise solutions cannot be found in the Balkans, and this is particularily true of Kosovo. Compromise with the Albanians is therefore vital.'[7] Other mainstream opposition parties were also prepared to contemplate some form of negotiated agreement with the Albanians. The DS stated that it was willing to engage in a process of dialogue with the Albanians which could lead to the institution of an autonomous government in Kosovo. The DSS proposed that the formation of a regional government in Kosovo should take place as part of an overall process of decentralisation and democratisation covering the whole of Serbia 'on the model of a modern European regional state such as Spain'.[8]

In spite of the attempt by the Serbian Resistance Movement to mobilise opinion in the province most Kosovo Serbs continued to offer their support to Milošević and the SPS. When in December 1996 Milošević had sought to summon his supporters to Belgrade to defend him against the growing pressure of anti-government protests, many of those who answered his call were Kosovo Serbs. However, there was an element of desperation in their loyalty. The more precarious their position became, the more firmly they sought to align themselves with the centre of power in Belgrade. But there were indications that the Milošević government was concerned that it could lose its grip on the loyalties of the Kosovo Serbs. The re-activation of the long-dormant Božur organisation at the start of 1998 was an attempt to channel the energies and anxieties of the Kosovo Serbs into a grouping which was basically of a pro-regime orientation. Božur's leader Bogdan Kecman had spent the 1990s working as a director of Jugopetrol in Priština. In September 1997, however, he had publicly quarrelled with his superiors, accusing Dragan Tomić of using his position as head of Jugopetrol to appropriate large quantities of oil for his own personal profit. Kecman, however, stated that he continued to regard Slobodan Milošević as an 'honest man'.[9] This dispute with such a senior member of the political-economic elite might well have been seen as giving a 'dissident' gloss to Božur's government-supporting activities. Božur's initial meeting held on 13 January 1998 at Kosovo Polje, however, attracted only about 500 supporters. Interviewed after the rally Bogdan Kecman said: 'We are going to continue our protests. [...] We are going to hold rallies here in Kosovo-Metohija and we are going to stay here and fight, if need be.'[10] In a further illustration of the intra-communal competition for the loyalties of the Kosovo Serbs which had broken out, Kecman was attacked by Kosta Bulatović of the Serbian Resistance Movement who said: 'The Božur organisation has renewed its work, but all we hear from them is a call to follow the war option. But who will follow that call? The Serbian people do not want war and it is not true to say that they are representatives of the Serbian people or that the Serbian people supports their type of politics.'[11]

In spite of the deteriorating security situation, the period 1996-7 had not been distinguished by any significant political progress on the part of the leading Serbian and Albanian political forces. On 1 September 1996 Slobodan Milošević and Ibrahim Rugova had signed an agreement which was meant to facilitate the movement of Albanian students from their 'parallel' schools back to state-run institutions, but differences had quickly emerged between the two sides over interpretation of the agreement's somewhat vague terms. The Albanian leadership insisted that they should be allowed to issue diplomas to students bearing the inscription 'Republic of Kosova'. The Serbs, however, predictably refused to contemplate any such move. During 1997 as the Serbian government took on an increasingly nationalist position it became progressively less willing to contemplate any serious attempt at compromise on the Kosovo issue. On 10 December the Federal Yugoslav and Bosnian Serb delegations walked out of the Bonn conference on implementation of the Dayton agreement when an attempt was made to place Kosovo on the agenda. Following these events Ivica Dačić, the SPS spokesman, stated: 'The representatives of the FRY will walk out of all future meetings in which an attempt is made to interfere in the internal affairs of our land.' International observers noted that the conference walkout coincided with the need of the Socialists to appear to be taking a firm line on Kosovo in the run-up to the 21 December elections.[12]

In response to the stalemate over the education agreement an Albanian Students' Union, apparently organising independently from the LDK, began on 1 October to stage a series of protests demanding unconditional access to university facilities. Although the demonstration of some 20,000 students was initially peaceful some of the participants were later attacked by the police. While a subsequent demonstration on 27 October passed off peacefully, a further protest on 30 December was once again forcibly dispersed by the police. The Serbian Patriarch Pavle responded to these events by sending a letter to the leaders of the Albanian student movement which was notable for its conciliatory tone, its condemnation of the police action, and its equating of the sufferings of Albanian and Serbian students: 'I am sending you an expression of my deep sorrow and protest at the way in which the state defenders of order used violence to break up your demonstration. The beating and arrest of students is a grave error not only for the state authorities but also for the honour of the land in which we live. There is nothing worse than the use of violence against young people, I know that it has taken the greatest effort for you to endure such provocation. I said the same things last winter when your comrades, the students of Belgrade, were scattered by water cannon in the cold night and beaten with batons, and what happened to them then was no worse than what took place at yesterday's demonstration in the suburbs of Priština.'[13]

UČK attacks continued throughout 1996-7 with the organisation targetting policemen, Serbian refugees and Albanians who, due to the fact that they worked in some capacity for the authorities, were considered to be 'collaborators'. In the autumn of 1997, however, the hostilities in Kosovo began to escalate. On 25 November Serbian police made an attempt to enter the village of Vojnik in the Drenica region west of Priština in order to collect taxes in the area. As they approached the village, however, they came under fire from gunmen positioned in the surrounding hills. Unable to enter the village the police withdrew in order to await reinforcements. The next day fighting resumed with a gun-battle between the two sides that lasted for several hours before the police were once again forced to retreat. As the Serbian police vehicles left the village they opened fire on nearby buildings. In the village school an Albanian teacher, Halit Geci, was killed by the police fusillade, and his funeral was attended by 20,000 Albanians. Among the mourners were three masked men dressed in military fatigues and carrying automatic rifles, who identified themselves as members of the UČK. One of them said at the graveside: 'The UČK is the only force which is fighting for the liberation and national unity of Kosovo.' The mourners responded with cheers and chants of 'UČK! UČK!'. From this point onwards the Drenica region, consisting of Srbica, Klina, and Glogovac, effectively became a 'liberated zone' where real power lay not with the Serbian state but rather with the guerrillas of the UČK.[14]

The international community watched these events with increasing anxiety believing that they might signal the start of the long anticipated and feared war in Kosovo. The established leadership of the Kosovo Albanians also found cause for concern in this episode with Rugova and the rest of the LDK leadership no longer being able to dismiss the UČK as a fabrication of the Serbian authorities. In December Adem Demaci addressed an open letter to the UČK asking them to call a halt to their operations for a period of three months in order to allow time for the international community to use its influence to initiate dialogue between the Serbs and the Albanians. Between the end of November 1997 and 1 February 1998 there were nine instances of ethnically-motivated violence. On 22 January a Serbian local councillor was killed, reportedly as the result of a UČK attack. Apparently acting in retaliation the Serbian police then launched a raid on the village of Donji Prekaz in which one Albanian was killed and two women were injured.

In purely military terms the existence of this UČK – controlled area in western Kosovo did not necessarily constitute a threat to Milošević's overall control of the region. Although the Drenica area was only 35 km. from Priština it largely consisted of small villages in rural hill country. The area's long-standing tradition of resistance to central authority was at least in part a product of its 'remoteness' from the centres of power. Milošević's failure to maintain the authority of the state in the Drenica area did, however, serve to heighten his already acute credibility problem in the eyes of domestic public opinion. In January and February the plight of the Serbs in Kosovo was widely covered by the Belgrade press. Serbs from the village of Osojana, for instance, attested: 'The Šiptars [Albanians] are threatening us on all sides, they want to terrorise us and drive us out of here' and 'The state, our Serbia, has forgotten that we exist here. For more than thirty years we have been left on our own at the mercy or mercilessness of the separatists.'[15] Abbess Anastasija from the convent of Dević was interviewed, and lamented the fact that the surrounding countryside was alive with Albanian insurgents while the convent's telephone lines and electricity had been cut off. Milošević seemed to believe that decisive police/military action in the Drenica region would allow him once again to present himself as the defender of the Kosovo Serbs. He calculated that, as on previous occasions in his career, the rhetoric and symbolism of nationalism could be used to rally popular support behind him. However, he was aware that opting for the 'warpath' in Kosovo would put at risk the links that he had been cultivating with the international community. On 23 February, however, Robert Gelbard, the US envoy in the Balkans, gave a press conference in Priština in which he praised Milošević in lavish terms and described the UČK as a terrorist organisation. These comments were made shortly after Milorad Dodik had been appointed, with Milošević's backing, as Prime Minister in the Republika Srpska and Gelbard was apparently trying in these statements to highlight the 'positive' role played by Milošević in these events. Milošević, however, chose to interpret Gelbard's gesture as being a 'green light' for a security crackdown in Kosovo.[16]

On 28 February, according to the Serbian police, a 'routine patrol' was attacked by UČK guerillas near the village of Likošani. In the firefight which followed four policemen were killed and two seriously injured. Sixteen Albanians were reported to have been killed and nine arrested during the clash. This incident was followed by a major offensive by the Serbian police which aimed to wrest control of Drenica from the fighters of the UČK. Co-ordinated assaults involving tanks, artillery, and helicopters were launched against Donji Prekaz, Glogovac, Likošani, Srbica, Lauša and other villages which were believed to be strongholds of UČK. The fighting around Donji Prekaz was particularily fierce. On 5 March the Serbian authorities announced that the leader of the UČK in Prekaz, Adem Jašari, had been killed along with twenty-six other Albanians. This it was said, had 'destroyed the core' of the UČK in the area. Other sources, disputed Jašari's status suggesting that he was not particularily senior in the UČK hierarchy and was really a 'typical village idler' from a powerful local family. It was predicted, however, that his death in battle would have transformed him into a 'national hero' in the eyes of the Albanian population. Albanian sources claimed that the security forces had used indiscriminate violence against civillians during their attacks on the villages. In addition to those killed and injured the fighting also caused a wave of civillian refugees to flee from the scene of the conflict.[17]

The official version of events portrayed the situation in Drenica as a direct response to the Albanian attack initiated on 28 February. Independent Serbian sources, however, cast doubt on the suggestion that any 'routine' police activity would be taking place in an area which since November 1997 had effectively been a 'no-go' area for the security forces. The impression that these operations were in fact part of a pre-planned intervention was strengthened by the fact that the operations were reportedly spearheaded by members of the Special Anti-terrorist Unit (SAJ). Under the command of Franko Simatović the SAJ effectively acted as Milošević's personal praetorian guard within the state security apparatus. During the war in Bosnia the SAJ had organised the arming and training of paramilitaries, and had even co-operated with them in the field. During the opposition winter protests of 1996/7 members of the SAJ were reported to be roaming the streets of Belgrade looking for demonstrators to beat up. In the autumn of 1997 Simatović's men were back in Bosnia attempting, unsuccessfully, to engineer the overthrow of Biljana Plavšić. In Kosovo in early 1998 the SAJ were once again in the front rank acting as the trusted executors of Milošević's policies.[18] While the rival armed forces clashed both Albanian and Serbian populations in Kosovo began to mobilise. On the morning of 2 March around 30,000 Albanians attempted to march through the centre of Priština in protest at the police intervention, but their path through the town centre, was blocked by riot police and Interior Ministry units who dispersed the protesters using tear-gas, water-cannons and riot batons; 150 people were reportedly injured. In the area around Priština University fighting broke out between Serbian and Albanian students. That afternoon 1,000 Serbs gathered on the outskirts of Priština near Kosovo Polje to see one of the policemen killed in the previous day's fighting buried with military honours. The next day the Albanians buried their dead. At a mass burial near Likošani 40,000 mourners attended the funeral of twenty-one Albanians who had been killed in the local area. In the following days further demonstrations were held by the Albanian population in Priština and other towns which, unlike the previous protest, was not prevented from proceeding by the police. Some of these protests were clearly intended to bring their situation to the attention of the outside world with the slogans on their placards written in English. On 15 March thousands of Albanians walked through the centre of Priština to the Catholic church of Saint Ndou. Some of the marchers carried portraits of Mother Teresa. This religious procession/political demonstration was meant to counter the portrayal by the Serbian authorities of the Albanians as being part of an 'Islamic threat'. An Albanian journalist explained: 'Most Kosovars are Catholics, if anything. [...] Serb propaganda plays the Islamic card, as though they are fighting fundamentalism.'[19] In fact only about 55,000 of the 1.7

million Albanians in Kosovo were Catholics. On 10 March 30,000 Kosovo Serbs attended a demonstration in Priština in support of the Serbian government's attempt to crush the insurgents. The numbers of Serbs who had come out onto the streets surprised some Albanian political activists in the town. Western journalists observed that the 'atmosphere' at the Priština demonstration was similar to that at earlier Serbian demonstrations in Bosnia and Montenegro. It was suggested that as in these previous demonstrations operatives within the Interior Ministry had played a role in organising the already frightened and angry Kosovo Serbs.[20] The political/ethnic radicalisation of the Kosovo Serbs had been heightened by the fact that significant numbers of them were refugees from Bosnia and Croatia who feared that any Serbian abandonment of Kosovo would turn them into refugees again. As was the case in the Albanian demonstration, the iconography at the Serbian rally mixed religious and nationalist symbolism. Portraits of the Virgin Mary and Orthodox saints were carried along with posters of Radovan Karadžić and other political leaders. These patterns of mobilisation and counter-mobilisation clearly heightened the risks of intercommunal conflict.

The decision of the Serbian government on the 23 March to set in motion the long-postponed implementation of the education agreement raised the political temperature on the streets of Priština still further. The agreement was immediately denounced by the rector, Radovoje Papović, a senior figure in the SPS: 'The agreement is treason...it is unlawful and unconstitutional and at the same time it can certainly be said to represent a step towards the realisation of the separatists' basic aim – a Republic of Kosovo.' The rector, however, was himself condemned by Živko Šokolovač, a senior figure in JUL: 'Radovoje Papović is one of those who has fallen for national romanticism, who say they are leftists but are really nationalists.'[21] On the same day that the agreement was signed 20,000 Serbs demonstrated in support of the rector's 'revolt' against the authorities. In addition the rector appeared to have the support of other academics and the Serbian students at Priština University. The students who demonstrated against the agreement modelled their protests on the earlier student demonstrations which had taken place in Belgrade in the winter of 1996/7. The Priština students, for instance, accompanied their protests with the same blowing of whistles as had characterised the daily walks of their

Belgrade compatriots. In spite of these similarities in form the two sets of demonstrations differed considerably in their political content. While the Belgrade demonstrations were complex manifestations imbued with strong elements of civility the Priština protests were purely aimed at protecting collective national rights. One young Serbian woman demonstrator said: 'Serbia has no right to decide what happens in our lives. Only we who live here have the right to do that. We are demonstrating to show the world that there are Serbs in Kosovo and not only Albanians.'[22] Živojin Rakočević, one of the Priština student leaders, invoked the symbolism of the Kosovo myth in calling on the students to reject the agreement: 'Tsar Lazar lost Kosovo and his head, but he gained the heavenly kingdom...those who try to sell Kosovo will be remembered by the Serbian people as traitors.'[23] In addition, whereas in Belgrade one of the key student aims had been to remove the rector of Belgrade University, who was also an SPS appointee, the Priština students had dedicated themselves to protecting the position of their rector. Indeed when Čedomir Jovanović and a delegation from the Belgrade Students' Political Club travelled down to Priština, their request to meet the local student leaders was refused. Jovanović explained their reluctance to talk: 'I think they are exceptionally close to rector Papović, which means that the political line they are following is very bad. He has been at the head of the protest which, with the co-operation of the SPS, he has been promoting for the last two weeks.'[24] It remained unclear whether this suggestion that the rector's 'revolt' was being carried out as part of an agreement with the authorities was a correct evaluation of events. Such a planned academic 'insurrection' in response to implementation of the education agreement would, however, have served the government's purposes allowing it to officially act in a 'moderate' and 'conciliatory' way while at the same time 'covertly' cultivating ethnic tensions. Papović only agreed to call off the demonstrations following an intervention by the Serbian President, Milan Milutinović.

Outside Kosovo, however, the Serbian population showed less enthusiasm for renewed mobilisation around such ethnic issues. While the vast majority of Serbs believed that Kosovo should remain an integral part of Serbia there was little evidence amongst ordinary people of the nationalist passions which had been observable in 1991-3 during the war in Croatia and the first years of the war in Bosnia. Public opinion in Serbia was by the spring of 1998 characterised by political apathy, and social and economic exhaustion. A poll published in *Nedeljni telegraf* showed that more than 70 per cent of those asked would be against having their close relations sent to fight in Kosovo. Even Ljubomir Tadić, the veteran *Praxis* activist who ten years earlier had played a key role in opposing the 1974 constitution, said: 'I feel personally apathetic even though I understand the issue intellectually...People don't have pensions. The Americans have frozen our money. It is hard to get passionate about it.'[25]

The international community reacted with considerable alarm to the outbreak of violence in Kosovo. Central to their anxieties was the belief that the conflict in Kosovo could easily spill over into neighbouring countries such as Macedonia where relations between the Slav majority and the Albanian minority had become increasingly tense over the previous year. On 1 March the American ambassador in Belgrade issued a statement including the words 'the United States of America is deeply worried by the reports of violence in the Drenica region.' The United States was followed on 3 March by the British Foreign Office who, speaking on behalf of the European Union called for 'urgent negotiations between the government in Belgrade and the leaders of the Kosovo Albanians in order to work towards a peaceful solution to the crisis.'[26] On 5 March Robin Cook, the British Foreign Secretary, travelled to Belgrade to re-emphasise the EU message. Cook, however, found Milošević in an intransigent mood, refusing to accept the EU demand for immediate negotiations with the Albanian leadership. On the same day the United States withdrew the limited trade and diplomatic concessions made to the Federal Republic of Yugoslavia the previous week as an acknowledgment of his support for Dodik's premiership in the Republika Srpska. The diplomatic pressure on Milošević was increased on 9 March when the Contact Group countries, meeting in London, set a deadline of ten days by which time they expected the special police units to have been withdrawn from Kosovo and measures taken to begin dialogue with Rugova and the other Albanian leaders. It was specified that if these points were not complied with, the Federal Republic of Yugoslavia would find itself subject to 'real and biting economic sanctions'. Encouraged by this apparent diplomatic support Ibrahim Rugova stated that acceptance of independence for Kosovo was a precondition for his involvement in any negotiations with the Serbs. On 12 March the Serbian government sent a delegation headed by Ratko Marković, the Deputy Prime Minister, to Priština in an attempt to start negotiations. The Albanian political figures who had been invited to take part in the inter-ethnic dialogue, however, did not turn up. International observers regarded this visit by the Serbian government officials as a public relations gesture rather than a genuine attempt to find a solution to the crisis. Nevertheless international pressure was also exerted on the Albanian leadership in order to persuade them to support a negotiating platform which stopped short of outright independence. On 25 March the Contact Group met again in Bonn and decided that although the conditions they had set out on 10 March had not been adhered to Milošević would be given a further four weeks in which to produce real progress in Kosovo. If at the end of this period no positive movement had been witnessed then Yugoslav assets and money held abroad would be frozen. In addition the Contact Group resolved to work for the adoption of an United Nations arms embargo on both the Yugoslav government and the UČK. The Contact Group appointed the former Spanish Prime Minister, Felipe Gonzáles, as the international special envoy on Kosovo. During the winter 1996/7 demonstrations Gonzáles had headed the OSCE delegation to Belgrade investigating the disputed local election results. The decision by the Contact Group to postpone any decisive action against the FRY was seen inside and outside of Yugoslavia as a weakening of the group's stance. The Contact Group resolution proposing an arms embargo was passed by the United Nations Security Council on 31 March. The British envoy at the UN, David Redmond, stated that the resolution 'says to Belgrade that repression in Kosovo will not be tolerated by the international community' and was a signal to the Kosovo Albanians 'that terrorism – in whatever guise and for whatever end – is unacceptable'.[27] The measure, however, was largely symbolic as both the Serbian government forces and the UČK were both known to be well armed. A large arms deal involving fighter aircraft, attack helicopters, missiles, and tanks, had been agreed between the Russian and Yugoslav governments in December 1997. As the arms embargo was not considered retroactive, this deal was deemed to be legal under the terms of the resolution.

This slackening in the pace of international pressure on the Yugoslav government corresponded to the decline in the intensity of fighting on the ground in Kosovo. The region, however, remained in a state of high tension with daily small-scale clashes and shooting incidents taking place. The Serbian special forces remained firmly entrenched in the area while the UČK, although driven out of their bases in the Drenica villages, had regrouped and were increasingly well armed with imported weaponry. Observers noted that in the area on both sides of the border between Kosovo and Albania the UČK insurrection was being used as a cover for the activities of various criminal gangs adding to the generally lawless climate in the province. On 6 April the bodies of six Albanians who had been shot repeatedly were found near the Kosovan village of Carevac. The Albanians were identified as being among a group who on 22 March had put their names to a letter, copies of which were sent to the Contact Group, OSCE and President Clinton, expressing their support for Serbian government policies in the province. The killings were apparently part of the UČK policy of liquidating those it classed as 'domestic traitors' or 'collaborators.'[28] Reports carried by the Belgrade press on 15 April of Serbian and Montenegrin villagers fleeing from the Dečani region after the arrival of a force of armed and uniformed UČK fighters made it clear to the Serbian public that the 'intervention' of early March had not provided a swift solution to the problem of the Kosovo insurgency.[29] It appeared doubtful, even if meaningful talks did begin between the Serbian government and Ibrahim Rugova's LDK, whether the increasingly radicalised and battle-hardened UČK would see any value in such negotiations.

During early 1998 the regime had continued in its attempts to pressurise and harrass the independent media. On 25 February inspectors from the Federal Inspectorate for Transport and Communications accompanied by police entered the premises of Feman TV in Jagodina and ordered it to cease broadcasting. Although the authorities stated that they were acting to enforce broadcasting regulations the journalists and management of Feman TV saw their closure as a purely political act. It was suggested that the authorities had taken exception to the fact that Feman's owner was Miodrag Nikolić, a local businessman and DS leader, and noted that the police incursion came the day after the station had carried an interview with the economist Mladjan Dinkić who had made wide-ranging criticisms of the Serbian government.[30] The onset of the crisis in Kosovo provided the authorities with an opportunity to intensify their offensive against the media. On 8 March the Belgrade District Attorney announced that he was ready to take action against five independent newspapers – *Blic, Naša borba, Demokratija, Danas* and *Dnevni telegraf* – whose reporting of the situation in Kosovo was judged by the authorities to be 'unpatriotic'.[31] Ivica Dačić, the SPS spokesman, reinforced this message: 'The so-called independent media are in fact the most dependent media because they depend on those who have never wished this people well.'[32] In response Miloš Vasić, head of the Independent Association of Journalists of Serbia, described the authorities as wanting to introduce 'compulsory lying' for the media. The most vigorous prosecutors of this state-sanctioned 'war' against the media, however, were senior figures within JUL. On 25 March Mirjana Marković at a party meeting in Zemun spoke of the 'evil forces' which were conspiring against Yugoslavia. These 'centres of political power', she said, were being aided by groups and individuals who supported foreign intervention in Serbia's internal affairs. She identified these 'collaborators' as being 'present in the so-called independent media, in certain publishing houses; they are the leaders of certain right-wing political parties and occasional right-wing politicians or opportunists installed in the left. They are present in a part of the corrupt or manipulated intellectuals, experts, public figures and young people....'[33] The sentiments expressed in this diatribe were echoed on 2 April by Ivan Marković, the Deputy Chairman of JUL, who said that a 'special psychological war' was being waged against Yugoslavia aided by a journalistic 'fifth column'. Several journalists from independent newspapers and radio stations subsequently reported that they were being denied access to government press conferences. Veran Matić, the editor-in-chief of Radio B-92, saw these moves and the 'conspiracy'-centred rhetoric prevalent among the government parties as an ominous sign that they were preparing a 'platform for dictatorship'.[34]

The commencement of hostilities in Kosovo facilitated a fundamental change in the Serbian political landscape. Although the negotiations between the SPS and the SPO continued during early March they had effectively become deadlocked over a number of 'material' and 'symbolic' issues. As the negotiations progressed the SPO had significantly raised the level of their demands. They apparently believed that their earlier failure to obtain the position of Prime Minister entitled them to strengthen their overall position within the government. During the final round of consultations the SPO reportedly demanded that they should receive eighteen ministerial places in the new government. This proposal was clearly unacceptable to the SPS as it would have given the SPO more representatives than them within the ranks of the new government. Problems had also arisen over Vuk Drašković's insistence that the entry of the SPO into the government should be accompanied by a 'Declaration of National Reconciliation' signalling an end to the historic conflict between Četniks and Partisans. Drašković's promotion of this declaration was based partly on the strong personal ideological beliefs held by himself and his wife. In addition, however, he regarded it as vital that he should be able to claim some sort of 'symbolic' victory in order to counter the accusations of the other opposition parties that he had abandoned his anti-communist heritage. On 13 March the SPO appeared to have been successful when Mirko Marjanović signed an agreement which recognised the equality of the Četnik and Partisan traditions saying that it 'celebrates and thanks all those who fought against the foreign invaders in the expectation that they will no longer consider each other to be enemies.' This declaration, however, was the cause of considerable unhappiness within the ranks of the 'left coalition' and particularily amongst the ideological circle surrounding Mirjana Marković. One senior official within the SPS warned that if the declaration was adopted by parliament it would cause serious disquiet among the 400,000 voters for the 'left coalition' who were former Partisan fighters or their family members.[35]

Analysts in Belgrade speculated that Milošević's decision to launch the offensive in Kosovo may have been influenced by the desire to 'create a psychology and illusion of acute threat' which would open up new political options and possibilities.[36] In the months since the 21 December election any rapprochement between the SPS-JUL and the Radicals had appeared impossible. In the new atmosphere of 'national crisis' over Kosovo, however, the Socialists and the Radicals began to draw close together again. On 12 March when the Serbian government sent representatives to Priština in an unsuccessful attempt to talk to Albanian political leaders the SPO refused to take part in the delegation on the grounds that no common Serbian position had been worked out in advance. By contrast the Radicals were represented by Tomislav Nikolić, and JUL by Milovan Bojić.[37] Drašković's refusal to back the Serbian government earned him a sharp rebuke from the Socialists with Ivica Dačić suggesting: 'Vuk Drašković refused to take part in negotiations with the Kosovo Albanians on the orders of his foreign mentors.'[38] In spite of all this bad blood between the SPO and the SPS on the issue of Kosovo Drašković continued to believe that Milošević would be unwilling to endure the international condemnation which would certainly follow any alliance with the Radicals. As late as 23 March the Serbian President, Milan Milutinović, told journalists that he was 'still hoping' for an agreement with the SPO and affirmed that an alliance with Šešelj was considered to be 'out of the question.'[39]

Later that same day, however, an intensive series of consultations began between Milutinović and Marjanović, and Šešelj's Radicals. In dramatic contrast with the SPO-SPS negotiations the talks between the Socialists and the Radicals were swiftly concluded. On 24 March the formation of a new government was announced. In this administration fifteen ministerial places were taken by the Socialists and five by JUL. The Radicals received fifteen places in the new government. Vojislav Šešelj and Tomislav Nikolić were both named as Deputy Prime Ministers while the Minister for Information was Aleksandar Vučić (SRS). The Minister of the Interior was Vlajko Stojiljković (SPS) and Dragoljub Janković (JUL) was appointed as Minister of Justice. Janković was the President of the Belgrade District Court and in November 1996 he had been responsible for the attempt to annul the local election results in the capital city. Milan Beko remained in the government but was now a Minister without Portfolio with his former position as Privatisation Minister being taken by Jorgovanka Tabaković (SRS). New Democracy, whose representatives had ensured the survival of the Socialist government from 1994-7, was excluded from the new government. The first act of the latter was to pass a 'Declaration of National Unity' by 169 votes (SPS-JUL-SRS) to 49 (SPO). The declaration stated: 'Serbia, Montenegro, and the Republika Srpska are the three pillars of national unity. [...] This time demands unity and togetherness. It is our responsibility consciously to reject all divisions from the past and consign them to history.' While this declaration resembled the one which had been agreed between Marjanović and Drašković all the explicit references to the reconciliation of Četnik and Partisan traditions had been deleted.

The opposition greeted the news of this new government with expressions of anguish and despair. Even in the period 1992-3 when the war in Bosnia had been at its height Milošević and the Socialists had not been willing to offer the Radicals the direct share of power to which they had now agreed. Dragan Veselinov stated: 'I think the Socialists have decided that there will be strife in Kosovo and renewed conflict with the international community. This government is a government of national catastrophe and the greatest threat to the unity of the state. This is a war government. This government cannot guarantee peace or economic progress.'[40] For Nenad Čanak the new administration was one of 'fascists and national socialists'.[41] Miroljub Labus of the Democratic Party said: 'This new Serbian government will follow populist economic policies. It has been formed on the assumption that this country will be subject to economic sanctions.'[42]

Although the Socialists and the Radicals had found it relatively easy to agree on the division of offices few observers believed that this harmonious situation would last for long. The desire of the Socialists to retain heir hold on power would at some point come into conflict with Šešelj's political ambitions. The initial co-operation between the parties would then be replaced by a fierce intra-governmental competition for control of material resources and access to the state media sector.

Following the formation of the Socialist-Radical government Vuk Drašković attempted to put a brave face on the situation saying that he was 'not in the least' bit disappointed by the fact that the SPO had been left out of the government and predicted that the future held 'grim days indeed for our country and our people'.[43] Such words, however, could not disguise the fact that Drašković, after having abandoned the opposition to negotiate with the Socialists, had now been unceremoniously abandoned by the Socialists themselves. One political analyst commented on the situation: 'For more than three months he was publicly involved in negotiations, but then he was left in disgrace because he remained without anything. Some people have already been been calling Drašković the "Judas of the democratic opposition", but in the end he turned out to be "Judas without his pieces of silver". He attempted over a period of months to give legitimacy to the government, but in the end he was not paid anything for that service.'[44] Vesna Pešić, however, predicted that even after Drašković's rejection by the regime as a suitable coalition partner the SPO might not abandon its pro-government policy. She said: 'There are various reasons for this. On the one hand they will want to retain control of the Belgrade city government. On the other hand they may be waiting for the Socialists to change course again, to call in Gonzàlez and throw Šešelj out of the government. It appears that they have made a lasting decision to take the side of the regime, and not to work with the opposition.'[45]

The new Socialist-Radical government was formed as Serbia continued its downward economic slide. On 1 April the dinar was devalued from 3.3 to 6 to the mark. The black market street money-changers however were exchanging money at a rate far higher than this official level. The devaluation produced an immediate inflationary jump of 10-20 per cent in the prices paid for imported goods such as cigarettes, fuel and alcohol. Shortages occurred in basic commodities such as milk, sugar and cooking oil. Supplies were apparently being held back in anticipation of imminent price rises. These shortages encouraged panic buying of food by ordinary Serbs. The regime-supporting newspaper *Politika* was also known to be stockpiling newsprint. In an attempt to prevent an inflationary spiral the government sought to impose a strict limit on the amount of money in circulation. This monetary control resulted in a number of Belgrade banks running out of money in the days immediately after the devaluation. While officials of the National Bank of Yugoslavia appeared confident that they could control any inflationary pressures building up in the economy, other observers doubted this. Mladjan Dinkić predicted that inflation would exceed the government target of 25 per cent and rise to over 60 per cent during 1998.[46] On 9 April Danko Djunić, the 'reformist' federal Deputy Prime Minister, resigned from the government. His 'reformist' position had been becoming steadily more difficult to maintain, and his isolation had only been increased when, after the Montenegrin Presidential elections, he had publicly called for the recognition of Djukanović's victory. In departing from the government Djunić became part of a succession of Serbian technocratic reformers, including Panić and Avramović, who had believed that they could change the government from within only to see their reformist plans come to nothing.[47] The sense of gathering economic crisis was heightened by the fear that the international community might impose further economic sanctions on the FRY.

The entry of the Radicals into positions of power meant that there would be no moderation in the government's stance on the issue of Kosovo. Faced with increasing pressure from the outside world the government sought to gain 'democratic' and 'popular' legitimacy by asking the electorate to endorse its position through a referendum. Voters were asked to respond to the question 'Will you accept the participation of foreign representatives in resolving the Kosovo problem?' The proposal of a referendum with a question framed in these terms was a classic example of Milošević's cunning and manipulative abilities. It linked in the minds of the electorate a response which supported Serbian state sovereignty with one which supported the regime. It was also a question, posed in essentially abstract terms, with the electors being asked to decide on a policy without the consequences of that policy being considered. Critics of the referendum observed that the question should have been put to the people in such a way that the results of their choice were fully explained. In its most simple terms this would be 'Do you want war or not?'[48] In certain respects the use of this referendum tactic was reminiscent of the way in which during the 1/2 July 1990 referendum on the constitution, acceptance of the state authorities' right to frame the constitution before elections was equated with the need to defend the integrity of the state. The referendum would also, it was believed, provide Milošević with a response to the demands of the international community that he should show 'moderation' and 'flexibility'. He would be able to stand by his position that the Kosovo issue was an internal Serbian affair, confidently proclaiming that his capacity for compromise was constrained by the directly expressed 'will of the people'.

The arrangements for the referendum were instituted with remarkable speed. Milošević had first set out his proposal for a referendum on 2 April in a letter to Mirko Marjanović, Milan Milutinović and Dragan Tomić. The referendum was discussed in parliament on 7 April, and there was no real opposition to its being held. Instead the discussions came to be centred on which of the parliamentary factions could most effectively invoke national symbolism in support of the proposition. Mirko Marjanović called on the representatives to reject 'blind submissiveness to the world powers' just as the people of Serbia had done on 6 April 1941 when they chose to defy the Nazi invaders. Aleksandar Vučić speaking for the Radicals declared that they 'should not dare to allow their centuries-old hearths to be lost again as they were in the RSK'.[49] The SPO supported the referendum and added that it should also be used to consult the people on whether the traditional symbols of Serbian statehood should be restored on the flag and coat of arms.[50] The motion fixing the referendum for 23 April was passed by 193 votes to 4. The only opposition to the holding of the referendum came from the extra-parliamentary political parties (DS,DSS,GSS) They maintained that the referendum had little real connection with providing a solution to the Kosovo problem but was simply a device to provide a 'cover' for the failure of Milošević's policies and cast the blame for the consequences of that failure onto the people. It was further pointed out that even the minimal systems of control which were normally counted on to supervise Serbia's fraud-ridden elections would not be in place for this hurriedly-organised poll. In the event the 23 April referendum yielded the result which Milošević had wanted and expected, with 95 per cent of those who voted rejecting international participation in the resolution of the Kosovo crisis. According to the Referendum Election Commission, 73 per cent of the electorate had voted in the poll. The fact that Milošević had put such effort into engineering this electoral snub to the international community was further confirmation that Milošević had opted for an isolationist and nationalist course. Even while voting was underway, further fighting was taking place in Kosovo. According to Yugoslav Army sources they had intercepted a group of 200 UČK guerillas as they were crossing the border into Kosovo from Albania near the village of Kosare in the Dečani region.[50] In the ensuing firefight nineteen of the insurgents were killed. The Yugoslav government accused Albania of allowing the UČK to use it territory as a staging point for operations in western Kosovo while the Albanian authorities countered by stating that Yugoslav aircraft had violated Albanian airspace.

Notes

1. Shkelzen Maliqui, 'Broken April', *War Report*, May 1996.
2. Dejan Anastasijević, 'Jedan sat terora', *Vreme*, 27 April 1996.
3. Steve Crawshaw, 'Milošević Turns Up the Heat in Kosovo', *Independent*, 30 January 1997.
4. Dukagjin Gorani, 'Belgrade Stays Silent', *War Report*, June 1996.
5. 'Kosovski Srbi više nisu za Miloševića', *Naša borba*, 7 July 1997.
6. SRNA, 22 June 1996 in *SWB EE/2646 A/12*, 24 June 1996.
7. *Naša borba*, 7 July 1997.
8. Vojislav Koštunica, 'Srbi u magli', *Vreme*, 22 March 1997.
9. Miloš Antić, 'Od Tomićevog dolaska na čelo Jugopetrola "isparilo" je osam miliona litara goriva', *Nedeljni telegraf*, 1 October 1996.
10. *Blic*, 14 January 1998 in *SWB EE/3126 A/12*, 16 January 1998.
11. 'Prodaja i izdaja', Kosta Bulatović interviewed in *NIN*, 15 January 1998.
12. 'Glup potez preti veća izolacija', *Dnevni telegraf*, 12 December 1997.
13. Patriarch Pavle, 'Država nije isto što i njeni režimi', *NIN*, 8 January 1998.
14. Guy Dinmore, 'Kosovo's Albanian Rebels Take Up Arms', *Financial Times*, 20 December 1997.
15. Miloš Antić, 'Nema noćnih straža ni okupiranih i oslobodjenih teritorija ali i Albanci i Srbi Strepe od Najgoreg', *Nedeljni telegraf*, 18 February 1998.
16. James Pettifer, 'We Have Been Here Before', *World Today*, April 1998.
17. Dejan Anastasijević, 'Kravi vikend u Drenici', *Vreme*, 7 March 1998; Dejan Anastasijević, 'Mrtvački ples', *Vreme*, 14 March 1998.
18. Tom Walker, 'Massacre by the "ethnic cleansers"', *The Times*, 4 March 1998; Dejan Anastasijević, 'Batinaši', *Vreme*, 11 January 1997; Filip Švarm, 'Idite na Kosovo, *Vreme*, 28 March 1998.
19. 'Kosovar March to Catholic Church Belies Belgrade's "Islamic Card"', *Guardian*, 16 March 1998.
20. Karen Coleman, 'Newsday', BBC World Service, 20 March 1998.
21. Sandra Petrušić, 'Pobuna crvenog rektora', *NIN*, 2 April 1998.
22. Marijana Milosavljević, 'Tesna koža', *NIN*, 26 March 1998.
23. Zoran B. Nikolić, 'Čekanje i strah', *Vreme*, 28 March 1998.
24. Sandra Petrušić, *NIN*, 2 April 1998.
25. Jane Perlez, 'Few Serbs Supporting Milošević on Kosovo', *International Herald Tribune*, 13 March 1998.
26. Dragoslav Grujić, 'Kosovska hronika', *Vreme*, 14 March 1998.
27. Robert H. Reid, 'Conflict in Kosovo Brings UN Arms Ban', *Independent*, 1 April 1998.
28. Zoran B. Nikolić, 'Šumari za odstrel', *Vreme*, 11 April 1998.
29. 'Srbi panično napuštaju sela oko Dečana, teroristi prave bunkere, kopaju rovove', *Dnevni telegraf*, 15 April 1998.
30. *Beta*, 25 February 1998 in *SWB EE/3162 A/13*, 27 February 1998.
31. Jansmina Teodosijević, 'Counting the Dead', *Transitions*, April 1998.
32. 'Protiv nacionalnih interesa', *Dnevni telegraf*, 13 March 1998.
33. RTS SAT TV, 25 March 1998 in *SWB EE/3186 A/3*, 27 March 1998.
34. Radio B-92, 3 April 1998 in *SWB EE/3195 A/5*, 7 April 1998.

35. Milan Milošević, 'Stara Ijubav', *Vreme*, 28 March 1998.
36. Olivera Zekić, 'Vanredni izbori zavise od Kosova, posle njih SPO nestaje sa scene', *Dnevni telegraf*, 13 March 1998.
37. Sandra Petrušić, 'Pet puta ništa', *NIN*, 19 March 1998.
38. 'Dačić: Drašković pod potpunom stranom kontrolom', *Dnevni telegraf*, 20 March 1998.
39. *Beta*, 26 March 1998 in *SWB EE/3186 A/3*, 27 March 1998.
40. Sandra Petrušić, 'Ponoćno deljenje', *NIN*, 26 March 1998.
41. *Beta*, 25 March 1998 in *SWB EE/3186 A/4*, 27 March 1998.
42. 'Radikali u koaliciji sa SPS Drašković i ND ispali iz igre', *Dnevni telegraf*, 25 March 1998.
43. *Beta*, 24 March 1998 in *SWB EE/3185 A/5*, 26 March 1998.
44. Slobodan Antonić quoted in: Nenad LJ Stefanović, 'Elastične kičme', *Vreme*, 4 April 1998.
45. 'Novi bolje vide', Vesna Pešić interviewed by Nenad LJ Stefanović, *Vreme*, 18 April 1998.
46. Guy Dinmore, 'Money Joins Serbs' List of Shortages', *Financial Times*, 3 April 1998.
47. 'Zamerili se levici radiualinim zahtevima za transformaciju društvene svojine', *Dnevni telegraf*, 17 April 1998.
48. This formulation was suggested by George Ninković, a member of the DSS, in a discussion organised by the Royal Institute for International Affairs, London, on 7 April 1998.
49. Roksanda Ninčić, 'Unutrašnje sagorevanje', *Vreme*, 11 April 1998.
50. *Beta*, 3 April 1998 in *SWB EE/3194 A/6*, 6 April 1998.

30. Conclusion

The hegemony exercised by Slobodan Milošević and the Socialist Party of Serbia over the political landscape in the period from 1990-8 arose out of his ability to command potent sources of material and ideological strength.

The 'anti-bureaucratic revolution' of the late 1980s left the Serbian ruling party and its leader Slobodan Milošević firmly in control of the political institutions. By utilising the tensions and ambiguities of the federal constitution, Milošević's faction of the ruling elite had been able to bypass the processes of 'transition' which were taking root in the other countries of Central and Eastern Europe. Indeed Milošević and his party had made use of the same energies of popular alienation which had in other countries served to dismantle the old order in order to strengthen the defences of the regime. When during the 1990s a 'pluralist' system took shape in Serbia it was a strange, distorted, hybrid creature. The formal structures of a democracy, such as the existence of multiple parties, the holding of elections and the formation of an operational parliament, had come into being. The nature of the political system, however, meant that none of these institutions functioned properly. Major inequalities existed between the ruling SPS and the newly-created opposition parties. As a 'new' political force the SPS based it appeal as much on its capacity to dispense patronage as its ability to articulate a coherent ideology. The SPS had inherited all the structures and the financial/material resources of the old League of Communists. More importantly the new 'pluralist' system had not effected a separation between the state and the party. Indeed the SPS lacked the key features of a political party in the normal sense, but rather functioned as a state-dependent agency of power. The SPS remained interconnected with all the main institutions of the state. The state media in particular remained faithful to the party line, and was a key element in the Socialist election victories from 1990 onwards. The extent of SPS control was illustrated by the fact that between 1991 and 1995 Milorad Vučelić acted simultaneously as head of state television and leader of the SPS parliamentary group. The police also remained under the control of the SPS. In particular Slobodan Milošević sought, through a trusted clique of security service operatives, to construct, within the framework of the police force, his own paramilitary private army or 'praetorian guard'. The army, whose loyalty Milošević considered suspect, was systematically purged and denuded of funds. In addition the key appointments within the judiciary and the diplomatic service fell under the control of the ruling Socialist elite. The power of the Socialist Party also rested on its ability to control the economy. Officials, managers and bureaucrats exerted direct control over the large state sector. Alongside this direct state power a major sector of the economy was controlled by 'private' businessmen who owed their position to the patronage of the state oligarchy. In some well-known cases such 'businessmen' were prominent government officials or politicians.

The formal structures of parliament were effectively a hollow shell. Real power was located with the Serbian President and in the political-economic bureaucracy. The opposition, understanding the limited nature of parliamentary power would on a number of occasions resort to tactics which involved a boycott of parliament or the organisation of 'parallel parliaments'. The refusal to participate in parliamentary business, however, meant that the opposition would be denying itself access to a forum, no matter how flawed, for criticism of the government. The opposition would repeatedly face a similar dilemma regarding participation in elections. With the SPS controlling the state apparatus it was able to determine the conditions under which elections were fought. These conditions were designed to guarantee a continued Socialist grip on power. The opposition were faced with a choice between participating in elections in which they would, in all probability, be defeated once again or boycotting the elections in which case they would risk political marginalisation. The flawed nature of parliamentarism was demonstrated by the fact that the defining moments in Serbian political life during this period occurred not within the debating chamber but rather on the streets, on 9 March 1991, during the Vidovdan Sabor of June 1992, the demonstrations of June 1993, the winter protests of 1996/7, and the violent confrontation in Belgrade on the night of 30 September 1997.

For all the entrenched power of the ruling elite, Serbia under Milošević was not a dictatorship in the *totalitarian* sense of the word. Opposition political parties, and civic organisations, continued to operate throughout this period, and the independent media continued to publish and broadcast. These freedoms 'granted' to the opposition groupings and the media were, however, symptomatic of the strength of the ruling party and the *authoritarian* nature of its rule rather than its tolerance and a belief in democratic practice. While Milošević and his associates were safe within the institutional citadel they had created, they showed little concern over the activities of the various opposition groups which existed below those commanding heights. When, however, elements in the opposition or the media took actions which were considered to be a threat, the state reacted in ways which were both arbitary and unchecked by any legal restraint. Prime examples of such coercive actions by the authorities were the arrest and beating of Vuk and Danica Drašković, the arrest of Vojislav Šešelj on the 3 June 1995 at Gnjilane in Kosovo, and the trial of Zoran Djindjić in 1996 after he had been accused of slandering the Prime Minister, Mirko Marjanović. The independent media were also on the receiving end of such political justice with the suppression of *Borba* in December 1994 and the stifling of Studio B in February 1995. All these actions were clothed in the language of legality, but it was understood by all those concerned that they were in essence manifestations of the naked power of the state. In this sense Serbia was a country where the laws had fallen silent.

The role of Slobodan Milošević as an individual was critical to the persistence of the *ancien régime* in Serbia. He had created around himself a highly personal web of *extra-institutional* political, economic, and coercive power (*sultanism*). The personalised nature of politics with an oligarchic power-clique clustering around Milošević was replicated at a lower regional level and in areas such as the Republika Srspka where local hierarchical elites flourished. Any reform of the political system would have severed critical strands in this web. For this reason the SPS could not, while Milošević was at its head, transform itself into a social democratic force along the lines undertaken by the communist parties in Poland and Hungary. The SPS image-makers and spokesmen sought, both at the party's inception and through the processes of cadre change, to clothe itself in the outward garb of 'modernity'. In spite of the deployment of these presentational techniques there was never a fundamental shift towards a 'democratic left' path.

The SPS had inherited, and made no attempt to abandon, the socialist cultural/political tradition. This 'leftism', however, was mixed with the the resentments which had long been nurtured by socialist cadres and preserved as a form of 'secret history' to produce a national/socialist political amalgam. The tradition was, however, preserved in its purest form by such neo-communist factions as the SK-PJ and later JUL. This tradition celebrated the Partisan victory over the forces of 'occupation' and 'reaction' as its *foundation myth*. This mythic cycle was invoked by senior members of the SPS and JUL at key moments of political crisis. In this way during the March 1991 demonstrations the government-controlled press sought to stigmatise the opposition protesters as 'collaborationist' Četniks. Similarly the demonstrations of 1996 prompted Ljubiša Ristić to recall, in apocalyptic terms, the measures taken during the Partisan struggle against Četniks and their sympathisers. The conspicuous celebration of Partisan anniversaries was also resumed during the period of the rift between Belgrade and Pale when Milošević's government felt it necessary to put political/symbolic distance between itself and the Bosnian Serb leadership.

Such 'left/revolutionary' symbols and myths, referring back to a divided wartime past, could appeal only to a segment of the Serbian population. Aware of this, Milošević utilised unifying national symbols which blurred or crossed ideological boundaries. By adopting such symbols, and particularly the Kosovo 'master-symbol', Milošević was able to transcend the normal, profane considerations of politics. He rose to power by exploiting the plight of the Serbian minority in Kosovo and maintained himself by utilising the situation of the Serb populations in Croatia and Bosnia. When he felt that the capital of nationalism had been expended he, in alliance with his wife's JUL grouping, again adopted a 'neo-communist' agenda (1994-6). In 1997-8 when this 'leftist' experiment appeared to falter he played the nationalist card once again, trying to use the deteriorating security situation in Kosovo to bolster his political power.

Milošević's personal role within the state/party elite was demonstrated by the fact that while during the demonstrations of November 1996 to February 1997 the elite came under severe pressure, there was no general breakdown of authority. This can be contrasted with the rapid collapse in January 1997 of the socialist government in neighbouring Bulgaria, which lacked a central figure of authority comparable to Milošević, when faced by similar street demonstrations although these were of shorter duration and involved fewer people.

By taking a decisive leadership role at the time of his 1987 intervention in the affairs of Kosovo and the 'anti-bureaucratic revolution', Milošević was able to implant himself in the consciousness of a wide section of Serbian opinion. He became a *supra-political* figure whose actions were not judged by normal political criteria and whose popularity was largely detached from the reputation of the political organisation of which he was the leader. Although his standing as a modern political icon suffered from a process of ongoing decline in the eyes of particular groups such as the urban population, he maintained a high degree of loyalty among a certain core of the electorate in spite of the increasing economic misery in Serbia and the failure of his national policies. Milošević's support remained strongest among the rural population and industrial workers of Serbia whose political loyalties were determined more by the attraction of 'symbols of power' than by the merits of policy in the civic marketplace of ideas.

The formidable strengths of the SPS political machine were paralleled by weaknesses among the opposition. Lacking a strong institutional and ideological framework, the opposition parties were fatally prone to fragmentation, with splits and divisions arising over issues of policy, strategy and personality. The opposition leaders were, of course, aware of the need to create an opposition force strong enough to take on the SPS, but attempts to construct such a coalition, as with DEPOS in 1992-3 and Zajedno in 1996-7, suffered from the same sources of division and dissension. The diversity of opposition forces on the political scene meant that a situation of 'multi-polar' opposition developed. In this situation the opposition frequently expended as much or more energy, opposing each other than acting in opposition to the government.

Differences in political culture, tradition and symbolism not only existed between the government and opposition, but also within the opposition itself. There was a clear distinction in the language used in political discourse and identity between the *rationalists/modernists* and the *national romantics/neo-traditionalists*.

These divisions were external to and supplemented divisions over issues of policy such as the national question. Individuals with links to the *Praxis* group, such as Mihailo Marković (SPS), Ljubomir Tadić (DS) and Dobrica Ćosić (unaffiliated), drew their ideas from within a dissident socialist stream of thought which expressed itself as both 'left/rationalist' and strongly nationalistic. Others such as Dragoljub-Mićunović and the Civic Alliance of Serbia represented a stream of thought which was 'liberal-rationalist' in its understanding of politics and placed less emphasis on the national issue, or was actively anti-nationalist. Vuk Drašković and the SPO, by contrast, spoke a political language which was strongly 'national romantic', placing great emphasis on Serbian tradition and historic symbolism (Orthodox church, monarchy, Ravna Gora heritage). The emphasis on national tradition and history did not mean that the SPO necessarily took a more radical national line than some of the other ('rationalist') political forces. Indeed for a significant proportion of its existence the SPO opposed some of the more radical expressions of nationalism prevalent on the Serbian political scene. The Serbian Radical Party, as might be expected from an ultra-nationalist force, utilised traditional symbolism and language, but its dedication to such traditions was superficial and Šešelj placed much emphasis on the way in which his party represented a 'modern' interpretation of the Serbian 'national' interest unchecked by the constraints of tradition. His authoritarian populism should, considering his intellectual origins, be seen as a deviant branch of the 'rationalist' ideological stream. The poorly-defined and amorphous nature of his nationalist identity was politically useful, allowing him to project a *populist* message which could appeal to disaffected voters from both opposition and government camps. The Democratic Party of Serbia followed what can be defined as a 'right/rationalist' path where an emphasis on constitutional 'modernity' and rationalism was mixed with reverence for aspects of 'tradition.' In the case of Zoran Djindjić his political origins were within the *Praxis* 'left/rationalist' tradition. On assuming control of the DS in 1993/4 he sought to take the party down a path which can be described as 'right/rationalist', but where the ideological emphasis was shown in the interpretation of economic and social rather than constitutional issues.

These 'rationalist'/'national romantic' or 'modern'/'neo-traditional' distinctions were not simply differences in ideological expression, but rather provided the language by which the various opposition forces distinguished themselves from each other and fought for space on the political spectrum. The SPO and the DS, particularly in the period 1994-5 fiercely contested each other's right to represent the 'centre ground' of Serbian politics. The DS in support of their claim drew attention to their 'modern' identity in contrast to the use of neo-traditional symbolism by the SPO. The SPO by contrast sought to bolster its own 'centrist' image by drawing attention to the 'nationalism' of the DS. The competitive exchanges between the SPO and the DSS, with each emphasising its attachment to the national tradition, took on a different form as both parties sought to challenge the fidelity of the other to the tenets of that tradition. Koštunica, for instance, sought to portray the SPO's ostentatious use of traditional symbolism as a 'caricatured' and false version of the national tradition. The SPO also sought to contest the legitimacy of its rivals' claims suggesting that the emphasis the DSS placed on support for the Serbs outside Serbia compromised their links with the Srbijanci constituency. When, in the spring of 1997, the Zajedno coalition began to collapse this was expressed as a conflict between Drašković's political vision, with its symbolic emphasis on Ravna Gora and the monarchy, and the more 'rationalist' strategy favoured by the leaders of the DS and the GSS.

The considerable depth and bitterness of the divisions between the 'democratic' opposition forces with their discordant identities also ensured that a collective gathering of their forces under one banner did not necessarily result in a precise mathematical accumulation of opposition votes. The Zajedno coalition at the time of the November 1996 federal elections (SPO, DS, DSS, GSS), appeared to lose votes as individual supporters of these parties apparently judged that the placing of these diverse groups on one electoral slate lacked credibility. The creation of an opposition 'grand coalition' did not therefore of itself provide a 'magic key' to electoral success.

At a fundamental level the ability of the opposition in Serbia to create and maintain effective coalitions was weak in comparison with the situation in other Balkan countries. In Bulgaria and Romania the opposition coalitions, respectively the Union of Democratic Forces and the Democratic Convention, suffered between 1990 and 1997 from an almost constant process of division and fragmentation, but they always ultimately remained in existence, acting as the principal focus for opposition loyalties. Their continued survival, in spite of the level of internal conflict, owed much to the fact that they retained a degree of respect and status for the role that they had played as *pre-political* coalitions involved in the first battles against the socialists. The Serbian coalitions (DEPOS, Zajedno) by contrast tended to fall apart, being unable to contain their internal tensions. The fragility of the Serbian coalitions can in part be accounted for by the fact that, unlike their neighbours, they lacked any of that inherited memory of *pre-political unity* which would have given the coalition an identity of its own. The fact that Milošević himself had been the one who had first succeeded in mobilising the *pre-political* energies of the Serbian people during the 'happening of the people', had the effect of denying the opposition this vital moral and psychological resource.

The balance of forces among the opposition also tended to frustrate attempts at sustained unity and co-operation. With no single political party enjoying undisputed dominance within the opposition ranks there was a constant competitive urge operating between the rival parties, even when they were theoretically working together in the same coalition. This quest for superiority by the parties bedevilled relations between the SPO and the DSS (DEPOS) in the period 1992-3 and between the SPO and DS in 1996-7 (Zajedno).

At the level of policy the opposition suffered from the political agenda in the 1990s being dominated by national issues and the resolution of the Serbian question. Differing attitudes to the national question divided the opposition against itself and prevented it from focusing its energies against the regime. The importance of national issues in Serbian politics cannot simply be seen in terms of the prevalence of 'blood and soil' patterns of thought. Even political parties which were self-consciously 'civic and 'democratic' in orientation felt themselves compelled to define and set limits on the borders of the state in which those values should operate. The perception that the primary political imperative was to provide an answer to the conundrum of the Serbian national question meant that for many such politicians it appeared 'natural' or 'rational' if the borders of such a national state should correspond to the boundaries of the national group.

The conflict between the various opposition groups was most

pronounced during the period after the Belgrade-Pale schism when the various opposition forces took up positions determined by their attitudes to the Contact Group peace plan. The SPO-GSS which supported acceptance of the plan, and the SRS, DS and DSS which maintained links with the Bosnian Serbs, launched bitter attacks on each other over this issue. The earlier Vance-Owen peace plan was similarly divisive, encouraging the growth of splits within the SPO and in the wider DEPOS. In this way the external diplomatic developments helped to crystallise the existing internal divisions within the parties themselves.

On the fragmented Serbian political scene forces also developed which were contemptuous of democracy and followed a *populist* and *authoritarian* ultra-nationalist path. Vojislav Šešelj's Serbian Radical Party maintained a symbiotic relationship with the ruling party and the state. The SRS had originally been cultivated by the state authorities but later took on a life of its own, putting down roots among the alienated and dispossessed in Serbia's urban centres. Even when the SRS was not publicly allied with the government and presented itself instead as an 'opposition' party it continued to serve the interests of the ruling party by complicating the political situation and ensuring that there could be no simple confrontation between the 'democratic' opposition and the 'anti-democratic' regime. *Populist* nationalist parties external to but connected with the regime were not peculiar to Serbia. In both Romania and Bulgaria ultra-nationalist groupings emerged: these were described as parties of the 'red right' because while their message was one of *populist* ultra-nationalism they were strongly connected with the former state security apparatus and their leadership cadres consisted largely of former communist officials. However, the radicalised and economically devastated atmosphere in wartime Serbia meant that Šešelj's ultra-nationalist movement grew to be far stronger and to put down firmer roots than other such organisations in neighbouring countries. By the end of 1997 and the beginning of 1998 it appeared that Šešelj's Radicals would be better placed to take advantage of the growing weakness of the Milošević government than the divided 'democratic' opposition. In this grim scenario Milošević's *populist* ultra-nationalism was being 'challenged' by a party which was imbued with those same values.

The prospects for the development of democracy in Serbia

were also inhibited by the poor integration of ethnic minorities, which made up 34 per cent of Serbia's population, into Serbia's public life. The Albanians of Kosovo had withdrawn completely from the political process refusing to take part in elections and setting up their own parallel institutions. Slobodan Milošević made no serious attempt to seek conciliation with them, but instead throughout this period he chose to utilise the issue to strengthen his position in the short term. He had risen to power in the late 1980s by exploiting Serbian dissatisfaction over the status of Kosovo. The Albanian election boycott during the 1990s, by allowing a small number of Serbian voters to unfailingly return a relatively large number of pro-government representatives in an area where they faced little real opposition, served his purposes. The existence of a large state security establishment in Kosovo acted to strengthen the overall coercive power available to the state. While these forces where ostensibly meant to respond to manifestations of Albanian 'secessionism', they also provided a police 'standing army' ready to counter manifestations of popular opposition to the regime from among the Serbs themselves. In November 1996, when anti-government demonstrations began in the south Serbian town of Niš, one of the first acts of the regime was to reinforce the police presence in the city with units drafted in from Kosovo. The Kosovo Serbs also provided Milošević with a source of reliable if increasingly anxious supporters. In December 1996, when he called on Serbs to come to Belgrade to demonstrate their support for his government, relatively few people answered his summons. Many of those who did were Kosovo Serbs eager to defend the integrity of Kosovo on the steets of Belgrade. In the winter of 1997 Kosovo was the scene of barely-concealed electoral fraud in which the authorities maintained that the Albanian population had come out to vote *en masse* for the Socialist candidate. In the spring of 1998 Milošević exploited the Kosovo issue again, being apparently ready to risk a new conflict in the region in order to strengthen his ailing regime. The 'boycotting' tactics pursued by the Albanian leadership under Ibrahim Rugova effectively played into the hands of Milošević and the Socialist regime; withdrawal from political life consigned the Albanians to the margins of public life where Milošević felt he could safely ignore them. The strategy pursued by the Albanians in Kosovo can be contrasted with that of the Turkish population in Bulgaria, who by organising themselves into their own political party, the Movement for Rights and Freedoms, were able to transform themselves from an oppressed minority into being the 'kingmakers' of Bulgarian politics. Rugova's insistence that independence for Kosovo was the only solution to the confrontation with the Serbian state also made meaningful dialogue with the Serbian opposition difficult despite the fact that all of the latter had by the end of the 1990s accepted that the Albanian population should enjoy some form of political autonomy. The limited capacity of either side to contemplate compromise served to make conflict a more likely outcome in the area than political progress.

By the spring of 1998 the prospects for democratic development in Serbia appeared bleak. The Zajedno coalition, which in early 1997 had seemed to have the momentum necessary to achieve real change, had fallen apart leaving many ordinary Serbs deeply disillusioned. The anti-democratic Serbian Radical Party had risen to prominence and filled the vacuum created by the failures of both government and opposition. Milošević was trying to regain the political initiative by using a combination of personal guile, institutional strength and the exploitation of issues with which for the Serbs had the deepest national and symbolic resonance. As Milošević's position became more fragile and the political elite around him more restive, his tactics became more dangerous as he showed himself willing to risk conflict in Kosovo and confrontation with Montenegro.

In spite of the bleakness of the political landscape, the demonstrations of 1996/7 had provided a clear demonstration that a large pro-reform constituency existed among Serbia's population. In Montenegro Milošević had lost control to political leaders who, in spite of what they might have said or done in the past, appeared ready to follow a 'reformist' and 'democratising' path. The challenge faced by the democratic opposition in Serbia was to build an organisation and present policies which could restore their credibility and present a viable alternative to the competitive use of rhetoric and symbolism which had characterised Serbian politics in the previous decade.

Index